D1706843

Economic Crisis and Policy Choice

Economic Crisis and Policy Choice

THE POLITICS OF ADJUSTMENT
IN THE THIRD WORLD

Edited by
Joan M. Nelson

PRINCETON UNIVERSITY PRESS

PRINCETON, NEW JERSEY

Library of Congress Cataloging-in-Publication Data

Economic crisis and policy choice : the politics of adjustment in
developing countries / edited by Joan M. Nelson.
p.   cm.
ISBN 0-691-07821-1 (alk. paper)
ISBN 0-691-02310-7 (pbk. : alk. paper)
1. Economic stabilization—Developing countries—Case studies.
2. Developing countries—Economic policy—Case studies. 3. Economic
indicators—Developing countries—Case studies. 4. Business cycles—
Developing countries—Case studies. I. Nelson, Joan M.
HC59.7.E276   1990
338.9′009172′4—dc20   89-10790

Contents

List of Figures and Tables   vii

Contributors   ix

Preface   xi

CHAPTER ONE
Introduction: The Politics of Economic Adjustment in Developing
Nations   3
  Joan M. Nelson

CHAPTER TWO
Orthodoxy and Its Alternatives: Explaining Approaches to
Stabilization and Adjustment   33
  Miles Kahler

CHAPTER THREE
Stabilization and Adjustment in Argentina, Brazil, and Mexico   63
  Robert R. Kaufman

CHAPTER FOUR
Politics and Economic Crisis: A Comparative Study of Chile, Peru,
and Colombia   113
  Barbara Stallings

CHAPTER FIVE
The Politics of Adjustment in Small Democracies: Costa Rica, the
Dominican Republic, and Jamaica   169
  Joan M. Nelson

CHAPTER SIX
The Political Economy of the Philippine Debt Crisis   215
  Stephan Haggard

CHAPTER SEVEN
Lost Between State and Market: The Politics of Economic
Adjustment in Ghana, Zambia, and Nigeria   257
  Thomas M. Callaghy

CHAPTER EIGHT
Conclusions   321
  Joan M. Nelson

Statistical Appendix: Thirteen Countries, 1979–1988   363

Index   371

Figures and Tables

FIGURES

1.1	External Shocks in Thirty Countries (1979–1982)	20
3.1	Monthly Inflation Rates, Argentina (January 1985–April 1987) and Brazil (January 1984–January 1987)	81

TABLES

1.1	Selected Indicators of Economic Trends and Structure	14
1.2	Selected Indicators of Social Structure	15
1.3	Regime Types: Nineteen Governments	23
1.4	Net Official Development Assistance	26
1.5	Net Long-term Capital Transfers	27
1.6	Policy-based Loans from the International Monetary Fund and the World Bank, 1979–1988	28
3.1	Argentina and Brazil: Economic Performance in the 1980s	77
3.2	Mexico, Argentina, and Brazil: Annual Rates of GDP Growth and Inflation, 1946–1970	93
3.3	Changes in Mexican Minimum Daily Wage Levels, 1945–1966	94
3.4	Mexican Economic Performance in the 1980s	101
3.5	Mexico, Argentina, and Brazil: Average Real Wages, 1982–1987	103
4.1	Peru: Growth, Inflation, Balance of Payments, 1955–1985	120
4.2	Chile: Growth, Inflation, Balance of Payments, 1955–1985	121
4.3	Chile and Peru: Foreign Debt Indicators, 1980–1987	123
4.4	Chile and Peru: Macroeconomic Indicators, 1980–1988	127
4.5	Colombia: Growth, Inflation, Balance of Payments, 1955–1985	152
4.6	Colombia: Foreign Debt Indicators, 1980–1987	153
4.7	Colombia: Macroeconomic Indicators, 1980–1988	156
5.1	Costa Rica, Dominican Republic, Jamaica: Selected Economic and Social Indicators, 1980	171
5.2	Costa Rica, Dominican Republic, Jamaica: Macroeconomic Trends, 1965–1980	173
5.3	Costa Rica, Dominican Republic, Jamaica: External Shock Indicators, 1979–1986	175
5.4	Costa Rica, Dominican Republic, Jamaica: Macroeconomic Trends, 1980–1987	177
6.1	The Evolution of Philippine External Debt, 1972–1987	227

6.2 Chronology of Major Philippine Political Events of the Marcos
Period, 1973–1986 229
6.3 Philippine Export Performance under Martial Law 231
6.4 Philippine Economic Crisis Indicators, 1980–1985 235
6.5 Philippine Business Views of the Aquino Government, March–
July 1986 246
7.1 Ghana, Zambia, Nigeria: Macroeconomic Indicators, 1980–1987 267
8.1 Adjustment Decisions and Implementation: A Rough Typology 322

APPENDIX

A.1 Real GDP Growth 363
A.2 Real Per Capita GDP Growth 364
A.3 Current Account Balance as Percentage of GDP 364
A.4 Terms of Trade 365
A.5 Real Effective Exchange Rate 365
A.6 Trade Ratio 366
A.7 Service on Public and Publicly Guaranteed Debt as Percentage
of Exports of Goods and Services 366
A.8 Interest on Public and Publicly Guaranteed Debt as Percentage
of Exports of Goods and Services 367
A.9 Total External Debt as Percentage of GNP 367
A.10 Short-term Debt as Percentage of Total Debt 368
A.11 Public and Publicly Guaranteed Debt as a Percentage of Long-
term Debt 368
A.12 Money plus Quasi-money: Annual Growth 369
A.13 Consumer Price Changes 369

Contributors

THOMAS M. CALLAGHY is associate professor of political science at the University of Pennsylvania. He is author of *The State-Society Struggle: Zaire in Comparative Perspective* (1984) and articles and book chapters on state formation, capitalism, and the debt crisis in Africa.

STEPHAN HAGGARD is associate professor of government and faculty associate of the Center for International Affairs at Harvard. He is coauthor with Tun-jen Cheng of *Newly Industrializing Asia in Transition: Policy Reform and American Response* (1987); *Pathways from the Periphery: The Politics of Growth in the Newly Industrializing Countries* (in press); and coeditor with Chung-in Moon of *Pacific Dynamics: The International Politics of Industrial Change* (1989).

MILES KAHLER is professor at the Graduate School of International Relations and Pacific Studies, University of California, San Diego, and chairs the Committee on Foreign Policy Studies of the Social Science Research Council. He is author of *Decolonization in Britain and France: The Domestic Consequences of International Relations* (1984); and editor of *The Politics of International Debt* (1986).

ROBERT R. KAUFMAN is professor of political science at Rutgers University, specializing in Latin American political economy. Recent writings include "Democratic and Authoritarian Responses to the Debt Issue," in Miles Kahler, editor, *The Politics of International Debt* (1986); *The Politics of Debt in Argentina, Brazil, and Mexico: Economic Stabilization in the 1980s* (1988); and *Debt and Democracy in Latin America*, coedited with Barbara Stallings (1988).

JOAN NELSON is senior associate at the Overseas Development Council. She is author of *Access to Power: Politics and the Urban Poor in Developing Nations* (Princeton, 1979); coauthor with Samuel Huntington of *No Easy Choice: Political Participation in Developing Contries* (1976); and has written several recent articles on the politics of economic adjustment and on policy-based lending.

BARBARA STALLINGS is professor of political science and former director of the Latin American Studies Program at the University of Wisconsin in Madison. She is author of *Class Conflict and Economic Development in Chile, 1958-73* (Stanford, 1978); *Banker to the Third World: U.S. Portfolio Investment in Latin America, 1900–86* (1987); and coeditor with Robert Kaufman of *Debt and Democracy in Latin America* (1988).

Preface

ECONOMIC ADJUSTMENT poses complex technical and economic issues and perhaps still more intractable political challenges. Strikes and demonstrations in response to increased food prices and falling real wages are only the most visible repercussions. Less open but equally bitter and more tenacious struggles rage inside governments and between governments and interest groups over issues such as liberalizing trade, reallocating government expenditures, or reducing governmental regulation and subsidization of private economy activity. Not only vested economic and political interests, but also fundamental ideological convictions are engaged. All these domestic pressures interact with an array of international demands, advice, and bargaining.

By 1984, each author of this volume was already engaged in research on political dimensions of adjustment. Several members of the group met at the series of workshops organized by Miles Kahler at the Lehrman Institute in autumn 1984 that led to his volume on *The Politics of International Debt.* In late May 1985, most of us met again at a cross-disciplinary conference on the political economy of stabilization sponsored by the Yale Center for International and Area Studies and the Institution for Social and Policy Studies. The conference underscored both the importance of the topic and its relative neglect compared with economic dimensions of adjustment. A collegial effort, we agreed, might combine the intensive knowledge crucial to understanding individual countries' experiences with a large enough set of cases to permit some rough generalizations.

The project that emerged has three phases: a series of country studies and cross-national analyses reported in this volume; a set of studies of key issues that cut across countries and geographic regions, which will constitute a second volume; and a policy-oriented distillation of our work that appeared in the Policy Perspectives series of the Overseas Development Council.

As individual scholars, each member of the group benefited from the information and perspectives of the many informants and critics acknowledged in our separate chapters. We want to draw attention to the support and counsel crucial to the project as a whole. The project was financed by the Ford and Rockefeller foundations, and we owe special thanks to Tom Bayard, then at the Ford Foundation, and Catherine Gwin of the Rockefeller Foundation for their early encouragement and helpful advice. Christine Bogdanowicz-Bindert, Hollis Chenery, Gerry Helleiner, Daniel Schydlowsky, and John Williamson provided constructive counsel at an initial workshop. Chenery, Gwin, and Williamson with Max Corden, Richard Feinberg, Robert Liebenthal, Azizali Mohammed, and John Toye took part in a mid-course workshop to review the country analyses and attempt to distill broader generalizations; Vittorio Corbo, Richard Erb, and Jacques Polak joined the workshop for the session focusing on Kahler's essay, "Orthodoxy and its Alternatives." Those who met with us did so in their individual capacities and not as representatives of the organizations to which they belonged.

In October 1987, El Colegio de México hosted a lively conference, bringing together social scientists from the nine countries discussed in chapters 3, 4, and 5 to discuss the draft case studies and Kahler's study. That same month the Political Science Department of the University of Nairobi hosted a smaller gathering to discuss chapter 7. We are grateful to the two institutions and their staffs, and to Carlos Roces and Blanca Torres of El Colegio and Michael Chege, then at the University of Nairobi, for their key roles in organizing the conferences.

The manuscript as a whole has also benefited greatly from detailed and thoughtful written comments from Thomas Biersteker, Gerry Helleiner, Tony Killick, Azizali Mohammed and Robert Russell, and John Sheahan.

Because each member of the research group is located at a different institution, we needed an organization to administer the project and host its workshops. During its first year, the Lehrman Institute of New York served that role with grace and skill. When changes at the institute led us to seek another arrangement, the Overseas Development Council offered a home base, and since mid-1987 has provided intellectual stimulation and helpful contacts as well as invaluable administrative support. We thank both organizations.

Financial and administrative support have made the project feasible; constructive criticism has greatly improved the first-phase studies that comprise this volume. Responsibility for the studies, of course, remains entirely our own.

Economic Crisis and Policy Choice

CHAPTER ONE

Introduction: The Politics of Economic Adjustment in Developing Nations

Joan M. Nelson

HISTORIANS will record the 1980s as an extraordinary and largely perverse era in economic relations between North and South. International financial collapse was averted, but the price was high and mainly paid by the poorer nations. In most of Africa and Latin America, growth stopped or reversed. In some nations, the gains of a decade or more in real per capita gross national product (GNP) were erased. Net flows of capital between North and South reversed; from 1984 through 1988 developing nations transferred about $143 billion to industrialized creditor nations.[1] With the downward trend of most nonoil commodity prices, the brunt of the resource shift fell on imports and domestic investment. In many developing countries, the repercussions are likely to slow growth for many years.

The crisis was originally perceived in industrial nations and international financial circles as a temporary shock to be resolved mainly by short-run measures in the debtor nations. It gradually became clear that much longer-term, more complex issues were involved. Their resolution demands changes within and between industrialized nations, innovations in international institutions and arrangements, and adjustment within the developing nations. By early 1989, more serious attention was being focused on possible reforms in international arrangements, including guided rather than wholly voluntary debt relief and closer coordination of domestic policies among rich nations, but little action has been taken. From the outset of the crisis, however, creditor nations and banks and international financial institutions pressed the developing nations to take adaptive measures.

The adjustment of individual nations usually comprises two distinct though intertwined tasks. The first is *stabilization*, that is, reducing balance of payments deficits and inflation to levels compatible with resumed and sustainable growth. The debt crisis abruptly and dramatically increased the need to export while virtually eliminating new commercial finance. In many countries this new and acute pressure was added to long-evolving weaknesses in trade and fiscal accounts. The core of conventional short-run stabilization efforts is re-

---

[1] World Bank, *World Debt Tables: 1988–89*, vol. 1, *Analysis and Summary Tables* (Washington, D.C.: World Bank, 1989), tab. 1, p. xii.

duction of aggregate demand through macroeconomic management, that is, through fiscal and monetary measures often accompanied by devaluation. Stabilization programs normally aim at relatively quick results, typically within one or two years.

The second aspect of adjustment is *structural change* designed to encourage foreign exchange earning or saving activities and, more generally, to improve incentives and efficiency for sustainable growth. The specific measures needed vary widely with individual country circumstances. Structural changes require longer time horizons than stabilization efforts; typical programs are designed for three to five years, often with still longer plans in mind.

Both stabilization and structural change provoke intense controversy. Old debates on stabilization between monetarists and structuralists over causes and, therefore, cures of inflation (particularly in Latin America) have been modified as each camp has accepted some of the other's points. But deep differences remain about the conditions under which demand restraint should be the major thrust of stabilization efforts, the time frame within which deficits should be contained, the costs and benefits for longer-term growth prospects of austerity programs sustained over many years, and the realistic alternatives to such programs as long as commercial banks and the governments of industrialized nations do not take more effective action to staunch flows of capital out of the indebted nations.

The bitterest debates on structural change focus on the pace and sequencing of measures to open economies to international markets, the appropriate roles and limits of states and markets in promoting growth and other national objectives, and the allocation of transitional costs. The decade has seen considerable narrowing of differences on these issues in technical circles, as discussed later in this chapter and in detail in chapter 2. But among economists, and in less technical circles, disagreements still rage over the timing, phasing, and extent of structural reforms needed to restore growth in the new and rapidly changing international economic context of the 1990s.

Many of the debates, of course, are driven not only by differences regarding national values and priorities and disagreements over how specific national economies work, but also by the efforts of groups within and between countries to protect themselves and shift the burdens of adjustment onto others. Adjustment, in short, is complex and controversial at a technical level and immensely conflictual at ideological and political levels. While the crisis of the 1980s promptly generated a flood of economic analyses in North and South ranging from broad theory to highly specific and operational issues, the political dimensions received much less attention.

Historical experience in Latin America is an exception to this neglect. Albert O. Hirschman and Thomas Skidmore, among others, analyzed the political economy of inflation (and, in Hirschman's case, other structural issues) long before the crisis of the 1980s.[2] Just as the crisis was gathering, Alejandro Foxley and Laurence Whitehead organized a series of case studies on the political economy of stabilization in Latin America, touching many of the themes with which we are concerned.[3] Other recent studies have tended to focus on whether authoritarian regimes are better suited than democracies to carry out adjustment measures,[4] or on links between stabilization efforts and political instability.[5] Stephan Haggard and Joan Nelson explored political factors affecting adjustment programs, in samples of thirty and five countries respectively.[6]

This volume seeks a broader and more systematic comparative analysis of the political economy of adjustment. We focus on the political factors shaping governments' adjustment choices and on the implementation of those choices. Why do some governments respond promptly to signs of economic difficulty, while others muddle indecisively for years? What factors enter the choice (explicit, or by default) to treat difficulties as short-term only, or to adopt a longer-term strategy of adjustment? Why have some countries experimented with heterodox approaches, while most have, however reluctantly, pursued neoorthodox courses? Why have structural reforms failed to get off the ground in some countries and forged ahead in others? And why, when confronted with heated political protest, have some governments persisted, while others have modified or abandoned their courses? The answers to these questions are mainly political, not economic.

[2] Albert O. Hirschman, *Journeys Toward Progress* (New York: Greenwood Press, 1968); Thomas Skidmore, "The Politics of Economic Stabilization in Postwar Latin America," in James M. Malloy, ed., *Authoritarianism and Corporatism in Latin America* (Pittsburgh: University of Pittsburgh Press, 1977), pp. 149–90.

[3] Alejandro Foxley and Laurence Whitehead, "Economic Stabilization in Latin America: Political Dimensions—Editor's Introduction," *World Development*, 8, special issue (November 1980).

[4] John Sheahan, "Market-Oriented Economic Policies and Political Repression in Latin America," *Economic Development and Cultural Change*, 28, no. 2 (1980): 267–91; Carlos Diaz-Alejandro, "Open Economy, Closed Polity?," in Diana Tussie, ed., *Latin America in the World Economy: New Perspectives* (London: Gower, 1983), pp. 21–54; Robert Kaufman, "Democratic and Authoritarian Responses to the Debt Issue: Brazil and Mexico," in Miles Kahler, ed., *The Politics of International Debt* (Ithaca, N.Y.: Cornell University Press, 1986), pp. 187–218; Karen Remmer, "The Politics of Economic Stabilization: IMF Standby Programs in Latin America, 1954–1984," *Comparative Politics*, 19, no. 1 (October 1986): 1–24; Jonathan Hartlyn and Samuel Morley, *Latin American Political Economy: Financial Crisis and Political Change* (Boulder, Colo.: Westview Press, 1986). This collection offers eight case studies plus several cross-cutting essays focused in part on a related issue, the record of military compared with civilian regimes.

[5] Henry S. Bienen and Mark Gersovotz, "Economic Stabilization, Conditionality, and Political Stability," *International Organization* 39, no. 4 (1985): 729–54; Scott Siddel, *The IMF and Third-World Political Instability* (London: MacMillan, 1987).

[6] Stephan Haggard, "The Politics of Adjustment: Lessons from the IMF's Extended Fund Facility," in Miles Kahler, ed., *Politics of International Debt* pp. 157–186; Joan Nelson, "The Political Economy of Stabilization: Commitment, Capacity, and Public Response," *World Development* 12, no. 10 (October 1984): 983–1006.

In pursuing these questions, we assume that it is neither necessary nor useful to enter the continuing debates about the appropriate design of adjustment programs. Like most analysts of adjustment efforts during the 1980s, including many within the international financial institutions, we believe that continued economic stagnation or decay in much of Latin America and Africa makes imperative some reassessment of approaches to date, including program design and levels of financing as well as countries' efforts to carry out policies and reforms. But redesigned, more gradual, and more generously financed programs would still require politically controversial policy adjustments. The 1990s will see continuing intellectual debate and political conflict over how to adjust to the shocks of the early 1980s, their repercussions, and the ongoing technological and other forces changing the international economic setting. A better understanding of the political forces at work may contribute to more realistic and sustainable approaches to these challenges.

The Global Setting: Crisis and Response

The trends and events contributing to the crisis of the 1980s have been discussed extensively, and only the briefest summary is needed here. The most obvious triggers that contributed to the massive realignments of the late 1970s and early 1980s were the two oil price increases: quadrupling in 1974 and more than doubling again in 1979. The surge in petroleum producers' earnings coupled with changes in international financial markets produced dramatic increases in the flow of commercial bank credit to developing countries, especially those at intermediate stages of industrialization. Much of the lending carried maturities of five to ten years, and floating interest rates tied to the London Inter Bank Offer Rate or the U.S. prime rate.

The reactions of industrialized nations to the second oil shock compounded the effects of increased debt in the developing nations. The United States and other advanced nations promptly tightened macroeconomic policies, especially monetary policy. By the end of 1980 the U.S. prime rate was 21 percent. Further boosted by large U.S. fiscal deficits from 1981 on, real interest rates reached a fifty-year peak by 1982. Nations with large debts at variable interest rates suddenly found debt service devouring much of export earnings.

At the same time, demand for and prices of their exports declined. High interest rates contributed to the most severe recession in the industrialized nations since the 1930s. Nonfuel commodity prices of importance to the developing countries, after a period of buoyancy in the late 1970s, began to slip in 1980 and by 1982 were lower in real terms than at any time since World War II.[7]

---

[7] World Bank, *World Development Report* (Washington, D.C.: World Bank, 1983), pp. 9–11.

Responses in the North

Mexico's announcement in August 1982 that it could no longer service its massive external debt focused international attention on the implications of these trends for the global financial system. The international financial community initially viewed the crisis as a short-term liquidity problem. Rescue packages linked to stringent stabilization measures were rapidly put together for Mexico and other major debtors. The International Monetary Fund (IMF) and the U.S. government played central roles in these efforts and strongly pressed commercial creditor banks to participate. The efforts averted a major international financial collapse. By 1983, the industrial nations were beginning to recover from the deep recession of 1981–1982. Commodity prices turned up at the end of 1982. By 1984, a number of countries seemed to be on the road to recovery.

However, the apparent revival was short-lived in most countries. Moreover, commercial lending did not resume, and capital flows reversed dramatically. Mexico, Brazil, Argentina, and other major debtors, as well as smaller debtors like Costa Rica, were paying out considerably more to meet their debt obligations than they were receiving in financial relief. Real growth continued to be elusive.

In October 1985, U.S. Secretary of the Treasury James Baker III signalled a second phase in international reactions, stressing the need for growth as well as stabilization. The Baker Plan called for increased financing from international institutions and commercial banks and redoubled adjustment efforts with more emphasis on longer-run structural reforms in the developing countries themselves. It implicitly assigned the World Bank a more central role, especially through increased use of structural and sector adjustment loans linked to policy reforms, which the Bank had introduced at the beginning of the decade. Loans financing commodity imports (rather than specific projects) were desperately needed in many countries that depended on imported fuel, spare parts, and materials for industrial and agricultural production. Banks and multilateral agencies naturally wished to assure that such financing supported policies and programs that would help correct internal imbalances. Extensive conditionality and coordination among major financing agencies produced external pressure on internal economic policies historically unprecedented in scope and detail and in the number of countries affected.[8]

---

[8] External intervention in domestic economic policies and even in institutional organization and administration, is hardly new. In the nineteenth and early twentieth centuries, European creditor nations imposed virtual receiverships upon the Ottoman Empire and some other chronic debtor nations, sending in agents to take over financial and customs administration. Financial missions to a number of debt-distressed Latin American nations during the 1930s restructured governmental financial organization. The Alliance for Progress in the 1960s sought to link financial support to a broad agenda of economic and social reforms, with multilateral arrangements for advice and

Many poorer nations, especially in sub-Saharan Africa, posed little threat to international economic stability but faced still more overwhelming problems relative to their resources and capabilities. To assist them, the World Bank in 1985 established a special facility for sub-Saharan Africa, and the IMF created a structural adjustment facility for the lowest-income nations in March 1986, augmented in December 1987 by the enhanced structural adjustment facility. Increased support was linked to countries' own adjustment efforts spelled out in policy framework papers prepared by borrowing governments with the joint assistance of the two Bretton Woods agencies.

These changes in emphasis and approach produced improvements in some countries, but overall trends continued disappointing. By 1987, the moderate international economic recovery that started in 1983 was slowing down. Real interest rates were still high by historical standards, though well below their late 1982 peak. Ironically, the dramatic success of some major debtor nations, including Brazil, in expanding exports in 1983 and 1984 had been accomplished at the price of shrinking domestic consumption and investment, with adverse longer-run effects on growth that were becoming clear by the late 1980s.[9]

With the exception of a brief spurt in 1985, commercial banks had not resumed new lending to developing nations despite the exhortations of the Baker Plan and a variety of innovative devices to encourage resumed lending.[10] IMF operations now began to swell the drain on developing nations' resources. IMF net lending had increased dramatically in the early 1980s, peaking at over $11 billion in 1983. Repayments on many of those loans fell due in the second half of the decade. By 1986, net lending from the IMF to developing countries was negative, and in 1987 those countries repaid $6.1 billion more to the IMF than they received from it. The drain continued, though at much lower levels, in 1988.[11] In both the newly industrializing and the poorest nations, different combinations of all these factors added up to chronic severe fiscal and balance of payments constraints, import shortages, and slow or negative growth.

By the late 1980s, the unrelieved problems were prompting calls for a third, post-Baker Plan round of responses from the North. A variety of initiatives sought to whittle down the debt burden, including experiments with debt-for-equity swaps, U.S. Treasury Secretary Nicholas Brady's recognition of the

---

continuing review of reforms. IMF stand-by arrangements have long linked specific policy measures to financial support. But the policy-based lending of the 1980s is directed to a much broader range of policies than traditional IMF stand-bys (and the pre-World War II arrangements), is considerably more directive, and affects more countries than the Alliance for Progress.

[9] World Bank, *World Development Report 1987* (Washington, D.C.: World Bank, 1987), p. 19.

[10] John W. Sewell, Stuart K. Tucker, comps., *Agenda 1988: Growth, Exports, and Jobs in a Changing World Economy*, Overseas Development Council, U.S., Third World Policy Perspectives no. 9 (New Brunswick: Transaction Press, 1988), app. tab. B-4.

[11] International Monetary Fund, *World Economic Outlook* (Washington D.C.: International Monetary Fund, October 1988), tab. A45.

need for debt reduction in some cases, and the possibility of outright debt forgiveness for poor African nations. Proposals for more comprehensive and less voluntary debt relief continued to come from private voluntary agencies, religious groups and even from U.S. legislators, but by early 1989 had not prevailed.

Responses in the South

From the perspective of individual developing countries, the external shocks of the 1980s struck at different times and with varying intensity. Nations entered the decade with diverse legacies from the past with respect to debt, reserves, propensities for inflation, and growth.

It is difficult to assess nations' "responses" unambiguously. The most readily available data record economic performance. But performance is only in part a result of governments' efforts. Both international economic trends and events and internal factors beyond the control of the government, such as weather, often influence performance as much or more than deliberate policies.

Almost all developing nations adopted one or more conventional stabilization packages in the 1980s, mostly with IMF guidance and financial support. These programs varied somewhat with country circumstances, but their common core was restraint of public and private demand, to bring use of resources into closer alignment with available internal and external resources. A handful of developing countries—Argentina, Brazil, Peru—experimented with heterodox approaches that did not hinge primarily on demand restraint to contain hyperinflation and stabilize their economies.

In addition to these immediate crisis-management measures, with the urging of the external agencies many countries adopted reforms aimed at medium-term structural reform. These were generally neoorthodox in inspiration, promoting greater reliance on market mechanisms and fuller integration into the international economy, although old or new more heterodox elements were often part of the policy package. Among the most frequent measures were flexible exchange rate arrangements, increased real interest rates, incentives for export promotion, rationalization of public sector investment programs, tightened revenue collection, and sharply increased prices (reduced subsidies) for public utilities and publicly distributed commodities (including gasoline and other petroleum products). Trade liberalization usually encountered stiff resistance, although some major developing nations dismantled quantitative restrictions and reduced tariffs. Tax reforms, privatization of state enterprises, and cuts in public sector employment were part of the reform agenda in many nations, but were still less often carried through.[12] In most countries, structural

[12] World Bank, *Adjustment Lending: An Evaluation of Ten Years of Experience*, Policy and

reforms were adopted piecemeal, rather than as parts of a more comprehensive development strategy to which the government was dedicated.

Developing countries' responses to the crisis with respect to their external obligations initially were similarly conservative. Despite creditors' early fears, there was no debtors' cartel, in part because the crisis hit different countries at different times. More importantly, the larger debtors felt they had more to gain by negotiating singly than jointly. Almost all debtors initially tried to honor their obligations. Those that fell behind, such as Sudan and Bolivia, did so more as a result of incoherent economic management than as a deliberate strategic choice.

But as the decade wore on, the inability to resume sustained growth, growing internal pressures, further drops in terms of trade or demand for key exports for some countries, and above all, the failure of even "good performers" to regain normal access to commercial credit led more governments to reassess their policies regarding debt obligations. As prospects for substantial new financing faded, so did incentives for continuing to play by conventional international rules. In the absence of new net funding, a growing number of governments concluded they must choose between growth and debt service. Some simply quietly fell into arrears. Others, like Peru in autumn 1985 or Brazil in February 1987, dramatically declared a moratorium or cap on debt service, weighting the domestic political advantages of such an announcement more heavily than the probable external repercussions and the potential for future domestic political embarrassment. Between 1985 and 1988, in addition to Peru and Brazil, Bolivia, Costa Rica, the Dominican Republic, Ecuador, and Honduras unilaterally suspended part or most of their debt service. In Africa, the Ivory Coast, Nigeria, Tanzania, Zaire, Zambia, and a half-dozen other nations were also in serious arrears by late 1988.[13] The main factor inhibiting fuller default is no longer the hope of resumed long-term private flows, but fear that public bilateral and multilateral support might be affected. Nevertheless, the number of governments in serious arrears to the World Bank and the IMF, while still small, also rose in 1988.

Continued economic stagnation or deterioration in many countries and slow growth accompanied by continuing austerity in others are fueling not only quiet or noisy rebellion against the debt burden, but also growing internal challenges to stabilization and economic liberalization. The World Bank estimates that per capita incomes in highly indebted countries have dropped by a seventh and in sub-Saharan Africa by nearly a quarter in the course of the decade.[14] Increased poverty has been accompanied by erosion of health and education services and the deterioration of roads, factories, and other produc-

Research Series no. 1 (Washington, D.C.: World Bank, 1988), pp. 33–67. See especially chapters 3 and 4 for a broad survey of policy reforms during adjustment in the 1980s.

[13] Jeffrey D. Sachs, "The Debt Crisis at a Turning Point," *Challenge* (May–June 1988), p. 21.

[14] World Bank, *World Debt Tables: External Debt of Developing Countries, 1988*, vol. 1, *Analysis and Summary Tables* (Washington, D.C.: World Bank, 1988), p. ix.

tive facilities, posing fresh obstacles to resumed growth. One result is growing popular political unrest in many countries. A second effect is intellectual: among both Northern and Southern analysts, not only old opponents but some of the advocates of neoorthodoxy are raising questions with increasing urgency.

Evolving International Ideological Currents

Miles Kahler traces in chapter 2 the older monetarist approach to stabilization dominant in international financial and development circles, which gave way during the 1970s to a considerably broader "neoorthodox" approach.[15] The newer outlook assumed that trade and fiscal imbalances often reflect causes deeper than excess demand. It, therefore, called not only for corrective macroeconomic policies but also for medium-term structural reforms, including shifts towards outward-oriented trade policies, reductions in the role of the state, and public sector reforms. The broadened neoorthodox approach was based in good part on growing evidence—and some misinterpretation—of East Asian successes in the 1960s and 1970s, contrasted with the increasing difficulties of both Latin American and much less-advanced African nations.

Despite wholly different origins, this new conventional wisdom in international development circles coincided neatly with the rising tide of opposition to "big government" in the United States and the United Kingdom. The convergence reinforced technical reassessment with ideological commitment, at least in U.S. official circles. Neoorthodox assumptions wholly dominated the reactions of the Bretton Woods institutions and of the United States, Germany, and Japan. Linked to balance of payments support through the new emphasis on policy-based lending and backed by formal or informal cross-conditionality among creditors and donors, neoorthodox prescriptions were urged on governments in all regions and in varied situations.

As the crisis persisted into the latter half of the decade, neoorthodoxy drew increasing criticism on three grounds: welfare costs, economic effectiveness, and political implications.

As it became clear that adjustment was not a short-term proposition, social costs could no longer be viewed as unfortunate but transitory. Demands mounted for "adjustment with a human face."[16]

Moreover, the neoorthodox formula was increasingly challenged as inadequate to rekindle sustainable growth. Criticism focused partly on trade-offs and conflicts between stabilization and longer-run adjustment. Not only officials from developing countries but also many staff members of bilateral aid

[15] International Monetary Fund, "Theoretical Aspects of the Design of Fund-supported Adjustment Programs," Research Department occasional paper 55 (Washington, D.C., September 1987); see for a discussion of current IMF perspectives.

[16] Giovanni Andrea Cornea, Richard Jolly, and Frances Stewart, *Adjustment with a Human Face: Protecting the Vulnerable and Promoting Growth* (Oxford: Oxford University Press, 1987).

agencies and international organizations argued bluntly that while stabilization was a crucial element of adjustment, fiscal stringency and balance of payments and debt constraints increasingly compromised crucial longer-term investment.

Neoorthodox formulas for structural change also were questioned. Many smaller countries, especially in Africa, were skeptical of export-oriented strategies and viewed pressure for early import liberalization as a formula for destroying their small manufacturing sectors. In Africa these doubts were reinforced by fears of reestablishing colonial economic patterns based almost wholly on raw materials exports. Among economic scholars, more recent and careful assessments of East Asian experience, touted as a model for Latin American and Southeast Asian newly industrializing nations, suggested a much more active state role and much more gradual and phased reform than current neoorthodoxy was prescribing.[17]

As Kahler indicates in chapter 2, no clear-cut "heterodox" alternative to neoorthodoxy has emerged. The dramatic heterodox experiments in Argentina, Brazil, and Peru are widely regarded as having failed to achieve lasting gains.[18] Many critics of neoorthodoxy endorse many of its principles, including fuller recognition of the economic costs of subsidies, overvalued exchange rates, and other price distortions. Indeed, acceptance of many basic neoorthodox tenets is probably greater now in diverse countries around the globe than at any time in the post-World War II era. But the critics urge more flexible application of the neoorthodox approach: more careful attention to sequencing and more realistic time horizons, greater priority to production and less emphasis on containing demand. To succeed, they argue, adjustment programs must give more priority to growth and equity as well as short-run current account balance. They note that market mechanisms, despite considerable potential, have their limits. They question the legitimacy of highly detailed conditionality and external intervention. And they insist that the North should shoulder more of the global adjustment burden.[19]

Industrialized nations and the international financial community increasingly recognize the genuine political constraints in the developing nations to the pace and pattern of adjustment measures. The issue is slippery. It is clearly inadequate analysis to collapse issues of political feasibility into simplistic formulas of "political will." Indeed, in view of the human suffering entailed

---

[17] See, for example, Jeffrey D. Sachs, "Trade and Exchange Rate Policies in Growth-Oriented Adjustment Programs," in Vittorio Corbo, Morris Goldstein, and Mohsin Khan, eds., *Growth-Oriented Adjustment Programs* (Washington, D.C.: International Monetary Fund and World Bank, 1987), pp. 295–307 especially.

[18] The heterodox shock approach was more successful in Israel.

[19] See, in addition to the UNICEF studies already cited: Cornia, Jolly, and Stewart, *Adjustment with a Human Face*; World Institute for Development Economics Research (WIDER), "Stabilization and Adjustment Policies and Programmes Country Study Series" (Helsinki: United Nations University); Lance Taylor, *Varieties of Stabilization Experience: Toward Sensible Macroeconomics in the Third World* (New York: Oxford University Press, July 1987).

in failed or ineffective adjustment efforts, it is morally unacceptable to do so. But governments are strongly tempted to point to political risks to justify inaction. Political analysts tend to emphasize political obstacles to adjustment measures without considering whether or how it might be possible to work around those obstacles. After the fact, it is easy to identify a great many political pressures shaping the outcome of policy debates and government action (or inaction) and to conclude that the outcome was inevitable. More strongly put, undoubtedly in some situations, given realistic limits on external resources, no set of economic measures adequate to tackle current problems is politically sustainable. Yet in many instances, skillful political strategy and tactics combined with leaders' courage and vision have put in place and sustained effective policies and programs.

THE APPROACH AND FRAMEWORK OF THIS STUDY

What We Seek to Explain

This volume examines the adjustment efforts of nineteen governments in thirteen countries. Our sample of cases is not systematic, but the set is not unrepresentative; it is not strongly skewed with respect to major characteristics. Tables 1.1 and 1.2 provide a concise overview of some major social and economic features of our cases. The tables in the Appendix to this volume provide more detailed data on their economic performance during the 1980s.

Policy responses among the nineteen governments ranged from the broad-gauged and sustained neoorthodox approaches of Mexico and Chile to the outright rejection of these strategies in Peru and Zambia. Stances toward the international community similarly varied from cooperation to confrontation. Several of the cases were selected to capture particularly striking experiences such as the heterodox shock programs in Argentina and Brazil or dramatic policy reversals (in opposite directions) in Ghana and Zambia.

Our focus in this volume is to understand the factors that explain divergent adjustment choices and implementation. Adjustment decisions vary along three dimensions: *timing, scope,* and *content.*

Economists repeatedly point out that if emerging problems are addressed early, they can usually be resolved much more easily than if action is delayed. Yet behavior in many industrialized as well as developing nations demonstrates that most governments postpone action. From a political perspective, up to a point the reasons for delay are obvious; what needs explaining is inordinate postponement, or (at the opposite extreme) preemptive action before economic problems have become truly severe.

Governments tend also to define their problems restrictively and approach them in terms of crisis management rather than more fundamental structural change. Again, what calls for explanation is departures from the norm: pursuit

TABLE 1.1
Selected Indicators of Economic Trends and Structure

	Average Annual Growth of GDP:		Per Capita GNP, 1986 ($ U.S.)	Percentage of GDP in 1986 from:		Trade Ratio[d] (Avg. 1985–1986)
	1965–1980	1980–1986		Agriculture	Manufacturing	
A. UMIC[a]	6.7	2.5	1,890	10	25	
Argentina	3.4	(0.8)	2,350	13	31	17.6
Mexico	6.5	0.4	1,860	9	26	21.0
Brazil	9.0	2.7	1,810	11	28	19.7
B. LMIC[b]	6.5	1.8	750	22	17	
Chile	1.9	0.0	1,320	—	—	45.1
Colombia	5.7	2.4	1,230	20	18	26.4
Peru	3.9	(0.4)	1,090	11	20	24.5
Costa Rica	6.2	1.3	1,480	21	—	54.0
Jamaica	1.3	0.0	840	6	22	73.3
Dominican Republic	7.3	1.1	710	17	16	42.9
Philippines	5.9	(1.0)	560	26	25	32.0
Nigeria			640	41	8	27.4
C. LIC[c]	3.1	2.9	200	38	11	
Ghana	1.4	0.7	390	45	12	34.3
Zambia	1.8	(0.1)	300	11	20	72.0

Source: World Bank, World Development Report 1988 (New York: Oxford University Press, 1988), except where noted; (hereafter cited as World Development Report 1988), tables 1, 2, 3, pp. 222–27.

[a] Weighted average for upper middle-income countries.

[b] Weighted average for lower middle-income countries.

[c] Weighted average for low-income countries excluding China and India.

[d] Sum of imports and exports (1985 and 1986) divided by GNP (1985 and 1986). Calculated from data in World Bank, World Tables 1987, 4th ed. (Washington, D.C.: World Bank and International Finances Corporation, 1987), (hereafter cited as World Tables 1987).

of medium-term reform strategies in addition to immediate crisis management.

We draw an admittedly rough distinction between "narrow" policy packages focused solely or mainly on stabilization and "broader" sets of measures to encourage structural change. In some instances, the distinction is fairly easy. In several cases, probably most clearly the Dominican Republic, adjustment efforts were almost entirely confined to stabilization. In other cases, the sets of choices were sequential; stabilization fairly clearly preceded longer-term structural reforms. The de la Madrid government that took office in Mexico in 1982 envisioned a two-stage process of stabilization followed by reform. Somewhat similarly, the Monge government that entered office the same year in Costa Rica tackled stabilization first.

But in other countries, political leaders and groups believed that decisions about short-run stabilization entailed major implications for longer-run development strategy. The two stages were not separated in the minds of decision-

TABLE 1.2
Selected Indicators of Social Structure

	Population 1986 (millions)	Population Growth Rate 1986	Percentage Population Urban 1985	Percentage Labor in Agriculture 1980	Life Expectancy[d] 1986 (years)	Infant Mortality[e] 1986 (per thousand)	Secondary Education Ratio[f] 1985 (%)
A. UMIC[a]		1.8	65	29	66	56	56
Argentina	31.0	1.2	84	13	70	34	70
Mexico	79.6	2.2	69	37	67	50	55
Brazil	138.5	1.8	72	31	65	67	36
Chile	12.4	1.2	83	16	70	22	65
B. LMIC[b]		2.3	36	55	58	52	40
Colombia	29.2	1.7	67	34	65	48	49
Peru	20.2	2.0	68	40	59	94	65
Costa Rica	2.7	1.9	45	31	73	19	44
Jamaica	2.4	1.5	53	31	73	20	58
Dominican Republic	6.4	2.0	56	46	64	70	45
Philippines	55.0	2.2	39	52	63	48	68
C. SSA[c]		3.3	25	75	—	104	21
Nigeria	98.5	3.4	30	68	50	21	29
Zambia	6.9	3.5	48	73	52	84	17
Ghana	14.0	3.0	32	56	53	94	36

Sources: Population and growth rate: International Monetary Fund, *International Financial Statistics Yearbook* (Washington, D.C.: International Monetary Fund, 1987), (hereafter cited as *International Financial Statistics Yearbook*). All other items: World Bank, *World Development Report, 1988*, tables 1, 30–33.

[a] Weighted average for upper middle-income countries.
[b] Weighted average for lower middle-income countries.
[c] Weighted average for sub-Saharan Africa.
[d] Life expectancy at birth, in years.
[e] Infant mortality per thousand infants aged 0–1 years.
[f] Percentage of children in secondary school age group attending secondary school.

makers and politically important groups, nor can they be neatly dissected by ex post analysis. Moreover, because fiscal and balance of payments pressures have persisted through the 1980s, most developing countries have had no practical alternative to simultaneous pursuit of short-run macroeconomic stabilization measures and longer-run reforms, whether or not they earlier adopted a sequential approach.

Nevertheless, the distinction remains a useful first approximation for the scope of adjustment efforts. As discussed in chapter 8, the inherent political dynamics of "pure stabilization" programs differ from those of longer-run structural changes, and the major international financial institutions, the IMF and the World Bank, define their roles and divide responsibilities largely in terms of the distinction.

The content of governments' adjustment choices can be described along several dimensions, including the internal consistency or inconsistency of the decisions, the pace and sequencing of measures, and the degree to which the policy package adheres to or departs from neoorthodox prescriptions. We focus mainly on the question of orthodoxy.

As the 1980s end, the distinction between neoorthodox and heterodox approaches to stabilization may have outlived its validity.[20] The terms tend to generate more heat than light. The "orthodox" label for some connotes a rigid or unimaginative approach, while others may assume that measures labeled "heterodox" are irresponsible or utopian. However, much of the thinking about adjustment approaches during the 1980s was cast largely in terms of the orthodox/heterodox distinctions. Though future debate would probably gain from dropping the labels in favor of more fine-grained and less emotive ways to describe the substance of adjustment programs, the terms remain useful as broad characterizations of past programs. We use them without implying either praise or criticism.

We assume, tentatively, a built-in bias towards neoorthodox approaches to short-run stabilization. Only a small number of policy instruments is available to cope with short-run crises—that is, instruments that are readily manipulable and likely to produce fairly quick effects. Moreover, the general principles and instruments of neoorthodox theory on stabilization are well known, while heterodox alternatives are less clearly defined and require more innovation. Equally important, in the 1980s pressure to service ballooning debts left many countries little room to manuever. Therefore, the predominance of neoorthodox approaches to short-run stabilization is no surprise. The more challenging questions concern the factors leading to heterodox stabilization efforts and those shaping choices regarding longer-run structural change.

We are concerned not only with policy choices, but also with *implementation*. Many adjustment decisions die stillborn, or are diluted, or abandoned in midstream. This is indicated by the high proportion of stabilization efforts undertaken within the guidelines of agreements with the IMF that break down before they are completed. Failure to meet agreed targets and, more clearly, cancellation of agreements usually, though not always, reflect implementation difficulties. During the 1978–1981 period, for instance, 40 percent of stand-bys and 56 percent of extended fund facility programs "suffered from major breaches of performance criteria."[21] Of thirty-four extended fund facility arrangements entered between July 1975 and April 1987, nineteen were cancelled before completion.[22] Thirty of 180 stand-by

---

[20] John Williamson argues this point forcefully in comments on an earlier draft of this study.

[21] Tony Killick, ed., *The Quest for Economic Stabilization: The IMF and the Third World* (London: Gower in association with the Overseas Development Institute, 1984), p.247.

[22] International Monetary Fund, *Annual Report 1987* (Washington, D.C.: International Monetary Fund, 1987), tab. II.7, p. 82. Some of the cancelled EFFs were replaced with shorter-term stand-by arrangements. With the exceptions of Chile, Ghana, and Tunisia there have been no new EFFs since 1984.

arrangements entered between 1980 and 1987 similarly were cancelled before completion.[23]

Structural reforms are implemented over a longer period and seek a wider range of objectives than stabilization packages. Therefore, the extent to which decisions are executed is still harder to assess. The most careful available appraisal of experience with World Bank structural and sector loans concludes that on average, 60 percent of the formal conditions attached to the loans were fully implemented during the loan period, with considerable variation around the average according to the category of reform.[24] The same study indicates that implementation rates for most types of reforms rose slightly if the period since the expiration of the loan was also taken into account, although implementation of industrial policies and exchange rate reforms declined, which suggests backsliding.

In principle, we focus on the extent to which different governments carried out adjustment decisions, rather than economic outcomes. Outcomes always reflect not only the government's actions but also the responses of other economic actors (for example, potential private investors) and trends and events beyond the government's control (such as international prices or weather). In practice, it is extremely hard to untangle implementation from outcomes. Economic trends may or may not be largely caused by government policies, but they always influence both public responses and subsequent adjustment decisions. Our studies take this feedback very much into account. But we do not try to systematically or fully explain the economic trends themselves or assess the extent to which they are the result of government policies.

Determinants of Adjustment Choices and Action

Our approach to analyzing experience in these cases is inductive. There is no general theory of the politics of adjustment. A number of different theories and bodies of research are relevant to one aspect or another of our topic, but fall well short of an overarching conceptual scheme or theory. Premature theory building is likely to produce either generalizations so broad and vague that they have limited value or sharper propositions that illuminate some cases but miss crucial aspects of others. Rather than specify a theory a priori, we set out to sharpen concepts of both dependent and independent variables and to specify more precisely some of the causal mechanisms at work and the circumstances in which they are more or less important. Our goal was to put in place building blocks and to offer some significant insights for future theory building.

[23] Calculated from IMF *Annual Reports*, 1982–1987 appendixes discussing Fund activities in the course of each fiscal year.

[24] World Bank, *Adjustment Lending: An Evaluation of Ten Years of Experience*, Policy and Research series no. 1 (Washington D.C., 1988), table 3, p. 9.

For each case, we traced adjustment experience as it unfolded in three arenas: decision-making circles (usually quite small), the interaction between the
government and external creditors, and the broader arena of domestic politics.
Our studies weave back and forth between these arenas, each with its own
internal dynamics, and each interacting with the others.[25] We also occasionally
touch on a fourth arena, the relations between external actors, to the degree
important for understanding events in specific countries.[26]

We seek explanations for different adjustment choices and implementation
efforts among governments in five broad sets of causal factors:

1. The economic crisis itself, as it was interpreted in the light of prior experience
   and precrisis trends
2. The technical and administrative capacity of states to formulate and execute adjustment measures
3. The structure of political institutions and rules of the political game, including
   general regime type and more specific variations
4. The more circumstantial patterns of leadership, support bases, and political coalitions
5. The roles of external agencies including the international financial institutions,
   governments of creditor nations, and commercial creditors

Clearly, these factors interact and at points overlap, but they provide a
framework for analyzing individual cases and for drawing comparisons within
chapters and across the full set of cases.

VARIATION IN THE NATURE OF THE ECONOMIC CRISIS

The economic crisis of the early 1980s affected the thirteen nations considered in this study with varying speed. For some, such as Costa Rica and the

[25] See Robert Putnam, "Diplomacy and Domestic Politics," *International Organization* 42,
no. 3 (Summer 1988): 427–60. Our image is quite similar to Robert Putnam's metaphor of the
decision makers playing simultaneously at two tables, domestic and international. But because
many of our cases entail weak and divided executives, we devote a good deal of attention to the
internal dynamics of the decision-making circle, including top political leaders and senior advisors.

[26] This fourth arena of relations among the external agencies themselves may strongly influence
their interaction with individual governments and can indirectly affect the internal politics of
adjustment. The international financial institutions are not free agents; they are subject to various
pressures, particularly on behalf of clients of the major powers or to the detriment of countries
those powers disapprove. Intricate cross-currents of support and rivalry exist between the IMF and
the World Bank, between both Bretton Woods institutions and the regional multilateral banks and
specialized United Nations agencies, between the international institutions and the major bilateral
aid agencies, and among various wealthy nations' programs and goals in particular developing
countries. There is a complex world of politics among commercial banks, and between them and
their own governments and the international institutions. We did not consider this fourth arena in
its own right; to do so would have made the scope of this study quite unmanageable. But we did
try to note where specific aspects of the fourth arena directly affected our cases.

Dominican Republic, the crisis came as an abrupt shock that terminated long periods of satisfactory growth. Others, most notably Zambia, Jamaica, and above all Ghana, had been in economic decline before or since the early 1970s. The crisis also hit with varying intensity. Bela Balassa and F. Desmond McCarthy analyzed the effects of shifts in terms of trade, volume of exports, and interest rate increases for thirty countries, including ten of our cases, for the period 1979 through 1982. Figure 1.1, adapted from their analysis, measures the combined impact for each country as a percentage of its annual GNP. The ten of our cases included in Balassa and McCarthy's analysis were spread across the spectrum from most severely to comparatively lightly affected.[27] The nations we considered may be somewhat biased towards the more heavily indebted: ten are among the World Bank's list of seventeen "highly indebted countries," including Argentina, Brazil, Chile, Colombia, Costa Rica, Jamaica, Mexico, Nigeria, Peru, and the Philippines.[28] Four of our cases were among the six assessed by Donald R. Lessard and John Williamson as clearly suffering heavy capital flight.[29]

How might we expect the characteristics of the external shock to shape adjustment responses? The probability that a government will adopt a stabilization package clearly increases with the severity of the crisis as reserves dwindle and arrears mount, imports dry up, and inflation soars. We are concerned, however, not with the general connection between mounting economic pressure and governmental reactions, but with the variation in the timing, scope, and content of adjustment responses. In some countries the same or successive governments have failed to act decisively not just for years, but for decades.

In principle, unsustainable fiscal and balance of payments gaps and/or rapid inflation confront governments with a logical series of judgments, a four-pronged decision tree.

> Are the causes of the problems single-shot or self-correcting, with temporary compensatory financing the main response required?[30] Or, are the internal or external causes unlikely to be self-correcting, with more active government intervention needed?

[27] Bela Balassa and F. Desmond McCarthy, "Adjustment Policies in Developing Countries, 1979–83: An Update," World Bank Staff working paper no. 675 (Washington, D.C.; 1984), p. 3. The impact on specific countries would, of course, be different if the period after 1982 were covered.

[28] World Bank, *World Debt Tables:* vol. 1, *Analysis and Summary Tables* (Washington, D.C.: World Bank, 1988), xlviii.

[29] Donald Lessard and John Williamson, *Capital Flight and Third World Debt* (Washington, D.C.: Institute of International Economics, 1987) pp. 205–13; ibid., p. 213. An additional seven of our cases were among the twenty-three Lessard and Williamson listed as often cited as experiencing large-scale capital flight.

[30] A government may conclude its problems fall in this category. Yet, if adequate compensatory finance is not available, it may have to resort to more active intervention as if the problem were not potentially self-correcting.

If the problems are not self-correcting, what short-run measures will most
effectively restore balance?

Is the economy's broad course sustainable and desirable, after short-run
corrections? Or, are more basic structural changes necessary?

If structural changes are needed, what should be the country's medium-term
strategy?

FIGURE 1.1: External Shocks in Thirty Countries (1979–1982)

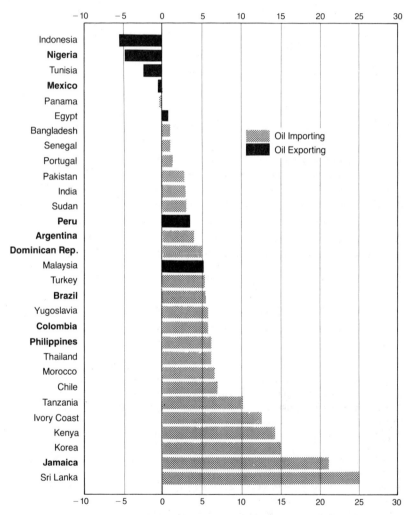

Source: Adapted from Bela Balassa and F. Desmond McCarthy, ''Adjustment Policies in Developing Countries, 1979–83: An Update,'' World Bank staff working paper no. 675 (Washington, D.C., 1984), p. 3; reprinted with permission.

At a technical level, the answers to these questions should determine the scope and content of adjustment decisions. But each step in the logical series calls for difficult interpretations of an often fast-evolving situation. Interpretations are shaped not only by the facts available, which are often partial, inaccurate, or outdated, but also by assessments of previous adjustment experiences and value judgments about precrisis progress and future priorities. We hypothesized that the probability of adopting broad programs of reform is higher in countries where economic trends have been widely viewed as unsatisfactory for a long time than in countries with precrisis records of fairly rapid growth, not only because economic decisionmakers are more likely to perceive structural problems at work, but also because the key interest groups and the public are likely to be more receptive to extensive reforms.

In principle, not only the nature of the economic crisis, but also the scale and development level of the economy should shape the content of adjustment responses. Small countries, for example, have few realistic alternatives to heavy reliance on trade. Again, interpretations and assessments rather than "objective facts" are crucial. Governments and publics may be slow to recognize such constraints; the characteristics of the economy are, therefore, more certain to affect outcomes than choices.

STATE CAPACITY

Capacity to generate informed and objective analyses of economic problems ' and options obviously affects the speed and coherence of adjustment responses. To some extent this capacity is determined by very basic features: the number of well-trained and experienced analytic staff in central economic agencies and whether they are largely in agreement or deeply divided. Broadly, we expected small and/or inexperienced economic staffs to be preoccupied with day-to-day economic management, with little time or perspective to consider broader reforms. Stephen Haggard and Chung-in Moon, reviewing Korean experience, pointed to a further crucial feature: the degree to which technical staff are insulated from legislative, interbureaucratic, and interest group pressures. Reasonable autonomy is probably essential to the ability to propose and follow through on politically painful measures.[31]

At least as important as the ability to formulate coherent policies are the instruments and institutions that permit implementation. In some countries, economic managers are rather like pilots pulling levers that do not connect, or connect only loosely, to the actual steering equipment. Even in countries with potentially adequate institutions and procedures, the authority of central economic agencies may be sharply circumscribed by constitutional and legal allocations of power to operating ministries, semiautonomous public sector agencies, the legislature, or lower levels of government. Separate from cen-

[31] Stephen Haggard and Chung-in Moon, "Institutions and Economic Policy: Theory and a Korean Case Study" (draft manuscript, Cambridge, Mass., 1988).

tralization, but also important for implementation, is the depth of managerial capacity in operating agencies.

These dimensions of state capacity are partly matters of technical training and experience, administrative organization, and legal authority, but they are also intertwined with regime type and political structure, interest groups, and political support bases. Unity or dispute within the economic team, for instance, often reflects wider political consensus or conflict. The role of state officials and public sector employees as a powerful interest group or groups is also a political factor that strongly affects the capacity of the state to formulate and execute adjustment measures.

The countries in this study vary widely with respect to these dimensions of state capacity. The depth and sophistication of economic staff available to decision makers range from the impressive capabilities in Chile or Colombia to the small, harried, and comparatively inexperienced economic staffs (despite outstanding individual exceptions) in Ghana, Zambia, the Dominican Republic, or Peru. Similarly, there are important contrasts among our cases in economic staffs' autonomy and insulation from societal pressures, the degree to which they and the chief executives exercise effective financial and substantive control over major public sector agencies, and the strength of the state apparatus as an interest group.

THE STRUCTURE OF POLITICAL INSTITUTIONS

The governments in this study run the gamut of regime types, as indicated in table 1.3. At least since the 1970s, the assumption has been widespread that authoritarian governments are more likely than democracies to decide upon and enforce unpopular economic stabilization and adjustment measures. Authoritarian governments, it was hypothesized, are better able to make long-run plans than are governments tied to electoral cycles. They may also have less rapid turnover at staff levels, which facilitates implementation. Further, authoritarian regimes have less need to respond to either broad popular pressures or vested interests; they can more readily base their decisions on criteria of economic rationality. And, authoritarian regimes are better able than democratic governments to forestall protest through anticipated repression and to suppress protest if it occurs.[32]

Recent studies cast considerable doubt on these assumptions. Karen Remmer surveyed 114 stabilization programs in nine Latin American countries over the thirty years from 1954 to 1984; Stephan Haggard analyzed thirty extended fund facility programs in twenty-four countries.[33] Neither found any systematic association between regime type and the ability to stabilize. Stall-

---

[32] See the sources cited in note 4. The theory was developed almost entirely with reference to rightist authoritarian systems, but applies also to leftist authoritarian regimes.

[33] Remmer, "Politics of Economic Stabilization"; Haggard, "Politics of Adjustment."

TABLE 1.3
Regime Types: Nineteen Governments

Military/ Authoritarian	Single party/ Dominant Party	Transitional Democracy	Established Democracy
Pinochet (Chile)	de la Madrid (Mexico)	Belaúnde (Peru)	Betancur (Colombia)
Rawlings (Ghana)	Kaunda (Zambia)	Sarney (Brazil)	Carazo (Costa Rica)
Babangida (Nigeria)	Marcos (Philippines)	Alfonsin (Argentina)	Monge (Costa Rica)
		Limann (Ghana)	Arias (Costa Rica)
		Aquino (Philippines)	Seaga (Jamaica)
		García (Peru)	Guzmán (Dominican Republic)
			Jorge Blanco (Dominican Republic)

ings and Kaufman, in their more recent review of adjustment efforts in nine Latin American nations, found evidence that regime type does relate to the scope and content of programs. They suggested that authoritarian regimes are most likely to adopt strongly orthodox programs, not only for stabilization but also for longer-term structural change. Regimes in transition to democracy are most likely to adopt heterodox programs. Established democracies, they concluded, are likely to pursue orthodox stabilization programs but have difficulty sustaining longer-run programs of orthodox structural change.[34]

More sharply specified institutional and procedural variables almost surely have more impact than broad regime type, both on ability to formulate coherent and consistent adjustment policies and on capacity to implement them. One such variable is electoral cycles. It is well-documented that the approach of elections hampers adoption and implementation of stabilization programs and structural reforms.[35] Fiscal and monetary policies often loosen in the run-up to elections, not only in competitive democratic systems but also in more authoritarian systems where elections serve important legitimating functions.

[34] Barbara Stallings and Robert Kaufman, eds., *Debt and Democracy in Latin America* (Boulder, Colo.: Westview, 1989), pp. 205–12.
[35] See, among other sources, Barry Ames, *Politics and Survival: Politicians and Public Policy in Latin America* (Berkeley: University of California Press, 1987).

Governments also become more sensitive to opposition criticisms; governments in office may split into pro- and antiadjustment factions.[36] Conversely, stabilization and structural changes are most likely to be adopted just after elections (or unscheduled changes of government), when the new government is likely to have high legitimacy and/or opposition groups are in disarray.

Other kinds of formal and informal institutional features also modify the crude authoritarian-democratic distinction. For example, governments that depend for much of their support on patronage (which may be true of democracies or weak authoritarian systems) are unlikely to adopt or implement structural changes that shift the allocation of resources to impersonal market mechanisms.

We treat coalitions and interest groups as a separate variable that shapes adjustment responses, but a combination of regime type and support base may be more helpful than either variable taken separately. Thus established or transitional democratic systems that depend on business (and sometimes also on military groups) may behave in some ways like similarly based authoritarian systems, although they are unlikely to be as repressive. Conversely, authoritarian regimes that draw a substantial degree of support from popular forces (including though not necessarily confined to organized labor) may respond to adjustment pressures somewhat like similarly based transitional or established democracies.

POLITICAL LEADERSHIP, COALITION POLITICS, AND SUPPORT BASES

The importance of political leadership in economic adjustment is hotly contested. Two extreme positions mark the outer bounds of debate.

1. Political will is the major determinant of capacity to adopt and implement adjustment measures; where the political leadership has the required will, the program will carry; where will is lacking, the program will fail.
2. The commitment and skill of political leaders are largely irrelevant to whether adjustment measures succeed or fail; what counts is the constellation of key pressure groups and political circumstances.

Few would defend either proposition so baldly stated. Yet views fairly close to the first position are not uncommon in international financial circles and among commercial creditor banks. The opposite extreme is more often implied than stated, perhaps mainly in political analyses that trace, ex post, the multiple factors leading to the downfall of a program. Clearly, leadership, tactics, and political configurations all are important. Leaders are far from free

[36] Stephan Haggard and Robert Kaufman, "The Politics of Stabilization and Structural Adjustment," in Jeffrey D. Sachs, ed., *Developing Country Debt and Economic Performance* (Chicago: University of Chicago, 1989), pp. 239–43 review various versions of electoral cycle theories with respect to stabilization.

agents, yet the case histories in chapters 3 through 7 demonstrate that imagination and skill have often succeeded against long odds.

The chapters also suggest that broad scope in adjustment programs is usually a product of a combination of committed leadership and a high degree of centralized control and authority. Concentrated authority directly facilitates implementation; it also heightens the credibility of programs, crucially shaping both political and economic responses. Such control and authority can result from military rule, or from civilian institutions that accord the chief executive dominant power, or from more transient circumstances such as overwhelming popular election and/or temporarily suspended or disabled opposition.

Turning from the scope to the content of adjustment programs, the balance of interests among the government's supporters obviously is likely to influence its adjustment choices. Governments depending mainly on labor and popular support are more likely to adopt heterodox programs; those relying on business and financial support to favor neoorthodox prescriptions.[37] It is widely assumed that organized labor is the most likely interest group to derail adjustment efforts, whether from within or outside the governing coalition. Haggard and Kaufman, reviewing recent research on this point, suggested a variant: unions pose the sharpest threat to stabilization not simply where they are strongest, but where they are moderately strong, lack secure access to decision makers, and are vulnerable to periodic repression.[38]

EXTERNAL AGENCIES

The extent of external finance and involvement in adjustment policy varied greatly among the governments and countries discussed in this study. Tables 1.4 and 1.5 provide data on concessional assistance and net capital flows. Net per capita concessional aid ranged from over a hundred U.S. dollars for some years in Costa Rica to pennies in Nigeria. Net capital flow is, in principle, a better indicator of external finance, because concessional aid is unimportant in several of our cases. But such flows are more complex to calculate and fluctuate sharply from year to year.

The intensity of external advice and guidance is still harder to gauge. However, high-conditionality (stand-by and extended fund facility) agreements with the IMF, and structural or sectoral adjustment loans with the World Bank inevitably entail considerable policy dialogue, advice, and some pressure. Table 1.6 lists such agreements with our thirteen countries, for the period 1980–1988. A few of our cases, including Jamaica, Costa Rica, and Ghana, received

---

[37] An alternate approach would distinguish between business and labor interests in tradable and nontradable sectors or subsectors and within the tradables category between export-oriented and import-substitution interests. That approach calls for more fine-grained data on patterns of support and opposition than are usually available.

[38] Haggard and Kaufman, "Politics of Stabilization," p. 226.

TABLE 1.4
Net Official Development Assistance (U.S. dollars per capita)

	1980	1981	1982	1983	1984	1985	1986
A. UMIC[a]	—	—	—	—	4.80	6.60	7.10
Argentina	.64	1.53	1.03	1.62	1.60	1.30	2.80
Mexico	.81	1.39	1.92	1.76	1.10	1.80	3.10
Brazil	.70	1.89	1.64	.78	1.20	0.90	1.30
B. LMIC[b]	—	—	—	—	15.00	14.60	14.50
Chile	(0.90)	(0.62)	(0.70)	0.0	0.20	3.30	(0.40)
Colombia	3.48	3.87	3.61	3.14	3.10	2.20	2.20
Peru	12.22	13.71	10.82	16.70	17.00	17.00	13.70
Costa Rica	28.52	23.47	33.25	102.02	86.00	107.70	76.50
Jamaica	65.86	73.95	84.59	83.76	77.60	76.00	74.70
Dominican Republic	21.94	18.00	22.93	16.84	32.40	34.60	16.10
Philippines	6.21	7.59	6.56	8.24	7.40	8.90	16.70
Nigeria	0.42	0.47	0.41	0.51	0.30	0.30	0.60
C. LIC[c]	—	—	—	—	14.20	16.20	19.60
Ghana	17.73	13.24	12.21	9.23	17.50	16.10	28.20
Zambia	56.31	39.70	52.41	34.67	37.10	49.10	66.80

Source: World Bank, *World Development Report 1986*, pp. 220–21; *1987*, pp. 244–45; *1988*, pp. 264–65.

[a] Weighted average for upper middle-income countries.

[b] Weighted average for lower middle-income countries.

[c] Weighted average for low-income countries excluding China and India.

detailed and continuous advice, pressure, and support from the Bretton Woods agencies and from the Agency for International Development in Jamaica and Costa Rica, for most of the decade. At the opposite pole, several governments held the IMF at arm's length or cut relations, and/or agreed to little or no policy-based lending from the World Bank.

How are these sharp contrasts in the extent of external financial support and involvement reflected in governments' adjustment decisions and actions? A good deal of past research focused on factors that determine the relative bargaining strength of debtor governments and external creditors as reflected in the amount, terms, and conditions of financing. The evidence through the mid-1980s supported the generalization that the largest debtors, broadly speaking, received more favorable rescheduling terms and conditions than smaller debtors. Some small countries, whose debts were large relative to their economies but small in the global picture, managed to extract favorable terms by exploiting geopolitical importance.[39] More recently, with continued negative flows

[39] Haggard and Kaufman, "Politics of Stabilization," pp. 211–13. See also Christine Bog-

TABLE 1.5
Net Long-term Capital Transfers

	Capital Transfers[a] as a Percentage of GNP						
	1980	1981	1982	1983	1984	1985	1986
Argentina	3.7	9.1	6.7	(1.3)	(4.2)	(1.2)	(3.3)
Brazil	(0.1)	1.2	0.4	(0.8)	0.6	2.6	2.6
Mexico	2.5	3.9	1.2	(4.0)	(5.1)	(5.6)	(4.8)
Chile	5.2	7.5	(0.6)	(0.8)	(1.2)	(3.9)	(4.9)
Colombia	1.7	3.2	2.3	2.5	3.5	4.4	4.4
Peru	(1.5)	(1.1)	3.1	4.3	(1.7)	(0.8)	(0.7)
Costa Rica	5.3	5.1	2.1	(4.8)	0.5	2.0	—
Jamaica	6.5	6.7	10.3	3.7	4.6	0.0	(6.1)
Dominican Republic	4.9	1.5	2.0	0.1	3.1	(0.1)	(1.4)
Philippines	2.0	2.2	1.6	2.6	0.2	0.2	(1.3)
Nigeria	0.2	3.0	3.3	4.1	(1.4)	(2.9)	(0.4)
Zambia[b]	12.3	12.0	4.2	6.0	9.7	9.3	—
Ghana	2.1	1.8	0.9	2.4	3.7	3.3	—

Sources: Net long-term transfers and GNP: World Bank, *World Debt Tables*, vol. 2 (Washington, D.C.: World Bank, 1987–1988), (cited hereafter as *World Debt Tables*). Direct investment and official capital grants: World Bank, *World Tables 1987*.

[a] Net long-term transfers plus direct investment plus official capital grants.

[b] Calculations exclude net transfers of private, nonguaranteed debt.

from many debtor nations, Mary Williamson and Richard Feinberg have argued that the main source of bargaining power for both debtors and creditors is no longer the size of the debt and the financing offered, but creditors' apparent willingness to provide positive flows.[40]

For this study, however, the key dependent variable is not relative bargaining power, but external impact on governments' economic decisions and implementation. This second set of issues has been much less explored for several reasons. The notion of influence is slippery. It must be defined in contrast with a counterfactual: in what ways have governments' choices and actions been altered from what would probably have occurred without external intervention? Moreover, the process of ongoing influence is much harder to observe than the process and especially the outcomes of negotiations.

danowitz-Bindert, "Small Debtors, Big Problems: The Quiet Crisis," Overseas Development Council *Policy Focus Series, 1985* no. 5 (Washington D.C., 1985); John Williamson, "IMF Conditionality in Small Countries" (Paper presented to the Conference on External Debt of Small Latin American Countries, San José, Costa Rica, 9–11 December 1985).

[40] Mary Williamson and Richard Feinberg, "Debt and Power in Latin America: The Net Transfer of Resources as a Determinant of Bargaining Power among Creditors and Debtors" (Paper prepared for the Sistema Económico Latinamericano (SELA), Caracas, Venezuela, 4–8 May 1987).

Nevertheless, it is widely assumed that external agencies powerfully influence the timing, scope, and content of adjustment decisions and action, particularly where they are providing high levels of finance relative to the recipient's economy. Sizable support increases a government's incentive to comply with creditors' advice and permits compensating "losers." Moreover, such support should facilitate broader economic improvements, which in turn stimulate domestic confidence and political support. However, where financing is partic-

TABLE 1.6

Policy-based Loans from the International Monetary Fund and the World Bank, 1979–1988

	IMF Standbys and Extended Fund Facilities			World Bank Structural and Sector Adjustment Loans	
Argentina	SBA	1/83– 4/84	(1/84)[a]	Agriculture	4/86
	SBA	12/84– 2/86		Trade Sector	5/87
	SBA	7/87– 9/88		Banking Sector	3/88
				Trade Policy	10/88
Brazil	EFF	3/83– 2/86		Agriculture & Exports	10/83
				Export Development	10/83
				Agriculture	6/86
Mexico	EFF	1/83–12/85		Export Development	6/83
	SBA	11/86– 4/88		Trade Policy	7/86
				Trade Sector	11/87
				Agriculture Sector	3/88
				Fertilizer	3/88
Chile	SBA	1/83– 1/85		SAL I	10/85
	EFF	8/85– 8/88		SAL II	11/86
				SAL III	12/87
Peru	EFF	6/82– 6/85	(5/84)[a]		
	SBA	4/84– 7/85	(4/85)[a]		
Colombia				Trade Sector	5/85
				Trade & Agriculture	4/86
				Power Sector	12/87
Costa Rica	EFF	6/81– 6/84	(12/82)[a]		
	SBA	12/82–12/83		Export Development	5/83
	SBA	3/85– 4/86		SAL I	4/85
	SBA	10/87– 3/89		SAL II	12/88
Jamaica	EFF	6/79– 6/81	(4/81)[a]	Export Development I	5/79
	EFF	4/81– 4/84		Export Development II	4/81
	SBA	3/87– 5/88		SAL I	3/82
	SBA	6/84– 6/85		SAL II	6/83
	SBA	7/85– 5/87	(7/86)[a]	Export Development III	6/83
	SBA	3/87– 5/88		SAL III	11/84
				Public Enterprises	6/87
				Trade & Finance	6/87
Dominican Republic	EFF	1/83– 1/86	(1/85)[a]		
	SBA	4/85– 4/86			

TABLE 1.6 (*cont.*)

	IMF Standbys and Extended Fund Facilities			World Bank Structural and Sector Adjustment Loans	
Philippines	EFF	4/76– 4/79		SAL I	9/80
	SBA	2/83– 2/84		SAL II	4/83
	SBA	12/84– 6/86	(6/86)[a]	Agriculture	9/84
	SBA	10/86– 8/88		Economic Recovery	3/87
				Public Enterprise Reform	6/88
Ghana	SBA	8/83– 8/84		Reconstruction	6/83
	SBA	8/84–12/85		Export Rehabilitation	1/84
	SBA	10/86–10/87		Reconstruction	3/85
	EFF + SAF[b]	11/87–11/90[c]		Industry	3/86
	ESAF	11/88–11/91		Education	12/86
				SAL	4/87
				Financial Sector	5/88
Nigeria	SBA	1/87– 1/88		Fertilizer	9/83
				Trade	10/86
				Trade and Investment Policy	12/88
Zambia	EFF	5/81– 5/84	(8/82)[a]	Export Rehabilitation	3/84
	SBA	4/83– 4/84		Agriculture	1/85
	SBA	7/84– 4/86	(2/86)[a]	Industry	10/85
	SBA	2/86– 2/88	(5/87)[a]	Recovery Credit	6/86

Sources: SBA (Stand-by Agreement) and EFF (Extended Fund Facility): International Monetary Fund, *Annual Reports, 1980–1988*. SAL (Structural Adjustment Loan) and Sector Loans: World Bank, *Annual Reports, 1980–1988*.
[a] Cancelled.
[b] Structural Adjustment Facility.
[c] Converted into an Extended Structural Adjustment Facility (ESAF).

ularly generous, it often reflects creditors' or donors' political or strategic motivations. These may undercut the use of financing to influence economic policy. Generous assistance may also relieve the sense of crisis among political leaders and politically important pressure groups, thereby perversely undermining commitment to adjustment.[41] It may well be that above some minimum level creditor influence varies with willingness to adjust funding in response to adjustment effort, rather than with an absolute level.

A BRIEF OVERVIEW

Responses to economic crises are shaped by a range of political pressures, but they are also strongly influenced by the intellectual lenses through which economic advisors and political leaders perceive the crisis and the available options. Miles Kahler's essay lays out the competing perspectives on stabiliza-

[41] Nelson, "Political Economy of Stabilization," pp. 1000–1001 discusses the "donors' dilemma." Haggard, "Politics of Adjustment"; and Haggard and Kaufman, "Politics of Stabilization," pp. 216–17 also discuss the "temptation" problem.

tion and longer-run growth strategies as these evolved and eventually, in part, converged over the past several decades.

Chapters 3 through 7, the case studies, share a common concern to trace the effects of the five sets of causal factors on adjustment choices and implementation. They also reflect the diversity of our cases; each raises its own themes and issues.

Democratic transitions and the heterodox shock experiments of the mid-1980s are at the heart of Kaufman's analysis of Argentina and Brazil. Despite the broad parallels between the two, contrasts in their political and economic situations produced important differences in design and implementation of the Cruzado and Austral programs. Kaufman's discussion together with Stallings' analysis of García's heterodox program in Peru suggests that such programs may generate political dynamics that militate against their success. Kaufman contrasts adjustment efforts in Argentina and Brazil with those of Mexico, which persistently pursued a strongly orthodox, broad-gauged adjustment program. Of particular interest is the way in which varying domestic business interests in the three countries affected choices about cooperation with the international financial community.

Stallings' examination of Chile, Peru, and Colombia highlights the extreme contrasts in the trio's adjustment responses. Chile, even more than Mexico, pursued a strongly orthodox strategy, with praise from private bankers and international agencies. Yet its economic success was purchased at a price in social suffering that few civilian governments could have tolerated. At the opposite end of the scale, Peru in 1985 attempted a far-reaching heterodox approach, including open confrontation with the international economic community. The economic collapse that followed, however, is probably traceable more to economic mismanagement than to the decision to cap debt payments.[42] Colombia, long characterized by political stability and conservative economic management, avoided severe economic difficulties and handled those that arose in a comparatively consensual and cautious manner. The causes of these contrasts are the central theme of Stallings' essay.

Like Colombia, Costa Rica, Jamaica, and the Dominican Republic are established democracies. They also share certain broad similarities of small scale and economic vulnerability. But their adjustment responses ranged from the Dominican Republic's brief, bitter, and isolated stabilization effort of 1984–1985 to Jamaica's substantial structural reforms over eight rocky years. Nelson traces these contrasts in adjustment effort scope to two main causes: contrasting earlier economic trends and their effects on interpretations of the 1980s' crises, and variation in the concentration of executive authority flowing from differences in political institutions and circumstances within the demo-

---

[42] See Peter Hakim and Richard Feinberg, "The Lessons from Chile and Peru," *Financial Times*, 30 November 1988, p. 21, for a capsule discussion of these points.

cratic framework. Costa Rica and Jamaica also received extraordinarily high levels of external assistance coupled with intense outside advice and pressure. Along with Zambia and Ghana, where external agencies were also deeply involved, their experience offers insights about the potential and the limits of external influence on adjustment in small nations.

The Philippines, like Brazil and Argentina, confronted both economic crisis and political transition in the 1980s. Haggard deals with both the Marcos government and the first eighteen months of Aquino's rule. The major theme under Marcos was the mounting, and ultimately crippling, effects of the crony network on which Marcos increasingly depended for political support. To the extent that structural change entailed dismantling that network, Aquino's government launched vigorous action. But other aspects of the reform agenda were constrained by Aquino's own dependence on business and military groups. Philippine experience in late 1986–1987, taken jointly with earlier chapters' discussions of Argentina, Brazil, and Peru, point towards both opportunities and constraints on adjustment choices inherent in the transition to democracy.

Zambia and Ghana pose dramatic contrasts in Callaghy's essay. By 1983, both had been in severe economic decline for at least a decade. In Ghana, the most recent of a series of electoral and nonelectoral changes in government plus the widespread perception that the country was in desperate straits paved the way for a far-reaching neoorthodox adjustment effort closely shepherded by the World Bank and the IMF. Zambia launched a program of stabilization and structural change in the same year and with similar guidance. But, as in the Philippines under Marcos, structural change threatened the very interests at the core of the long-established but eroding support for the government. The program sputtered, then foundered. Nigeria started its adjustment effort somewhat later and the outcome is unclear, though Nigeria's traditionally vociferous interest groups and the mounting pressures of a phased political liberalization pose formidable challenges. In all three countries, state capacity also emerges as a more crucial limitation than in the other cases discussed in the volume.

Chapter 8 seeks to pull together the diverse threads of all the cases. The chapter first examines the causes of divergent timing, scope, and content of adjustment choices among our cases and the reasons why those choices were pursued in some cases with dogged determination, elsewhere halfheartedly or not at all. The cases where broad reforms were adopted and substantially implemented are apparently diverse: Mexico and Chile are conservative military or semiauthoritarian systems; Rawlings' regime in Ghana was launched as a radical military coup; Aquino's first eighteen months represented a transitional democracy dependent on a center-right power base; Seaga's government was similarly based in an established democracy; García's Peru was most fairly described as a still-transitional democracy with strong populist support. Yet these cases share two core features: the widespread perception of the need for far-reaching reforms (resulting from a legacy of economic decline and political decay or acute challenge) and an executive empowered by some combination of established political institutions and more transient circumstances with an unusual concentration of authority. Contrasting cases of halfhearted reform, narrow stabilization efforts, or failure to attempt adjustment at all departed from this syndrome in varying degrees. The role of external agencies, while important to the details of particular cases, is less important than these essentially internal factors as a determinant of adjustment choices and action. The chapter also surveys the roles of major interest groups as political forces shaping adjustment. Two groups emerge as powerful actors: business interests and the state machinery itself. Organized labor and agricultural interests play much less important roles.

The debt crisis and its repercussions have raised an array of broader analytic and policy questions that chapter 8 touches lightly or not at all. Among these are the criteria and mechanisms for more equitable burden-sharing between North and South; the most effective modes and appropriate limits for international financial agencies' influence on countries' policy choices; the links between the crisis and the emergence of new or renewed democracies, and the tensions between continued adjustment and consolidation of democracy; the interplay between developing countries' domestic political and economic policies and their strategies vis-à-vis the international financial community; the constraints on adjustment posed by state capacity; and the relationship between the domestic equity and the political sustainability of adjustment efforts. The case material in this volume, we believe, offers provocative if partial evidence on many of these issues. We plan to use that evidence and supplement it from additional cases and sources to address these issues more directly in a later study.

CHAPTER TWO

Orthodoxy and Its Alternatives: Explaining Approaches to Stabilization and Adjustment

Miles Kahler

THE 1980s, a decade of economic crisis for many developing countries and slow growth for industrialized countries, is often portrayed as a decade in which the "supply" of economic ideas and policy prescriptions has been heavily tilted toward a resurgent orthodoxy. That supply shift, it is argued, has had a profound impact on economic outcomes in the industrialized economies—leading to fiscal and monetary stringency (often at the expense of high unemployment and lower growth), a shrinking of government involvement in the economy (marketization and privatization), and external liberalization, far clearer in capital movements than trade in goods and services. The orthodox consensus of the larger industrialized countries was also reflected in the policies pursued by developing countries, particularly after the onset of the debt crisis, when many developing countries undertook programs of adjustment supported by the International Monetary Fund (IMF) or the World Bank.

This reading of recent history points to two very different views of the importance of economic ideas in shaping policy. For many in the South, the triumph of orthodox prescriptions in the developing world is a simple result of power relations. The "new influentials" of the 1970s have lost their bargaining leverage in the dramatically different external circumstances of the 1980s. The developing countries have not been convinced by the failure of their previous strategies: the pressure of events and the economic weight of a unified industrial country bloc have cowed, but not converted them. Any apparent consensus on orthodox policy prescriptions in this view is a false consensus.

The second reading takes ideas seriously and views the shift in internationally accepted policy prescriptions as an example of social learning. The results of the alternatives to orthodoxy in the 1960s and 1970s had been disastrous; even socialist economies have become intrigued by market-oriented alternatives. In contrast to statist failures, economies pursuing policies applauded by the new orthodoxy, particularly those of East Asia, had succeeded. Orthodox ideas in practice produced economic success; even short-sighted political elites could not avoid that conclusion.

The author thanks Peter Hall, Albert Hirschman, David Finch, and the Mexico City and Washington workshop participants for their helpful comments on earlier drafts.

Both of these explanations are inadequate: power is involved, but in a much more subtle way than the bargaining model allows; an evolution in intellectual consensus is involved, but not in the way that some of the orthodox would have us believe. Each view is also more profoundly inaccurate: the orthodox view of stabilization and adjustment and the alternatives to it were never identified exclusively with North or South. Heterodoxy has always found important intellectual support in the North, and some of the most severe orthodox experiments were indigenous to the South. Nor is the outcome—portrayed as a triumph of orthodoxy—so clear-cut. Skeptics abound, and the mediocre economic performance of many developing countries in the 1980s has led to a resurgence of alternative approaches to adjustment that may produce a consensus less orthodox than that existing in the early 1980s.

This chapter maps the evolution of orthodox and alternative thinking on stabilization and adjustment during the postwar period, emphasizing the 1970s and 1980s. Simply describing the evolving "orthodoxy" and its rivals is a complicated task, but an effort will also be made to piece together an account of the production of the alternatives, North and South: in the universities, in international organizations, and in governments.[1]

The presence or absence of consensual knowledge may in its own right play a role, albeit a minor one, in the evolution of cooperative solutions internationally.[2] (This is particularly true if the social learning model holds.) The case studies completed for this project and other studies in the transmission of economic ideas suggest that such a technocratic view of policy formulation must be tempered by attention to politics. This discussion adds politics to the argument in two steps: first, by examining the political assumptions that are implicit in orthodox and heterodox prescriptions, and second, by suggesting the political circumstances in which these clusters of ideas have had influence over policy outcomes.

MONETARIST ORTHODOXY AND THE STRUCTURALIST ALTERNATIVE

While legend portrays the 1930s as a staging ground for alternatives to orthodox policies of laissez-faire and deflation in the face of international economic

---

[1] Many discussions of "ideas" or "knowledge" are vague in their definition of the study subject. Here I will be concerned with the evolution of models of economic reality (how the world works) and the prescriptions that flow from those models (what policy makers should do). I will largely sidestep the question of whether evolution of knowledge in the social sciences is best explained by an "internalist" (relying on the internal logic and argumentation of a discipline) or "externalist" (suggesting external social influences on scientific change) model.

[2] See Ernst Haas, "Is There a Hole in the Whole? Knowledge, Technology, Interdependence and the Construction of International Regimes," *International Organization* 29 (Summer 1975): 827–76; Stephan Haggard and Beth A. Simmons, "Theories of International Regimes," *International Organization* 41, 3 (Summer 1987): pp. 509–13; for examples where consensual knowledge has been employed by some to explain the evolution of international regimes.

crisis, the developing world of that time did not present a coherent intellectual alternative. The impact of the Great Depression differed from region to region, and, of course, much of the Third World lacked the sovereignty to institute policy experimentation because it was locked into colonial empires.[3] Even in Latin America, where the scope of policy experimentation was wide, innovations in economic policy were not influenced by a novel and coherent view of economic circumstances and strategy. As Diaz-Alejandro suggested, the move from orthodoxy "was not due to new theoretical insights, but to the pressure of circumstances," producing an "exhilarated creativity," but not one that embodied a new set of rules.[4] Innovation in the developing countries during the 1930s was an innovation of desperation rather than design.

Two particular contrasts with the 1980s are worth noting: a crisis in confidence and a turn to experimentation took place at the center in the 1930s as well, encouraging the burst of change in Latin America; financial links were severed early in most cases, with little reaction from the industrialized countries. In the 1980s, the center, despite a deep recession (followed by relatively speedy recovery), did not lose its intellectual confidence; and the center was far more activist in negotiating means to keep the Latin American and other developing economies within the rules of the game.

The "lessons" of the 1930s were embodied in doctrine only with a lag, as import-substituting industrialization and the structuralist arguments that underpinned it were defined as an economic strategy . The role of Raúl Prebisch and the Economic Commission for Latin America in propagating these ideas is an oft-told story. Only in the late 1950s and 1960s, however, did structuralism enter directly into controversies over stabilization.[5] In dealing with repeated balance-of-payments crises and persistent inflationary tendencies in the economies of the region, a structuralist position on inflation and adjustment was elaborated in opposition to the prescriptions of the International Monetary Fund. Those arguments, emphasizing supply-side rigidities and bottlenecks as sources of inflation in developing economies, would reappear in later debates with the advocates of orthodoxy. As Osvaldo Sunkel declared in 1957,

[3] Angus Maddison, *Two Crises: Latin America and Asia, 1929–38 and 1973–83* (Paris: Organization for Economic Cooperation and Development, 1985), pt. 3; on the differential impact of the Great Depression on Latin America and Asia, and particularly the highly orthodox policies imposed on such colonial territories as India and Indonesia.

[4] Carlos F. Diaz-Alejandro, "Latin America in the 1930s," in Rosemary Thorp, ed., *Latin America in the 1930s* (London: Macmillan, 1984), pp. 22, 49; ibid., 68, confirmation for the case of Chile; ibid., 238, for Mexico; Vittorio Corbo, "Problems, Development Theory and Strategies of Latin America" (World Bank discussion paper, report no. DRD190, September 1986), pp. 7-12.

[5] Albert Hirschman, "Ideologies of Economic Development," in *A Bias for Hope* (New Haven: Yale University Press, 1971), pp. 279–291; Corbo, "Problems, Development Theory, and Strategies," p. 20–21, for summaries.

the inelasticity of some productive sectors to adjust to changes in demand—or, in short, the lack of mobility of productive resources and the defective functioning of the price system—are chiefly responsible for structural inflationary disequilibria.[6]

While arguing that their monetarist opponents had misdiagnosed the roots of inflation, the original structuralists have been criticized in turn for offering yet another purely economic interpretation of inflation, sidestepping both concrete policy recommendations and the possible political underpinnings of the phenomena that they described. Ian Little, for example, argues that they were unwilling "to understand and admit that many of the inelasticities were caused by policy and by inflation itself."[7]

Although structuralist stabilization prescriptions were seldom clear-cut, the political and policy conclusions drawn from structuralist analysis were usually taken to imply greater state intervention to relieve supply bottlenecks. In later elaborations of structuralism, the foreign exchange constraint was also to be relieved by an increase in planning (which had arrived later in Latin America than in India and other developing countries) and through export expansion within schemes of regional economic integration.[8]

The orthodoxy assailed by the structuralists, symbolized by the conditionality of the International Monetary Fund, remains a part of the broadened orthodoxy of the 1980s. The policy "packages" endorsed by the Fund in the 1950s incorporated policies that would remain central to the Fund's perception of how to establish balance-of-payments equilbrium and stabilize the price level: reduction in the fiscal deficit, controls on domestic credit expansion and credit extended to the public sector, and establishment of a realistic exchange rate. During this period, the Fund emphasized the anti-inflationary elements of its mandate, and it directly confronted those in the developing countries who argued for higher rates of inflation as a necessary part of unbalanced growth. A final point of continuity was the Fund's emphasis on the internal sources of disequilbrium at a time when structuralists and others were pointing to declining terms of trade and other external sources of persistent deficits.

Although the Fund had developed a coherent analysis of developing country deficits, the origins of this early orthodoxy have been misconstrued. The Fund's analysis was not based on theories derived in the North and then applied indiscriminately to developing economies. Much of the key research at the International Monetary Fund was based on detailed studies of developing country experience after 1945. Both the absorption approach and the early

[6] Cited in H. W. Arndt, "The Origins of Structuralism," *World Development* 13, no. 2 (February 1985): p. 155. Mary Sutton, in Tony Killick, ed., *The IMF and Stabilisation: Developing Country Experiences* (London: Heinemann, 1984), pp. 20–24 gives a summary of structuralist arguments.

[7] Ian M.D. Little, *Economic Development* (New York: Basic Books, 1982), p. 81.

[8] Corbo, "Problems, Development Theory and Strategies," pp. 21–23.

monetary approach (Polak model) to the balance of payments owed their shape to experience with stabilization programs in Latin America.[9] Particularly important was the Fund's work with Latin American central banks, many of which were sympathetic to the Fund's approach. Mexico's devaluations (1948,1949, and 1954) served as a major building block in the construction of Fund theory. Although the Polak model and the monetary approach to the balance of payments became a standard part of the Fund's financial programming methodology, the Fund's analysis remained eclectic (within the limits described above).[10] Reliance on the monetary approach was driven by practical as well as intellectual considerations: statistics necessary for the design of such programs were available from the central banks, and the quantitative analysis required was not overly complex for a precomputer age. In emphasizing controls on domestic credit, the Fund employed an instrument already in use in many developing countries.[11] Reliance on a single model for all countries undertaking a Fund program—whether Guatemala or Great Britain—served to underpin Fund claims of uniformity of treatment.

The Fund did not engage its structuralist critics in this first debate over stabilization policy. As one participant recalled, the Fund designed its programs according to its own lights and did not attempt to proselytize; eventually, the intellectual turbulence dissipated. In failing to confront its structuralist critics, however, the Fund set a pattern that would persist. The first generation at the Fund, under Edward M. Bernstein, crafted a Fund approach to stabilization that was firmly accepted within the organization. With few links to outside specialists on the developing economies, however, the organization at times seemed impervious to alternative points of view.

This first confrontation between orthodoxy and an alternative view based in the developing countries should not be misconceived. The lines of intellectual debate were never clearly North versus South. Many of the key ideas of structuralism in its broadest sense—emphasizing market failure and "elasticity

[9] Interview with author, 26 June 1987; see Margaret Garritsen de Vries, *Balance of Payments Adjustment, 1945 to 1986* (Washington, D.C.: International Monetary Fund, 1987), pp. 9–30 for a detailed account of the evolution of Fund approaches to stabilization in this period; Mohsin S. Khan, Peter Montiel, and Nadeem U. Haque, *Adjustment with Growth: Relating the Analytical Approaches of the World Bank and the IMF* (Washington, D.C.: World Bank, 1986), pp. 7–21 for a recent exposition of the Polak model; idem, ibid., p. 45 also emphasize the "large gap between the formal models and the actual policy packages that are implemented by the Bank and the Fund."

[10] The limits of the Fund's eclecticism is clearly a function of one's view of the "mainstream" according to heterodox critics. In support of the view given here, see John Williamson, *The Lending Policies of the International Monetary Fund* (Washington, D.C. : Institute for International Economics, 1982), p. 53.

[11] Rudolf R. Rhomberg and H. Robert Heller, "Introductory Survey," in International Monetary Fund, *The Monetary Approach to the Balance of Payments* (Washington, D.C.: International Monetary Fund, 1977), pp. 6–7.

pessimism''—were found in Europe after World War II. The first generation of development economists often shared these views, and most of those economists were not from the South.[12] Nor was the structuralist view dominant within the developing world. As Little described, India, for all its emphasis on planning, stood outside the debate. East and Southeast Asia, from the Dodge Plan in Japan to the Indonesian stabilization of the 1960s, were far more receptive to orthodox stabilization advice from international organizations and the United States. Africa in the 1960s had recently achieved independence and had not yet found a regional voice in economic affairs. (The contrast between the Economic Commission for Latin America (ECLA) and the Economic Commission for Africa, headed by Robert Gardiner, was stark.)[13]

Even within Latin America, the structuralist perspective was not uncontested. Hirschman noted two foci of opposition: the business community and certain economists, such as the Brazilian, Roberto Campos.[14] Some countries in the region continued to pursue export-oriented development patterns after World War II, and by the 1960s, some that had accepted the prescriptions of import-substituting industrialization were embarked on programs of economic stabilization and liberalization: Chile under Frei (1964–1970), Colombia after 1967.[15] Finally, the apparent coherence of arguments concerning economic strategy and stabilization should not lead to an exaggeration of the coherence or power of economic ideas. Development strategies informed by structuralism and import substitution were compatible with macroeconomic policies that combined an orthodox fiscal and monetary stance with a fixed exchange rate. (Mexico is the best example.) ECLA and its ideas should not be blamed (or praised) for industrialization behind a protective carapace that often owed more to wartime experience and to recurrent balance-of-payments crises than to an intellectual strategy.[16] Structuralist ideas on stabilization and adjustment were handy for elites that saw the political risks in stabilization. Their skepticism about orthodox prescriptions often had political rather than theoretical origins.

The structuralist-monetarist debate faded in the 1960s in part because the industrialized countries conceded some developing country arguments about the sources of deficits. The IMF's Compensatory Financing Facility—backed

[12] On Northern influences in structuralism, see Arndt, ''Origins of Structuralism,'' pp. 150–55.

[13] Isebill V. Gruhn, ''The Economic Commission for Africa,'' in Domenico Mazzeo, ed., *African Regional Organizations* (Cambridge: Cambridge University Press, 1984), pp. 34–37.

[14] Hirschman, ''Ideologies of Economic Development,'' pp. 291–97.

[15] Corbo, ''Problems, Development theory and Strategies,'' pp. 28–29; see Sutton in Killick, ed., *IMF and Stabilisation*, pp. 24–29, for a discussion of the Frei episode that was also influenced by structuralist analysis.

[16] Even Little concedes that controls were instituted for other reasons, producing a pattern of protection that was ''haphazard, unrelated to any economic rationale for protection, and certainly excessive'' (Little, *Economic Development*, p. 72).

by the United States and designed by the IMF staff—was a symbol of new attention to the particular problems of the developing countries. A more significant reason for less vocal developing country discontent was the generally buoyant conditions of world trade in the last decade of the postwar boom from 1963 to 1973. By the early 1970s, the number of stand-by arrangements requested by developing members had declined, and most of the arrangements entailed low conditionality.[17]

The original monetarist-structuralist debate reflected two trends that would intensify after 1960. The debate depended on a new institutionalization of economic policy advice in the United Nations system, in the Bretton Woods organizations, and in countless aid agencies and development research institutes. Institutionalization at first produced regional divisions and differences in policy prescriptions. But institutionalization preceded a second feature that would erode such divisions: the internationalization of training and policy advice, which would eventually reduce intellectual divergence between center and periphery. The growing number of Latin American and Asian economists trained in the United States and Europe was a precursor of intellectual internationalization.

The most significant substantive effects of the structuralist-monetarist debate were a broadening of the context of stabilization policies and a deepening of the diagnosis of inflation in developing economies. The structuralists linked questions of stabilization and adjustment to broader questions of economic strategy. Stabilization was not narrowly conceived as the simple manipulation of a few policy instruments; to do so would risk stunting economic development. Balance-of-payments crises were seen as a predictable feature of economic development and one rooted in the rigidities of developing societies. In the hands of the structuralists, this linkage pointed to an intensification of government intervention to ease bottlenecks by supply-side action. The outcome of the structuralist debate suggested deep-seated social and political—rather than purely economic—explanations for the inflationary bias in Latin American economies. Such sociological, "tug-of-war," theories of inflation had been an early target of the structuralists. By the early 1970s, however, the spiraling competition of groups and classes for economic shares seemed a convincing explanation of the resilience of inflation in Latin America.[18]

With the resumption of orthodox and neoclassical interest in developing economies, these structuralist assumptions were picked up by a reviving orthodoxy and stood on their heads: stabilization and adjustment policies were linked to a shift in economic strategy through broadening orthodoxy to encompass trade policy, public sector reform, and deregulation. The new orthodoxy

---

[17] De Vries, *Balance of Payments Adjustment*, pp. 112–13.

[18] See Arndt, "Origins of Structuralism," p. 156 on the importance of the "spiral mechanism"; Albert Hirschman, "The Social and Political Matrix of Inflation," in *Essays in Trespassing* (Cambridge: Cambridge University Press, 1981), pp. 183–85, on the tug-of-war thesis.

would accept that the source of economic ills lay deeper than had been implied by the old orthodoxy. For the neoorthodox, however, bottlenecks or social impasses that produced inflation and balance-of-payments crises would be alleviated, not by additional government intervention but by radically reducing the role of government. As Hirschman noted,

> Whereas the Latin American economists who had first advanced the structuralist thesis were in general identified with the Left, it now appears that structuralist theorizing is a game at which all kinds of believers in the need for "fundamental" reform and change can and do play. The more persistent and intractable the inflation, the more likely are all of these parties to come forward with their favorite "deep" diagnosis and cure.[19]

THE BROADENING OF ORTHODOXY: FROM STABILIZATION TO STRUCTURAL ADJUSTMENT

By the late 1960s, structuralism seemed to be in retreat intellectually, a retreat that would be reinforced by the apparent failure of economic policies in Chile (1970–1973) and Peru (1968–1975) that were influenced by structuralist analysis.[20] Among mainstream economists in the North, a renewed interest in trade regimes and the significance of trade liberalization in spurring growth produced a series of studies that were highly critical of the import substitution model.[21] This consensus, which was to become a firm part of the new orthodoxy, held that outward orientation—trade and exchange rate policies that were not biased against exports—was likely to ensure more successful adjustment to external shocks and a higher rate of economic growth.[22]

A second element in the creation of the new orthodoxy—overlapping the first concern over liberalized trade and payments regimes—was renewed in-

[19] Hirschman, "Social and Political Matrix," pp. 181–82.

[20] See Sutton in Killick, ed., *IMF and Stabilisation*, p. 41; this judgment is shared by those who are not orthodox in their inclinations.

[21] Major studies that appeared in the 1970s were Ian M. D. Little, Tibor Scitovsky, and Maurice Scott, *Industry and Trade in Some Developing Countries* (London: Oxford University Press, 1970); National Bureau of Economic Research, *Foreign Trade Regimes and Economic Development* a special conference series (New York, 1974, 1975, 1976); see Anne O. Krueger, *Liberalization Attempts and Consequences* (New York: National Bureau of Economic Research, 1978); and Jagdish N. Bhagwati, *Anatomy and Consequences of Exchange Control* (Cambridge: Ballinger Publishing Company, 1978) for summaries of the findings in the preceding series. Bela Balassa and associates, *The Structure of Protection in Developing Countries* (Baltimore: Johns Hopkins University Press, 1971). Max Corden, *Trade Policy and Economic Welfare* (Oxford: Clarendon Press, 1974) was an influential treatise critical of protectionist arguments.

[22] See Jagdish Bhagwati, "Outward Orientation: Trade Issues," in Vittorio Corbo, Morris Goldstein, and Mohsin Khan, eds., *Growth-Oriented Adjustment Programs* (Washington, D.C.: International Monetary Fund and World Bank, 1987), pp. 257–90, for a recent succinct defense of outward orientation.

terest in government policy and its economic effects. The prevalence of protectionist trade regimes and other market-inhibiting devices had to be explained. Economic rationality appeared absent, but a political rationale could perhaps be discovered. For many economists, that rationale was found in the burgeoning public choice literature, which suggested an inevitable tendency on the part of the public sector to expand, and in the concept of rent-seeking and directly unproductive profit-seeking (DUP). One of the additional charges levied against an import-substituting trade regime, with its weight of exchange and trade restrictions, was precisely that this type of regime would engender such inefficient activities.

Finally, the growing attraction of monetarism in the industrialized countries during the 1970s reinforced the turn against expansionary demand management and focused attention on the costs that persistent high levels of inflation imposed on an economy. The rise of monetarism coupled with the end of fixed parities under the Bretton Woods monetary regime also reinforced the role of exchange rate measures (typically devaluation) within adjustment programs.[23]

Each of these elements—external liberalization, a reduced role for the state, and disinflation—clashed not only with structuralist argumentation, but also with elite preferences in many developing countries. In one respect, the new orthodoxy that took shape in the 1970s accepted structuralist arguments. The links between stabilization (the short-term), structural adjustment (the medium-term) and economic strategy (the long-term) were tightened. The scale of the external shocks that the developing countries suffered in the 1970s and 1980s convinced even mainstream development economists that all had to be considered concomitantly. Hollis Chenery declared that

> The conventional separation between stabilization and development, or short-term and long-term policies, has become increasingly inappropriate to the international economic problems of this decade, in which the adjustment policies of individual countries must be assessed over periods of five to ten years and are heavily dependent on actions by other countries.[24]

A second assumption of the emerging new orthodoxy was less congenial for structuralism and development economics. Hirschman labeled this assumption monoeconomics, "rejection of . . . the view that underdeveloped countries as a group are set apart, through a number of specific economic characteristics

---

[23] Within both the orthodox and heterodox camps, exchange rate management has been a point of division; the later phases of the Southern Cone programs described below used preannounced exchange rates as an anti-inflation instrument. Among those endorsing alternative approaches to adjustment, some (John Williamson) take a position on devaluation that is much closer to orthodoxy than others (such as Lance Taylor).

[24] Hollis Chenery, "Comments," in William R. Cline and Sidney Weintraub, editors, *Economic Stabilization in Developing Countries* (Washington, D. C.: Brookings Institution, 1981), p. 115.

common to them, from the advanced industrial countries and that traditional economic analysis . . . must therefore be recast in significant respects when dealing with underdeveloped countries.''[25] The resurgent neoclassical view asserted that only one economics applied to both developed and industrialized countries.

During the 1970s, the emerging, broadened orthodoxy began to find its way into the international development institutions—not the United Nations system, which, by and large, remained hostile—but the World Bank and the International Monetary Fund. These institutions found themselves in a curious position, facing both the demands of developing countries that reflected past structuralist criticisms and the broadening neoclassical orthodoxy of intellectual (and increasingly governmental) circles in the industrialized countries.

The Fund and the Bank at first attempted to square the circle by responding to the "structural" demands of each side. The extended fund facility (EFF) in the IMF, for example, was regarded as a concession to the developing countries, offering a longer period of Fund support (and a longer term of adjustment) for programs attacking structural shortcomings. In the decision establishing the EFF, two types were mentioned, one focused on structural maladjustment, the second on a weak balance of payments that prevents pursuit of a development program. The second was clearly of greatest interest to the developing countries, but the EFF as implemented reflected far more the new "structuralism" of the industrialized countries: structural adjustment with widened conditionality, often affecting a broader range of policies than traditional Fund programs.

The EFF reflected greater IMF emphasis on "supply side" elements in the conditionality of its programs: once again, an emphasis (even a terminology) that could strike chords among structuralists. The types of measures that were included, however, reflected the new orthodoxy: particularly trade liberalization, public sector pricing and subsidies, and policies affecting interest rates and the exchange rate.[26] By the late 1970s the composition of Fund programs—whether stand-bys or EFFs—reflected the broadening of orthodoxy. In 1980, for example, over half the stand-by arrangements included public enterprise rationalization and a quarter included trade liberalization measures. The proportion of structural elements in EFFs tended to be higher.[27]

Structural adjustment lending by the World Bank also reflected the new orthodoxy and represented an even more dramatic departure for that institution than the new emphasis in Fund conditionality. If the Fund moved toward more microeconomic considerations, the Bank's SALs emphasized policy-based

---

[25] Albert Hirschman, "The Rise and Decline of Development Economics," in *Essays in Trespassing* (Cambridge: Cambridge University Press, 1981), p. 3.

[26] Manuel Guitian, *Fund Conditionality* (Washington, D.C.: International Monetary Fund, 1981), pp. 26–27.

[27] Morris Goldstein, *The Global Effects of Fund-Supported Adjustment Programs* (Washington, D.C.: International Monetary Fund, 1986), tab. 5, p. 9.

lending on an unprecedented scale. Structural adjustment lending reflected an awareness that government policy could influence growth in the developing countries, a key element in the emerging consensus. At first, structural adjustment loans were justified by external shocks that beset the developing countries after 1979, but gradually "inappropriate domestic policies" were added as bars to better economic performance.[28] Such emphasis on policy change involved the Bank in conditionality and bargaining with governments that came to resemble the experience of the Fund, with the same mixed results.

The two "structuralisms," the old structuralism of the developing countries and the new neoorthodox structuralism of the industrialized countries, could be bridged during the 1970s because of the ready availability of finance for most developing countries, either from the burgeoning Euromarkets (for middle-income countries) or the special facilities established by the Bretton Woods institutions. The implicit bargain was one between a broadened conditionality desired by the industrialized countries and the developing country goal of a lengthier period of adjustment with greater commitment of external resources. With the onset of the debt crisis in the 1980s, however, the new orthodoxy and its definition of structural adjustment seemed firmly in command as levels of external finance dropped precipitously and the period of adjustment was shortened: adjustment would of necessity be relatively rapid and according to market-oriented prescriptions.[29] The apparent dominance of this international program was due in large measure to the preferences of the G-5 governments, which, apart from France, endorsed the prescriptions being offered and were in the course of implementing them in their own countries (with certain glaring exceptions, such as the fiscal stance of the United States). The new orthodoxy seemed secure, then, by the early 1980s, not only among economists, but in G-5 government attitudes and in the major international lending institutions. John Lewis captured key elements of the new policy paradigm in the United States:

> The kind of adjustment now being favored goes beyond austere demand management. The mood is to press for greater efficiency—to give precedence to optimal uses of scarce resources—throughout the economic system. . . . Their "orthodoxy" is, as to economics, neoclassical. It carries forward with redoubled vigor the liberalizing, pro-market strains of the thinking of the 1960s and 1970s. It is very mindful of the limits of governments. It is emphatic in advocating export-oriented growth to virtually all comers. And it places heavier-than-ever reliance on policy dialoguing, especially between aid donors and recipients.[30]

[28] Elliot Berg and Alan Batchelder, "Structural Adjustment Lending: A Critical View" World Bank CPD discussion paper no. 1985–21 (January 1985), pp. 9–11.

[29] Williamson, *Lending Policies*, pp. 44–49, for the documentation of tougher conditionality in programs after mid-1981.

[30] John Lewis, in John Lewis and Valeriana Kallab, editors, *Development Strategies Reconsidered* (New Brunswick, N.J.: Transaction Books, 1985), p. 9.

CHINKS IN THE ARMOR OF ORTHODOXY: ASIAN NICS AND
THE SOUTHERN CONE

The 1980s, which seemed to witness the triumph of orthodoxy, also produced
new grounds for skepticism. The overarching grounds for skepticism were
those that challenged the hold of import-substitution twenty years before: economic performance. Whether measured as growth in Gross Domestic Product (GDP) or in GDP per capita, the 1980s were a lost decade for many developing countries.[31] One prevalent explanation for relatively poor performance
was the international environment, and at least one element of that environment—protectionism in the industrialized countries—did elicit condemnations
from the proponents of orthodoxy. Two other external explanations, however,
posed greater problems. Low industrial country growth brought calls for reflation from the developing countries, but, particularly in Western Europe, the
new policy consensus replied that higher growth without renewed inflation
was impossible. The rapid dropping off in external finance and, in many cases,
a net capital outflow was explained by the need for further adjustment; adjustment, it was predicted, would bring renewed commercial bank lending and
flows of foreign direct investment. Neither, by the mid-1980s, had material-
ized in substantial quantities.

Increased dependence on an uncertain international economic environment,
one in which markets might be closed or growing very slowly, was a further
source of skepticism concerning the new orthodoxy. Its proponents replied
that those countries following the new policy prescriptions performed better,
even in mediocre international conditions. Such arguments in favor of outward
orientation and liberalization opened new chinks, however, because two
groups of developing countries were difficult to explain by the new orthodox
canons. One set of economic successes—the East Asian exporters of manufactures—were often portrayed as prime exemplars of orthodox prescriptions,
but closer scrutiny demonstrated that their pattern of policy hardly fitted the
neoclassical mold. Although their exchange rate policies were not biased
against exports and fiscal and monetary policy was prudent, these dynamic
exporters displayed high levels of protection in their import-competing industries, substantial public sectors, and interventionist governments.[32]

[31] On these measures, in World Bank classifications, only low-income Asian countries performed better in 1980–1985 than in the preceding two decades. And that group, particularly in
South Asia, was hardly representative of orthodox policy prescriptions.

[32] See Jeffrey D. Sachs, "External Debt and Macroeconomic Performance in Latin America
and East Asia," *Brookings Papers on Economic Activity* 2 (1985): 523–73, for an economist's
treatment of these issues; idem, "Trade and Exchange Rate Policies in Growth-Oriented Adjustment Programs," in Vittorio Corbo, Morris Goldstein, and Mohsin Khan, eds., *Growth-Oriented
Adjustment Programs* (Washington, D.C.: International Monetary Fund and World Bank, 1987),
pp. 291–325.

A source of even greater unease was a set of countries that was not anomalous successes, but apparent failures: the Southern Cone economies (Chile, Argentina, Uruguay) that had enacted liberalization experiments in the late 1970s and suffered economic collapse in the early 1980s. For orthodox economists, these cases have become objects of endless scrutiny and debate. Chile, which came closest to pursuing orthodox prescriptions from 1973 to 1981, has been subjected to microscopic analysis: how could a country that moved so quickly in the orthodox direction—"the purest example of a comprehensive economic liberalization in the Third World"[33]—suffer the sort of economic collapse that Chile experienced in 1981–1982?

Given the significance that the orthodox have given to these cases, evaluations have typically varied according to initial sympathies.[34] Even the criteria of judgment are not uniform: those sympathetic to orthodox prescriptions generally omit any consideration of income distribution or concentration of wealth. Although the lessons of the Southern Cone are still being assimilated, tentative assessments point to some significant revision of the broadened orthodoxy that was endorsed in the 1970s and 1980s. First, although the three regimes did share a similar commitment to the neoorthodox agenda, their experiences highlight variation within orthodox experience (as John Toye has suggested).[35] Chile was by far the most thoroughgoing in its implementation of the orthodox program; Uruguay and Argentina delayed trade liberalization and maintained levels of public investment in the first phase of the program.[36] Initial "old" orthodox adjustment measures (devaluation, cutting the fiscal deficit, control of the money supply) did have a rapid impact on the balance

[33] Ronald McKinnon, "Comments," in Cline and Weintraub, eds., *Economic Stabilization*, p. 146.

[34] Carlos F. Diaz-Alejandro, "Southern Cone Stabilization Plans," in Cline and Weintraub, eds., *Economic Stabilization*, pp. 119–48; Guillermo Calvo, "Fractured Liberalism: Argentina under Martinez de Hoz," *Economic Development and Cultural Change*, (*EDCC*) 35 (April 1986): 511–33; Vittorio Corbo and Jaime de Melo, "Lessons from the Southern Cone Policy Reforms," *The World Bank Research Observer* 2 (July 1987): 111–42; Vittorio Corbo, Jaime de Melo, and James Tybout, "What Went Wrong with the Recent Reforms in the Southern Cone," Economic Development and Cultural Change *EDCC* 35 (April 1986): 607–40; Sebastian Edwards, "Monetarism in Chile, 1973–1983: Some Economic Puzzles," Economic Development and Cultural Change *EDCC*, 35 (April 1986): 535–60; Alejandro Foxley, *Latin American Experiments in Neoconservative Economics* (Berkeley: University of California Press, 1983); Nicolas Ardito Barletta, Mario I. Blejer, and Luis Landau, eds., *Economic Liberalization and Stabilization Policies in Argentina, Chile, and Uruguay* (Washington, D.C.: World Bank, 1983); Joseph Ramos, *Neoconservative Economics in the Southern Cone of Latin America, 1973–1983* (Baltimore: Johns Hopkins University Press, 1986); Sebastian Edwards and Alejandra Cox Edwards, *Monetarism and Liberalization: The Chilean Experiment* (Cambridge: Ballinger, 1987), among the vast outpouring of analysis on these cases.

[35] John Toye, "Varieties of Stabilisation Experience: A Comment," mimeographed (Institute of Development Studies, University of Sussex, Brighton, England, 1987).

[36] Ramos, *Neoconservative Economics*, chaps. 2–4.

of payments when they were implemented; in Chile, nontraditional exports showed dramatic growth. Success in achieving external balance, however, was matched by failure in reducing unemployment, which remained highest in Chile (above the historic maximum) and very low in Argentina (which made the least progress in reducing its fiscal deficit). Uruguay displayed the most positive record in productivity improvement and growth. Another indicator, inflation, was far more intractable: in part, because Argentina and Uruguay did not pursue the first phase of stabilization energetically enough (particularly reduction of the fiscal deficit); in part, because of the inertial character of inflation (wage indexation in Chile), a feature that would impress proponents of heterodox shock policies in the 1980s.

The resilience of inflation pushed political elites in these countries toward a second phase of experimentation: using preannounced exchange rate changes as a means of controlling inflation. This latter, global monetarist phase is far more controversial, and the reasons for its ultimate collapse, at least in Chile, are still debated. Some focus on this exchange rate innovation as the principal "macroeconomic disturbance" that led, given the slow convergence of domestic inflation levels with the international level, to an appreciation in the exchange rate, a widening current account deficit, and final collapse when external capital flows that had covered the deficit reversed in 1981–1982. Others point to liberalization of the capital account as equally important, arguing that exchange rate appreciation began with liberalization and consequent capital inflows; wage indexation (in Chile) was a second key inconsistency that prevented planned adjustment along global monetarist lines.[37]

Orthodox analysts of the Southern Cone experiments do not award external shocks a very large role in the collapse of 1981–1982. Policy mistakes are given pride of place, and it is policy errors associated with the broadened new orthodoxy that are emphasized. The old orthodoxy of fiscal and monetary restraint coupled with devaluation was, in their eyes, successful in improving external balance. Edwards even compares Chilean policy with the recommendations of the Klein-Saks mission in 1955, arguing that if the Chilean military had implemented the recommendations of the "old" monetarists of the 1950s—reducing indexation and maintaining a flexible exchange rate—the economy would not have risked collapse. While internal marketization of these highly controlled economies is regarded as successful, the timing of capital account liberalization and excessive deregulation in the financial sector are questioned. Indeed, the benefits of financial liberalization are hard to enumerate: domestic savings and investment did not increase in Chile throughout the period in question. In contrast, trade liberalization, to the degree that it was

[37] Edwards and Calvo emphasize capital account liberalization; Corbo focuses on the change in exchange rate policy. Uruguay liberalized the capital account early on, but did not witness exchange rate appreciation until the new exchange rate policy was introduced.

implemented, is widely regarded as successful, even by those who are skeptical of orthodox arguments. Ramos, for example, does not assign much weight to tariff liberalization in explaining Chile's decline in industrial production or loss of competitiveness. The Southern Cone experiences have thus produced a new orthodox consensus that the sequencing of liberalization is significant: trade liberalization should in general precede liberalization of the capital account.[38] They have also influenced a renewed belief by some in the need to separate stabilization and broader measures of liberalization, a reversal of "structuralist" assumptions in the new orthodoxy.

The Southern Cone experiments have received a remarkable degree of attention because of the risk that their collapse will call into question the entire orthodox agenda. A final threat to that agenda in the 1980s arose from the role played by the Bretton Woods institutions. Uneasy collaboration between the Bank and the Fund raised the question of whether the two institutions comprehended adjustment in the same way. To some observers, the Fund seemed ill-equipped to deal with policy changes that ranged beyond its traditional demand management and exchange rate policies. In an effort to impose conditions that ensured significant change in a broad range of economic policies, the policy conditionality associated with World Bank structural adjustment loans had, in the eyes of some, become so broad as to be unmeasurable.[39] Indeed, the difficulties that the IMF and the World Bank have had in their policy dialogues with governments raises a core dilemma of implementation for the broadened orthodox approach, what might be called the orthodox paradox: how does one convince governments to change policies that are economically damaging or irrational but politically rational? Since state policy and political preferences produce many of the economic distortions under attack, the orthodox approach has been unable to produce a strong "theory of reform."[40]

All of these weaknesses within orthodoxy, however, return to the key criterion of growth. Here, once again, change in a key G-5 government, the United States, has revived debate and lent credibility to critics of the new orthodoxy. With announcement of the Baker Plan in October 1985, the American government publicly endorsed "adjustment with growth," signaling that positive results should be expected sooner rather than in the very long run. Despite this American rhetorical pivot, the concept of "adjustment with growth," like "structuralism," could be filled with very different meanings. In the context of the Baker Plan, it appeared to be a renewal and extension of the bargain—stringent adjustment for a modest amount of financing—that had been established at the beginning of the debt crisis. All that was added was

---

[38] See, for example, Sebastian Edwards, *The Order of Liberalization of the External Sector in Developing Countries*, Princeton University, International Finance Section, Essays in International Finance (Princeton, N.J., 1984).

[39] Berg and Batchelder, "Structural Adjustment Lending," pp. 33–46.

[40] *Ibid.*, pp. 22–32.

hope that growth would result. For others, however, adjustment with growth became a convenient opening for a more profound questioning of the orthodox prescriptions.

ALTERNATIVES TO THE NEW ORTHODOXY: CHIPPING AT THE MARGINS

If the dominant orthodoxy has often erected a monolithic facade over diverse country experiences, heterodoxy in the 1980s has not disguised its fragmentation. Full-blown, old-style structuralist arguments no longer unite either academic critics or developing country governments. Instead, one can detect three clusters of critics, united in their skepticism concerning orthodox prescriptions for stabilization and adjustment in the developing countries. Their work has often been supported by the United Nations system, which was more attuned than the Bretton Woods institutions to the concerns of developing countries ... the 1980s. Their degree of disagreement with orthodox analysis and prescriptions varies, as does the coherence of the economic programs that they endorse.

The first group are the neostructuralists, such as Lance Taylor, whose arguments have recently been placed beside orthodox claims in a set of country studies sponsored by the World Institute for Development Economics Research.[41] The aim of Taylor and his team of country specialists is to present an alternative to orthodox stabilization programs in the interest of goals other than simply achieving sustainable external balance: goals such as economic growth, a more desirable distribution of income, and self-reliance. The neostructuralist aim is not simply to reassert a broader array of legitimate policy goals, however; neostructuralism also claims to present a different model of how developing economies work from which its policy prescriptions can be derived. Those claims should not be overstated. Perhaps the strongest empirical assertion made by Taylor is to reassert (against orthodox monoeconomics) that developing economies *are* structurally different as a group and that each developing economy deserves independent analysis of its economic and institutional parameters. Neostructuralism is not willing to go far beyond that claim of specificity. Taylor admits that orthodox analysis and prescriptions may fit some developing economies, particularly those with economies characterized by flex prices, an orthodox assumption that neostructuralists treat as a hypothesis. As he noted in an earlier volume:

> the structuralist view emphasizes complexity and the need for wisdom and receptiveness to how the economy at hand seems to work. A structuralist stabilization package would no doubt include many of the [orthodox] policies listed . . . Not many others are known. But it would not apply them all in the usual directions, and

[41] Lance Taylor, *Varieties of Stabilization Experience: Toward Sensible Macroeconomics in the Third World* (Manuscript, Massachusetts Institute of Technology, July 1987)

would also incorporate distributional considerations and nomarket interventions explicitly.[42]

If specific prescriptions are examined, the neostructuralist program is particularly skeptical of certain elements of orthodox adjustment policies. The contractionary and inflationary consequences of devaluation are emphasized; the ability of devaluation to improve performance in the tradable goods sector without prior intervention or a well-established industrial base is regarded as unlikely. The anti-inflationary effects of trade liberalization are estimated as overrated in Bretton Woods orthodoxy; neostructuralism claims that direct controls (import quotas and export subsidies) often produce positive effects. Financial liberalization may also have unforeseen negative effects, inflationary (through higher interest rates) and destabilizing. In sum, the WIDER analysis suggests that orthodox policies may have perverse (lowering growth, increasing inflation) effects in *some* cases.[43]

Many of these arguments are well within the mainstream (the contractionary effects of devaluation, for example). The disagreement between neostructuralism and orthodoxy seems to reduce to how prevalent structuralist conditions are in developing countries (*when* structuralist analysis is more accurate than orthodox analysis) and whether those conditions point toward liberalization to increase flex price behavior or accommodation in the form of direct state action. Critics could well argue, however, that neostructuralism offers a useful critique of orthodoxy, but does not present a full-fledged alternative to the policies of the Fund and the World Bank.[44] In addition, though Taylor contests this, neostructuralist programs would require considerably more financing to achieve adjustment than the standard IMF recipe. Critics allege that it is the additional financing that supplies the growth, not novel policies.

Heterodox shock programs of stabilization in Israel, Argentina, and Brazil, claimed as intellectual descendants by neostructuralism, represent a second alternative to orthodoxy. Their neostructuralist lineage is based on an analysis of inertial inflation that suggested the usefulness of incomes policies (direct wage and price controls) as a means of breaking inflationary expectations with relatively low cost for economic growth. In Brazil, income redistribution toward wage earners was a part of the initial package, a striking contrast to many orthodox efforts to lower inflation.[45]

---

[42] Lance Taylor, *Structuralist Macroeconomics* (New York: Basic Books, 1983), p. 202.

[43] This summary is drawn from Taylor, *Varieties of Stabilization Experience*, pp. 154–61.

[44] See, for example, Gerald K. Helleiner, editor, *Africa and the International Monetary Fund*, (Washington, D.C.: International Monetary Fund, 1986), p. 251, for the comments of John Williamson on John Loxley's proposals.

[45] Useful summaries are given in Stanley Fischer, "The Israeli Stabilization Program, 1985–86," *American Economic Review* 77, no. 2 (May 1987): 275–78; Daniel Heymann, "The Austral Plan," *American Economic Review* 77, no. 2 (May 1987): 284–87; Eliana A. Cardoso and Rudiger Dornbusch, "Brazil's Tropical Plan," *American Economic Review* 77, no. 2 (May 1987):

In fact, these programs were narrow in scope—aimed at very high levels of inflation—and less heterodox than they appear at first glance. The key political constraint in all three cases was the absolute necessity to avoid a recession (defined as an increase in unemployment). The programs instituted wage-price freezes with partial or total deindexation and currency reform, but also orthodox measures such as a devaluation and substantial budget cuts. In examining the course of the programs since 1985–1986, the old orthodox standby, controlling the fiscal deficit, appears as a central element in determining success or failure. However, these programs have been incapable of moving beyond disinflation toward broader measures of structural change in their economies. In many respects, they resemble the old orthodoxy in their limited ends and in many of their instruments.[46] It should also be noted that the clearest case of heterodox shock success, Israel, is the beneficiary of very high levels of external finance, while Brazil and Argentina were seriously constrained in implementing fiscal consolidation by the need to make payments on their external debts.[47] Once again, successful alternative programs appear dependent on increased levels of external finance.

A third alternative to orthodoxy endorses much of the neostructuralist critique of orthodox prescriptions and the search for programs that combine adjustment with growth. More clearly than the preceding approaches, however, those who propose "adjustment with a human face," are concerned with the distributional consequences of orthodox adjustment.[48] They differ from other heterodox proponents, however, in constructing a set of alternative policies that are targeted on particular "vulnerable groups"—children and the poor—and in arguing that these policies can be implemented, in the short-run at least, without increased growth. To more expansionary and gradualist macroeconomic policies, they add meso policies (setting priorities in government expenditure) and sectoral policies that are of particular importance for the welfare of vulnerable groups. In this way, the UNICEF study sidesteps knottier questions of measuring the overall distributional effects of adjustment programs. By suggesting that such programs can be undertaken within an orthodox framework, the UNICEF team also provides an opening for policy change

288–292; Eliana A. Cardoso, "Inflation and Stabilization in Latin America: Orthodoxy versus Heterodoxy" (Paper prepared for the Conference on Stabilization Policies, Quito, Ecuador, 5–6 October 1987, mimeographed); and Eduardo Marco Modiano, "The Cruzado Plan: Theoretical Foundations and Practical Limitations" (PUC/RJ Departamento de Economía, January 1987), on the Brazilian experience.

[46] See Mario I. Blejer and Nissan Liviatan, "Fighting Hyperinflation: Stabilization Strategies in Argentina and Israel, 1985–86," *IMF Staff Papers*, 34 (September 1987): 409–438. An analysis by the Fund staff emphasizes precisely the need for orthodox fiscal support for such programs.

[47] Cardoso, "Inflation and Stabilization," p. 23.

[48] Giovanni Andrea Cornea, Richard Jolly, and Frances Stewart, *Adjustment with a Human Face*, vol. I (Oxford: Clarendon Press, 1987).

by governments and international organizations that might balk at heterodox macroeconomic prescriptions.

Although these three groups have provided the most significant critiques of orthodoxy in the 1980s, others, whose prescriptions deviate less from the orthodox consensus, have also contributed to the debate. The real economy approach developed by Tony Killick extends and consolidates the supply-side measures and longer adjustment periods that many had hoped would characterize EFF programs when they were instituted in the 1970s. The debate over adjustment has also been joined in the 1980s by economists who might be called émigrés from orthodoxy: mainstream macroeconomists, such as Jeffrey Sachs, whose firsthand encounter with developing economies has made them skeptics of the orthodox program, if not orthodox analysis. Given their acceptance of key elements in the orthodox argument, such as the superiority of outward-oriented development strategies, they could be regarded as the left wing of orthodoxy or the right wing of its critics. Sachs' concern with income distribution (for reasons of efficient policy as well as equity) and a willingness to contemplate a negotiated resolution of the debt crisis places him with the critics of orthodoxy; on the other hand, the instruments he recommends are conventional, although he disagrees with the orthodox programs that combine stabilization with wholesale external liberalization.[49]

Finally, in the recent Group of 24 Report, developing country governments have voiced their own critiques of adjustment policies in the 1980s.[50] Because the consultants to the Group included many of the critics of orthodoxy (Tony Killick, for example), it is hardly surprising that the report resembles a compendium of those criticisms. Like many alternative adjustment scenarios, the Group's recommendations devote substantial attention to increasing levels of finance and argue, somewhat gingerly, for "debt reconstruction." Like the mildly heterodox, the Group's expressed economic assumptions do not deviate substantially from those of the IMF; they argue instead for more explicit and realistic attention to those assumptions and to additional goals, such as income distribution (but only at the request of the country involved). The mildness of the report's recommendations illustrates a central point of consensus: acceptance of Hirschman's "mutual gain" hypothesis, the belief that involvement in the international economy does provide greater benefits for developing countries than a delinking strategy.

Is there a coherent, alternative approach to adjustment that can be pieced together from these critics of orthodoxy? The construction of such an alternative is hindered by one of the key arguments made by the critics of orthodoxy: that adjustment programs must be shaped according to national economic cir-

---

[49] Sachs, "Trade and Exchange Rate Policies," in Corbo, Goldstein, and Khan, eds., *Growth-Oriented Adjustment Programs*, pp. 291–325.

[50] The report, "The Role of the IMF in Adjustment with Growth," is reprinted in *IMF Survey*, 10 August 1987.

cumstances, not according to a rigid international template. Many alternative prescriptions are, as a result, voiced as criticisms of particular country programs or particular instruments, such as devaluation. Nevertheless, four themes link the alternatives: a higher priority to goals other than achieving external equilibrium in the short run, particularly economic growth and distributional or poverty alleviation goals; a more cautious and selective approach to the use of the market (though market mechanisms are not rejected); a questioning of the legitimacy of detailed, external policy intervention; and a refusal to take the international environment as given, arguing for greater symmetry in adjustment between North and South and for a different resolution of the debt crisis.[51]

Orthodoxy and the Alternatives: Points of Convergence

The chipping away at orthodox claims during the 1980s would be unlikely to shift the discourse on adjustment if key international political changes had not first produced an opening. The change in position of the United States under Treasury Secretary Baker has been particularly important: even if adjustment with growth is still defined in orthodox vocabulary, one of the criticisms leveled at orthodox approaches has been implicitly accepted. The managing director at the Fund, Michel Camdessus, has also made an emphasis on growth clear in his statements.

Less apparent are internal changes and initiatives at the Fund that suggest an opening to alternative approaches. Under Jacob Frenkel, the Research Department renewed its ties to the universities and embarked in directions that intersect with the interests of those presenting alternatives to Fund prescriptions. The Group of 24 Report spurred the department to begin considering financial programming exercises with growth targets, although it is some distance from having usable models. The Research Department assumed a more important role in evaluating Fund programs and in considering the effectiveness of particular policy instruments across programs. In undertaking its expanded mandate, the department also enlisted types of expertise—specialists in labor economics and industrial organization—who would have been unlikely participants in the past. Critics of the Fund approach detected an edging toward questions of income distribution (the Fiscal Affairs Department has already published two studies on this issue), although methodological and data problems are cited as serious obstacles.[52] The former managing director, Jacques de Larosière, declared in July 1986 that "adjustment that pays atten-

---

[51] I owe several of these common themes to a conversation with Frances Stewart.

[52] International Monetary Fund, "Fund-Supported Programs, Fiscal Policy, and Income Distribution," occasional paper no. 46 (Washington, D.C.: International Monetary Fund, 1986); International Monetary Fund, "The Implications of Fund-Supported Adjustment Programs for Poverty: Experiences in Selected Countries," occasional paper no. 58 (Washington, D.C., International Monetary Fund, 1988).

tion to the health, nutrition and educational requirements of the most vulnerable groups is going to protect the human condition better than adjustment that ignores them.''[53]

At a World Bank in the throes of reorganization, the picture has been more obscure, although there are signs that the critical arguments have been heard. Shortcomings in Bank expertise related to its policy-based lending are widely acknowledged within the organization: whether this points toward building that expertise or toward closer collaboration with the IMF is less clear. Pressure for closer collaboration has been a constant theme of the executive boards of both organizations for several years, and efforts to develop a common analytical approach, particularly regarding the poorest nations, indicate that cooperation may deepen operationally. Under Barber Conable, the Bank's commitment to policy-based lending seems certain to continue, although some structural adjustment loans (SALs) are disaggregated into more manageable sectoral programs. Both outsiders and insiders confirm that the Bank is returning in the design of adjustment programs to its earlier substantial concern with poverty alleviation.

If the Bretton Woods organizations have stirred in response to criticism of the orthodox approach to adjustment, what are the likely constituents of an evolving consensus? In stabilization programs, many elements of the old orthodoxy remain central in programs to reduce inflation and achieve external balance. Southern Cone experiments and the Brazilian heterodox shock program foundered in the absence of a reduction in the fiscal deficit. The manner of closing that deficit—through increasing taxes or reducing public spending—is likely to remain a point of contention. Devaluation to a realistic exchange rate, despite the cautions of the neostructuralists, does seem effective in increasing nontraditional exports in semi-industrialized countries. The need for maxi-devaluations that are believed to ''stick'' seems less clear, however. The principal change in orthodox positions in any new consensus on short-term stabilization programs will come, less in the composition of programs than in incorporating additional objectives in program design (beginning with growth), ensuring the increased resources to meet those goals, and accepting a lengthier adjustment period if structural change is a goal.

The question of longer-term development strategy is one in which the heterodox have presented fewer arguments and even less of a clear alternative to the favored Bretton Woods model of outward orientation.[54] Given the neostructuralist critique of orthodox stabilization as too short-term and in conflict with longer-run development goals, this is a peculiar state of affairs. Both sides would agree on the importance of supply-side measures in ensuring adjust-

---

[53] *IMF Survey*, 14 July 1986, p. 220.

[54] See Rosemary Thorps, ''Is There Life in Heterodoxy Yet? The Lessons from the Peruvian Experience'' (Oxford: International Development Centre, Queen Elizabeth House, 1988), pp. 5–6. In her review of the Peruvian heterodox experiment under Alan García, Rosemary Thorp emphasizes the weakness of the program with regard to long-term and structural issues.

ment with growth, but the content of those supply-side measures would differ in orthodox and alternative programs. Neostructuralists are far more willing to see value in a prominent public sector role; they see public investment in particular as complementary to private investment. Externally, reconsideration of the East Asian newly industrializing countries (NICs) and the Southern Cone experiences suggests a convergence toward prudent and gradual liberalization, externally and internally, as a plausible goal.[55] Heterodox recommendations no longer include a delinking alternative; the gains to be made from ties to the international economy—on some terms at least—are accepted. In orthodox discourse, emphasis on wholesale and rapid liberalization has faded. Most agree that stabilization should come first, and only then should the risks of trade liberalization and financial liberalization be undertaken.[56] In a sense, the broadened orthodoxy has been qualified; stabilization is once again considered independently of questions of broader economic orientation. The arguments of structuralism and neoorthodoxy on this point have been substantially revised.

Finally, consensus on the international requirements of adjustment with growth is considerable. Orthodox and heterodox agree that higher levels of growth among the industrialized countries will be necessary for any improvement in adjustment outcomes. While the potentially destabilizing effects of private financial flows are accepted by many orthodox analysts, it is equally clear that the support offered by large public inflows—bilateral and multilateral assistance—has been crucial to many of the most successful stabilization and liberalization episodes: Indonesia and Turkey on the orthodox side, Israel on the heterodox.[57] Some argue that the principal divide between orthodox and heterodox lies, not in models of the economy or policy prescription, but in assumptions about the amount of financing necessary to support an adjustment program. Here the shift in orthodox (G-5) positions has recently been toward increased financing from public sources: endorsing a capital increase for the World Bank, establishing a structural adjustment facility and enhanced structural adjustment facility targeted on the poorest countries. Equally significant is growing agreement on the need for a resolution of the debt crisis and a reduction in the large debt overhang of many developing countries. The obstacle that debt servicing requirements posed for the heterodox shock programs has been noted on all sides. Debt overhang makes most adjustment with growth scenarios implausible, even in analyses from the Bretton Woods insti-

[55] It is a tribute to South Korea that its successful adjustment is claimed by both the heterdox and the orthodox.

[56] See also Max Corden, *Protection and Liberalization: A Review of Analytical Issues* (Washington, D.C.: International Monetary Fund, 1987), p. 21, although Sachs makes this point most forcefully.

[57] George Kopits, *Structural Reform, Stabilization, and Growth in Turkey* (Washington, D.C.: International Monetary Fund, May 1987), pp. 26–27, explicitly notes the importance of that external support, particularly for a supply-side program in its early stages in a Fund analysis of the Turkish program.

tutions.[58] Conflict here centers on the role that public institutions should play in a resolution. While the United States and other G-5 governments have been willing to expand the "menu of options" set before a debtor country and its private creditors, they have balked at any public role in purchasing discounted developing country debt.

ORTHODOXY, HETERODOXY, AND POLITICS

In painting this portrait of possible intellectual convergence, a final element common to both orthodox and heterodox prescriptions should be explored: unwillingness to consider the political assumptions and requirements of their economic prescriptions. A few examples can be offered here. The qualities of "coherence and credibility" that are regarded as central to influencing expectations in orthodox programs are not simply abstracted features of programs; they are highly dependent on political context. The failed Southern Cone programs were certainly coherent by the standards of most adjustment efforts and authoritarian governments made clear commitments over a period of years to the program goals. The macroeconomic inconsistencies that undermined their credibility owed a great deal to political constraints (particularly the need to avoid urban unemployment). In assessing the credibility of their policies, political elites must estimate the level of political sustainability that the population awards those policy initiatives. If, according to past experience, the estimate of political sustainability is low, expectations may well undermine the implementation of the program. Such an analysis may well point toward a gradualist program that meets clear targets, rather than the shock treatment that was often favored in neoorthodox analysis. In other instances, the success of orthodox prescriptions may depend on effective depoliticization, shielding key prices, especially the exchange rate, from the vagaries of domestic political conflict. In Latin America, Colombia is a rare example of a country that has usually managed such a feat in the context of democratic politics. Much of the prudent management of exchange rate policy in East and Southeast Asian political economies depends on the effectiveness of such institutional mechanisms, which are not entirely dependent on an authoritarian political system.

A more serious political shortcoming of the orthodox case has already been mentioned: the question of implementation is both a theoretical and empirical embarrassment. Orthodoxy has not dealt successfully with the paradox of using the state—its only instrument—to change policy in a less statist direction. While orthodox prescriptions have clearly affected the policy advice embodied in Fund and Bank adjustment programs, the record of implementation for those programs is less than stellar.[59]

[58] See Marcelo Selowsky and Herman G. Van Der Tak, "The Debt Problem and Growth," *World Development*, 14, no. 9, pp. 1107–24, for example.

[59] See Tony Killick, ed., *The Quest for Economic Stabilization* (London: Heinemann, 1984), pp. 251–57, for one summary.

Alternative approaches to adjustment have less difficulty in explaining the political incentives for choosing their programs; it is a plausible assumption that politicians will choose economic growth if it is offered as the probable outcome of a set of policies. Alternative approaches are less successful in explaining the political incentives for pursuing goals other than growth—particularly those that are part of "adjustment with a human face." The UNICEF study alludes to powerful political interests that may oppose such a redirection of economic policy and social expenditures, but offers few clues as to how that political resistance can be overcome. Reliance on "political determination and courage" becomes nearly as mysterious as the appeals to "political will" that pervade orthodox exhortations.

Other elements of alternative programs seem less difficult to implement, because they do not require overcoming political resistance. Indeed, alternative approaches often accept the possibility of political resistance as a justification for the policy status quo; the existing winners and losers represent the only political equilibrium that is possible. Although alternative approaches endorse a wider role for the state and for public policy than orthodoxy, they face a mirror image of the implementation issues that plague orthodox prescriptions: determining the "comparative advantage" of public over private (market) solutions in particular developing societies. The African cases described by Thomas Callaghy in this project illustrate that weak administrative capabilities may hinder the implementation of internationally dominant orthodoxy, but also prevent a retreat to older, heterodox and statist patterns.[60] In denouncing a wholesale bonfire of the public sector, alternative approaches offer little guide for judging the efficacy of a political instrument rather than one based on the market. Conceding the errors of their structuralist ancestors and continuing to endorse an activist state (often pointing to East Asian models), they sidestep the question of how to turn state action that hinders economic growth into state intervention that forwards economic and social goals.[61]

KNOWLEDGE AND POWER IN ADJUSTMENT ALTERNATIVES

Having traced the development of orthodoxy and its alternatives, the importance of new intellectual alternatives (or a possible convergence of old ones) must be assessed. In the future, would the reconstruction of a different intellectual consensus on stabilization and adjustment affect economic outcomes in the developing countries?

[60] Thomas Callaghy, "Lost between State and Market: The Politics of Economic Adjustment in Ghana, Zambia, and Nigeria," chap. 7 in this volume, pp. 257–319.

[61] Joseph Ramos, "Planning and the Market during the Next Ten Years in Latin America," *CEPAL Review* no. 31 (April 1987): pp. 145–52 is one effort to define the boundaries of state and market, incorporating recent lessons from Latin American experience.

One reigning hypothesis awards international power relations a principal role in answering that question. An argument based on power configurations suggests that alternative intellectual formulations are subsidiary to, and perhaps rationalizations of, national interests. Orthodoxy served the interests—internal and external—of most G-5 governments in the 1980s. Until that definition of interests changes, the international dominance of orthodoxy is likely to remain, however intellectually tattered it becomes. Such a realist position does capture a part of the recent history described above: the shift toward tougher conditionality in the early 1980s, support for broadened orthodoxy in both the IMF and the World Bank, the relatively small number of heterodox programs that were undertaken in the decade, and the opening for alternative arguments provided by a more flexible American ideological stance. It does not explain why orthodoxy began its intellectual long march through the international institutions well before 1981, nor does it explain why the G-5 governments defined their interests in terms of orthodox prescriptions. In the United States, it was clear that the international banks had an interest in an orthodox outcome after 1982 (though some would argue theirs was a short-sighted definition of interests), but the stance of other groups was less clear. Fund conditionality was attacked by both the liberal left and the populist right in the United States because of its consequences for growth in developing countries. The availability of plausible alternative arguments to orthodoxy may also have affected the American redefinition of interests under Baker after 1985.

An emphasis on bargaining power and control over external finance can explain only a part of the pattern that emerges from the cases in this volume. Only in a few divided governments did external pressure provide essential support adherents of orthodoxy. Other paralyzed governments in small countries, such as the Carazo government in Costa Rica and the Guzman government in the Dominican Republic, did not respond to clear external signals.

The pattern of heterodox programs, at first glance, might seem to support a power relations model; two of the largest countries in the sample—Brazil and Argentina—were among the few countries to undertake such programs. The association between bargaining power and program content is called into question by Peru, however, a much weaker country that attempted the most sweeping heterodox program among the countries examined.

Power asymmetries did influence the degree to which the international financial institutions intervened in the implementation of stabilization and structural adjustment programs. External agencies were far more willing to exercise detailed oversight in smaller countries with weak state capabilities. The degree of success in implementation, however, was influenced far more by features of internal politics than by fluctuations in external advice and conditionality.

As a guide in answering such questions on the power of economic ideas, a model developed by Peter Hall to explain the cross-national influence of

Keynesian ideas is particularly useful.[62] Hall does enter the impact of international relations in his model, but it is assumed that, among the industrialized countries in his set, domestic variables best explain the relative acceptance or rejection of Keynesian policies. He organizes the explanation into three categories: economic viability (the theoretical appeal and problem-solving ability of a set of ideas for economic professionals), administrative viability (the degree to which a set of ideas accorded with existing administrative institutions and was feasible to implement) and political viability (the degree to which a doctrine served as an instrument for politicians in coalition-building and retaining political support).[63] Through these categories, Hall explains the career of Keynesian ideas in an array of societies, thereby giving empirical meaning to the concept of social learning.

Two historical episodes closer to our subject demonstrate the usefulness of this model in explaining the diffusion of economic ideas from North to South and within the South. In his study of Edwin Kemmerer, the "money doctor" who dispensed advice to Latin American and other developing countries during the interwar period, Paul Drake points to many of the same features that Hall employs in explaining the relative success of Kemmerer's programs.[64] While power relations (the hegemonic power of the United States and the desire for international finance) played a major role in the formal acceptance of Kemmerer's orthodox prescriptions, other domestic considerations also came into play. Economic viability was seldom at issue, given the absence of competing intellectual models during this period, but Kemmerer increased the adminstrative viability of his ideas by building institutions, particularly central banks, that might incorporate and sustain his economic program. The political viability of his ideas was more tenuous, tied to the progressive image of the United States at the time and buoyant external economic conditions. Drake carefully delineates the way in which economic prosperity permitted the construction of an unusually broad coalition in support of "Kemmererization," in particular by compensating traditional elites who might have opposed his reforms. With the onset of the Great Depression and a radical deterioration in economic progress, that coalition disintegrated, orthodoxy was called into question, and many of Kemmerer's prescriptions were thrown out.

Kathryn Sikkink's study of Raúl Prebisch and his economic prescriptions for Argentine economic policy is a second confirmation of Hall's findings.[65]

[62] Peter Hall, ed., *The Political Power of Economic Ideas* (Princeton, N.J.: Princeton University Press, 1989).

[63] Ibid., pp. 9, 13

[64] Paul Drake, *The Money Doctor in the Andes: US Advisors, Investors, and Dependent Development in Latin America from World War I to the Great Depression* (Durham, N.C.: Duke University Press, 1989).

[65] Kathryn Sikkink, "The Influence of Raúl Prebisch on Economic Policy Making in Argen-

Prebisch's developmentalist ideas clearly had economic viability in Argentina when he arrived there in the mid-1950s to recommend a stabilization program and head a team from ECLA that would produce a longer-term development strategy. Developmentalist ideas close to those of Prebisch had emerged as important strands of the economic debate in Argentina after the fall of Perón. Nevertheless, the political viability of Prebisch's program—despite its similarity to those of certain Argentinian political factions—was nil: he was regarded by many as an outsider and was associated, not with the structuralist ideas of ECLA, but with the orthodox programs of the pre-Perón years, when he headed the Argentine Central Bank. His political position was further weakened by association with the military government that succeeded Perón, a government that was opposed by his likely intellectual allies in the Radical party. Finally, the administrative viability of his ideas was reduced by the fact that the ECLA team was unable to create any lasting institutions to implement his program (in contrast to Brazil and other Latin American countries).

How do the fortunes of contemporary orthodoxy and heterodoxy appear in light of this model of influence? The internationalization of economic training, through the Bretton Woods institutions and the graduate departments of American and European universities, has clearly increased the economic viability of orthodoxy by creating a cadre of economists in many developing economies who can understand its outlines and are attracted (in part) to its coherence. Their influence on policy has certainly been greater in Latin America than in sub-Saharan Africa. Heterodoxy in Latin America has benefited as well, however, from local émigrés from orthodoxy who are conversant with the prevalent vocabulary and debates in the economics profession. Their transnational contacts and international standing increased the influence of those economists who developed heterodox shock approaches to stabilization in Argentina and Brazil. In Africa, Callaghy suggested that despite the absence of a clear heterodox alternative, the economic viability of the orthodox model—its acceptability to political elites and intellectuals as a representation of economic reality—remains in question.

The administrative viability of each set of ideas is affected by institutional histories in many developing countries (the links between central banks and finance ministries and international financial organizations) and by the problems of implementation described. Kaufman, for example, describes the key role of Central Bank and treasury economists in Mexico in ensuring respect for orthodox macroeconomic policies in postwar Mexico (though not orthodox outward-oriented development strategy).[66] In Africa, as Callaghy notes, the orthodox paradox is most pressing and the adminstrative viability of orthodox

tina, 1950–1962 (Paper presented at the LASA Thirteenth International Congress, Boston, Mass., 23–26 October 1986).

[66] Robert Kaufman, "Stabilization and Adjustment in Argentina, Brazil, and Mexico," chap. 3, in this volume, pp. 63–111.

ideas is most uncertain, because administrative capabilities for implementing economic policy are limited. The World Bank, in particular, has tried to strengthen economic analysis and administrative capabilities, but institutional development is a slow process. In proposing fairly intricate administrative controls in place of market mechanisms, the alternative approaches must also face the test of administrative viability; although they do not threaten the role of the state in the same way as orthodoxy, successful heterodox approaches must attempt to change administrative procedures (in adjustment with a human face) or set new goals for entrenched bureaucracies. The administrative obstacles to such strategies are noted in Barbara Stalling's description of the Peruvian experiment with an alternative strategy after 1985.[67]

Of greatest interest in our cases, however, is the political viability of the two sets of ideas. A few politicians (the "economic strategists") have some sense of the overall direction of economic policy that they wish to take—Stallings suggests that Pinochet may be one example and Alan García another. In most other cases, however, the political leaders can be regarded as "political maximizers" seeking to retain power in uncertain political circumstances. As the country cases illustrate, orthodoxy's principal political asset is typically the international financial support that it can bring; secondarily, it may fit the preferences of certain domestic groups, particularly internationally connected business groups. Its political liabilities with much of the population are great, however, which is one reason for the appeal of heterodoxy in situations of democratization.

Alternative approaches often seem to promise adjustment without political pain, a much greater attraction for many politicians than the intellectual content of alternative programs. The danger for advisors designing such a program lies in the "heterodoxy of politicians," the abandonment of key elements of a program as political costs rise (the pattern in Brazil). A further limitation on the viability of a coherent and more radical alternative to orthodox prescriptions is the social base of democratizing regimes in the newly-industrializing countries (not only Latin America, but in Korea and the Philippines as well). The core support of these governments remains the middle class, a middle class that would reject an economic strategy based on delinking from the international economy. Contemporary heterodox programs, less statist than those in the past, may also depend on the support of private business; maintaining and directing that support was one of the persistent weaknesses in Peru's alternative program.

In his study of Keynesianism, Peter Hall emphasized the importance of past national experience and its interpretation in determining the political viability of economic ideas. For many developing countries, statist heterodoxy has

[67] Barbara Stallings, "Politics and Economic Crisis: A Comparative Study of Chile, Peru, and Columbia," chap. 4, in this volume, pp. 113–67.

been called into question, but recent experiences with orthodox prescriptions are considered failures as well, particularly in Latin America. What Max Corden calls guilt by association ties the failure of certain elements in the economic package with others that may not have been related causally to the economic outcome. Thus, the coherence of an economic package, which may improve its economic viability with professionals, might undermine its political viability.

The cases in this project suggest that, absent international constraints, neither orthodoxy nor the alternative approaches has guaranteed long-term viability within the policy making of the developing countries. Institution building in the 1980s has been weak, hindering the consolidation of new policies. The political viability of each is limited by a fragmented social base and by an association, in Latin America at least, with external influence and past economic disasters (both orthodox and heterodox). This void could be filled by a new international consensus that modified orthodoxy in the directions described above, or, more likely on the evidence of these cases, with variants of national policy that will not satisfy the purer proponents of either view.[68] If one were to draw a final conclusion, based on the more successful Asian experiences, it may well be that the polar sets of ideas that have confronted each other for much of the postwar era are not politically viable guides to stable and successful economic policies in the developing economies.

[68] At least one seasoned observer of Latin America has concluded that Latin Americans "have become skeptical of their former sets of certainties and 'solutions' " (Albert Hirschman, "The Political Economy of Latin American Development: Seven Exercises in Retrospection," *Latin American Research Review* 22, 3: 34).

CHAPTER THREE

Stabilization and Adjustment in Argentina, Brazil, and Mexico

Robert R. Kaufman

IN ONE WAY or another, the sharp contraction of private international lending during the 1980s has forced severe economic austerity on most of the countries of Latin America. During this bleak decade, however, Argentina, Brazil, and Mexico—the three largest debtor states in the region—have pursued quite distinctive lines of adjustment. New civilian governments in Argentina and Brazil, each attempting to manage transitions from authoritarian to constitutional regimes, have experimented with a range of policy approaches, including widely publicized "heterodox shock" packages in the mid-1980s and the Brazilian moratorium on servicing its medium- and long-term commercial debt during 1987 and 1988. Conversely, the stabilization and adjustment policies adopted under Mexico's president Miguel de la Madrid (1982–1988) moved more consistently along orthodox lines. Conventional monetary and fiscal austerity, more extensive trade liberalization, and a less confrontational approach toward the IMF and international creditors were emphasized.

From the perspective of the late 1980s, unfortunately, it was clear that all of these approaches to adjustment had fallen well short of initial hopes and expectations. Brief economic recoveries did follow the sharp recessions of the early 1980s; but as the decade drew to an end, each of the large-debtor countries had again entered a new round of crisis. With such generally disappointing outcomes, it seems apparent that no government had dealt effectively with constraints that had been underestimated or ignored during the "first round" of the crisis: the resource drains associated with the huge debt overhang and major weaknesses in the institutional capacity to generate fiscal and private savings at home.

But if routes out of contemporary dilemmas are to be found, it is essential

This chapter has benefited from criticisms by participants in seminars at El Colegio de México, Columbia University, the Kellogg Institute at the University of Notre Dame, Rutgers, and UCLA. I would like to thank the following individuals for assistance during various research and writing phases of the project: Todd Appel; Eliana Cardoso; David and Ruth Collier; Jose Maria Dagnino Pastore; Eric Davis; José María Fanelli; Cheryl Eschbach; Nancy Llach; Emilio Sacristan; Steven Sanderson. An earlier version of this chapter's text was published as *The Politics of Debt in Argentina, Brazil, and Mexico: Economic Stabilization in the 1980s* (Berkeley: Institute of International Studies, University of California, 1988).

to examine the divergent paths already traveled. In this chapter, we analyze the political determinants of choices regarding three sets of issues confronted by each government during the 1980s. The first was how to stabilize external accounts and domestic prices. The heterodoxy/orthodoxy distinction used in this chapter refers primarily to variations in the way governments dealt with this problem, specifically, the emphasis placed on direct administration of prices and currency as contrasted with more conventional forms of fiscal and monetary demand-management approaches. A second key issue was how to bargain with external creditors. Contrasting degrees of confrontation and collaboration with these creditors, as we shall see, was closely linked to stabilization policies. A third set of choices concerned the liberalization of trade, reduction of the public sector, and reform of the fiscal system. During the time period covered, from the early 1980s to 1987, top decision makers generally gave less time and attention to these structural reform issues than to stabilization and external bargaining. We must consider not only the heterodoxy or orthodoxy of the choices in structural reform issues, but also the circumstances in which these issues moved onto policy-making agenda at all.

Woven into our description of the responses to these policy issues will be five explanatory factors already discussed in the introduction to this volume:[1]

1. The way the crisis itself shaped the agenda and perceptions of policy makers
2. The organization of the state's decision-making apparatus—the orientations and cohesion of the technocratic elite, the backing it receives from the head of state, and its capacity to coordinate the state apparatus as a whole
3. Relations with external financial agencies, including the IMF, private commercial banks, and the creditor governments
4. The combined influence of regime type and distributional coalitions among political groups and economic interests
5. The role of electoral cycles and other "situational" variables in affecting the time horizons and security of the principal decision-makers

Of course, these are not the only factors—political or economic—that have conditioned responses to the crisis of the 1980s. Brazil's huge economy, for example, has been less vulnerable to capital flight than the economies of Argentina and Mexico; its financial system is less closely linked to the dollar; and its diversified export sector can adapt relatively quickly to changes in world trade flows. This has provided the Sarney government with considerable space to engage in heterodox experiments. Tighter constraints in the other two countries have encouraged greater macroeconomic caution—particularly in Mexico, with its geographic and economic proximity to the United States. Yet ongoing structural constraints have not prevented alternating periods of orthodoxy and heterodoxy in any of the three countries considered in this chapter;

[1] Joan M. Nelson, chap. 1, in this volume.

and these policy shifts, as well as the cross-national contrasts mentioned above, seem attributable, at least in part, to the way political conflicts and institutions have structured perceptions of policy alternatives. Our primary objective here is to trace the main dimensions of these political influences, leaving to another time the much more difficult task of assessing their relative importance for a fuller explanatory theory of policy behavior and economic outcomes.

Despite important differences in economic structure, moreover, we assume sufficient socioeconomic parallels among the three countries to provide a useful basis for a comparative discussion of policy choice. Argentina, Brazil, and Mexico (the ABM countries) are not only the largest debtors in the region, but the largest and most advanced industrial economies. Compared to most other Latin American countries, each society is also characterized by a powerful financial/industrial business class, a politically important popular sector, and a relatively sophisticated and professionalized state apparatus. Finally, although developmental paths began to diverge after the mid-1970s, earlier patterns ran along similar lines, characterized by import-substitution industrialization and the emergence of a large state enterprise sector.[2]

The cross-national comparisons undertaken against this backdrop are intended to serve two purposes. In keeping with the inductive approach of this volume, one goal is to sharpen our understanding of the distinctive features of each national political context.[3] To further this objective, the five sets of explanatory factors listed above serve as reference points to highlight the differences within each political system as each responded to the debt shocks of the 1980s. Given the importance of the role that the ABM countries have played in

---

[2] References on general development patterns of ABM countries. For Argentina: Carlos F. Diaz-Alejandro, *Essays on the Economic History of the Argentine Republic* (New Haven, Conn.: Yale University Press, 1970); Richard D. Mallon and Juan V. Sourrouille, *Economic Policy Making in a Conflict Society: The Argentine Case* (Cambridge, Mass.: Harvard University Press, 1975); Laura Randall, *An Economic History of Argentina in the Twentieth Century* (New York: Columbia University Press, 1978); Javier Villanueva, *The Inflationary Process in Argentina, 1943–1960*. For Brazil: Joel Bergsman, *Brazil: Industrialization and Trade Policies* (New York: Oxford University Press, 1970); Werner Baer, *Industrialization and Economic Develompent in Brazil* (Homewood, Ill.: Economic Growth Center, Yale University, 1965); Nathaniel H. Leff, *Economic Policy Making and Development in Brazil* (New York: John Wiley and Sons, 1968); Wilson Suzigan et al., *Crecimento Industrial no Brasil, Incentivos e Desempenho Recente* (Rio de Janeiro: IPEA/INPES, 1974); Raouf Kahil, *Inflation and Economic Development in Brazil* (Oxford: Oxford University Press, 1973). For Mexico: Timothy King, *Mexico: Industrialization and Trade Policies since 1940* (New York: Oxford University Press, 1970); Roger Hansen, *The Politics of Mexican Development* (Baltimore: Johns Hopkins University Press, 1971); Sylvia Ann Hewlitt and Richard S. Weinert, eds., *Brazil and Mexico: Patterns in Late Development* (Philadelphia: Institute for the Study of Human Issues, 1982).

[3] Theda Skocpol, "Emerging Agendas and Recurrent Strategies in Historical Sociology," in Skocpol, ed., *Vision and Method in Historical Sociology* (Cambridge: Cambridge University Press, 1984), pp. 356–91.

international debt politics, a fuller understanding of their internal systems is directly relevant to an understanding of broader aspects of the debt crisis itself.

The second purpose of the comparison is to contribute to an understanding of some of the more general relationships that will be explored across a broader range of cases in the second phase of this project. Because the debt crisis coincided with democratic openings in Argentina and Brazil, it seems appropriate to emphasize the impact of changing political regimes (i.e., a combination of the fourth and fifth "explanatory factors" listed previously). First we compare the policy choices of the transitional democratic governments in Argentina and Brazil, with particular attention to the "heterodox" packages of price controls and currency reforms (the Austral and Cruzado programs) adopted in the mid-1980s in response to rapidly escalating inflation. With the Argentine and Brazilian experiences as a reference point, we then analyze the more orthodox policies framed in the context of Mexico's more centralized and controlled political system.

ARGENTINA AND BRAZIL: ECONOMIC DECISION MAKING IN TRANSITIONAL DEMOCRACIES

Historical Antecedents: Populism and Regime Change in the Postwar Era

Unlike Mexico, changes of political regime have long been a feature of political life in Argentina and Brazil. Since the 1930s, these changes have been linked to recurrent attempts to mobilize nationalist-populist coalitions and the reaction of conservative military and business sectors. Underlying these parallels, however, are long-standing cross-national differences in the intensity of these struggles and the relative power of the actors involved. In Argentina, distributive politics of the post-World War II era have been shaped by a strong union movement and evenly balanced struggles along both class and sectoral lines. In Brazil, unions have been far more vulnerable to state manipulation or repression, and distributive struggles have gone more consistently in favor of agrarian oligarchies, large industrialists, and upper civilian and military strata of the state itself.

To understand the economic and political challenges confronting the constitutional regimes of the 1980s, the major implications of these contrasting historical patterns must be sketched more fully. We look first at the general pattern of distributive conflicts that preceded the rise of the bureaucratic-authoritarian regimes of the 1960s and 1970s. We then turn to a review of the impact of these regimes, and to the economic and political crises that preceded the current efforts at redemocratization.

DISTRIBUTIVE STRUGGLES AND THE STATE: 1940S TO THE 1960S

Contrasting patterns of distributive conflict in Argentina and Brazil are rooted in different modes of popular-sector incorporation undertaken under

Perón and Vargas during the 1930s and 1940s.[4] Alignments changed after that time, of course, in both countries. Yet like the Roosevelt era in the United States, certain basic patterns established during those decades persisted throughout most of the postwar period. In Brazil, workers were initially mobilized within the state corporatist framework of Vargas' Estado Nôvo. Despite waves of populist electoral militancy that followed the collapse of that system after 1945, state officials continued to deploy this framework to restrict the financial and political independence of organized unions, during the constitutional period from 1945 to 1964 as well as the military regime from 1964 to 1985. In Argentina, the popularly based Peronist regime of the 1940s engaged in much more radical appeals to urban working class and small business groups and far more direct challenges to export and big business interests. Despite a turn toward more orthodox policies in the years immediately preceding Perón's overthrow by the military in 1955, this left a far more polarized political legacy than in Brazil.

Each of these patterns of domestic conflict affected the capacity of state elites to sustain consistent developmental policies and to mediate relations with international economic forces. For our purposes, it is necessary to point to three long-term consequences.

Conservative Reactions to Import-substituting Models. Industrialists and military nationalists generally supported import-substituting models in both countries after 1945. In Argentina, however, the profound antagonism toward the Peronist movement frequently led these sectors into political alliances with financial and agro-export elites that advocated more liberal models of development.[5] Thus, although import-substitution remained the basic approach until the Martinez de Hoz period (1976–1980), laissez-faire ideologies remained strong among established business groups and were frequently reflected in periodic attempts at orthodox stabilization.

In Brazil, where the Estado Nôvo provided important benefits to industrialists and established export oligarchies, conservatives were much less inclined to react against the expansion of the state apparatus under Vargas. Moreover, because popular-sector groups remained comparatively weak, the danger was less in Brazil than in Argentina that they might eventually seize control of the state for redistributive purposes. Consequently, by the middle of the 1950s, most business and military sectors had come to share in the broad consensus over state-driven models of industrialization. More than in Argen-

[4] Ruth Berins Collier and David Collier, "Shaping the Political Arena: Critical Junctures, Trade Unions, and the State in Latin America" (Manuscript, Berkeley, University of California, Institute for International Studies and Department of Political Science, July 1988).

[5] Marcelo Cavarozzi, "Political Cycles in Argentina Since 1955," in Guillermo O'Donnell, Philippe C. Schmitter, and Laurence Whitehead, eds., part 2 of *Transitions from Authoritarian Rule in Latin America* (Baltimore: Johns Hopkins University Press, 1986), pp. 19–48.

tina, "developmentalism" became firmly entrenched as a feature of the Brazilian orientation to economic policy.[6]

Relations with External Capital. The conflicts over economic ideology also affected relations with external investors. As a result of Perón's strident nationalism of the 1940s, Argentina entered the postwar period far more isolated than Brazil (or Mexico) from diverse sources of financial aid and direct investment. As prices for agrarian exports slumped in the 1950s, the limited availability of external financial assistance made it more difficult for Argentine governments to soften the effects of recurrent foreign exchange bottlenecks and sharp stop-go cycles. As they ran out of reserves, governments of many different political orientations (including the Peronist regime of the early 1950s) were impelled to adopt highly orthodox stabilization packages to reduce external accounts deficits and establish credibility within international financial groups.[7]

On the other hand, despite some bitter controversies over foreign investment, both Vargas and his successors generally maintained more collaborative relations with international lending and investment forces. From the late 1940s until the early 1960s, and then again during the late 1960s and 1970s, this made it much easier for Brazilian governments to prolong expansionary policies despite deteriorations in the external accounts position. In this respect, the industrial boom experienced under Juscelino Kubitschek (1956–1960) was a prototype of later experiences under military rule. From about 1956 to 1958, the boom was fueled by a massive inflow of direct investment and long-term credits, which offset a sharp drop in the rise of coffee. Then, as current accounts balances began to deteriorate still more in the period 1958–1960, the government was able to postpone the exchange crisis by turning to suppliers' credits and other forms of short-term private lending.[8] In the early 1960s, as even these sources of exchange became exhausted, economic crisis could no longer be avoided. By that point, however, Brazil had already experienced close to a decade of very rapid industrial expansion.

Cumulative Effects on Relations between State and Society. These general patterns of conflict among competing political forces had important long-term implications for the overall types of relations that developed between state and society. In Argentina, between the overthrow of Perón in 1955 and the military takeover of 1976, Argentina had experienced two minority Radical governments (1958–1962 and 1963–1966), two military regimes (1955–1958 and

[6] Thomas E. Skidmore, *Politics in Brazil 1930–1964* (New York: Oxford University Press, 1967), pp. 164–70.

[7] Until the 1970s, the two most orthodox and prolonged stabilization episodes were under Perón (1951–1952) and Arturo Frondizi (December 1959 to April 1961).

[8] See Skidmore, *Politics in Brazil.*

1966–1973), a brief quasi-civil war (1962–1963), and a return of the Peronists (1973–1976). In a society so deeply divided, each change of regime brought major shifts of personnel and policy. Each failure, in turn, weakened the authority of the state and left civil society more fragmented than before.[9] Among industrialists and financial interests, the lack of predictability compressed time horizons and reinforced tendencies to engage in short-term financial speculation. Within the political parties, especially the Peronists, internal conflicts also intensified. Beginning in the late 1960s and early 1970s, the general crisis began to take on new dimensions, as Peronist and Marxist terrorist groups began to threaten the personal security of military officers, business executives, and Peronist officials themselves.

In Brazil, notwithstanding the economic and political crisis that followed Kubitschek's industrial boom, the long-term trends were in quite different directions. The military threats and coups of the 1950s did not, as in Argentina, produce wholesale displacements of the "developmentalist" technocrats in the state banks and planning agencies, and changes of government did not, on the whole, produce disruptive shifts in policy orientation.[10] On the contrary, the consistently expansionist approaches pursued during the early postwar decades helped to mute distributional conflicts among elites and to consolidate the ties between the state apparatus and key business interests.

BUREAUCRATIC AUTHORITARIAN EXPERIENCES: 1960s AND 1970s

The military-backed regimes that seized power after the mid-1960s reflected these divergent historical patterns of development and extended them. There were, to be sure, important cross-national parallels as well: military authorities in each country sought to purge their respective societies of populist forces and to rationalize their capitalist economies. In the next section, we will consider some of the common implications of these "exclusionary" experiences.[11] Here, however, we will consider some of the distinctive aspects of each authoritarian legacy.

In Brazil, as suggested, much of the "infrastructure" of the post-1964 authoritarian state already had been established by the time the military seized control of the government. Between 1964 and 1967, in response to the external accounts crisis that followed the Kubitschek boom, the new government did impose the first sustained IMF-backed stabilization plan in Brazil's postwar history. The promotion of manufactured exports was also an important new

[9] Guillermo O'Donnell, "State and Alliances in Argentina, 1956–1976," *Journal of Development Studies* 15, 1 (October 1978): pp. 3–33.

[10] Leff, *Economic Policy Making*, pp. 132–54.

[11] See Guillermo O'Donnell, *Modernization and Bureaucratic Authoritarianism: Studies in South American Politics* (Berkeley: Institute of International Studies, University of California, 1973); David Collier, ed., *The New Authoritarianism in Latin America* (Princeton, N.J.: Princeton University Press, 1979).

feature of the post-1964 era. After 1967, however, the primary long-term emphasis was on extensions of the "inward-oriented" developmental models of the Kubitschek years. The main engines of growth were massive state and foreign investments in heavy industry, infrastructure, and consumer durables.

There was also considerable continuity in the political sphere. Unlike Argentina, unions had already been weakened by corporatist controls; the new Brazilian regime did not have to rely as heavily on massive official terrorism to consolidate its authority. Brazilian repression did increase markedly in the late 1960s—a "hardline" response to an upsurge in guerrilla activities and wildcat strikes; but after the early 1970s, military presidents initiated a process of political liberalization, aimed at a controlled opening of the system to political debate and party competition. By the late 1970s, opposition movements had gained substantial space within the framework of the existing system and began to exert considerable pressure for a negotiated transition to civilian constitutional government.

In Argentina, authoritarian attempts to follow a comparably moderate course under Juan Carlos Onganía (1966–1970) were undermined by more profound divisions among industrialists, exporters, union leaders, and the military itself.[12] This episode was followed by the brief, disastrous Peronist interlude of 1973–1976, and then by a second, much more radical version of authoritarianism under Videla from 1976 to 1980. Although the military-controlled state enterprise system was left relatively intact during the 1970s, in all other respects, the economic project put into effect under Finance Minister Martinez de Hoz constituted one of the most drastic attempts in the region to dismantle the regulatory apparatus of state-led import-substitution industrialization (ISI) models. The IMF shock treatment of the mid-1970s was far more severe in fiscal and monetary terms than the Brazilian version from 1964 to 1967, and the Argentine regime went much farther in lifting controls on both capital movements and trade.[13] Canitrot has suggested that the underlying purpose of the post-1976 economic policies was to implement a "cultural revolution," aimed at forcing capitalists as well as workers into more "rational" market-oriented forms of behavior.[14] But by the early 1980s, the industrial sector shrank from about 28 to about 22 percent of GDP, while private economic power became increasingly concentrated in the hands of a narrow financial-industrial elite that could utilize its links to international credit to profit from short-term speculative activities.

[12] Guillermo O'Donnell, *El Estado Burocratico Autoritario, 1966–73 Triunfos, Derrotas y Crisis* (Buenos Aires: Editorial de Belgrano, 1982), pp. 229–308.

[13] Alejandro Foxley, *Latin American Experiments in Neoconservative Economics* (Berkeley: University of California Press, 1983).

[14] Adolfo Canitrot, "Discipline as the Central Objective of Economic Policy: An Essay on the Economic Programme of the Argentine Government Since 1976," *World Development* 8, 11 (November 1980): 913–28.

Much more than in Brazil, extreme concentrations of executive authority and extensive repression were also integral parts of this economic model in Argentina. Economic policy making became virtually the exclusive domain of the neoconservative technocrats, with the big industrial establishment as well as other civilian elites excluded from the ruling coalition. Party and union activity was also driven more deeply underground than ever before. And official terrorism, directed indiscrimately at a wide range of suspected "political enemies," was carried to unprecedented extremes.

ECONOMIC CRISIS AND POLITICAL TRANSITION

Severe problems in both the Brazilian and Argentinian models began to emerge well before Mexico's "declaration of bankruptcy" triggered a general freeze on credit to the region in August 1982. In Brazil, as in the 1950s, the main difficulty lay in the strain that developmentalist policies placed on fiscal resources and external accounts. Although deficits began to accelerate after the oil crises of 1973 and 1979, both the Geisel and Figueiredo administrations attempted to push ahead with externally financed capital goods and infrastructural investment, fearing that fiscal and monetary contractions would interfere with their projects of political liberalization. As in the 1950s, this allowed the regime to expand the industrial economy—as well as to keep the political opposition somewhat off balance. The costs, however, were a major buildup of external debt, annual inflation rates of about 50 percent, and eventually a severe decline in the creditor confidence required to sustain the process.

By the end of the 1970s, financial pressures began to close in, and as the government sought both to manage the deteriorating economy and to defend itself from a growing coalition of political opponents, its policy behavior became increasingly erratic. In their initial response to the 1979 oil shock, astonishingly, authorities attempted to step up the pace of growth and investment, hoping that a big devaluation would stimulate exports enough to offset the growing external deficit. When this instead produced a big jump in inflation, the government turned 180 degrees. Although it insisted it needed no help from the IMF (thus closing off an important source of external financing), it imposed one of the most severe stabilization packages since 1964. After private external lending collapsed entirely in late 1982, the regime turned at last to the IMF, yet failed repeatedly to meet the targets established during 1983 and 1984.[15]

Dissatisfaction with the economic crisis was undoubtedly also a factor in spurring the withdrawal of the military from government. Local industrialists, bitterly critical of the credit squeeze imposed under Figueiredo, stepped up

[15] Bolivar Lamounier and Alkimar R. Moura, "Economic Policy and Political Opening in Brazil," in *Latin American Political Economy Financial Crisis and Political Change* (Boulder, Colo.: Westview Press, 1986), pp. 174–77.

their demands for political reform, in many instances as members or financial backers of the opposition Party of the Brazilian Democratic Movement (PMDB).[16] In the direct gubernatorial elections of 1982, the first such elections since 1964, the PMDB won major victories in the depressed southern industrial states, which in turn augmented the leverage of the party leadership in leading massive popular movements for political change.

In typical Brazilian fashion, however, the change itself was incremental, flowing through official channels originally established under the military's policy of controlled liberalization. The eventual selection of a civilian president occurred in the framework of electoral college negotiations between moderate leaders of the PMDB opposition and a breakaway faction of the promilitary party headed by José Sarney. Sarney, who had initially been the choice for vice president, became head of state when Tancredo Neves, the PMDB president-elect, died before being able to assume office. As with earlier regime changes in Brazil, this incremental process insured substantial continuity in the power of the military establishment and in the business and professional interests represented in the state bureaucracy.

In Argentina, the main weakness of the economic model stemmed from the decision to allow peso devaluations to lag behind domestic price increases.[17] In combination with deregulation of interest rates and capital flows, this measure was intended to bring down domestic inflation, force import-competing capital into more cost-effective investment, and increase hard currency savings. By the year 1980–1981, however, the plan began to backfire badly, as local investors began to speculate against the peso and capital flight accelerated. The short administration of Roberto Viola attempted to reverse these developments by reimposing controls on capital movements and pumping new public resources into the financial sector. By this time, however, it was too late to stem the tide, and the government was forced to assume direct responsibility for most of the private external debt.

The 1982 Malvinas/Falkland adventure, launched as a desperate attempt to divert attention away from this collapsing house of cards, compounded these earlier miscalculations and quickly led to the demoralization and collapse of the military regime in 1983. In contrast to Brazil's negotiated transition, this

[16] Jeffry A. Frieden, "The Brazilian Borrowing Experience: From Miracle to Debacle and Back," *Latin American Research Review* 22, 1 (1987): pp. 95–132.

[17] For critiques from various perspectives: David Felix, "On Financial Blowups and Authoritarian Regimes in Latin America," Department of Economics, Washington University, working paper no. 60 (St. Louis, Mo., October 1983); Rudiger Dornbusch, "Argentina since Martinez de Hoz," National Bureau of Economic Research, working paper no. 1486 (September 1984); Adalbert Krieger Vasena and Enrique Szewach, "Inflation and Indexation: Argentina," in John Williamson, ed., *Inflation and Indexation: Argentina, Brazil, and Israel* (Washington, D.C.: Institute for International Economics, March 1985). Roberto Frenkel, José María Fanelli, Carlos Winograd, "Stabilization and Adjustment Programmes and Policies in Argentina," Centro de Estudios de Estado y Sociedad—CEDES (Buenos Aires, August 1986).

occurred in a characteristically sweeping and unplanned fashion.[18] Faced with an upsurge of popular demonstrations and public protest, the military establishment acquiesced unconditionally to direct presidential elections. To the surprise of most observers (and the participants themselves) the results of the elections also revealed the weakness of the Peronists, the military's great historic adversary. Still deeply divided internally, the party suffered the first free-election defeat in its history, and Alfonsín's hastily constituted Radical team was swept into office.

What were the chances that the new government could deal with the economic crisis within a constitutional framework? A major disadvantage, relative to Brazil, was the structural weakness and financial disarray of the Argentine economy. In many ways the experience of still another sweeping regime transition compounded this problem by increasing still more the uncertainty of private investors. Yet the new officials of the Alfonsín administration did have some advantages. After the violence, military defeat, and economic roller coasters of the past decades, expectations were low—at least relative to the past. Moreover, the political vacuum left by the military's external defeat and hasty retreat from office meant that, for the time being, macroeconomic policies could be framed by the incoming administration without immediate fear of a military backlash. Finally, new, more moderate leadership currents within both the Peronists and Radicals seemed anxious to avoid the kinds of bitter antagonisms that had led in the past to such mutually destructive consequences. Thus, although the discontinuities of the contemporary change in Argentina was in some respects a familiar extension of earlier patterns, there was some room for hope that the old vicious circles had "bottomed out."

Democratic Transitions and Economic Adjustments

We turn now to the policy-making process within the new democratic frameworks established in the mid-1980s. As with earlier regime changes, important contrasts in policy choices reflected differences in the alignments among the main political groups operating within each national framework and in the relation of each system to international political and economic forces. Yet the parallels in the experimentation with heterodox shock policies also indicate that the governments of the new transitional democracies to some extent were responding to common sets of challenges. Four important parallels in the two transitional situations are highlighted here.

[18] On transitions: Eduardo Viola and Scott Mainwaring, "Transitions to Democracy: Brazil and Argentina in the 1980's," The Kellogg Institute for International Studies, working paper no. 21 (July 1984); Scott Mainwaring, "The Transition to Democracy in Brazil," *Journal of Inter-American Studies and World Affairs* 28, 1 (Spring 1986): 149–80; William C. Smith, "The 'New Republic' and the Brazilian Transition?" (Paper delivered at the Eighth International Congress of the Latin American Studies Association, Boston, 23–26 October 1986).

THE RESURGENCE OF POPULAR FORCES AND THE PURSUIT OF EXPANSIONIST POLICIES

In both Argentina and Brazil, the restoration of electoral politics was closely linked to an increase in distributive claims on the state and a turn toward expansionist policies. Such pressures appeared directly related to the fact that popular parties and unions were the main targets of the outgoing exclusionary regimes. Where this was not the case—as in the Philippines under Marcos—distributive pressures were not as strong.[19] In Peru, where conservative business groups were the main opponents of the Velasco regime (1968–1975), the first elected government under Fernando Belaunde (1980–1985) attempted to adopt a very orthodox policy approach.[20] In Argentina and Brazil, on the other hand, previously repressed popular-sector groups filled the spaces vacated by retreating military governments. Both for these governments and their constitutional successors, it became difficult to separate the objectives of redemocratization from substantive policies aimed at a rapid improvement of depressed living standards.

Outgoing military administrations were the first to respond to these pressures. In an attempt to ward off civilian reprisals, Argentina's Bignone government acquiesced during 1983 to substantial real wage hikes and a major infusion of subsidized credit to highly indebted industrial firms. The Figueiredo government, less threatened by the possibility of reprisals, held somewhat more firm, entering into an IMF agreement at the end of 1982. Yet the austerity program was relaxed substantially in 1984 and 1985 as labor protests mounted and the transfer to civilian government drew increasingly near.

Expansionist orientations continued after civilian governments took power. Popular-sector groups that had moved into opposition—the Peronists in Argentina and assorted left politicians and union groups in Brazil—provided one important source of resistance to orthodox macroeconomic policy. But both Sarney and Alfonsín also faced major expansionist pressures within their own support coalitions. In Argentina, most segments of the Radical party advocated policies that were virtually identical to those of their Peronist rivals. Under Bernardo Grinspun, Alfonsín's first finance minister, the new democratic government adopted highly stimulative wage and credit measures for its first twelve months in office, until declining reserves and mounting confrontations with creditors forced the economy into recession in the last quarter of 1984.

In Brazil, the complex negotiations that led to the formation of the Sarney administration at first produced a stand-off between economic conservatives and more expansionist sectors of the governing coalition. During Sarney's first five months in office, the most important cabinet proponent of an orthodox approach was Francisco Dornelles, Tancredo Neves' choice as finance minis-

[19] Stephan Haggard, chap. 7, this vol.
[20] Barbara Stallings, chap. 4, this vol.

ter, who attempted to steer the regime into a renegotiated IMF agreement. The main opposition within the cabinet came from Planning Minister João Sayad, a developmental economist linked closely to the PMDB. As the new governing party, finally, the PMDB had evolved into a huge catchall majority, with a large left wing, an important base of support within the official labor movement, and a substantial appetite for federal and state patronage. In August 1985, the stalemate was broken by a presidential decision to replace Dornelles with Dilson Funaro, a São Paulo industrialist who shared the developmentalist orientations of the majority party. One of Funaro's first moves was to announce that the administration would break off negotiations with the IMF. During the last quarter of 1985, credit eased, interest rates turned negative, and growth (along with inflation) accelerated substantially.

PLEBISCITARY DECISION MAKING

Stephan Haggard has noted in the case of the Philippines that transitional democratic governments may preserve for a considerable period the highly concentrated forms of executive power inherited from the outgoing dictatorships.[21] Although Alfonsín and Sarney did not, like Aquino, rule solely by decree, each president did retain substantial discretionary authority. National legislatures had little technical staff support, lacked clearly defined decision-making procedures, and were uncertain of their role vis-à-vis the executive branch. Organized labor and business groups also had a minimal input into executive decision making, in part as a result of their own internal divisions and in part because government officials were reluctant to "tie their own hands" by widening the circle of participants in the decision-making process.

Yet, although the new civilian presidents retained some of the authority of their military predecessors, they depended much more on popular support to sustain their legitimacy. In combination with the weakness of formal representational mechanisms, this created a strong incentive for top executives to focus on highly visible macroeconomic problems (such as inflation and growth), to make policies that would maximize their prestige within the population at large, and to dramatize their personal responsibility for such choices through televised speeches and dramatic public announcements. Sarney and Alfonsín, along with many of their top advisors, engaged frequently in such direct appeals. As we shall see, both the Austral and Cruzado packages bore the imprint of this plebiscitary style.

AVOIDANCE OF STRUCTURAL REFORM ISSUES

The situation of political transition also discouraged attention to more divisive "structural reform" issues that had less immediate political payoff. Neither the Alfonsín nor the Sarney governments took significant action along

---

[21] Haggard, chap. 7, this vol.

these lines during the period under consideration. In Brazil, notwithstanding some conservative appeals for economic liberalization, the Sarney government held to the assumption that there was no need to change the developmentalist orientations that had characterized policy making for so many decades. Indeed, the formal developmental plan made public in 1986 (Plano do Metas) outlined an ambitious program of public investment that evoked strong memories of both the Kubitschek and Geisel eras. Alfonsín's government was more willing to acknowledge a need for export promotion and a reduction of the state enterprise sector, but as of 1987, it also had failed to take extensive action on either front.

What specific features of the Argentine and Brazilian transitions worked against such policies? A brief comparison with the Philippine transition— where significant trade liberalization did go foward under Aquino—indicates that much depended on the political orientations and policies of the preceding authoritarian regimes. In the Philippines, Haggard argued, IMF-backed stabilization policies imposed under Marcos had already brought inflation and external accounts pressures under control by the time Aquino came to power, clearing the way for more sustained attention to structural reforms. Just as important, a significant portion of the Aquino coalition viewed trade liberalization as a means of dismantling a highly corrupt system of economic cronyism established in the Marcos era.[22]

In Argentina and Brazil, new democratic governments faced just the opposite set of conditions. First, the outgoing authoritarian regimes had been widely identified (in rhetoric, if not in fact) with shifts away from traditional import-substituting approaches, while their popular-sector opponents—the main backers of the incoming democratic governments—had long identified with more inward-oriented policies. In this context, the question of economic liberalization had highly divisive political and ideological implications. It is not surprising, therefore, that "plebiscitary" politicians in these transitional democracies were predisposed to avoid them.

Second, in contrast to the Philippines, the outgoing military regimes in Argentina and Brazil had not effectively dealt with stabilization. Although the economic contractions of the early 1980s did temporarily relieve balance-of-payments pressures, problems of inflation had grown to crisis proportions by the time of each democratic transition (see table 3.1 and figure 3.1). In Argentina, annual inflation rates soared from 160 percent in 1982 to almost 400 percent during the election campaign of 1983. By the time of the Austral decree in June 1985, the monthly prices were increasing at an annual rate of nearly 800 percent. In Brazil, annual inflation persisted at about 100 percent from 1981–1983 despite austere monetary policies, then jumped to about 200 percent after a big devaluation in 1983. By the time of the Cruzado decree,

[22] Ibid.

TABLE 3.1
Argentina and Brazil: Economic Performance in the 1980s

	GDP[a]		Inflation[b]		Trade Balance[b]		Median Wage Index[d]	
	Argentina	Brazil	Argentina	Brazil	Argentina	Brazil	Argentina	Brazil
1979	11.1	7.2	159.5	52.7	1782	−2717		
1980	1.5	9.1	100.8	82.8	−1373	−2823		
1981	−6.7	−3.3	104.5	105.6	712	1185		
1982	−5.0	0.9	164.8	97.8	2764	778	80.1	121.6
1983	2.9	−2.5	343.8	142.1	3716	6469	100.5	112.7
1984	2.5	5.7	626.7	197.0	3982	13086	127.1	105.1
1985	−4.4	8.3	672.1	226.9	4878	12466	107.8	112.7
1986	5.4	8.2	90.1	145.2	2446	8348	109.5	121.8
1987	—	—	131.3	229.7	1000	—	100.3	105.8

Sources: GDP, Inflation, and Trade Balance: International Monetary Fund, *International Financial Statistics Yearbook, 1988* (Washington, D.C.: International Monetary Fund, 1988), pp. 167, 119, 141.
Average Median Wage Index: United Nations Commission for Latin America and the Caribbean, *Preliminary Overview of the Latin American Economy, 1987* (Santiago, Chile: 31 December 1987, LC/G. 1485), p. 17.
[a] Annual rate of growth
[b] Consumer price index
[c] Millions of U.S. dollars
[d] 1980 = 100

monthly inflation rates were at 15 percent, then an all-time high for Brazil. With fears of hyperinflation mounting, concerns about structural reform were even more susceptible to being shoved onto the back burner.

THE INITIATION OF THE AUSTRAL AND THE CRUZADO

It was under these circumstances that the Austral and the Cruzado packages, decreed in June 1985 and February 1986, became the policy centerpieces of the Alfonsín and Sarney governments. The intellectual leadership for these programs came from a relatively small group of young U.S.-trained Ph.D.'s in economics who had returned to professional research careers in their own countries.[23] During the early 1980s, these academics contributed to a growing body of research which indicated that a reduction of the Brazilian and Argentine triple-digit inflations required the breaking of inertial cycles of wage/price readjustments linked to the price increases of each preceding contract period. Although this research by no means implied the abandonment of fiscal or monetary restraint, it did suggest that inflationary problems would be insensitive to demand management alone, and it indicated the need for short-term price freezes and/or currency reforms as a way to break the inertial spirals.[24]

[23] Judith Evans and James Bruce, "Fresh Faces in Third-World Finance," in *Institutional Investor* (International Edition, September 1986): 167–72.
[24] See the working paper series ("Texto para Discussão") of the Departamento de Economía,

For our purposes, it is not necessary to trace the analytical intricacies of these arguments further—although they did gain considerable currency within high-prestige international academic networks. The key issue is how, and in what form, such ideas became converted into governmental programs. During 1985, several leading heterodox economists themselves became important protagonists in the decision-making bureaucracy as high-level advisors to the new finance ministers, Juan Sourrouille and Dilson Funaro. Nevertheless, they were not the decisive factors in the policy process. What counted far more were the interests and political resources of each president, and the kinds of pressures and opportunities they faced within the larger political arena.

As inflationary problems closed in, the stabilization strategies advocated by the heterodox economists served three highly important political purposes for the political executives. First, they seemed to offer a more sophisticated alternative to the expansionist programs being advocated by populist groups and the left. In Argentina, as noted, such programs had already led into a recessionary cul-de-sac under Grinspun, and they appeared to be leading into dangerous directions in Brazil as well. At the same time, the Austral and Cruzado propsals were framed explicitly as "nonrecessive" approaches to stabilization, which could avoid the short-term contractions associated with more conventional demand-management approaches. For Alfonsín, this meant an opportunity to dig out of the recession that had hit at the end of 1984. For Sarney and Funaro, it offered hope that inflation could be brought under control without slowing already high rates of growth. Finally, precisely because these proposals focused intensively on issues of stabilization and growth, they postponed the need to choose immediately among longer-term strategies of structural reform. Indeed, in Brazil, the economists pushing the Cruzado Plan implied strongly that the economy was already "structurally sound," and that a sharp break in the cycle of inertial inflation would clear the way for a new wave of investment and expansion.

Having gained executive backing, both programs moved along the general "plebiscitary" lines already discussed above. The packages were prepared secretly within the executive bureaucracy, announced without legislative approval, and implemented over the vigorous criticism of the heads of the major unions. During the first several months following each decree, however, the apparent economic success of each program squelched most signs of organized opposition. With inflation rates quickly dropping to nearly zero, the price

Pontifícia Universidade, Católica do Rio de Janeiro: André Lara-Resende, "A moneda indexada: Uma proposita para eliminar a inflacão inercial," no. 75 (September 1984); Pérsio Arida and André Lara-Resende, "Inertial Inflation and Monetary Reform in Brazil," no. 85 (January 1985), subsequently published in Williamson, ed., *Inflation and Indexation* pp. 27–44; Franciso Lafaiete Lopes, "Inflação inercial hiperinflação e desinflação: Notas a conjecturas," no. 77 (October 1984). Articles of Francisco Lopes are published in *O choque heterodoxo, combate a inflação e reforma monetária* (Rio de Janeiro: Editoria Campus Ltda., 1986)

freezes enjoyed immense popularity. At the same time, these measures did not appear to jeopardize expansion. By the fourth quarter of 1985, the Argentine economy had begun a process of reactivation that continued at a brisk pace throughout 1986. The Brazilian economy, already in high gear by the time of the Cruzado decree, accelerated still more—spurred by a big wage increase which had accompanied the announcement of the package. Between March 1985 and March 1986, consumption increased by an incredible 30 percent, and the industrial sector expanded at a rate of about 12 percent.[25]

For the incumbent executives, this brought an immense upsurge in grass-roots popularity. In Argentina, popular approval ratings of the Alfonsín administration increased from 35 to 57 percent after mid-1985, while Alfonsín's already-high personal popularity went from 64 to 74 percent.[26] In Brazil, Sarney's personal approval rating (percent favorable minus percent unfavorable) jumped from a negative 36 percent in January 1986 to plus 68 percent in March, while confidence in the government leaped from 40 percent in September 1985 to 72 percent a year later.[27] In November 1985 and 1986 respectively, major Radical and PMDB congressional victories appeared to enhance presidential prestige still more. In the meantime, throughout most of this honeymoon period efforts by union leaders to organize protest strikes fizzled or were abandoned ahead of time, while other critics on both the right and left were drowned out by a chorus of approving comment from the press, business leaders, and even their own associates.

The Austral and Cruzado Compared: Contrasts in Design and Implementation

These broad similarities in focus, decision-making style, and initial impacts, notwithstanding, there were also important contrasts in the design and implementation of the two heterodox programs. In Brazil, the Cruzado reflected an especially high priority for distributive and expansionist objectives. Large wage increases were built into the initial package, public tariffs and key consumer prices were frozen at relatively low levels, and workers were guaranteed automatic wage adjustments at any point when price increases reached twenty percent. In the months following the decree, the Sarney government proved unwilling to make corrections in this expansionist course; as a consequence, the entire anti-inflation program unravelled quickly at the beginning of 1987. In designing and implementing the Austral, on the other hand, the Alfonsín administration relied more heavily on conventional fiscal and monetary controls. Although price stability was eventually undermined by a failure to follow through with more fundamental fiscal and trade reforms, this con-

---

[25] "O gigante volta as compras," *Conjuctura Econômica*, 15 July 1986, p. 9.
[26] Data provided by Encuesto Socmerc, Buenos Aires.
[27] *Veja*, 14 Janeiro 1987, p. 29; *Veja*, 17 December 1986, p. 42.

tributed to significantly lower rates of inflation for the next several years (see figure 3.1).

Why the differences in the designs and outcomes of these two programs? In the next two sections, we provide some details on the way the policy process unfolded in each country. Before turning to these descriptions, however, we need to extend our earlier discussion of the contrasting political and economic circumstances in which each democratic transition occurred. As in past decades, presidential choices were conditioned not only by the dynamics of regime change, but also by specific alignments of domestic and international political forces.

BARGAINING LEVERAGE TOWARD EXTERNAL CREDITORS

As large debtors with potential capacity to disrupt the international financial system, both the Argentine and Brazilian governments were in a comparatively good position to resist orthodox pressures from abroad. During the first half of 1985, Argentina used this leverage to enlist the support of the U.S. government and the IMF for the heterodox features of its anti-inflationary program. Compared to Brazil, however, Argentina's external room for maneuver was extremely limited. During 1985 and 1986, the Brazilian economy was rolling up monthly trade surpluses of about $1 billion, more than enough to cover interest payments without IMF assistance. In contrast, although its trade balance had improved after the early 1980s, Argentina was in a much more vulnerable position. By the end of 1984, in fact, Grinspun's acrimonious relations with creditors had backed the government into a corner—more than $1.6 billion in arrears on external interest payments, facing a suspension of previously negotiated U.S. treasury loans, and a clear refusal by Paris Club authorities to step into the breach.[28] Under these circumstances, Alfonsín and Sourrouille were under considerable pressure to normalize external economic relations, a step that required a fuller incorporation of conventional monetary and fiscal measures into its Austral package.

PRESSURE FROM DOMESTIC FINANCIAL AND INDUSTRIAL SECTORS

The orthodoxy of governmental policy choices was also influenced by cross-national differences in the composition and political position of strategic "big business" groups. In Argentina, the challenge of providing reassurances to economically conservative sectors of the business class was especially great. After so many decades of social conflict, most business groups tended to become frightened by the political implications of economic nationalism. Moreover, the weight of orthodox banking sectors within the business community had increased substantially during the era of financial liberalism in the

[28] Roberto Bouzas and Saul Keifman, "Argentina: El plan austral y las negociaciónes financieras externas," *America Latina/Internacional* 2, 6 (October–December 1985): 113–19.

FIGURE 3.1: Monthly Inflation Rates, Argentina (January 1985–April 1987) and Brazil (January 1984–January 1987)

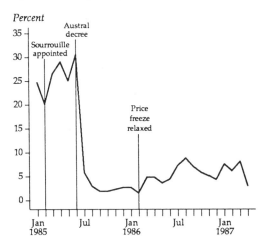

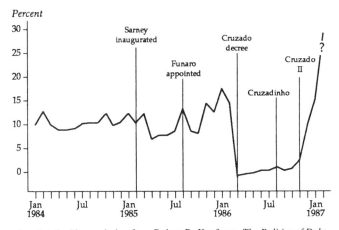

Sources: Reprinted with permission from Robert R. Kaufman, *The Politics of Debt in Argentina, Brazil, and Mexico: Economic Stabilization in the 1980s* (Berkeley: Institute of International Studies, University of California, 1988), p. 3, copyright 1988 by the Regents of the University of California. Original sources: Argentina—*Conjunctura y desarrollo* 92 (April 1986); Economist Intelligence Unit Report, *Economist*; Brazil—Eliana Cardoso and Albert Fishlow, ''The Macroeconomics of the Brazilian External Debt,'' in Jeffrey D. Sachs, ed., *Developing Country Debt* (Washington, D.C.: National Bureau of Economic Research, 1988).

late 1970s. Finally, many large industrial firms had also entered short-term money market activities, which weakened their historic opposition to orthodox monetary and trade policies. For the Alfonsín administration, coaxing long-term investment from such groups was viewed as a key to the chances for an overall economic recovery. This, in turn, depended on restoring collaborative relations with the IMF and other major centers of international business.

The Sarney administration had much greater room for maneuver in these respects. Because Brazilian capitalists in general had not been as threatened by regime changes and political conflicts, they were less inclined than the Argentines to engage in financial speculation and banking activities. Consequently, orthodox economic currents were not as strong within the Brazilian private sector as they were in Argentina and not as inclined to react to uncertainty with capital flight. Between 1976 and 1986, according to one estimate, approximately $10 billion dollars left Brazil, as compared with $26 billion for the much smaller Argentine economy.[29] Conversely, the powerful São Paulo business elite, with fixed investments in industrial plants and equipment, was inclined to push hard for easy credit policies and to resist orthodox approaches.[30] Though these groups eventually began to complain bitterly about the price freeze imposed under the Cruzado, they provided substantial support to the developmentalist policies that led Funaro to break with the IMF.

THE SECURITY OF THE PRESIDENTIAL TENURE

Tendencies toward orthodoxy, finally, also varied with the political vulnerability of the chief executive to popular protest and his capacity to dominate his own governing coalition. Alfonsín, in this respect, was in a much stronger position than Sarney to resist populist pressures. As Argentina's first directly elected president in almost a decade, he enjoyed great personal popularity. As the only Radical presidential candidate ever to defeat the Peronists, he had immense authority within his own party. With the armed forces temporarily weakened by the Malvinas debacle, there was less chance that his term of office would be threatened by a military backlash against strike activity and other forms of popular opposition. Although the president remained under considerable pressure to relax fiscal and monetary controls, particularly as the October 1987 midterm elections drew closer, he was for the time being in a relatively good position to throw his weight behind the comparatively cautious macroeconomic policies linked to the Austral.

Sarney's hold on office was far more precarious, the accidental outcome of

[29] Sylvia Maxfield, "National Business, Debt-led Growth, and Political Transitions in Latin America," in Barbara Stallings and Robert R. Kaufman, eds., *Debt and Democracy in Latin America* (Boulder, Colo.: Westview Press, 1989), pp. 75–91.

[30] Jeffry Frieden, "Debt, Development, and Democracy in Latin America: Classes, Sectors, and the International Financial Relations of Mexico, Brazil, Argentina, and Chile," *Comparative Politics* 21, 1 (October 1988): 1–20.

a negotiated political transition. As a former head of the old promilitary party, he was viewed with suspicion by the powerful notables who controlled the PMDB. Moreover, because Tancredo Neves had died before actually assuming office, there was no clear constitutional basis for Sarney's incumbency or for the length of his term of office. Finally, Sarney faced a much greater danger of a military threat to his authority. This was not a context that facilitated hard economic decisions. Even with presidential backing, Funaro and his economic team were not in a position to dominate the cabinet in the same way as Sourrouille; with Sarney's position so uncertain, it was difficult to obtain firm presidential support for a coherent economic program.

These factors became more and more important as inflationary tendencies began to reappear and economic advisors began to call for tighter monetary and fiscal adjustments. The increasingly divergent policy paths pursued from those points onward were directly related to the way political executives responded to this advice.

Brazil: From Honeymoon to Polarization

In Brazil, emerging problems of excess demand had become evident to economists inside and outside the Sarney administration within months of the Cruzado decree. Although the official price index showed almost zero rates of inflation, shortages and illegal surcharges had become widespread, with long queues to buy automobiles and other consumer durables. Although the money supply had tightened somewhat by the second quarter of 1986, fiscal deficits remained a serious problem.[31] Originally projected at only one percent of GDP, estimates reached 5 percent by the middle of 1986. Deteriorating trade balances, finally, began to set in after the middle of the year. In September 1986, the monthly balance fell below $1 billion for the first time in the past year to $840 million. By October and November, it had fallen to $210 and $131 million.

As early as April and May 1986, Pérsio Arida and André Lara-Resende, the leading figures in the initial drafting of the Cruzado, began to press strongly within the administration for an adjustment in price levels and a tightening of fiscal and monetary controls. By July, moderately orthodox economists associated with the prestigious Getulio Vargas Institute had also publicly begun to express concern. Business leaders, though publicly praising the success of the plan, also argued vigorously for adjstments in the freeze on relative prices.[32]

An important turning point came in a presidential conclave held in the town

[31] Eliana A. Cardoso and Albert Fishlow, "The Macroeconomics of the Brazilian External Debt," in Jeffrey Sachs, ed., *Developing Country Debt and the World Economy* (Chicago: University of Chicago Press, 1989), pp. 88–92.

[32] "O gigante volta as compras," *Conjuctura Econômica*, 15 July 1986, p. 9.

of Carajas at the end of May.[33] After several days of discussion with Funaro, Sayad, Arida, Lara-Resende and other high-level advisors, the president decided against a major tightening of the program. Part of the problem lay in disagreements among the advisors about the urgency and type of adjustment necessary. Planning Minister Sayad, by then locked in a bitter bureaucratic rivalry with Funaro, was less inclined than Arida and Lara-Resende to emphasize the dangers implied by the surge in domestic demand. Funaro, in turn, strongly resisted a relaxation of the price freeze that had brought him such immense personal prestige. Such disagreements did not entirely drown out the warnings about the overheated economy, but they did add considerable noise to the messages reaching Sarney's ears.

The decisive factor, however, was the approaching congressional election scheduled for November 1986. For Sarney, the stakes of this election were particularly high because the new legislature was also mandated to act as a constituent assembly, with authority to define the length of the presidential term and the scope of presidential power. With Sarney's legitimacy and base of party support already precarious, the president was under considerable pressure to avoid economic measures that might jeopardize prospects for a PMDB victory.

For most of the second half of 1986, therefore, the government's response to the excess demand problem was confined to a largely ineffective patchwork of measures. In July, the administration did decree "compulsory savings" fees on various middle-class consumption items, including air fares, gasoline, and automobiles. Although the new package (the Cruzadinho) angered middle-class consumers, it made only a slight dent in the fiscal deficit or the consumption boom. Follow-up efforts over the next several months concentrated primarily on highly publicized, but equally ineffectual supply-side attempts to relieve food shortages, such as arranging for large-scale imports or (at one point) sending government trucks to try to find herds of cattle being hoarded in the interior.

In late November, a few weeks after the PMDB's landslide congressional victory, the government finally decreed a new "surprise package" (again without warning or consultation) that attempted a more decisive tightening of fiscal and monetary controls. "Cruzado II" provided for major increases in public tariffs and new excise taxes on cigarettes and beer. It allowed interest rates on treasury bonds to float upward (nominal sixty-day rates hit 300 percent by January) and it reintroduced minidevaluations of the currency. In a move that infuriated the unions, it also attempted to soften the wage trigger provisions of the original Cruzado by creating a new inflation index, showing lower price rises. Although the government attempted to maintain the general price freeze,

[33] Alex Solnik, ed., *Por que não deu certo* (São Paulo, Brazil: L&PM Editores S/A, 1987).

it did authorize selective increases in a number of specific prices, including an 80 percent increase for automobiles.

By this time, opportunities for effective policy adjustments had been narrowed substantially by the buildup of speculative pressures and the deterioration in external accounts. Nevertheless, the rapid unraveling of the government's package over the next several months owed at least as much to the firestorm of political protest as to economic constraint. Criticisms came from every quarter of the political system. PMDB notables, fresh from their landslide victories, now began to express outrage at the fact that they had not been consulted about the government's shift in direction. Meanwhile, Sarney's popularity rating, at a high point only months before, plummeted disastrously.[34]

On the labor front, despite attempts at conciliation by Labor Minister Pazzionatti, relations with the unions became still more confrontational. A United Confederation of Labor (CUT) march held in Brasília in late November, organized to protest the government's blatant manipulation of the inflation index, ended in violence, with the police using tear gas and mobs setting fire to automobiles and banks. By early 1987, as price increases began to roll over the 20 percent mark, the wage trigger began to fire. But the government's attempt to hold the line on wages had alienated both the independent CUT and the more moderate unions linked to the official structure. As protests mounted, intimidation became an important part of the official response, with Sarney acquiescing to military occupations of port facilities and oil refineries when strikes threatened to shut them down.

In the meantime, business protests against the price freeze also became increasingly public. In January and February, the heads of the São Paulo Industrial Federation (FIESP) began strident threats that they would disobey government price regulations.[35] Faced with an open challenge of civil disobedience from the most powerful sectors of the business community, the administration capitulated. The freeze was lifted, and the dam burst. In February and March, monthly price increases escalated toward pre-Cruzado highs, while hard currency reserves sank to dangerously low levels. By this time, policy discord and internal recrimination had led, one by one, to the resignation of all the original architects of the Cruzado policy, with Funaro finally departing in March 1987.

The most visible and dramatic aspect of the next phase of the story occurred on the "external side," with the government's announcement in February that

[34] *Veja*, 14 January 1987, p. 29. Sarney's approval ratings, which had gone from minus 36 percent in January 1986 to plus 68 percent in March, plunged again to minus 22 percent by December 1986.

[35] "Confronto em aberto: críticas de Sarney a Mario Amato e a FIESP desagradam aos empresários, que já se mobilizam contra a nova ofensiva do governo," *Veja*, 21 January 1987, pp. 84–86.

it intended to suspend interest payments on its medium- and long-term external private debt. The decision, made during Funaro's last weeks as finance minister, was widely viewed as an ad hoc response to the collapse of the Cruzado and the deterioration of reserves—an effort to avoid a "return to the Fund," undertaken without any clear idea of how to deal with domestic price stabilization. A relatively coherent package of domestic adjustments did begin to take shape, however, after the appointment of the new finance minister, Luiz Carlos Bresser Pereira, a left-of-center economist associated with the PMDB. Once again, a heterodox wage/price freeze was a central component of the package—this time, however, with an explicit ninety-day limit and without the compensatory wage "sweeteners" provided by the Cruzado. The new finance minister also expressed determination to reduce the fiscal deficit through a combination of spending reductions, increases in public tariffs, and tax increases.

This time, there was no honeymoon period. Although the moratorium decision did receive some support from the PMDB, most party leaders continued to increase their distance from Sarney. Opposition leaders on the left generally viewed the moratorium as too little and too late. All it proved, remarked "Lula," the leader of the new independent union movement, "is that the government is broke."[36] Business reactions were also negative, even among groups that earlier had approved the break with the IMF. Comments summarized in *Veja*, a leading weekly newsmagazine, emphasized the "jump into the void" and expressed serious concern over the disruption of trade credits and key imports.[37] Finally, although the government expressed the hope of finding a new modus vivendi with the private banks, it met with a predictably hostile response from creditors. To Bresser's supreme embarrassment, U.S. Treasury Secretary Baker immediately dismissed a proposal to swap debt for discounted bonds as a "nonstarter." Negotiations with the private banks remained stalled throughout 1987, a time when (not coincidentally) Mexico and Argentina were concluding highly favorable new credit packages.

As with the Cruzado, however, the most difficult political problems centered on aspects of domestic adjustment policy. Bresser quickly found that there would be no presidential backing for reducing fiscal expenditures. Sarney (along with the military) declined to abandon plans for an ambitious railroad construction project conceived in earlier years, and governors allied to Sarney were able to insist on subsidies and bailouts for private firms in their states.

Although the unions and the left were not strong enough to prevent a substantial deterioration in general wage levels, a strike within the Bank of Brazil,

[36] *Veja*, 25 February 1987, p. 34.
[37] Ibid.

nominally under Bresser's direct authority, triggered a crippling round of salary increases for strategically placed public employees.

Finally, as they did under the Cruzado package, the business sector mounted a fierce attack on the price freeze and eventually dealt the fatal blows to the program as a whole. In September, the automobile giant Autolatina won a crucial court case against Bresser's ruling on automobile prices. Other companies simply ignored the restrictions entirely, and by the fourth quarter of 1987, monthly inflation rates were hurtling toward the 20-percent mark. The coup de grace came in December 1987, when bitter protests by FIESP induced Sarney to withdraw his support for a capital gains tax proposed by Bresser and forced the latter's resignation.

The new finance minister was Maílson Pereira da Nóbrega, a moderately conservative technocrat who had no ties to the PMDB. Although it was unlikely that he would be able to steer Brazil in a consistently orthodox direction, his appointment may well have marked the end of attempts to extend Brazil's traditional "developmentalist" approaches through the 1980s. Even with a dynamic export sector, it no longer seemed possible to avoid the constraints produced by the collapse of external financial markets. By early 1988, Maílson had embarked on efforts to negotiate an IMF agreement and to restore Brazil's standing with private creditors. Whatever the success of these efforts, this was an acknowledgment of diminished opportunities to mute domestic distributive struggles by stretching periods of economic expansion.

The "solution" reached under somewhat similar conditions in the period 1964–1967 was to transfer the costs of orthodox fiscal and monetary austerity onto the wage and salary sector. With the fierce business resistance to tax increases and price freeze, this is a course that again may become attractive to business groups that have otherwise resisted economic orthodoxy. For the time being, however, the viability of this option is limited by tentative military and business inclinations to operate within a constitutional framework. A much stronger and more independent workers' movement—compared to the 1960s—may be an even more important impediment. Such a movement may still be too weak to block a wage-repressive stabilization program backed by the military. But the political costs and long-term scars are likely to be much greater than they were twenty years ago.

It may be possible eventually to use the mechanisms of political democracy to mobilize backing for a more equitably designed stabilization program. In some respects, this was the inspiration behind both the Cruzado and Bresser Pereira programs. As we have just seen, however, the upper strata of Brazilian society have reacted strongly against even mildly redistributive adjustments; even with more extensive channels of consultation, high expectations on the workers' side would impede the task of winning their cooperation. Much more than in Argentina, a government seeking to implement a major redistribution of burdens within a democratic context would have to face the potential veto of a strong, cohesive military establishment that still claims the authority to arbitrate political struggles.

Under these circumstances, the power equation in Brazil appears to point toward more stalemated and inconclusive conflicts over stablization and adjustment—more "characteristically" Argentine than Brazilian. As long as such conflict continues to be played in a constitutional context, the door remains open to the possibility of political compromises and creative problem solving. But the risk is considerable that stop-go cycles will be shorter and sharper than in the past and that the military will not stay far from the political surface. A new round of military dictatorship, operating under much more severe international and domestic political constraints, can be expected to be much more repressive politically and less sucessful economically than the version between 1964 and 1985.

Argentina and the Austral: The Search for a Middle Ground

By the end of 1985, as the Argentine economy began to emerge from its long recession, the Alfonsín administration also confronted problems of overheating. For reasons already discussed, the group assembled under Sourrouille was in a better position than the economic team in Brazil to cope with such pressures by making adjustments in the Austral package. The government opened up a new phase in the program in March 1986, when it decided to begin an upward adjustment in price levels and to devalue the Austral/dollar exchange rate. This move to end the absolute price freeze was a crucial step, which helped to deter the hoarding and illegal surcharges that had begun to plague Brazil at about the same time; but it also raised the spector of a renewed inflationary spiral. The Sourrouille group responded with incremental efforts to steer the system away from crisis by tightening monetary controls, containing wage demands, and renegotiating its position with external creditors. For reasons already discussed, until about the middle of 1987, these efforts yielded noteworthy gains on all three fronts.

Negotiating wage adjustments involved restructuring the government's political relations with the Peronist-dominated unions. The Alfonsín administration had gotten off to a terrible start in early 1984 by proposing union reform legislation that offended virtually every faction of the Peronist movement. Labor protest, moreover, placed the administration increasingly on the defensive as Alfonsín's term wore on. General strikes and wage strikes surged in 1984 and early 1985, subsided briefly during the Alfonsín honeymoon, then started to surge again at the end of 1985.

In important respects, however, Argentine authorities fared somewhat better in negotiating these conflicts than their Brazilian counterparts, who had begun to rely increasingly on confrontation and intimidation.[38] In May 1986, after a number of half-hearted attempts to negotiate a general "social pact" with the unions, the Sourrouille group began to bypass the militant Peronist peak association, the General Confederation of Labor (CGT), and to bargain directly with the heads of key industrial federations, most dominated by old-line Peronist bosses. From the government's viewpoint, the new approach successfully helped contain wage pressures. A band of officially designated minimum and maximum wage levels established a range within which bargaining would be conducted. Agreements were then negotiated on a sector-by-sector basis, and by the middle of 1986 contracts had been concluded in such strategic areas as metallurgy, plastics, textiles, and the civil service. Some of these wage settlements did add to inflationary pressures; but most of the contracts stayed within government guidelines, and all contained commitments not to seek new adjustments for a six-month period—a crucial step for slowing the momentum of the inertial spiral. Thus, although the CGT continued to mobilize protests throughout 1986 and 1987, this round of agreements marked an important improvement in the uneasy relations between the government and the union movement.

A second major political battle emerged over the rediscount policies of the Central Bank, headed since 1983 by the Radical economist Alfredo Concepción. To hold the line on monetary policy, Sourrouille sought to limit Central Bank lending to politically influential provincial banks that had been hit hard by the financial crisis. But since these banks were linked closely to local political machines and smaller businesses, threats to their liquidity provoked strong protests from most segments of the Radical leadership. The internecine conflicts over this issue seesawed back and forth for the next several years. Despite substantial opposition from his own party, however, Alfonsín did back Sourrouille's effort to gain control of the Central Bank during 1986 and early 1987. In mid-1986, Sourrouille vetoed Radical party attempts to fill key vacancies on the board of directors. In August, he won an even more significant victory when Concepción himself was replaced as head of the Central Bank by José Luis Machinea, one of the finance minister's closest allies. For the time being, these victories were important to reaffirm and strengthen the cautious monetary directions charted at the inception of the Austral program.

On the "external front," finally, the Alfonsín government continued, unlike Sarney's, to adopt an essentially collaborative position with international creditor groups as a means of shoring up its deteriorating external accounts position. The response of official lending authorities and private banks was generally positive. Despite shortfalls on a range of targets during 1986, the IMF continued to disburse stand-by funds. IMF-World Bank agreements con-

[38] Marcelo Cavarozzi, Liliana de Riz, Jorge Feldman, "Concertación, Estado, y Sindicatos en la Argentina Contemporanea," (unpublished manuscript, CEDES, Buenos Aires, April 1986).

cluded in 1987 (in the context of the Brazilian moratorium) totalled $3.35 billion, and included a Mexican-style contingency fund to cover slowdowns in expansion. Subsequent agreements with the private banks were reported to include almost $2 billion in new money, at a spread that had previously been granted to Mexico on a "one-time only" basis.

Despite these victories, however, it became increasingly difficult by the middle of 1987 for the Alfonsín government to sustain its recovery. Growth rates slowed, the trade balance continued to deteriorate, and—after a new attempt at a price freeze—prices began to edge up toward 200 percent. Compared to the catastrophic collapse of the Cruzado, this was still not a bad performance. Yet it fell well short of what most sectors of Argentine society had hoped.

An important part of the problem was the approaching gubernatorial and congressional elections of 1987, which made it harder politically for Alfonsín to maintain anti-inflationary controls. In early 1987, for example, the appointment of a Peronist to head the Labor Ministry—an effort to draw closer to the union movement—injected a major note of dissension within the Cabinet over Sourrouille's wage policy. Similarly, despite the finance minister's earlier victory in the struggle over the Central Bank, it became increasingly difficult for the administration to resist Radical demands for a liberalization of rediscount lending. As with Sarney a year earlier, such decisions appeared to backfire both politically and economically. Many observers interpreted the Radicals' subsequent defeat in the midterm elections to popular disappointment over the resurgence of inflation.

In addition to the timing of the midterm elections, the Alfonsín administration faced two structural problems that loomed larger as the presidential term wore on. The fiscal weakness of the Argentine state was a major issue. During 1985, the fiscal gap had been narrowed by increases in public tariffs and by the gains in the real value of tax revenues that stemmed from the price freeze. But the public enterprise sector continued to be a major drain on public resources, and tax capacity remained considerably weaker than in either Brazil or Mexico. In 1986, consequently, deficits were somewhat higher than original targets, and in 1987, they widened even more. Tax and expenditure reforms thus remained one of the major unresolved issues on the political agenda.[39] During the initial honeymoon period of the Austral, it might have been possible to push such reforms through the Argentine legislature. Especially after the Radical party's midterm losses in 1987, however, time appeared to be working against the Alfonsín administration on this matter.

The second set of issues concerned the relation between the state and the private sector. On one hand, small Argentine banks and firms, already con-

---

[39] Rudiger Dornbusch and Juan Carlos De Pablo, "Debt and Macroeconomic Instability in Argentina," in Jeffrey D. Sachs, *Developing Country Debt and the World Economy* (Chicago: University of Chicago Press, 1989), pp. 37–57.

tending with very high interest rates, operated on the margin of bankruptcy. On the other hand, much more than in Brazil, the large-scale financial-industrial groups that were able to tolerate high interest rates remained heavily involved in short-term speculative activities and were inclined to wait for a clearer picture of follow-up policies before engaging in long-term investments. As had happened so often in the past, the relative ease with which such firms could move funds across sectors and abroad placed the government in an especially precarious position in handling both its monetary and fiscal policy.[40] The major question confronting new democratic governments in Argentina was still whether the guarantees required for increased investment by such groups could be made compatible with ongoing rivalries and bargaining within the union and party system.

MEXICO: ECONOMIC ORTHODOXY

For most of the 1980s, Mexico's durable authoritarian system provided a very different institutional setting for addressing the types of policy dilemmas discussed in the previous section. In contrast to the military-backed regimes that rose and fell in South America, the Mexican regime rested on firmer foundations—the Institutional Revolutionary Party (PRI) and its allied union and peasant organizations, a powerful political machine that based its claim to power on its roots in Mexico's revolutionary past. Between the 1920s and the 1980s, governmental elites deployed this machinery to mobilize electoral legitimation and co-opt competing labor and business interests, combining highly concentrated executive authority with considerable tolerance for public debate and dissent. During the early 1970s, however, the growing complexity of the interests contending within this framework began to make it increasingly difficult for state officials to manage the political process. By the 1980s, political conflicts in both civil society and the state itself had escalated into a crisis that appeared likely to produce fundamental changes in the nature of the system.

This section places the stabilization and adjustment policies of the 1980s in the context of these conflicts. Our point of departure is the unraveling of the political equilibrium established from the early 1950s to the late 1960s (the "stabilizing development" period), and the controversial efforts to reform the system in the 1970s. We then turn to the sharp shift to more orthodox approaches adopted during the presidency of Miguel de la Madrid (1982–1988) and to the way these approaches interacted with changes in the underlying balance of political power. We conclude with considerations of the principal contrasts between the Mexican experience and those of Argentina and Brazil.

---

[40] Jorge Schvarzer, "El Estado y su Mecanismo de Regulación frente a Diferentes Situaciónes Macroeconómicas" (Paper presented in the conference, "Crisis y Opciónes Societales ante Ella," CLASCO, Pôrto Alegre, Brasil, July 1986).

Historical Background: The Stabilizing Development Model and the Reforms of the 1970s

Between about 1955 and 1970, Mexico experienced a long period of unusually high growth with one of the lowest rates of domestic inflation in the region (see table 3.2). In economic terms, this "stabilizing development" period was based on a strategy of state-led import-substitution combined with highly restrained credit and fiscal policies implemented by technocrats of Mexico's powerful Central Bank and Treasury Departments.[41]

Politically, the period reflected two important priorities. One was to consolidate the increasingly cooperative relations initiated during the 1940s with the United States and domestic private capital, a major turn away from the social reformism and nationalism of earlier decades. The other was to shore up the position of the official unions and the organized white-collar sector, the most powerful segments of the PRI's popular base. Real wages of these groups, which had deteriorated badly during the 1940s, began to rise in the mid-1950s and continued to do so until the end of the 1970s (see table 3.3). Underlying this political balancing act were four sets of tacit understandings that served as important reference points for the growing conflicts of subsequent decades.

1. Macroeconomic policy authority would be concentrated within the treasury and the Bank of Mexico. In the aftermath of the civil wars of the 1910s, these institutions gained a privileged place within the state apparatus and established strong traditions of technocratic competence and financial orthodoxy.[42]
2. In exchange for the establishment of a "suitable investment climate," business groups would sustain a relatively low profile in national politics, relying for political access on informal contacts and formal consultations conducted through officially recognized associational groups.[43]
3. In exchange for their collaboration in the task of social control and electoral mobilization, the heads of the Mexican Worker's Confederation (CTM) and other allied groups of unionized workers would be provided with the political backing of the state and expanding material resources to distribute to their members.
4. The government would deal with resource constraints by shifting spending priorities and attention away from social services and distributive programs aimed

[41] John K. Thompson, *Inflation, Financial Markets, and Economic Development: The Experience of Mexico* (Greenwich, Conn.: Jai Press, 1979).

[42] Charles W. Anderson, "Bankers as Revolutionaries: Politics and Development Banking in Mexico," in *The Political Economy of Mexico*, William P. Glade and Charles W. Anderson, eds. (Madison: University of Wisconsin Press, 1963), pp. 113–14.

[43] Sylvia Maxfield and Ricardo Anzaldua Montoyo, eds., *Government and Private Sector in Contemporary Mexico*, Center for U.S.-Mexican Studies, Monograph series no. 20 (San Diego: University of California, 1987): Sylvia Maxfield, "Introduction," pp. 1–12; Matilde Luna, Ricardo Tirado, Francisco Valdes, "Businessmen and Politics in Mexico, 1982–1986," trans. Carmen R. Graizbord, pp. 13–44; Celso Garrido Noguero, Enrique Quintana López, "Financial Relations and Economic Power in Mexico," trans. Sandra de Castillo, pp. 105–26.

TABLE 3.2
Mexico, Argentina, Brazil: Annual Rates of GDP Growth and Inflation, 1946–1970

Year	Mexico GDP[a]	Inflation	Argentina GDP[b]	Inflation	Brazil GDP[c]	Inflation
1946	6.6	25.0	—	17.1	—	27.3
1947	4.0	12.6	—	12.2	—	5.8
1948	4.5	6.2	—	13.0	7.4	3.5
1949	6.1	5.4	—	32.7	6.6	6.0
1950	9.7	10.6	—	24.6	6.5	11.4
1951	7.7	12.6	3.8	37.2	6.0	10.8
1952	3.9	14.5	−5.0	38.1	8.7	20.4
1953	0.2	−1.7	5.4	4.3	2.5	17.6
1954	10.5	25.9	4.1	3.5	10.1	25.6
1955	8.8	16.0	7.1	12.5	6.9	18.9
1956	6.6	4.9	2.8	13.1	3.2	21.8
1957	7.6	5.8	5.1	25.0	8.1	13.4
1958	5.5	11.5	6.3	31.4	7.7	17.3
1959	−0.1	2.4	−6.4	113.9	5.6	51.9
1960	11.2	4.9	7.9	27.3	9.7	23.8
1961	3.5	1.7	7.1	13.5	10.3	42.9
1962	6.3	1.2	−1.7	28.1	5.3	55.8
1963	5.0	0.7	−2.4	24.0	1.5	80.2
1964	10.2	2.2	10.4	22.1	2.9	86.6
1965	5.3	3.7	9.1	28.6	2.7	45.5
1966	7.7	4.2	0.7	31.9	5.1	41.2
1967	6.5	3.0	2.5	29.2	4.8	24.1
1968	—	2.3	4.6	16.2	9.3	24.5
1969	—	3.7	7.9	7.6	9.0	24.3
1970	—	5.2	4.1	13.6	9.5	20.9

Source: Thomas E. Skidmore, "The Politics of Economic Stabilization in Postwar Latin America," in Authoritarianism and Corporatism in Latin America, James M. Malloy, ed. (Pittsburgh: University of Pittsburgh Press, 1977), tabs. 1, 8, 11, 14.
[a] In 1950 pesos.
[b] At 1960 factor prices.
[c] At 1949 prices.

at the PRI's traditional peasant constituency and at the growing urban underclass.[44]

These underlying rules of the game worked quite well as mechanisms for sustaining the stability of the Mexican regime. By the end of the 1960s, however, indications of strain were increasing. The rapid growth of preceding decades had generated accumulating infrastructural and capital-goods bottle-

[44] Hansen, Politics of Mexican Development, pp. 85–87.

TABLE 3.3
Changes in Mexican Minimum Daily Wage Levels, 1945–1966

Year	Urban Average[a]	Rural Average[a]
1945	5.41	3.41
1946	5.51	3.56
1947	4.89	3.17
1948	5.25	3.61
1949	4.99	3.42
1950	5.41	3.81
1951	4.79	3.38
1952	5.88	3.99
1953	5.97	4.06
1954	8.22	5.71
1955	7.08	5.78
1956	6.94	5.05
1957	6.56	4.77
1958	6.87	4.96
1959	6.69	4.84
1960	7.60	5.48
1961	7.48	5.40
1962	9.02	6.17
1963	8.96	6.13
1964	11.02	7.80
1965	10.63	7.52
1966	10.60	8.77

Source: Timothy King, *Mexico: Industrialization & Trade Policies since 1940* (London: Oxford University Press, 1970), tab. 2.10.

[a] Pesos, 1954 prices.

necks that required urgent attention if expansion was to be maintained in the future. Even more important was the growing evidence of dissatisfaction over the turn away from the reformist orientations of the past: bitter student protests, a decline in electoral turnout, an upsurge in rural land seizures, and guerilla activity.

These developments provided strong signals to Mexican elites that they could not avoid significant changes in the prevailing economic and political model. The turn in more reformist directions during the 1970s was primarily an attempt to address these issues from above. The flamboyant Luis Echeverría (1970–1976) inaugurated these changes with a controversial land reform program, major increases in health and education expenditures, a shift to the left in foreign policy, and greater bargaining latitude for both official and independent unions. Although the more moderate José López Portillo (1976–1982) ended the land reform, he added a reform of the electoral system aimed at providing greater representation for opposition parties, and he continued the trends in the area of labor policy and social spending. Without jeopardizing the essential structures of PRI domination, most of these reforms did help to deflect or co-opt the most radical pressures on the system, and in this respect, they were at least partially successful in accomplishing their goals. Yet these achievements came at the cost of upsetting the other arrangements that had contributed to the stability of the earlier period. For our purpose, three developments are particularly relevant to an understanding of the crisis of the 1980s.

FISCAL PRESSURES ASSOCIATED WITH STATE ENTERPRISE SECTOR GROWTH

Although public investment grew steadily throughout the stabilizing development period, a new "shared development" strategy announced under Echeverría in the early 1970s marked an important shift in emphasis for the state's role in the accumulation process. The overall level of public expenditure, comparatively low in 1970, became one of the highest in the region by 1982. The state's share of all fixed capital formation, about a third in the 1950s and 40 percent in the 1960s, had risen to over 50 percent by the early 1980s, with particular emphasis on petroleum, electricity, and steel.[45]

The revenue side of this equation, however, constituted a serious weakness for the model as a whole. Initiatives to increase Mexico's low tax rates, an important component of the earlier stabilizing development model, were blocked under Echeverría by strong behind-the-scenes pressure from business elites.[46] For the next decade, the results of this political standoff bore some resemblance to the developmentalist pattern experienced in Brazil in the late 1950s and again in the 1970s. A continued high rate of expansion, necessary for mitigating distributive conflicts, was accompanied by growing fiscal and external accounts deficits, resurgent inflation, and an expanding external debt. In 1975–1976, a speculative run on the peso triggered a major economic crisis, forcing the outgoing Echeverría administration into an IMF stabilization agreement and Mexico's first devaluation since 1954. Although the onset of the oil boom in 1978 rather quickly dissolved the immediate crisis, the underlying structural problems were essentially the same as those contributing to the post-1982 collapse.

DECLINE IN INFLUENCE OF BANK AND TREASURY TECHNOCRATS

The onset of the Echeverría period also brought a major shift in the correlation of factional forces within the state apparatus and the PRI leadership. Although Bank of Mexico and treasury officials remained extremely powerful players in the policy process, they lost the hegemony they had previous exer-

---

[45] E.V.K. Fitzgerald, "Capital Accumulation in Mexico," *Journal of Latin American Studies* 10, 2 (November 1978): 277.

[46] Leopoldo Solís, *Economic Policy Reform in Mexico: A Case Study for Developing Countries* (Elmsford, N.Y., Pergamon, 1981).

cised. Conversely, structuralist and neo-Keynesian economists, who played a major role in shaping the shared development doctrines of the early 1970s, continued to have significant policy-making influence until the advent of de la Madrid. Bank and treasury influence was also diminished by the emergence of new bureaucratic centers of power in the cabinet and within the state enterprise sector. One of the most important was the Secretaría de Programación y Presupuesto (SPP), a new superministry formed in 1977 with responsibilities for investment planning and public expenditures.[47] Although conservative technocrats often controlled this agency, it nevertheless tended to tilt in more expansionist directions than the bank and the treasury, and on occasion it provided an important foothold for economists with less orthodox perspectives.

BREAKDOWN OF SOCIAL CONTRACT WITH BUSINESS

An important corollary of the developments just described was the introduction of major new uncertainties into the relations between the state and large business groups that had grown increasingly powerful during previous decades.[48] The private sector, to be sure, was deeply divided over such issues as trade policy and foreign investment, and reactions to specific government initiatives were far from monolithic. Many industrialists profited substantially, for example, from the subsidized inputs and lucrative contracts provided by the expanding state enterprise sector. But business interests in general were uneasy about the new populist directions assumed by the governments of the 1970s, particularly when the decline of the bank and treasury technocrats seemed to be reducing their most important access point. The "central tendency" among these groups was thus to expand their political activity and organizational resources in ways that would reduce their dependence on the good will of governmental authorities.

Special note must be taken at this point of the role played by the powerful industrial-financial elites based mainly in the north of Mexico. With economic and political antecedents that predated the 1910 Revolution, this group stood out as the most orthodox and politically militant component of the private sector, more extensively linked than most other Mexican business groups to U.S. capital and export markets and in a reasonably good position to profit from the liberalization of trade and capital flows. Particularly after the mid-1970s, they also provided the cutting edge of business demands for greater political power: spearheading publicity campaigns, sponsoring the formation of a major new peak association (the Consejo Coordinador Empresarial, or

[47] John J. Baily, "Public Budgeting in Mexico, 1970–1982," *Public Budgeting and Finance* (Spring 1984) pp. 76–90; idem, "Presidency, Bureaucracy, and Administrative Reform in Mexico: The Secratariat of Programming and Budget,"*InterAmerican Economic Affairs*, 34, 1 (Summer 1980): 27–60.

[48] Saul David Escobar, "Rifts in the Mexican Power Elite, 1976–1986," trans. Sandra del Castillo, in Maxfield and Anzaldua Montoyo, eds., *Government and Private Sector*, pp. 65–88.

CCE), and providing increasing financial backing for the right wing PAN opposition party.

Confrontations between these hardline groups and the government fluctuated considerably under Echeverría and López Portillo. It reached a high point during Echeverría's land reform in the mid-1970s, subsided considerably for most of López Portillo's term, and then surged again after the decision to nationalize the private banking sector in 1982. Even during the quiet periods, however, it was clear that there would be no return to the norms of the stabilizing development era. By the beginning of the 1980s, the state-business relationship had irreversibly politicized.

Crisis of the 1980s and the Rise of de la Madrid

Towards the end of 1980, a sharp rise in U.S. interest rates and a decline in the price of Mexican oil exports marked the onset of the developments that eventually led to the crisis of 1982. For our purposes, it is not necessary to weigh precisely the relative importance of "external" and "internal" causes; clearly both were important. The tightening of U.S. monetary policy—the most immediate source of Mexico's debt-service squeeze—was obviously well beyond the control of the Mexican government, as was the subsequent evolution of U.S. trade, fiscal, and monetary policy. But Mexican fiscal and trade policies compounded the vulnerability of the system to such shocks, particularly after oil prices began to slump in 1980–1981. In an attempt to sustain the expansion of the late 1970s, the government stepped up external borrowing activity, relying on an expanding volume of short-term credits to finance the growing fiscal and trade deficits and allowing the peso to become increasingly overvalued.

In 1982, speculative pressures on the peso intensified, and the government began to engage in an increasingly desperate series of efforts to stem the outflow of capital. In February, the Central Bank allowed the dollar price of the peso to double in an effort to halt foreign exchange speculation. Next came the establishment of a two-tier exchange market, which established a fixed peso/dollar rate for priority transactions, but an unregulated rate for all others. When such measures proved ineffective, however, the crisis broke into the open. In August, the government fired the shot heard round the world, announcing that it could not meet interest payments coming due within the next few days and initiating negotiations for bridge loans and rescheduling agreements with the U.S. Treasury, the IMF, and the private commercial banks. In September, during the final months of the presidential transition period, continued speculation against the peso triggered the controversial decision to nationalize the domestic banking system, evoking another sharp wave of private sector protest. The year ended with the conclusion of an IMF agreement in November and the inauguration of de la Madrid in December.

The orthodox policies followed since the inauguration of the Miguel de la Madrid administration generally followed directions already signaled by the emergency negotiations with the banks and the signing of the IMF agreement. Strong international pressures—close ties to the United States, diminished access to international credit, and the need to induce flight capital back into the country—combined to push the regime in more orthodox directions. Yet the change in policy approach by no means flowed automatically from the crisis itself; indeed, the September bank nationalization reflected the presence within the regime of politically influential forces that sought to respond to the crisis with more heterodox measures.

Why did more orthodox views prevail during the 1980s? Obviously, the designation of de la Madrid as López Portillo's successor was pivotal in tipping the scales in an orthodox direction. De la Madrid was among the leaders of the conservative faction based in the treasury and the Central Bank, and as president, he strongly backed the resurgence of this faction within the governing elite. Thirteen of his initial eighteen cabinet appointments were from this background.[49] These included the heads of the three command centers of the economic bureaucracy: Jesús Silva Herzog in the treasury, Miguel Mancera at the Central Bank, and Carlos Salinas, eventually designated as president, in the SPP.

But why the choice of de la Madrid? What enabled him to sponsor such an extensive technocratic "takeover" of the administrative summit? In a system where deliberations over such issues are so thoroughly shrouded in secrecy, definitive answers are impossible.[50] Yet we can gain some insight into these changes by considering larger processes of political transformation in Mexican society and the way these interacted with key features of Mexico's authoritarian system.

Within the larger society, the most important development was the emergence of the northern financial-industrial sector as a major political force. Well before the beginning of the de la Madrid term, the bitter polarization of the mid-1970s had already imparted considerable momentum to their demands for economic liberalization and changes in the political system. After the post-1982 crisis closed in, several additional factors tended to augment the weight of these business hardliners and to increase their capacity to deter the de la Madrid government from straying too far from its orthodox commitments.

The first was the September 1982 bank nationalization. Although compensation issues were quickly settled under de la Madrid, the decree reinforced the hardline thesis that the PRI dominated system could not be trusted to refrain from the temptation of arbitrary and demagogic initiatives. This was the sec-

[49] Oscar Hinojosa, "Banco de Mexico y Hacienda, Manantiales de los Hombres del Presidente," *Proceso*, 507 (21 July 1986): 6–11.

[50] Steven E. Sandersen, "Presidential Succession and Political Reality in Mexico," *World Politics*, 35, 3 (April 1983), pp. 315–334.

ond time since the land reform of the mid-1970s, argued the business radicals, that the regime had instituted a major assault on private property. This, they argued, placed a special burden on de la Madrid to demonstrate that during his term, there would be no more surprises.[51]

The international financial crisis also tended to shift the balance of power within the Mexican business community and to increase the leverage that orthodox hardliners could use against the state. On one hand, interruption of the flow of external credit weakened the capacity of the state enterprise sector to deliver subsidies and public contracts to more inward-oriented business groups. On the other hand, although most northern sectors had also fed at the public trough, their control over liquid assets and their links to foreign markets placed them in a better position to ride out the credit austerity, capitalize on peso devaluation, or if necessary, get their money out of the country entirely.

Factional shifts within the inner circles of the government paralleled these larger trends. Because the choice of de la Madrid was made in late 1981, it seems likely that elite opinion was already moving in a more conservative direction even before the crisis. After 1982, a number of features of the authoritarian system added to the momentum.

First, in its responses to the challenges posed by an increasingly independent and militant business class, the political elite could turn to conservative technocrats that already occupied important roles within government. Although their influence had declined during the 1970s, these technocrats had remained important players in the policy process. Indeed, Silva Herzog and Mancera, the heads of the treasury and Central Bank, had occupied exactly the same positions under López Portillo. Thus, although the orthodox resurgence marked an important political change *within* the institutional framework, it did not require the kinds of disruptive military takeovers that had carried conservative technocrats to power in Argentina and Brazil during previous decades.

The highly concentrated system of executive authority was also crucial in consolidating these shifts. Regardless of their own factional links, most earlier presidents had typically made high-level appointments with a view toward balancing competing segments of the political elite. In contrast, de la Madrid deployed his power of appointment to push more heterodox economists from virtually all positions of authority and to diminish sharply the role of the political left. More importantly, the president appeared determined to extend this trend over a longer period by choosing Carlos Salinas, his closest advisor, to be his successor. Although this exercise of presidential power did not fully end the balancing act of earlier decades, it was important in establishing the basis for the implementation of a tough austerity program and a comparatively comprehensive program of trade liberalization.

---

[51] Luna, Tirado, and Valdes, "Businessmen and Politics," pp. 13–45.

Finally, the powerful social control mechanisms built into the Mexican system clearly facilitated the government's decision to move toward more austere and outward-oriented economic policies. Although long-term risks were connected with ignoring popular-sector opposition to such policies—risks increasingly evident after the presidential elections of 1988—de la Madrid could worry far less than his Argentine and Brazilian counterparts about the immediate claims of unions and opposition parties. On the other hand, big business groups were in a position to pose much more clear and present dangers to the stability of the system. Earlier waves of business protest, especially in the mid-1970s, demonstrated clearly that these groups had substantial capacity to disrupt the political process. As had long been the case in Mexico, the threat of massive capital flight loomed continuously over the heads of decision makers. Much more than in the democratizing regimes of Argentina and Brazil, this stacked the deck heavily against populist responses to the crisis.

Policy Responses to the Crisis of the 1980s

In the context of these developments, the Mexican government effected a sharp right turn in economic policy that persisted until the end of the de la Madrid term. The principal features of the new recovery strategy—austerity, greater attention to structural reform, and collaborative relations with external creditors—all differed in orthodoxy and comprehensiveness from the strategies described previously in Argentina and Brazil. Rightly or wrongly, moreover, the de la Madrid administration pursued its initial course with considerable consistency, despite an important change in tactics and emphasis that came with the initiation of the "solidarity pact" in the last year of the presidential term. In this section, we examine at the main features of these policies as well as some of their principal economic and political outcomes.

STABILIZATION POLICIES

The evolution of stabilization policy in Mexico can be subdivided into three time periods: from the end of 1982 to about mid-1985; from 1985 to the end of 1987; and the presidential transition year of 1988, always a time of considerable political and economic uncertainty in Mexico. The first of these periods was inaugurated with considerable hope that IMF-backed stabilization measures agreed on at the end of 1982 would be quickly followed by a restoration of international credit and a speedy economic recovery.[52] This hope was dashed, however, in the course of the next several years. After a crushing domestic recession in 1983, a slight easing of fiscal and monetary controls led

[52] Nora Lustig and Jaime Ros, *Stabilization and Adjustment in Mexico: 1982–1985* (Paper for the UNU/WINDER conference on "Stabilization and Adjustment Programs and Policies," Helsinki, 19–21 August 1986).

to a brief reactivation from mid-1984 to mid-1985. But as the trade deficit again began to widen and oil prices plunged, the government turned to a harsh new credit freeze and the economy plunged back into severe recession.

The second phase of government policy dates from the onset of this new crisis period during the second half of 1985. It was marked in general by continued reliance on demand-management policies, but a disappearance of the élan and certainty that characterized the earlier period. One reflection of this uncertainty was the sudden departure of Treasury Minister Jesús Silva Herzog, the chief rival of Carlos Salinas for the presidential succession and the strongest advocate within the administration of even greater fiscal austerity. Though Silva's departure produced no significant changes in the government's basic strategy, it paved the way for a cautious attempt to ease the economy out of its recession through a slight easing of credit to the private sector.

Growing debate over fiscal problems was a second important aspect of the new period, which continued to loom large throughout the rest of the de la Madrid era. The principal concern of many orthodox economists outside the government was the growth of the "financial" deficit, i.e., the difference between revenues and all expenditures, including interest payments on past debt. After having come down substantially in 1983 and 1984, this began to rise steeply again in subsequent years (see table 3.4). In late 1985, this development prompted the IMF to suspend payments on its EFF agreement, setting into motion a difficult new round of negotiations that lasted well into the next year.

TABLE 3.4
Mexican Economic Performance in the 1980s

	1981	1982	1983	1984	1985	1986	1987
GDP[a]	8.0	−0.6	−4.2	3.6	2.6	−4.0	1.0
Consumer Prices	28.7	98.8	80.8	59.2	63.7	105.7	143.6
Urban Minimum Wage[b]	101.9	92.7	76.6	72.3	71.1	64.9	55.9
Interest Payment on External Debt[c]	29.0	47.2	37.5	39.0	36.0	37.9	27.9
Fiscal Deficit[d]	14.8	17.7	8.9	8.7	10.0	16.3	
Current Accounts[e]	−5.8	−3.7	3.8	2.5	0.7	−1.3	
Gross Fixed Capital Formation[f]	25.7	21.0	16.1	16.3	16.9	15.4	
Private	14.5	11.7	9.4	9.9	10.9	10.2	
Public	11.2	9.3	6.6	6.4	6.0	5.2	

Sources: GDP, Consumer Prices, Urban Minimum Wage, Interest Payment on External Debt: United Nations Economic Commission for Latin America and the Caribbean, *Preliminary Overview of the Latin American Economy, 1987* (Santiago, Chile: 31 December 1987, LC/G. 1485), pp. 15, 17, 18, 24.

Fiscal deficit and Gross Fixed Capital Formation: Eduard F. Buffie, with the assistance of Allen Sangines Krause, "Mexico 1958–1986: From Stabilizing Development to the Debt Crisis," in Jeffrey D. Sachs, ed., *Developing Country Debt and the World Economy* (Chicago: University of Chicago Press, 1989), pp. 156, 159.

Current Accounts: International Monetary Fund, *International Financial Statistics Yearbook, 1988* (Washington, D.C.: International Monetary Fund, 1988), p. 155.

By 1987, however, financial deficits had grown to approximately the same size (as a percentage of GDP) as in 1982, the peak year, which lent fuel to the charge that the government had allowed public sector borrowing requirements to drive up interest rates and spur inflation.

Mexican officials, on the other hand, began to argue with considerable plausibility that the financial deficit was driven by forces beyond their control—that it was primarily the reflection of servicing external and domestic debt contracted in previous years at interest rates indexed to previous rates of inflation. As more accurate indicators of current efforts to impose fiscal discipline, they pointed to the "operational" budget, which corrected for the inflationary components of interest payments, and the "primary" budget, which deleted interest payments entirely. Whereas the financial deficit had grown, operational deficits remained low in comparison to earlier years. More importantly, from 1983 to 1988, the primary budget actually registered *surpluses* between 2 to 6 percent of GDP—a major turnaround from primary deficits that had reached over 8 percent of GDP at the beginning of the decade. As Stephen Quick has argued, this represented "an extraordinary willingness of [the] government to cut discretionary spending and provides the strongest evidence that fiscal austerity ha[d] taken deep root inside the Administration."[53]

In the meantime, despite strong political pressures to pump up the domestic economy, the administration stuck quite closely to other key aspects of its initial stabilization strategy. Credit to the private sector remained extremely tight even after the ouster of Silva Herzog in 1986. The general thrust of exchange rate policy was toward prolonged and painful increases in the dollar price of the peso. Wage policy remained particularly tough throughout the presidential term. Whereas workers in Argentina and Brazil managed to stay more or less even with inflation during the 1980s, the PRI-controlled tripartite bargaining commissions generally set wage adjustments at levels well below escalating prices (see table 3.5). This produced a drop of over 30 percent in the average real wage between 1982 and 1986, a sharp reversal of the twenty-five year trend toward steady improvement.

As inflation continued to surge during 1986 and 1987, the government entered a third phase of stabilization policy with the initiation in December 1987 of a "solidaridity pact" on wage and price controls. The anti-inflation pact, endorsed by the heads of the orthodox CCE as well as the official unions, reflected growing concern within both the government elite and big business sectors about the possibility of an election-year financial panic and, as 1988 wore on, about the increasing strength of the populist protest candidate, Cuauhtémoc Cárdenas. Significantly, another big devaluation and a steep in-

[53] Stephen A. Quick, "Mexico's Economic Revolution: Implications for the United States," (Staff study for the Joint Economic Committee, U.S. Congress, October 1988), p. 27; World Bank, *World Development Report 1988* (Oxford, England: Oxford University Press, 1988), pp. 56, 63.

TABLE 3.5
Mexico, Argentina, and Brazil: Average Real Wages, 1982–1987

	1982[b]	1983	1984	1985	1986	1987
Mexico	104.2	80.7	75.4	76.6	72.8	—
Argentina	80.1	100.5	127.1	107.8	109.5	100.3
Brazil[a]	121.6	112.7	105.1	112.7	121.8	105.8

Source: United Nations Economic Commission for Latin America and the Caribbean, *Preliminary Overview of the Latin American Economy, 1987* (Santiago: U.N. Publications); (1987 figures are preliminary estimates).

[a] Brazilian figures are for Rio de Janeiro.
[b] Data for all years adjusted: 1980 = 100.

crease in the price of government services preceded the announcement, indicating a strong continuing commitment to maintain the underlying austerity program. The pact, which was to be renegotiated at three-month intervals, then provided for holding both price and wage increases to targeted levels, freezing the exchange rate, and commitments to new cuts in fiscal expenditures. By the middle of 1988, these measures had successfully reduced monthly inflation rates from around 15 percent in January to less than 2 percent in July.[54]

With the decision to move toward wage/price controls, the Mexican government finally acted on the inertial inflation assumptions that had guided Argentine and Brazilian policy-makers several years earlier. The Mexican version, however, reflected important differences in political alignments and institutional frameworks. First, in contrast to Argentina and Brazil, Mexico's technocratic elite linked its program closely to an extension of the trade liberalization and privatization measures it had begun in earlier years—programs we will discuss at greater length. Second, as implied, the Mexican government generally resisted the election-year temptation to reactivate the economy and clamped down hard again on credit to the private sector after having eased slightly in 1987. (The decision to maintain a fixed exchange, however, was an important exception to this general pattern; sooner or later, it virtually guaranteed strong speculative pressure against the peso.)

Most importantly, the program of the Mexican government continued to reflect a very high priority for accommodating the interests of its orthodox critics within the Mexican private sector. The Mexican package, in contrast to that of Argentina and Brazil, was the product of ongoing negotiations with the CCE, one of the most powerful business proponents of economic orthodoxy. Conversely, although the heads of the CTM also participated in the agreements, they did little to hide the fact that they were collaborating under considerable

[54] "Mexico: 'Pact' is Renewed amid Rising Doubts," *Latin American Weekly Report* (London, England: Latin American Newsletters Ltd.), no. 6, September 1, 1988, p. 4.

pressure from the government. Throughout the process of negotiation and re-negotiation, they were generally impelled to swallow a continuation of the policy that lagged wages behind inflation.

REFORMS OF ECONOMIC STRUCTURES: TRADE LIBERALIZATION AND PRIVATIZATION

Although the government moved more slowly than anticipated in its original plans for structural adjustment, significant changes occurred in this area as well, especially after the deepening of the general economic crisis in 1985–1986. Several important foundation stones—aimed at restoring private sector confidence and strengthening private capital markets—were set in place during the first year of de la Madrid's term. The government settled rapidly on compensation for the private bank nationalization of 1982, and it offered private firms the opportunity to service dollar debts at favorable rates of exchange. It also permitted the establishment of private brokerage houses with wide latitude for financing transactions in domestic capital markets, and by 1987, these measures laid the groundwork for the growth of the first significant stock market in Mexican history.

With the de la Madrid administration initially facing a severe foreign exchange shortage, trade restrictions were initially increased in 1983. By 1984, however, import controls were relaxed substantially, and in subsequent years progress was significant in replacing the import licensing system with a generalized tariff system. By 1985, the proportion of imports covered by licensing requirements had been reduced from 75 to only 38 percent.[55] In 1986, the government signed the GATT treaty, ending more than a decade of bitter debate over whether to accept the liberalized trade provisions embodied in that system of agreements.[56] In 1987, it agreed to a framework for expanding bilateral trade relations with the United States, and in 1988, in connection with the solidarity pact, additional moves were made to eliminate quantitative import restrictions to protect local industry. In the meantime—and perhaps most significantly as changes in the structure of the Mexican economy—the peso devaluations of the preceding years had led to a significant expansion of nonoil exports led by rapidly growing investments in the maquiladora plants along the northern border.

Progress was more limited in the public enterprise sector, where the major giants proved highly resistant to rationalization or reduction. Strategically placed public-sector unions posed perhaps the most difficult roadblock. In the Mexican petroleum company PEMEX, for example, the extremely powerful petroleum union used threats of sabotage and massive resistance to force the government to back down on its plan to eliminate the union's control over

[55] Lustig and Ros, *Stabilization and Adjustment*.
[56] Dale Story, *Industry, the State, and Public Policy in Mexico* (Austin: University of Texas Press, 1986).

subcontracting—a lucrative but expensive source of political patronage.[57] Rationalization was also impeded by the capacity of state enterprise managers to manipulate the information available to fiscal authorities. Calculating asset and revenue flows between such enterprises, for example, posed major accounting problems that could be used in bureaucratic infighting; high inflation with unstable exchange rates compounded the difficulty of estimating real resource flows within the state sector.

Nevertheless, by the end of the de la Madrid era, the government had managed to sell or close a substantial number of medium and smaller public firms, and at least in some areas it had proved willing to confront powerful vested interests. Over the bitter protest of the steelworkers' union, it closed Fundidora, the oldest steel complex in the country, and at various points it used unusually strict interpretations of the labor code to crack down on striking electrical workers, teachers, and steel workers in Altos Hornos. In 1988, again in connection with the solidarity pact, the government engineered a highly controversial restructuring of Aeroméxico, one of the major public airlines, and sold the Minetas Cananea copper mine—the largest company in the region to be turned over to private investors.[58]

BARGAINING WITH EXTERNAL CREDITORS

At the onset of the debt crisis in 1982–1983, two assumptions governed the negotiating stance adopted by the Mexican regime toward external creditors. First, the risks of confrontation were higher than those implied by an orderly rescheduling of the debt—a view that continued to guide the government's policy throughout de la Madrid's term. Second, that a rapid resumption of private voluntary lending would allow the economy to grow out of its debt burden. As the Mexican economy began to enter its new round of crisis in 1985–1986 this second assumption became increasingly untenable; indeed, the total debt burden had actually increased as a percentage of GDP during that period (from 65 to over 77 percent).[59] From about 1985 onward, therefore, Mexico's relations with its creditors began to reflect the tensions between its continued adherence to the first assumption and its changing views on the second. During 1986–1988, this implied increasing demands for concessions and relief extracted in difficult, often acrimonious rounds of bargaining with creditors. At the same time, although the government sometimes appeared to approach the brink of a moratorium during these negotiations, it invariably stopped short and did not step over the edge.

The IMF and commercial bank agreements reached in 1986 are illustrative of the general process. During 1985 and 1986, the long period of bitter stale-

[57] Jeffrey Bortz, "The Dilemma of Mexican Labor," *Current History*, 86, 518 (March 1987): 105–8, 129–30.
[58] Quick, "Mexico's Economic Revolution," p. 31.
[59] Sachs, ed., *Developing Country Debt*, p. 158.

mate that preceded these agreements triggered an extensive debate within the Mexican government about the possibilties of a more radical approach to the debt. In March 1986, an internal report prepared under Leopoldo Solís, head of the Council of Economic Advisors, argued that neither the exchange rate nor domestic inflation would be controllable as long as inconclusive negotiations with the IMF and the banks encouraged speculation against the peso. The government, it suggested, should therefore consider bypassing the IMF and taking unilateral action on debt relief if it could not reach agreements with the banks. Treasury Secretary Silva Herzog, a strong advocate of fiscal austerity at home, also began to hint at a much more militant external bargaining stance in the months prior to his dismissal.

A confrontation with creditors was finally averted by the conclusion of a new IMF agreement in July 1986, followed by a rescheduling agreement with the banks a few months later. The specific terms of both agreements involved some unprecedented concessions by the creditors. The IMF, under strong U.S. government pressure to head off a crisis, acquiesced to the Mexican interpretations of its fiscal budget deficits and, in an even more novel step, agreed to peg lending levels to fluctuations in the price of oil. Likewise, in agreements with the commercial banks, the Mexican government obtained a rescheduling at unusually low interest rates and a commitment for additional lending if the economy fell below growth levels targeted for the coming year.[60]

Within the parameters of the existing international "debt regime," such concessions represented important victories for the Mexican negotiators. Even so, it appeared unlikely that they would be sufficient to permit the economy to do more than tread water during the remaining years of the decade. Even with the agreements described above, Mexico remained a net exporter of capital, and external interest payments continued to absorb a major percentage of both fiscal expenditures and export earnings. The issue thus remained open as to whether the risks of a more militant bargaining position were worth taking. By 1986–1987, even relatively orthodox economists began to argue that, one way or another, the Mexican government should seek more extensive forms of debt relief, generally in the form of local currency bonds to be paid on a reduced fraction of the total debt.

ECONOMIC OUTCOMES AND POLITICAL REACTIONS

By the end of the de la Madrid administration, the economic consequences of the comparatively orthodox approach adopted by the outgoing government remained unclear. Despite the prolonged recession in Mexico, defenders of the administration argue that outcomes would have been still worse with more heterodox policies. It is possible, moreover, that some of the structural changes imposed in the 1980s may have laid the groundwork for increased

[60] *Wall Street Journal*, 23 July 1986, p. 25.

growth in the future—for example, the increase in nonoil exports linked to the painful devaluations of the peso. The fact remains, however, that as of 1988, de la Madrid's orthodox strategy had been no more successful than the heterodox policies in generating a sustained recovery. The zero growth rate recorded between 1982 and 1988 represented the worst six-year performance since the civil war period of the 1910s, and real wage levels deteriorated far more drastically than in either Argentina or Brazil. If anything, the most visible success of the de la Madrid administration came in its fight against inflation in 1988 when it at last began to experiment cautiously with "heterodox" wage and price controls.

The reasons why this was so will undoubtedly be debated for a long time to come. Whatever the "economic logic" of the Mexican stabilization and adjustment strategies, however, it seems clear that their implementation has carried a high political cost for the governmental elites themselves. Throughout virtually all of de la Madrid's term, the machinery of the PRI quite effectively bottled popular-sector protest; yet even before the 1988 elections there were important signs of strain. One was the restriction of the bargaining space previously opened to powerful sectors of the union movement. Work conflicts with steel, electrical workers, and telephone unions were terminated by unusually strict applications of the labor code and threats of mass layoffs. Although CTM leaders were unable to break formally with the dominant party, by 1985–1986 they began to express unprecedently sharp and public criticism of the administration's policy.[61]

Dissent also grew among left-of-center PRI activists and middle-class supporters. Until the end of 1987, this was reflected primarily in efforts to open up the PRI itself to broader "grassroots" influence. After Carlos Salinas was designated the presidential successor, however, a substantial portion of the PRI's moderate and left wing broke away to support the populist electoral challenge launched by Cuauhtémoc Cárdenas, son of the famous reformer of the 1930s. Even by the much-disputed official vote count, the popular protest vote mobilized by Cárdenas (about 37 percent compared to about 50 percent for the PRI) shook the foundations of the dominant party, which had routinely rolled up majorities between 70 and 90 percent. At the same time, despite the collaboration between the government and the CCE, the PAN opposition continued to receive considerable backing from powerful conservative business interests and remained an important challenger to the PRI's domination of the northern states.

Like the changes in the economy itself, the long-run implications of the challenges to the PRI's dominance were highly ambiguous. The best hope,

[61] Bortz, "Dilemma"; Salvador Corro, "En Materia Económica, Gobierno y Obreros en Dirección Contraria," *Proceso*, 507, 21 July 1986, pp. 22–23. Not a single member of the decision-making team attended this congress. The report was received by de la Madrid with cold, noncommittal formality.

shared by many in the new Salinas government, was that these challenges had opened opportunities to construct a more pluralistic political system, in which the PRI itself would be impelled to reduce its emphasis on patronage and corporatist controls, to "modernize" its relationship with its own base, and to share power with its political opponents.

Yet with economic adjustment options so limited, polarization remained at least as strong a possibility as pluralism. On the external side, the debt service drain continued to pose a major, and perhaps insuperable obstacle to recovery; yet there were no clear solutions that could be unilaterally imposed by the Mexican government itself. Domestically, it was not clear how the government could reconcile a continuation of a highly unpopular recovery strategy with the democratic reform of a dominant-party machinery that had enabled it to initiate and sustain this strategy in the first place. The dilemma was sharpened by the fact that low-wage workers in the informal sector, and not the PRI's unionized blue-collar base, were the ones most likely to benefit from the employment-creating effects of an export-led recovery.

To contribute to a successful democratic transition, in other words, an economic recovery (*if* it actually materializes) would have to be accompanied by a more extensive renegotiation of the understandings that once regulated conflict within the Mexican system: the consolidation of a new framework of relations with the private sector that either neutralizes or accommodates its more conservative components; the reestablishment of stable financial and commercial ties to the United States; and the rebuilding of the system's legitimacy through the broadening of access to political power and material resources. These are daunting and contradictory challenges. But if they are not resolved, an economic recovery could well compound the obstacles to democratization by raising expectations, shifting the balance among social forces, and increasing conflicts over distributive shares.

Perspectives on the Determinants of Stabilization and Adjustment Policies

What conclusions can we draw about the forces that have shaped governmental responses to the stabilization and adjustment dilemmas of the 1980s? Since chapter 8 deals with this issue in an extended and general way, our observations can be confined more specifically to the three case studies just presented, with particular attention to the role of the five explanatory factors listed at the beginning of this chapter.

THE ECONOMIC CRISIS

In all three cases, the economic shocks that hit in the early 1980s played an important role, speeding the demise of military governments in Argentina and Brazil and altering the balance of forces among contending governmental factions and business groups in Mexico. At several points, policy makers were galvanized into action by specific aspects of these crises (for example, the inflationary surges in Argentina and Brazil). Nevertheless, the range of policy initiatives adopted within and between nations suggest that patterns of response did not derive directly from "objective" features of the crises themselves. Surging inflations encountered in Brazil and Argentina, for example, might well have encouraged more orthodox shocks like those imposed earlier under military regimes. Although the Mexican government followed a more orthodox pattern, its initial response to the 1982 shock involved bank nationalization as well as an IMF stabilization agreement. Economic constraints may well have shaped the outcome of such choices, but the policies themselves derived more directly from the way political forces and institutions influenced the perceptions and interests of the policy makers. Some of the most important of these forces are subsumed in the remaining categories.

BARGAINING LEVERAGE VIS-À-VIS EXTERNAL CREDITORS

Bargaining leverage appeared to have a substantial impact on choices regarding stabilization policy, particularly the extent to which governments emphasized restrictions on domestic demand. As the Brazil/Argentina comparison emphasized, this was the case even among governments that had incorporated direct wage/price controls as components of their anti-inflation packages. More generally, it seems quite likely that Brazil's effort during the mid-1980s to combine "developmentalism" at home with a comparatively confrontational approach toward external creditors depended directly on the capacity of its robust export sector to accumulate reserves. On the other hand, the pressure of relatively orthodox domestic business groups also played an important role in encouraging both the Argentine and Mexican governments to seek cooperative arrangments with the IMF.[62] And in general, the case studies suggest that domestic factors were complementary or even decisive influences on policy choices.

THE ORGANIZATION OF THE STATE APPARATUS

Our case studies indicate at least three important points at which the organization of the state apparatus influenced policy choices. First, the heterodoxy of stabilization policies depended directly on the training and economic ideologies of the technical staffs. Second, the cohesion of the technical team played an important role in the subsequent politics of implementation. The eventual collapse of the Cruzado program, for example, was partially attributable to divisions among Brazilian technical advisors about whether to tighten fiscal and monetary controls during the third quarter of 1986. Third, in

[62] Robert R. Kaufman, *The Politics of Debt in Argentina, Brazil, and Mexico: Economic Stabilization in the 1980s* (Berkeley: Institute of International Studies, University of California at Berkeley and Los Angeles, 1988), pp. 119–24.

Mexico, the capacity of the government to engage in a fairly comprehensive series of structural adjustment measures cannot be understood without taking into account the long-standing influence of the bank and treasury technocrats in the state apparatus and their broad ideological commitments to "economic reform" in the 1980s.

How did such "state-centered" influences interact with other explanatory factors considered in this chapter? With respect to the three cases considered here, their primary importance appears to be as variables that mediated (without being fully reducible to) broader interactions between the state and civil society. Whatever their respective weaknesses, none of the governmental bureaucracies in our societies was as penetrated as those of the African countries discussed by Thomas Callaghy, where effective policy of any kind was impeded by the virtual absence of a technical staff and overwhelming difficulties of bureaucratic coordination.[63] On the other hand, the states in Argentina, Brazil, and Mexico also did not approximate the degree of insulation achieved in Pinochet's Chile, where powerful authoritarian controls allowed a cohesive cadre of orthodox technocrats to become the decisive force behind broad adjustment strategies.[64] Even in Mexico, the "strongest" of the three states considered here, the influence of the bank and treasury officials fluctuated quite directly with the changing political pressures confronting successive presidents. In Argentina and Brazil, of course, the recruitment of heterodox economists into the state bureaucracy could not have occurred without a change of regime.

POLITICAL SITUATIONS: ELECTORAL CYCLES

Influences stemming from "domestic politics," more broadly understood, can be subdivided into two categories: short-term "situational" factors that affect the time horizons and opportunities of the heads of state; and more durable power relations shaped by organized interests and political regimes.

The timing of the electoral cycle constituted the most important component of the immediate political situation within each country. In Brazil, the congressional elections of 1986 played a crucial role in delaying adjustments to the Cruzado package. A relaxation of fiscal and monetary controls was also associated with presidential and midterm campaigns in Argentina in 1983 and 1987 and in Mexico in 1982 and 1985. This is consistent with Barry Ames's seventeen-country study of Latin American fiscal policies between 1965 and 1975, which found that fiscal expenditures consistently increased in the years preceding elections.[65] While such cycles appear to have exerted a powerful influence, however, they were by no means inevitable. Alfonsín maintained

[63] Thomas Callaghy, chap. 6, this vol.

[64] Stallings, chap. 4, this vol.

[65] Barry Ames, *Politics of Survival: Politicians and Public Policy in Latin America* (Berkeley: University of California Press, 1987).

an extremely tight monetary and fiscal policy in the months prior to the 1985 congressional elections, and by drawing on the substantial power of the Mexican presidency, de la Madrid managed during the 1988 election to avoid the financial turmoil that had accompanied each of the two preceding contests.

THE ROLE OF POLITICAL REGIMES

The other important features of domestic politics concerned the way political regimes structured the relations among competing sociopolitical forces and their access to the state. As has been noted at several other points in this volume, a simple dichotomy between "authoritarianism" and "democracy" is not sufficient to capture the complexity of these institutional/political relationships. Policy making in the transitional democracies of Argentina and Brazil can be expected to differ not only from authoritarian regimes, but also from the more institutionalized constitutional systems such as Costa Rica or Colombia, where more established norms govern the role of the legislature, party competition, and interest group representation.[66] In a similar vein, Mexico's party-based authoritarianism should not be lumped with other authoritarian regimes discussed in this volume—for example, Pinochet's Chile, or Zambia, or Marcos' Philippines.[67] Yet the degree of popular influence over government and the channels through which this influence is exercised have made a major difference in the three societies considered here. In this respect, the distinction among political regimes has remained as a centerpiece of the analysis. Of all the influences contributing to policy choices in Argentina and Brazil, the one that stands in sharpest relief is the expansion of distributive expectations associated with an attempted transition from a labor-repressive authoritarian regime to a more democratic one. In the Mexico of Miguel de la Madrid, the key factor was the authoritarian mechanisms of control that the dominant party placed in the hands of the executive.

[66] Joan M. Nelson, chap. 5, this vol.; Stallings, chap. 4, this vol.
[67] Haggard, chap. 7, this vol. for discussion of authoritarian regimes.

CHAPTER FOUR

Politics and Economic Crisis: A Comparative Study of Chile, Peru, and Colombia

Barbara Stallings

THE RESPONSES of Chile, Peru, and Colombia to the economic crisis that has gripped Latin America since the early 1980s represent three extreme cases. Chile has followed the most orthodox adjustment strategy in the region and received the highest praise from private bankers and international agencies. Peru has been the only Latin American nation to adopt an openly confrontational stance and policies that have led it to be considered a virtual international economic outlaw. Colombia, partly because of its conservative economic policies in the 1970s, avoided the severe crises that befell its neighbors and now is trying to return to "voluntary" lending in international capital markets. At some risk of caricature, then, this chapter can be seen as a comparison of the "good debtor," the "bad debtor," and the "nondebtor."

Three principal questions will be addressed. First, what factors determined these diverging policy choices to deal with the economic crisis of the 1980s? For convenience of discussion, policy choice will be dichotomized into orthodox and heterodox approaches, in which the former is characterized by a relatively open economy and low state intervention and the latter a more closed economy and a greater state role. These descriptions will be very broad because both stabilization policies and economic development strategies must be included. Second, what factors determined whether the policy choices were actually implemented? Third, what factors determined the "success" or "failure" of the chosen policy packages? Success will be defined in terms of traditional macroeconomic indicators including growth, inflation, and distribution of income.

In answering these three questions, a model will be employed that involves increasingly complex sets of political and economic variables.

Policy choice has the simplest explanatory framework. It is hypothesized that decisions will be based on the nature of the political coalition that provides the main

I would like to thank the people in Chile, Peru, Colombia, and elsewhere who shared their information and ideas with me, thus making this study possible. In addition, I am grateful to those who provided comments on earlier drafts, especially the other members of the research group and participants in the workshop in Mexico City in October 1987. The latter included Carlos Portales and Juan Guillermo Espinosa from Chile; Richard Webb, Leonel Figueroa, and Jürgen Schuldt from Peru; and Eduardo Lora and Fernando Rojas from Colombia.

114 · Chapter Four

support for a government, given its diagnosis of the political-economic situation. The importance of the coalition variable is magnified in highly polarized, multi-party societies. Under such circumstances, coalitions are more likely to have firm economic programs than in less polarized, two-party systems.

Implementation of initial policy choices is more complex than the decisions them-selves, because it involves several sets of factors outside the immediate control of the government. (1) *Characteristics of the state inherited by the government.* A highly centralized state will increase the chances of implementation of preferred policies, as will a state with a high level of technical capacity. (2) *Characteristics of domestic political groups.* The support of powerful organized groups and the disorganization of opponents will increase chances of implementation. The partic-ular type of program and the rules under which the state operates will determine which groups are most powerful, but in general business, labor, political parties, and the military are especially important. (3) *Activities of international actors.* International groups can increase the possibility of implementation of policies by providing essential resources. Just how important outside resources are will de-pend on initial conditions, especially the balance of payments, and the economic strategy being followed.

Success in terms of macroeconomic outcomes depends on both previous sets of fac-tors, plus others exogenous to the model. On the one hand, the degree to which a set of policy choices has been implemented will clearly affect outcomes. On the other hand, the viability of the policy choices will become a factor sooner or later. Viability, of course, depends on the objective circumstances facing a country at a given time. Beyond implementation and viability of the original choices, exoge-nous factors—such as prices of exports and imports, availability and terms of finance, and the state of the world economy—will also play a role in determining outcomes. The outcomes, in turn, will affect policy choice at a second round, either reinforcing existing policies or stimulating change.

Depending on the particular time period chosen and the variables under con-sideration, Chile, Peru, and Colombia either have been quite similar or very different. The point of maximum political similarity occurred in the mid-to-late 1960s, when centrist democratic governments ruled in all three—Eduardo Frei's Christian Democrats in Chile, Fernando Belaunde's Popular Action in Peru, and Carlos Lleras Restrepo's Liberal Party in Colombia. All saw a need for the state in Latin America to play an important role in the economy but not to the exclusion of the private sector. They also generally agreed that foreign capital, although necessary for the development process, had to be restrained in its activities and required to serve national interests. Furthermore, the three countries began to see themselves as a unit forming the heart of the Andean Pact, one of the most important integration movements in Latin American history.

From a longer perspective, however, political differences have predominated over similarities. In particular, differences have tended to separate Chile and Peru from Colombia. In Colombia, a quasi-democratic system of power sharing has been in place since the formation of the National Front in 1958. The National Front, together with the informal arrangements to perpetuate the system after 1974, resulted in substantial consensus and continuity on economic policy questions as well as personnel. In Chile and Peru, by contrast, little if any agreement has existed on basic economic issues among groups with political influence. Both societies became increasingly polarized from the 1960s on, and military regimes eventually displaced the earlier democracies. In Peru, a return to democracy occurred in 1980, while the process of redemocratization still continues in Chile. Not surprisingly, sharp policy swings accompanied the various political shifts.

A very general economic comparability prevailed in that all three are medium-sized countries with a medium level of development in the Latin American context. This middle ranking contrasts with Brazil, Argentina and Mexico at the larger, more developed end of the spectrum and the Central American and Caribbean nations at the smaller, less developed end. Thus, the GDPs of Chile, Peru and Colombia were roughly similar in size—around $15 billion in 1970—and populations ranged between 10 and 20 million. Their industrial sectors were likewise of comparable quantitative and qualitative status. Value added by manufacturing was around $3.5 billion in each case, and all had advanced consumer and intermediate goods industries but not much in the way of capital goods.[1] In fact, the Andean Pact was seen as one way in which a capital goods sector could be fostered among the medium-sized countries as the third stage of the import-substitution process that all had followed.

Nevertheless, significant economic differences again tended to separate Chile and Peru from Colombia. Minerals dominated exports in both Chile and Peru, while coffee was the principal export product of Colombia, meaning that the terms of trade behaved in quite different ways. Foreign borrowing patterns during the 1970s also diverged. Both Chile and Peru borrowed heavily from the private international banks, while Colombia was a reluctant borrower at least until the end of the decade. Growth patterns were different; Chile and Peru had very uneven growth and Colombia had a modest but fairly constant rate.

Given these differences and similarities, this chapter will first compare Chile and Peru as "most similar" cases until 1985. After the historical and structural similarities between Chile and Peru are identified, the diverging policies adopted after 1985 will be analyzed. Colombia will be introduced as a

---

[1] Statistics are calculated from Interamerican Development Bank, *Economic and Social Progress in Latin America, 1975 Report* (Washington, D.C.: Interamerican Development Bank, 1975), pp. 378–83.

"most different" case when compared to Chile and Peru in historical-structural terms. The contrast provided by Colombia is useful in several ways: it highlights the subjective notion of "crisis"; it shows the advantages and disadvantages of continuity in economic policy, and it demonstrates the power of the political system to limit economic policy choice.

As will become apparent, the role of stabilization policies varies significantly within the Chile/Peru and Colombia contexts. In the former, where fundamental disagreement persists among important actors on basic issues of economic approach, attempts at stabilization are inherently subordinate to larger economic strategy questions. In the latter, where consensus on general approach reigns among politically relevant actors, stabilization can become important in its own right.

CHILE AND PERU: RESPONSES TO SEVERE CRISIS

To explain the diverging policies now being followed by Chile and Peru, it is necessary to understand the historical trends in economic policy and political mobilization in the two countries. This section will begin with an overview of the three decades between the mid-1950s and mid-1980s. In this context, the current crisis appears as a continuation of the longer-term pattern despite the greater severity of recent problems. After the overview, we will examine in more detail the 1980s crisis in the two countries, the initial attempts at stabilization, and the different paths followed since 1985.

Historical Patterns

During the postwar period, Chile and Peru were marked by a common inability to achieve long-term economic development. Inflation, balance-of-payments crises, and uneven growth patterns characterized both economies. Political similarities also existed; different political coalitions had different diagnoses and policies for dealing with the economic problems. In each case, political allegiance was so dispersed that no coalition gained sufficient hegemony to implement its preferred policies over a long period. The result was alternating coalitions in power and shifting policies.

POLITICAL COALITIONS AND ECONOMIC STRATEGIES

The particular pattern of coalitions and strategies resulted in similar long-term trends in the two countries. The trends consisted of increasingly leftward movements, greater state intervention and a more closed economy, from the mid-1950s until the mid-1970s, and then a shift to the right until the mid-1980s. The Chilean shift was extremely abrupt whereas that of Peru was more gradual, but the general trajectory was the same.

In the early 1950s, Chile faced a series of choices.[2] The economic strategy of import-substitution industrialization that had provided the dynamic for growth since the 1930s had exhausted itself. The middle-class political coalition that had governed during that period had lost its hold on the electorate. There was no agreed-upon solution to these dilemmas. Proponents of at least three alternatives fought among themselves and tried each option, in turn, over the period 1958 to 1973.

The first alternative was the government of Jorge Alessandri (1958–1964), which was based on a coalition of rightist political parties and followed what were considered at the time to be orthodox economic policies. The private sector was given extensive privileges and allowed to dominate the economy. Foreign investment was invited in as a welcome partner, and wages and consumption were constrained in favor of investment. Nevertheless, the state maintained an important role in regulating the economy and assisting the private sector.

Fears of a leftist victory in 1964 led to a coalition of right and center that produced an electoral majority for Eduardo Frei and the Christian Democrats. As was typical of "reformist" governments in Latin America in that era, the Frei administration (1964–1970) wanted to "modernize" the economy. The state assumed a more important role, while still relying on the private sector for the bulk of production and investment. Foreign capital was sought but forced to operate within government guidelines. Certain structural reforms were also seen as necessary prerequisites for such a strategy to work; they included an agrarian reform and state ownership of the crucial copper industry.

The Frei strategy further polarized and radicalized Chilean society. By the end of the 1960s, the three alternative coalitions were again in contention, but the weight had shifted toward the left. The Popular Unity alliance, oriented around the Socialist and Communist parties and supporting the candidacy of Salvador Allende, won the 1970 election by a narrow plurality. This victory led to a government (1970–1973) committed to preparation for a transition to socialism. The agrarian reform and control of foreign capital were stepped up. The state increased its domestic strength as well through takeovers of certain strategic firms, increased regulation of others, and higher public expenditure for both consumption and investment.

The Peruvian trajectory was similar during these years.[3] In 1956, what has been described as the last oligarchic government took power in Peru with Manuel Prado as president. Like the Alessandri government in Chile, Prado's basic view of economic development pointed to the private sector, both do-

[2] See Barbara Stallings, *Class Conflict and Economic Development in Chile, 1958–73* (Stanford, Calif.: Stanford University Press, 1978), for a comparison of Chilean development strategies in the period 1958–1973.

[3] See E.V.K. FitzGerald, *The Political Economy of Peru, 1958–78* (Cambridge: Cambridge University Press, 1979), for a comparison of Peruvian development strategies.

mestic and foreign, as the leading actor. The Peruvian state, however, was smaller and less developed than its Chilean counterpart, and the economy was more open to international trade. Prado's government continued the liberal economic policies that had prevailed during most of the century and a half of independence, despite growing pressures for change.

In 1963, following a brief military interregnum, the centrist Popular Action Party won control of the presidency. Led by Fernando Belaunde Terry, Popular Action advocated reformist policies not dissimilar from those of Eduardo Frei. They included modernization of the industrial sector and more equal distribution through public-sector expenditures in education and housing. Structural changes through agrarian and tax reforms were also advocated. Belaunde's proposals had little success, however, because the rightist opposition had a majority in congress.

The lack of effective change led to a coup in 1968 directed by General Juan Velasco Alvarado, which produced a government quite unlike the typical military regime in Latin America. Its major goals were an increase and reorientation of production, a redistribution of income, and greater international independence. One of its first acts was an agrarian reform even more radical than that of Allende. After a period of trying to induce the private sector to undertake a policy of rapid industrialization, the government itself took the lead.

By 1973 in Chile and 1975 in Peru, opposition to the progressive, nationalist governments had gained sufficient strength to overthrow them. The coup in Chile, a bloody one, installed a military government in power, while that in Peru was a nonviolent change within the military itself. In both cases, the new regimes opened the way for a shift in the direction of economic policy. The increasingly leftward orientation of the preceding two decades ended, and a turn to the right began.

After the Chilean coup, economic policy was indecisive, and it was not until 1976 that a coherent line emerged around the group of economists who came to be known as the "Chicago Boys."[4] Based in the Catholic University in Santiago but with close ties to the University of Chicago, the group had been preparing an alternative economic program since the late 1960s. Their extreme free-market ideas were revolutionary within the Chilean tradition of a strong state and protected economy, and after 1976 they were applied in almost textbook fashion under the leadership of Finance Minister Sergio de Castro. Government expenditure was cut so dramatically that the large deficit was eliminated. Many public firms were returned to their previous owners or sold at

[4] See Alejandro Foxley, *Latin American Experiments in Neoconservative Economics* (Berkeley: University of California Press, 1983); Sebastian Edwards and Alejandra Cox Edwards, *Monetarism and Liberalization: The Chilean Experiment* (Cambridge, Mass.: Ballinger, 1987); Samuel Valenzuela and Arturo Valenzuela, eds., *Military Rule in Chile: Dictatorship and Oppositions* (Baltimore: Johns Hopkins University Press, 1986), for several perspectives on Chile since the coup.

bargain-basement prices. Tariffs were lowered from an average of 100 percent to a uniform 10 percent, and the capital markets were deregulated. Moreover, the exchange rate was pegged to the dollar in mid-1979, which encouraged foreign borrowing by the private sector and resulted in a vast foreign debt.

The Peruvian shift to the right was more gradual.[5] In fact, the new military government, under the leadership of General Francisco Morales Bermúdez, claimed that it differed little from its predecessor, but more orthodox economic policies were quickly introduced. In 1979, a civilian economic team was appointed that began a concerted effort to open up the economy. The reelection of Belaunde in 1980 continued the rightist trend. Tariffs and quotas were lowered, more favorable terms were offered to foreign capital, and plans were announced (but never implemented) to sell off state firms. Government spending soared, however, as the president insisted on carrying out his construction projects. As a consequence, foreign borrowing also rose in Peru, although in the Peruvian case the government, not the private sector, was the main borrower.

STABILIZATION CRISES

Superimposed on these long-term trends was a series of short-term crises of fairly standard character.[6] The resulting patterns of economic indicators can be seen in tables 4.1 and 4.2. In general, these crises were triggered by balance-of-payments problems as imports increased in the face of stagnant or even falling export revenues. The result was a set of stabilization policies that slowed growth rates. Increased inflation was also generally part of the process although the exact relationship varied between the two countries and over time.

The Peruvian pattern was more consistent. As can be seen in table 4.1, inflation generally followed the stabilization measures when a large devaluation and the lifting of controls led to price rises. This was the case in the late 1950s, mid-1970s, and early 1980s. The relationship in the mid-1960s was somewhat more ambiguous. In Chile (table 4.2), inflation per se stimulated stabilization measures in the late 1950s. In the early 1960s and early 1970s, inflation and balance-of-payments problems appear to have been simultaneous phenomena, while in the early 1980s, inflation increased during the crisis but never to the level of earlier periods.

[5] See Cynthia McClintock and Abraham Lowenthal, eds., *The Peruvian Experiment Reconsidered* (Princeton, N.J.: Princeton University Press, 1983), on the transition from the Velasco to Morales Bermúdez period; Martin Scurrah, "El estado latinoamericano y las políticas de austeridad: Perú 1980–85," *Apuntes* 20 (1987): 15–32, for one of the few analyses of the Belaunde years.

[6] See Ricardo Ffrench-Davis, *Políticas económicas en Chile, 1952–70* (Santiago: CEPLAN, 1973); Enrique Sierra, *Tres ensayos de estabilización en Chile* (Santiago: Editorial Universitaria, 1969), on stabilization crises in Chile. John Dragisic, "Peruvian Stabilization Policies, 1939–68" (Ph.D. diss., University of Wisconsin, 1971), on Peru.

TABLE 4.1
Peru: Growth, Inflation, Balance of Payments, 1955–1985

Year	GDP[a] (%)	Inflation[b] (%)	Balance of Payments[c] ($ millions)
1955	5.0	4.9	−37
1956	4.6	7.0	−87
1957	1.0	8.6	−130
1958	3.4	7.7	−99
1959	3.5	12.9	−25
1960	9.1	10.1	+8
1961	8.4	3.7	−8
1962	9.0	5.4	−37
1963	4.1	5.8	−81
1964	7.1	13.0	+14
1965	4.9	13.4	−148
1966	7.1	12.3	−233
1967	1.6	12.2	−282
1968	0	17.9	−22
1969	4.1	7.8	+3
1970	7.3	6.6	+202
1971	5.1	3.8	−34
1972	5.8	4.9	−31
1973	6.2	14.7	−262
1974	6.9	16.6	−725
1975	2.4	20.0	−1541
1976	3.3	33.5	−1072
1977	−0.3	38.0	−783
1978	−1.8	57.8	−164
1979	4.3	67.7	+953
1980	2.9	59.2	−101
1981	3.1	75.4	−1728
1982	0.9	64.5	−1609
1983	−12.0	111.1	−872
1984	4.7	110.2	−221
1985	1.6	163.4	+125

Sources: E.V.K. FitzGerald, *The Political Economy of Peru, 1956–78* (Cambridge: Cambridge University Press, 1978), pp. 310–11; Banco Central de Reserva del Perú, *Memoria Anual* (various issues) (Lima); International Monetary Fund, *International Financial Statistics* (various issues) (Washington, D.C.: International Monetary Fund, 1987).

[a] Annual growth rate.

[b] GDP deflator (1955–1975), consumer price index (1976–1985), twelve-month average increase.

[c] Current account.

TABLE 4.2
Chile: Growth, Inflation, Balance of Payments, 1955–1985

Year	GDP[a] (%)	Inflation[b] (%)	Balance of Payments[c] ($ millions)
1955	2.7	83.8	24
1956	1.2	37.7	− 13
1957	0.9	17.3	− 93
1958	2.5	32.5	− 82
1959	1.7	33.3	− 19
1960	3.7	5.5	− 130
1961	6.1	9.6	− 278
1962	5.7	27.7	− 211
1963	4.0	45.3	− 202
1964	4.8	38.5	− 133
1965	6.5	25.8	− 43
1966	10.1	17.0	− 93
1967	1.2	21.9	− 62
1968	3.5	27.9	− 138
1969	5.5	29.3	+ 89
1970	3.4	34.9	− 91
1971	9.0	22.1	− 198
1972	− 1.2	163.4	− 471
1973	− 5.6	508.1	− 279
1974	1.0	375.9	− 292
1975	− 12.9	340.7	− 490
1976	3.5	174.3	+ 148
1977	9.9	63.5	− 551
1978	8.2	30.3	− 1088
1979	8.3	38.9	− 1189
1980	7.8	31.2	− 1971
1981	5.5	9.5	− 4733
1982	− 14.1	20.7	− 2304
1983	− 0.7	23.1	− 1117
1984	6.3	23.0	− 2060
1985	2.4	26.4	− 1307

Sources: Ricardo Ffrench-Davis, *Políticas económicas en Chile, 1952–70* (Santiago: CEPLAN, 1973), pp. 247, 252; Banco Central de Chile, *Indicadores económicos y sociales, 1960–85* (Santiago), pp. 24, 148; International Monetary Fund, *International Financial Statistics* (various issues).

[a] Annual growth rate.
[b] Consumer price index, December-December.
[c] Current account.

With the single exception of the Allende government in Chile, all stabilization programs were orthodox, operating under the assumption that inflation and balance-of-payments problems had to be dealt with by cutting demand. Thus government spending was reduced, credit to the private sector was cut, and wage increases were held down. The currency was devalued to increase export competitiveness and/or cut real wages, and some gesture toward lowering controls was usually undertaken. International credit was sought through agreements with the International Monetary Fund, which reinforced support for demand-reduction policies. Although local industry was hurt by these measures, much of the cost was borne by workers, who saw their wages decline or who were thrown out of work.

ROLE OF INTERNATIONAL ACTORS

Another similarity between the two countries was the important role played by international actors, both private and public. At the end of World War II, foreign corporations owned the crucial minerals industries, and they gradually moved into manufacturing too. Gaining control over these firms' activities, or even displacing them, was increasingly on the agenda in Chile and Peru. The Frei government "chileanized" the copper industry, while the Allende administration nationalized it outright and took over other foreign firms as well. During the first Belaunde period, attempts were made to control the Standard Oil subsidiary (IPC) in Peru; the Velasco government nationalized that firm and others. Both the Pinochet and the second Belaunde governments backtracked to the nationalistic stands of their predecessors to some extent, but neither returned to the status quo ante of the early postwar years.[7]

Of more import for the politics of economic adjustment, the private international banks became very active in both countries during the 1970s and early 1980s. Table 4.3 shows the particular characteristics of that foreign lending with the quantitative and qualitative variations in the resulting debt burdens by 1982. The Chilean debt was larger, both in absolute terms and as a percentage of exports. In addition, a majority of the Chilean debt belonged to the private sector, while almost all the Peruvian debt was the responsibility of the public sector. Eventually, however, the Chilean government was forced to guarantee much of the private sector's debt as can be seen by comparing data for 1982 and later. Finally, a much larger portion of the Chilean debt was owed to private banks rather than public agencies, thus carrying more stringent terms.

The activities of public-sector agencies, both bilateral and multilateral, were closely correlated with those of the private-sector firms. The U.S. government was strongly supportive of the Frei government, despite the chileanization policies, since the alternative was a more leftist coalition. Once the Popular Unity won the 1970 election, the well-known actions designed to undermine that government began. More surprising was the U.S. opposition to

[7] Stallings, *Class Conflict*; FitzGerald, *Political Economy*.

TABLE 4.3
Chile and Peru: Foreign Debt Indicators, 1980–1987

	1980	1982	1984	1986	1987
Total Debt[a]					
Chile	12.1	17.3	19.8	20.2	21.2
Peru	10.0	12.3	13.2	16.0[g]	18.0[g]
Debt/Exports[b]					
Chile	192.5	335.9	412.2	378.3	327.4
Peru	207.4	293.5	331.1	469.6	503.3
Public-Sector Share[c]					
Chile	50.2	37.7	62.8	84.3	86.1
Peru	83.0	80.7	86.8	89.2	89.7
Share Owed to Banks[d]					
Chile	58.6	70.1	81.1	76.8	72.5
Peru	38.1	42.3	44.8	38.9	36.2
Interest/Exports[e]					
Chile	7.7	10.6	19.2	23.2	18.2
Peru	11.3	13.1	9.3	6.2	5.5
Amortization/Exports[f]					
Chile	14.2	9.2	6.5	5.4	2.9
Peru	20.0	23.2	6.6	8.2	7.0

Source: World Bank, *World Debt Tables*, vol. 2, 1988–1989, pp. 74–77, 306–9.

[a] Total disbursed debt (long and short-term, public and private in U.S. dollars billions).

[b] Debt as share of exports of goods and services.

[c] Public-sector share of long-term debt only.

[d] Percentage of public-sector long-term debt owed to private banks.

[e] Interest payments on long-term public-sector debt as percentage of exports of goods and services.

[f] Amortization of long-term public-sector debt as percentage of exports of goods and services.

[g] These figures are substantially larger than Peruvian government figures or those of the U.N. Economic Commission for Latin America; it is unclear whether capitalization of interest arrears accounts for the difference.

the first Belaunde government, which stemmed from its treatment of IPC. The U.S. boycott of loans to Belaunde drove Peru to private-bank finance much earlier than most third world countries. Later the boycott was reimposed against the Velasco government, but the banks ignored it and lent in any case. The multilateral agencies tended to get involved in the two countries when a balance-of-payments crisis erupted. In addition, the United States persuaded most of the multilaterals to go along with its various boycotts.[8]

[8] See James Petras and Morris Morley, *The United States and Chile* (New York: Monthly Review Press, 1975), on U.S. political conflicts with Chile; Jessica Einhorn, *Expropriation Politics* (Lexington, Mass.: Lexington Books, 1974), on Peru.

Despite the important financial role played by international actors—the heavy reliance on external finance provided crucial leverage for foreign influence in domestic policy making in both countries—there was never any equivalent of the decision-making role that expatriates performed in many African countries (see chapter 6). Even in Peru with its less developed state, domestic personnel had sufficient skills and institutional capacity; foreigners were generally confined to exercising indirect influence.

POLITICAL REGIME AND POLITICAL MOBILIZATION

While economic strategies were moving in similar directions in the two countries, the political contexts within which they operated showed important differences in timing. The entire period of the leftward movement in Chile, from the mid-1950s to 1973, occurred within a liberal democratic system. In fact, democracy was one of the most salient characteristics of that country, distinguishing it from most of its neighbors. Only a half-dozen years since independence in 1818 had seen military rule, and the military was seen as professional and apolitical. In relative terms, Chile's democratic system provided for extensive civil liberties and political participation. Parties ranged from the far right to the far left (although the Communist party was banned in some periods and its members imprisoned or harassed). Labor unions dated from the end of the nineteenth century, and the business class was organized as well. By 1973, it was safe to say that Chile was one of the most mobilized—and polarized—societies in the world.

This mobilization, if not the polarization, ended abruptly with the coup of September 1973.[9] The coup was originally carried out as a combined move by the four branches of the armed forces, but it rapidly degenerated into a personal dictatorship of army chief Augusto Pinochet. Although many of its civilian supporters had expected the military government to be of short duration, followed by new elections within a period of months, the military had a longer-term project in mind—to depoliticize the country and, in particular, to eliminate the power of labor and the left. The demobilization campaign was relatively successful for a decade, as thousands of Popular Unity leaders and supporters were killed, put in concentration camps, exiled, or fired from their jobs. Congress was closed, political parties disbanded, and labor organizations made illegal. The initial success was based mainly on fear, but economic expansion was later accepted by many as a substitute for political freedoms. It was thus not until the economic crisis that mobilization began to reemerge. In 1982–1983, business groups began to push for a change in economic policy. Better known were the monthly ''days of protest'' that began in May 1983 to demand a return to democracy. The protests became massive, leading to tem-

[9] Arturo Valenzuela, *The Breakdown of Democratic Regimes: Chile* (Baltimore: Johns Hopkins University Press, 1978), describes the background to the coup.

porary changes in government policies and personnel. The lack of concrete results, disunity of the opposition, and selective use of repression, however, eventually led to a new decline in political activity and enabled the government to move back toward its previous line.[10]

In contrast to Chile, the peak of the leftist period in Peru was led by the military itself. Peru's military was different from that of Chile in at least two ways.[11] First, it had a history of more frequent involvement in politics, although generally involvements were short term. For example, the military intervened in the 1962 presidential election to prevent its archenemy, the Alianza Popular Revolucionaria Americana (APRA), from winning; it stayed in power for a year and then called for new elections. Second, by the latter half of the twentieth century, the Peruvian military had become more nationalistic and more progressive than its counterparts elsewhere in the region. These traits were already observable in the 1962 interregnum, but they became especially notable during the Velasco period.

The pattern of political mobilization in Peru was also different. The most important mobilization prior to the late 1970s was a peasant rebellion in the central highlands during the first Belaunde government. Being a relatively isolated movement, it was soon eliminated, and no comparable urban phenomenon emerged. During the Velasco period, whose Chilean counterpart saw a very high level of mobilization, there was a conscious attempt to prevent autonomous political activity. Nevertheless, the number of unions nearly doubled, and strike activities increased in both frequency and breadth. The frequency slowed under Morales Bermúdez, with the use of repression and mass firings, but the breadth of participation persisted. Two general strikes were called, and repeated street demonstrations brought together labor unions, shantytown dwellers and students in Lima as well as provincial cities.[12] Although the expectation was that mobilization would escalate with the new democratic government, the opposite occurred until the economic crisis reached full swing in 1983. At that point, both labor and business organizational activity increased.[13] Electoral support for the Belaunde government

[10] Guillermo Campero, *Los gremios empresariales en el período 1970–83* (Santiago: Estudios ILET, 1984); Gonzalo de la Maza and Mario Garcés, *La explosión de las mayorías* (Santiago: ECO, 1985); Manuel Antonio Garretón, "Protests and Politics in Chile," in Susan Eckstein, ed., *Power and Popular Protest: Latin American Social Movements* (Berkeley: University of California Press, 1988), pp. 259–77, describe various aspects of the protest movements of this period.

[11] See Victor Villanueva, *Cien años del ejército peruano: frustraciones y cambios* (Lima: Juan Mejía Baca, 1972), on the Peruvian military.

[12] Evelyne Stephens, "The Peruvian Military Government, Labor Mobilization, and the Political Strength of the Left," *Latin American Research Review* 18, 2 (1983): 57–93.

[13] Francisco Durand, *Los empresarios y la concertación* (Lima: Fundación Friedrich Ebert, 1987), discusses protest by business groups in Peru; see Jorge Parodi, "Los sindicatos en la democracia vacia," in Luis Pásara and Jorge Parodi, eds., *Democracia, sociedad y gobierno en el Perú* (Lima: CEDYS, 1988), pp. 79–124, on labor.

evaporated, and, in rural areas, a more sinister type of mobilization emerged as Sendero Luminoso managed to channel centuries of peasant resentment into demands for a violent overthrow of the entire system. This insurgency formed an increasingly important part of the context in which policy decisions were made in Peru.

SUMMARY

The crucial year 1985 arrived in the two countries at the end of a similar thirty-year economic trajectory. Both had seen increasingly progressive political coalitions take control of the presidency and at least partially implement programs that expanded the state role and turned the economy inward. Then, in the mid-1970s, both experienced shifts to the right and a reversal of some of the effects of the previous period. Generalized frustration prevailed, however, because none of the coalitions had managed to restore the countries to a long-term growth path.

Despite these economic similarities, some political characteristics were substantially different in the two countries as of 1985. Although both governments were rightist regimes, following orthodox development strategies, Chile was under authoritarian military rule, whereas Peru had a multiparty liberal democracy. Furthermore, the Peruvian population was highly mobilized and had the vote as a weapon. In Chile, mobilization had declined as its lack of effectiveness became apparent. These differences will play a major role in the explanation of the post-1985 policies.

Nature of the Crises

Given the strong international component of the 1980s crisis, it is often assumed that the problems of individual countries have been quite similar. Superficially, this assumption is true because the current crises are but severe examples of the stabilization problems that have periodically struck Latin American countries. A look beneath the surface, however, reveals some important differences. Table 4.4 presents a set of macroeconomic indicators for Chile and Peru during the period 1980–1988. It suggests that the same variables were problematic in the two countries, but their relative importance varied. The timing also varied slightly, with the worst year of the Chilean crisis occurring in 1982 and that of Peru a year later.

In Chile, inflation more than doubled between 1981 and 1982, from 9.5 to 20.7 percent, while the budget deficit went from a surplus to a deficit equivalent to 3.4 percent of GDP. Neither of these figures was especially high, however, either by historical or cross-national standards. The plunge in growth and the rise in unemployment, by contrast, were extraordinary. Chile's GDP fell by 13 percent in 1982, and unemployment increased to 20 percent of the labor force (27 percent if participants in the government's minimum employ-

TABLE 4.4

Chile and Peru: Macroeconomic Indicators, 1980–1988

	1980	1981	1982	1983	1984	1985	1986	1987	1988[j]
GDP[a]									
Chile	7.8	5.5	−13.1	−0.5	6.0	2.4	5.3	5.4	65
Peru	2.9	3.1	0.3	−11.8	4.7	2.3	8.9	6.5	−7.5
Inflation[b]									
Chile	31.2	9.5	20.7	23.6	23.0	26.4	17.4	21.5	10.9
Peru	59.7	72.7	72.9	125.1	111.5	158.3	62.9	114.5	1307.1
Wages[c]									
Chile	9.0	8.9	−0.2	−10.7	0.1	−3.8	1.7	−0.3	6.7
Peru	12.4	−1.7	2.3	−16.7	−15.5	−15.0	26.7	6.0	−34.5
Unemployment[d]									
Chile	11.8	9.0	20.0	18.9	18.5	17.2	13.1	11.9	11.2
Peru	7.1	6.8	6.6	9.0	8.9	10.1	5.3	4.8	—
Government Budget[e]									
Chile	+5.5	+0.8	−3.4	−2.8	−4.4	−2.6	−1.9	−0.8	—
Peru	−4.7	−8.4	−9.5	−12.1	−7.6	−3.0	−10.0	−10.0	—
Trade Balance[f]									
Chile	−2.8	−8.2	+0.3	+5.0	−1.5	+5.3	+6.5	+6.3	—
Peru	+4.9	−2.7	−2.1	+1.8	+5.9	+8.6	−0.1	−1.0	—
Current Account[g]									
Chile	−7.1	−14.5	−9.5	−5.7	−10.7	−8.3	−6.7	−4.8	—
Peru	−0.6	−8.6	−7.9	−5.4	−1.3	+0.9	−5.3	−7.0	—
Reserves[h]									
Chile	5.9	4.5	4.1	5.2	4.8	5.8	5.4	5.2	—
Peru	6.6	3.4	4.0	4.6	5.7	7.5	6.0	3.2	—
Investment[i]									
Chile	21.0	22.7	11.3	9.8	13.6	13.7	14.6	16.9	—
Peru	17.7	22.1	22.6	17.0	16.1	14.7	14.2	15.0	—

Sources: UNECLA, *Preliminary Overview of the Latin American Economy, 1988*, pp. 15–25; International Monetary Fund, *International Financial Statistics Yearbook, 1988*, pp. 286–89, 574–77; World Bank, *World Debt Tables*, vol. 2, 1988–1989; Banco Central de Chile, *Boletín Mensual*; Banco Central de Reserva del Perú, *Memoria Anual*.

[a] Annual growth rate.

[b] Consumer price index, December-December.

[c] Wages of nonagricultural workers (Chile)/private-sector workers in metropolitan Lima (Peru), annual averages.

[d] Unemployment as percentage of labor force in greater Santiago/metropolitan Lima, annual averages.

[e] Public-sector surplus/deficit as percentage of GDP.

[f] Merchandise balance as percentage of GDP.

[g] Current account as percentage of GDP.

[h] Reserves in months of imports of goods and services.

[i] Gross domestic investment as percentage of GDP.

[j] Preliminary estimates, inflation November-November.

ment program are included). Likewise, a balance-of-payments crisis manifested itself in a large loss of reserves, even though the trade balance moved into a small surplus. The problem was a rise in the debt-service ratio, combined with a sudden fall in capital inflow and an increase in capital flight. In addition, a domestic financial crisis of enormous proportions involved the largest banks in the country and many industrial firms.[14]

The most obvious similarity between Chile and Peru was economic contraction. The 12 percent fall in Peru's GDP in 1983 was almost as dramatic as Chile's crash the previous year. No other major Latin American country approached these figures.[15] On other indicators, however, opposing patterns prevailed; Chile's problems were worst in areas where Peru's were less severe and vice-versa. Inflation in Peru reached a historic high in 1983 of 125 percent, although this rate was still low by comparison with some other Latin American countries. The government deficit was also at a peak: 12 percent of GDP for the overall public sector. Unemployment and the balance of payments, by contrast, were only moderately problematic. Although Peru also faced a domestic financial crisis, it was less serious than the situation in Chile.

These varying patterns were largely determined by the differing causes and responses to the crises. In the Chilean case, the relative importance of domestic compared to international factors has been debated a great deal.[16] External shocks did hit Chile especially hard through a fall in the terms of trade and a rise in interest rates, but government policy decisions were at least as important. The balance-of-payments problems, for instance, were not solely due to international prices and interest rates. The dramatic reduction of tariffs, the elimination of capital controls, and the fixed exchange rate were also key causal factors. Likewise, the domestic financial crisis came about because the central bank withdrew from its normal regulatory functions and encouraged massive foreign borrowing by the private sector. These initial policies, undertaken in the 1976–1981 period, were extended once the crisis hit because the government refused to intervene. The belief in "automatic adjustment" will be discussed in the next section.

Peru had some similar although milder factors at play.[17] The lowering of

---

[14] See José Pablo Arellano, "De la liberalización a la intervención: el mercado de capitales en Chile, 1974–83," *Colección Estudios CIEPLAN* 11 (December 1983): 5–49; José Pablo Arellano and Manuel Marfán, "Ahorro-inversión y relaciones financieras en la actual crisis económica chilena," *Colección Estudios CIEPLAN* 20 (December 1986): 61–93, on the financial crisis.

[15] Average figures for GDP in the Latin American region as a whole for 1982 and 1983 were − 2.5 and + 3.5 percent, respectively. Among the major countries, the only one that neared Peru and Chile in terms of economic contraction was Uruguay, where GDP fell 10 percent in 1982.

[16] See Laurence Whitehead, "The Adjustment Process in Chile: A Comparative Perspective," in Rosemary Thorp and Laurence Whitehead, eds., *Latin American Debt and the Adjustment Crisis* (London: Macmillan, 1987), pp. 117–61, for a summary of this discussion.

[17] See Rosemary Thorp, "Peruvian Adjustment Policies in Peru, 1978–85: The Effects of Prolonged Crisis," in Thorp and Whitehead, eds., *Latin American Debt*, pp. 208–38; and Richard

tariffs and other trade barriers in 1979–1982 led to a large trade deficit, but the trend had already been reversed by 1983. Financial liberalization had been attempted, but interest rates did not even become positive, much less attain the extraordinarily high real rates seen in Chile. The main macroeconomic problem in Peru centered on an unwillingness to match government revenues and expenditures, which was closely related to the general issue of political manipulation of economic policy by the president and other party leaders. The new finance minister who took office in January 1983 saw traditional austerity and devaluation as the only way to reequilibrate the economy. These policies combined with the natural disasters that struck Peru in 1983 led to the contraction/inflation outcome.

Similar Attempts at Stabilization

Despite the differing origins, characteristics, and timing of the 1980s crises in Chile and Peru, the responses were remarkably similar during the first three years. In both cases, there was an initial attempt to maintain, or even reinforce, the reigning orthodox model as a way of dealing with the new problems. When this *economic* approach proved *politically* nonviable, deviations from orthodoxy began to emerge. By 1985, these ad hoc stabilization attempts had ended, and new development strategies were in place.

CHILE: FROM "AUTOMATIC ADJUSTMENT" TO REFLATION

From the viewpoint of the economic team in Chile, any governmental response to the crisis was at least as traumatic as the crisis itself because of the near-total commitment to market mechanisms, including an "automatic adjustment" to macroeconomic disequilibria. Thus government intervention was seen as tantamount to admitting that the model had failed. These proclivities of the economists, who had enjoyed an extraordinary amount of autonomy under the military, finally ran up against the political limits of the system by early 1982. Allowing the crisis to run its course would have threatened the government's very survival; rebellion could have been expected from business, the military, and opposition groups. To prevent such a scenario, Pinochet and his political advisors began to take a more active role in economic policy making. Over the next few years, they frequently changed finance ministers and allowed or even encouraged policies that deviated from the laissez-faire model of the "Chicago Boys."

With the dismissal of Sergio de Castro from the finance ministry in April 1982, a number of policies began to be questioned. The most important was the fixed exchange rate, which had been pegged at 39 pesos per dollar since

Webb, *Stabilization and Adjustment Policies and Programmes: Country Study, Peru* (Helsinki: WIDER, 1987), on the Peruvian case.

mid-1979.[18] Those who wanted to maintain the fixed exchange system argued that a preferable way to deal with the macroeconomic disequilibria was to lower nominal wages. The alternative positions were presented to Pinochet, who felt that the size of the wage drop needed to reequilibrate the economy was politically impossible. Thus, the economic team was ordered to devalue the peso in June 1982. In combination with the recession, the devaluation slashed imports, leading to a small trade surplus in 1982 and a much larger one in 1983.

The devaluation exacerbated the financial crisis, because much of the private-sector debt was in dollars. Many businesses became insolvent and were unable to service their loans from Chilean banks, which were already in trouble because of speculative activities. The two banks in greatest difficulty were the Banco de Chile and the Banco de Santiago, leaders of the largest conglomerates in the country.[19] Rather than allow them to go bankrupt, the government "intervened" the large banks (i.e., took them over on a temporary basis), while several smaller banks were scheduled for liquidation.[20] The latter led to additional problems, because some of the losers in the transaction were foreign banks that had lent money to the smaller institutions. Through various types of leverage, the foreign banks eventually forced the government to take responsibility for the debt of the private financial sector.[21]

Following the intervention, it fell to a new finance minister, Carlos Cáceres, to deal with the aftermath and the other problems of the economy. In his own view, these included external financial difficulties and a possible resurgence of inflation in addition to the domestic financial crisis. The challenge, as he saw it, was to get out of the critical situation that still faced the economy without changing the basic economic model. Although not part of the "Chicago Boys" group per se, Cáceres nevertheless shared their basic approach.[22]

The decision to intervene the banks left the government in a truly anomalous position. Firm proponents of a small state, they found themselves with more control over the economy than even Allende had had. Although the long-run issue was how to return the firms to the private sector, the immediate problem was how to rescue the ailing private sector. The means chosen represented huge subsidies to the banks and largest corporations, including the purchase of bad loans by the central bank, a preferential exchange rate for holders of dollar debt, the option to turn dollar debt into pesos, and ultimately, a govern-

[18] The exchange rate issue has been extensively discussed because it constitutes one of the main explanations for the economic crisis in Chile. See, for example, Edwards and Edwards, *Monetarism and Liberalization*, pp. 53–92, 109–34; and Whitehead, "Adjustment Process," pp. 126–42.

[19] See Andrés Sanfuentes, "Los grupos económicos: control y política," *Colección Estudios CIEPLAN* 15 (December 1984): 131–70, on the conglomerates in general.

[20] Interviews with former Chilean government officials, Santiago, Chile, August 1987. Other options considered for dealing with the banks included allowing them to go bankrupt and providing them with additional resources to remain solvent and refinance the corporate debtors.

[21] Interviews with former Chilean government officials, Santiago, Chile, August 1987.

[22] Ibid.

ment guarantee for a substantial part of the privately contracted foreign debt. It is estimated that these policies cost the government some $7 billion between 1982 and 1985, equivalent to 44 percent of the GDP in the latter year. Smaller debtors had to make do with much less, and their problems are still pending.[23]

International financial problems were also high on Cáceres' agenda. His predecessor had negotiated a two-year standby agreement with the IMF as the typical first step toward a renegotiation of the foreign debt, but the bank rescue measures made the program inoperable even before it began. The government, therefore, decided to follow austerity policies to curb the current account deficit, the public-sector deficit, and inflation to return to the originally agreed economic targets. The agreement made it possible to proceed with a renegotiation of the foreign debt due for repayment in 1983–1984.[24] The IMF agreement and the government's own preferences meant that austerity measures continued. GDP fell again in 1983, although by less than 1 percent. Real wages fell by 11 percent, however, while median family income in Greater Santiago plunged by 28 percent.[25] Given the previous year's crash in GDP and indications that policy was not about to change, the situation became politically explosive.

The Chilean protests were of several types. A movement was initiated by small businesses, especially farmers in the south, to demand changes in economic policy to alleviate the growing bankruptcies. By 1982, these groups were holding public demonstrations and forcibly attempting to prevent banks from taking possession of bankrupt firms. The larger firms were more cautious, but by mid-1982 the severity of the crisis led to new leadership for the umbrella organization, the Confederation of Production and Commerce (CPC). Its incoming president, Jorge Fontaine, surprised observers during his inaugural address by saying: "Either we unite and work together or we will all go under together." In July 1983, the CPC presented a document to the government that called for lowered interest rates on all debts to 5 percent; transformation of dollar debts into pesos; increased government expenditure, including labor-intensive public investment projects; and greater flexibility in dealing with the IMF.[26]

[23] On the "resolution" of the financial crisis, see Arellano and Marfán, "Ahorro-inversión"; Jorge Leiva, "Reformulación y rescate del modelo económico," *Coyuntura Económica* 13 (August 1986): 51–124; Sergio Infante, "Los claroscuros de la normalización bancaria," Programa de Empleo del Trabajo, working paper (Santiago, 1986).

[24] Ricardo Ffrench-Davis and José de Gregorio, "La renegociación de la deuda externa de Chile en 1985: antecedentes y comentarios," *Colección Estudios CIEPLAN* 17 (September 1985): 9–32, discuss the first debt restructurings. Chilean terms were similar to those obtained elsewhere in Latin America, except that the government agreed to guarantee the debt of the private financial sector and assumed responsibility for the debt of bankrupt financial institutions.

[25] Banco Central de Chile, *Indicadores económicos y sociales, 1960–85* (Santiago: Banco Central de Chile, 1986).

[26] See Campero, *Los gremios empresariales*, for the most extensive analysis of the relationship between the government and the business sector under the military.

Another type of protest was openly political. In May 1983, the copper workers' union called for a national "day of protest" that saw participation by workers, students, shantytown dwellers, and the population in general. Despite government repression, the protest days became monthly events involving partial labor strikes, school absenteeism, commercial boycotts, demonstrations in downtown streets, and barricades in the shantytowns. Sponsorship spread to the political parties and party alliances, and the demand for a return to democracy became the central issue.[27]

On August 10, after three monthly "days of protest," Pinochet announced a cabinet shuffle that centered around the appointment of Sergio Onofre Jarpa as minister of interior. Jarpa was a veteran politician from the right wing National party that favored a controlled return to democracy; his assignment was to provide an opening to the "respectable" opposition. One of Jarpa's main themes was the need for a change in economic policy and, thus, a change in finance ministers. Finally, in April 1984, Luis Escobar Cerda, a minister during the Alessandri government, was appointed to replace Cáceres.

The usual interpretation is that Escobar's ten months in office represented an important break with the "Chicago-style" policies. To some extent that was true. He definitely favored reflation and greater protectionism and introduced policies to bring them about. Nevertheless, many of the policies often attributed to Escobar were actually instituted earlier. For example, the special price and credit policies for agriculture, the subsidies for housing, and tariff increases from 10 to 20 percent preceded the change in finance ministers. Moreover, Escobar saw himself obliged to carry out certain measures that were inconsistent with his own policy preferences. Monetary policy, for instance, became quite contractionary in the latter part of 1984, and his elevation of tariffs to an even higher 35 percent was scheduled for rollback.[28]

These conflicting trends were manifestations of the diverse views within the government about how to deal with the crisis. In general, the orthodox positions prevailed, but small victories were won by officials connected with business, which introduced some flexibility into the system and improved performance. At the same time, the austerity policies prevented the resurgence of inflation and with the devaluation brought the balance of payments under control. The economy began to revive; not surprisingly, the protests diminished as well.

PERU: DISINTEGRATION OF BELAUNDE'S ECONOMIC POLICIES

As in Chile, the initial Peruvian response to the crisis was to maintain the existing orthodox economic policies. Indeed, in the Peruvian case, an attempt was made to intensify the orthodoxy, an approach that came about through a

---

[27] See de la Maza and Garcés, *La explosión*, for detailed information on the protests in the period 1983–1984; Garretón, "Protests and Politics," for an interpretation.

[28] Interviews with former Chilean government officials, Santiago, August 1987.

change in finance ministers in January 1983. The new minister was Carlos Rodríguez-Pastor, then international vice president of Wells Fargo Bank. Rodríguez-Pastor had been a high official of the Central Bank during the first Belaunde government and was hired by Wells Fargo to build up its international business.

Arriving in Peru after a fourteen-year absence, Rodríguez-Pastor identified the balance of payments and lack of international credit as the main problems facing the country in the short run. His general approach was quickly specified at a press conference where he said, "Don't fool yourselves into thinking that I am here to reactivate the economy. . . . It is impossible to reduce inflation if wages continue high, if sales continue high, and if public works continue full steam ahead."[29] Although he later denied having said that wages were too high, the statement was indicative of two important points: Rodríguez-Pastor favored an even more orthodox economic policy than his predecessor, and he was totally lacking in political sensitivity. The combination—in a climate of increased economic crisis and political debate—made his fifteen months in the ministry a continually escalating conflict.

Having been brought in to deal with external financial problems, Rodríguez-Pastor wasted no time. By mid-February, he already had an agreement with the IMF. At stake were new terms for the second year of an Extended Fund Facility negotiated the previous year. Because Peru had failed to meet the 1982 targets, there was some surprise that a renewal was granted.[30] Given that the Fund's main concern was Belaunde's spending proclivities, however, the IMF considered the best alternative to be support for Rodríguez-Pastor and his team of fiscal conservatives.[31]

Another indication of the new economic team's orthodoxy was its position with respect to the foreign debt. While even the Chileans agreed they were unable to pay in early 1983, a key member of Rodríguez-Pastor's group stated, "All of the other countries are throwing in the towel. We, by contrast, are determined to continue with full service of our debt."[32] In keeping with this stance, Peru did not ask for a restructuring, but an $850 million loan. About half ($400 million) was to pay amortization due through March 1984, whereas the rest was to pay interest and finance the government's budget deficit.

In the meantime, the extent of the economic crisis gradually was becoming clear as output fell 10 percent in just six months due to austerity policies and natural disasters. By the second half of 1983, what the then Central Bank President called "a commonsense rebellion against orthodoxy" ensued.[33] He identified three components of that rebellion: reductions in the rate of increase

[29] Carlos Rodríguez-Pastor, cited in *Caretas*, 10 January 1983, Lima, p. 13.

[30] *Peru Económico*, June 1983, Lima, p. 1.

[31] Interviews with IMF economists, Washington, D.C., September 1987.

[32] Augusto Blacker cited in *Andean Report*, March 1983, p. 34.

[33] Webb, *Stabilization*, p. 29.

of key prices, including the exchange rate (by the Congress and Central Bank); refusal to raise interest rates (Central Bank); and a substantial increase in Central Bank lending. Consequently, the finance minister first lost control of fiscal policy and was able to meet June IMF targets only by "creative accounting." During the second half of the year, additional economic problems emerged, and finally the IMF agreement was abandoned.

Although the rebellious policies undoubtedly softened the crisis to some extent, the economy continued in deep recession throughout 1983. As in neighboring Chile, protest began to appear. Strikes by individual unions increased through 1982. By 1983, however, they began to fall off because firms were perceived too weak to improve benefits, and the more politically oriented general strike reemerged. In March 1983, some three hundred thousand workers participated in a general strike to protest the new cabinet that had declared itself in favor of the same economic policies as before, "but with even greater aggressivity," according to the strike call. Another large general strike occurred in March 1984 to protest a set of price increases, while two others had less participation. None had much effect on policy.[34]

While labor tried to improve its situation, business also protested government policy, especially the decrease in protectionism. Until 1983, most of the protest was by atomized groups, and the government was able to keep them separated. With the onset of the crisis, however, the need to unify became apparent. At the annual meeting of business executives in November 1983, the idea of an alternative economic strategy was suggested. The resulting document, "The Business Consensus for a National Development Plan," was presented to the major presidential candidates a year later. At the same time, various sectorial organizations began to jointly present public communications about economic policies, culminating in the formation in late 1984 of the Confederation of Private Business Institutions (CONFIEP) to increase business influence in economic policy.[35]

What Peru had that Chile did not, of course, was elections. Presidential and congressional elections were held simultaneously every five years, but municipal elections were held on a separate cycle and could serve as referendums on government policy. In the municipal elections of November 1983, the Belaunde government suffered an overwhelming defeat. Of particular note was the rejection of the Popular Action candidate for mayor of Lima. He came in fourth, receiving only 11 percent of the vote, compared to 35 percent for the Marxist candidate and 28 percent for the APRA.[36]

[34] The most serious analysis of the labor movement in Peru in the 1980s is Parodi, "Los sindicatos."

[35] Durand, *Los empresarios*, discusses recent relations between business and government in Peru; idem, *Los industriales, el liberalismo y la democracia* (Lima: DESCO, 1984), for the earlier part of the decade.

[36] See Fernando Tuesta, *El nuevo rostro electoral: las municipales del 83* (Lima: DESCO, 1985), on the municipal elections.

The immediate casualty of the election was Carlos Rodríguez-Pastor. At the annual meeting of business executives shortly after the election, Belaunde announced that he was firing his finance minister and presumably changing economic policy. Nevertheless, Rodríguez-Pastor stayed in office for another four months to draft a new IMF accord and prepare the way for a debt renegotiation. These were almost in place when Belaunde finally appointed a new cabinet, including a finance minister who knew nothing about economics. The move was widely interpreted to mean that Belaunde—who also knew nothing about economics and had very little interest in the subject—would become his own finance minister. His main goal was to get enough money to complete his construction projects before leaving office in mid-1985. To do so, he thought it necessary to appease international creditors, including the IMF.[37] Belaunde's intentions were compatible with those of other leaders of his party, who were eager to enhance their electoral possibilities by short-term improvements in the economy, but they were not compatible with the new aims of Central Bank president, Richard Webb.

Webb, once a staunch supporter of the orthodox policies espoused by the original economic team, had already begun to shift position by 1983. In 1984, he embarked on a collision course with Belaunde and Popular Action that was played out daily in the press, revealing the complete shambles into which the government had fallen. Webb declared publicly that the new IMF agreement was nonviable and that full debt service was incompatible with economic growth. The government responded by demanding his resignation, which was not forthcoming.[38] When Webb's prediction proved correct, Belaunde had to choose between his investment program and debt payments. Because he did not want to precipitate an open break with the banks and other lenders, a non-policy evolved. Arrears began to accumulate in mid-1984 without any consistent explanation; by early 1985, they amounted to $300 million, mostly owed to private banks. The banks cut short-term credits, but resigned themselves to wait until a new government was elected in hopes they would receive more favorable treatment.[39]

SUMMARY

Despite the difference in regime type, political protests in both Chile and Peru forced governments to abandon their preferred orthodox economic policies. Although the types of protest varied, they had similar short-term impacts in both countries. The difference came in the longer run. The authoritarian government in Chile could wait out the protests and then return to a modified version of its previous policies; its democratic counterpart in Peru had no such opportunity. Rejection in the municipal elections was followed by defeat in

[37] Interviews with former Peruvian government officials, Lima, July 1987.
[38] Webb, *Stabilization*, pp. 34–35.
[39] *Andean Report*, March 1985, p. 23.

the 1985 presidential contest, and the change in government resulted in a turn toward heterodoxy.

The economic results of the stabilization attempts also played a part in determining the future course of policy in the two countries. As table 4.4 indicated, the fiscal and current account deficits in Chile had come down in 1982 and 1983, but rose again during the Escobar reactivation in 1984. Although inflation remained under control, Chilean policy makers concluded that reflation should be abandoned as soon as it was politically feasible. In Peru, the deficits were slashed more dramatically than in Chile. The current account recorded a small surplus by 1985 (due entirely to a fall in imports), and the public-sector deficit had been cut from 12 percent of GDP in 1983 to only 3 percent in 1985. Although wages were tumbling rapidly and unemployment was on the rise, inflation still reached an all-time high. These trends were interpreted by the incoming government as evidence that orthodox policies were not viable in the Peruvian context.

Diverging Development Strategies

By 1985, the ad hoc attempts at stabilization in Chile and Peru were over. Over also, at least temporarily, were the similar economic trajectories followed by the two countries since the 1950s. In 1985, Chile and Peru embarked on new development strategies that took them in near-opposing directions. This section will describe the new policies and discuss some of the political and economic results.

CHILE AND THE RETURN TO ORTHODOXY

The combination of economic recovery, repression and serious divisions within opposition ranks meant that Pinochet was able to survive the crisis, unlike his counterparts elsewhere in the region. The political protests petered out, and the business groups were placated by the favors they received. Putting these factors together, Pinochet and his advisors concluded that they could risk a return toward the precrisis economic model—which they still believed was best for the country, even if particular aspects had gone awry previously—and in February both Jarpa and Escobar were dismissed. Escobar's replacement was Hernán Büchi, an engineer who had served in various economic posts under the military: secretary general of the economics ministry, director of the planning agency, and superintendent of banks. The holder of a master's from Columbia University, Büchi was a nonconventional figure in a military government. Nevertheless, he was widely respected as a technocrat and had the full confidence of Pinochet.[40]

[40] Interviews with Chilean economists and former government officials, Santiago, Chile, July 1986 and August 1987.

Büchi's appointment resolved many problems facing the government. His policies combined the earlier laissez-faire model with the more interventionist approach of Escobar. The almost universal shorthand was that Büchi was a more "pragmatic" and "flexible" version of the "Chicago Boys." As one observer with close government connections said: Büchi favored the business organizations' line but was friends with the Catholic University people. Thus, he was able to unite the two factions in the government.[41] Perhaps the most useful way of expressing the synthesis was a long-term model resting on a small state and open economy, but a short-term model that was more interventionist. In other words, the former did not change much from the precrisis period, but the latter looked quite different.

The style of the economic team changed as well. While de Castro refused even to receive Chilean business leaders and appeared to hold them in complete disdain, Büchi listened to them and tried to obtain their backing for government policies. The combination regained the support of most of the business class as well as the international actors. Furthermore, it united the government itself, eliminating the tensions and divisions of the 1982–1984 period.[42]

The macroeconomic model in place since February 1985 has been aimed at a moderate rate of growth and low inflation through promotion of investment and exports and containment of public and private consumption.[43] Within this panorama, a tight fiscal policy has played a key role. The main emphasis has been on cutting social expenditure, since public investment has been increased while taxes have been lowered. Public-sector firms have also raised their prices, thus creating surpluses that have been transferred to the central government coffers. Through this combination, the fiscal deficit was lowered to only 1.9 percent of GDP in 1986 and was virtually eliminated by 1987. Monetary policy has also been restrictive, but the important innovation in this area is an active policy—including "suggested" interest rates—rather than the completely passive stance in vogue during the 1970s.

Another basic component of the short-term model is the limit on private consumption in general and wages in particular. Private-sector wages have been left to be determined by firm-level agreements, while public-sector wages have been kept down as part of the campaign to cut government expenditure. As a result, real wages fell by an average of 2.2 percent per year between 1982 and 1987. The minimum wage stayed far behind inflation as did wages in the government minimum-employment programs.

Trade policy has centered on two main instruments—the exchange rate and

[41] Interview with Chilean economist, Santiago, Chile, August 1987.

[42] Interviews with former Chilean government officials, Santiago, Chile, August 1987.

[43] See Leiva, "Reformulación y rescate," for the most useful overall discussion of the "new" economic model in Chile. Additional references on this topic can be found in *Colección Estudios CIEPLAN* and *Coyuntura Económica*.

tariffs. The peso has been gradually lowered in value through a crawling peg combined with occasional larger devaluations to maintain an expensive dollar, which is considered to be the best incentive for exports and import substitution. In addition, the low tariff level cheapens inputs needed for production. When Büchi became finance minister, tariffs were 35 percent. They were soon returned to a flat 20 percent rate (and later 15 percent), although the use of surcharges was continued in special cases. Other incentives for nontraditional exports also existed: rebate of the 10 percent value-added tax, exemption from other taxes, special credit facilities, and help from Pro-Chile, the government's export promotion office.

Prices for most goods remained market-determined with the important exception of agriculture. The special treatment provided agriculture after the protests in 1982–1983 was continued, including subsidized prices and special credit facilities. The new exchange rate policy also helped agriculture. The other sector with special help was construction, which benefited from the subsidies offered to homebuyers. Through this plan, people could obtain different types of subsidized credit, depending on their income levels. The original aim was to reduce the stock of unsold housing units that built up during the crisis, but more recently it has also benefited new construction.

This more interventionist set of macroeconomic policies has been linked to a medium-term "structural adjustment" strategy. The strategy stressed an increase in investment and a reorientation of production toward exports. In addition, both as a complement to these objectives and as an aim in itself, the emphasis on strengthening the private sector was increased. The policies to deal with the insolvency of banks and industrial firms have already been discussed. Beyond the question of debts, there remained the issue of property rights, both with respect to the banks themselves and the firms they had controlled. In 1984, while Hernán Büchi was still superintendent of banks, a plan evolved to sell the two main problem banks to the public through the process of "people's capitalism."[44] Stock in firms was sold, making it possible for the banks to get the additional capital they needed and the state to leave its undesired ownership situation. Generous credit facilities were provided, and supposedly a limit existed on the quantity of stock that any one individual could purchase. According to a former minister of economy, some one hundred thousand new stockholders bought into the two banks and two affiliated pension funds.[45]

The success of the bank sales encouraged the main structural change that has occurred since 1985—a significant increase in privatization. Following the coup in 1973, firms that had been under temporary government control were

[44] See Enrique Errázuriz and Jacqueline Weinstein, "Capitalismo popular y privatización de las empresas," Programa de Empleo del Trabajo, working paper (Santiago, Chile, 1986), on "people's capitalism" in Chile.

[45] Interview with former Chilean minister of economy, Santiago, Chile, August 1987.

returned to their owners, but a large number remained public because of military veto over their sale.[46] By 1985, the economic and, especially, the political conjunctures were different. Privatization via people's capitalism had two major political advantages for the government. On the one hand, it would increase the number of small property owners, who might then become government supporters. On the other hand, the shrinking of the public sector would limit the room for maneuver of a successor government, whenever one might take over. The economic benefits of privatization were more dubious. Little money would be obtained, and a major source of revenue would be lost. According to late-1988 figures, fourteen nonfinancial firms have been completely privatized, and fourteen more will be all or partially sold. The twenty-eight firms include the main providers of steel, communications, transportation, electricity, paper, and chemicals.[47]

The other important initiative to reduce the size of the state has been the lowering of taxes. From 1983 to 1988, reforms cut taxes by approximately $1 billion annually, compared to what they would have been, which is about 20 percent of government revenue (excluding public enterprises). These reforms included (1) an income tax cut for corporations and high-income groups; (2) cuts in various indirect taxes including tariffs, gasoline, and dividends; and (3) a cut in the value-added tax from 20 to 16 percent. Unlike the U.S. tax cuts of the 1980s, these are not projected to lead to government deficits, but are already being compensated by higher tax collection and expenditure cuts. The alternative to lowering taxes would have been using some or all of the surplus to increase social services, which were substantially reduced during the military government, but this alternative was rejected to reduce the size of the state.[48]

These domestic changes were not unrelated to Chile's international economic problems, although the exact nature of the link is debated. The government claims its policies represent its own ideas, whereas the opposition points to the IMF, World Bank, and private banks as the source of many of the policies.[49] It is undeniable that Chile's foreign debt makes the balance of payments a major constraint on economic policy, now that private bank loans have virtually dried up. Nearly half of export revenues have gone for debt service since the crisis began. The government's basic stance in favor of pri-

[46] Interviews with former Chilean government officials, Santiago, Chile, August 1987; see Cristián Larroulet, "El estado empresario en Chile," *Estudios Públicos* 14 (1984), for data on the trends in public sector ownership between 1965 and 1981. Larroulet was the main advisor to Finance Minister Büchi.

[47] Data are from Mario Marcel, "Privatización de las empresas públicas en Chile, 1985–87" (unpublished ms., CIEPLAN, Santiago, Chile, 1988).

[48] See Mario Marcel and Manuel Marfán, "La cuestión tributaria," *Revista de CIEPLAN* 13 (July 1988): 8–12, for a discussion of the tax cuts.

[49] See Leiva, "Reformulación y rescate," pp. 79–81, for a denunciation of Chile's inability to make policy decisions because of the restrictions of the IMF and World Bank agreements.

vate enterprise and an open economy means that the debt must be serviced, but government negotiators have sought the best deal possible. Under Büchi, relations with both the international agencies and the private banks were extremely cordial. Since 1985, the government has signed an extended financing facility (EFF) with the International Monetary Fund and three structural adjustment loans (SALS) with the World Bank. In addition, three sets of negotiations have been completed with private bank creditors. These negotiations have brought in some $3 billion, which has been crucial in enabling the government to meet its debt-servicing obligations.

The goals of the $775 million EFF were basically the same as the earlier stand-by—reducing the current account deficit and equilibrating public finance in the context of moderate growth and somewhat lower inflation. The change in finance ministers actually increased the speed of the adjustment by cutting the growth target and devaluing the currency. While the IMF conditionality relates to short-term macroeconomic policy, the World Bank negotiations focused on long-term structural adjustment. A first SAL (for $250 million) was signed in October 1985, while a second and third (for $300 million each) were approved in 1986 and 1987.

The first goal of the SALS is export promotion via exchange rate policy, a copper stabilization fund, and strengthening of governmental promotion agencies. Second, the SAL strategy aims to raise Chile's traditionally low investment rate. Stress is placed on public savings and investment, mainly in infrastructure related to export activities. Third, the continuing process of cleaning up the domestic debt is underlined as a prerequisite to export-led growth. A fourth goal of employment generation appears to have little relationship to other aims, because it relies on government emergency employment programs in the absence of job possibilities in the export sector.[50]

Negotiations with the private banks began shortly after the EFF was signed in 1985. These negotiations were to reschedule principal falling due in 1985–1987 and to renew short-term trade credits. New funds of $785 million were obtained for 1985–1986. One portion of this sum was guaranteed by the World Bank. Other than the World Bank participation, Chile's terms have been quite similar to those of other Latin American debtors. In 1987, Chile was again at the bargaining table to extend maturities for 1988–1991. Because the government negotiators expected more difficulties in obtaining new money in this round, a strategy of "re-timing" was developed. Rather than pay twice a year, a once-a-year payment was proposed that would save $450 million over two years. (The difference would later be repaid.) The banks initially opposed the re-timing scheme, but they eventually accepted it as preferable to providing

[50] See José Pablo Arellano, René Cortazar, and Andrés Solimano, *Stabilization and Adjustment Policies and Programmes: Country Study, Chile* (Helsinki: WIDER, 1987), pp. 25–30, on the aims of the IMF and World Bank programs.

new funds. Most recently, Chile received permission to repurchase a small amount of its debt on the secondary market.[51]

Chile also eliminated $4 billion from its external debt through the controversial debt-equity swaps. This program enables foreign corporations, or Chilean citizens who hold foreign currency, to purchase Chilean debt at a discount and then exchange it for the full face value equivalent of local currency to make direct investments. The resulting profits cannot be remitted for four years and then only in a phased manner. Critics charge that these mechanisms provide a cheap means to make investments that would be made in any case and lead to increased denationalization of assets. Often debt-equity swaps have been used to purchase companies sold by the government.[52]

All of the international financial negotiations, of course, have been affected by Chile's relations with the United States.[53] The most appropriate words to describe these relations are "inconsistent" or even "contradictory." The basic conflict juxtaposes concern over Chile's human rights record with strong approval of its economic policy. The contradiction came into play most sharply with the second World Bank loan, which the United States considered voting against. Ultimately, it abstained and the loan was approved with a 51 percent majority. The ambivalent position of the United States has enabled Chile to continue its authoritarian stance, but still deal adequately with its potentially debilitating foreign exchange constraint.

In October 1988, a new phase began in Chile, which will have profound political and economic ramifications. In an attempt to legitimize the authoritarian state, the 1980 constitution scheduled a plebiscite for 1988 to decide whether Pinochet would continue as president for another eight years. Economic policy figured prominently in the brief campaign. Government supporters not only lauded the economic model, but claimed that it could not survive a "no" vote in the plebiscite. The opposition also praised the basic elements of the model—especially the balanced accounts, the low inflation, and the emphasis on promoting exports—but criticized its distributional impact and the management of the debt. The victory of the "no" option means that the government must call open elections for president and congress by December 1989. In the meantime, the government seems determined to push ahead with its structural reforms (especially privatization) and to maintain the same macroeconomic policy. Whoever wins the upcoming elections, then,

[51] Interviews with Chilean debt negotiator, Santiago, Chile, August 1987 and August 1988.

[52] See Ricardo Ffrench-Davis, "Conversión de págares de la deuda externa en Chile," *Colección Estudios CIEPLAN* 22 (December 1987): 41–62, for a critique of debt-equity swaps from the Chilean perspective.

[53] See Heraldo Muñoz and Carlos Portales, *Una amistad esquiva: las relaciones de Estados Unidos y Chile* (Santiago: Pehuén, 1987), on U.S.-Chile relations; *Cono Sur* for a bimonthly chronology; *AID Memo*, Center for International Policy, Washington, D.C., 20 July 1987, for data on U.S. votes on loans to Chile in multilateral agencies.

will inherit a smaller state, but one whose balanced accounts will provide certain room for maneuver.[54]

While 1985 saw the Chilean regime re-embrace the major elements of an orthodox economic model, 1985 in Peru brought a turn toward a self-proclaimed heterodoxy. The change came through the presidential election in April, when the APRA's Alan García won an easy plurality with 48 percent of the vote. In second place, with 22 percent, was Alfonso Barrantes of the United Left coalition. Far behind were the right-wing contenders with 18 percent between them. Since García did not have an absolute majority, a second round was originally scheduled but avoided when Barrantes withdrew. Thus, on July 28, 1985, Belaunde fulfilled one of his major goals and transferred power to a democratically elected successor.

That transfer represented the first time the APRA had ever assumed the presidency; its previous victories had been annulled by the military.[55] Since the country's largest party had been waiting some sixty years to run the government, it was a disagreeable shock for veteran party leaders to discover that they were to have little role in governing, especially in the key economic area. García's victory was not a triumph for the traditional APRA, which is an antiquated center-right organization, but for its modern center-left faction. The new president's tendency toward personalistic rule further distanced party leaders as did the fact that many of his closest confidants were independents. These proclivities were apparent in cabinet choices and even more obvious in the economic team that surrounded the new president.

Like the Chileans in 1985, García also looked back to an earlier model, but his came from the leftist phase of the historical trajectory. In particular, he embraced an economic model that had been developed by a group of Velasco supporters, centered in a Lima research institute called Centro de Estudios para el Desarrollo y la Participación (CEDEP). A number of people associated with CEDEP would later become economic advisors, but the most important was Daniel Carbonetto, an Argentine engineer educated at Louvain. As early

[54] See International Commission of the Latin American Studies Association to Observe the Chilean Plebiscite, "The Chilean Plebiscite: A First Step toward Redemocratization," *LASA Forum* 19, 4 (Winter 1989), for an analysis of the plebiscite; Barbara Stallings, "The Political Economy of Democratic Transition: Chile in the 1980s," in Barbara Stallings and Robert Kaufman, eds., *Debt and Democracy in Latin America* (Boulder, Colo.: Westview Press, 1989), pp. 181–99 for a discussion of the differences in the political conjuncture during the 1983 protests and the plebiscite.

[55] See Peter Klaren, *Modernization, Dislocation, and Aprismo: Origins of the Peruvian Aprista Party, 1870–1932* (Austin: University of Texas Press, 1973), on the general background and history of the APRA; Victor Villanueva, *El APRA en busca del poder* (Lima: Editorial Horizonte, 1975); Heraclio Bonilla and Paul W. Drake, eds., *El APRA de la ideologia a la praxis* (Lima: Editorial Nuevo Mundo, 1989).

as 1982, Carbonetto had published a model in CEDEP's journal that was quite similar to what would later become government policy. García contacted Carbonetto and the others at CEDEP in 1982 and brought them together with CONAPLAN, an APRA group working on the electoral program. By the election, a "heterodox" plan was in place—at least to deal with short-term measures.[56]

The political process of the adoption of Peru's heterodox model thus differed from that in Argentina and Brazil (see chapter 3). In Peru, the model was developed in close collaboration with the president; it did not have to be "sold" to him after the election or have to compete with alternative programs. The characteristics of the model were also quite different, although the three plans were often seen as similar. The main difference was that Peru's heterodoxy was not just a stabilization program, but a long-term development strategy that included measures to deal with short-term disequilibria.[57]

The heart of the Peruvian program was to increase economic growth, with greater equality of distribution across both income groups and regions.[58] Carbonetto was very blunt when explaining at least one part of the rationale: "We must continually grow at an annual rate above six percent beyond the year 2000 if we do not want to be overtaken by Sendero Luminoso."[59] The original idea of the approach was to focus growth-stimulating policies on traditional agriculture and the informal sector, the areas whose poverty nourished the insurgency movement, but subsequently there was an implicit switch in the direction of industry. In direct opposition to the Chilean model, Peru aimed for demand-led growth. Consumption, and especially wage increases, were supposed to create reactivation through the use of idle capacity and then to stimulate investment. The foreign sector would be brought into long-run equilibrium by import substitution and export promotion, but in the short run restrictions on capital outflow were seen as the only way to deal with the foreign exchange constraint.

The short-term stabilization measures derived from the conviction that neither inflation nor balance-of-payments problems in Peru were caused by ex-

[56] "Metiendo Carbonetto," *SI*, 30 June 1987, pp. 20–21; and interviews with former Peruvian government officials, Lima, Peru, July 1987.

[57] Pérsio Arida, ed., *Inflacion ceró* (Bogotá: Editorial Oveja Negra, 1986) contains articles on the Peruvian, Brazilian, Argentine, and Israeli cases. A direct comparison is made in José Pablo Arellano, "Comparación de los planes de estabilización de Argentina, Brasil y Perú," *Apuntes* 20 (1987): 3–13.

[58] General descriptions of the Peruvian heterodox program can be found in Jürgen Schuldt, "Desinflación y reestructuración económica en el Perú, 1985–86: 119–98, un modelo para armar," Arida, ed., Inflación cero; Rosemary Thorp, "The APRA Alternative in Peru," *Peru Report*, June 1987, 5-1, to 5-23; and Cesar Herrera, Oscar Dancourt, and German Alarco, *Reactivación y política económica heterodoxa, 1985–86* (Lima: Fundación Friedrich Ebert, 1987). Daniel Carbonetto et al., *El Perú heterodoxo: un modelo económico* (Lima: Instituto Nacional de Planificación, 1987) is a key volume containing articles by most of the government's top economists.

[59] "Metiendo Carbonetto," p. 21.

cess demand. Large amounts of idle capacity combined with high rates of unemployment and depressed wages constituted the evidence. The analysis suggested that inflation was cost-induced through government-controlled prices, including the exchange rate, interest rates, public utility prices, and some food prices. Balance-of-payments problems came from long-term supply and price constraints for exports, high import propensities of domestic production and consumption, and capital flight. Recession actually worsened inflation by increasing unit costs, tax evasion, and welfare payments. With respect to the balance of payments, recession cut imports temporarily but also stimulated capital flight.[60]

The initial package of economic measures in August–September 1985 was aimed at slowing inflation and speeding up growth. It included freezing prices (after some initial adjustments), increasing wages, lowering interest rates and some taxes, freezing the exchange rate and increasing import controls, and limiting debt payments. The general idea was that higher production levels would lower unit costs, and the rise in wages could be offset by a frozen exchange rate, lower interest rates, and lower taxes. Thus a price freeze was viable without cutting profit margins, and it would also affect expectations positively. Later packages were similar in spirit, while making some modifications to deal with problems that arose. Most prices, for example, became regulated rather than frozen. The exchange rate moved to a complicated multitier system combined with a crawling peg. Fiscal and monetary policy throughout were to be accommodating rather than taking a leading role.[61]

The crucial question, to which many commentators complained that the government did not devote enough attention, was how these short-term measures related to a long-term strategy. One set of problems, pointed out by British economist Rosemary Thorp, was primarily technical: heterodoxy is such that short-term and long-term measures are often contradictory and must be carried out with extreme care in timing. For example, a frozen exchange rate is useful for slowing inflation but damaging for promotion of investment in nontraditional exports; thus it can only be used for a limited period.[62] Other problems were directly political: (1) Should the public sector or private business take the lead in the investment process? (2) Is the state capable of being the leading actor? (3) What should be done about the foreign sector?

The public-private issue was debated extensively by García's small group of trusted advisors. The president took an active part, demanded alternative positions, and made the final decision himself. A program was drawn up for nationalizing key firms, including the banks and financial houses, to be announced in the July 28 speech in 1986, but at the last minute García decided

[60] Thorp, "APRA Alternative," pp. 5-1 to 5-6.

[61] See "Síntesis de los paquetes," *Actualidad Económica*, (Suplemento Especial), June 1987, pp. 1–4, for an outline of the various "paquetes" introduced since July 1985.

[62] Thorp, "APRA Alternative," p. 5-2.

to pursue a "concertation" strategy instead.[63] Shortly before his annual message to the nation, he met with leading members of the local business class and began the effort to persuade them to invest. Various incentives were offered: concessions on the exchange rate, credit, prices, and taxes.[64]

The government's decision to rely on the private sector as the main engine of the economy was consistent with the APRAS historical position and García's own earlier writings.[65] Indeed, many industrialists and other business figures had supported the APRA in the 1985 election. The unexpected twist was the particular form that concertation assumed—primarily negotiations with the largest business conglomerates in the country, popularly known as the "twelve apostles." CONFIEP, the umbrella business association formed in 1984, was bypassed in favor of "selective concertation" with large business, in the hope that smaller entrepreneurs would follow suit.[66]

Several institutional innovations were developed to try to attract participation of the economic groups and others from the private sector. In January 1987, a National Investment Council was created. Of the four executive directors, three were from the major groups and the fourth was to represent the rest of the private sector. Another type of institutional innovation was the establishment in April of the Fund for Investment and Employment (FIE). FIE was an arrangement whereby an investor who bought a bond could exchange it for a share in an approved project. The government would then increase the value of the investment by 50 percent. Poor planning meant that FIE was announced simultaneously with the requirement that companies purchase compulsory government bonds at a very low yield. The latter plan was later abrogated, but served to undermine the government's credibility with the private sector.

A much more serious break in the government's strategy vis-à-vis the private sector occurred with the July 28 address in 1987. For a combination of political and economic reasons, the president announced that all of the financial institutions in the country, except for foreign bank branches, would be nationalized. Since the Banco de Crédito, the largest private bank in Peru, belonged to the most important of the "twelve apostles," the move clearly seemed to limit the possibility of selective concertation as the basis of long-term strategy. Some commentators say that the lack of investment response led the president to make his decision; others attribute the move to an attempt to revive his flagging popularity.[67] The move aroused enormous controversy. The United Left supported the nationalization, because they had long advocated it. The rightist opposition saw the nationalization as a perfect opportu-

[63] Interviews with former Peruvian government officials, Lima, July 1987.

[64] *Oiga*, 4 August 1986.

[65] See Alan García, *El futuro diferente: la tarea histórica del APRA* (Lima: Editorial e Imprenta DESA, 1982).

[66] Durand, *Los empresarios*, pp. 53–56.

[67] *Caretas*, 3 August 1987, pp. 12–19.

nity to increase its own political support and attacked the government in the courts, in the Congress, and in street rallies. The government eventually back-tracked considerably and a resolution was reached, but the consequences were extremely negative, in both political and economic terms.

The other side of the question about the role of the private sector concerned the role of the state. Even if the concertation strategy were to go forward, the very notion of heterodoxy assigns an important role to economic policy makers and thus imposes substantial requirements in state capacity. In this respect, the García government faced serious problems.

First, the APRA as a party had never had a strong group of technocrats among its members. This was recognized all along, and it was assumed that García would bring in a prominent group of independent economists. To some extent this happened at the top levels, and some ambitious individuals joined the party. Nevertheless, it proved very difficult to fill the hundreds of upper-middle and upper level positions with people who were both competent and trusted by García's core group of advisors.

A second problem, which partially explained the inability to attract high-quality people, was the low salary structure in the public sector. Public service has never been considered a high-prestige occupation in Peru. This historical problem was made more difficult by the Belaunde government's explicit attempt to devalue the state. Real wages in the public sector fell by much more than the average,[68] and it was typical for government employees to have multiple jobs. In some areas, corruption further discredited the image of the public sector.

Third, sectarianism and infighting limited the possibility of attracting competent people. Honest disagreement, even on relatively minor details of policy, could result in one being considered an enemy. Virtually the entire Central Bank staff, which included the majority of trained economists in the public sector, was marginalized on suspicion of being "monetarists." Symbolic of this attitude was the dismissal of Leonel Figueroa as president of the Central Bank—although in Figueroa's case the countervailing complaint was that he was too "statist."[69] Filling the central bank presidency and various other top jobs proved difficult, and an ever-smaller group of advisors had to manage ever-greater responsibilities. A comment by one of them, after legal complications arose in connection with the bank nationalization, summarized the situation well: "There aren't many of us in the team, and we overlooked the legal aspect."[70] The sectarianism was compounded by García's desire to keep power concentrated in his own hands.

---

[68] Calculated from Instituto Nacional de Estadísticas, *Perú: compendio estadístico 1985* (Lima: Instituto Nacional de Estadísticas, 1986), pp. 141, 151. Remunerations in the public sector fell by 57 percent between 1980 and 1985, while comparable salaries in the private sector declined by 22 percent.

[69] Interviews with former Peruvian government officials, Lima, July 1987.

[70] *Latin America Weekly Report*, 20 August 1987, p. 11.

All of the policies discussed thus far—the short-term stabilization measures, the concertation with the private sector, and the nationalization of the banks—were related to Peru's international situation. García's economic team came to a decision substantially different than its Chilean counterpart about foreign capital. The team concluded that Peru was unlikely to get much new money, even if the arrears accumulated under Belaunde were paid, and that playing by the rules would leave them with a large net outflow of foreign exchange. This was especially true for the private banks, but it could occur with public-sector lenders as well. To make matters more difficult, a formal renegotiation of the debt would require an agreement with the IMF (Peru had tried to negotiate without the Fund in the 1970s and the attempt had backfired), which was opposed to Peru's version of heterodox policies. Thus the economic team saw no alternative to redefining the rules if they wanted to carry out their plans.[71]

The basic plank in the international economic strategy was announced in García's inaugural address: the limit of debt-service payments to 10 percent of export earnings. Strong attacks were also made on the IMF. Various exceptions to the 10 percent rule were gradually cut back, and profit repatriation was eventually barred as well. Nonetheless, it should be noted that the confrontational nature of this policy—more so than any other in the hemisphere—did not represent a complete break with the international financial system. Peru did not repudiate its debt; it simply said that it would pay slowly. Likewise, it did not withdraw from the IMF even after being declared ineligible for further loans. The same occurred with other international agencies, including the World Bank and the Interamerican Development Bank. Conversations continued on an occasional basis with the banks and the Paris Club. Some banks, working through intermediaries, accepted the government's offer to pay in kind with a variety of products.[72]

Despite the limitation on debt service and various stopgap measures, such as purchasing reserves from drug dealers in the jungle region, the foreign exchange constraint reached emergency levels by the end of 1987. The rapid growth of 1986 and 1987 had spurred imports, creating a trade deficit and depleting reserves. Net international reserves became negative in early 1988, which meant that imports had to be cut, crippling many parts of the industrial sector and boosting inflation.

The initial response of the García government was to continue the heterodox approach through a "selective growth" model. The basis of the model was the distinction between "social" and "nonessential" products. Producers of the former—including basic consumer goods, exports, and items with low import content and/or high employment-generation capacity—were to be

[71] Interviews with former Peruvian government officials, Lima, July 1987.

[72] Barbara Stallings, "Self-Destruction of an Auspicious Initiative: Peruvian Debt Policy under Alan García," in Bonilla, *El APRA*, pp. 293–319.

given incentives to grow about 5 percent per year, while the other products would be allowed to stagnate or even decline in output. Various wage, price, and exchange rate policies were introduced to support the new economic model and stem the loss of reserves.[73]

When García's popularity plummeted as a result of the economic crisis, with his "approval rating" in the polls dropping from 96 percent in August 1985 to 16 percent in September 1988,[74] the leaders of the APRA finally felt emboldened to move. They had already managed to get party veterans into key positions, but by the second half of 1988, they intervened in policy issues as well. García's confidants were sent packing, the heterodox model was replaced by an orthodox shock treatment, and negotiations were opened with the IMF and World Bank in order to regain Peru's access to international credit.

The result of two poorly planned and poorly implemented packages of orthodox measures, on top of the previous heterodoxy, created even greater economic chaos. Inflation moved into four digits, and the economy began to contract rapidly. Talk abounded of a military coup, moving up the 1990 elections, or a "supercabinet" that would make decisions with García as a figurehead president, but none of these scenarios has come to pass, and García retains enough control to water down the various measures being taken. While the current trends seem to imply the end to heterodoxy in Peru, no one is yet willing to count out the president.

SUMMARY

By 1989, four years into the new development strategies, the economies of Chile and Peru were in very different conditions. As can be seen in table 4.4, growth in Chile continued at its moderate pace, inflation had declined substantially, and real wages had consequently increased. The budget and balance of payments were equilibrated, and investment was on the rise. Although the growth figures were not impressive in terms of historical trajectory—the positive growth only signified a recovery of levels from fifteen years earlier—Chile's performance nevertheless put it at the top of the Latin American region in comparative terms. Peru, by contrast, was near the bottom of regional league tables. Growth had ceased after two years of rapid advance based on use of idle capacity; inflation was out of control; and the size of the external and internal deficits meant that no relief was in sight. Even the distributional gains were in jeopardy as inflation far outstripped nominal wage increases.

Throughout the crisis period, the political institutions of the two countries had also differed substantially: authoritarianism compared to multiparty liberal democracy. The Chilean government's resulting ability to limit wages and social spending was an important factor in its economic performance. García's

---

[73] Javier Tantaleán Arbulu, "APRA's Economic Policy," in Bonilla, *El APRA*, pp. 201–13, describes the selective growth model; Tantaleán was the head of the National Planning Institute.

[74] *The Peru Report*, October 1988, pp. 7-1 to 7-4.

populism, however, cannot be solely attributed to Peru's democratic institutions, although recent evidence suggests some "elective affinity" between populism and transitional democracy. The nature of the coalition that supported him, and the power of the left including Sendero Luminoso in the background, clearly provided some of the motivation for his policies, just as the guerrilla movement would stimulate Betancur's populism in Colombia.

The main similarity between Chile and Peru was that, by 1988, neither the authors of Chile's relatively successful economic strategy, nor Peru's disastrous one, were popular among their constituents. The differences, of course, in the extent and nature of the opposition were important. In Chile, the government had strong support from business and other traditionally conservative sectors, while opposition was strongest among lower-class groups who had not shared in the benefits of the orthodox model. In Peru, the situation was more blurred, because García's popularity had eroded both among the lower classes and among business people.

A potential similarity also derives from the long-awaited beginning of Chile's transition back to democracy. Citizens in that country will again be able to use elections to change economic policy orientation, and the new institutional framework will privilege different groups than under the fifteen years of authoritarian rule. In theory, Chile and Peru will both have newly elected governments in 1990. It remains to be seen whether the two countries will return to the similar political-economic trajectories that characterized them until 1985 or whether their paths will continue to diverge.

COLOMBIA: STABILITY AMID CHAOS

Colombia is a great enigma in Latin America, differing in many ways from Chile and Peru. On the one hand, its macroeconomic stability during the 1980s contrasts with the economic chaos elsewhere in the region. On the other hand, Colombia's economic stability also contrasts with the political chaos inside the country itself. The insurgency in Colombia is even more serious than in Peru, but its macroeconomic performance is as smooth as in Büchi's Chile. To explain these contrasts and understand developments in the 1980s, it is essential to begin with the political-economic history of Colombia.[75]

[75] Many people believe that these paradoxes are related through the varying facets of the drug trade in Colombia. Clearly drug traffickers contribute to the political violence, but their economic impact is less clear. Two recent studies have tried to estimate the volume of foreign exchange returning to Colombia as a result of drugs. See Hernando José Gómez, "La economía ilegal en Colombia: tamaño, evolución, características e impacto económico" *Coyuntura Económica* 13, 3 (September 1988): 93–113; Carlos Caballero, "La economía de la cocaina: algunos estimativos para 1988," pp. 179–83. They calculate that the amount ranges between $300 million and $1 billion, or between 1 and 3 percent of GDP. Any positive effect on the balance of payments would have to be mostly on top of the existing figures. Gómez suggests that the drug money may actually have a negative macroeconomic (as opposed to regional) effect on growth by encouraging contra-

Historical Background

The post-World War II period in Colombia witnessed an extraordinary wave of violence. Some two hundred thousand people lost their lives in the decade following the April 1948 assassination of Liberal party leader Jorge Eliécer Gaitán. Deaths resulted both through "official" violence against Liberal civilians and guerrilla actions against Conservative civilians and government authorities. The violence that wracked Colombian society was primarily a rural phenomenon and mainly political in motivation, pitting supporters of the two parties against each other. The partisan fighting was brought under control through agreements between party leaders and ratified by a national plebiscite to create a National Front.[76]

Going into effect in 1958, the National Front was a defensive measure to avoid further serious conflict by integrating two sets of actors. On the one hand, the political parties agreed to share power rather than fight over it. The arrangement called for alternation in the presidency and parity in the executive, legislative, and judiciary branches through 1974. At that point, although competitive elections were reestablished, an amendment to the constitution provided that the party receiving the second largest number of votes was to receive "adequate and equitable" representation.[77] On the other hand, the public and private elites were merged as well. The most obvious example is the inclusion of the coffee growers, the most powerful of the private sector groups, in many of the official organs of the state.[78] In addition, alternation between positions in the state itself and the business associations is a long tradition.

The flip side of these practices is that significant parts of the population have been marginalized from participation in political institutions. Labor is especially impotent in Colombia, and significant political opposition has been driven outside the system. Broad "civic movements" call general strikes to protest, and a guerrilla insurgency poses a serious military challenge to the

---

band trade and thus hurting industry. The drug money also has driven up real estate prices and stimulated speculative activity.

[76] See Francisco Leal, *Estado y política en Colombia* (Bogotá: Siglo 21, 1984), especially chap. 4, pp. 136–70; R. Albert Berry, Ronald Hellman, and Mauricio Solaún, eds., *The Politics of Compromise: Coalition Government in Colombia* (New Brunswick, N.J.: Transaction Books, 1980); and Bruce Bagley, "Colombia: National Front and Economic Development," in Robert Wesson, ed., *Politics, Policies, and Economic Development in Latin America* (Stanford, Calif.: Hoover Institution, 1984): 124–60, on the background and operation of the National Front.

[77] Bagley, "Colombia," p. 149 and note 74 above.

[78] See Edgar Revéiz, ed., *La cuestión cafetera: su impacto económico, social y político* (Bogotá: Universidad de los Andes, 1980), on the coffee issue; see Guillermo Gallón, *Concertación simple y concertación ampliada* (Bogotá: CINEP, Controversia no. 105, 1978); idem, *Crisis y reajuste del esquema de concertación económica en Colombia, 1980–85* (Bogota: CINEP, Controversia no. 130, 1986), on more general issues of relations between the public and private sectors in Colombia.

establishment. At the same time, shifting coalitions of guerrillas, drug traffickers, right-wing death squads, and the army battle each other in small-scale operations on a daily basis.[79]

These challenges have furthered the unity of the two dominant parties. Their quasi-democratic system has put severe limits on the type of economic policies that can be followed, because they have to receive approval from all participant economic and political groups. Hence, it is not surprising that fairly conservative policies have resulted, especially since Colombian history has legitimized such policies in the past. Inflation, for example, was regarded with such fear and antipathy at the turn of the century that a 1910 constitutional amendment prohibited further emissions of paper money.[80] In addition, Colombia has a long tradition of close reliance on international financial institutions, particularly the World Bank, which has reinforced the tendency toward moderate and continuous macroeconomic policy.[81]

Like Chile and Peru, stabilization crises interrupted long-term growth trends in Colombia, but these were less severe as can be seen by comparing tables 4.1, 4.2, and 4.5.[82] Colombia's growth rate never became negative and was not below 2 percent until the 1980s. Likewise, the inflation rate never exceeded 35 percent and was generally below 15 percent until the mid-1970s. The most important stabilization episode occurred in 1967, when the IMF was urging President Lleras Restrepo to devalue the peso. He went on television to denounce the external pressure and broke off negotiations with the Fund. As an alternative policy, he instituted import and exchange controls rather than a devaluation, which eventually led to an overall package that included a crawling peg exchange rate and promotion of manufactured exports. Political support for the government increased significantly as a result of these actions, and the IMF emerged with a severely tarnished image among Colombians.[83]

[79] See Víctor Manuel Moncayo, Camilo Gonzáles Passo, and Eduardo Pizarro, *Entre la guerra y la paz* (Bogotá: CINEP, Controversia 141, 1987), for an overview of the antigovernment struggles; see Olga Behar, *Las guerras de la paz* (Bogotá: Planeta, 1985), on the guerrilla movement and its background in particular.

[80] Paul Drake, *The Money Doctor in the Andes: U.S. Expansion in Latin America from World War I to the Great Depression* (Durham, N.C.: Duke University Press, 1989), chap. 2, pp. 30–75.

[81] Juan Luis Londoño and Guillermo Perry, "El Banco Mundial, el Fondo Monetario y Colombia: análisis crítico de sus relaciones," *Coyuntura Económica* 15, 3 (October 1985): 209–43.

[82] On the pre-1980 period, see José Antonio Ocampo, ed., *Historia económica de Colombia* (Bogotá: Siglo XXI/Fedesarrollo, 1987); Salomón Kalmanovitz, *Economía y nación, una breve historia de Colombia* (Bogotá: Siglo XXI/CINEP, 1985); and Edgar Revéiz and María José Pérez, "Colombia: Moderate Economic Growth, Political Stability, and Social Welfare," in Jonathan Hartlyn and Samual Morley, eds., *Latin American Political Economy* (Boulder, Colo.: Westview Press, 1986), pp. 265–91.

[83] Kalmanovitz, *Economía y nación*, pp. 439–40. See also David Mares, "State Leadership in Foreign Economic Policy: Suggestions from the Public Choice Literature with Illustrations from Colombia," (unpublished ms., Political Science Department, University of California at San Diego, 1988).

TABLE 4.5
Colombia: Growth, Inflation, Balance of Payments, 1955–1985

Year	GDP[a] (%)	Inflation[b] (%)	Balance of Payments[c] ($ millions)
1955	3.9	0.0	− 141
1956	4.0	6.1	− 42
1957	2.2	14.3	+ 70
1958	2.5	15.0	+ 52
1959	7.2	6.5	+ 49
1960	4.3	4.1	− 94
1961	5.1	7.8	− 149
1962	5.4	3.6	− 175
1963	3.3	31.6	− 139
1964	6.2	17.3	− 142
1965	3.6	3.4	− 21
1966	5.4	19.8	− 288
1967	4.2	8.3	− 73
1968	6.1	5.9	− 164
1969	6.3	10.4	− 175
1970	6.6	6.5	− 293
1971	6.0	9.5	− 454
1972	7.7	13.0	− 190
1973	6.7	20.9	− 55
1974	5.7	24.5	− 350
1975	2.3	22.6	− 109
1976	4.7	20.2	+ 207
1977	4.2	33.2	+ 440
1978	8.5	17.8	+ 322
1979	5.4	24.6	+ 491
1980	4.1	26.6	− 159
1981	2.3	27.5	− 1895
1982	0.9	24.5	− 2895
1983	0.8	19.8	− 2826
1984	3.2	16.1	− 2050
1985	2.3	24.0	− 1220

Source: International Monetary Fund, *International Financial Statistics* (various issues).
[a] Annual growth rates.
[b] Consumer price index, twelve-month average increase.
[c] Current account.

During the 1970s, a moderate version of the liberalization seen in Chile and Peru was followed, as import restrictions were lifted and the financial markets opened up. Substantially different from the other two countries, however, was the restraint in foreign borrowing, especially from the private banks. It was not until the Turbay government (1978–1982) that heavy borrowing began, but even then the Colombian debt remained small in comparison to other Latin American countries. Statistics on the debt, in table 4.6, indicate that the initial share owed to the private banks was small. Combined with the small size of the debt, this limited the impact of debt service, making it possible for Colombia to deviate from the Latin American pattern and avoid rescheduling.

In the latter half of the 1970s, Colombia enjoyed an economic boom due to the high price of coffee. Reserves increased rapidly as the balance of payments went into a rare surplus phase. As a consequence, the exchange rate became overvalued and nontraditional exports stagnated. When many import controls were lifted, these factors set the stage for a large balance-of-payments deficit and resulting recession when coffee prices dropped in the early 1980s. The problems in the real economy were exacerbated by a growing financial crisis as the new institutions became overextended.

Despite these incipient problems, the economy was not a major issue in the 1982 electoral campaign.[84] Political issues were the key focus of the quadrennial contest between Liberals and Conservatives, with special emphasis on the various proposals for dealing with the guerrilla insurgency that was a growing challenge to the existing system. Divisions among the Liberals opened the way for Belisario Betancur—lawyer, poet, politician, and renegade Conservative, who had been the party's candidate several times previously—to win the pres-

TABLE 4.6
Colombia: Foreign Debt Indicators, 1980–1987

	1980	1982	1984	1986	1987
Total Debt[a]	6.9	10.3	12.0	15.4	17.0
Debt/Exports[b]	117.1	204.3	223.0	219.3	220.3
Public-Sector Share[c]	88.8	83.4	84.3	88.5	90.1
Share Owed to Banks[d]	36.2	45.0	44.7	38.9	35.3
Interest/Exports[e]	4.8	11.5	10.2	13.4	14.4
Amortization/Exports[f]	4.2	6.2	10.2	14.2	16.3

Source: World Bank, *World Debt Tables*, vol. 2, 1988–1989, pp. 82–85.

[a] Total disbursed debt (long- and short-term, public and private) in U.S. dollars billions.

[b] Debt as share of exports of goods and services.

[c] Public-sector share of long-term debt only.

[d] Percentage of public-sector long-term debt owed to private banks.

[e] Interest payments on long-term public-sector debt as percentage of exports of goods and services.

[f] Amortization on long-term public-sector debt as percentage of exports of goods and services.

[84] Francisco de Roux, *Candidatos, programas, y compromisos* (Bogotá: CINEP, Controversia no. 103, 1982), provides an overview of the issues in the 1982 campaign.

idency. Although he received a 47 percent plurality, the Liberals retained control of the congress.[85]

Crisis, Colombian Style

In some interesting ways, Betancur was a preview of Alan García three years later in Peru. Like García, Betancur had a populist style, an alienation from the traditional apparatus of his party, and the ambition to become a third world leader. Both also shared an economic approach to dealing with the major guerrilla insurgencies in their respective countries, but the willingness to use force when they deemed it necessary. Furthermore, the two presidents followed economic policies with some minimal similarities in their initial periods in office, although the historical-structural contexts differed in important ways and led to different outcomes.

The first two years of the Betancur administration have also been described as a "heterodox" period, but the policies were more ad hoc and more cautious than in Peru.[86] Since Betancur did not have much interest in economic issues per se—although he needed a growing economy to provide the resources to fulfill his international and domestic political goals[87]—the details were left to his finance minister, Edgar Gutiérrez Castro. Gutiérrez Castro was a Liberal from the industrial stronghold of Antioquia and had two main concerns. One was reactivating the economy, especially the industrial sector; the other was resolving the domestic financial crisis. Despite the large deficit, the balance of payments was not seen as a problem because the coffee boom and the rising drug trade had left a large volume of reserves.

The initial plan was to reactivate the economy through credit to the private sector, but this failed when the credit facilities went unused. At approximately the same time that the credit policy failure became evident, the devaluation of the currency in Venezuela, Colombia's main market for industrial products, called attention to the balance-of-payments problems in Colombia itself. The combination of deepening recession and loss of reserves provided the opportunity for the heterodox stabilization policies.

In the Colombian case, unlike Peru, heterodoxy was a set of short-term

[85] See Mario Latorre, *Hechos y crítica política* (Bogota: Universidad Nacional de Colombia, 1986); Ricardo Santamaría and Gabriel Silva Luján, *Proceso político en Colombia*, 2d ed. (Bogotá: Fondo Editorial CEREC, 1986) on Colombian elections.

[86] José Antonio Ocampo and Eduardo Lora, *Stabilization and Adjustment Policies and Programmes: Country Study, Colombia* (Helsinki: WIDER, 1987), use this term.

[87] Gabriel Silva Luján, "La dinámica del sector externo, la política exterior y la estrategia de paz," *Estrategia* (August 1984), pp. 44–48; Ricardo Pardo García-Peña, "Colombia: potencia regional en crisis de endeudamiento," *Ciencia Política* 4 (1986), pp. 79–95, are two articles on the interrelationship of Betancur's political and economic goals.

stabilization policies rather than a long-term development strategy.[88] The centerpiece was rejection of demand-cutting austerity measures as the way to deal with the disequilibria in the economy. On the contrary, the idea was to increase growth, both through expanded credit to the public sector to finance a higher level of spending and through a rise in real wages. Any problems with the public-sector deficit were to be resolved through increased taxes rather than spending cuts, and much of Gutiérrez Castro's time was devoted to a tax reform focusing on a value-added tax. Measures to deal with the balance-of-payments deficit were complementary to the reactivation policy. They emphasized import controls to partially counteract the liberalization of the 1970s. In this way, it was hoped that the industrial sector would be able to get back on its feet through less international competition. At the same time, the exchange rate continued to be managed by a policy of minidevaluations—the traditional Colombian crawling peg.

Competing with macroeconomic disequilibria for the finance minister's attention was the financial crisis that also resulted from the liberalizing philosophy of the 1970s.[89] A large number of new financial institutions had been created, and a variety of problems had resulted. Some derived from illegal activities and others from poor management, so the government took a differential approach to deal with them. One bank was liquidated, another was nationalized, and several were intervened (put under temporary state control), including the country's largest bank, the Banco de Colombia. The latter was eventually nationalized in 1986. Other banks were recapitalized, using government resources. Although the measures were in some ways similar to those taken in Chile, the losses to the state and the subsidies to the private sector did not reach the same proportions.

By early 1984, the financial crisis appeared to be receding, and the results of the macroeconomic policies were mostly positive as can be seen in table 4.7. Growth increased, especially in the industrial sector. The balance of trade had gone into surplus, although a deficit remained on the current account, and the rate of inflation had dropped significantly. Nevertheless, by mid-1984, Gutiérrez Castro had been dismissed; Roberto Junguito, the new finance minister with more orthodox views, announced that the country was in a crisis and had to sign an agreement with the IMF. What had happened?

The explanation must be sought in both the political and economic realms. Economically, some problems offset the positive results outlined. In particular, despite the improving trade balance, a large fall in reserves was caused by capital flight and the fall in trade credits. (The decline in long-term loans was

---

[88] Ocampo and Lora, *Stabilization*, pp. 18–25; interviews with former Colombian government officials, Bogotá, July 1987.

[89] See Salomón Kalmanovitz, *La crisis financiera en Colombia: autonomía de una evolución* (Bogota: CINEP, Controversia no. 131, 1986), on the financial crisis; see also interviews with current and former Colombian government officials, Bogotá, July 1986 and July 1987.

TABLE 4.7
Colombia: Macroeconomic Indicators, 1980–1988

	1980	1981	1982	1983	1984	1985	1986	1987	1988ʲ
GDPᵃ	4.1	2.3	1.0	1.9	3.8	3.8	5.9	5.4	4.0
Inflationᵇ	26.5	27.5	24.1	16.5	18.3	22.3	21.0	24.0	27.7
Wagesᶜ	0.8	1.4	3.7	5.0	7.3	−3.0	4.9	−0.4	−0.6
Unemploymentᵈ	9.7	8.2	9.3	11.8	13.5	14.1	13.8	11.7	11.4
Government Budgetᵉ	−3.3	−6.3	−8.1	−8.0	−7.2	−5.1	+0.6	−1.6	—
Trade Balanceᶠ	−0.9	−4.3	−5.7	−3.9	+0.6	−0.1	+5.5	+5.0	—
Current Accountᵍ	−0.6	−5.4	−7.8	−7.8	−3.7	−5.2	+0.9	+0.7	—
Reservesʰ	12.5	10.1	8.2	5.8	3.0	3.8	5.9	5.2	—
Investmentⁱ	19.1	20.6	20.5	19.9	18.6	18.5	17.5	—	—

Sources: UNECLA, *Preliminary Overview of the Latin American Economy, 1988*, pp. 15–25; International Monetary Fund, *International Financial Statistics, Yearbook, 1988*; pp. 294–97; World Bank, *World Debt Tables*, vol. 2, 1988–1989; Fedesarrollo, *Coyuntura Económica* (various issues); DANE, *Boletín de Estadística*.

ᵃ Annual growth rate.
ᵇ Consumer price index, December-December.
ᶜ Real wages in manufacturing, annual average increase/decrease.
ᵈ Unemployment as percentage of labor force in major cities, annual average.
ᵉ Consolidated public sector as percentage of GDP.
ᶠ Merchandise balance as percentage of GDP.
ᵍ Current account as percentage of GDP.
ʰ Reserves in months of imports of goods and services.
ⁱ Gross domestic investment as percentage of GDP.
ʲ Preliminary estimates; inflation November-November.

compensated by an increase in direct foreign investment.) In addition, the government deficit was large by Colombian standards and unemployment was on the rise. At the same time, the view in government circles was that Gutiérrez Castro was incompetent and/or too liberal.[90] Indeed the heterodox policies had not been introduced as a coherent package, but emerged piecemeal as problems forced themselves onto the agenda. Business confidence in the government was low because of doubts about the peace initiatives to the guerrillas that dominated the news, and some of the president's more conservative advisors took the opportunity to persuade him to name a new finance minister. The man chosen was an archtypical representative of the Colombian elite—a Bogotá economist who was the former director of the country's main research institute, former president of the National Agricultural Society, and a frequent consultant to the international financial institutions.

[90] Interviews with former Colombian government officials, Bogotá, July 1987.

Although Junguito did not reverse all of the individual measures in place when he took over in July 1984, and in fact, reinforced some of them, he did superimpose an orthodox approach based on demand management.[91] On the fiscal side, taxes continued to be raised as before, but government expenditure was also cut, including investment and wages in the public sector. To deal with the balance of payments, the rate of devaluation was sharply increased although the effect on imports was partially offset by lowering import controls. It is interesting to note that even orthodox measures to resolve a crisis "were to be gradual, in line with the tradition of Colombian economic policy," in the words of the new finance minister.[92]

Gradual or not, the measures were unpopular. Opposition came from the cabinet, the business associations, and the labor movement, especially the public sector union that was among the most militant. Unlike Carlos Rodríguez-Pastor in Peru, however, Junguito proved to be an astute politician. His first success was convincing the president to get behind the measures despite their political cost. One way to convince him was to be flexible in dealing with Betancur's particular objections. For example, the 10 percent wage increase (well below inflation) was weighted so that the highest paid workers would receive less than 10 percent, and the minimum wage would actually rise in real terms. As will be discussed, Betancur's refusal to sign a standby agreement with the IMF was honored through an unusual set of arrangements. Beyond his relationship with the president, Junguito was also skillful in his dealings with the Congress and the unions. In addition to extensive discussion with congressional leaders, Junguito also called in union leaders to discuss alternatives, an unusual move in the elite-dominated politics of Colombia. Ultimately, the unions were co-opted through the sliding scale wage increase and Betancur's appointment of a union leader as minister of labor.[93]

The international arrangements to complement the domestic austerity measures have been widely publicized, but they are often misunderstood.[94] For reasons of political image, Betancur did not want to sign a stand-by agreement with the the IMF. Much of this had to do with the legacy of the conflict between Lleras Restrepo and the Fund nearly two decades earlier, but he also had honest concerns about the negative effects of IMF policies on growth and distribution. Nevertheless, it was clearly agreed by all that Colombia needed new international capital that would not be easy to obtain. Unlike its neighbors, the issue was not that the government could not meet its payment obligations, but

---

[91] See Roberto Junguito, *Memoria del Ministro de Hacienda, Julio 1984–Septiembre 1985* (Bogotá: Ministerio de Hacienda, 1985) for Junguito's own account of his policies and their implementation.

[92] Ibid., pp. 10–11.

[93] Interviews with former Colombian government officials, Bogotá, July 1987.

[94] An example is found in the otherwise excellent paper of Ocampo and Lora, *Stabilization*, p. 26, when they refer to the Colombian negotiation strategy as "radically different" than the other Latin American countries.

that large-scale new investment projects needed finance. Thus, a "jumbo" loan of $1 billion was sought from the private banks; the question concerned the conditions that would be attached.

Negotiations began at the IMF/World Bank annual meetings in September 1984. There the Colombian delegation held discussions with international agency officials as well as representatives of the U.S. Treasury, Federal Reserve, and private banks. Upon returning to Bogotá, Junguito wrote a memo to Betancur recommending a formal standby agreement as the essential precondition for getting the loan.[95] When Betancur refused to follow the advice, a lengthy process ensued to find an alternative that all parties would accept.

The initial idea was that the World Bank, which had long and close relations with the Colombian government, would monitor the economy. That plan was scuttled, however, when the private banks declared they had no confidence in the World Bank in this particular role.[96] The eventual proposal was that the IMF would provide monitoring services, but without a formal standby and without a request for money from Colombia. This arrangement reportedly was strongly opposed by the Fund's managing director, Jacques de Larosiere, and only agreed to under heavy pressure from the Federal Reserve's Paul Volcker. Volcker was sympathetic to the Colombians and saw their proposal as a model for other third world countries, once the most severe debt problems had subsided.[97] Even George Schultz and Ronald Reagan were brought into the negotiations when Betancur visited Washington in April 1985. Reagan reportedly agreed to support the Colombian proposal in return for that country's increased cooperation with U.S. policy on Central America and drugs.[98]

Whatever the combination of events, a deal was eventually struck, and the bank steering committee agreed to raise $1 billion, contingent on informal reports from the IMF. The credit agreement was signed in December 1985, but actual disbursement was delayed until late 1986 after a new government had taken office. Although appearances suggest that the Colombians had won a sigificant victory in maintaining their autonomy, the victory was more symbolic than real. In actual policies followed, the Colombian measures did not differ much from those of other countries. In fact, some economists suggest that Colombian policies were more strict than usual because de Larosiere wanted to make sure that other countries would not follow suit.[99]

---

[95] This memo was published in the Colombian press as were most of the later documents relating to the international negotiations. See "Colombia y el FMI," in *Economía Colombiana*, Serie documentos, Separata No. 6 (March–April 1985); "Memorando del Ministro de Hacienda al Banco Mundial," *Economía Colombiana* 171 (July 1985), pp. 77–82; "Cartas y memorando del Gobierno de Colombia al Fondo Monetario International," *Revista del Banco de la República* (April 1986), pp. 33–40; and Junguito, *Memoria*, pp. 99–110.

[96] Interviews with former Colombian government officials, Bogotá, July 1986 and July 1987.

[97] Ibid.

[98] Ibid.

[99] See Londoño and Perry, "El Banco Mundial," for example.

Although the disbursement of the $1 billion was delayed, the new direction of the economy had been established by mid-1985 and Junguito resigned. He was replaced by Hugo Palacios, the head of the central bank (Banco de la República), just as Colombia's international fortunes changed again. In late 1985, coffee prices headed up, and any vestige of an external crisis ended. Palacios' main policy decision was whether to stick with the restrictive measures in the face of another bonanza. It is indicative of Colombian tradition that he did so, and even more indicative that the new Liberal government elected in May 1986 did the same.

In terms of macroeconomic policy, it is hard to distinguish between the last half of the Betancur government and that of the new president, Virgilio Barco. For both, fiscal policy was a key area of concern, with an emphasis on limiting government spending and improving tax collection. The public-sector deficit was turned into a surplus in 1986 and remained low in 1987. Trade policy also continued along similar lines. The goal was to keep the exchange rate constant in real terms by equating inflation and devaluation. Import controls continued their slow decline, as agreed with the World Bank in 1985 in connection with an export promotion loan. The main change in economic policy during the Barco government involved higher spending on social development, including a war on "absolute poverty," to try to deal with economic inequalities exacerbated by political exclusion.[100]

As in the past, international financial policy constituted a controversial aspect of Barco's economic program. Although Colombia's foreign debt is still modest, despite the increase in the 1980s, large payments will be falling due in the next few years, and a major debate has developed over how to deal with these external problems. Leading economic officials from the past and current governments argue that Colombia should continue to exploit its status as the only Latin American country to maintain payments and attempt to return to "voluntary" private lending and to tap the international agencies. Many other groups—on the right as well as the left—insist that a rescheduling would be more advantageous.[101]

All these economic issues continue to be seen as secondary to the political struggles. Prominent political figures of all stripes have been kidnapped and/ or murdered, while hundreds, perhaps thousands, of ordinary citizens die in battles between guerrillas, drug traffickers, right-wing death squads, and the

[100] Eduardo Lora, "Las políticas económicas del nuevo gobierno," *Economía Colombiana* 189 (January 1987). Additional references on this topic can be found in *Coyuntura Económica* issues for 1987–1989.

[101] See, for example, Carlos Caballero et al., "La política de endeudamiento externo," *Debates de Coyuntura Económica* 6 (June 1987) and *Economía Colombiana* 195–96 (July-August 1987): 33–87. Discussion of the differences between the terms on the Colombian loans and the restructuring agreements in other Latin American countries is found in *Coyuntura Económica* 18, 3 (September 1988): 42–45.

military. Of course, the fact that the macroeconomy continues to function reasonably well makes it possible—unlike the situation in Peru—to divert attention from the economy. The political chaos has its greatest effects on the microeconomy, frightening off potential investors, limiting growth in certain regions of the country, and slowing exports as transportation facilities are disrupted. Eventually, these microphenomena may begin to play havoc with the macroeconomy, and stagnation may result.

Summary

The political alliance created in 1958 in Colombia set the stage for several processes that distinguish that country from Chile and Peru. In political terms, it perpetuated a closed elite of Liberals and Conservatives that ran the country with substantial consensus. Conflict was avoided by disallowing participation by those who did not share the basic approach, at the cost of a profound anti-system struggle. Economically, this quasi-democratic alliance placed boundaries on the types of policies that could be followed, preventing the violent economic swings that typified Chile and Peru.

The advantage of these cautious policies became clear in the 1980s. The previous lack of economic excesses meant that the crisis in Colombia was much less severe than elsewhere in the region. The debt was smaller, in both relative and absolute terms, and the terms were easier because a larger part was owed to public sector agencies. Consequently, debt service could be maintained without creating a massive recession. Growth slowed in the early 1980s, but it never became negative. Inflation remained within acceptable bounds. And, in spite of large current account and budget deficits, the economy did not seem to be out of control in the same way as the Chilean and Peruvian economies in the early 1980s and Peru again in 1988.

The fact that Belisario Betancur nonetheless agreed to a change in policy—despite heavy costs to his own political ambitions—demonstrates the difference in meaning of the term "crisis" across countries. While García refused to switch course until reserves were gone and inflation was well into three digits, Betancur capitulated under much less serious circumstances. This difference was partly due to historical tradition. As one economist and former government official put it, "Colombia is very conservative. If reserves go below four months of imports or inflation above 30 percent, there is panic."[102] Political differences were also relevant. Betancur had no powerful support that he could count on. His party was much more conservative than he himself; the opposition controlled Congress; and even the economic bureaucracy opposed his policies. Labor might have been a source of support, but unions had no power. Business was divided and opposed Betancur for other reasons. In ad-

[102] Interview with Colombian economist, Bogotá, July 1986.

dition, all saw the stabilization measures as short term and so were more inclined to go along.

This brings us to another important difference in the Colombian case. The decision in mid-1984 to change finance ministers and policy direction was not a decision on development strategy but on short-term stabilization measures to deal with external and internal disequilibria. The economy was not seen to be in need of major restructuring, despite obvious problems like high unemployment. In part, this view derived from objective circumstances, because the Colombian economy had clearly performed better than the rest of the region. In addition, given the basic continuity of political alliances in Colombia, major change would have been difficult to bring about regardless of whether Liberals or Conservatives were nominally in power. As has been happening in Mexico recently (see chapter 3), restructuring might endanger the whole set of explicit and implicit agreements in place since 1958.

CONCLUDING COMMENTS

This section returns to the questions posed in the introduction and considers them in light of the evidence from the Chilean, Peruvian, and Colombian cases. As will be recalled, the questions were (1) Why were particular policy packages selected in each country? (2) Why were these policies implemented, or not? and (3) Why were the outcomes successful, or not? In the Chilean/Peruvian cases, the main focus will be on the period beginning with the new policy initiatives in 1985, whereas the Colombian discussion will begin with the new government elected in 1982.

Policy Choice

In the introduction, it was hypothesized that policy choices are basically attributable to the political coalition that supports a government. It was further suggested that the political coalition variable is especially powerful in highly polarized multiparty systems because parties are more likely to have firm economic policy preferences under those conditions. Both Chile and Peru fit into this category, although, of course, parties were formally suppressed in Chile. In Colombia, by contrast, the two-party system produced smaller differences in economic programs and thus less attention to economic issues.

In both Chile and Peru, the decisions made in 1985 were about long-term development strategies that incorporated short-term stabilization policies but were not limited to them. The sharp divergence in the strategies selected is interesting for two reasons. One is the similar pattern of strategies in the preceding decades, extending to the general approach followed after the international crisis began in 1982. Thus the sudden divergence in 1985 is especially noteworthy. The other is the extreme nature of the two decisions. Chile went with the prevailing line among international financial institutions and advanced industrial countries (see chapter 2), but in an especially exaggerated form. Peru, by contrast, embarked upon a strategy that went against international trends, including those in other Latin American countries in the 1980s.

Both of these policy packages reflected the interests of the respective governments' supporters. The decision in Chile in early 1985 was to adopt a more flexible variant of the previous orthodox policies. The rigid version in place from 1976 to 1981 had aroused growing protests from local business and middle-class groups, the main source of support on which a right-wing government must rely. The new policies continued the approach that required tight fiscal and wage policies and timely debt payments, but also retained the special measures for agriculture and construction and somewhat more protectionist trade policies. The government style changed too as business was given greater entrée to policy makers.

In Peru, the orthodox approach of the Belaunde government had been soundly defeated by Alan García. His campaign promises had centered on a heterodox strategy, featuring consumption-led growth financed by a limit on debt service. García, it should be noted, was located between the right-wing outgoing government coalition and the Marxist left. While the latter advocated a dominant role for the state in the economy, García went less far. He had been supported by a substantial share of Peruvian business, which had been alienated by Belaunde's policies, and he clearly wanted to reward them as well as his lower-class constituencies. Thus, the package was aimed to maintain profit margins *and* raise consumption. The purest form of this package was followed in his first two years, but even after the bank nationalization an attempt was made to keep business support.

The lesser emphasis on economic issues in the 1982 election in Colombia, and the lack of differentiation between the two parties, meant that Belisario Betancur could be less specific in his campaign. Nevertheless, he too followed a populist stance, emphasizing reflation with special support for the industrial sector. This economic policy was a necessary complement to the key issue on which Betancur was elected—a promise to reincorporate the guerrilla opposition into civil society.

Policy Implementation

While the nature of a government's chosen political coalition is the crucial variable in explaining policy decisions, implementation involves additional factors that are not within the government's short-term control. The characteristics of the state, the nature and mobilization of the political opposition, and the role of international actors are all important at the implementation stage. These three sets of variables together led to a substantial degree of implementation of the Chilean policies, but reversals in the other two countries.

The authoritarian regime in Chile allowed Pinochet to survive the crisis period in spite of the protests that were mounted. Selective repression and the freedom to channel economic rewards and punishments were effective weapons. What distinguished the Chilean situation from those of Brazil and Argentina, however, was the unity of the armed forces and the divisions within the opposition, which undermined the protest movement. Once it died down, Pinochet was free to return to the previous approach, but in a way to maintain the support of his business constituency. With the new economic team in place, the authoritarian system again gave them substantial autonomy to carry out their policies coherently. The high level of state capacity in developed institutions and skilled personnel was another important advantage in policy implementation.

The essence of providing space to the economic team was keeping civilian groups at bay. Different tactics were used. The opposition was dealt with through authoritarian means. Labor, for example, had little room to press demands for salary increases or greater social spending. Its organizational capacity had been severely limited by the coup and aftermath in the early 1970s, and the failure of the 1983 protests reinforced their weakness. Business groups were generally pleased with the Büchi program, compared with the 1976–1981 and 1982–1983 policies, so little opposition arose from their ranks. It was only with the approach of the plebiscite called by the military themselves that opposition forces began to mobilize. The success of the opposition in the plebiscite reflected the change in the political rules of the game, which limited the government's ability to take advantage of its authoritarian powers.

International actors were also important in enabling the Chilean government to implement its chosen policies from 1985. A key aspect of its program was to maintain an open economy, to attract foreign investment, and to work toward a return to ''voluntary'' access to the international capital markets. The latter two goals required prompt service of the debt, which was possible only because of new loans from the multilateral agencies. Despite Chile's efforts, the private banks were not willing to put new money into the country although some did participate in debt-equity swap arrangements. Ironically, the United States was the biggest obstacle to Chilean plans. In an attempt to promote a more open political system, and thus forestall the strengthening of the far-left opposition, the United States eliminated Chile's trade preferences and abstained on key votes for multilateral loans. Nevertheless, the U.S. attitude was ambivalent enough that it did not block access to international finance.

Peru's multiparty democratic system potentially provided much more space for opposition to pressure the government and a greater need to heed public opinion. In the first two years of the García government, however, the president's popularity was so high that it permitted him to rule in an extremely autocratic way. Until the bank nationalization of July 1987, García's popularity did not go below 60 percent in the polls, and the November 1986 municipal elections reconfirmed his political domination of the country. As a consequence, the rightist opposition was virtually silenced, especially since their business constituency largely defected to García. Equally as important, García's own party was cowed as the triumphant president made clear that APRA veterans were to stay clear of economic issues. Thus, the only organized and active political forces were on the left, and García played to them as well as to business.

He used his political popularity to provide autonomy to his economic team, which struggled to implement his chosen policies. Two obstacles, however, stood in the way. One was the government's own sectarianism, compounded by the president's desire to maintain control over decision making. This led to increasing marginalization of potential team members and the consequent lack of people to do any long-term planning. A second, related problem was a general lack of state capacity in Peru. Unlike neighboring Chile, there was no reservoir of institutional or personal skills to draw on. The bureaucracy below the economic team was not up to the task of running the economy, a serious difficulty since the heterodox strategy put an especially heavy burden on state management capacity.

International actors initially went along with the new government, despite reservations about García's debt policy. With the exception of the IMF, the government tried to maintain good relations with the multilateral agencies and foreign governments. The main effect of the 10 percent limit on debt payments fell on the private banks. Even the United States was not willing to force a confrontation because of the threat from Sendero Luminoso and García's general willingness to cooperate against drug trafficking. Thus, new money flowed in, and international reserves actually increased until March 1986. Foreign exchange did not constitute a serious limitation to policy implementation until after mid-1987.

All these variables changed in the year following the bank nationalization. García's popularity tumbled, leaving him and his team vulnerable to opposition. Simultaneously, the opposition became reinvigorated. Although the left initially supported the nationalization, disagreements over details broke any incipient alliance. The rightist parties saw the opportunity to reconstitute their political space and fought the government in various arenas. Even García's hold on his own party began to falter. Furthermore, private-sector investment, the key to the long-term aspect of his heterodox strategy, disappeared as the bank nationalization convinced entrepreneurs that the government was antibusiness after all. Ironically, the opposition to his policies at home led García to make some international overtures, but he was unwilling to go far enough to regain access to foreign credit and prevent the depletion of Peru's foreign exchange reserves.

By mid-1988, the heterodox strategy was over. The main factor was aggressive action by the APRA hierarchy, which took advantage of García's new weakness. He was forced to appoint APRA veterans to key posts, dismiss his personal confidants, change policy direction internally, and sue for peace with the international financial community. Although political factors were the immediate cause of the about-face, serious problems with the economic strategy provided the opportunity for it.

In Colombia, too, a policy change occurred, although it was less dramatic than in Peru. The characteristics of the political system also played an important role. Like Chile's authoritarian regime and García's popularity within a democratic one, the Colombian two-party system provided support for top-down government. In this instance, however, it was turned against an isolated president when the reactivation strategy of Betancur's first finance minister went beyond the bounds set by the Liberal-Conservative consensus. The increased budget deficit and the loss of reserves were not necessarily crippling in an absolute sense, but they were more than a president without much political support could get away with. Betancur's own party was not willing to back him, the economic bureaucracy opposed his policies, and neither business nor labor was willing to come to his defense.

Likewise, international actors helped to push for a change. The World Bank delayed disbursements; the banks cut trade lines; and the IMF produced a very negative report on the economy. When the Colombian delegation to the IMF/World Bank annual meetings returned to Bogotá in October 1984, and reported that no one was willing to help without a prior change in policies, Betancur acquiesced—although with a face-saving formula—and orthodox stabilization policies were introduced.

Policy Outcomes

The introduction stated that traditional macroeconomic outcomes, such as those shown in tables 4.4 and 4.7, can be traced to degree of implementation, viability of the strategy being followed, and exogenous shocks such as international prices and interest rates. Furthermore, it was hypothesized that these outcomes will have a feedback effect on later rounds of policy choices.

Although Chile's economic policies in the 1970s and early 1980s led to a disastrous crisis, the policies after 1985 were much more successful. Growth averaged more than 5 percent per year between 1986 and 1988; inflation was relatively low; the budget was balanced; and the current account deficit was able to be financed, so reserves were stable. Two main variables were nonetheless troublesome. One was investment. Although investment was rising, it was still not high enough to sustain a 5 percent growth rate, given the existing capital/output ratios. The other problem was wages and consumption in general. Workers were not sharing in the new prosperity, and this was an important factor in the government's defeat in the plebiscite. Especially with positive exogenous shocks (high prices for copper and falling oil prices and interest rates), the strategy was economically viable, but with the change in political rules surrounding the plebiscite, it was no longer politically viable. The resulting change in institutions can be expected to have a significant effect on the economic strategy itself, regardless of who wins the presidential election in 1989.

Economic outcomes in Peru had some success during the first two years of the García government. Growth recovered, investment rose, and inflation fell. Nevertheless, the strategy was not sustainable. The balance of payments went into deficit, so that reserves were depleted despite the limit on debt service, and there was no program to replenish them. The growing budget deficit fueled inflation once price controls were loosened. After the bank nationalization, investment fell off as the private sector ceased to invest and the government had no money to step in. The negative outcomes in early 1988 were largely responsible for the president's decline in popularity and, therefore, the APRA's decision to enforce a change in strategy. But it was poorly planned and poorly executed orthodox policies on top of the previous heterodoxy that produced the four-digit inflation and economic contraction of 7.5 percent.

Colombia's case falls in between the other two outcomes. Some economic indicators had improved by 1984; growth had resumed, inflation remained under control, and the trade balance had improved substantially. Nonetheless, the growing budget deficit and falling reserves were crucial in stimulating the change in policy in late 1984. Those changes improved economic performance, but the bonanza from higher coffee prices and the coming onstream of new export projects were more important factors. Given the consensus on economic policy in Colombia, however, the more orthodox policy stance was maintained, despite the improvement in the international situation. The positive results were interpreted to mean that the country was on the right track economically despite the growing political conflicts.

It is important to analyze accurately the outcomes of these three cases, because they have implications beyond their own borders. Many are saying, for example, that the macroeconmic success in Chile and Colombia means that countries can grow and pay their debts at the same time. Likewise, the disintegration of the Peruvian model is held up as proof that nonpayment leads to disaster. Closer analysis suggests that Chile's model was viable only under an authoritarian state, although how far it will deviate under democracy remains to be seen. Colombia's insistence on maintaining payments of principal has forced tradeoffs that have worsened its political problems and may ultimately undermine the political system itself. Interestingly, neither Chile nor Colombia has had notable success in returning to voluntary lending—one of the main justifications for "good debtor" policies. Peru's unilateral decision to spend only a fixed percentage of its export revenues on debt service is a very different approach. The key point here is that the link between this debt policy and the negative economic outcomes was not a necessary one. A less expansionary growth policy, combined with a plan for financing government expenditure and replenishing reserves, could have led to different results. All three cases illustrate the very difficult trade-offs that debt-burdened countries must face. Negative political consequences will likely continue until a solution to the economic crisis is found.

CHAPTER FIVE

The Politics of Adjustment in Small Democracies: Costa Rica, the Dominican Republic, Jamaica

Joan M. Nelson

WHEN THE DEBT CRISIS erupted in the early 1980s, it was widely believed that economic adjustment would prove more difficult for democracies than for authoritarian regimes. Yet clearly, some democratic governments have successfully pursued stabilization and reform, while many authoritarian governments have performed poorly. Nonpolitical factors, of course, partly determine the success of such attempts. But to the extent that outcomes are influenced by political institutions and relationships, broad regime type is too crude a proxy for the forces at work. We need to understand better the particular features of political systems—both institutional arrangements, and less formal relationships and attitudes—that facilitate or permit stabilization and structural change, or sabotage those goals.

This chapter focuses on three competitive democracies: Costa Rica, the Dominican Republic, and Jamaica. In all three, the media are independent and outspoken, governments are chosen by elections, and parties alternate in power. Jamaica and Costa Rica are both long-established, highly participatory democracies, though their institutions and political traditions are quite different. Dominican democracy is more recent and fragile.

Like many other countries, the three democracies considered in this chapter initially responded to emerging economic troubles by postponing corrective action and seeking finance to cover trade and fiscal deficits. All eventually adopted harsh austerity measures in an effort to restore economic balance. But here their paths diverged.

Field research for this study was facilitated by the gracious hospitality of the Central Bank of Costa Rica, the economics faculty of the Universidad Católica Madre y Maestra in Santo Domingo, and the Institute of Social and Economic Research of the University of the West Indies, Mona. I thank the directors and staffs for their invaluble assistance. I am also indebted to the many officials and private individuals in all three countries, and to staff of the IMF, the World Bank, AID, and the Inter-American Development Bank, who generously provided information and interpretations, and in some cases also commented on earlier drafts. The study benefited greatly from the suggestions of other members of the research group and participants in the workshop in Mexico City in October 1987, including Omar Davies from Jamaica, José Luis Aleman from the Dominican Republic, and Jorge Guárdia Quiros and Francisco Gutiérrez from Costa Rica. I would also like to acknowledge the assistance of Carol Graham in early stages of the research.

The initial Dominican effort, abrupt and ill-prepared, ignited a political explosion in April 1984. A more carefully prepared austerity program later in 1984 and 1985 succeeded in temporarily restoring economic balance and growth. But the program remained an isolated episode, followed neither by structural change nor disciplined economic management.

Costa Rica's stabilization effort during 1982–1983 succeeded more rapidly than even its designers had expected. But it proved far harder to gain consensus on a new growth strategy to cope with the changing international economic setting, including the decay of the Central American Common Market. Some structural reforms progressed; but most faced adamant political opposition.

In Jamaica, economic decline and political polarization in the 1970s set the stage for a shift in 1980 to a much more market-oriented, open strategy under a new government and with massive external aid. Eight years later, Jamaica had indeed carried out more far-reaching reforms than Costa Rica. But the speed and direction of further changes were intensely debated in the 1988–1989 electoral campaign, and continue to be deeply controversial under the new government. The main theme of this chapter is how variations among these three democracies with respect to their institutions, historical legacies, and political circumstances resulted in adjustment efforts of such varied scope.

A second, subordinate theme is the implications of small scale for adjustment. Costa Rica and Jamaica are both quite small, with 1987 populations of 2.8 and 2.4 million, respectively. The Dominican Republic, with 6.7 million, is considerably larger, but still small in an international perspective. Scale clearly influences economic structure, international economic relations, and options for development strategy. The implications of small scale for political relationships and dynamics are much less clear.[1]

The chapter first briefly sketches aspects of the economic and social structure and recent economic and political development within each country that set the stage for the adjustment efforts of the 1980s. Those efforts are then traced in broad outline. The third section of the chapter seeks explanations for contrasting adjustment choices and action in earlier economic trends and in the ways the economic crisis affected each of the three countries; in their varying political institutions and situations; and in the roles of external agencies. The final section returns to the themes of the effects of democratic politics and small scale on economic adjustment.

[1] See B. Jahan, ed., *Problems and Policies in Small Economies* (New York: St. Martin's Press, 1982), for reviews of knowledge and issues on the economic implications of small size; E.A.G. Robinson, *Economic Consequences of the Size of Nations* (London: Macmillan, 1963), an older but still helpful volume; Robert A. Dahl and Edward R. Tufte, *Size and Democracy* (Palo Alto, California: Stanford University Press, 1973), on political implications of scale.

ECONOMIC STRUCTURE AND HISTORY

Structural Similarities

At the outset of the 1980s, Costa Rica, the Dominican Republic, and Jamaica shared certain broad economic features (see table 5.1). Despite the spread between Costa Rica and the Dominican Republic, all were middle-income, near the center of the World Bank's array of per capita income in 168 coun-

TABLE 5.1
Costa Rica, Dominican Republic, Jamaica:
Selected Economic and Social Indicators, 1980

	Costa Rica	*Jamaica*	*Dominican Republic*
GNP Per Capita[a]	1,900	1,200	1,000
Sectoral Origins of GDP[b]			
Agriculture	17	8	18
Manufacturing	20	15	15
Services	54	55	55
Trade Ratio (1980–1982)[c]	102.9	127.5	53.3
Urban Population[d]	43	41	51
Labor Force[e]			
Agriculture	29	21	49
Industry	23	25	18
Life Expectancy[f]	70	71	61
Infant Mortality[g]	24	16	68
School Enrollment Ratio[h]			
Primary	108	99	106
Secondary	48	57	32
Higher	26	6	10

Source: All data from World Bank, *World Development Report 1982* (New York: Oxford University Press, 1982) unless otherwise indicated.

[a] World Bank, *World Tables 1987*, 4th ed. (Washington, D.C.: World Bank and International Finance Corporation, 1987), pp. 109, 129, 133.

[b] Percentage; *WDR* 1982, table 3, pp. 114–15.

[c] Exports plus imports as a percentage of GNP, three-year average; *WDR* 1982, table 8, pp. 124–25; *WDR* 1983, table 9, pp. 164–65; *WDR* 1984, table 9, pp. 234–35.

[d] Percentage; *WDR* 1982, table 20, pp. 148–49.

[e] Percentage; *WDR* 1982, table 19, pp. 146–47.

[f] At birth, in years; *WDR* 1982, table 1, pp. 110–11.

[g] Deaths per thousand infants aged 0–1 years; *WDR* 1982, table 21, pp. 150–51.

[h] Children of relevant age range in school as a percentage of the population in that age range; *WDR* 1982, table 23, pp. 154–55.

tries. The scale of the economy as measured by GDP was similar in Jamaica and Costa Rica, and both were highly trade dependent, with average ratios of trade to GDP for 1980–1982 of over 127 percent for Costa Rica and 102 percent for Jamaica. Dominican GDP, at roughly $6.5 million, was about twice the level of the other two nations', and the Republic was less trade dependent.[2]

All three nations depended on primary products for the great bulk of export earnings. Aluminum and bauxite provided 70 percent of Jamaica's export earnings on average from 1978 through 1980; in the same period, coffee, bananas, and beef accounted for 57 percent of Costa Rican exports; sugar, ferronickel, and coffee for 53 percent of Dominican trade earnings. Manufacturing contributed 15 percent of GDP in Jamaica and the Dominican Republic, 20 percent in Costa Rica; most manufacturing was highly protected and heavily import-dependent. Jamaica and Costa Rica were very similar with respect to health and education indicators; the Dominican Republic lagged behind the other two in social progress.

The three countries shared (and share) another characteristic: all are squarely in the U.S. economic and cultural sphere of influence. The United States is the major trading partner of all three, the major source of investment and concessional assistance, and the primary destination of outmigration and (in times of uncertainty) capital flight. Exposure to U.S. media, ties between emigrants and those they left behind, and tens of thousands of U.S. tourists shape life-styles and expectations.

These multiple ties have two implications for stabilization and adjustment efforts. Political changes in Washington and economic trends in the United States powerfully affect the economies of all three countries. Their internal social and political pressures in part reflect aspirations to U.S. life-styles and the relative ease of outmigration.

The Legacy of Recent Economic Trends

Despite certain broadbrush structural similarities, the recent economic and political histories of the three nations are quite different. As table 5.2 indicates, Costa Rica grew steadily and briskly from the creation of the Central American Common Market in the early 1960s. From 1948 on, economic and social policy followed a broadly social democratic path, and by the late 1970s, Costa Rica had created an advanced social welfare state—by developing country standards—that was internationally admired for its equity, civil liberty, and stability.

But apparent success masked emerging weaknesses. By the late 1970s, growth of manufactured exports was slowing and the trade deficit widening.

[2] World Bank, *World Tables 1987* (Washington, D.C.: World Bank and International Finance Corporation, 1987).

TABLE 5.2
Costa Rica, Dominican Republic, Jamaica: Macroeconomic Trends, 1965–1980

	Costa Rica			Dominican Republic			Jamaica		
	GDP[a]	Inflation[b]	Current Account[c]	GDP[a]	Inflation[b]	Current Account[c]	GDP[a]	Inflation[b]	Current Account[c]
1965	9.8	−0.7	−68	−10.9	−1.9	43	5.6	2.8	−30
1966	7.9	0.2	−44	13.1	0.3	−75	2.3	2.0	−42
1967	5.7	1.2	−50	3.4	1.2	−66	4.7	2.9	−81
1968	8.5	4.0	−43	0.5	0.1	−75	4.8	5.9	−92
1969	5.5	2.7	−50	12.2	0.9[d]	−85	3.2	6.3	−124
1970	7.5	4.7	−74	8.5	3.8	−102	11.9	7.7[d]	−153
1971	6.8	3.1	−114	10.9	4.3	−129	3.1	5.3	−172
1972	8.2	4.6	−100	10.4	7.8	−47	9.2	5.4	−197
1973	7.7	15.2	−112	12.9	15.1	−97	1.4	17.7	−248
1974	5.5	30.1	−266	6.0	13.2	−241	−4.6	27.2	−92
1975	2.1	17.4[d]	−218	5.2	14.5	−73	−0.3	17.4	−283
1976	5.5	3.5	−201	6.7	7.8	−129	−6.5	9.8	−303
1977	8.9	4.2	−226	5.0	12.8	−129	−2.4	11.2	−42
1978	6.3	6.0	−363	2.1	3.5[d]	−312	0.5	34.9	−50
1979	4.9	9.2	−558	4.5	9.2	−331	−1.7	29.1	−139
1980	0.8	18.1	−664	6.1	16.8	−720	−5.8	27.3	−166

Sources: International Monetary Fund, *International Financial Statistics Yearbook*, 1987. Data are from *World Tables 1987*: GDP, pp. 166–67; inflation, pp. 118–19; current account, pp. 154–55.

[a] Percentage change over previous years, GDP at constant prices.

[b] CPI.

[c] Current account balance excluding exceptional financing, U.S. $ millions.

[d] A break in the statistical series.

Manufacturing, geared to domestic markets and the Central American Common Market, was highly protected and highly dependent on imported inputs. The economy as a whole remained vulnerable to swings in international prices for coffee and bananas. The dominant Party of National Liberation (PLN) was dedicated to a strategy of state-led growth in a mixed economy; the public sector accounted for 40 percent of investment and 20 percent of employment. The 1970s had seen rapid expansion of public economic enterprises, many operating at a loss and adding to growing budget deficits. A pervasive system of direct and indirect business and agricultural subsidies mushroomed, further straining the budget and distorting investment incentives. Trade and fiscal deficits were covered by borrowing. External debt increased six-fold between 1970 and 1978. Thus, even before the crisis, some Costa Ricans were pointing to the need for structural reforms. But most saw decades of steady progress topped with the high coffee prices of 1977–1978; they expected only further gains.[3]

[3] Useful sources for Costa Rican economic and political evolution during the 1960s and 1970s include Claudio Gonzáles Vega, "Fear of Adjusting: The Social Costs of Economic Policies in Costa Rica in the 1970s," in Donald E. Schultz and Douglas H. Graham, eds., *Revolution and*

In stark contrast, Jamaica in the late 1970s was in economic decline and political turmoil. Fifteen years earlier, in the mid 1960s, Jamaica's per capita income had been somewhat higher than Costa Rica's and almost twice that of the Dominican Republic. The 1960s saw a bauxite-led economic boom, but growing social tensions. The 1972 electoral victory of Michael Manley and the People's National party (PNP) ushered in an eight-year search for more equitable and participatory growth.

Domestic policies plus global shifts in the bauxite industry tipped the economy into decline from 1974 on. The government and ruling party were divided between moderate and radical wings. In 1977, as economic difficulties deepened, the moderates temporarily prevailed and Jamaica turned reluctantly to the IMF. An abortive agreement in that year was followed by a more ambitious and tougher Extended Fund Facility agreement in mid-1978, entailing a 30 percent drop in real wages for formal sector workers and instituting a system of mini-devaluations, among other measures to stabilize and reorient the economy.

The economy did respond, but not swiftly enough. By spring 1979, political pressures were mounting strongly and Manley distanced himself from the program, which essentially collapsed later that year. By 1980, battered further by two severe hurricanes, per capita income was 62 percent of Costa Rica's, and only marginally above that of the Dominican Republic. Bitter divisions over economic, social, and political strategy had polarized the nation and political violence was rampant.[4]

The traditionally poor and isolated Dominican Republic had entered a new era in the mid-1960s, after the 1961 assassination of Trujillo and ensuing turmoil and political reconstruction. The economy expanded rapidly from 1966 to 1978, under the tight and highly personalistic (though formally democratic) management of President Balaguer. Real GDP increased on average 11 percent a year from 1968 to 1974. But by the mid 1970s, growth slowed and, as in Costa Rica, signs of trouble emerged. As in many other countries, the easy initial returns from import-substitution industrialization were dwindling, and continued high investment rates yielded lower returns. State enterprises accounted for a growing proportion of expenditures, and many regularly ran losses. The costs of maintaining and operating the infrastructure and facilities constructed since 1968 were also mounting rapidly. But revenues were shrink-

Counterrevolution in Central America and the Caribbean (Boulder, Colo.: Westview Press, 1986), pp. 351–84; Charles D. Ameringer, *Democracy in Costa Rica* (New York: Praeger, 1982); Charles Denton, *Patterns of Costa Rican Politics* (Boston: Allyn and Bacon, 1971); Harold D. Nelson, ed., *Costa Rica: A Country Study*, American University Foreign Area Studies Series (Washington D.C., 1984); Morris J. Blachman and Ronald G. Hellman, "Costa Rica," in Morris J. Blachman, William M. LeoGrande, and Kenneth E. Sharpe, *Confronting Revolution: Security Through Diplomacy in Central America* (New York: Pantheon Books, 1986), pp. 156–67.

[4] Evelyne Huber Stephens and John D. Stephens, *Democratic Socialism in Jamaica* (Princeton, N.J.: Princeton University Press, 1986), present the most thorough discussion of economic and political trends and debates during the 1970s.

ing, due partly to adverse terms of trade and partly to erosion of the tax base through concessions to attract investment.

At the same time, pressures mounted for a more thoroughgoing democracy and for measures to address glaring economic and social inequities. In 1978, Balaguer and his Reformist party (PR) were defeated by Antonio Guzmán and the Revolutionary Democratic party (PRD), despite attempted military interference. Unlike Costa Rica, there was certainly no broadbased social consensus. But most Dominicans expected continued economic progress and hoped a new and more open political era was beginning.[5]

External Shocks

All three countries suffered severe external shocks in the late 1970s and 1980s, but the differences in timing, nature and degree were important (see table 5.3). Bela Balassa and F. Desmond McCarthy calculated the balance of payments effect of external shocks—adverse terms of trade, reduced export vol-

TABLE 5.3
Costa Rica, Dominican Republic, Jamaica: External Shock Indicators, 1979–1986

	1979	1980	1981	1982	1983	1984	1985	1986	1987
Terms of Trade									
Costa Rica	111.8	100.0	93.6	94.2	97.5	96.5	96.3	105.5	
Jamaica	111.3	100.0	94.2	93.6	94.5	94.8	93.9	108.6	
Dominican Republic	106.5	100.0	88.2	81.9	86.9	88.3	82.6	103.9	
Export Volume[a]									
Jamaica	95.6	100.0	101.6	72.2	74.6	72.2	62.2	62.9	64.0
Dominican Republic	136.0	100.0	111.0	109.0	124.0	123.0	110.0	92.6	109.0
Debt Service Ratio[b]									
Costa Rica	23.1	16.8	16.6	11.7	51.6	25.0	35.2	26.6	12.1
Jamaica	15.9	14.0	15.1	16.7	19.2	19.2	29.1	29.7	25.8
Dominican Republic	13.9	10.3	13.4	19.2	15.3	10.1	12.7	16.3	n.a.
Debt Service to GNP[c]									
Costa Rica	0.4	4.5	8.6	6.1	21.5	9.7	12.5	9.3	4.5
Jamaica	8.8	8.3	9.1	8.6	8.4	12.2	22.7	20.3	17.3
Dominican Republic	2.4	2.6	3.5	3.9	3.6	3.3	4.9	5.5	3.5

Sources: Terms of trade index—World Bank, *World Tables 1987*, 4th ed.; export volume index—International Monetary Fund, *International Financial Statistics Yearbook*, 1988; debt service—*World Debt Tables*, vol. 2, 1988–1989.

[a] Index is not calculated for Costa Rica.

[b] Total service on public and publicly guaranteed debt as a percentage of exports of goods and services.

[c] Total service on public and publicly guaranteed debt service as a percentage of gross national product.

[5] See Ian Bell, *The Dominican Republic* (Boulder, Colo.: Westview Press, 1981), for recent Dominican economic and political history.

ume, and increased interest rates—for thirty developing nations for 1979–1982; among these, Jamaica was the second most severely harmed, exceeded only by Sri Lanka (see figure 1.1 in chapter 1).[6] Jamaica suffered roughly equally from worsened terms of trade (due largely to a decline in bauxite prices and an increase in oil prices) and from the dwindling volume of bauxite and alumina exports (due to international recession, increased competition from newer sources of supply, and the multinational corporations' reactions to Jamaican tax and other policies). The Dominican Republic was initially affected most strongly by higher interest rates coming just as foreign borrowing had soared, but terms of trade also dropped by over a third from 1979 through 1982. Costa Rica, which was not part of the Balassa and McCarthy sample, was hit early and abruptly by the global drop in coffee prices in 1978–1979, followed promptly by soaring oil prices and the disruption of her important Central American markets by civil war and revolution. Having run up high private external debts in the mid-1970s, Costa Rica was also one of the earliest casualities of increases in international interest rates that began in the late 1970s.

ADJUSTMENT EXPERIENCE

From these different points of departure, the three countries considered in this chapter traced sharply contrasting courses of attempted adjustment. Dominican efforts were essentially confined to stabilization. Costa Rica combined stabilization with some reform, but structural changes moved very slowly. By the late 1980s, Jamaican reforms had made more progress. Table 5.4 provides basic data on economic performance during the 1980s in the three nations, but the indices available do not capture significant institutional changes.

The Dominican Republic 1978–1986: Reluctant Stabilization

The 1978 elections marked a watershed for the Dominican Republic; they brought to power the first elected president other than Joaquín Balaguer, who had dominated politics and guided economic growth since 1966.[7] The elec-

---

[6] Bela Balassa and F. Desmond McCarthy, *Adjustment Policies in Developing Countries, 1979–1983: An Update*, World Bank staff working papers no. 675 (Washington, D.C., 1984), p. 3.

[7] The following account of stabilization efforts in the Dominican Republic draws on Andres Dauhajre, Jr., "The Dominican Economy in the Light of the Stabilization Programmes of the International Monetary Fund" (Paper delivered at SELA (Sistema Económico Latino Americano) meeting, Caracas, 6–8 December 1985); Hugo Guiliani Cury, *Deuda externa: un proceso de renegociación* (Santo Domingo: Centro de Estudios Monetarios y Bancarios, June 1986); idem, *Stabilization Policies* (Santo Domingo: Central Bank of the Dominican Republic, October 1985); Jonathan Hartlyn, "The Dominican Republic," in Abraham F. Lowenthal, ed., *Latin America and Caribbean Contemporary Record*, vol. 5 (New York: Holmes and Meier, 1987), pp. B507–

TABLE 5.4

Costa Rica, Dominican Republic, Jamaica: Macroeconomic Trends, 1980–1987

	1980	1981	1982	1983	1984	1985	1986	1987
GDP[a]								
Costa Rica	0.8	−2.3	−7.3	2.9	8.0	0.7	5.4	3.9
Dominican Republic	6.1	4.1	1.6	4.9	1.0	−3.6	3.2	8.1
Jamaica[b]	−5.8	2.5	1.0	2.0	−0.4	−4.6	2.3	5.5
Inflation[c]								
Costa Rica	18.1	37.1	90.1	32.6	12.0	15.1	11.8	16.8
Dominican Republic	16.8	7.5	7.6	4.8	27.0	37.5	9.7	—
Jamaica	27.3	12.7	6.5	11.6	27.8	25.7	15.1	6.7
Public sector deficit[d]								
Costa Rica		−14.2	−8.9	−8.0	−6.2	−7.0	−5.4	−3.2
Dominican Republic								
First data series	−6.1	−5.4	−6.6	−4.9	−3.4			
Second data series					−7.3	−3.5	−6.8	−5.7
Jamaica			−15.7	−19.6	−15.1	−13.8	−5.6	−3.4
Real Effective Exchange Rate								
Costa Rica	100	63	73	83	82	81	73	66
Dominican Republic	100	101	103	97	71	78	73	61
Jamaica	100	107	111	104	73	64	69	68
Balance of Payments[e]								
Costa Rica	−13.7	−15.6	−10.4	−10.3	−7.0	−7.5	−3.7	—
Dominican Republic	−10.9	−5.4	−5.6	−4.8	−1.6	−2.4	−2.2	—
Jamaica	−6.2	−11.4	−12.5	−10.0	−14.1	−15.0	−1.6	—
Reserves[f]								
Costa Rica	1.2	1.0	2.1	2.7	3.1	3.9	3.9	3.3
Dominican Republic	1.5	1.6	1.1	1.3	1.7	2.3	2.5	—
Jamaica	0.8	0.5	0.7	0.4	0.7	1.1	0.7	1.1
Investment[g]								
Costa Rica	26.6	29.0	24.7	24.7	22.7	25.4	23.7	23.9
Dominican Republic	24.9	23.4	20.0	21.2	21.3	19.5	—	—
Jamaica	15.9	20.5	20.8	21.6	23.7	24.9	19.3	22.6[a]

Sources: GDP, inflation, current account, investment: International Financial Statistics Yearbook, 1988.

Fiscal deficit (including central bank losses): Costa Rica, Central Bank; Dominican Republic, World Bank staff documents; Jamaica, IMF staff documents.

Reserves: World Bank World Debt Tables, vol. 2, 1988–1989.

Real effective exchange rates: background data for World Bank, Adjustment Lending: An Evaluation of Ten Years of Experience, 1989.

[a] Percentage change.

[b] Jamaican 1987 investment: preliminary World Bank data.

[c] Consumer Price Index.

[d] Consolidated public sector deficit as a percentage of GDP.

[e] Balance of payments (current account) as a percentage of GDP.

[f] Months of imports covered.

[g] As a percentage of GDP.

tions were a severe test for the nation's fragile democratic institutions. When early returns indicated that Antonio Guzmán amd his Democratic Revolutionary party (PRD) were defeating Balaguer, the police and military moved to block the count. The Church and the United States government intervened to permit the count to resume and Guzmán to take office. Manipulation of the results of senatorial contests left Balaguer's party in control of the Senate.

Guzmán's understandable first concern was assuring control of the military, but acute economic problems shortly pressed his government. The 1979 oil price increase was compounded by plummeting sugar prices and by two severe autumn hurricanes. These shocks were not only obviously external, but could appropriately be viewed as cyclical or random. The government's reaction was to seek ways to ride out the storm with the least injury to social stability and a fragile democracy. Deficit spending and borrowing were the result. Less understandable was the decision in 1980 to bolster political support by virtually doubling public sector employment through creation of tens of thousands of public sector jobs; this evidenced failure to grasp the increasingly serious medium-term economic situation.

The Central Bank was virtually the sole voice within the government counseling financial caution in this period. One Central Bank governor was dismissed for protesting too vigorously the sharp jump in deficit spending. His replacement, Carlos Despradel, struggled for two years to contain spending pressures. By the last year of Guzmán's administration, recession in the industrial nations and falling sugar prices had cut exports by a third, triggering corresponding losses of revenues. The economy stalled, and public borrowing almost tripled in the first half of 1982.

In the 1982 elections, the new PRD candidate, Salvador Jorge Blanco, campaigned on a platform of economic expansion. Elected with 47 percent of the popular vote to Balaguer's 39 percent, Jorge Blanco was immediately counseled by his Central Bank governor-designate, Bernardo Vega, to seek a standby agreement with the IMF as a prerequisite to rescheduling external debt.[8] The Dominican Republic had virtually no history of relations with the IMF, and the experience of U.S. intervention during the 1960s (and earlier in the nation's history) had left a legacy of profound suspicion of any external agency's influence. But the advice of Vega, and of outgoing Central Bank Governor Carlos Despradel, now named as Dominican ambassador to the United States, took on added urgency when Mexico defaulted two days after Jorge Blanco took

B524; idem, "Dominican Republic," in Lowenthal, ed., *Contemporary Record*, vol. 6, pp. B477–B492; Bernardo Vega, "Crisis del sector externo y política cambiaria," in *Estrategias para la superación de la crisis económica dominicana*, Primer Congreso Nacional de Economistas (Colegio Dominicano de Economistas, Santo Domingo, 1986), pp. 291–315; interviews with members of the Jorge Blanco government economic team; staff members of AID, the IMF, and the World Bank; businessmen, journalists, and academic analysts in Santo Domingo, March 1987.

[8] Vega, "Crisis del sector externo."

office. The prompt freezing of new commercial bank credits to Latin America further heightened pressure. In his inaugural address in August 1983, the new president announced a short-term austerity program. A three-year extended fund facility agreement was negotiated with the IMF in the autumn.

Perhaps in part recognizing the special sensitivities of Dominican opinion, the agreement worked out with the IMF during the autumn was rather generous and envisioned a gradual adjustment process. A three-year extended fund facility (EFF) made available $408 million, of which $140 million (plus $47 million from the compensatory fund facility) was provided the first year. The program sought a modest recovery of real growth plus significant adjustments in external imbalances. It set goals for reduced fiscal deficits and slower growth of domestic credit combined with increased savings and public and private investment. The government agreed to increase revenues considerably through new taxes, including a property tax and introduction of a value-added tax (VAT). The Dominican Republic had long used a dual exchange market, regulating the effective exchange rate by changing the composition of transactions allowed under the higher official rate (pegged for decades at par with the U.S. dollar) and the flexible parallel rate. When Jorge Blanco took office, the free-market rate, covering roughly a fifth of all transactions, was about 1.46:1.[9] The Fund staff proposed a unified rate of 1.25:1, but yielded to government concerns and agreed to a plan to gradually transfer various categories of transactions from the official to the free-exchange rate over the three-year period.

The government did, in fact, pursue fairly stringent policies in the autumn of 1982 and the early winter of 1983. But neither the president nor most of his cabinet had any real grasp of the nation's economic problems, nor any serious commitment to a three-year program of reforms. The legislature refused to consider the property tax, a proposed 50 percent cap on income tax deductions for investment in favored sectors, or the VAT; the cabinet delayed proposing the VAT for many months after the schedule discussed with the IMF. Meanwhile, pressures built within the cabinet for increased spending. By December 1983, the targets agreed under the EFF had been missed, inflation was accelerating, and the Dominican peso was rapidly losing value.

Fund staff, concerned that so little had been accomplished in the first year of the agreement and alarmed over the rapid economic deterioration, demanded much more vigorous action. In particular, the Fund now insisted that at least half of the import bill, including petroleum, should be transferred to the flexible market exchange rate in the coming year, along with tightened fiscal and monetary measures. Political leaders in the cabinet and the legislature vehemently rejected these demands, but they were divided and uncertain on how to cope with the deepening crisis. Attempts in late 1983 to halt the

[9] Vega, "Crisis del sector externo," p. 296.

peso's drop by controls failed. By March 1984, prices were rising 10 percent a month, spurring popular and union protests and scathing criticism from the Church. Larger business interests were pressing, through the Monetary Council, for a floating peso.[10] The United States had made it clear that U.S. balance of payments assistance was contingent on agreement with the Fund regarding the second year of the EFF. Debate within the cabinet shifted from whether to deal with the IMF to when and how to do so.

The government had unrealistically high hopes that transfers of major import categories to the market exchange rate would be accompanied by generous U.S. financial aid. Traveling to Washington in March 1984, Jorge Blanco stated that the Dominican government was prepared to act, but warned of political risks and asked for U.S. aid. President Reagan was noncommittal, and Jorge Blanco returned home empty-handed.

What happened next is all too well known. During Holy Week, Jorge Blanco announced the transfer of most imports to the free exchange rate, with petroleum imports to follow in May. Prices of many food staples soared. Massive protests erupted the following Monday, mainly in the capital. The toll was at least 55 lives.

The government retreated, rolling back the price increases and postponing the transfer of petroleum imports to the market exchange rate, but the basic predicament remained. All external financial support was contingent on an agreement with the IMF. Any faint hopes for alternative options died with the failure of the Latin Americans debtors' conference at Cartagena in June. During the summer of 1984, a partly revamped economic team reopened discussions with the Fund. The government was now prepared to transfer oil imports to the free rate, but shied away from the corresponding increase in electricity rates recommended by the Fund. New Minister of Finance Hugo Guiliani Cury, therefore, negotiated an unorthodox "bridge" or "shadow" agreement, similar to the later "enhanced surveillance" arrangement between the IMF and Colombia which entailed informal IMF endorsement but no financial support. The government hoped for U.S. financial support at this stage, but the U.S. Treasury was wary of providing funds for so unconventional an arrangement. The Dominican Republic again would have to proceed with the blessing but without the financial support of Washington.

At the end of August 1984, petroleum imports were transferred to the free exchange rate. Thanks largely to much more careful political preparations than those of the previous spring (discussed later), there was no major protest. But the IMF now required, as a prerequisite for a stand-by agreement, a complete shift to a unified and floating exchange rate plus a commitment to reduce the public sector deficit from 7.5 percent of GDP in 1984 to 4.9 percent in 1985, which entailed a cut in food subsidies and a prompt 50 percent increase in

[10] *Latin American Weekly Review*, January 27, 1984.

electricity rates.[11] Intense negotiations through the autumn, facilitated by further changes in the economic team, produced agreement just before Christmas.

On January 23, 1985 the new package was announced. The exchange rate was unified, and debt service was shifted to the floating rate. To help cover increased costs of oil and debt service, a temporary 36 percent surcharge was imposed on traditional exports (above all sugar), to be phased down to 18 percent in 1986 and then eliminated. Increases in electricity rates were less than the Fund had advised and were graduated to buffer small users. As in August/September 1984, political and security precautions prevented serious immediate protests.

The Dominican Republic had received no external financial support throughout 1984. Five days after the January 1985 measures were announced, $50 million in U.S. balance-of-payments support was deposited to the Dominican account in a New York bank. IMF funds under the agreement signed in January became available in April, and Paris Club rescheduling of public debt followed in May. Commercial bank negotiations took much longer, but a multiyear rescheduling was finally approved in February 1986, contingent on approval of a new stand-by by that time under discussion.

As feared, the January 1985 package initially sharply increased inflation and cut incomes. Real per capita GNP had dropped 1.9 percent in 1984 and slid an additional 4.5 percent in 1985; real wages almost surely eroded considerably more. Major strikes and protests erupted in March and June of 1985. But by midyear the real economy, with the help of external aid and some return of flight capital, was showing signs of a turnaround. Inflation dropped sharply.[12] The exchange rate, having overshot, appreciated somewhat. Revenues from import taxes jumped with the increase in the peso value of imports, helping to cover continuing public enterprise deficits. With fairly tight monetary and fiscal policies through the first quarter of 1986, the immediate financial crisis was largely resolved. In 1986, real GNP increased somewhat, though real per capita incomes still dwindled slightly. A unified and flexible exchange rate was in place, orderly relations had been restored with the nation's creditors, and the near-term debt burden was substantially reduced.

However, the hard-won stabilization proved fleeting. Many of the more basic structural reforms envisioned in the EFF had hardly been addressed. Moreover, rising electoral pressures loosened macroeconomic restraint, and post-election economic management failed even to preserve the stability achieved by the end of 1985.

Jorge Blanco's economic team that had carried through the Dominican sta-

---

[11] Economist Intelligence Unit, *Quarterly Economic Reports*, 1st quarter 1985, p. 18.

[12] Central Bank data indicate that the consumer price index actually declined in August 1985 and also in four of the first eight months of 1986.

bilization of 1984–1985 knew that the nation faced longer-term structural problems. Academic and government economists and some businessmen had debated these problems since the late 1970s.[13] The IMF, World Bank and AID had all stressed structural issues. As already noted, Jorge Blanco (and Guzmán earlier) had proposed some steps to address these problems, especially the eroding tax base, but business and legislative opposition promptly scuttled the attempts.[14] The Jorge Blanco government initially indicated some interest in a World Bank structural adjustment loan, but backed away when it became clear that conditions in addition to those in the agreement with the IMF were entailed.[15]

By late 1985, when the stabilization program began to produce some economic improvements, time had run out for the Jorge Blanco government. Attention and energies turned increasingly to the elections scheduled for spring 1986, and fiscal and monetary management loosened under the pressures of politics and patronage, eroding some of the economic gains so painfully achieved.

The May 1986 elections were a resounding defeat for the PRD, reflecting blame for economic hardship, recognition that the party was so divided that it was unable to govern, and above all, evidence of pervasive corruption. Dominicans turned again to Balaguer, still feared and respected despite his age and infirmities. Balaguer promptly put into effect two of the reforms on the unfinished agenda of the previous economic team: a cap of 50 percent of tax liability on exemptions claimed under industrial incentives provisions, and virtual elimination of the overall rice subsidy.[16] But his broader economic management did not sustain the precarious economic balance he inherited. Inflation accelerated from mid-1987, placing increasing pressure on the exchange rate. By mid-1988 the unified and flexible exchange rate was replaced by a managed rate.[17] Arrears mounted reflecting an undeclared partial mora-

[13] An excellent record of debate on many economic policy issues is available in the series of volumes published since early 1982 by Forum, a nonprofit Dominican organization supported by the Friedrich Ebert Foundation. Frank Moya Pons is executive secretary.

[14] Jonathan Hartlyn, "The Politics of Economic Crisis in the Dominican Republic, 1978–1986" (Paper presented at the SECOLAS conference, Mérida, Mexico, April 1987), p. 11.

[15] Interviews with World Bank staff, Washington, D.C., 1987.

[16] As part of a broader effort to reduce subsidies, INESPRE was returned to its original role of stabilizing agricultural prices for the consumer. The tasks of purchasing, storing, and distributing rice were transferred to the Agricultural Bank. The overall rice subsidy was eliminated, but the price of the lowest grade of rice was reduced, while prices for better grades were raised considerably. The reform was applauded as combining social justice and fiscal rationality. But it shortly became obvious that supplies of the cheapest rice were inadequate, for reasons that are not clear.

[17] By the end of the Jorge Blanco term, business elites were persuaded of the merits of the flexible rate. Even commercial importers found the impartiality of the new arrangements an improvement over the old system, which had generated a constant competitive scramble for discretionary, hence unpredictable, exemptions and favors. (Interview with Dominican business representative, Santo Domingo, March 1987.) In early 1987, when Balaguer's Central Bank Governor

torium on debt service. As the economy deteriorated, speculation mounted that a new agreement with the IMF would be unavoidable, but no such agreement had been reached by mid-1989. The painful measures of 1984–1985 remained an isolated episode, and most of the Dominican Republic's adjustment issues remained not only unresolved but unaddressed.

Costa Rica 1979–1988: Disintegration, Stabilization, Contested Reforms

Over the decade from 1979 through 1988, Costa Rica both attempted and achieved considerably more reform than the Dominican Republic, but much of the reform agenda was strongly resisted and moved very slowly.[18] Costa Rican adjustment experience can be divided into three major phases: three years of rapid economic disintegration coinciding with most of the presidential term of Rodrigo Carazo Odio; a vigorous and effective stabilization program launched shortly after the new government of Alberto Monge Alvarez took office in mid-1982 that continued through 1983; and thereafter, a protracted struggle to maintain stability and promote structural reforms and sustainable growth.

Rodrigo Carazo became president of Costa Rica in spring 1978, at a moment when extremely high coffee prices had lifted national income to record levels. But coffee prices promptly dropped while the cost of oil soared in 1979; Costa Rica's terms of trade fell by a third between 1977 and 1981. Flexible interest rates on debt already outstanding plus new borrowing in response to the crisis quadrupled debt service between 1977 and 1981. By 1981, total debt service amounted to 8.6 percent of GNP. Inflation and capital flight accelerated rapidly, as did pressure on Costa Rica's currency, the colon.

Handicapped by a divided cabinet and a fragile plurality in the Assembly, for two years the government took only scattered and indecisive stabilization

Julian Pérez hinted he might restore the Dominican peso to its traditional parity with the dollar, according to interviews, businessmen discretely discouraged the idea. But the system was abandoned 24 June 1988, and replaced by a managed rate in August (Economist Intelligence Unit, *Quarterly Report*, no. 4 [1988] p. 16).

[18] Particularly useful discussions of Costa Rican stabilization experience under Carazo and during the first eighteen months of the Monge administration include Mitchell Seligson, "Costa Rica," in *Latin America and Caribbean Contemporary Record*, vol. 1, 1981–1982 (New York: Holmes and Meier), pp. 399–408; idem, "Costa Rica," in Lowenthal, ed., *Contemporary Record*, vol. 2, 1982–1983, pp. 460–74; Carlos Manuel Castillo, "The Costa Rican Experience with the International Debt Crisis" (Paper delivered at the Inter-American Dialogue, CIEPLAN meeting 17–19 March 1986, Santiago, Chile); Victor Hugo Cespedes, *Costa Rica: estabilidad sin crecimiento: evolución de la económia en 1983* (San José: Academia de Centro America, 1984); Richard Feinberg, "Costa Rica: The End of the Fiesta," in Richard Newfarmer, ed., *From Gunboats to Diplomacy* (Baltimore: Johns Hopkins Press, 1984), pp. 102–15; Sol Sanders, *The Costa Rican Laboratory* (New York: Priority Press for the Twentieth Century Fund, 1986); Marc Edelman, "Back from the Brink," *Report on the Americas*, 19, no. 6 (November–December 1985), pp. 37–48.

measures. The initial (1979) response was an expansionist fiscal policy including an ambitious infrastructure construction program; the legislature balked at proposed tax increases and the public sector deficit jumped to 12 percent of GDP. Efforts to tighten economic management in 1980 were not enough to prevent the collapse of an attempted stand-by agreement with the IMF. Frightened businessmen moved capital out of the country at a quickened pace. By mid-1980, reserves covered a week's imports. Carazo viewed devaluation as politically suicidal, but by autumn 1980 a de facto dual exchange rate was announced, and at the year's end the colon was floated.

Early in 1981, Minister of Finance Hernán Sáenz Jiménez persuaded the IMF to consider a three-year extended fund facility program and overcame intense resistance within the cabinet to announce a package of reforms meeting the Fund's stiff preconditions. But in April, as Sáenz was traveling in Europe to raise additional financial support, the Chambers of Industry and Commerce held a large public meeting in San José, protesting the new decrees and particularly the requirement that they purchase foreign exchange on the free market to repay obligations incurred earlier at the much lower official rate. President Carazo revoked the key decrees. Sáenz promptly resigned.

By autumn 1981, the foreign exchange market was in chaos. The colon had plunged from its official value of 8.54 to the dollar to a free rate of roughly 65:1. Carazo announced drastic import controls and a debt moratorium; actual debt payments had ceased earlier. Real per capita GDP fell at an increasing rate from 1980; real wages dropped considerably faster.

By the elections of February 1982, Costa Ricans feared not only for their standard of living but for their deeply valued political and social institutions. Not surprisingly, the opposition National Liberation party won two-thirds of the seats in the unicameral Assembly, while PLN presidential candidate Monge won a 59 percent majority. The new economic team, led by Central Bank Governor Carlos Manuel Castillo, moved rapidly to regain economic control. Within months strict foreign exchange controls were combined with measures designed to stabilize and eventually unify the official and free-market rates. The fiscal deficit, which had reached 14.3 percent of GDP in 1981 and was headed higher when Monge took office, was slashed to 9 percent in 1982 and 3.4 percent in 1983,[19] entailing draconian utility rate and sizable tax increases. More popular action could be taken regarding the exchange rate. Judging the rate had overshot, the government somewhat appreciated the colon to about 40 to the dollar, which proved highly effective in curbing inflation and reversing capital flight.

The program was supported by an IMF stand-by arranged late in 1982, com-

[19] Central Bank of Costa Rica, "Costa Rica: Economic and Financial Situation," part 6 of *Republic of Costa Rica: Economic and Financial Program*, memorandum prepared by the [commercial banks'] Coordinating Committee for Costa Rica (San José: January 1985), table 1.

mitting the government to continued wage restraint, further utility hikes, and somewhat increased interest rates. The stand-by paved the way for a Paris Club rescheduling of public external debt in January 1983.

Rescheduling commercial bank debt was more complex. Costa Rica's problems had preceded the general debt crisis, and the banks initially viewed her problems as evidence of particular incompetence. The Mexican default in August 1982 led them to take a more systemic view of the issues, but also initially distracted their attention and later led them to weigh any settlement with Costa Rica in terms of possible precedents for larger debtors. Nevertheless, by September 1983 an agreement was finally signed covering a substantial fraction of the public external debt.

The stabilization program was also supported by large-scale concessional assistance. The United States channeled $175.7 million in balance-of-payments support to Costa Rica in 1982 and 1983. The IMF stand-by agreement approved in December 1982 provided $106 million in 1983. These flows were in large part intended to facilitate payments to creditors. Interest payments on public and publicly guaranteed debt soared in 1983, increasing to more than $500 million from $78 million the previous year. In 1984 and 1985 the interest burden dwindled, but remained heavy.

Despite the debt service drain, the economy responded considerably more rapidly than anticipated. By late 1983, inflation had cooled to roughly 10 percent, far better than the standby target of 30 percent. After contracting 7.3 percent in 1982, GDP increased 2.9 percent in 1983. Average real wages rose roughly 10 to 15 percent (though they remained well below their peaks in the late 1970s); open unemployment dropped from 9.5 percent in 1982 to 9.0 percent in 1983.[20] Perhaps as much as $100 million of flight capital returned in the same year.[21] The exchange rate was unified and reasonably stable. Relations with external creditors were once again on a contractual footing. The turnaround was impressive, but the battle for sustainable growth was just beginning.

Even before the crisis began, many Costa Ricans had been increasingly concerned with widening fiscal and balance-of-payments deficits and mounting debt, and with the structural problems underlying those symptoms. By the late 1970s, some drew anxious analogies with Uruguay, another small democracy where an expensive welfare system, overgrown bureaucracy, and low productivity had led to breakdown and military rule.[22] Before his administration was

[20] Gary S. Fields, ''Employment and Economic Growth in Costa Rica'' (Report prepared for U.S. Agency for International Development, Cornell University, February 1986), p. 39; Victor Hugo Cespedes et al., *Costa Rica: estabilidad sin crecimiento* (San José: Academia de Centroamerica, 1984), p. 86.

[21] USAID, ''Annex 2: Economic Trends and Problems: January 1985'' (Memorandum, San José, U.S. Embassy), p. 3.

[22] Ameringer, *Democracy in Costa Rica*, pp. 108, 127.

overwhelmed by the debt crisis, Carazo tried to initiate some modest structural reforms, provoking heated resistance within his own business-based coalition as well as from unions and the opposition PLN.[23] As the economic crisis deepened, short-run economic management seized center stage, and issues of national development strategy and reform were essentially shelved for the next four years, from 1980 through 1983.

By the end of 1983, with the stabilization effort a clear success, twenty-seven months remained in Monge's term of office. Unlike Jorge Blanco's government at the end of 1985, the Monge government had time plus general popular approval for its economic management. For the reform-minded, the moment seemed ripe to work out an agenda of structural changes needed to correct long-standing weaknesses, adjust to the changed international economic environment, and put Costa Rica on a sustainable growth path. With strong encouragement from the AID mission, a commission was established in late 1983 to draw up such a plan. But cabinet-level reviews in early 1984 so gutted the plan that the final version was virtually ignored.[24]

Three factors probably contributed to the fate of the comprehensive reform plan. In early 1984, Carlos Manuel Castillo, governor of the Central Bank and chief architect of the stabilization program, resigned to seek the PLN nomination for the 1986 presidential campaign. His departure and other changes left a semivacuum in economic policy leadership for six months during 1984 until late August. The substantially external impetus for the plan undoubtedly also weakened it. More importantly, by late 1983 the public mood was shifting from relief that the crisis had been brought under control to demands for rapid restoration of precrisis incomes and services. The crisis was blamed on external forces plus the mismanagement of the Carazo government; most of the electorate (and much of the cabinet) saw no need for painful structural reforms to reestablish economic health.

Indeed, the shift in mood coupled with the lapse in economic leadership threatened not only reform initiatives but also the hard-won stability itself. The original 1984 budget, as submitted to the legislature in autumn 1983, had a deficit so large that the IMF insisted it be cut by legislative action. The Assembly reluctantly complied in the Emergency Economic Law of 1984. But by mid-1984 loosened credit restrictions caused imports to surge, reserves to dwindle, and arrears once again to build. A second stand-by agreement had been almost agreed upon in March, but the new trends led the IMF to stiffen its

---

[23] See Edgar Fuerst Weigand, "Crisis económica, medidas de estabilización y políticas industriales durante la administración Carazo: 1978–1982," final research report, Universidad Nacional, Departamento de Economía (San José, May 1986), for an account of Carazo's industrial reform plan and its reception.

[24] Robert Adler, "Policy Dialogue and Economic Recovery in Costa Rica: Leverage and Guile in a Democracy" (Memorandum, San José, U.S. Agency for International Development, December 10, 1984), p. 4.

conditions. Legislative resistance and lack of economic leadership contributed to a long stalemate in discussions with the Fund.

By August 1984, however, a new economic team was in place, capped with the appointment of highly respected academic economist Eduardo Lizano as new governor of the Central Bank. For the remainder of Monge's term, and continuing in the term of his successor, Oscar Arias Sánchez, Lizano became the chief architect and lobbyist for measures to liberalize the Costa Rican economy. Working with a few allies within the cabinet and with strong backing, often verging into pressure, from AID and the World Bank, a number of reforms were begun.[25] Despite the recent stormy history of resistance to devaluation, the introduction of a crawling peg in autumn 1984 caused barely a murmur, testimony to the business community's confidence in Lizano. In late 1984, financial sector reforms urged for some time by AID were forced through the Assembly after heated debate and under strong pressure from the external agencies, especially AID. In addition to a variety of export promotion measures, the tariff structure shared with Costa Rica's partners in the Central American Common Market (CACM) was renegotiated. With persistent prompting from AID, the massive state holding company CODESA was dismantled and in small part privatized. Again with outside pressure, the National Production Council (CNP), responsible for encouraging production and controlling distribution of basic grains, began to trim its losses in part by confining payment of highly subsidized producer prices for rice to purchases for domestic needs.

However, on many of these issues initial steps were only partially implemented, or the measures needed to consolidate the reforms were not taken. As of late 1988, new reforms for the troubled financial sector were stalled in the Assembly. There was little response to World Bank calls for reduction in the variation and overall level of tariff protection for more than two hundred locally manufactured items. Privatization of some parts of CODESA similarly moved very slowly. Efforts to reduce subsidies for agricultural credit and crop prices prompted major farmers' protests in mid-1987 and again in 1988. Capping or reducing public sector employment was also deeply contentious. The first World Bank structural adjustment loan had called for a cap on public sector employment and reduced CNP losses. When instead the losses grew and employment increased by many thousands (the precise figure is disputed), the Bank delayed release of the second tranche of the SAL for many months. The resulting financial shortfalls contributed to failure to meet IMF targets, in turn causing delays in expected flows from bilateral donors and the commercial

---

[25] The sharp distinction between the initial "stabilization phase" of the Monge administration and the subsequent "reform phase" is exaggerated. A number of reform initiatives were launched in 1983. Of course, stabilization measures continued to be necessary after the conclusion of the initial drive. Nonetheless, by early 1984 macroeconomic management questions were less dominant, and proposals for longer-term structural reform were more evident.

banks. To qualify for release of the funds, the government imposed import surcharges earlier agreed upon, but lifted them after the funds were in hand.[26]

Structural reforms were, of course, resisted by the interests most immediately and obviously threatened. But other obstacles were also important. A pervasive and complex system of administrative regulations and laws, mostly designed to protect individual rights, raised countless roadblocks to reform. Many PLN leaders and most PLN legislators were ideologically committed to the long-established social priorities and statist principles of the party and saw no compelling need to rethink their approaches. As the Monge term drew to a close, many believed the Minister of Planning's statement that Costa Rica was "out of the woods."

The new PLN presidential candidate, Oscar Arias, focused most of his attention during the electoral campaign of 1986 and after his election on promoting regional stability. His main domestic economic plank was a massive housing program. Perhaps in order to keep the confidence of external agencies, Arias did retain Lizano and Minister of Finance Fernando Naranjo. These and a few allies tried to continue the gradual liberalization of the economy and to encourage debate on new development strategies. The reform effort neither died nor forged ahead, but inched forward fitfully.

Economic recovery similarly sputtered. Real GDP surged 8 percent in 1984, then stagnated (and declined on a per capita basis) in 1985 and resumed more moderate growth in 1986 and 1987. Inflation continued to be contained at 12–15 percent, but savings and investment were too low to sustain both rising real incomes and employment and debt service.

The struggle over internal reforms was constantly shadowed by the massive debt burden. Debt service in 1983 claimed more than half the value of exported goods and services. In March 1985, the long-delayed stand-by originally scheduled for a year earlier was concluded, followed by Paris Club rescheduling of public debt, a new agreement with commercial banks, and the signing of a long-gestating structural adjustment loan (SAL) with the World Bank. Even after reschedulings, service on long-term public and publicly guaranteed debt in 1984 and 1985 absorbed 25 percent and 35 percent of export earnings or about 10–13 percent of GDP.[27] The outflow more than counterbalanced concessional aid and IMF lending. While poll data showed most Costa Ricans in principle favored paying the debt,[28] it was increasingly seen as the main obstacle to resumed growth.

Shortly after taking office in June 1986, Oscar Arias' government suspended interest payments on commercial long-term debt to maintain a mini-

---

[26] Interview with World Bank staff, Washington, D.C., October 1988.

[27] World Bank, *World Debt Tables*, vol. 2, Country Tables (Washington, D.C.: World Bank, 1988–1989), p. 97.

[28] Consultoria Interdisciplinaria en Desarrollo S.A., *Encuesta de opinion publica*, Heredia, Costa Rica, July 1986.

mum level of reserves. Partial payments were resumed in the autumn.[29] Between September 1986 and summer 1988, discussions with the commercial banks shifted from harsh acrimony to more pragmatic exploration of possible solutions. The banks were reluctant to radically reschedule Costa Rican debt before settling their problems with larger debtors, above all Brazil. Differences between the major banks also delayed agreement. Repeating the by now familar pattern of interaction among key funders, inability to reach agreement with the banks delayed finalization of a standby agreement with the IMF, which in turn prevented disbursement of AID balance-of-payments aid. In October 1987, the IMF did finally sign an agreement despite a continued stalemate with the commercial banks. But the chronic, complex and often acrimonious negotiations kept Costa Rican policy in a constant state of precarious balance, both complicating and reducing incentive for careful appraisal of long-run prospects and appropriate reforms.

Stabilization and Structural Change in Jamaica: 1980–88

In Costa Rica and the Dominican Republic, the economic blows of the late 1970s and early 1980s rudely interrupted economic growth; adjustment called for a basic shift in psychology. For Jamaica, in contrast, the troubles of the 1980s were a continuation of much longer trends.[30] Edward Seaga took charge in late 1980 of an economy fundamentally in much worse condition than Costa Rica's at the time of Monge's 1982 election. His adjustment strategy moved through four main phases over the next eight years: an initial two years (1981–1982) of aid-financed, import-primed economic recovery accompanied by limited reforms; three years (1983–1985) of harsh austerity, again accompanied by some reforms; a partial break with neoorthodoxy that started in October 1985 and merged in 1986 into a new phase of economic recovery as a result of favorable international trends and earlier reforms.

The 1980 elections seemed to mark a clear watershed in Jamaican history.

---

[29] Inter-American Development Bank, *Economic and Social Progress in Latin America: 1987* (Washington, D.C.: Inter-American Development Bank, 1987), p. 273.

[30] Helpful sources on Jamaican stabilization efforts include Omar Davies, "An Analysis of the Management of the Jamaican Economy, 1972–1985," *Social and Economic Studies*, 35, no.1 (March 1986): pp. 73–109; Locksley Edmondson, "Jamaica," in Jack Hopkins, ed., *Contemporary Record*, vol. 1, 1981–1982; idem, "Jamaica," in Hopkins, ed., *Contemporary Record*, vol. 2, 1982–1983; John D. Forbes, "Jamaica: Managing Political and Economic Change" (Washington, D.C.: American Enterprise Institute, 1985); Evelyne Huber Stephens and John D. Stephens, *Democratic Socialism in Jamaica* (Princeton, N.J.: Princeton University Press, 1986), especially chap. 7, "Seaga's Return to Dependent Capitalism," pp. 251–269; Carl Stone, "Jamaica, from Manley to Seaga," in Donald E. Schultz and Douglas Graham, eds., *Revolution and Counterrevolution in Central America and the Caribbean* (Boulder, Colo., Westview Press, 1984), pp. 385–419; Carl Stone, "Political Trends in Jamaica in the Nineteen Eighties" (Paper presented to the intercampus social sciences faculty conference at Mona, June 30, 1986).

The campaign posed an unusually sharp series of fundamental choices regarding development paths: "the merits of the mixed vs. market economy; the democratic socialist (populist type) vs. the Puerto Rican model; an independent self-reliant approach vs. an IMF-guided path; diversifying links to the socialist world vs. entrenching ties with the West; and aligning with anti-imperialist militants or moderates in the Third World movement."[31] In the October election Edward Seaga won 58 percent of the popular vote—the largest electoral margin in the nation's history; his Jamaica Labour party (JLP) took 51 out of 60 seats in Parliament.[32]

Unlike the Monge and Jorge Blanco governments, then, Seaga entered office apparently committed to focus on structural change. The Reagan administration, also recently elected, and the Bretton Woods institutions certainly viewed Seaga's resounding victory as a mandate for such change. Reagan saw in Seaga a leader who shared his own intense antistate, free-market convictions. The IMF and the World Bank held high hopes that Seaga, with his extensive economic experience and known abilities, would reorient the Jamaican economy along lines they viewed as sounder and more promising. U.S. assistance began flowing within weeks and continued at high levels. An IMF extended fund facility with no "negative features" (that is, no devaluation or public sector layoffs) was concluded by April 1981. The first World Bank structural adjustment loan took a year longer to arrange, but was followed by two more, and then by two sector adjustment loans, during the next five years.

Seaga's own economic strategy was not identical with the external agencies' agenda, a point discussed more later. His initial program was guided by several basic assumptions.

> The economy could be rekindled by putting unused capacity to work. More specifically, the bauxite industry could be restored to 1974 levels or better, i.e., from its 1980 production level of 12 million tons to as much as 16 million tons.
> The key to starting the process was increased availability of imports. Not only bauxite, but also tourism, manufacturing, and even agriculture were highly import-dependent, and the economy had been starved for spare parts, raw materials, and fuel as well as consumption goods.
> As the Reagan government was predicting, the U.S. economy would respond to "supply-side economics" with 6 percent growth, providing a bouyant market for Jamaican goods and services.
> Investment, particularly foreign investment, would respond rapidly and strongly to improved economic management and a brightened general outlook.

With generous external assistance, the first two years of the JLP government were, in fact, expansionist. There was no devaluation. The budget deficit con-

---

[31] Edmondson, "Jamaica 1981–82," vol. 1, 1981–1982, p. 589.

[32] See Carl Stone, "Jamaica's 1980 Elections," *Caribbean Review* 10, no. 2 (Spring 1981), for more detail on the elections.

tinued roughly 14–15 percent of GDP, as in the late 1970s. Imports expanded sharply, financed by extensive aid. Investment increased from 16 to 21 percent of GDP. Private capital registered a sizable net inflow in 1981 for the first time in years. The rate of increase in the consumer price index dropped dramatically, from almost 29 percent in 1980 to 4.6 percent in 1981,[33] mainly reflecting the surge of imports.

However, the recovery shortly wilted. By mid-1982 it was clear that the balance of payments was deteriorating, investment and production were not increasing as expected, and inflation was accelerating. Three of Seaga's four initial assumptions had proved incorrect. The U.S. economy declined in 1981 and 1982. Investors proved cautious. Bauxite and alumina exports, far from increasing, dropped 40 percent in value between 1980 and 1982. The IMF, the World Bank, and AID all began to urge serious consideration of devaluation and tightened monetary and fiscal management. In August 1982, the Mexican debt crisis abruptly dried up foreign bank credit available to Jamaica, as had happened also in the Dominican Republic.

On New Year's Day 1983, declaring that Jamaica had been "blown off course," Seaga announced the beginning of a new austerity phase. For the next three years, stabilization dominated the economic agenda. Exchange rate management was the initial focus. Through much of 1982, Jamaica had operated a de facto dual exchange rate with informal IMF sanction. As in the Dominican Republic a little later, the intent was to gradually transfer transactions to the lower, floating rate, aiming for eventual reunification. Delays in expected capital inflows in early 1983 forced a sharp acceleration of the process. In mid-1983, most merchandise trade was shifted to the floating rate. In October, the rate was unified and a system of biweekly auctions was launched for allocating foreign exchange. The step entailed a 77 percent nominal devaluation.[34] The prior transfer of most items to the floating rate plus continued subsidized prices for some basic foods muffled the immediate impact on consumer prices. In the course of 1983, however, consumer prices increased 16.7 percent.[35] The auction system was modified and opened to more participants in 1984.

Anticipating the need for more stringent austerity measures and reacting to clear signs that the opposition PNP was recovering from its crushing defeat of 1980, Seaga called a snap general election in December 1983. The timing probably also reflected the popularity in Jamaica of Seaga's support for the

[33] Statistical Institute of Jamaica, *Consumer Price Indices: Annual Review 1985* (Kingston, 1985), p. i.

[34] "Movements in the Jamaican Dollar Exchange Rate," app. 1, in Bank of Jamaica, *Statistical Digest* (Kingston, September 1986), p. 109.

[35] Statistical Institute of Jamaica, *Consumer Price Indices*, 1985, table 1.3, p. 5 and table 1.4, p. 6. The all-Jamaica Consumer Price Index rose only 3 percent between September and December 1983, but the December-on-December increase was 16.7 percent.

U.S. invasion of Grenada in October 1983.[36] But Seaga had earlier promised that new elections would not be held until the electoral rolls were updated to include the large number of young voters who had come of age since the last election, many of whom were PNP supporters. The PNP decided to boycott the elections. Seaga thus won an unopposed mandate for another five years in power. But the anomaly of a one-party parliament fueled opposition accusations that Jamaican democracy was being eroded.

Having won time to manuever, Seaga returned to immediate economic problems with almost frightening determination. The fiscal year 1984–1985 budget announced in April 1984 set out to slash the public sector deficit from 16 to less than 8 percent of GDP. Roughly 4,000 public sector employees were dismissed; subsidies were cut; some state factories were closed. Taxes were sharply increased.

Meanwhile, hopes that bauxite would revive were rapidly fading. Reynolds had withdrawn from Jamaica in 1984. Alcoa, contradicting earlier assurances, announced in February 1985 that it would close its operations in Jamaica. Bauxite exports continued to contract in 1984 and 1985. The 1985–1986 budget was still more draconian than that of the previous year. Thousands of additional public sector positions were eliminated, and steep new import stamp duties were imposed. Shying away from further increases in prices of petroleum, food, and utilities, much of the burden of demand restraint shifted to monetary policy; interest rates were sharply hiked and credit restricted.

In contrast to experience in both Costa Rica and the Dominican Republic, vigorous austerity measures failed to stabilize the economy. Real GDP dropped 0.4 percent in 1984 and 4.6 percent in 1985, while inflation accelerated. As discouraging or more so than bauxite/alumina trends were increases in debt service. Total debt service had hovered around 19 percent of exports of goods and services from 1982 through 1984, but in 1985 suddenly shot up to 29 percent (equivalent to 23 percent of GNP).[37] The nonfinancial public sector deficit had been slashed to 3.8 percent of GDP in 1985–1986, but debt service swelled the operating losses of the Bank of Jamaica, keeping the consolidated public sector debt in the neighborhood of 14 percent of GNP. (The government and the international financial agencies disagreed regarding the precise figure.)

The view spread that Seaga had permitted a spending spree during his first two years in office, purchased at the price of greatly increased debt. The austerity that followed seemed to be accomplishing little, while spreading much misery. In January 1985, two days of nationwide demonstrations erupted, triggered by oil price increases, with a costly aftermath of cancelled tourist bookings. A crescendo of strikes in spring 1985 peaked in an unprecedented gen-

---

[36] Stephens and Stephens, *Democratic Socialism*, pp. 267–68.

[37] World Bank, *World Debt Tables*, vol. 2, Country Tables (Washington, D.C.:'World Bank, 1988), p. 201.

eral strike in June, with union federations affiliated with both major parties taking part. Seaga faced down the strikers, but the mounting unrest was obvious. Criticism from business, church, and other quarters also escalated. Municipal elections, originally due in 1984 and twice postponed, were now scheduled for July 1986.

At this point Seaga again changed course, diverging somewhat from the neoorthodox line. The real exchange rate had been dropping since the introduction of the auction in late 1983; by October 1985 it had dropped at least 40 percent.[38] In that month its decline suddenly accelerated, in part reflecting pre-Christmas importers' demand. This triggered a decision that must have been under consideration for some time. The Bank of Jamaica began to manage the auction, reflating the Jamaican dollar from a low of about 6.40 to 5.50 and thereafter pegging it at that rate. The decision responded to political pressures but also reflected a new economic appraisal. The government argued that real depreciation since the auction was introduced was adequate to make Jamaica's exports, especially its nontraditional items, competitive; further devaluation would merely fuel additional inflation.[39]

A few weeks earlier, at the joint World Bank-IMF meetings held that year in Seoul, Korea, Seaga had seized on the announcement of the Baker Plan to deliver an eloquent plea for a more humane pace of adjustment. Now, having in effect frozen the exchange rate, Seaga requested a special tripartite mission representing the IMF, the World Bank, and the U.S. government, to take a fresh look at Jamaica's situation and make new recommendations. The tripartite mission worked intensively through the first four months of 1986, but its report, submitted to the government in April, deeply disappointed Seaga. The mission argued that Jamaica had very little room for manuever. The exchange rate could be held constant only at the cost of very tight monetary and fiscal measures, and probably import controls, which would throttle investment and growth. Instead, the team urged a return to flexible exchange rate management and considerably relaxed monetary policy.[40]

The report was never officially released. The long-postponed municipal elections were held in July 1986, and as expected strongly favored the opposition PNP. Michael Manley promptly launched an accelerating campaign to force general elections as soon as possible, but Seaga made clear his intention to delay. His incentive to do so was reinforced by the first positive economic trends since the short-lived surge of 1981–1982. In 1986, real GDP growth was

[38] World Bank data on real effective exchange rates. The Tripartite Commission estimated the fall as close to 50 percent (Constantine Michalopoulos, Azizali Mohammed, and Widney Weintraub, *Jamaica: A Medium-Term Assessment*, Report of the Tripartite Mission (cited hereafter as "Report Tripartite Mission" [Washington D.C.: 1986], table 4, p. 20).

[39] Inter-American Development Bank, *Economic and Social Progress*, p. 337.

[40] Report Tripartite Commission, especially section 4, "Macro-economic Policies," pp. 17–30.

2.3 percent; the 1987 rate was approximately 5.5 percent. Consumer price inflation slowed from almost 26 percent in 1985 to just over 15 percent in 1986, then was held to 6.7 percent in 1987. The improvement owed much to exogenous trends: some strengthening in demand for and the volume of bauxite/alumina exports, an easing of international interest rates, and more importantly, the sharp drop in the price of oil. Tourism and nontraditional exports also boomed, in good part reflecting domestic reforms. The current account deficit narrowed dramatically.

Though disappointed with the outcome of the "Fresh Look" (tripartite) study, the government resumed discussions with the IMF after the mid-1986 municipal elections. The discussions stalled for some months on the question of devaluation, but as the drop in the U.S. dollar mitigated the effects of Jamaica's exchange rate freeze, the Fund yielded. A stand-by agreement with no requirement for a devaluation (unless certain triggering conditions occurred) was announced in January 1987 and was generally viewed as a David-defeats-Goliath victory for Seaga. Jamaica had emerged from its three years of harsh austerity. But elections had to be held, at the latest, by spring 1989. Mounting campaign debate focused heavily on whether recent economic gains were durable, whether the associated costs were acceptable, and whether better alternatives were available.

Despite its preoccupation with immediate stabilization issues from 1983 through 1985, the JLP government had introduced a broad array of structural reforms since taking office. Most of the extensive price controls established during the PNP era were removed fairly quickly. In 1982, Seaga announced the gradual abolition over five years of quantitative restrictions on imports plus simplification of the cumbersome licensing scheme. By 1985, administrative restrictions were limited mainly to consumer imports. State monopolies on the export of major agricultural crops were substantially loosened. Parliament early approved a range of incentives for industry and especially exports, including free ports in Kingston and Montego Bay and a one-stop agency to help foreign investors through the maze of regulations. Of course, the depreciation and unification of the exchange rate was in principle a major incentive to exports.

On the revenue side, utility rates were raised and tax collection tightened. After three years of intensive analysis and review, a sweeping reform of the individual income tax structure went into effect at the beginning of 1986 and was followed a year later by new corporate tax arrangements. Management studies were completed for most major public enterprises, and initial steps were taken toward reform of the core staff ministries of Finance and Public Service.[41] Far more controversially, under pressure of austerity, perhaps

[41] Unclassified AID and World Bank staff reports, interviews, and press reports, 1982–1988; Report Tripartite Commission; Davies, "Management of Jamaican Economy"; Stephens and Ste-

20,000 positions were cut from the public sector. In 1978, public sector workers comprised 15.7 percent of the labor force; by October 1985 that ratio had dropped to 10.4 percent.[42] Reflecting these and other steps, the central government deficit dropped from a peak of 15.8 percent of GDP in 1983–1984 to about 1.4 percent in 1986–1987, and was projected to move into surplus in 1987–1988; the overall public sector deficit shrank almost as dramatically in the same years from 19.6 percent to 5.6 percent of GDP and continued to decline in 1987.[43] Nontraditional exports to markets outside the Caribbean Economic Community (CARICOM) increased from 11 percent of total exports in 1982 to 27 percent in 1986. Business confidence, long half-hearted, by 1988 was responding strongly. Investment levels rose in both 1987 and 1988, and there was evidence of considerable capital flight reversal.[44]

Nevertheless, liberalization remained partial and precarious. The import structure was still riddled with concessions to special interests. Resistance to import liberalization continued unabated; in 1986 some sixty items reverted to import licensing pending studies of comparative advantage. The Jamaica Commodities Trading Corporation (JCTC) continued to monopolize imports of certain staples and to subsidize their prices to consumers. Divestment of various state activities, a goal AID pressed with particular vigor, crawled save for a brief flurry of activity in late 1986. Management studies of public enterprises often were not followed by action.[45]

Was the glass half full or half empty? The answer depends in good part on initial expectations. With hindsight, the external agencies' early expectations were clearly overblown, in part reflecting a misreading of Seaga's commitment to the reforms they regarded as crucial. The prime minister shared the donors' emphasis on encouraging private and foreign investment, but his game plan emphasized renewed confidence, access to imported inputs (initially through concessional aid), and increased government efficiency more than structural changes. Trade liberalization was not high on his list of priorities. Divestment was still lower. As was evident from his earlier record in the late 1960s and early 1970s, the prime minister did not object on principle to an active state role. He was skeptical about the magic of the marketplace and especially, perhaps, about the enterprise of the Jamaican business and industrial communities.[46]

phens, *Democratic Socialism*, chap. 7, are the basis for information in this and previous paragraphs on structural reforms.

[42] Statistical Institute of Jamaica, *The Labour Force* (Kingston, 1985), table 3.5, pp. 70–71. The estimate of cuts in public sector positions is from the Report Tripartite Commission p. 78. Technical issues, such as how to count part-time positions, complicate the estimate.

[43] IMF data, February 1988.

[44] Interview with World Bank staff, 1989.

[45] Report Tripartite Commission; AID and World Bank memorandums.

[46] Stephens and Stephens, *Democratic Socialism*, p. 253; interview with former senior Jamaican official, 1988.

Nor was it as clear as outsiders believed that the JLP had been given a mandate for structural change in October 1980. Despite the ideological rhetoric of the campaign, for most ordinary Jamaicans the overriding issue was probably economic management. The Manley government was regarded as having disastrously mismanaged the economy. Seaga had been minister of finance in the previous JLP government and had the reputation of a financial wizard. It was certainly more comfortable to assume that a thorough housecleaning and good management would correct Jamaica's ills, rather than contemplate deeper surgery. At least by implication, Jamaicans also got the message that a foreign policy reoriented towards the West would attract much greater aid and investment. Thus, Seaga's sweeping victory was probably not so much a mandate in favor of structural reforms, as a judgment on the relative capabilities of the two candidates to manage the economy and attract external support.[47]

In addition to some misinterpretation of Seaga's own commitment and his electoral mandate, external agencies underestimated both the tenacity of resistance from vested interests and the administrative complications of implementing many of the desired reforms. Higher levels of the civil service were demoralized and decimated by years of dwindling real salaries. Donor agencies provided extensive technical assistance with specific reforms including the tax measures, but dependence on foreign advisors became a focus of criticism. Seaga's insistence on personally controlling many details of administration also constituted a bottleneck, according to many Jamaicans and foreigners.

The approach of elections in 1989 spurred intense debate over development strategies appropriate for the island. The opposition challenged even those aspects of performance that the government claimed as clear accomplishments. The reduced role of the state and the narrowed public sector deficit, they argued, had been purchased at the price of long-term neglect of education, health, and basic infrastructure, hurting all Jamaicans but most of all the poor. Three-quarters of the increase in nontraditional exports, they noted, was concentrated in "Section 807" manufactures of garments from textiles woven and cut in the United States and destined for U.S. markets. Not only was this a kind of enclave industry with few upstream or downstream ties to other Jamaican enterprises, but it also depended on extremely low wages to an almost wholly female work force. Labor protest in the free zones was already putting serious pressure on these industries. Many Jamaicans were uneasy about the long-term social and cultural implications of heavy and growing reliance on tourism. Import liberalization under the Seaga government was viewed as having already destroyed some local industries, and as in Costa Rica, further opening was deeply controversial. The debt overhang now meant little room for large new net inflows; in 1986 net long-term capital transfers turned neg-

---

[47] Stone, "Jamaica's 1980 Elections."

ative. These and related issues prompted proposals for strategies that relied less on export promotion—proposals not wholly confined to the opposition.

Yet for all the frustrations of partial reform and for all the pre-election debate and rhetoric, there was more consensus across party lines in Jamaica by early 1989 than in the past two decades. Within the PNP appreciation of the importance of careful macroeconomic management was much greater. While the appropriate balance between state and markets was disputed, many conceded that the programs of the mid-1970s relied too heavily on the state. Increased investment in 1987 and 1988, despite the approach of elections, suggested increased underlying consensus and corresponding business confidence that a probable PNP victory would not bring radical shifts in policy. Similarly, while there was no agreement on the best mix of measures to expand internal markets compared to international trade, acceptance that external markets must play a major role was broader than in the 1970s. While the prospects for bauxite were unclear, most Jamaicans conceded that it could no longer be relied on as the engine of Jamaica's growth. Finally, there was a consensus that more must be done to protect the poorer and more vulnerable groups during Jamaica's continuing adjustment.

FACTORS SHAPING ADJUSTMENT CHOICES AND IMPLEMENTATION

The contrasting adjustment paths pursued in the three small democracies examined in this chapter in part reflect their different economic histories prior to the 1980s and the different timing and intensity of external shocks; the result was diverse interpretations of how much reform is necessary. Within the framework of competitive democracy, variations in political institutions and informal traditions, and contrasting political coalitions also shaped adjustment paths. While external agencies played prominent roles in all three countries and Jamaica and Costa Rica received extremely high levels of aid, domestic forces ultimately determined choices and action.

The Perceived Nature of the Economic Crisis

Interpretations of the nature of the crisis strongly affected both the timing and the scope of adjustment efforts. An economic crisis is easier to recognize after the fact than while it is emerging. When economic difficulties are substantially due to single-shot events (drought, hurricanes) or trends that can plausibly be viewed as cyclical (falling prices for a key export), it may be sound economics as well as tempting politics to finance current deficits rather than take painful stabilization measures. The governments of all three nations considered in this chapter postponed stabilization in part because of diagnoses that turned out to be mistaken. Neither the Guzmán nor Carazo administrations anticipated the extent to which oil prices would rise. Guzmán was further misled by the temporary surge in sugar prices in 1981–1982 and by false hopes that a major oil discovery was imminent.[48] Carazo expected coffee prices to recover quickly. And Seaga based his early strategy largely on the expectation that bauxite/alumina exports would recover and perhaps even exceed previous peaks in the early 1970s. The pattern was similar in countries discussed in other chapters of this volume, for instance, in Zambia.

Not only the nature of the immediate economic troubles, but also the earlier performance of the economy affected interpretations of how deep-rooted and durable the crisis was, and therefore, what responses were appropriate. In all three countries, some analysts were convinced of the need for lasting reforms as well as short-run macroeconomic adjustments. But in the Dominican Republic, there was little internal pressure for reform, and the obvious economic indicators were much less worrisome than in the other two nations. As indicated in table 5.4: growth was positive and inflation moderate in all years except 1985; the fiscal and current account deficits were much smaller, and the debt burden lighter. Some exogenous shocks, such as progressive cuts in the U.S. sugar quota, were not likely to be reversed, but neither these nor ongoing equity issues excited deep concern among influential economic elites.

In Costa Rica, the record of growth and social progress before 1979 had led most people to assume the traditional development formula continued to be valid. But public debate since the mid-1970s, the abortive Carazo reform program of 1978, and the disintegration of the Central American Common Market in the 1980s prompted broader recognition of basic structural problems than in the Dominican Republic. The sputtering program of reforms pursued reflected fairly accurately the tentative recognition of the need for such reforms.

In contrast to both the Dominican Republic and Costa Rica, economic trends in Jamaica had been anything but satisfactory. By 1980, the need for major changes was widely recognized, though whether these would be mainly in government management or would entail more far-reaching restructuring of the economy was not clear.

State Capacity: The Unity and Authority of the Economic Team

The unity and authority of the economic team, key aspects of the capacity of state machinery to formulate and implement economic policies, were also important factors that shaped both the timing and the scope of adjustment choices in the three countries. In Costa Rica under Carazo, Minister of Finance Sáenz fought a lonely battle for stabilization and reform measures. The Dominican Central Bank governors under Guzmán and under Jorge Blanco until mid-1984 were in similar positions. Divided cabinets contributed to a vicious circle of uncertainty, dwindling public and business confidence, falling free-market

---

[48] Jonathan Hartlyn, "Politics of Economic Crisis," p. 5.

exchange rates, accelerating capital flight, mounting labor and business protest, and governmental paralysis. In both Costa Rica and the Dominican Republic, sustained and coherent stabilization efforts were launched only after new teams were installed, with or without a change in administration. In Jamaica, the issues of unity within the economic team and trust between the team and the chief executive were finessed: Seaga took charge of the finance portfolio and essentially acted as his own economic team.

Structural reforms demand longer-run and more basic choices and often entail wider cooperation within the government than do most elements of short-run stabilization. Few such measures ever moved onto the agenda of the Jorge Blanco government; those that did were promptly scuttled by vested interests. In Costa Rica, the initial economic team under Monge worked well together to formulate a vigorous stabilization program. But the new team assembled during spring and summer 1984 was badly split regarding longer-term growth strategy and the desirability of the neoorthodox reforms being urged by the World Bank and AID. The minister of planning had views quite different from those of Central Bank Governor Lizano; most of the remainder of the cabinet were perhaps still less persuaded of the need for reforms. Jorge Manuel Dengo, who had smoothed the political path for Castillo's stabilization measures, became ill later in Monge's term.

Indeed, the key economic analysts for the ruling PLN were probably closer in their economic judgments to their counterparts for the opposition party than to their own party cadres. These splits carried over into the Arias administration and hampered most specific reform measures under both Monge and Arias. In contrast, Seaga's strong domination of his cabinet damped serious opposition within the government regarding structural changes as well as stabilization. However, more diffuse administrative weaknesses and bureaucratic resistance slowed reforms.

Political Structures and the Centralization of Authority

The broader authority of the chief executive and his top economic officials within the government as a whole was still more important than the coherence of the economic team and the larger cabinet in shaping the scope of adjustment efforts. The political and administrative institutions of the three countries provided their chief executives with sharply contrasting degrees of authority and control over economic (and other) policy.

In Costa Rica, formal and informal features of the system normally limit the authority of the president, diffuse power widely within the executive branch and between it and the legislature, and encourage factions in the governing party.[49] The president can act alone on rather few issues; on most mat-

[49] See, for example, Ameringer, *Democracy in Costa Rica*, pp. 40ff., 49, 52, 56; Denton,

ters the constitution assigns joint responsibility to the president and appropriate ministers. The financial and administrative autonomy of the very large semiautonomous public sector hampers central control. The constitution requires an active legislative role. Because the president may not be reelected, within a year or so his party breaks into rival factions led by contenders for the party's next presidential candidate.[50] Since deputies in the Assembly are barred from immediate reelection, parties cannot enforce discipline by threatening to withhold endorsement for the next election.

These features of the Costa Rican system contributed to paralysis during Carazo's tenure, exacerbated by the fragility of his coalition and its lack of a majority in the Assembly. His own coalition virtually never voted as a bloc. While Carazo failed to put forward adequate and integrated measures, the legislature consistently thwarted the efforts he did make, for example, to adjust taxes, increase the price of oil, and float the colon. When he resorted to executive action to change the exchange rate, the legislature won a ruling from the highest court that he was not entitled to do so.

By the time the Monge government took office, the sense of crisis prompted an informal and temporary concentration of authority. The initial strong economic team encountered little opposition from the rest of the cabinet. The legislature, with a strong PLN majority, criticized but passed crucial legislation. The crisis may also have somewhat muted and postponed the usual rivalries within the PLN for nomination for the next presidential election, until Castillo, who was a prime contender, resigned from the Central Bank in February 1984. But as the crisis eased, the familar diffusion of authority reemerged and hampered later efforts at medium-term adjustment.

Under Balaguer in the late 1960s and early 1970s, authority in the Dominican Republic was highly centralized. The president exercised ubiquitous personal control over government activities, utilizing various features of the system including the provision that permitted him to allocate unexpended funds. The Reformist party (PR) was his personal vehicle.

Under the PRD governments from 1978 to 1986, authority was much more diffused. Neither Guzmán nor Jorge Blanco was strongly supported by his own cabinet. Both could count on the loyalty of only certain segments of the party. In contrast to Balaguer's Reformist party, the PRD is comparatively institutionalized and is not the instrument of a single leader. Somewhat as in Costa Rica, the party tradition barring presidential renomination limits the president's authority within the party and breeds bitter factional rivalries. During both the Guzmán and Jorge Blanco governments, the legislature was bla-

Patterns of Costa Rican Politics, pp. 34ff., pp. 95–97; Jean R. Tartter, "Government and Politics," in Harold Nelson, ed., *Costa Rica: A Country Study*, pp. 183–240.

[50] Through the mid-1970s, the PLN usually had a designated "heir apparent"; more recently, however, contests for the party's nomination have been wide open.

tantly obstructionist (exacerbated in the Guzmán years by opposition control of the Senate).

The stabilization program constructed from mid-1984 through 1985 reflected these constraints. Congress repeatedly rejected tax bills, forcing reliance on revenue-increasing measures directly within executive control. In 1985, Congress mandated wage increases without corresponding revenues. The president's veto was politically unsustainable and he was twice (in 1985 and again in 1986) forced to use one-time windfall funds within executive discretion to cover public sector wage increases.[51]

In sharp contrast with both Costa Rica and the Dominican Republic under PRD rule, the Westminster parliamentary system in Jamaica gives great power to the prime minister. Both major parties are well established. Each has suffered periods of factional strife and demoralization, but for the most part the leaders of both government and opposition parties have substantial control of party affairs and positions. The flexible timing of elections, the traditional two-term pattern, and the long tenure of party standard-bearers reinforce that authority.

Personality and leadership style can intensify or dilute these institutional factors. Seaga further concentrated authority by holding key portfolios including Finance and delegating little authority to most other cabinet members. He held JLP parliamentarians and interest groups at arm's length. The uncontested 1983 election did away with organized parliamentary opposition. In the 1970s, Manley operated quite differently, relying on extensive dialogue and sharing power more widely. The system itself permits either highly concentrated or somewhat diffused authority. (In contrast, it is difficult to imagine a Seaga-style president in Costa Rica.) Given his semimonopoly of decision-making authority, Seaga had little difficulty initiating the measures he felt necessary and appropriate.

Interest Groups, Coalitions, and Political Legacies

During the periods considered in this chapter, more circumstantial political factors—support bases, patterns of coalition politics, and political legacies—reinforced the structural contrasts in the strength of chief executives in the three countries. In the Dominican Republic, business interests are much better organized and more influential regarding economic policy than any other group. The labor unions are fragmented among competing federations and have little access to decision makers. Large industrialists and merchants concentrated in Santo Domingo had benefited greatly from Balaguer's twelve years in office and were traditionally hostile to the PRD. They were particularly

---

[51] See Ian Bell, "Political Structure" chap. 13 in *Dominican Republic*, pp. 199–248, on the Dominican political system, also pp. 98ff. on President Balaguer; Hartlyn, "Politics of Economic Crisis."

antipathetic to Guzmán, a wealthy farmer from Santiago. Shortly after he took office in 1978, the moribund National Council of Businessmen (Consejo Nacional de Hombres de Empresa [CNHE]) was rebuilt into a highly effective peak organization modeled on the aggressive Mexican Consejo Coordinador Empresarial.[52] Business interests also financed and thereby controlled many legislators. The CNHE was less confrontational during the Jorge Blanco administration, but strongly and effectively resisted measures such as increased business taxes or the introduction of a property tax. However, big business interests represented on the Monetary Board of the Central Bank did encourage the initial agreement with the IMF, and by late 1983 had come to favor a floating peso.[53]

Jorge Blanco attempted to build a coterie of supporters in the business community by manipulating resources and concessions, somewhat akin to Marcos' creation of a "crony" support base in the Philippines. Like Marcos' strategy, this provoked anger among noncrony businessmen and energetic efforts to dismantle the web of favored arrangements after Jorge Blanco left office. Unlike Marcos' case, the "cronies" strategy did not succeed in greatly strengthening Jorge Blanco's position while in office.

In Costa Rica, representation of interests was considerably less unbalanced. In addition to numerous vocal business and agricultural associations, including well-organized peak associations, the fifth of the labor force in the public sector was organized into powerful though multiple and competing unions. Nevertheless, as in the Dominican Republic, the business community was most effective in pressing its views and protecting its interests.[54] Although the Carazo government had been elected with broad support from business and agricultural interests, the government rapidly lost the confidence of the private sector. The only serious attempt of the badly divided government to cope with the crisis—the package painfully negotiated with the IMF in late 1980 and early 1981—was effectively scuttled in response to protests from a massive meeting sponsored by the chambers of industry and commerce.

Monge entered office in 1982 with contingent support from business, which hoped for better economic management, and from unions, which hoped the new president's earlier association with the international labor movement and the PLN's closer ties with labor would work in their favor. All groups blamed the Carazo government for bungling the economic crisis: the Monge government was free of blame. Perhaps more important, because the de facto devaluation of the colon occurred before the 1982 elections, Monge had the much more popular task of partly reflating and stabilizing the colon. Rapid economic improvement confirmed initial hopes that the new government would be a bet-

---

[52] Hartlyn, "Politics of Economic Crisis," pp. 5, 14, 16.

[53] *Latin America Weekly Review*, January 27, 1984.

[54] Jean R. Tartter, "Government and Politics," p. 218.

ter manager of the economy, but also confirmed widespread assumptions that there was little need for more basic reforms. The broad consensus supporting vigorous government action to contain the crisis gave way to more normal interest group pressures to regain their precrisis positions. Public sector unions, long a major pillar of PLN support, particularly resisted attempts to contain the size or reduce the privileges of state employees. Within the PLN, both ''old guard'' ideology and the political concerns of younger cadres were formidable obstacles to proposals for economic liberalization.

Seaga's initial position in late 1980 was analogous in some respects to Monge's situation in 1982: virtually all groups blamed their acute economic problems on mismanagement by the prior government and were prepared to acquiesce in Seaga's highly centralized, take-charge approach. The 1980 election in Jamaica also signaled a major shift in core support bases. Both major parties in Jamaica draw support from all strata in society. But the business and commercial communities had felt deeply threatened by the Manley government. As in the Dominican Republic, they had established an aggressive peak association, the Private Sector Organization of Jamaica (PSOJ) in the mid-1970s. These groups heavily supported Seaga. After the 1980 elections, the defeated PNP was in near total disarray for more than two years, further enhancing Seaga's power. However, by the time economic difficulties were becoming obvious in mid-1983, some of Seaga's early advantages had faded. The need for austerity measures could no longer be blamed convincingly on the prior government. The opposition PNP was pulling itself together. And as in Costa Rica, an array of well-organized and vocal interests were poised to resist both austerity and many of the government's structural reforms.

Nevertheless, not only the institutional features of the Jamaican system already described, but also certain circumstantial factors helped sustain Seaga's highly centralized authority. In particular, Manley and much of the PNP leadership were convinced of the need to present a responsible, moderate image to Jamaican business, the U.S. government, and the international financial community. Thus, they did their best to contain and halt the islandwide demonstrations of January 1985, and more generally attempted to restrain their more aggressive followers.

External Agencies' Influence

External finance, policy dialogue, and conditionality played major roles in shaping adjustment responses in the three countries considered in this chapter. The roles varied in the different countries. Within each country, external support and pressure had a variety of effects, some working at cross-purposes with others.

Dominican relations with external agencies were problematical from the start. The main actors were the IMF and AID; aside from some project assistance, the World Bank was not involved. As in Costa Rica under Carazo, only a very narrow circle supported approaching the IMF at the beginning of Jorge Blanco's term. Failure to implement the first year's targets under the phased, fairly gradual plan worked out in early 1983 with the IMF caused the Fund to stiffen its requirements for the second year, but the specific steps announced in April 1984 were not those the IMF had recommended. Nevertheless, Dominicans viewed the Fund as responsible for the measures, and nationalist anger further inflamed public reactions. Throughout the remainder of 1984, both the U.S. government and the IMF insisted that financial support would come only after the Dominican government had adopted an adequate stabilization package. The sustained financial pressure undoubtedly strengthened the hands of the new economic team designing the package in autumn 1984. It is extremely doubtful that the measures would have been adopted without the external pressure.

In both Costa Rica and Jamaica, the external financial agencies were involved far more intimately and on a much broader array of issues than in the Dominican Republic. Relationships with the outsiders, especially in Costa Rica, entailed a great deal of tension and resentment, but there was also far more dialogue and cooperation than in the Dominican case.

In contrast to the Dominican tale, the initial Costa Rican stabilization effort of 1982–1983 and the Jamaican austerity period peaking in 1984–1985 were both presented by their governments and received by the public as largely internal initiatives, forced on the nations by external circumstances but not dictated by external agencies. Outside advice and pressure increased to the extent that internal political consensus and commitment wavered. Thus the IMF played a much larger role in Costa Rica's macroeconomic management decisions after 1983, starting in February 1984 with the Emergency Economic Law and continuing through the protracted and often acrimonious discussions over successive standby agreements. AID and the World Bank were extremely active in proposing, helping to design, and pressing for specific structural reforms. The banking and currency reform legislation of August 1984, for instance, was passed only after deputies of the National Assembly were cloistered over a weekend for a marathan twenty-hour debate, while AID apparently was delaying release of promised assistance.[55]

In Jamaica, because authority was highly centralized in Seaga's hands, there was less occasion for a broad and highly publicized debate spotlighting external initiatives or pressure. Outsiders dealt primarily with Seaga and a small circle around him, and decisions were presented as the government's. Nevertheless, given an active opposition and free media, speculation regard-

---

[55] AID funds had actually been released before the bill was approved, but this was kept secret to increase leverage on the Assembly (Marc Edelman, "How Washington Bailed Out Costa Rica," in *Report on the Americas*, 19, 6 [November–December 1985]: 37–48).

ing external influence was constant. Some measures, such as privatization of public enterprises, were quite clearly linked to specific outside agencies.

In both countries, advice, technical assistance, and financial support and pressure from AID, the World Bank, and the IMF clearly affected the timing and design of many reforms. The process also strengthened the ability of the governments to formulate and implement timely macroeconomic measures and structural reforms. While that effect may appear paradoxical at first glance, it was partly the result of extensive institution-bulding efforts by the external agencies. Moreover, the very process of ongoing discussion and negotiations provided an agendum, a timetable, and an incentive for agencies within the governments to improve their own forward planning and intragovernment coordination to be better prepared to deal with external pressures and to seize the initiative. In Costa Rica, negotiations for the second structural adjustment loan with the World Bank prompted a concerted attempt at better planning and coordination.[56]

The intensity and detail of external pressures also had a less constructive effect. Particularly in Costa Rica, cross-conditionality among the major donors (and the commercial banks) and repeated disagreements and delays in financing caused recurrent crises and preempted most of the time of the small circle of senior economic officials responsible for both day-to-day macroeconomic management and more durable structural reforms. Predictably, attention to longer-run reforms suffered.

Despite the scale of aid and the small size of the countries, the Bank and AID made only limited progress pushing reforms that threatened strong interests or deeply held ideological convictions.[57] The clearest examples are probably privatization of public enterprises (pressed hard by AID in both countries); import liberalization (on which the World Bank took the leading role); and capping public sector employment in Costa Rica. Several key conditions of SAL I in Costa Rica clearly were not fulfilled. Where political leaders and senior economic officials were convinced that a key measure was essential, both governments were prepared to act regardless of predictable displeasure in Washington. Thus Costa Rica seized the initiative in partially suspending debt service pending major debt relief, and Jamaica pegged the exchange rate. Both gambles worked, in the sense that after a period of strained relations, both nations negotiated new agreements with the IMF that essentially accepted their measures, while AID and the World Bank moved ahead with their programs.

In both countries, the greatest contribution of external pressure in the long run may well be the broadened scope and heightened sophistication of internal

[56] Interviews with Costa Rican officials, Washington, D.C., late 1988.

[57] See U.S. General Accounting Office, "Foreign Assistance: U.S. Use of conditions to Achieve Economic Reforms" (Washington, D.C.: 1986) for a more positive view of the success of U.S. conditionality. The report concentrates on the period 1982–1985 and reviews experience in all three countries discussed in this chapter.

policy debate. It bears noting that in both, economic staff in the resident AID missions systematically sought to stimulate internal debate, providing informal forums for discussion and sponsoring considerable economic research.

The very volume of assistance to Jamaica and Costa Rica raises a different issue. Large-scale aid is double-edged: it simultaneously supports and eases adjustment, yet undermines the urgency of reform. The problem may be particularly marked in small democracies. Both government officials and the general public in small countries view themselves as powerless to change substantially the international political and economic setting. But they recognize that their small scale makes them relatively inexpensive to help and support. Small democracies, and perhaps especially those in the U.S. sphere of influence, are prone to believe that they have a special moral claim on assistance, that they will not be permitted to fail. The attitude is a deterrent to self-help, a special kind of moral hazard.

The pattern clearly is relevant in both Jamaica and Costa Rica. Costa Rica was (and is) the showcase of democracy in Central America, under threat from Sandinista incursions. Jamaica was the "prodigal son" and potential showcase of free-market principles in the Caribbean. Concessional aid to Costa Rica averaged $95 per capita and 6.9 percent of GDP over the four years from 1983 through 1986; the parallel figures for Jamaica from 1981 through 1986 were $79 per capita and 7.2 percent of GDP.[58] In retrospect, many observers and some of those involved in the assistance programs in the two cases believe that the high levels of financial support constituted disincentives for reform. The generous aid to Jamaica in 1981–1982, it is now argued, provided a breathing space but also permitted postponing necessary measures while increasing the debt burden. In Costa Rica, the conviction that the United States would not desert such an attractive small democracy undercut efforts to liberalize trade and shrink public expenditures, including direct and indirect agricultural and industrial subsidies. At the same time, large-scale aid carries insidious overtones of political dependence.

Large-scale financing and intensive involvement may carry a more subtle cost from the perspective of the external agencies themselves, particularly the World Bank. Once an agency is extremely heavily invested in reforms in a specific country, its own reputation for effectiveness is on the line. In this sense, World Bank involvement in Jamaica and Costa Rica may be similar to its involvement in Ghana, discussed in Callaghy's chapter in this volume. In all these cases, the external agency itself comes to have a vested interest in effective reform in the country, perhaps impairing objective assessment and flexible reactions.

Both Costa Rica and Jamaica are likely to continue close ties with the

---

[58] World Bank, *World Development Reports* (Washington, D.C.: World Bank, 1985, 1986, 1987, 1988), Statistical appendix tables on "Official development assistance: receipts."

United States. But several factors suggest that the era of massive aid and intensive policy intervention may be waning. Among these factors are budget pressures in the United States, somewhat improved prospects for substantial debt relief, electoral shifts in Jamaica, and possible reduced tensions in Central America. Less aid and policy intervention will shift responsibility for charting development strategy and pursuing reform more fully to the governments and people of Costa Rica and Jamaica. That shift is appropriate, but will test their ability to forge at least a partial consensus.

POLITICAL CONSTRAINTS AND EVOLVING CONSENSUS IN SMALL DEMOCRACIES

We turn now from comparisons among the three countries to the clues they provide regarding economic adjustment in democracies more generally. Some effects of competitive democracy on economic policies are well recognized. The approach of elections swells public expenditures and prompts governments to postpone unpopular reforms.[59] The Costa Rican central government deficit jumped from 1.25 percent of GDP in 1985 to 4.45 percent in 1986.[60] In the Dominican Republic, fiscal discipline also loosened with the approach of the 1986 elections. In Jamaica, growing pressure for municipal elections almost surely influenced Seaga's decision in autumn 1985 to freeze the exchange rate, and election concerns were obvious in the inflated initial budget for 1986–1987 and the "growth budget" of 1987–1988. More broadly, the electoral cycle limits politicians' time horizon for planning reform strategy, particularly in fixed-term systems. In Costa Rica, it is commonplace to observe that any significant structural change must be well launched within the first months of a new administration, before maneuvering begins for the next election. The one-term rule also undermines continuity and experience within the bureaucracy. Jamaica's more flexible election timing and two-term tradition offers the executive more leeway.

The prospect of elections also serves as a safety valve, channeling disaffection into legal channels and encouraging patience, as in Jamaica from early 1985 to the 1989 elections. Even in Costa Rica, had the crisis reached its 1982 proportions earlier in Carazo's term, reactions might have been more explosive.

Where parties alternate in power, previous experience and the prospect of regaining power combine to promote realism in major opposition groups, in economic policy as in other matters. Again Jamaica illustrates the point: PNP positions (and debate within the party itself) give much greater weight to mac-

[59] Barry Ames, *Politics and Survival: Politicians and Public Policy in Latin America* (Berkeley: University of California Press, 1987), pp. 9–33, for example.

[60] International Monetary Fund, *International Financial Statistics* (Washington D.C.: International Monetary Fund, 1988), "Government Finance," p. 157.

208   ·   Chapter Five

roeconomic considerations and the need to maintain the confidence of both the
international financial community and domestic business interests than during
the 1970s.

Adjustment Tactics in Democracies

Electoral and institutional contraints might be expected to affect the tactics
and approaches used to implement unpopular policies in established democracies, as contrasted with authoritarian systems. The most obvious assumption
is that democracies will turn less readily to repressive measures, and therefore,
will have to rely more heavily on consultation and persuasion, partial compensation, and perhaps obfuscation to prevent or contain opposition. More
broadly, political competition might be expected to increase attention to equitable allocation of the costs of adjustment.

Yet the three cases considered in this chapter suggest that democracies can
employ very different tactics and styles to manage the political challenges of
adjustment. Costa Rica largely fits the democratic stereotype. One of the hall-
marks of the Costa Rican political system is its emphasis on consultation and
persuasion; indeed, impatient external agencies tended to feel this approach
hamstrung reform. As one small recent example, in response to farmers' demonstrations in mid-1988 protesting cuts in large agricultural subsidies, six
commissions were established with representation from all interested parties
to explore all dimensions of the planned changes.[61]

The Costa Rican governments also have been strongly concerned to protect
vulnerable groups and to allocate the burdens of adjustment equitably. The
Monge government initially asked workers to tighten their belts further: a
wage freeze and longer hours were promptly announced. Real wages continued to fall throughout 1982, and several lengthy strikes were put down without
concessions. But in September 1982, a form of partial wage indexing was
approved by the Assembly that provided for periodic adjustments to cover the
rising cost of a basic basket of twenty-one commodities (later repeatedly expanded). As noted earlier, other wage adjustments coupled with the dramatic
decline in inflation boosted average real wages in 1983 considerably faster
than GDP, with lower-paid workers making the greatest gains.[62]

In addition, during the harshest period of adjustment, a temporary food aid
program distributed monthly packets to some 40,000 needy households designated by local committees. The program probably was particularly helpful
in reaching the unemployed and self-employed who could not benefit from

[61] Economist Intelligence Unit, *Quarterly Reports*, 1988, no. 4, p. 17.
[62] Fields, "Employment and Growth," p. 23, calculates the average increase as 15 percent.
Victor Hugo Cespedes, Alberto Di Mare, and Ronulfo Jiménez, *Costa Rica: Recuperación sin
reactivación* (San José: Academia de Centroamerica, 1985), p. 71, gives the figure as over 10
percent.

wage increases. Other measures partly intended to protect the poor included highly subsidized credit (at 12 percent interest) for smaller farms and cattle ranchers. The government bargained hard and successfully with the IMF to permit this to continue. The poor had suffered most as Costa Rica's economy collapsed after 1979, but the Monge government's stabilization program sought to shift more of the burden to the middle classes.[63]

In contrast, the painful Dominican decisions of spring 1984 included little attention to political tactics, other than timing the announcement of the transfer of food imports to the free exchange rate during Holy Week, when a great many people were on vacation. The government itself was too divided to make consultation and persuasion credible. According to some accounts, Jorge Blanco's earlier attempts to explain the situation often sounded muddled and unconvincing, and key economic team members added to the confusion with conflicting and ill-considered comments.[64] Though low-grade staples were exempted from the price increases announced in April 1984, the measures were certainly seen as bearing mainly on the poor and lower-middle classes.

The April riots prompted considerably more attention to tactics from mid-1984 through the announcement of the January 1985 policy package. Jorge Blanco toured the country during the summer to explain the need for stabilization. Both the August 1984 and January 1985 policy packages included "sweeteners" for poorer and particularly middle-class groups: for example, prices for bottled gas for household use were increased much less than rates for large commercial users. A deal was arranged with jitney cab drivers of Santo Domingo permitting them to increase fares as soon as gas prices rose. Preemptive measures were taken before announcement of both packages; labor leaders and prominent leftist politicians were detained, and soldiers patrolled the streets.[65] The tactics did forestall immediate violence and permitted stabilization measures to take effect. But strikes and protest continued throughout 1985, even after the initial adverse impact of the measures was eased by slowed inflation.

In Jamaica, Manley's government during the 1970s had strongly emphasized consultation and participation. In sharp contrast, Seaga was convinced that extensive consultation would merely intensify complaint and slow or deflect necessary reforms. Even the Bustamente Industrial Trade Union (BITU)

[63] Probably in good part because of extensive U.S. aid, the impact on middle and upper–middle class living standards in absolute terms was not very harsh. The president of the Central Bank was cited as stating that in practice, for professional and business classes, austerity meant "vacationing in Costa Rica itself rather than Florida, and maintaining an automobile for a few years longer rather than buying a new one" (U.S. General Accounting Office, "Foreign Assistance: U.S. Use of Conditions to Achieve Economic Reforms," [August 1986], pp. 26–27). The effects on young people seeking housing and employment were more serious.

[64] Dauhajre, "Dominican Economy," p. 23.

[65] Interviews with members of the economic team during the Jorge Blanco administration, Santo Domingo, March 1987.

federation linked to the ruling JLP lacked access, though BITU president Hugh Shearer was appointed deputy prime minister. Limited contact through the Joint Trade Union Center faded after the first two years. Intimidated by the government's hard-line approach and by court decisions interpreting strikes as abandonment of jobs, the number of strikes dropped dramatically after 1983.[66] Business associations also felt they had little voice in decisions.[67]

Equity and protection of vulnerable groups also received less emphasis in Jamaica under Seaga than in Costa Rica under Monge. The task was also harder in the context of protracted economic decline and accelerating inflation between 1983 and 1986 in contrast to Costa Rica's rapid turnaround in 1983. Increases in the minimum wage, tax relief, and partial rent controls were among the measures used to try to protect the poor and near-poor. But the main focus was pricing policies for staple foods. Under the dual exchange rate in effect from 1981 to late 1983, the Jamaica Commodities Trading Corporation (JCTC) imported staples at the official exchange rate, thereby constituting an implicit subsidy. When the exchange rate was reunified in November 1983, the JCTC shifted to explicit subsidies. Many of these were reduced or removed in the 1984–1985 budget, but the JCTC continued to monopolize imports of a few key commodities and to enforce ceilings on retailers' markups for these items. To partly compensate for the withdrawal of explicit food subsidies, a food aid program was announced in mid-1984, providing milk and a fortified ''nutribun'' for school children and food stamps for the very poor, the elderly, and pregnant and nursing mothers with young children. But the level of benefits was very low, and the program initially encountered administrative problems.[68] Explicit price controls were reintroduced in 1986–1987, covering a wider range of foods.

[66] Stone, "Political Trends," pp. 32–33.

[67] Seaga's handling of income tax reform was an interesting exception to his usual nonconsultative pattern. A "blue ribbon" public commission representing all major interests was set up to review technical staff's proposals for a radical overhaul of the system. The commission proved remarkably effective in reversing initial skepticism and opposition from almost every quarter (Interview with Roy Bahl, director of technical assistance for the reform). But this particular reform was inherently suited to a multifaceted consultation process; all groups had vested interests in the existing system, and all, therefore, had to give up some advantages to achieve the broader gains of the proposed reform: increased simplicity and equity. When one or a few groups bear the brunt of reform, compromise is harder.

[68] See Derick Boyd, "The Impact of Adjustment Policies on Vulnerable Groups: The Case of Jamaica, 1973–1985," in Giovanni Andrea Cornia, Richard Jolly, and Frances Stewart, *Adjustment with a Human Face*, vol. 2, *Country Case Studies* (Oxford: Clarendon Press for UNICEF, 1988), pp. 140ff., for a description of the program. Food stamps for rice, cornmeal, and skim milk were provided in the amount of J$20 every two months.

Although this was only a small increment for most fairly poor households, survey data indicate it may have boosted buying power of the very poorest rural recipients by as much as 10 percent. See Barbara Diane Miller and Carl Stone, "Household Expenditure Effects of the Jamaican Food Stamp Programme," Maxwell School, Syracuse University and Board of Revenue, Government

These various measures were not adequate to protect low-income Jamaicans from the stagflation gripping the economy from 1983 on. Prices of necessities rose faster than the general price level despite the subsidies. Between December 1983 and July 1985 the costs of a basic basket as determined by the Ministry of Health rose by two-thirds. Households at the bottom of the income scale could no longer afford even the basic basket.[69] Falling real incomes and living standards were exacerbated by deteriorating education and health services. Hardships for the poor seemed more bitter because the wealthy and upper middle class strata were much less harmed. Indeed, many seemed to benefit from liberalization of the economy. Satellite "dish" antennae were sprouting in Kingston gardens. As of May 1986, Carl Stone's survey data showed that even among JLP supporters, only 4 percent thought their party defended the interests of the poor.[70] As pressures for general elections increased, the JLP image of indifference to the "little man" became ever more damaging politically. When the economy finally began to improve in 1986, and as the international community became increasingly concerned about the social costs of adjustment in developing countries, Seaga entered discussions with the World Bank for a massive program of social sector rehabiliation, which would benefit both middle and poorer strata.

The differences between the three small democracies in consultation and persuasion, partial compensation, and concern for equity in the course of adjustment suggests caution in generalizing about the effects of regime type. Established democratic institutions make unlikely any strong reliance on simple repression. But in the short run, competitive party systems guarantee neither the inclination nor the skill to use persuasion, engage in consultation, or design partial compensation to manage political pressures associated with adjustment. In the longer run, what may prove crucial is economic outcomes and the distribution of costs and gains.

Peter Katzenstein's analysis of the politics of economic adjustment in small Western European democracies is suggestive regarding the requirements of effective adjustment over longer periods. Since the 1930s, the Scandinavian nations, Austria, Switzerland, the Netherlands, and Belgium have adjusted their small open economies to rapid international change. Emphasis and details vary, but all have maintained open trade regimes. All have used state intervention to promote a middle course of incremental adaptation to changes in technology and the international environment, rather than either laissez-faire or drastic state-guided solutions. All have relied on extensive compensation of adversely affected groups. For the most part, this combination of measures has been highly successful in achieving and maintaining high stan-

---

of Jamaica, Jamaica Tax Structure Examination Project (staff paper no. 36, Syracuse and Kingston, August 1987) for an evaluation of program impact.

[69] Boyd, "Impact of Adjustment Policies," p. 198.

[70] Stone, "Political Trends," table 5, pp. 26–27.

dards of living and minimizing social conflict, despite these nations' open economies and vulnerability to external changes.

Katzenstein identifies several key features of social and political structure and tradition that have facilitated this pattern of adjusting to larger international forces.

> Concentration of political power in a fairly small number of decision makers (strong "oligarchic" tendencies)
>
> Interest groups organized into strong peak associations, helping to ensure that agreements reached among elites are accepted by the rank and file within each sector
>
> Overlapping governmental and business elites with a great deal of informal communication
>
> Close cooperation between government and all major interest groups in formulating policy
>
> A pervasive ideology of social partnership, resting less on social homogeneity than on a sense of shared vulnerability, underpinning the above[71]

Like the countries Katzenstein examined, Costa Rica, Jamaica, and the Dominican Republic are characterized by "oligarchic" decision making and by overlapping, extensive informal communication between business and political elites. But interest groups are generally less centralized. Labor federations in Costa Rica and the Dominican Republic are fragmented rather than centralized; Jamaica with its two strong federations more closely approaches Katzenstein's description. All three countries have peak business associations, but these may be less inclusive and have less influence over their own members than in the European democracies.

It is the sense of social partnership that most clearly distinguishes Katzenstein's cases from those here, with the exception of Costa Rica. That sense, Katzenstein suggested, grew out of the perception of acute vulnerability that emerged in the small European democracies in the 1930s and 1940s. Shared threat generated a consensus that domestic quarrels were "a luxury in a hostile and dangerous world."[72] In the postwar era, intensified international competition perpetuated that conviction.

The Dominican Republic clearly lacks these elements of the "small European democracies model." Most government and business elites feel no urgent need for major economic reforms, nor is there much evidence of any sense of social partnership. Costa Rica boasts a strong ideology of social partnership quite similar to the attitudes Katzenstein described. But, until very recently, that ideology was not harnessed to a sense of economic threat and

[71] Peter J. Katzenstein, *Small States in World Markets: Industrial Policy in Europe* (Ithaca, N.Y.: Cornell University Press, 1985).
[72] Katzenstein, *Small States*, p. 30.

vulnerability. As the implications of regional and global changes become clearer and, perhaps, as the comfortable assurance of indefinite U.S. aid comes into question, a broader consensus on the need for reforms may emerge.

Jamaica entered the 1980s deeply divided. But the experiences of the past dozen years may be modifying views in Jamaica. The desire never to return to the polarization of the late 1970s is widely shared and intense, a recognition of the high costs of unbridled social conflict. There is also, especially since early 1985, the recognition that bauxite is unlikely to serve again as the engine of the Jamaican economy. Without bauxite Jamaica's options are severely constrained. Partly converging views plus the shared sense of threat could generate a more collaborative search for solutions to Jamaica's dilemmas, solutions that seek a balance between economic efficiency and equity.

CHAPTER SIX

The Political Economy of the Philippine Debt Crisis

Stephan Haggard

THE POLITICS OF CRISIS, STABILIZATION, AND ADJUSTMENT

IN THE 1950s, the Philippines held greater economic promise than any developing country in the region. By the 1980s, Philippine economic performance had been surpassed not only by Korea and Taiwan, but by the Southeast Asian countries with comparable economic structures: Thailand, Malaysia, and Indonesia. In 1984 and 1985, the Philippines experienced the most wrenching stabilization episode in the region. Coming to power in 1986, the new democratic government of Corazon Aquino faced daunting economic as well as political problems, including the rehabilitation of the state-owned banking and public enterprise sectors, deregulation of agricultural markets, and land reform.

Diagnoses of the Philippines' economic crisis are plentiful. One view holds that it was the culmination of a long-standing pattern of import-substitution industrialization (ISI), compounded in the short-run by macroeconomic mismanagement.[1] A second view, advanced by the government of Ferdinand Marcos at the time, blames external shocks.[2] Critics on the left have argued that the country's problems stem from the adoption of outward-oriented policies at

In addition to the members of this project, I thank Houchang Chehabi, Rick Doner, Gary Hawes, Ted James, Bruce Koppel, Jamie Mackie, Robert Stauffer, Mark Thompson, Rigoberto Tiglao, Penny Walker, and David Wurfel for their assistance and comments on earlier drafts. Particular thanks are due to Robert Dohner, who shared his excellent manuscript with me and helped with a number of data problems. Rosan Siongco provided me with first-rate research assistance. In addition to the generous grants from the Ford and Rockefeller Foundations that financed this project, the Council on Foreign Relations assisted my research on privatization.

[1] General criticism of this sort is the theme of John H. Power and Gerardo P. Sicat, *The Philippines: Industrialization and Trade Policies* (New York: Oxford University Press, 1971); Robert E. Baldwin, *Foreign Trade Regimes and Economic Development: The Philippines* (New York: Columbia University Press, 1975); Romeo M. Bautista, John H. Power and Associates, *Industrial Promotion Policies in the Philippines* (Manila: Philippine Institute for Development Studies, 1979); Robert Dohner and Ponce S. Intal, Jr., "The Marcos Legacy: Economic Policy and Foreign Debt in the Philippines," in Jeffrey D. Sachs, ed., *Developing Country Debt and Economic Performance Vol. III: Country Studies* (Chicago: University of Chicago Press, in press), hereafter cited as "Marcos Legacy." Citations are to pages and chapters of the unpublished ms., National Bureau of Economic Research, Cambridge, Mass., 1988.

[2] See Dante B. Canlas et al., *The Philippine Economic Crisis: A Workshop Report* (Quezon City: University of the Philippines, School of Economics, June 1984), (heareafter cited as *Workshop Report*), for an examination of this argument.

the behest of the World Bank and IMF.[3] These three views each have some merit. Import substitution stunted export growth and crucial adjustment decisions were delayed, but these policy choices must themselves be explained. The Philippines did face severe external shocks, but other countries did too and managed better economic performances. The country's economic policies were influenced by the World Bank and IMF, but it is misleading to argue that Marcos opted for an outward-oriented development strategy.

This study analyzes the Philippine debt crisis by focusing on the relationship between domestic political structures, international bargaining, and economic policy choice during Marcos' lengthy rule and the first eighteen months of Aquino's presidency. Political coalitions and constraints on state capacity were closely intertwined with shifts in political structure.

The political system constructed by Marcos during the period of martial law conforms to an ideal-type I have called the "weak" authoritarian regime.[4] Unlike the bureaucratic-authoritarian governments of Latin America, such as Chile or Brazil, or the developmental states of East Asia, such as Korea,[5] "weak" authoritarian governments exhibit a number of political characteristics that limit their capacity to pursue coherent economic policies.

The first of these is the development of a class of "crony" capitalists dependent on preferential policies: the grant of monopoly powers, protection, guaranteed finance, and government contracts. Though cronyism in the Philippines was largely associated with private firms, it is also possible to think of the managers of state-owned enterprises in weak authoritarian regimes as crony capitalists. The creation or strengthening of domestic capitalist classes

[3] See Walden Bello, David Kinley and Elaine Elinson, *Development Debacle: The World Bank in the Philippines* (San Francisco: Institute for Food and Development Policy, 1982). See S. K. Jayasuriya, "The Politics of Economic Policy in the Philippines during the Marcos Era," in Richard Robison, Kevin Hewison, and Richard Higgot, eds., *Southeast Asia in the 1980s: The Politics of Economic Change* (Sydney: Allen and Unwin, 1987), pp. 80–112 an excellent study that critiques this perspective from the left.

[4] See Stephan Haggard, "The Politics of Adjustment: Lessons from the IMF's Extended Fund Facility," *International Organization* 39, 3 (Summer 1985): 505–34; Stephan Haggard and Robert Kaufman, "The Politics of Stabilization and Structural Adjustment," in Jeffrey D. Sachs, ed., *Foreign Debt and Economic Performance: Selected Issues* (Chicago: University of Chicago Press, in press). This formulation profited from the writings of Thomas Callaghy, particularly *The State-Society Struggle: Zaire in Comparative Perspective* (New York: Columbia University Press, 1984), chap. 1, pp. 3–80.

[5] See Guillermo O'Donnell, *Modernization and Bureaucratic Authoritarianism: Studies in South American Politics* (Berkeley: Institute of International Studies, University of California, 1973), for the original statement of the bureaucratic-authoritarian model; David Collier, ed., *The New Authoritarianism in Latin America* (Princeton, N.J.: Princeton University Press, 1979). See Stephan Haggard and Tun-jen Cheng, "The State and Foreign Capital in the East Asian NICs," in Fred Deyo, ed., *The Political Economy of the New East Asian Industrialism* (Ithaca, N.Y.: Cornell University Press, 1987), on the role of the developmental state in the economic development of the East Asian newly industrializing countries.

through state intervention or the creation of state-owned enterprises is certainly not unique to "weak" authoritarian regimes. Nor is rent seeking or corruption, though corruption in the Philippines reached unusual proportions. What distinguishes business-government relations in weak authoritarian regimes is the *personal stake* of the executive in the crony enterprise, and *the resulting breakdown of the boundary separating the public and private spheres*.

The second feature of weak authoritarian regimes, and one also characteristic of many populist democracies, is a broader network of patronage extending beyond those with immediate personal ties to the executive. In contrast to more "insulated" authoritarian regimes, such as Chile, which develop ideological, institutional or repressive means of social control, weak authoritarian governments rely heavily on instrumental, patron-client networks to cement societal support. Patronage systems assumed particular importance because of the continued importance of electoral politics, a curious feature of many authoritarian polities in the developing world. In the Philippines, martial law removed legal and congressional checks on presidential power, and Marcos was not averse to repression of the opposition. Like many authoritarian rulers, however, Marcos never achieved a legitimating formula or party structure that would institutionalize his rule. Quite early, Marcos sought to "normalize" political life through a controlled opening to opposition activity and elections. As he did, cronyism and patronage grew.

A third feature of weak authoritarian regimes concerns the *capacity* of the state, rather than its constituent base or the nature of political rule. In the ideal-typical bureaucratic-authoritarian or developmental state, economic technocrats ally with military elites, thus gaining independence from political constraints and the power to act decisively. The "new" authoritarianism differed from the old in that it emerged among the most advanced developing countries, and thus a threshold of bureaucratic capability was assumed.[6] Technocrats championed policies that had long-term benefits, but involved short-term political costs difficult to impose under democractic auspices. These included stabilization and a variety of market-oriented reforms. By allying with the technocrats, the military legitimated its rule—or at least softened opposition—by delivering economic performance.

In weak authoritarian regimes, by contrast, the power of the technocrats is circumscribed. This may happen because the bureaucracy lacks the personnel to implement certain types of policy. This is the crucial question of state capacity, particularly evident in the low-income African cases discussed by Callaghy in his study for this volume. Frequently, however, the technocrats are politically marginalized in the decision-making process. This may happen in one of three ways. Particularly in low-income developing countries, the num-

---

[6] O'Donnell, *Modernization and Bureaucratic-Authoritarianism*, pp. 79–87.

ber of technocrats may simply be insufficient to exert sustained influence on decision-making. Their programs may also be undermined by conflicts within the bureaucracy that the executive cannot or will not resolve. In the Philippines, liberal technocrats clashed with "import-substituting technocrats" drawn from the private sector; similar conflicts are also visible in bureaucratic-authoritarian regimes under stress, like those in Mexico described by Kaufman (see chapter 3). Finally, the executive can circumvent the technocrats through discretionary power over economic policy, such as presidential decrees that bypass the formal policy-making machinery or direct control over key implementing ministries. Technocrats may gain autonomy from interest group and legislative pressures under authoritarian rule, but they do not necessarily gain independence from the executive.[7]

These characteristics of Philippine authoritarianism help explain a number of aspects of the early 1980s' crisis. First, the growth of the crony sector increased the vulnerability of the entire economy to external shocks. Protection and disequilibrium financial markets encouraged rent seeking and the misallocation of resources, but the discretion inherent in cronyism added an additional layer of distortion. The preferential loans extended to crony firms encouraged inefficient investment and financial overextension. As the size of the crony sector expanded, the financial system as a whole became increasingly fragile, ultimately undergoing a crisis in 1981 that severely weakened state-owned banks and public finances.

Second, cronyism, the instrumental basis of Marcos' rule, and the high level of executive discretion combined to weaken auditing, oversight, and planning functions. Institutional checks on spending were effectively removed. The rapid expansion of the state-owned enterprise sector was the most important result of weak central control. After the lifting of martial law in 1981, the economy also became vulnerable to the electoral economic cycles that were typical of the premartial law period.

A third source of both political and economic vulnerability was the gradual disaffection of the noncrony private sector. The private sector largely supported the imposition of martial law, but over time, noncrony capitalists became vulnerable to a predatory state and the rise of the crony sector. The government could destroy firms through prejudicial policies, discretionary "taxation," extortion, and the redefinition of property rights. The result was increasing uncertainty, loss of confidence, a decline in productive investment, capital flight, and finally, open political opposition. Domestic business was not the only source of opposition, but the defection of the private sector created a particular bind for the regime that helps explain the policy vacillation following the Aquino assassination in August 1983. Maintaining private sec-

[7] Eliza Willis, "The State as Banker: The Expansion of the Public Sector in Brazil" (Ph.D. diss., University of Texas, 1986), pp. 25–30, makes this important point.

tor confidence was critical for short-term balance-of-payments management and longer-term growth, but business demands gradually included fundamental political reforms.

Finally, I follow Callaghy in chapter 7 in giving particular attention to how the dualistic policy-making structure of weak authoritarian regimes affects external relations with banks and multilateral institutions. Under an umbrella of strong political support from the United States, the Philippines developed close relations with the World Bank and IMF.[8] Commercial banks also considered the country an excellent risk. Agreements reached with the technocrats did not necessarily reflect political commitments, however. On the contrary, at a number of important junctures, the technocrats served the function of legitimating the system of economic management to external creditors.

Such a dualistic system is vulnerable to credibility crises. Within two months of the assassination of Benigno Aquino in August 1983, the country suffered an acute balance-of-payments crisis and suspended debt payments. The draconian nature of the stabilization program ultimately adopted was not solely a function of the depth of the balance-of-payments crisis; rather, it reflected a changed political relationship with sceptical external actors, who tightened conditionality, increased surveillance and demanded policy reform as a prior condition of further support.

The government of Corazon Aquino raises a different set of analytic issues, particularly the conditions under which new democracies can launch economic reform. Aquino came to office with a broad mandate, a buoyant revival of internal and external confidence, and the constitutional powers to act decisively. Unlike Argentina and Brazil, the Philippines faced its stabilization crisis prior to the transition to democratic rule. Aquino thus had the good fortune to preside over a fairly strong economic recovery and a relaxation of external constraints. The very economic difficulties and corruption associated with government intervention under Marcos and the broad political support and extraordinary constitutional powers Aquino enjoyed allowed the government to initiate structural reforms.

As with other democratic governments navigating the transition from authoritarian rule, however, the Aquino administration sat atop a diverse political coalition, ranging from portions of the military and the church hierarchy, to technocrats, businessmen, and the urban middle class, to social democrats and human rights activists. (For similar descriptions, see Kaufman on Brazil and Argentina; Stallings on Peru; Callaghy on Nigeria.) More importantly, the economic team was split between technocrats and businessmen on the one hand, and those pushing more fundamental social reform. Despite her populist

[8] Bello, Kinley, and Elinson, *Development Debacle*, pp. 41–66; Robin Broad, *Unequal Alliance: The World Bank, the International Monetary Fund, and the Philippines* (Berkeley: University of California Press, 1988), pp. 20–56.

image abroad and new freedom for the left to organize, the new government's economic strategy was fundamentally conservative. Aquino sought a rapprochement with the noncrony private sector and external creditors, granted new freedom to market-oriented technocrats, and proved unable or unwilling to confront the entrenched power of large landholders.

Given these preferences and the conflicts within the antiauthoritarian coalition, where could the new democracy successfully implement reform? Successes were most apparent where reform disenfranchised those closely associated with the previous regime, where the measures were within the immediate administrative power of the government, and where the reform was not politicized within the ruling coalition. Reform was more limited where it confronted "legitimate" opposition not tied to the previous regime, where prolonged implementation placed demands on a weak and divided bureaucracy, and where the reforms engaged divisions between market-oriented liberals and those advocating a more statist or populist line. Critics frequently underestimate the extent of change under Aquino and other new democratic leaders. It is true, however, that continuities in administrative capacity and social structure in new democracies are likely to place fundamental limits on reform.

The next section of this study outlines some historical features of the Philippine political economy and examines briefly the transition to martial law rule. The following sections discuss economic policy from 1972 through 1980, including the growth of cronyism and examine the period from 1981 through the end of the Marcos era in February 1986. I distinguish three crisis phases: a financial crisis that begins in 1981; the balance-of-payments crisis in 1983; and the stabilization episode in 1984–1985. The final section provides an overview of the Aquino administration's economic policies.

THE PHILIPPINE POLITICAL ECONOMY IN HISTORICAL PERSPECTIVE

The Philippines differ from other Southeast Asian countries and from Korea and Taiwan in the presence of a class of large landowners and the particularly decentralized nature of political power. Local and regional patron-client systems served as the building blocs of the Natonalist and Liberal parties, which were "quite identical—with respect to the social, occupational, and regional sources of their support as well as to their policies."[9] Elite affiliations with the two national parties were fluid and party organization was weak. Interest groups cultivated both parties in the struggle over the congressional pork bar-

---

[9] See Carl Lande, *Leaders, Factions and Parties: The Structure of Philippine Politics*, Yale University Southeast Asia Studies monograph series no. 6 (New Haven, 1965), p. 2. Lande was the first proponent of this view.

rel that dominated national politics.[10] Access to government resources provided independent bases of political power for members of Congress and the president, but given the nature of the political system, even centralizing presidents relied on patronage.

The centrifugal pressures from rural-based elites, the importance of patronage politics, and the relative weakness of the executive help explain several features of the postwar Philippine political economy. First, in contrast to Korea and Taiwan, rural elites were politically positioned to resist land reform, though at the cost of armed rural movements of which the current insurgency is only the most recent example. Second, Congress strongly opposed taxation of real property, and the size of the government was comparatively small. The instrumental basis of political competition contributed to a third feature of the policy system: a vulnerability to political business cycles.[11]

An important puzzle is how a political system dominated by rural-based elites generated an import-substituting policy regime. As with Taiwan, Korea, and the countries of Southeast Asia, postwar ISI was initially stimulated by controls imposed in response to balance-of-payments difficulties.[12] These controls and an overvalued exchange rate encouraged the formation of new domestic commercial and manufacturing enterprises, as well as foreign investment. Urban industrial interests gained a more important role in national politics through their ability to finance costly election campaigns for the presidency and upper house.[13] The decline in the relative power of purely agricultural elites, such as the sugar lobby, was thus a factor in explaining the emergence of ISI. A number of conditions muted overt sectoral conflict, however.

[10] See Amando Doronila, "The Transformation of Patron-Client Relations and Its Political Consequences in Postwar Philippines," *Journal of Southeast Asian Studies*, 16, 1 (March 1985): 99–116; Kit Machado, "Changing Aspects of Factionalism in Philippine Local Politics," *Asian Survey*, 11, 12 (December 1971): 1182–99; David Wurfel, "Elites of Wealth and Elites of Power: The Changing Dynamic," *Southeast Asian Affairs 1979* (Singapore: Institute of Southeast Asian Studies, 1979), pp. 233–45 on the transformation of patronage over time.

[11] See Baldwin, *Foreign Trade Regimes*, pp. 12–13, on the political economy of the 1949 election; Frank H. Golay, *The Philippines: Public Policy and National Economic Development* (Ithaca, N.Y.: Cornell University Press, 1961), pp. 95–96, on the 1957 election; Harvey A. Averich, John Koehler, and Frank Denton, *The Matrix of Policy in the Philippines* (Princeton, N.J.: Princeton University Press, 1971), pp. 98–109, for a more general test that finds evidence of an electoral business cycle over the 1960s.

[12] See Golay, *Philippines*, pp. 78ff., on the effects of American legislation. The Tydings-McDuffie Act of 1934, established the timetable for Philippine independence that was interrupted by the war. The Philippine, or Bell, Trade act of 1946 passed immediately prior to independence amended the Tydings-McDuffie Act. This legislation imposed a free trade and payments regime and a fixed exchange rate system, but a foreign exchange crisis in 1949 led to exchange controls and licensing. The Laurel-Langley agreement of 1955 guaranteed national treatment of U.S. foreign investment, but granted the country the right to increase tariffs.

[13] See Doronila, "Transformation of Patron-Client Relations," pp. 99–116; Wurfel, "Elites of Wealth," pp. 233–45.

Rural elites were effectively compensated by their ability to capture the benefits of government expenditure in the countryside and by their preferential access to the U.S. market for sugar and coconut oil. Links also developed between ''new'' commercial and financial enterprises launched by members of
old elite families and the manufacturing sector, in which Chinese entrepreneurs played a crucial role.[14]

By the late fifties, the corruption associated with trade and exchange controls became the target of political opposition, not only from the sugar lobby
and technocrats, but even from manufacturers. With the support of the IMF,
the government gradually liberalized the trade and exchange rate regime and
devalued between 1960 and 1962.[15] Traditional exports responded to the
changed incentives and investment flowed into agriculture, but industrial
growth slowed over the first half of the 1960s. The austerity and inflation in
food prices associated with the stabilization episode resulted in increased
strike activity and labor militancy.

Whatever its economic merits, the decontrol episode was a political failure
and produced demands for a more nationalist economic policy, including demands from the private sector. On taking office in 1966, Ferdinand Marcos
staked his political reputation on increased government spending on rural infrastructure, a relaxation of credit to the industrial sector, and a more deliberate state intervention in the ISI process.[16] The Board of Investments (BOI) was
created to support preferred areas of investment, furthering the development
of Manila-based manufacturing and financial interests, and cementing their
political relations with the executive. Marcos' policies increased budget and
current account deficits and foreign borrowing and forced the reimposition of
exchange and trade controls beginning in 1967.[17] Following a pattern discern-
able prior to the elections of 1957, 1961, and 1965, monetary and fiscal poli-

[14] John J. Carroll, *The Filipino Manufacturing Entrepreneur* (Ithaca, N.Y.: Cornell University
Press, 1965), chaps. 4, 5, pp. 60–147; and Dante Simbulan, ''A Study of the Socio-Economic
Elite in Philippine Politics and Government, 1946–1963'' (unpublished Ph.D., diss. Australian
National University, 1965), stress the integration, if not unity of the old and new elites. New
research underlines the importance of the Chinese in the manufacturing sector; see Yoshihara
Kunio, *Philippine Industrialization: Foreign and Domestic Capital* (New York: Oxford Univer-
sity Press, 1985), pp. 82–107.

[15] See Robert F. Emery, ''The Successful Philippine Decontrol and Devaluation,'' *Asian Survey*, 3, 6 (June 1963): pp. 274–84 on the short-term success of the decontrol period. Power and
Sicat, *Industrialization and Trade Policies*, pp. 38–50, offer an economic assessment. Florian
Alburo and Geoffrey Shepherd, ''Trade Liberalization: The Philippine Experience'' (Paper prepared for the World Bank Project on the Timing and Sequencing of Trade Liberalization Policy,
1986), chap. 2, offer an overview of the political economy of the decontrol.

[16] See Romeo B. Ocampo, ''Technocrats and Planning: Sketch and Exploration,'' *Philippine
Journal of Public Administration* 15 (January 1971): 31–64 on the rise of the technocrats under
Marcos.

[17] See Baldwin, *Foreign Trade Regimes*, chap. 4, pp. 65–83 on the Marcos administration's
economic policies prior to martial law.

cies in 1969 were highly expansionary. Marcos was reelected, but a foreign exchange crisis ensued. The government devalued in early 1970 under an IMF stand-by and commercial debt was rescheduled. The IMF program increased the prominence of technocrats, particularly in the Central Bank and led to the formation of a Consultative Group for the Philippines and a deepening involvement on the part of the World Bank and the IMF in the country's economic policy.

During his first two administrations, Marcos used patronage, rural infrastructure investment, and the new industrial policy to build a new political coalition and to expand the power of the executive at the expense of Congress.[18] These efforts to centralize power polarized the political system. Centralization naturally put him into conflict with congressional political elites and the oligarchy.[19] A left-nationalist urban political opposition criticized government corruption, poor economic performance, increasing income disparities, and continuing dependence on the United States. During the ''first quarter storm'' of 1970, students protested violently against electoral fraud, Philippine involvement in the Vietnam War, and the corruption of the convention called to rewrite the constitution. Though urban labor was weakly organized, the late 1960s saw an increase in strike activity and growing militancy among segments of the urban working class and poor. Secessionist and leftist insurgents posed an increasing challenge to the government in the countryside.[20]

On September 21, 1972, Marcos declared martial law. Robert Stauffer has argued that martial law was a prerequisite for a new, more outward-oriented development strategy.[21] Expanding the power of the liberal technocrats and opening the country to foreign investment, imports, and a greater role for the IMF and World Bank demanded taming the nationalist opposition within and outside of Congress. In fact, continuity in economic policy was greater between the pre- and postmartial law periods than Stauffer suggested. Foreign investment increased in the years immediately following the declaration of

[18] See Doronila, ''Transformation of Patron-Client Relations,'' p. 115, on rural patronage; Richard Doner, ''Domestic Coalitions and Japanese Auto Firms in Southeast Asia: A Comparative Bargaining Study'' (Ph.D. diss., University of California, Berkeley, 1987), chap. 5, on the Progressive Car Manufacturing Program and the origins of cronyism.

[19] Robert Stauffer, *The Philippine Congress: Causes of Structural Change*, Sage Research Paper 90–024, vol. 3 (Beverly Hills, 1975), pp. 14–21.

[20] See Jose Lacaba, *Days of Disquiet, Nights of Rage* (Manila: Salinlahi Publishing House, 1982), for a compelling account of the political events that preceded martial law; Justus M. van der Kroef, ''Communism and Reform in the Philippines,'' *Pacific Affairs* 46, 1 (Spring 1973): 29–58, on the link between the insurgency and the declaration of martial law.

[21] See Robert Stauffer, ''Philippine Authoritarianism: Framework for Peripheral 'Development,' '' *Pacific Affairs* 50, 3 (Fall 1977): 365–86; idem, ''The Political Economy of a Coup: Transnational Linkages and Philippine Political Response,'' *Journal of Peace Research* 11, 3 (1974): 161–77; idem, ''The Political Economy of Refeudalization,'' in David A. Rosenberg, ed., *Marcos and Martial Law in the Philippines* (Ithaca, N.Y.: Cornell University Press, 1979), pp. 180–218.

martial law, but policy remained quite restrictive.[22] If the coup was staged to launch a liberalizing project, one would expect protected domestic business to be sceptical and the land-based elite supportive. Import-substitution interests that were not the object of immediate attack by the government were strongly supportive of the coup, though, and members of the old elite were among Marcos' most vocal opponents.

Short-term economic conditions are more helpful in understanding regime change. As with the authoritarian installations in Argentina, Brazil, and Chile, the imposition of martial law occurred following a period of economic crisis and popular sector mobilization. There are noteworthy differences between the Philippines and the Latin American bureaucratic-authoritarian cases, however. In Latin America, new military governments pursued conservative economic programs, curbed inflation by targeting wages and budget deficits, and imposed market-oriented reforms. Marcos, by contrast, sought to blur the left-right distinction and promised initiatives that had a nationalist, antioligarchic and even populist cast, including land reform and the promotion of domestic industry.

The imposition of martial law is best understood in political as well as economic terms. The growth of urban and rural unrest provided an opportunity for Marcos by increasing the ambivalence of traditional politicians and the middle class who might otherwise have opposed martial law more actively. Important instances of urban violence used to justify martial law were, in fact, staged by the government.[23] The target of the coup was as much the traditional political elite as the left, and the closing of Congress was not an altogether unpopular act. Politicians in Congress and the constitutional convention and other elected officials were prominent among the initial martial law detentions.[24] Martial law would allow Marcos to consolidate his political power against an established elite through discretionary control of economic policy and the further restructuring of patron-client networks around the executive.

[22] Primitivo Mijares, *The Conjugal Dictatorship of Ferdinand and Imelda Marcos* (San Francisco: Union Square Publications, 1986), p. 408. In his gossipy memoir, Mijares, a confidant of the Marcoses, claimed that Marcos used the need to protect American property as an argument for martial law in his conversations with the American ambassador. See Raymond Bonner, *Waltzing with a Dictator* (New York: New York Times Books, 1987), prologue, pp. 3–7, and chap. 5, pp. 92–11; Carl Lande, "Authoritarian Rule in the Philippines: Some Critical Views," *Pacific Affairs*, 55, 1 (Spring 1982): 86; on U.S. knowledge of the coup. Mijares, *Conjugal Dictatorship*, p. 6, has Mrs. Marcos claiming that Nixon gave his "personal blessings" to the coup. According to Mijares, however, she also said that Nixon endorsed the coup "because he might find need for a model which he could adopt later on in the United States." Jayasuriya, "Politics of Economic Policy," pp. 104–10 provides a critique of the "externalist" hypothesis and a neat summary of the domestic political landscape.

[23] See Bonner, *Waltzing with a Dictator*, p. 100, on the staging of violence prior to the martial law announcement.

[24] John H. Adkins, "Philippines 1972: We'll Wait and See," *Asian Survey* 13, 2 (February 1973): 147.

ECONOMIC POLICY UNDER MARTIAL LAW 1973–1980

The Growth of the State and the Limits of Reform

The dramatic growth of the state during the martial law period served political as well as economic purposes. The creation of more centralized planning agencies concentrated resources at the center and weakened local government.[25] The use of the military for community development and law enforcement increased under martial law and provided Marcos an additional instrument of political control, patronage, and support.[26] Officers assumed positions as local officials, particularly in areas threatened by insurgency, and played a role in the development of Marcos' political party, the New Society Movement or KBL (Kilusang Bagong Lipunan). Finally, Marcos established a hierarchy of local (*barangay*), provincial, and national advisory councils, though these never developed into the corporatist system he envisioned.

The creation of the National Economic Development Authority (NEDA) appeared to provide an institutional locus for market-oriented reformers. NEDA's first director, economist Gerardo P. Sicat, defended martial law as a progressive "revolution from the top." Martial law would arrest the "social cancer" of the "false democracy" dominated by the oligarchy, in part through land reform.[27] Technocrats never achieved dominance within the economic bureaucracy, however. Industrial promotion was centered on the Board of Investments and Ministry of Trade and Industry, both of which maintained close links with the import-substitution private sector. Land reform was predictably modest in scope, excluding, for example, all sugar and coconut lands. Above all, the power of the formal decision-making machinery was limited by Marcos' discretionary control over the budget, the authority to make law through presidential decrees, letters of instruction, and a network of appointees in implementing agencies, including the Central Bank.

Limited capacity to extract resources remained a basic weakness of the martial law regime, but this weakness was initially concealed by favorable international price trends. The boom in international commodity prices of the early 1970s raised trade tax revenues and relieved Marcos from the constraints of

---

[25] Among the new institutions created were the Department of Local Government and Community Development and the National Economic Development Authority (NEDA). The share of local government expenditure in total government outlays dropped from 16 percent in 1972 to 9.5 percent in 1977. See Mohd. A. Nawawi, "Political Participation during the First Five Years of the New Society in the Philippines," *Journal of Southeast Asian Studies* 13, 2 (September 1982): 270–78 for an overview of the institutional changes.

[26] Felipe Miranda, "The Military," in R. J. May and Francisco Nemenzo, eds., *The Philippines After Marcos* (London: Croom Helm, 1985), pp. 90–109.

[27] Gerardo P. Sicat, *New Economic Directions in the Philippines* (Manila: National Economic Development Authority, 1974), chaps. 1, 2, pp. 1–31.

the 1970 stabilization plan.[28] In 1970, government expenditures as a share of GNP stood at 9.9 percent; by 1975, this had increased to 15.1 percent, with the growth wholly attributable to "capital expenditure" (from 1.8 percent to 5.0 percent of GNP) and "economic services" (from 1.5 percent to 4.5 percent of GNP).

With the oil shock and collapse of commodity prices, balance of payments pressures resurfaced, foreign borrowing grew, and IMF and World Bank involvement in the country increased. The programs of the late 1970s suggest that the influence of these organizations on Philippine economic policy was both more spotty and less orthodox than some analysts have suggested.[29] The multilateral agencies supported an expansion of the state's role and imposed only very light conditionality on the management of public resources.[30] A number of politically difficult structural reforms urged on the Philippines by the multilateral agencies were simply not implemented.

The IMF's involvement included an Extended Fund Facility agreement (2 April 1976–1 April 1979), the stand-by that followed in June 1979 and the two-year stand-by negotiated for 1980–1981. The EFF contained standard targets for inflation and the balance of payments, but also an ambitious investment program in the energy sector and reforms of tax and trade policy. In contrast to the rationalization of trade policy or raising revenue, the expansion of the public sector promised immediate political benefits. In an effort to emulate the heavy industry push in Korea and Taiwan, Minister of Industry Roberto Ongpin packaged a number of large investment projects into a major policy initiative in September 1979. The "Eleven Major Projects" carried an estimated price tag of $6 billion. By the time the projects were announced, World Bank enthusiasm for state investment had waned: "Unless [the projects] are financed solely by direct foreign investment, [they] would reduce by a very substantial margin the already limited scope for flexibility in the management of public finances and the balance of payments."[31] The size of the projects was far beyond any reasonable expected inflow of direct investment, however, which peaked at $216 million in 1977 and became very erratic thereafter. In 1980, disinvestment was $102 million.[32] A substantial portion of project costs were, therefore, met through foreign borrowing (table 6.1).

[28] Dohner and Intal, "The Marcos Legacy," Table 1.4, p. 380, for data on the growth of government.

[29] Contrast Bello, Kinley, and Elinson, *Development Debacle*, pp. 127–64, and Broad, *Unequal Alliance*, 162–71, with S. K. Jayasuriya, "Politics of Economic Policy," pp. 104–10.

[30] See World Bank, *The Philippines: Priorities and Prospects for Development* (Washington D.C.: World Bank, 1976), p. 31. For example, the World Bank argued in 1976 that "the Philippine economy will require even more participation by public corporations than in the past, not only by public utilities . . . but also by public enterprises in such areas as fertilizer production, steel making, and shipbuilding."

[31] "Marcos Pushes $6 bn Projects," *Financial Times*, 3 January 1980, p. 4.

[32] Data provided by the Central Bank.

TABLE 6.1
The Evolution of Philippine External Debt, 1972–1987

	Total Debt Outstanding ($U.S. billions)	Public[a] (%)	Short-Term[b] (%)	Debt Service Ratio[c] (%)
1972	2.73	42.1	14.5	26.4
1973	2.88	43.5	12.2	19.9
1974	3.75	43.7	12.1	14.6
1975	4.93	46.5	12.8	18.4
1976	6.76	53.3	14.0	17.2
1977	6.56	57.6	14.6	14.5
1978	10.69	62.9	15.4	20.1
1979	13.35	66.2	18.5	20.1
1980	17.25	66.8	20.8	20.8
1981	20.89	69.4	24.6	25.2
1982	24.67	69.4	25.5	38.1
1983	25.81	73.5	21.1	38.2
1984	25.41	76.0	21.4	43.4
1985	26.25	75.2	17.6	36.9
1986[d]	28.25	77.0	10.9	34.0
1987	28.64	80.2	6.9	35.3

Source: Dohner and Intal, "Marcos Legacy," tabs. 6.1, 6.2, 6.5.

[a] Public nonmonetary debt, including IMF obligations, as a share of total nonmonetary debt.

[b] Share of nonmonetary debt with maturity of one year or less.

[c] Total debt service of interest and principal as percentage of exports of goods and services.

[d] The classification system for nonmonetary debt differs slightly beginning in 1986. The figures for 1986 and 1987 therefore, are roughly, but not strictly, comparable to those for earlier years.

It is difficult to disentangle the effects of poor management, bad luck, and corruption on the state-owned enterprise sector, but it is clear that patronage and political intervention weakened monitoring and control.[33] Assuming it could secure an initial budget appropriation, any ministry could create an enterprise simply by listing it with the Securities and Exchange Commission. These companies could create their own subsidiaries. Between 1972 and 1984, the number of state-owned enterprises increased from 70 to 245, not counting those acquired through default. Mrs. Marcos' Ministry of Human Settlements, a notorious patronage machine, accumulated seventy-three subsidiaries. Once formed, a subsidiary's capital budget was determined internally and outside financing could be sought. Subsidiaries were subject to less cumbersome rules for disbursement and audit than their parents. In 1984, less

[33] See Stephan Haggard, "The Philippines: Picking Up After Marcos," in Raymond Vernon, ed., The Promise of Privatization (New York: Council on Foreign Relations, 1988), pp. 91–121; the following paragraphs on the public sector draw on this study.

than two-thirds of all government corporations were audited. Public corporations were also exempt from the personnel rules and pay scales governing the regular civil service, and served as a source of income for cabinet members, military officers, and cronies. In a listing by the Commission on Audit in 1985, thirty-nine persons were board directors of ten or more state companies, and an additional thirty-two had betweem five and nine directorships.

The ability of the government to borrow reduced the incentives to undertake reforms sought by the IMF, which concluded that progress in the structural aspects of the program was not evident.[34] The tax reform inaugurated under the EFF was particularly important because it would reconcile the objectives of increasing public investment while reducing the rate of increase of foreign borrowing. Marginal income tax rates were high, but the collection rate was extremely low. The corporate tax code was riddled with special exemptions. The system thus depended heavily on regressive indirect taxes and trade taxes that reinforced the bias against exports. Finance Minister Cesar Virata admitted that the delay of the tax reform in 1977 was tied to the election for an Interim National Assembly (Batasang Pambasa) in April 1978, but there was no progress on tax reform after the election either. During the period of the EFF, total tax revenue as a share of GNP remained roughly constant; and dropped steadily from 1980 through 1984.[35]

It is difficult to draw a strong causal link between politics and the decision to pursue a countercyclical response to the second oil shock; most developing countries placed the same bet. Nonetheless, difficult choices concerning adjustment strategy overlapped with a controlled opening of the political system and an expansion of opposition activity.[36] Prior to 1977, Marcos ruled by plebiscite. The elections for an Interim National Assembly in 1978 began a period of "normalization," with frequent elections (table 6.2). In 1978, opposition efforts were hamstrung by factional differences and disagreements over whether they should participate in elections at all. These divisions, Marcos' control over the media and tight restrictions on opposition campaign activity resulted in a virtual sweep for the KBL. On 15 December 1979, Marcos made the surprise announcement that there would be snap elections on 30 January 1980 for governors, vice governors, mayors, vice mayors and provincial, city,

[34] International Monetary Fund, "Supplementary Material for Prolonged Use of Fund Resources," 4 May 1984, as cited in Mark Thompson and Gregory W. Slayton, "An Essay on Credit Arrangements Between the IMF and the Republic of the Philippines: 1970–1983," *Philippine Review of Economics and Business* 22, nos. 1 and 2 (March–June 1985): 65; Broad, *Unequal Alliance*, pp. 222–28.

[35] Virata's comments were made to the *Asian Wall Street Journal*, 15 August 1979, p. 35; Dohner and Intal, "The Marcos Legacy," table 2.7, p. 396, data on tax revenues.

[36] On the emergence of the opposition, see Lela Garner Noble, "Politics in the Marcos Era," in John Bresnan, ed., *Crisis in the Philippines* (Princeton, N.J.: Princeton University Press, 1986), pp. 70–113; Robert L. Youngblood, "The Philippines in 1981: From 'New Society' to 'New Republic,'" *Asian Survey*, 22, 2 (February 1982): 226–35.

and barangay councilors. These positions had grown into a complex structure of patronage and central political control and were also swept by the KBL. One year later, Marcos announced that martial law would be lifted. Amendments to the constitution created a mixed presidential-parliamentary system along French lines, but Marcos retained an array of discretionary powers. A national plebiscite confirmed these constitutional changes, martial law was lifted on 17 January 1981, and the presidential election was held on 16 June 1981, boycotted by the major opposition groups.

The decision to borrow through the second global oil shock was accepted by the IMF. The performance criteria for the two-year stand-by covering 1980 and 1981 included limits on medium- and long-term foreign borrowing, but this cap simply encouraged shorter-term borrowing, which accelerated dramatically in 1980 and 1981 (see table 6.2). Ceilings on credit to the public sector and international reserves in the banking system were exceeded before the first review of the program in the summer of 1980, and no agreement was reached on the exchange rate despite evidence of overvaluation. Nonetheless, the program was not cancelled.[37]

TABLE 6.2
Chronology of Major Philippine Political Events of the Marcos Period, 1973–1986

15 January	1973	Indirect plebiscite on martial law constitution
15 July	1973	Plebiscite on continued martial law rule
27 February	1975	Plebiscite on continued martial law rule
16 October	1976	Plebiscite on constitutional changes
17 December	1977	Plebiscite on constitutional changes allowing Marcos to seek presidency
7 April	1978	Elections for Interim Batasang Pambasa
15 January	1980	Gubernatorial and mayoral elections
17 January	1981	Martial law lifted
7 April	1981	Plebiscite on constitutional changes
16 June	1981	Presidential election
17 May	1982	Barangay elections
27 January	1984	Plebiscite on constitutional changes
14 May	1984	Elections for Batasang Pambasa
7 February	1986	Presidential election

[37] Thompson and Slayton, "Essay on Credit Arrangements," pp. 67–73.

World Bank efforts to promote structural reform in the Philippines expanded after 1979. The main purpose of the first structural adjustment loan
(SAL) in 1980 was to improve the performance of the industrial sector and
promote exports by reducing and equalizing tariffs, lifting foreign exchange
restrictions, and reversing the exemptions that had crept back into the tariff
system following a reform in 1973.[38] Robin Broad's account of the bureaucratic politics of the trade reform showed how resistance from the Central
Bank and Import Office to the trade policy reforms was circumvented through
an alliance between the World Bank and technocrats in the ministries of finance (Cesar Virata), industry (Roberto Ongpin), and NEDA (Gerardo Sicat).
Their victory became "Manila's most talked about power play," and is used
by Broad to demonstrate the influence of the transnational alliance between
the World Bank and the technocrats.[39]

In fact, trade reform efforts revealed the *limits* on the power of the liberal
technocrats and their multilateral supporters. Nationalist technocrats continued to advance an import-substituting program, Marcos extended special tariff
exemptions to crony firms, and in 1983, an array of controls were reimposed
over the objection of the World Bank.[40] It is thus inaccurate to argue, as Bello
and others have done, that the Bank succeeded in "dismantling" ISI and
launching an export-oriented program.[41] The incentives to import-substitution
were hardly dismantled, and the government's commitment to export promotion was limited. Export enclaves such as the Bataan export-processing zones
remained just that; enclaves within an inward-oriented economy. Exchange
rate policy in no way reflected a commitment to exports; the real effective
exchange rate was virtually unchanged between 1972 and 1982. Most importantly, the dominant political coalition was not built around exports, as it was
in Korea and Taiwan.[42] Ongpin's commitment to heavy industry suggests the
continuing commitment to ISI within the bureaucracy, while cronyism funneled resources into the nontraded and import-substituting sectors. Policy interventions in agriculture undermined traditional exports.

Exports grew and diversified in the early years of martial law, but the share

[38] World Bank, "Program Performance Audit Report: Philippines First and Second Structural
Adjustment Loans," World Bank Operations Evaluation Division, report no. 5813 (Washington,
D.C., 31 July 1985) p. 4; Bautista, Power and Associates, *Industrial Promotion Policies*, which
was extremely influential within the government; Alburo and Shepherd, "Trade Liberalization,"
p. 131.

[39] Broad, *Unequal Alliance*, pp. 81–90.

[40] Alburo and Shepherd, "Trade Liberalization," p. 177.

[41] The World Bank's own optimistic assessments are partly responsible for the belief that the
Philippines had fundamentally changed course. See for example, Barend de Vries, "Transition
Toward More Rapid and Labor-Intensive Industrial Development: The Case of the Philippines,"
World Bank Staff Working Paper no. 424 (Washington, D.C., October 1980); Bello, Kinely, and
Elinson, *Development Debacle*, chap. 5, pp. 127–164; Broad, *Unequal Alliance*, pp. 178–201.

[42] Robert T. Snow, *The Bourgeois Opposition to Export-Oriented Industrialization in the Philippines* (Manila: Third World Studies Center, University of the Philippines, 1983).

of exports to GDP remained roughly constant over the 1970s and early 1980s and was the same in 1985 as it had been in 1950. As shown in table 6.3, this was in large part attributable to a steady deterioration in the Philippines' terms of trade over the 1970s. While terms of trade losses and higher interest payments were responsible for expanding the current account deficits and increasing debt, the Philippine experience must be viewed comparatively and attention paid to the domestic response. The external shocks of 1979–1982 were only slightly worse for the Philippines than the average for one sample of thirty developing countries.[43] Thailand closed larger investment gaps, government and current account deficits than the Philippines over the 1970s, and experienced similar external shocks from 1979 to 1982, but incurred a smaller foreign debt and grew more rapidly.[44] Domestic demand continued to grow at a relatively high rate despite a worsened external environment, and measures were not taken to control public sector deficits, adjust the exchange rate, and respond to the harder terms of foreign loans. To understand why demands a closer examination of domestic political structures, including the growth of cronyism.

The Rise of Cronyism

Defining and measuring cronyism presents a number of problems. The popular image of cronyism is the direct raiding of the public treasury.[45] Marcos did

TABLE 6.3
Philippine Export Performance under Martial Law

	Exports/GDP	Current Account/GDP	Export Quantum Index	Terms of Trade
1972	13.1	−0.1	100.0	100
1975	14.5	−5.6	101.9	88
1978	14.2	−4.9	152.6	78
1980	16.4	−5.4	201.3	69
1982	12.6	−8.1	215.0	59
1984	16.7	−3.5	199.4	60
1985	14.1	0.0	195.0	56

Sources: World Bank, *Philippines: A Framework for Economic Recovery* (Washington, D.C.: World Bank, 1987), pp. 76, 77, 79.

[43] Bela Balassa and F. Desmond McCarthy, "Adjustment Policies in Developing Countries, 1979–1983: An Update," World Bank Staff Working Paper no. 675 (Washington, D.C., 1984), p. 3.
[44] This point is also made in Canlas, *Workshop Report*, p. 13. See World Bank, "The Philippines: A Review of External Debt," report no. 4912-PH, 2 Nov. 1984, p. 3, on the role of external shocks; Eli M. Remolena, Mahar Mangahas, and Filologo Pante, Jr., "Foreign Debt, Balance of Payments and the Economic Crisis of the Philippines in 1983–1984," Report to the Group of Twenty-four, UNCTAD/MFD/TA/32/Add. 6 (16 July 1985), pp. 1–6.
[45] For overviews of cronyism see Belinda Aquino, *The Politics of Plunder: The Philippines*

authorize transfers from state-owned banks and the Central Bank for personal
purposes, such as his wife's shopping sprees, but cronyism *as a system* rested
on personal policy favors extended to firms in which Marcos and his family
frequently participated directly. Three areas of activity were central to the development of cronyism: the monopolization of key agricultural markets; the
development of conglomerates in protected and nontraded goods sectors
through the extension of preferential finance and government contracts; and
the opportunities provided by control of foreign borrowing, aid, and direct
investment.

A government sugar monopsony was formed in 1974 in an effort to capture
the benefits of rising world prices.[46] The trading company incurred large losses
when the sugar market turned down in 1975–1976. In 1977, trading responsibilities and previous losses were transferred to the National Sugar Trading
Corporation (NASUTRA). NASUTRA was regulated by the Philippine Sugar
Commission, headed by a close associate of Marcos. High marketing margins
and easy access to finance for the construction of mills resulted in large transfers to NASUTRA.

The effect of government intervention in the coconut sector was even more
wide-ranging.[47] After rice, coconuts are the most important crop in the Philippines, accounting for nearly one-fifth of all farms in the country. Government intervention began prior to martial law with the passage of a levy on
producers to finance integration into milling. In 1973, the Philippine Coconut
Authority monopolized export functions and increased the levy in order to
stabilize prices. The stabilization fund purchased the United Coconut Planters
Bank (UCPB) to finance a rationalization scheme. The bank gained control of
milling through the United Coconut Oil Millers (UNICOM), received the deposits from the stabilization fund interest free, and expanded into unrelated activities. These included the controversial purchase of a controlling interest in San

Under Marcos, College of Public Administration, University of the Philippines Occasional Paper
No. 87–1 (Quezon City, Philippines, 1987); Mijares, *Conjugal Dictatorship*, chaps. 7, 8, pp.
187–233; Patricia Mamot, *The Aquino Administration's Baptism of Fire* (Manila: National Book
Store, 1987), chap. 1, pp. 2–134, which outlines the activities of the PCGG; John F. Doherty, *A
Preliminary Study of Interlocking Directorates* (Manila: Regal Press, 1979); Anonymous, "Some
Are Smarter than Others" (mimeo., 1979), published by a foreign business group. "Some are
smarter than others," was the reply given by Mrs. Marcos to a reporter when asked about the
enrichment of friends and relatives under martial law. Marcos also used martial law powers to
extort assets from his political enemies. See Mijares, *Conjugal Dictatorship*, pp. 196–204, on the
attack on the Lopez family's property.

[46] See *Workshop Report*, 72–94 on the broader problem of monopolies; On sugar, see Gary
Hawes, *The Philippine State and the Marcos Regime: The Politics of Export* (Ithaca, N.Y.: Cornell University Press, 1987), chap. 3, pp. 83–101.

[47] On coconuts see Hawes, *Philippine State*, chap. 2; Rigoberto Tiglao, "The Political Economy of the Philippine Coconut Industry," Third World Studies Center, Commodities Studies no.
1 (mimeo., Quezon City, 1980), pp. 55–82.

Miguel enterprises in 1981, a move demonstrating the power of the cronies over noncrony entrepreneurs.

Government intervention in sugar and coconuts was characteristic of cronyism. In both cases, key institutions were managed by close Marcos associates and the lines between public regulatory agencies and private ventures blurred. The cronies enjoyed easy access to credit, but their operations escaped audit. Not only did the ventures provide political funds, but state intervention undercut the power of traditional politicians in the two industries by creating new sectorial "czars."[48] In both cases, intervention increased inefficiency and transferred resources away from producers.

The growth of Herminio Disini's business empire provides an example of the methods used to create crony firms in the manufacturing and service sectors.[49] In July 1975, a presidential decree imposed a 100 percent tax on the import of cigarette filters, but extended an exemption to Disini's Philippine Tobacco Filters Corporation that closed Disini's principal competitors and gave him a virtual monopoly on the local market for tobacco filters. His other interests included a 500,000-acre logging concession granted him by Marcos and a number of manufacturing enterprises acquired with "behest loans" from state-owned banks made at Marcos' personal request.

Government control over foreign borrowing and investment provided additional opportunities for the cronies. Disini borrowed abroad on the basis of guarantees from the Philippine National Bank to take over the Caterpillar tractor distributor. The guarantees were extended personally by Marcos on grounds of national security, over Finance Minister Cesar Virata's objections. Disini received "commissions" for securing a highly controversial nuclear reactor contract for Westinghouse, from which Marcos personally received an estimated $80 million.[50] A consortium led by Disini was awarded major construction contracts on the plant, though Disini had no prior experience in construction.

The size of the crony sector defies accurate measurement. The Presidential Commission on Good Government (PCGG) was established by Corazon Aquino to trace illicitly accumulated wealth.[51] By January 1987, it had sequestered 268 companies accused of prospering illicitly from connections with the Marcoses. These enterprises were valued at $1.5 billion, but did not include all the properties of the Marcoses or the wealthiest cronies.[52] Capital

[48] Hawes, *Philippine State*, p. 82.

[49] See Aquino, *Politics of Plunder*, p. 37, on Disini.

[50] See "Westinghouse's Nuclear Fiasco," *Fortune*, 1 September 1986, pp. 38–46 on the nuclear reactor project; *New York Times*, 7 March 1986; p. A1.

[51] On the activities of the PCGG see Mamot, *Baptism of Fire*, chap. 1; *Business Day*, 19 January 1987.

[52] See *Manila Times*, 17, 21, 22, 28, 31 July 1987, on the suits. A number of alleged cronies were still negotiating the status of their property with the Aquino government in 1988. Suits filed

flight is also a poor measure of Marcos and crony holdings. Estimates of capital flight do not include *domestic* assets acquired illicitly, and the share of capital flight that can be attributed to the cronies is unknown.[53]

The structure and operation of the financial system provide some clues to the extent of cronyism.[54] During the marital law period, the four major government-owned financial institutions captured a growing share of the total assets of the financial system, and another eight financial institutions were considered "political banks" with special access to Central Bank rediscounting. These twelve banks accounted for 53 percent of the assets of the commercial banking system. In a memo from Central Bank Governor Jaime Laya to Marcos on the crisis facing the Development Bank of the Philippines in 1983, Laya revealed that forty-four of eighty-seven nonperforming accounts larger than $5 million were made at the personal request of Marcos.[55]

After the failure of crony firms in 1981 and 1982, it became clear that a substantial share of the $5.5 billion of nonperforming assets of the state-owned banks, perhaps as high as one-fourth, were loans to inefficient crony operations.[56] Capital-intensive government projects contributed to the inefficiency of investment, but as the Westinghouse case showed, these were related to the crony system. One measure of the efficiency of investment is the incremental capital output ratio (ICOR); the ratio of the share of investment in GDP to the GDP growth rate—the lower the ICOR, the less investment required to achieve an increment of output. The Philippine ICOR for 1974–1980 was 17 percent higher than Korea's, 29 percent higher than Malaysia's, 31 percent higher than Thailand's, and 69 percent higher than Indonesia's. Moreover, the ICORS showed an accelerating upward trend: 5.22 in 1980; 6.72 in 1981; 8.24 in 1982, and a staggering 22.55 in 1983.[57]

CRISIS AND RESPONSE 1981–1985

The relationship between cronyism, politics, and economic decision making can be clarified by analyzing the economic crisis of the early 1980s. The crisis

---

in mid-1987 sought properties valued at over $10 billion, but these figures were probably inflated. On the relatively meagre amounts of money actually turned over to the government by the PCGG, see "Tainted Watchdogs," *Far Eastern Economic Review* (cited hereafter as *FEER*), 17 September 1987, pp. 22–25.

[53] Robert Dohner, "Capital Flight" (unpublished ms., Fletcher School, March 1987). The most careful estimates place total capital flight from 1970 through 1985 at $16.7 billion. While these are higher than some domestic estimates (*Business Day*, 1985 February 2), they suggest that some of the higher estimates of Marcos's externally held wealth are almost certainly exaggerated.

[54] See for example, Canlas et al., *Workshop Report*, pp. 65–72.

[55] Jaime Laya to President Marcos, "Development Bank of the Philippines" (Memorandum 11 August 1983), p. 2.

[56] *Business Day*, 8 September 1986.

[57] Report to the Group of Twenty-four, UNCTAD, p. 33.

unfolded in three stages. A financial crisis in 1981 led to a massive bailout of failing firms, many of them crony operations. Central Bank rescue operations and budgetary contributions to state-owned banks compounded the effect of external shocks on the balance of payments (table 6.4). Conflicts within the government between the technocrats and Marcos' political advisers diluted adjustment efforts. The assassination of Benigno Aquino on 21 August 1983 opened the second phase: the balance-of-payments crisis proper. On October 17 the country announced that it could not meet its debt obligations and declared a ninety-day moratorium. Facing regular demonstrations by the "parliament in the streets," the gradual defection of the private sector, and crucial elections, the administration resisted stabilization. The third phase began after the May 1984 elections. Under escalating external pressure, the government undertook a stabilization plan that paved the way for an agreement with the IMF and rescheduling with the banks.

From Financial Crisis to Debt Crisis

On January 9, 1981, a prominent Chinese businessman named Dewey Dee skipped the country, leaving corporate and personal debts totalling between $65 and $100 million.[58] Several investment houses declined to roll over debt as usual, resulting in runs on other investment houses and Chinese banks. The

TABLE 6.4
Philippine Economic Crisis Indicators, 1980–1985

	1975–1979	1980	1981	1982	1983	1984	1985
Real GNP Growth	6.4	5.0	3.4	1.9	1.1	−7.1	−4.1
Inflation[a]	9.9	17.6	12.4	10.4	10.0	50.3	24.9
Current Account/GNP	−4.6	−5.4	−5.4	−8.1	−8.1	−3.5	0.0
Fiscal Deficit/GNP[b]		3.0	5.7	5.4	3.2	2.8	2.2
Unemployment[c]		8.1	8.9	9.5	7.9	10.6	11.1
Capital Formation[d]		30.7	30.7	28.8	27.5	19.2	14.3

Source: All data from Dohner and Intal, "Marcos Legacy," p. 384, except unemployment rates from World Bank, *Philippines: A Framework for Economic Recovery* (Washington, D.C., World Bank, 1987), p. 73.

[a] Consumer price index, yearly average.

[b] Consolidated public sector deficit. Consolidated public sector balances include the deficits of the public sector corporations, which averaged 2.5 percent of GNP between 1979 and 1983.

[c] October of each year.

[d] Gross domestic capital formation/GNP.

[58] The following draws on coverage by the *FEER*, 30 January, 6 February, 13 February, 13 March, 3 April, 1 May, 31 July, and 4 September 1981.

crisis coincided with downturns in commodity prices and an increase in interest rates caused by a deregulation of the financial sector in 1980.[59] The new Central Bank governor, Jaime Laya and Finance Minister Cesar Virata sought to calm the financial markets by announcing a plan to lend to banks and investment houses. In April, the government also extended assistance to nonfinancial companies affected by the recession and financial uncertainty.[60]

The crony companies were among the largest firms seeking assistance. The Development Bank of the Philippines (DBP) and the Philippine National Bank (PNB) were increasingly involved in deals that converted loan exposure into equity.[61] The initial size of the industrial assistance fund was set at P1.5 billion ($190 million), to be expanded to P5 billion ($635 million) over two years. In June, the government announced that the entire P5 billion would be made available. That same month, the Construction and Development Corporation of the Philippines (CDCP), a crony construction firm and the sixth largest firm in the country in total assets, sought an injection of P1.5 billion *for itself alone*. Between 1981 and 1983, the government funneled P6.2 billion into CDCP, an amount equal to 30 percent of total tax collections in 1983 and roughly two percent of GNP. In 1983, P4 billion of those loans were converted from debt to equity. Herminio Disini's Herdis Group and various firms owned by Ricardo Silverio, including Delta Motors, also faced consolidation. Aggregate figures on the size of the bailout are difficult to obtain, but equity held by the two major state-owned banks and the National Development Corporation totaled about P11 billion, to which must be added approximately P3.8 billion of additional government expenditure.[62]

The crisis ultimately marked the downfall of a number of the most important industrial cronies, but at tremendous cost to public finances and to the overall credibility of economic decision making. In an effort to reverse perceptions, Marcos elevated Finance Minister Cesar Virata to the concurrent position of prime minister following the presidential elections in June. By the summer of 1981, however, the sixteenth IMF stand-by was clearly in trouble as a result of the surge in government spending associated with the plebiscite, the presidential election and the Dewey Dee bailout. Government contributions to state-owned banks and the operating losses of other state-owned enterprises produced large budget deficits for 1980 and 1981 and a surge in the government's short-term borrowing.

[59] See Broad, *Unequal Alliance*, pp. 128–61 on the financial reform. World Bank and International Monetary Fund, *The Philippines: Aspects of the Financial Sector* (Washington, D.C.: World Bank, 1980), pp. 70–83 spells out the objectives of the multilateral institutions.

[60] "A Blue Chip Goes Begging," *FEER*, 12 June 1981, pp. 80–81.

[61] Other agencies involved included the National Investment Development Corporation, the National Development Corporation and the Government Services Insurance Corporation, all of which effectively became holding companies.

[62] Dohner and Intal, "Marcos Legacy," pp. 66–73, 406.

External conditions alone might have warranted a revision of targets, but the 1981 IMF staff appraisal revealed a sanguine view of economic management. "Implementation of the various adjustment measures under the program had gone forward," according to the appraisal, and no change in targets was required.[63] In September, however, a new Philippine team took over at the IMF and quickly concluded that the sharp increase in short-term debt and the growth in monetary aggregates violated the stand-by.[64] A debate ensued over the veracity of data before Marcos signalled that agreement on a new program was impossible. Thus, 1982 was only the second year since 1962 during which the Philippines was not under an IMF stand-by. During that year, the country's fiscal, debt and balance-of-payments situation worsened substantially.

The failure to secure Fund support coincided with an upsurge in domestic political opposition. The lifting of martial law spawned new efforts to unite diverse and factionalized anti-Marcos politicians.[65] The Church adopted a more critical public posture. Strike activity and labor militancy increased in the urban areas, and the deterioration of the conditions of small farmers and landless laborers fueled the growing armed insurgency.[66]

A new source of opposition also began to emerge—the noncrony private sector. In 1981, Enrique Zobel formed the Makati Business Club to sponsor discussions of the economy among business organizations. Zobel was an example of landed wealth that had successfully moved into finance and urban real estate, but had been directly challenged by Marcos cronies.[67] The Makati Business Club denounced the inattention to agriculture, growing income disparities, and "graft and corruption" in government, all of which contributed to the strength of the left. Jaime Ongpin, the brother of Minister of Trade and Industry Roberto Ongpin, issued stinging indictments of the government's mismanagement of the Dewey Dee scandal.[68] Reports of Marcos' poor health

[63] As quoted in Thompson and Slayton, "Essay on Credit Arrangements," pp. 67–73.

[64] The IMF had been somewhat disadvantaged in monitoring events because of the departure of its resident representative in December 1980 following a clash with Central Bank Governor Licaros over the veracity of balance of payments and reserve data. Only in late 1981 did the executive board of the IMF informally send a new representative to restore a working relationship with the Central Bank.

[65] See Benjamin N. Muego, "The 'New Society' Five Years Later: The State of the Opposition," *Southeast Asian Affairs 1978* (Singapore: Institute of Southeast Asian Studies, 1978), on the growth of the opposition, pp. 215–26; David Wurfel, "The Succession Struggle," in May and Nemenzo, *Philippines After Marcos*, pp. 17–44.

[66] Hal Hill and Sisira Jayasuriya, "The Philippines: Growth, Debt and Crisis: Economic Performance During the Marcos Era," Development Studies Centre, Australian National University, Canberra, working paper 85/3 (1985), a comprehensive review of conditions in the countryside; Robert Youngblood, "The Philippines in 1982: Marcos Gets Tough with Domestic Critics," *Asian Survey*, 23, 2 (February 1983): 208–16 on the repressive response to labor.

[67] Wurfel, "Succession Struggle," p. 28.

[68] See the summary of an early report by Zobel in *Foreign Broadcast Information Service: Asia and the Pacific* (cited hereafter as *FBIS*) 2 September 1982, pp. P3–P6 for the Makati Business

and fears that Mrs. Marcos would attempt to succeed him led to demands for clarification of the lines of succession.

Because of the growth of the opposition and the gradual opening of electoral politics, Marcos' own political machine began to exert significant pressure on economic policy. By late 1982, the technocrats recognized that the counter-cyclical stance could not be sustained. A new stand-by was urgent, and prior action on the budget would probably be required to negotiate it. The left had long denounced the country's subservience to the IMF; in April 1983, Virata came under similar criticism from Marcos' own party, the KBL.[69] Open conflicts surfaced between Imelda Marcos and the technocrats over her control of aid funds channeled through her Ministry of Human Settlements and "People's Livelihood Program."[70] Criticism of the technocrats also came from the cronies, particularly sugar czar Roberto Benedicto, who used his connections to maintain access to preferential rediscounting over Central Bank objections.[71]

Though the balance-of-payments crisis of late 1983 appeared to be the direct result of the Aquino assassination, the deterioration of the current account had begun much earlier. By October 1982, the Central Bank was covering external payments shortfalls by overnight borrowing.[72] A new stand-by was negotiated that went into effect in February 1983 and was accompanied by additional funding that suggested political intervention from the United States: a second, rapidly disbursing SAL of $300 million; a $300 million package from major New York banks; and an IMF compensatory financing facility of 188 million SDRs.[73] By late March, however, it was clear that this program, too, was not working. A peculiar item in the monetary accounts suggested that the Central Bank was using short-term borrowings to overstate the country's reserve position, a practice known as "window dressing."[74] Though the full extent of the deception was not clear until later, the review of the program in June and the discussions at the Consultative Group meeting in July constituted almost

Club's (MBC) views; and in *MBC Economic Papers*, various issues, 1983–1985; Jaime Ongpin, "A Report on the Political Situation," *Business Day*, 1, 2 March 1984; idem, "A Report on the Economic Crisis," *Business Day*, 13, 14 August 1984; Ongpin's views went through an evolution, but these articles include full statements.

[69] *FEER*, 5 May 1983 and 19 June 1983.

[70] *FEER*, 29 October, 1982. Imelda Marcos' Kilusang Kabuhayan at Kaunlaran (KKK) or People's Livelihood Program, was launched amidst much fanfare in August 1981, but was seen primarily as a vehicle for consolidating Marcos' support at the barangay level.

[71] *FBIS*, 28 July 1983, pp. P1–P5.

[72] *FEER*, 29 March 1984, pp. 56–57. Virata later dated the erosion of confidence to the end of 1982 or beginning of 1983, when commercial banks began to withdraw lines of credit to the Central Bank.

[73] Thompson and Slayton, "Essay on Credit Arrangments," pp. 74–77, outline the February 1983 package.

[74] See *FEER*, 29 March 1984, pp. 56–59; *Business Day*, 7 March 1984, 21 August 1984, on the reserve overstatement.

an entirely new program negotiation, as a number of performance criteria, including the ceilings on net domestic assets and short-term debt, had been breached.[75]

Immediately following the Consultative Group meeting, a new round of actions was taken by the government.[76] The peso was devalued 7.3 percent, on top of the 10 percent fall that had occurred during 1982, and additional cuts were made in the budget, including the shelving of five of the Eleven Major Projects. A decontrol of certain prices was begun as a condition for the second SAL. The government also reimposed trade and exchange controls as an alternative to more costly domestic actions. The controls and the general decline in confidence led to a cancellation of the program, the first time in Philippine history that a Fund agreement had been terminated for noncompliance.

From the Aquino Assassination to the February "Revolution": Forced Adjustment

Economic decline, reports that Marcos' health was failing and new efforts to organize the opposition encouraged Benigno Aquino to return to Manila on 21 August 1983, where he was assassinated seconds after stepping off the plane.[77] Foreign credit, already tight, now dried up completely and capital flight increased. On 5 October, a new round of corrective measures were implemented, including a further devaluation of 21.4 percent, an increase in tariffs and a tightening of exchange controls. On 17 October, however, a ninety-day moratorium on payments of principal was declared, and the Philippines joined the club of troubled debtors.

Inflation emerged as a serious economic problem.[78] Emergency assistance to financial institutions and poor monitoring of investment by state-owned enterprises contributed to a particularly expansionary monetary policy in the second half of 1983. Devaluation, the emergence of a black market, the lifting of price controls on petroleum products, and panic buying all contributed to

[75] Much of this debt was going into continued investment by state-owned enterprises, including particularly the nuclear power project. The role of the state-owned enterprises in the country's fiscal problems was not revealed until 1984 in an important World Bank study, "The Philippines: Public Expenditures and their Financing," World Bank report no. 4919-PH (25 September 1984).

[76] Mario Lamberte, ed., *A Review and Appraisal of the Government Response to the 1983–84 Balance of Payments Crisis,* Philippine Institute for Development Studies monograph no. 8 (Manila, October 1985), (cited hereafter as *PIDS Report*), contains a comprehensive guide to policy actions in the stabilization period.

[77] See Lewis M. Simmons, *Worth Dying For* (New York: William Morrow, 1987), chaps. 8, 9, 12, pp. 121–58, 193–202. The investigation of the Aquino assassination was the central drama in Philippine politics in 1984. Simmons provides a compelling account.

[78] The *Workshop Report* provided an influential overview of the problems the economy faced in the aftermath of the Aquino assassination. The following also draws on *PIDS Report*; International Monetary Fund, "Philippines: Staff Report for the 1984 Article IV Consultation," EBS/84/117 (29 May 1984); Dohner and Intal, "Marcos Legacy."

strong inflationary pressures.[79] Inflation was not the only bad economic news, however. IMF missions also uncovered evidence that central government finances were much worse than had been known. Beginning in 1982, the Central Bank had entered a series of forward contracts and swaps to favored private sector firms. The depreciation in 1982 and the two devaluations in 1983 resulted in huge Central Bank losses. In January, it was discovered that the PNB and the DBP had guaranteed the loans of favored private borrowers. On an annual basis, these guarantees were the size of the total capital budget of the government! By early 1984, approximately 90 percent of the DBP's portfolio was nonperforming and 50 percent of the PNB's, a total of over $5.5 billion in nonperforming assets.

In December, the Central Bank's complex operations to manipulate the country's balance-of-payments position were revealed. This was a major watershed in the international negotiations, and several important changes in the strategy of the external creditors followed. First, the IMF and World Bank began coordinated efforts to link stabilization and structural adjustment measures into a more integrated package.[80] When agreement was reached on a new program in October 1984, for example, it included:

1. Substantial and comprehensive tax reform to redress long-run weaknesses in the level and pattern of public sector revenues
2. Reduction in the deficits of major nonfinancial public sector corporations and close monitoring of their accounts
3. Close scrutiny of the public sector investment program, including the national government as well as the major nonfinancial public corporations
4. Rehabilitation programs for the Philippine National Bank (PNB), the Development Bank of the Philippines (DBP); and the Philippines Export Guarantee Corporation (PGC)
5. Limits on Central Bank assistance to PNB
6. Policy reform in export agriculture, principally in the sugar and coconut sectors, to be implemented in consultation with the World Bank.[81]

These measures reflect not only concern about discrete policies, but the broader structure of economic decision-making and institutions.

The second change in bargaining strategy was the IMF's use of time pressure and control over access to other sources of external financing to force policy actions *prior* to reaching an agreement.[82] The rescheduling of the country's commercial debt was expected to be relatively smooth. A group of foreign

[79] Dohner and Intal, "Marcos Legacy," p. 219.

[80] Sources in the Philippines provided a confidential document that reviewed performance under the IMF Standby Agreement dated May 1985.

[81] Ibid.

[82] *FBIS*, 24 November 1982, p. P1. The IMF had done this before. In late 1982, "prior action" was demanded on the budget.

bankers met with Marcos at the end of October 1984 and issued a surprisingly strong vote of confidence.[83] Events in November and December undermined that confidence. Private sector representatives pressed Marcos publicly about the succession, the integrity of public administration, freedom of the press, and the independence of the judiciary.[84] Marcos' response was to blame business for tax evasion, hoarding, and capital flight. The government filed charges against thirty-three businessmen for smuggling and "dollar salting," including several active in the political opposition. A new wave of demonstrations erupted in Makati, Manila's financial district.

By the end of November, lack of clarity about the succession, the demonstrations, and the slow pace of the government in generating a proposal made the commercial banks sceptical about reaching quick agreement.[85] After the disclosure of the reserve overstatement, the banks refused to proceed until a program was signed with the IMF. The highly contentious negotiations with the banks were not concluded until May 1985. The amount of "new money" was reduced from the $1.6 billion the country had sought to $925 million, and virtually all of this went to settle outstanding arrears.

If the multilateral and commercial creditors showed increasing scepticism about Marcos, U.S. policy revealed conflicting imperatives and policy differences within the Reagan government.[86] In its first two and a half years, the Reagan administration retreated from Carter's emphasis on human rights and established a closer relationship with Marcos. In 1981, the administration accepted the lifting of martial law, plebiscite on constitutional changes, and presidential elections at face value, despite evidence of widespread fraud and Marcos' retention of broad discretionary powers. In a much-cited gaffe, Vice President George Bush toasted Marcos' "adherence to democratic principle and to the democratic process." In September 1982, the Marcoses went to Washington for a heavily publicized state visit, and in the summer of 1983, a new five-year, $900 million military bases agreement was negotiated.

The Aquino assassination generated pressure from Congress and the State Department for a new policy. Key to the reassessment that followed was a growing awareness of the strength of the armed insurgency. In November 1984, the State Department drafted a detailed National Security Study Directive that underlined the importance of comprehensive political, economic, and military reform for political stability.[87]

[83] *FBIS*, 2 November 1983, p. P4.

[84] *FBIS*, 14 November 1983, p. P1.

[85] *FBIS*, 29 November 1983, p. P6.

[86] See Ross Munro, "Dateline Manila: Moscow's Next Win?" *Foreign Policy* no. 56 (Fall 1984), pp. 173–90, on the Reagan administration's response to the crisis.

[87] National Security Council, *NSSD: U.S. Policy towards the Philippines Executive Summary*, prepared by National Security Council, leaked by State Department employees and released by Philippine Support Committee, mimeo., 12 March 1985.

The United States tied its agreement on bridging loans and the Paris Club rescheduling to an agreement with the IMF, backed the temporary suspension of IMF drawings in 1985 over failure to implement reform of the agricultural monopolies, and held up bilateral assistance when Marcos thwarted reforms in the food distribution system.[88] Overall, however, the Reagan administration rejected the use of aid as a lever for reform. Disbursements of previously committed aid accelerated during 1984 and additional money was granted under a continuing resolution and a $150 million export-import bank facility.[89]

The United States played a crucial role in finalizing the bank rescheduling. Various diplomatic missions designed to "send Marcos a message" were either too weak, rejected by Marcos, or undermined by other policy statements. In October 1985, for example, senior administration officials were testifying that the Philippines was headed toward "civil war on a massive scale" if reforms were not forthcoming, though at the same time, cabinet officers were urging bankers to continue to lend to the country for strategic reasons.[90]

Despite the pressure from the multilateral agencies, the government delayed the adjustments required to reach an agreement with the IMF. Economic circumstance was partly to blame. Swap losses, the continuing drain to public enterprises, and a major bank failure in mid-1984 helped account for the loss of control over fiscal and monetary policy. Nonetheless, the parliamentary elections of 14 May 1984 appear critical in explaining the timing of government actions.

In mid-March, after successfully securing $350 million in trade credits from the United States, Japan, and Korea, Marcos informed the IMF that he was not prepared to finalize the letter of intent until after the elections.[91] The government responded to increased labor activism with a series of wage concessions that largely offset the effects of the devaluation.[92] Classic pork barrel expenditures, such as Imelda Marcos' People's Livelihood Program and the activities of her Ministry of Human Settlements contributed to budgetary problems.[93] Other actions were even more transparently related to the elections,

---

[88] Charles Greenleaf, "Administration Review of U.S. Policy toward the Philippines," testimony, in *Hearings* before the Senate Foreign Relations Committee, 99th Congress, 1st session, (30 October 1985), (cited hereafter as *1985 Hearings*), pp. 2–57 provides an overview of American policy toward economic reform.

[89] Congress did succeed in shifting the balance of aid toward economic assistance, but because much of this was channeled through Mrs. Marcos' Ministry of Human Settlements, this can only be considered a symbolic victory.

[90] See Paul Wolfowitz, Assistant Secretary of State for East Asia and the Pacific, testimony in *1985 Hearings*, pp. 2–57: "U.S. Says It Fears Philippines Faces a Wide Civil War," *New York Times*, 31 October 1985, section A1.

[91] *FBIS*, 14 March 1984.

[92] *PIDS Report*, pp. 52–57.

[93] Sources in the Philippines provided a confidential document regarding 1984 Article IV consultations.

such as the announcement of wage increases for public employees on May 1 and Mrs. Marcos' announcement at a rally in Cebu City of "prizes" of P50,000 to each barangay and P100,000 to each town in the province that delivered a straight pro-Marcos vote.[94]

The importance of the May 14 elections in delaying adjustment measures becomes particularly clear in examining the actions that followed.[95] An increase in the tax on petroleum products was decreed only days after the election, and on 5 June, Marcos moved to institute a new round of adjustment measures, including a 22 percent devaluation and additional budget cuts. While wage adjustments between June 1983 and June 1984 were roughly commensurate with price rises, real wages fell steadily over the next year and a half. Once again, however, the government relied heavily on exchange and trade controls. The IMF balked at the control-oriented style of adjustment and demanded stiffer domestic action. In August, the Central Bank launched an open market operation by issuing high-yielding treasury bills. The intervention aimed at defending the exchange rate, keeping capital in the country, and meeting the IMF's demand that liquidity in the system be reduced prior to reaching an agreement. The need to reestablish creditworthiness was clearly paramount in this decision, and in October 1985 an IMF program was signed.

The economic consequences were sharp. The ninety-day treasury bill rate rose by over ten percentage points to a peak of 43 per cent at end-October. On a monthly basis by the end of 1984, inflation was at 65 percent. By early 1986, it had dropped to 3 percent, one of the sharpest drops in inflation outside of a hyperinflationary setting. The policy also resulted in a severe depression; real GNP declined 5.5 percent, employment declined 5.6 percent, and savings and investment fell from 27.5 to 18.5 percent of GNP. In May 1985, some targets were relaxed following internal debate within the Fund and Bank about the severity of the program. But a year earlier, the IMF had feared that without external pressure for strong action, the Philippines would fall into a devaluation-inflation cycle.

It is a sign of the low degree of confidence in Marcos that despite the program's success in reducing inflation and closing the current account deficit, external scrutiny of policy remained particularly close. The drawing of the second tranche of the stand-by in April 1985 was delayed by the failure to meet budget targets. Though Central Bank Governor José Fernandez and the technocrats had control over some areas of policy, large areas of policy were not integrated into overall economic management. Some of these, such as the coconut and sugar sectors, food distribution, and the complex of institutions that had been developed around Mrs. Marcos, were the result of cronyism and

---

[94] Charles W. Lindsey, "Economic Crisis in the Philippines," *Asian Survey* 24, 12 (December 1984): 1189.

[95] The following paragraphs draw on the *PIDS Report*, pp. 52–57.

the use of government resources for political objectives. Others, such as the control of the state-owned enterprises, are better explained by the generally lax system of management that was characteristic of the late Marcos period.

By 1985, the United States had moved toward the position that comprehensive reforms were necessary for political reasons. A full reform of the government financial institutions was temporarily waived, but largely due to U.S. pressure, the multilateral institutions insisted on reform of the agricultural monopolies. The IMF approved the release of the second tranche in July, but negotiations began immediately for a revision of the program to include tax reform, changes in the heavily subsidized rural credit system, and trade liberalization. An agreement in principle was reached concerning drawings on the third and fourth tranches in October, but the IMF and World Bank, despite persistent rumors, were unaware of Marcos' intention to announce snap elections. The pattern was predictable: a reversal on the commitment to tax reform; politicization of the trade liberalization proposals; a massive backsliding on monetary targets and continued failure to dismantle the monopolies.

Adjustment in a Weak Authoritarian Regime

International constraints were crucial in ultimately forcing the severe stabilization effort of 1984. Despite some bilateral and multilateral trade finance during the year following the Aquino assassination, the restoration of international credit was crucial for recovery. A second external constraint was a detailed surveillance that increasingly focused on the nature of economic policy making itself. Though the U.S. sent mixed signals, the commercial banks refused to negotiate until agreement was reached with the IMF. The IMF, in turn, refused to agree to a program until the Philippines demonstrated its commitment. The crisis had revealed the extent to which the creditors had been lulled into complacency by the dualistic policy structure. The technocrats had not only proved impotent in controlling economic policy, they had also engaged in deception. Every effort was taken to ensure that this did not happen again. Finally, the international financial constraint operated indirectly on the government by increasing the pressure from import-dependent businesses. The noncrony private sector increasingly saw its interests undermined by Marcos' mismanagement of the economy. Stabilization was thus also aimed at reestablishing domestic confidence.

If external constraints dictated the *nature* of the stabilization package, domestic factors explained the *timing* of the measures and their limited *scope*. The vacillating government response to the crisis is explained by the May 1984 elections, the growth of opposition, and pressures from within Marcos' own party to delay politically costly measures. These same factors, the continuing power of the cronies in the agriculture sector and the resulting dualistic policy-making structure limited the extent of structural reform.

THE AQUINO ADMINISTRATION THROUGH THE RECONVENING OF CONGRESS, JULY 1987

The Aquino Coalition

The coalition that brought Aquino to power was broad and heterogeneous.[96] After the assassination of her husband, Aquino endorsed the "parliament of the streets" in which the Bayan organization of left "cause-oriented" groups played a crucial role. In December 1985, however, Aquino rejected a set of conditions laid down by Bayan for their support. Bayan's subsequent boycott of the elections, later recognized as a major tactical blunder, created an uneasy relationship between the left and the new government. Willing to mobilize to support Aquino against the right, they also criticized Aquino for her cautious approach to reform and continued to press the interests of peasants and workers. Though Aquino broke formally with Bayan, a number of prominent human rights advocates entered her cabinet, constituting its left wing. These included Joker Arroyo, who held the crucial position of presidential secretary, and minister of Labor Augusto Sanchez, a strong advocate of labor rights who became the bête-noir of foreign and local business.

The most important group on the right was the military, represented in the cabinet by Minister of Defense General Juan Ponce Enrile. Enrile had been a prominent Marcos ally, chairman of the United Coconut Planters Bank and closely linked with the Cojuangco crony complex. It was the defection of Enrile, General Fidel Ramos and lower-ranking members of the Reform Armed Forces Movement that set up the dramatic four-day standoff around Camp Aquinaldo that constituted the February "revolution."[97] Enrile used his office and considerable personal fortune to develop a base of support among middle-ranking military officers, KBL loyalists, and regional political bosses.

Much of the political analysis of the Aquino administration has rightly focused on the two major challenges to the new regime's survival: destabilization from the right and the rural insurgency.[98] The insurgency and the entrée it provided to the right and the military help explain the rural emphasis in

[96] Peter Krinks, ed., *The Philippines Under Aquino* (Canberra: Australian Development Studies Network, 1987); Mark Turner, ed., *Regime Change in the Philippines: The Legitimation of the Aquino Government*, Department of Political and Social Change monograph no. 7, Australian National University (Canberra, 1987) are two useful studies of the politics of the Aquino administration.

[97] See Anne Mackenzie, "People Power or Palace Coup: The Fall of Marcos," in Turner, *Regime Change*, pp. 1–57 on the military's role in the Revolution.

[98] See Anne Mackenzie, "People Power or Palace Coup: The Fall of Marcos"; and Mark Turner, "The Quest for Political Legitimacy in the Philippines: The Constitutional Plebiscite of 1987," in Turner, ed., *Regime Change in the Philippines*, pp. 1–101; and Alfred W. McCoy, "After the Yellow Revolution: Filipino Elite Factions and the Struggle for Power," pp. 9–34, in Krinks, ed., *Philippines Under Aquino*.

Aquino's economic program. To understand the play of policy, however, equal weight must be given to the private sector and a group of Philippine economists.

When the "Convenor Group" was formed in late 1984 to coordinate opposition strategy, Aquino developed links with disaffected Makati businessmen. As her break with Bayan suggests, she had already moved toward the center-right before the election of 1986. All of the major economic portfolios with the exception of NEDA were controlled by representatives of the private sector opposition. Jaime Ongpin, the leader of the Convenor Group and chairman of a large mining concern, became minister of finance and the most powerful and consistent voice for policy reform. José Concepcion, Jr., also a businessman, became minister of trade and industry and the banker José Fernandez, the architect of the 1984 stabilization program, retained his position as head of the Central Bank, the sole holdover from the Marcos administration. The new relationship with business was reflected in a poll conducted from March to July 1986 by *Business Day* that covered 243 of the largest 1,200 companies (table 6.5). Half of the respondents were uncertain about the state of the economy, but the answers to questions on business-government relations reflected confidence and a new optimism.

A second set of influences on adjustment strategy came from local economists. The 1984 Workshop Report by a group of University of the Philippines

TABLE 6.5
Philippine Business Views of the Aquino Government, March–July 1986

	Yes	No	No Answer
1. Do you think the element of uncertainty that prevailed over the economy during the past 30 months has now been removed?	44.0	49.8	6.2
2. Under the new government, do you think the task of nation [sic] rebuilding would nonetheless be a slow and painful process for the country?	93.4	5.4	1.2
3. Under the new government, do you think confidence in the government has been restored?	84.8	12.8	2.4
4. Do you believe in the new government's ability to put the economy back on its feet?	82.3	13.2	4.5
5. Do you think the government and the private sector can still mend their severely tarnished relationship?	85.6	10.7	3.7
6. Do you think the government will lessen its presence in certain industries and in effect create a business environment where private enterprise will flourish?	81.9	11.5	6.6

Source: Ma. Carolina B. Ibanez, "Big Business Talks on How It Looks Now," in *1000 Top Corporations in the Philippines*, vol. 18 (1985–1986), (Manila: Business Day, 1986), p. 274.

Note: Unit of measurement = percentage of respondents.

economists had provided the analytic underpinning for the business opposition.[99] Solita Monsod, a University of the Philippines professor active in publicizing economic criticisms of the Marcos administration, was made head of NEDA. The "Jesuit mafia" centered on a number of Catholic universities, and the Center for Research and Communication, while identified with the right, also generated highly critical analyses of Marcos' economic policy.[100] Drawing on this work, input from the private sector and the research efforts of the Philippine Institute of Development Studies, NEDA released a comprehensive statement on economic policy in May 1986, subsequently known as the "yellow book."[101]

The influence of the "yellow book" should not be exaggerated, but it is revealing in its comprehensive combination of market-oriented policies, institutional reforms, and an explicit emphasis on redistribution. The call for a reintroduction of market forces and a more restricted government role might be interpreted as a response to the demands of the multilateral institutions. Export promotion received strong endorsement, as did a number of other reforms pushed by the World Bank and IMF: the dismantling of agricultural monopolies; tax reform; disposition of the nonperforming assets of the state-owned banks; privatization of other state-owned enterprises; trade liberalization and the pursuit of a more flexible exchange rate policy. To interpret these policies solely as a response to pressure from either the domestic private sector or outside creditors is to miss a crucial feature of the post-Marcos political context. Given the pervasive political intervention that had characterized economic management, *market-oriented policies took on a progressive cast.*

The political objectives underlying structural adjustment were visible in the attention given to institutional reform. Two principles were underlined: decentralization and accountability. The report argued for the independence of the Central Bank from the executive, decentralization of planning functions, the strengthening of regional and local levels within the decision-making structure, and a strengthening of oversight and audit of the public enterprise sector. The most striking feature of the report, however, was its effort to combine market-oriented and institutional reforms with a populist thrust designed to blunt the appeal of the left and the armed insurgency. The core of the new strategy was a shift in emphasis away from the capital-intensive, Manila-based

[99] Florian Alburo et al., *Towards Recovery and Sustainable Growth* (Quezon City: University of the Philippines School of Economics, 1985). The workshop report was followed in September 1985 by this second and equally critical study.

[100] The Center for Research and Communication's views are spelled out in two serial publications, *Economics and Society* and *Staff Memos*. The CRC's critique of the Marcos administration is contained in Bernardo Villegas et al., *The Philippinies at the Crossroads: Some Visions for the Nation: Summary Report* (Manila: Center for Research and Communication, 1985).

[101] Philippine Institute for Development Studies, *Economic Recovery and Long-term Growth: Agenda for Reforms,* vol. 1, *Main Report* (Manila: Philippine Institute for Development Studies, 1986), cited hereafter as *Yellow Book.*

industries towards small agricultural and industrial enterprises in the rural areas. In the short run, the government would launch an employment-generating rural public works program. This strategy demanded a relaxation of fiscal and monetary policy, to be achieved in part through a more aggressive stance vis-à-vis both the IMF and the commercial banks.[102]

The report recognized, however, that the fundamental goal of poverty alleviation could not be accomplished through growth alone; "a meaningful redistribution of wealth and incomes," including particularly land reform, was required.[103] The report argued that "it is not the system of private property that is fundamentally at fault,"[104] but was explicit in drawing links between political and social structure and economic reform. The "minimum requirements for successful land reform" included:

1. The dismantling of private armed groups; the forces of the state should be for the protection of all without discrimination.
2. Democratically based, and noneconomically based selection of local government officials, whose loyalties would be more to the masses of their constituents than to the economic powers in their areas.
3. Effective administrative separation of the function of promoting agricultural and natural resource productivity from the function of promoting land justice.[105]

Implementing Structural Reform

Several factors favored a wide-ranging reform effort. The most important condition for the reform effort was a change in the external environment. The government took advantage of its unique political and moral position to press for increased aid. Total foreign assistance in 1985 was just over $1 billion; in 1986, this nearly doubled to $1.8 billion.[106] The current account, which had been virtually balanced in 1985 as a result of the stabilization program, showed a $1 billion surplus in 1986 and foreign exchange reserves were replenished. Terms of trade also improved as a result of the drop in oil prices and, beginning in late 1986, improvements in copra prices.

The change of government also improved relations with the World Bank and IMF. Spending related to the 1986 elections had again pushed the Philippines over IMF targets, blocking drawings under the stand-by and the banks'

[102] The report defended "selective repudiation" of external debts, arguing "we should first aim for reasonable economic growth and only then work out a debt restructuring plan consistent with that" (*Yellow Book*, p. 17).

[103] Ibid., p. 5.

[104] Ibid., p. 115.

[105] Ibid., p. 117.

[106] See Richard Kessler, "The Philippines Under Corazon Aquino: An Assessment of the First Two Years and the Challenges Ahead," February 1988, Asia Society Media Briefing (New York: Asia Society, 1988), p. 26. The United States accounted for only 27 percent of the total; new multilateral, European and Japanese assistance was also important.

"new money" facility. Rather than work within the old program by seeking a waiver, the IMF agreed to cancel the program. A new stand-by was signed in October 1986. The letter of intent included virtually all of the initiatives that the IMF and World Bank had sought unsuccessfully from Marcos, including rehabiliation of the state-owned banking sector, tax reform, privatization, reform of the coconut and sugar sectors, and trade liberalization. At the same time, the IMF allowed the election-related increases in the money supply to stand and validated the government's expansionary Community Employment and Development Program (CEDP).[107] The CEDP was designed to spur demand, but also reflected the new focus on the rural areas. CEDP spending was also politically useful in the campaigns for the constitutional plebiscite and the congressional elections, resembling in many ways the pork-barrel projects of the past.

In contrast to the improvement in relations with the IMF and World Bank, bargaining with the banks became more politicized.[108] Members of the cabinet and outside critics argued that greater leeway for domestic reform could be gained through an aggressive bargaining stance. Ongpin and Fernandez argued strongly against "selective repudiation," advocated by Solita Monsod, and won Aquino to a public statement that the government would honor all debts.[109] This victory increased the pressure to extract good terms in the rescheduling negotiations, however, particularly since Mexico had just received an unusually generous package. Though the banks insisted that the Mexican deal was sui generis, Ongpin believed that the Philippines deserved a package at least as good; the country was seeking no new money and had successfully undertaken both stabilization and structural reform.

In March 1987, an agreement was signed that restructured $3.6 billion in debt falling due between 1987 and 1992 and $5.9 billion from the 1985 agreement. The Philippines settled for a spread of 7/8 over LIBOR, though the amortization period was a generous seventeen years, with seven and one-half years of grace. In comparative terms, the agreement was favorable and immediately reduced debt servicing cost. Nonetheless, the agreement was the source of substantial political controversy and was one factor leading to Ongpin's tragic fall from power.[110]

[107] "Memorandum on Economic Policy," enclosed with the letter from Fernandez and Ongpin to Camdessus (IMF), 1987 March 10; FEER, 6 August 1987.
[108] Dohner and Intal,"Marcos Legacy," pp. 289–94.
[109] "Painful Prescriptions," FEER, 2 July 1987, p. 22. Ongpin and Fernandez also won the debate about new money, arguing that none was required.
[110] Economic and Political Monthly, Third World Studies Center, vol. 1 (Manila, April 1987), for a critical analysis of the rescheduling. See Claudia Rosett, "Jimmy Ongpin's Last Words," Wall Street Journal, 29 February 1988, p. 20; idem, "The Trials of Jaime Ongpin," Wall Street Journal, 1 March 1988, p. 38; idem, "Aquino's Embattled Democracy," Wall Street Journal, 2 March 1988, p. 28. Ongpin committed suicide shortly after leaving government in December 1987.

The political power of the new government was a second factor propitious for reform. Not only did Aquino enjoy broad support, she also held unusual powers. Ironically, the first acts of Aquino's presidency resembled closely Marcos' actions on declaring martial law: the dissolution of the National Assembly; a deep purge of regional and local governments, the judiciary, and to a lesser extent, the armed forces; the replacement of ousted officials by Aquino loyalists; and the sequestration of the assets of political opponents. Aquino quickly established a timetable for the normalization of politics, convened a Constitutional Convention and was publicly committed to ensuring civil liberties. Nonetheless, during her first eighteen months she ruled through presidential decree.

Yet the formal powers of government were ultimately less important than Aquino's caution, which in turn could be traced to underlying coalitional constraints. The very breadth of the support Aquino enjoyed, her own commitment to representative government, and the resulting factionalism within the cabinet checked the reform process. The events of February legitimated Aquino's rule. But the "revolution" of February was political rather than social. It validated the claims of a diverse array of backers, but left fundamental social structures unchanged. Reforms that imposed costs on "legitimate," i.e., non-Marcos, groups proved difficult to implement; this is the perennial dilemma of democratic reformism. Reforms that pitted the nationalist left against the center-right within the Cabinet also stalled, particularly given the control over the flow of policy exercised by Joker Arroyo, the presidential secretary, and a key figure on the left.

A full review of Aquino's economic policy goes beyond the scope of this chapter, but these points may be demonstrated briefly by comparing four areas in which the government achieved some success—tax reform, the elimination of the monopolies, a new investment code, and trade liberalization—with two policy areas in which both policy formation and implementation lagged: privatization and land reform.

Tax reform and the elimination of monopolies are examples of structural reform that could be initiated by fiat. Marcos reversed his commitment to tax reform prior to the 1986 elections, but shortly after coming to power, the Aquino government began work with the World Bank and IMF on a comprehensive change in tax policy. The objectives of the reform were not solely to raise revenues, but to eliminate trade taxes, improve collection, reduce regressive taxes, and eliminate the numerous special exemptions granted by Marcos.[111] In June 1986, twenty-nine separate tax measures were approved, with others, including a value-added tax, undertaken in conjunction with a World Bank "Economic Recovery Loan" of $300 million. The only major

---

[111] *Euromoney*, Karen Witcher interview with Jaime Ongpin, July 1987, p. 122; "Memorandum on Economic Policy," enclosed with Fernandez and Ongpin to Camdessus (IMF), 10 March 1987.

measure meeting effective opposition in the policy formulation stage was an effort to raise real estate tax rates. The problems of strengthening tax administration remained daunting, however, and would affect ultimate *implementation* of the tax reform, particularly in the area of strengthening collection.[112]

Minister of Finance Ongpin noted that "abolishing the monopolies was basically a stroke of the pen. It didn't really require any involved implementation."[113] Both reforms also provided visible benefits to growers. The marketing monopoly on sugar and the Philippine Sugar Commission were abolished, and though export quotas were retained because of international agreements in the sugar sector, these quotas were made tradable. The freeing of coconut oil exports and milling from monopoly control resulted in a diversification of exporters and the entry of new millers. In both sectors, audits of the monopolies were undertaken with the aim of sequestering illicitly accumulated assets.

The drafting of a new investment code and trade liberalization suggest how the extraordinary powers of the government were used to preempt wider opposition to reform. The Constitutional Convention convened in June 1986 heard heated debates over economic policy. A "Coalition for a Constitutional Provision on Industrialization, Economic Protectionism and Filipinization of the Economy" was formed. Several delegates walked out before a compromise balanced nationalist concerns on natural resources and foreign investment with provisions stressing the integrity of private property and the importance of a market-oriented economy.[114] Just prior to the convening of Congress, Aquino signed a new investment code. The code departed in only marginal ways from the previous codes. For example, it maintained the limit of 40 percent foreign ownership in joint ventures, but its introduction upheld reforms of the system of industrial incentives undertaken by Marcos in 1983 and reduced the chances that politicians would ally with nationalist business interests to draft an even more restrictive code.[115]

One of the most controversial reforms was the resumption of the trade liberalization program.[116] Marcos succeeded in reforming the the tariff structure by 1985, but backed away from his commitment to remove quantitative restrictions, the more serious instrument of protection. The new government

[112] *FEER*, 29 September 1986. See Louis Berger, International, Development Economics Group, "Assessment of the Philippine Economic Reform Program: Evaluation of Past USAID Program Assistance and Future Recommendations" (mimeo., 10 October 1988), (hereafter cited as *Berger Report*), chap. 5, p. 7, on the problems of implementing administrative reforms.

[113] *Euromoney*, interview with Jaime Ongpin, July 1987, p. 122.

[114] *The Constitution of the Republic of the Philippines*, "National Economy and Patrimony," article 22.

[115] *Business World*, 29 February 1988, for a comprehensive analysis of the investment code; See *Berger Report*, chap. 4.

[116] See *IBON Facts and Figures* no. 196 (15 October 1986), on import liberalization; *Manila Chronicle*, 27 July 1986, on the IMF's role in pressing import liberalization.

resumed the program, which was to proceed in two stages: the lifting of quantitative restrictions and their replacement by tariffs; and a further reduction of levels of protection. By April 1988, import bans and quantitative restrictions had been lifted on 637 of 1,232 items scheduled for liberalization. Though these categories represented only 17 percent of total Philippine imports, this compared favorably with the less than one percent in the early 1980s. Minister of Trade and Industry Jose Concepcion sided with the Philippine Chamber of Commerce and Industry in arguing for gradualism in lifting quantitative restrictions on remaining items, among which were a number of major intermediate products likely to provoke controversy. Nonetheless, the government did commit itself to a schedule for the remainder of the program, limited most replacement tariffs to 50 percent, and advanced significantly beyond what Marcos had accomplished.[117]

Privatization and land reform represented structural reforms that involved both resistance in the formulation of policy and a more complex and daunting process of implementation. Privatization in the Philippines moved along two, somewhat distinct tracks.[118] The first was the disposition of the nonperforming assets acquired by the state-owned banking sector. This effort was linked to the rehabilitation of the two largest government-owned banks, the Development Bank of the Philippines and the Philippine National Bank.

The second track was the sale of state-owned enterprises and an effort to improve the management of those state-owned enterprises being retained. Over time, a number of barriers to rapid privatization emerged and implementation lagged behind stated intentions. These barriers included the sheer administrative and legal complexity of preparing the nonperforming assets for sale as well as political and legal conflicts over the rights of previous owners. In the state-owned enterprises, political barriers also emerged.

The Philippine National Oil Company provides the clearest case. The company had been prepared for sale by outside consultants, but privatization was blocked when an Arroyo appointment took over the company and defended continued state ownership. Advocates and opponents of privatization in the cabinet argued over a range of particular issues such as the pricing of the enterprise, but the debate also reflected deeper ideological and institutional differences. Arroyo was able to delay the signing of crucial executive orders on privatization, thus guaranteeing that the debates would be reopened in the legislature.

Because of its perceived importance in stemming the insurgency, land reform was the central political issue in the Philippines in 1986 and 1987.[119] A

---

[117] See *Berger Report*, chap. 4, p. 10. The World Bank subsequently allowed adjustments above 50 percent on a case by case basis.

[118] The following draws from Haggard, "Picking Up After Marcos," pp. 104–15.

[119] I have benefited from comments by John Thomas in this section. See *FEER*, 5 March 1987, pp. 32–34; ibid., 11 June 1987, pp. 22–23; ibid., 2 July 1987, p. 21.

cabinet action committee delayed formulation of a reform strategy because of conflicts between a relatively weak minister of agrarian reform and a more powerful minister of agriculture who had reservations about the effects of reform on agricultural growth and productivity. Action was spurred by a demonstration for land reform in Manila in January 1987 in which a number of protestors were killed.

The Comprehensive Agrarian Reform Program (CARP) that was signed in July 1987 had four components. Program A, to be implemented in 1987–1989, would complete Marcos' early-1970s land reform plan in corn and rice land, covering 557,000 hectares. Program B (1987–1989) would distribute sequestered, foreclosed, idle, and abandoned lands and covered 600,000 hectares. Program C (1989–1992) would distribute 1.3 million hectares of private land, mostly in sugar and coconuts, while the fourth phase, Program D (1987–1992) covered 1.3 million hectares of land in the public domain.

A World Bank study immediately noted a number of defects in the program, including the high price per hectare that farmers would have to pay, the inclusion of a "transitional" voluntary land-sharing agreement that would have been distinctly inferior to the initial plan, and the unnecessary sequencing of the various reforms. Protests to the draft program came immediately from both sugar planters and local government in Negros Occidental; alternative formulas surfaced that limited redistribution and increased compensation.[120] The CARP also failed to address two politically critical issues: the size of maximum holdings, or "retention limit," and the timing of redistribution.

These issues were thrown onto Congress. Nearly half the members of the House of Representatives, in which landowners are heavily represented, sponsored a bill that would allow higher retention limits and defer the distribution of nongrain lands until other phases of the program were completed. Outside the legislature, landowners reacted in predictable ways by dividing up estates among family members and forming private armies to resist the takeover of their lands, suggesting the powerful constraints that will operate on the pursuit of a redistributionist project.

CONCLUSION

The central arguments of this study may be restated by discussing the significance of four clusters of variables on Philippine decision making: the role of external agencies; state structure and capacity; political cycles; and coalitions and interest groups.

When analyzing policy choice, I underlined the interaction between the creditors and multilateral institutions and domestic political structures. The

---

[120] The most important of these is the comprehensive plan developed by the government of Negros Occidental. See "Poverty and Adjustment in Negros Occidental, Philippines," April 1988, processed.

stance of the creditors went through four distinct stages. From 1972 until 1980, the commercial banks considered the Philippines a good risk, and the IMF and World Bank were relatively lax in imposing conditionality, particularly over public finances. As elsewhere in the developing world, external credit supported an expanded state role in the economy. This approach changed in the early eighties, when the multilaterals made greater efforts to introduce structural reforms and to limit borrowing and government spending in response to external shocks. Beginning in 1983, confidence in the country's economic management plummeted, opening a third stage of severely strained relations between the Philippines and external actors. Deceived by Marcos in the past, the IMF and the World Bank forced a particularly severe stabilization program on the country and widened their demands to include a comprehensive set of structural reforms. The change of government in 1986 ushered in the most recent phase, during which the objectives of the IMF and World Bank and domestic policymakers converged. A relaxation of external economic constraints was certainly important in providing the space for Aquino's reformism, but the easing of those constraints was itself a function of renewed confidence on the part of external creditors and donors. The *politics* of these relations mattered.

A central argument of this study is that definitions of regime type limited to the formal arrangements governing representation conflate authoritarian regimes of very different sorts; the equation of "authoritarianism" with the capacity to institute reforms is overly facile. Marcos' "authoritarianism" was built around extensive state patronage networks and the creation of a class of rent-seeking capitalists. Because the political system rested on a high degree of discretion, independent planning and oversight functions atrophied. In addition, the Philippines lacked the bureaucratic depth of the more developed Latin American debtors. Even with a change of political regime, fundamental administrative reforms were required if the Philippines was to implement many components of the structural reform, such as a strengthening of tax collection.

"Democratization" must also be perceived with some care. Aquino clearly won a popular mandate with the election and demonstrations that followed it. But during the first eighteen months in office, Aquino retained extraordinary powers and politics was "democratic" primarily because of Aquino's own commitments rather than because of an immediate change in political form. On the whole, Aquino used her powers to introduce accountability, consultation, and the rule of law into economic policy making, but in the introduction of several structural reforms, such as import liberalization and tax reform, the government's autonomy helped.

Electoral cycles played an important role in the late Marcos years. The transition from formal authoritarian rule opened a period of controlled electoral contestation. Given the instrumental nature of Marcos' rule and the generally

low level of legitimacy the regime enjoyed, patronage and politically motivated spending assumed particular importance. Electoral pressures, emanating
from Marcos' political supporters as much as from the opposition, were important in explaining the delay in the adoption of reform measures from 1981
through 1984.

Coalition politics played out differently in the Philippines under Aquino
than in Brazil, Argentina, and Peru. New democratic regimes should be vulnerable to the temptation to maintain broad support and guarantee the democratic experiment against destabilization through expansionist policies. As the
studies by Kaufman and Stallings showed, new democracies also have a pro-
clivity for heterdox programs. Aquino faced serious challenges from both left
and right, and the centerpiece of economic policy was an expansionist rural
public works program. Two interrelated factors explain why the Philippines
differed from the heterodox experiments in Latin America. First, the difficult
task of stabilization had already been achieved by the previous government
and the external financial constraint had been reduced, leaving the new government room for political maneuver.

The second reason, however, had to do with the center-right political coalition that supported Aquino and the legacy of Marcos' interventionism. In
the early 1980s, Marcos ruled through a political strategy that relied heavily
on expansionary policies and the distribution of favors to cronies and through
new state-patronage networks. Over time, the corruption, predation, and social instability associated with Marcos' rule generated resistance from the private sector. The Philippine private sector was by no means economically liberal; they had developed under a prolonged ISI regime. Nonetheless,
manufacturing, financial, and commercial interests supported some rationalization of economic policy. The Aquino government responded to these business interests in formulating its program and only weakly to calls for a more
basic transformation in the social structure.[121]

Wide-ranging reform confronted two additional political barriers that will
shape economic policy in the future. The Philippine bureaucracy lacked the
depth and independence to carry out reforms that taxed administrative capacity
or demanded insulation from local social pressures. More fundamentally, the
reconvening of Congress opened a new political phase. Established social
forces regained entry to government, raising the well-known dilemmas of
democratic reformism.

[121] *Philippine Daily Inquirer*, 24 October 1987. For a clear statement of Aquino's tilt toward
business by the end of her first two years, see her speech before a group of businessmen, 20
October 1987.

CHAPTER 7

Lost Between State and Market:
The Politics of Economic Adjustment in Ghana, Zambia, and Nigeria

Thomas M. Callaghy

> Nkrumah once said "Seek ye first the political kingdom and every-
> thing else will be added unto you." And it seemed so plausible then.
> It was only 30 years ago, and look! We sought the "political king-
> dom" and nothing has been added unto us; a lot has been taken
> away.
>
> —Chinua Achebe

THE SYNDROME

As INDEPENDENCE came to Africa, beginning in the late 1950s, political rather
than economic logics prevailed. Despite their diversity, most of the new countries developed a deeply rooted syndrome of quite common political and economic characteristics, which has dominated much of the last thirty years. In
the context of low levels of economic development and very dependent mineral and agricultural primary product export economies, new and insecure ruling groups came to power with liberal democratic political structures inherited
at the last minute from their former colonial masters. From the first, their
primary concerns were political—how to stay in power and build a base for
themselves and their allies.[1]

In addition to the members of this project, I thank all the people in Ghana, Zambia, Nigeria,
and elsewhere who shared their time and thoughts. I am also grateful for the support and wisdom
of the following people: Thomas Biersteker, Naomi Chazan, Michael Chege, Betsy Frost, Ravi
Gulhati, Peter Lewis, Matthew Martin, James Scarritt, Michael Shafer, and Tina West. Much of
the data for this chapter comes from confidential interviews conducted in Accra, Lusaka, Lagos,
Nairobi, and London in January, February, and October 1987 and in Washington, D.C. and New
York between October 1986 and December 1988.

The epigraph was taken from an interview with Chinua Achebe by Anne Belsover, *African
Events*, November 1987, p. 77. It concerned his new novel *Anthills of the Savannah* (London:
Heinemann, 1987).

[1] On the syndrome see Thomas M. Callaghy, "The State and the Development of Capitalism in
Africa" in Donald Rothchild and Naomi Chazan, eds., *The Precarious Balance* (Boulder, Colo.:
Westview, 1988), pp. 67–99; idem, "The State as Lame Leviathan" in Zaki Ergas, ed., *The*

A new political class began to emerge that used the state as its arena of action and source of power, status, rents, and other forms of wealth. The state was used to begin to build an economic base for itself. All groups concentrated on the weak, but newly autonomous, state as the major avenue to power, status, and wealth because other avenues of upward mobility, such as private capitalist activity, were much more difficult, constrained, time consuming, and uncertain. As political rather than economic logics prevailed, the dominant form of political economy became a crony statism consisting of three interrelated characteristics: (1) clientelist networks used to build support through the extraction and distribution of rents, (2) expansion of state size, including the creation of an extensive parastatal sector, and (3) purchase of primarily urban support via state welfare services and subsidies. In some cases, a parallel indigenous crony or patrimonial capitalism also emerged alongside the state and existing foreign enterprises. The result was neither an effective socialism or state capitalism nor a viable autonomous capitalism. Both state and market were weak. At the same time, the new rulers strongly distrusted anything that could not be controlled politically, especially relatively free market forces and autonomous business groups, either domestic or foreign. As a result, African countries were no less statist than the rest of the Third World, but their dominant statism was less effectively developmental. Neither was the form of indigenous capitalism particularly productive. Both were deeply permeated with the political logics of cronyism.

The new political groups attempted to use rents from the state to reward allies and, at the same time, crosscut and control complicated ethnic, regional, religious, clientelistic, and emerging class ties. Patrimonial, rentier, and prebendal forms of politics and administration defined the political economy. All major social groups put heavy demands on the new states. Liberal democratic structures quickly became more authoritarian, but not necessarily more secure, and military and single-party regimes came to predominate. Most African states were transformed into highly personalistic authoritarian, but weak, administrative states—lame Leviathans—in which crony statism and a subordinate crony capitalism prevailed.

This syndrome was reinforced by precolonial politico-cultural predispositions favoring clientelist structures and political office as the primary avenue

African State in Transition (New York: St. Martin's, 1987), pp. 87–116; idem, "Debt and Structural Adjustment in Africa," *Issue*, 16, 2 (1988): 11–18; John Ravenhill, ed., *Africa in Economic Crisis* (New York: Columbia University Press, 1986); Paul Kennedy, *African Capitalism: The Struggle for Ascendency* (Cambridge: Cambridge University Press, 1988); Goran Hyden, *No Shortcuts to Progress* (Berkeley: University of California Press, 1983); Richard Sandbrook, *The Politics of Africa's Economic Stagnation* (New York: Cambridge University Press, 1985); Harvey Glickman, ed., *The Crisis and Challenge of African Development* (New York: Greenwood, 1988); Sara Berry, *Fathers Work for Their Sons* (Berkeley: University of California Press, 1985); Robert H. Bates, *Markets and States in Tropical Africa* (Berkeley: University of California Press, 1981).

to attain wealth, status, and power. These predispositions were further strengthened by African observations of the behavior of their European colonial rulers.[2]

The new political syndrome had a clear welfare or distributional thrust. The major arena for political combat was urban. In an attempt to maintain political control and satisfy the most urgent demands upon them, the new rulers created a system of food, transport, fuel, health, and education subsidies and services, paid for out of state revenue. This natural statecraft reaction was strongly reinforced by the existence of multiparty electoral systems in the early independence period and by the nature of the decolonization process itself. Africans had struggled against the exploitation and capitalism of their colonial masters. Very strong welfare expectations were created during the independence struggles, which were reinforced by socialist, or at least statist, ideological trends.

To pay for this structure of political control, the new elites, drawing on colonial traditions, began to extract a surplus from their peasant producers and/or their country's mineral wealth. In the agricultural sector, marketing boards were created to buy crops at artificially low prices. Agriculture was accorded major development attention in rhetoric, but not in reality. It was both exploited and neglected at the same time. In the mineral sectors, existing foreign operations were nationalized or controlled in varying degrees, but again, despite the rhetoric, real diversification was not practiced and a maintenance culture was not established to protect existing productive capacity. In both the agricultural and mineral sectors, the intent was to extract a surplus to undergird the state and the needs of Africa's new political class, especially building an economic base for it, to pay for the expanded state, and to fund primarily urban-based welfare services and subsidies.

The lifeblood of this new political class was foreign exchange. To support themselves as an emerging class and the expanded state with its concomitant welfare subsidies and parastatal sectors upon which they were dependent, the new rulers maintained overvalued exchange rates, import controls, and foreign exchange licensing systems. In other words, political control of the acquisition and allocation of foreign exchange was central to this syndrome.

The creation of sizable parastatal sectors led to weak, inefficient, and, because no intermediate and capital goods sectors existed, heavily import-dependent import substitution activity. The statist strategy was congruent with much of the existing international wisdom about development paths, but it was also highly congruent with the political logics of Africa's new and insecure, but increasingly authoritarian rulers. Investment decisions were politically

[2] Robert M. Price, *Society and Bureaucracy in Contemporary Ghana* (Berkeley: University of California Press, 1975); idem, "Politics and Culture in Contemporary Ghana," *Journal of Modern African Studies*, 1, 2 (1974): 173–204; Thomas M. Callaghy, *Culture and Politics in Zaire* (Ann Arbor: Center for Political Studies, University of Michigan, 1987).

determined, usually haphazard, and rarely based on clear economic logic. Investment in politically inspired prestige projects often aggravated this aspect of the syndrome.

In this highly political, often arbitrary and unpredictable context, private investment in long-term production was rarely rational or productive. As a result, the crony capitalism that emerged concentrated on commercial and service forms of business, real estate investment, consumption, and capital flight. Liquidity preferences remained high. Occasionally, investment would be made in productive activity, but only with heavy reliance on crony political participation, protection, and particularistic policy making. Thus, this syndrome did not result in efficient and productive property rights, either state or private. Political rather than economic logics clearly prevailed.

The outcome was what economic historian Douglass North has called a predatory state, as opposed to a contract state. A predatory state concentrates on maximizing rents accruing to the rulers; it "would specify a set of property rights that maximized revenue of the group in power, regardless of its impact on the wealth of society as a whole."[3] Corruption, fraud, appropriation of state and private property, extraction of all kinds, and arbitrary and particularistic administration became dominant features of African life. Politically derived and dependent property rights resulted in inefficient economic outcomes in the long term, but higher rents and political payoffs in the short term. The enormous "transaction costs" and constrained opportunity structure of other, more productive, forms of economic activity made them almost irrational. It was simply much easier and more profitable in the short run to pursue the political logics of the crony and clientelist rentier state.

As a result, no powerful and productive indigenous private sector emerged to push the political logics in the direction of a contract state. In addition, given the existing low level of development, the ideological context of these recently decolonized countries, and the crony statist logic of nationalization, foreign capital could not push very hard in the direction of a contract state either. It was too busy playing the crony capitalist games that were necessary for its own entry or survival. Eventually external capital began to exit or refrained from entering, preferring more propitious regions of the world in which the overall climate was more conducive to long-term productive investment.

The postcolonial syndrome began to constrain Africa's rulers as well. With weak and constrained private sectors, they had to favor the "property rights" of their most powerful constituents—state and party officials and the crony capitalists linked to them, the military, students, urban labor, and the urban population more generally. These new and insecure rulers came to establish

[3] Douglass C. North, *Structure and Change in Economic History* (New York: W. W. Norton, 1981), p. 22.

"a property rights structure favorable to those groups, regardless of its effects on efficiency. . . . In effect, the property rights structure that will maximize rents to the ruler (or ruling class) is in conflict with that that would produce economic growth." In short, "relatively inefficient forms of organization will survive if more efficient forms threaten the survival of the ruler from within or without."[4] Lastly, unlike other regions and other times, no external military or other threat was strong enough to override the inefficient political logics of the syndrome. Only with the advent of major debt and economic crises in the mid-1970s was any serious consideration given to the weaknesses and contradictions of the syndrome. Even then, this happened only under certain facilitating circumstances.

Given the nature and brevity of colonial rule, Africa's new rulers found themselves in control of states with very weak administrative capabilities. This situation was aggravated by the rapid expansion of the state and the political logics that directed it. In addition, existing economic infrastructure was weak and not maintained while reliable economic and administrative data were almost nonexistent.

The syndrome had a direct impact on all types of decision making, but particularly on economic policy making. African governments developed even more dualistic decision-making structures than the other cases discussed in this volume. Clearly the political half was dominant, as in the Philippines under Marcos, but the technocratic half was even weaker, smaller, and, with individual exceptions, less skilled. A thin technocratic staff emerged in the main economic units of these governments—the finance, economic, and planning ministries; the central bank; and parts of the parastatal sector. Given the dominant political logics, the technocratic decision-making structure was insecure and had very little administrative depth. Weak data collection and analysis capabilities were a major constraint. In addition, this already small technocratic stratum was often badly shaken by political and regime changes.

At crisis points, the new rulers felt they had to take corrective measures, a view often reinforced by external pressure. The result was partial, but usually temporary, reliance on the small technocratic stratum. During noncrisis periods, the technocrats often argued quietly for corrective measures, including more rational fiscal policies, the establishment of a maintenance culture, diversification, and more attention to agriculture. Such views appeared in planning statements and documents, but had very little impact on real decisions, much less on administrative practice. When the long-simmering debt and economic crises exploded in the late 1970s and early 1980s, the small technocratic strata emerged into more continuous prominence and influence. How important they became in policy formulation, much less implementation, de-

---

[4] Ibid., pp. 28, 43.

pended, however, on the ongoing play of the deeply rooted political logics of this dominant African syndrome.

Thus, it took nearly twenty years for world economic forces to catch up with Africa's crony statism and crony capitalism and for their negative aspects to result in quite pervasive economic decline. While not caused by external factors, this decline was aggravated greatly by unfavorable external economic shocks, especially falling commodity prices and the oil price increases of the 1970s. Even in countries that benefited greatly from the oil shock, such as Nigeria, the newly abundant foreign exchange merely intensified the negative aspects of the syndrome—a sort of crony hyperinflation. Being so heavily dependent on foreign exchange and imports, African economies were particularly sensitive to the external shocks. The shocks resulted in accelerated deterioration of both urban and rural productive capacity and international competitiveness. Monetary expansion, budget deficits, and debt, while long important, became the easy answers to this crisis.

Because Africa was suffering from severe and simultaneous stabilization and structural difficulties, the hard answers involved deep austerity and major economic restructuring. These answers were seen, however, as too threatening and difficult to contemplate seriously. In addition, most African rulers believed that these problems were cyclical or that external actors would bail them out. The result was an increasing preoccupation with control of a shrinking productive base. The interrelated debt and economic crises led to substantial dependence on external actors, especially the International Monetary Fund (IMF), the World Bank, and the Paris Club countries. The overall economic and structural adjustment crisis long predated the debt difficulties, however. It had begun to emerge almost immediately after independence. The debt crisis merely brought the structural adjustment crisis to a head and moved external actors even more to the center of Africa's stage.

At the same time, increasingly powerful informal or parallel economies that were largely beyond the reach of the state emerged as a major internal reaction to these interlocking crises. Not only did the state now have a smaller formal productive base, but it also had only minimal control over new and important arenas of economic activity. Because of the triumph of the political kingdom and its logics, Africa really had become lost between state and market.

THE ARGUMENT

How do we explain the varied ability of African governments, caught as they are between strong and often contradictory internal and external pressures, to engage in sustained economic adjustment? The argument, briefly sketched here and elaborated in the three cases, is that the degree to which an African government can adjust is determined by its ability to insulate itself from the political logics, characteristics, and effects of the postcolonial syndrome just discussed. The *ability to insulate* is affected principally by the following variables: (1) how the *economic crisis* is perceived by African rulers and how this perception affects the level of commitment to reform; (2) the degree to which decision making is influenced by the technocratic half of the *dualistic decision-making structure*—that is, by economic rather than political logic; (3) the degree of government *autonomy* from the powerful sociopolitical forces of the syndrome as affected by political structure and context and the statecraft skill of the rulers; (4) the *capacity of the state* apparatus and the overall level of economic development; (5) the nature, dependence on, and extent of *external influence*, support, and resource flows, including the market forces of the world economy.

Economic Crisis

The perception of the economic crisis by Africa's rulers is affected by its nature, duration, and severity. The deeper the socioeconomic "trough" and the more serious, deeply rooted, and traumatic it is perceived to be, the more likely the rulers will commit to systematic efforts at economic adjustment. Their perception of the crisis, or trough, is influenced by whether they think it is caused primarily by external and cyclical factors or also by internal factors linked to the syndrome. The ideology, or worldview, of the leadership, often greatly determined by the anticolonial struggle, also influences their perception of the crisis, as does sociopolitical *shredding*, another important variable. As used in this chapter, shredding refers to the degree to which elements of the syndrome and its cohesiveness have been weakened by frequent and debilitating regime change. How the crisis is perceived influences the commitment of the rulers to weather the inherent costs of attempting to alter the syndrome by efforts to restructure the economy. The perception also helps to determine the government's willingness to use external advice and the timing and scope of reform efforts.

Dualistic Decision Making

Sustained reform is greatly affected by the degree to which decision making is dominated by the economic logics of the technocratic staff rather than the political logics more common to the postcolonial syndrome. Rulers need to use, insulate, and protect the technocratic staff while keeping them informed of the political consequences of their reform policies. The more serious and inherent the crisis is perceived to be, the more the technocratic staff will be allowed to dominate decision making. In addition to insulation, the ability of the technocratic staff to operate effectively is largely determined by staff size, technical and administrative capabilities, depth, cohesiveness, continuity over time, and the degree to which they are allowed to interact and bargain with external actors. Here, African choices are severely constrained. The essential data, analytic skills, and other capabilities required to formulate and implement adjustment policies are quite limited.

Given these constraints and the great need for external resources, rulers often feel that they have little choice but to rely on external actors for advice and accept the conditions that go with it, whether or not they understand the advice or feel it to be appropriate. The technocratic staff's insulation, influence, and level of interaction with external actors will vary over time given the statecraft skills of the rulers and the political impact of attempted reforms on the groups most affected by them—state and party officials, the military, state employees, parastatal enterprises, students, labor, and the urban population.

Degree of Sociopolitical Autonomy

The ability to implement economic reforms is primarily influenced by the government's degree of autonomy or insulation from the powerful sociopolitical pressures of the syndrome. This autonomy is determined by the extent to which these forces are coherent and have formal and informal lines of influence to the top leadership and middle-level officials responsible for implementing reforms. The level of insulation is also affected by the nature of the trough and the degree of prior shredding. The statecraft skill of rulers can significantly influence the creation and effective management of given or changing levels of insulation.

New centralized military regimes committed to change have some advantages in this regard. Older authoritarian regimes (whether military or single-party) and democratic regimes tend to have less insulation. Legitimacy given to new regimes may help increase the level of insulation, at least in the initial period. In either authoritarian or democratic regimes, elections tend to diminish insulation and weaken economic reform efforts. Transitions back to democracy can seriously threaten the existing insulation of authoritarian regimes and diminish the sustainability of reform endeavors. This does not rule out successful economic reform under democratic or transitional conditions, but it becomes much more difficult under them. Such regimes require fairly significant centralized authority, elite consensus, and considerable statecraft skill. Even then, democratic governments are more likely to achieve more economic stabilization than structural change.

Insulation or autonomy can be fortified by support from groups that benefit from reform. Given the statist and urban biases of the African syndrome, however, and the overall level of development, a major dilemma of economic reform is that few viable coalitional supporters exist. Noncrony private domestic entreprenuers are weak and few. Africa's feeble formal markets and low level of development also delay the emergence of viable domestic private sector coalitional partners, which takes time under the best conditions. Resident foreign businessmen—Asians, for example—and multinational firms could benefit from the reforms, but they are rarely viable coalitional partners because of existing political sensitivities. While peasant farmers are major potential beneficiaries of reform efforts, they are difficult to mobilize effectively. In regimes with low levels of autonomy, support coalitions need to be stronger and appear sooner to be effective. This has rarely been the case in Africa.

State Capacity

The ability to implement economic reforms is also greatly affected by the quality and depth of state technical, administrative, data gathering, and analytic capabilities beyond those of the technocratic staff, as well as by the nature and effectiveness of external efforts to support and strengthen them. Given the nature of the syndrome, domestic capabilities are quite weak; whereas foreign efforts to support them, although highly sensitive politically, are often useful in the short run, their long-term utility is more questionable.

External Actors and Resources

The capacity to formulate, implement, and monitor economic reforms in Africa is strongly influenced by external actors, particularly the IMF and the World Bank—"the terrible twins" as African officials call them. These officials react strongly to their dependence on external actors and the high-handedness and heavy policy conditionality that often result from it. The more external actors and African officials engage in effective dialogue and learn to pay attention to the conditionality load and timing, policy pace, sequencing, and policy fine tuning, the higher the chances of sustained implementation. While proper crisis perception, leadership commitment, capable and insulated technocrats, effective state capacity, and insulation from sociopolitical pressures all facilitate successful policy formulation and implementation, sufficient and timely external resource flows are also required. They can come from export earnings, the IMF and World Bank, bilaterial assistance, debt rescheduling, new lending, and indigenous and external investment, but they must come if reform is to be sustained.

This argument maintains a balance between voluntarist perspectives that stress "political will," so common to external actors, and pessimistic perspectives that stress structural constraints, so common to academic and African analyses. Adequate levels of understanding, commitment, and statecraft skill are necessary but not sufficient; state capacity, sociopolitical insulation, and adequate external resources are also necessary but not sufficient. Some combination of both sets of factors is required. Given this argument, and the nature of the postcolonial syndrome, it is not surprising that examples of sustained neoorthodox reform in Africa have been few. The three cases in this chapter—Ghana, Zambia, and Nigeria—cover the spectrum relatively well.

To facilitate clear comparison, a brief sketch of the argument for each of the three cases will be presented first; each case then will be explored in greater detail.

THE CASES

Ghana

The radical populist military government of Jerry Rawlings in Ghana has successfully implemented a neoorthodox reform effort since April 1983. Ghana had a very deep socioeconomic trough combined with considerable shredding of its sociopolitical fabric following twenty-five years of chronic regime instability and ineffectiveness. At first the Rawlings regime tried radical populist mobilizational efforts to cope with the severe crisis, but it soon came to believe that Ghana's problems were very deeply rooted and had both internal and external causes. With limited capabilities and resources, the military government felt quite constrained and turned eventually to the IMF and the World Bank. It set aside many of its ideological and policy predispositions in the process. The government demonstrated strong commitment to quite substantial change, a willingness to take the advice, conditions, and resources of the IMF and the World Bank, and an ability to act quickly and very broadly in scope.

In the process, a small and thin but remarkable technocratic economic team was assembled and given considerable autonomy and freedom to work with external actors. This team remained very stable over time and received substantial external help, ranging from data gathering through systematic sector studies to general analysis and monitoring. Given the severity of Ghana's trough and the high degree of shredding over the previous decade, the Rawlings government operated with significant initial legitimacy and insulation. As policies were implemented, this insulation began to shrink and opposition from state employees, labor, students, and the general urban population increased. Using its statecraft skills and authoritarian capabilities, the government pursued its course, however.

The major beneficiaries were cocoa farmers and other rural groups and expatriate businesses. Rural beneficiaries proved difficult to mobilize and use as coalitional partners despite repeated government efforts to find appropriate political formulas and structures. Expatriate business success proved embarrassing and generated considerable political sensitivities. The local indigenous private sector was weak. Much of it was quite antagonistic to the Rawlings' regime and withheld support despite the fact that many of the reforms were congruent with private sector interests.

The radical character of the regime slowed development of external support from other than the IMF and the World Bank. Eventually, as the coherence and seriousness of the reform effort became obvious, and few other such cases appeared in Africa, external resource flows increased significantly. The additional resources helped mitigate increasing opposition while all actors began to adjust policies and conditionality to make the reform effort more sustainable.

TABLE 7.1
Ghana, Zambia, Nigeria: Macroeconomic Indicators, 1980–1987

	1980	1981	1982	1983	1984	1985	1986	1987
GDP[a]								
Ghana	0.0	(1.8)	(7.2)	0.7	8.7	5.1	5.3	4.0
Zambia	3.0	6.2	(2.8)	(2.0)	(1.3)	4.4	0.5	(0.2)
Nigeria	5.3	(8.4)	(3.2)	(6.3)	(5.2)	5.3	(3.3)	1.2
GDP Per Capita[b]								
Ghana	(4.1)	(5.3)	(9.7)	(3.1)	6.0	3.3	—	—
Zambia	(0.2)	6.2	(6.2)	(5.5)	(4.7)	1.0	(2.9)	—
Nigeria	(0.6)	(6.3)	(3.4)	(11.9)	(8.9)	(2.1)	(6.2)	—
Inflation[c]								
Ghana	50.1	116.5	22.3	122.9	39.7	10.3	24.6	—
Zambia	11.7	14.0	12.5	19.6	20.0	37.4	51.6	—
Nigeria	10.0	20.8	7.7	23.2	39.6	5.5	1.1	—
Wages[d]								
Ghana	100.0	64.2	68.3	63.8	—	—	—	—
Zambia	100.0	109.0	103.5	95.6	89.0	72.3	—	—
Nigeria	100.0	94.0	101.5	74.9	42.3	41.8	—	—
Terms of Trade[e]								
Ghana	100.0	81.4	73.1	88.1	98.1	90.3	88.0	—
Zambia	100.0	79.8	70.9	77.9	70.1	71.5	70.0	—
Nigeria	—	—	—	—	—	—	—	—
Exchange Rate[f]								
Ghana	100.0	222.0	278.0	187.0	72.0	52.0	30.0	23.0
Zambia	100.0	102.0	114.0	106.0	91.0	84.0	40.0	43.0
Nigeria	100.0	111.0	114.0	134.0	185.0	166.0	91.0	29.0
Debt/GNP[g]								
Ghana	29.6	34.7	34.7	39.8	43.7	49.1	47.5	63.3
Zambia	90.5	92.9	101.9	120.3	151.5	195.2	398.6	334.4
Nigeria	8.9	13.0	14.1	21.1	20.5	22.1	53.1	122.6
Reserves[h]								
Ghana	3.1	2.4	4.2	4.8	6.4	6.8	7.1	—
Zambia	1.2	1.0	1.1	1.3	0.6	2.5	0.4	—
Nigeria	5.8	2.0	1.2	1.0	1.7	2.0	1.9	—
Investment[i]								
Ghana	5.5	4.6	3.4	3.7	6.9	9.5	—	—
Zambia	23.3	9.3	16.8	13.8	14.7	14.9	14.8	—
Nigeria	21.8	27.5	21.6	16.8	12.3	9.6	—	—

TABLE 7.1 (*cont.*)

	1980	1981	1982	1983	1984	1985	1986	1987
Current Account[j]								
Ghana	0.2	(1.6)	(0.3)	(0.8)	(0.5)	(2.1)	—	—
Zambia	(13.8)	(18.5)	(14.6)	(8.2)	(5.6)	(9.0)	(18.2)	—
Nigeria	5.6	(7.4)	(8.8)	(5.7)	0.2	1.7	—	—

Sources: International Monetary Fund, *International Financial Statistics Yearbook*, 1987, 1988; World Bank, *World Tables 1987*; World Bank, *Adjustment Lending*, 1989; World Bank, *World Debt Tables*, vol. 2, 1984–1985, 1986–1987, 1988–1989; various estimates.

[a] Real GDP growth based on 1980 local currency.
[b] Real per capita GDP growth based on 1980 local currency.
[c] CPI, percentage change over previous year.
[d] Real minimum wage index, 1980 = 100.
[e] Terms of trade, 1980 = 100.
[f] Real effective exchange rate, 1980 = 100.
[g] Total external debt as percentage of GNP.
[h] Average month's coverage of reserves.
[i] Total investment as percentage of GDP.
[j] Current account balance as percentage of GDP.

In sum, Ghana had a deep crisis; considerable shredding, understanding and commitment; a thin but competent technocratic team; substantial insulation; external advice and support; internal and external learning and experimentation; and eventually, important resource flows. The result was a quite sustained economic reform effort.

Zambia

Reform came late and grudgingly to the single-party regime that has ruled Zambia since independence in 1964. Despite a serious economic trough and evaporating copper deposits, the regime perceived the crisis to be temporary, cyclical, and caused almost exclusively by external factors. This perception was reinforced by ideological views quite antipathetic to market economics and the IMF. In addition, Zambia had a huge parastatal sector, even by regional standards, and the highest urbanization in sub-Saharan Africa. Despite considerable debt and resource constraints and strong external pressure, the government resisted serious, systematic change until 1985. As the economic crisis mounted, President Kenneth Kaunda finally agreed to attempt a broad reform effort formulated and pushed by the IMF and the World Bank. This program received almost unanimous disapproval from key officials and major sociopolitical groups.

In place since 1964, the regime in the mid-1980s, despite its authoritarian character, had very little sociopolitical insulation and had undergone almost no shredding. All groups took advantage of this fact and used their multiple formal and informal lines of access to express dislike for the reform endeavor. The technocratic team was very small and uninfluential. In the middle of the reform effort its composition was dramatically altered; officials opposed to the IMF and the reforms were put in charge of implementing them. Political logic and crony statism prevailed. Key policies were manipulated, with significant negative consequences, and other reforms were simply not implemented because of extremely weak administrative capabilities and opposition at all levels of the state.

Beneficiaries of the reforms were almost nonexistent because agricultural policy changes were not fully implemented. An African private business sector barely existed, and Asian and other foreign businessmen eventually became scapegoats of the reform effort.

Sceptical about the government's commitment to reform, external actors were ambivalent and hedged their resource support, all in the context of extreme foreign exchange scarcity. Many of the resources that were committed were slow to be disbursed. Effort to fine-tune policies was limited and the government offered no real cooperation in doing so.

Through poor statecraft, pervasive opposition culminated in riots that led eventually to the collapse of the reform program in 1987 and the departure of the IMF. Fears about upcoming presidential and parliamentary elections, perceived to be important to the legitimacy of the single-party regime, were also a factor in the collapse. The neoorthodox reform endeavor was replaced by a homegrown adjustment program. Despite the rhetoric, it amounted to a return to the same old crony statism and its political logics.

In sum, Zambia had a deep crisis but little sociopolitical shredding, poor understanding and very limited commitment, a thin and uninfluential technocratic stratum, no insulation, very strong opposition, extremely weak state capability, strong external pressure with heavy conditionality but ambivalent support, and limited and uneven resource flows. The result was the collapse of the reform effort and a return to crony statism.

Nigeria

Nigeria is an intermediate case. Under several military regimes and one democratic government, the massive oil revenues of the 1970s and early 1980s intensified rather than mitigated all the negative aspects of the postcolonial syndrome. The civilian regime seriously aggravated the economic crisis and took only limited action to correct it. A military regime overthrew it in 1983, only to be replaced itself in 1985 by another military government headed by General Ibrahim Babangida. Given its oil wealth, Nigeria had a less intense trough and an ambivalent assessment of the need for serious internal restructuring. Nevertheless, the Babangida regime appeared committed to serious reform despite vehement popular antipathy for the IMF. Through clever statecraft, a way was found around this dilemma. A broad reform program was put together by the World Bank and a small, but skilled, stable, and protected technocratic group of officials. This reform package was quietly transformed into an IMF program in 1986, but with a government commitment not to draw on the available resources attached to it.

The military regime had substantial initial legitimacy and insulation. It also had, however, a serious commitment to returning Nigeria to democracy by 1992. This would happen under a structure determined, after widespread consultation, ultimately by the military. Much of the population remained uncommitted to the necessity of economic reform, especially given the perpetual hope of higher oil prices. An incoherent agricultural policy did not lead to substantial rural support. The relatively large, by African standards, indigenous private sector initially supported the reform endeavor, only to back away as its negative consequences became apparent. Over time, opposition increased, particularly among students, labor groups, and the general urban population. It culminated in serious strikes, demonstrations, and riots in the spring of 1988.

The strength of the reform effort was the commitment of the Babangida government to change and its military-induced insulation. Its potential weaknesses had to do with the transition back to democracy in a staged five-year process with several sets of elections at various levels. The early stages of this process made it clear that little sociopolitical shredding had taken place and that most groups had a limited understanding of the need to sustain restructuring activities. Despite its quite good statecraft skills, the military government's efforts to prevent the old sociopolitical forces of the syndrome from recoalescing with the return to democratic rule appeared to be limited. In the face of mounting opposition, a major wobble in the reform effort occurred in 1988. The transition back to democracy and, despite very high expectations, weak external resource flows from oil, rescheduling, new commercial lending, and external investment, clouded the prospects for sustained implementation of the restructuring program, but did not rule it out.

In sum, Nigeria had a moderate crisis, little shredding, important regime understanding but limited societal understanding, a skilled and protected technocratic team, extensive and quite creative external advice, substantial but weakening insulation due to the transition to democracy, and quite modest external resource flows. The result was an important but wobbly reform effort with uncertain prospects.

Each of the three cases will now be explored in more detail, first through an examination of each version of the postcolonial syndrome and then through an analysis of each reform effort and the attendant politics.[5]

---

[5] Major sources used for all three cases over the period 1982–1988 include: Economist Intelli-

GHANA: RADICAL POPULISM AND NEOCLASSICAL ECONOMICS

The Ghanaian Syndrome

In 1957 Ghana became the first African country to achieve independence, and Ghanaians had very high expectations about what it would mean. Instead, "the regressive cycle of Ghanaian politics"[6] shredded these early hopes and much sociopolitical life besides. One regime succeeded another as the decline deepened in the face of incoherent and ineffective action. From 1957 to 1966 Kwame Nkrumah ruled Ghana, transforming it from a multiparty democracy into a personalized and quite authoritarian single-party state. He declared Ghana to be a socialist state, but the ultimate result was a nonproductive form of crony statism.

The military overthrew Nkrumah in February 1966 and established the National Liberation Council, committing itself in the process to curing the evils of the former regime and returning the country to multiparty democracy. This was achieved in 1969 with the advent of the Second Republic under Dr. K. A. Busia. His civilian government was in turn overthrown by a military coup in 1972 led by Colonel J. K. Acheampong. After accelerated decline and massive corruption, an intramilitary coup brought General Fred Akuffo to power in 1978. Akuffo's Supreme Military Council was in its turn overthrown by Flight Lieutenant Jerry Rawlings in a mid-1979 coup. Rawlings permitted the transition back to democratic rule that was already underway to continue, while attempting to cleanse Ghana once again of corruption. With Rawlings looking over his shoulder, Dr. Hilla Limann became the first president of Ghana's Third Republic in September 1979, only to be removed by Rawlings on the last day of 1981.

The focus in this chapter will be on the principal reasons for Ghana's sustained inability to cope with its progressive decline over more than two decades. Of particular importance was Ghana's dualistic decision-making structure and its lack of insulation from the pressures of the postcolonial syndrome that had become firmly rooted under Nkrumah.

The National Liberation Council switched decision making from the political side, where it had been under Nkrumah's political kingdom, to the tech-

---

gence Unit's quarterly "Country Reports"; *West Africa; Africa Confidential; Financial Times* (London); *Africa News,* and *Africa Report.*

[6] Deborah Pellow and Naomi Chazan, *Ghana: Coping with Uncertainty* (Boulder, Colo.: Westview, 1986), p. 88. On Ghana's version of the syndrome, also see Naomi Chazan, *An Anatomy of Ghanaian Politics* (Boulder, Colo.: Westview, 1983); Tony Killick, *Development Economics in Action: A Study of Economic Policies in Ghana* (London: Heinemann, 1978); and two very fine unpublished policy analyses, Joan Nelson, "Ghana: 1967–72" in "The Political Economy of Stabilization in Small, Low Income, Trade-Dependent Nations" (Washington, D.C., July 1983); idem, "Political Factors Shaping the Economic Policies of the Limann Administration, Ghana, September 1979–December 1981" (Washington, D.C., September 1985).

nocratic side. Supported by IMF and World Bank advice, some stabilization was achieved, but at the cost of a painful recession. The stabilization measures included a 30 percent devaluation, which was not fully reinforced by proper fiscal and monetary changes. Much of the public believed that Nkrumah's external debts were the root of the economic problem, and calls for debt repudiation were very strong. Most groups were vehemently opposed to the devaluation and viewed it as a failure.

This legacy was to stalk Busia's new democratic government. His technocratic economic team lacked consensus, with its key player strongly opposed to another devaluation. Intense political doubts about the need to make any economic adjustments existed among key regime and party officials. Lacking any insulation, and rapidly losing its legitimacy, the democratic government was besieged by pressures from all sides, particularly from labor and state employees. By 1970, for example, the real minimum wage was only 55 percent of its 1960 level. The military also viewed the new democratic regime with considerable disdain. Above all, most Ghanaians had powerful, but conflicting expectations. On the one hand, they wanted the government to take general measures that would bring economic growth, but, at the same time, they expected particularistic help and exceptions via the pervasive patron-client networks. Finally, in the context of accelerating decline and political shock, confusion, and misunderstanding, Busia announced another devaluation in December 1971. The next month the military seized power again.

While the coup had other roots, its timing and justification and the early actions of the new government, which included revaluation and debt repudiation, only intensified the negative devaluation legacy. This legacy had serious implications for the viability of technocratic decision making and the use of economic rather than political logic. Under Acheampong's National Redemption Council, Ghana's social and economic slide continued, with no clear economic policy and a substantial increase in corruption and political incompetence. By 1978, the situation had become so serious that General Akuffo staged an intramilitary palace coup against Acheampong.

Akuffo brought back a technocratic economic team, initially headed by Dr. Joseph Abbey. The team introduced strong stabilization measures, with some IMF support, but they proved to be too little, too late, and prompted strong popular reaction. The demand for a return to democracy was too strong to be ignored, and such a transition was started, only to be interrupted by the four-month Rawlings interregnum. In a very popular move, he executed the leader of the 1966 coup and Acheampong and Akuffo and vowed to rid the country of corruption before allowing the transition to democracy to resume.

Thus, in the context of major socioeconomic decline and political shredding, the Limann government took power in September 1979, with Rawlings looking very closely over its shoulder. While the brief Rawlings interregnum had not made any fundamental changes, it had begun to lay the groundwork for them. This included bringing Abbey back as commissioner of finance and economic planning. During the short life of the Rawlings' Armed Forces Revolutionary Council, Abbey worked closely with Dr. Amon Nikoi, Limann's prospective finance minister. These two worked quietly with the IMF, and, at the technical level, prepared strong neoorthodox measures with which to attack Ghana's problems. But it was not to be. For political reasons, no real action was taken. Only halfhearted measures emerged as the Limann government tried to avoid a formal IMF program. Lacking a strong political base of his own, Limann was pushed around by his party's political barons, whose political networks dated back to the 1960s. The government ignored the groundwork laid by Abbey and Nikoi, as political decision making predominated. Negotiations with the Fund did continue, and agreement appeared to be close a couple of times. The technocrats became less and less influential, however, and Nikoi was finally removed in November 1980.

Factional disputes within the government and fears of popular opposition to stabilization measures meant that economic logic was not taken seriously. The 1981 budget, for example, included a deficit equal to 40 percent of proposed spending. Stabilization measures seriously threatened key groups and the functioning of the all-important patron-client networks controlled by the party's old guard. Members of the old guard felt that they had been out in the cold and away from their state rents for far too long under the military. Devaluation was to be avoided at all costs. Under democratic conditions, the government had very little insulation from a whole array of sociopolitical groups, all of which were very vocal. The statecraft skills of the Limann government were quite modest as it became increasingly preoccupied by the fear of a new Rawlings coup. It delayed action on the severe economic problems until its support had almost completely evaporated. On New Year's Eve 1981, as corruption ran rampant again, the economy approached collapse, and the government was rumored, out of desperation, to be close to an agreement with the IMF, Jerry Rawlings stepped in again. An exhausted, humiliated, and impoverished population awaited a miracle from its returning hero, "Junior Jesus" as it called him. Rawlings ultimately gave it to them, but not in the form that they expected.

The Program and the Politics

Ghana thus presents the intriguing contrast of a radical populist regime with an IMF and World Bank-sponsored neoorthodox economic recovery program, which, against enormous odds, proved to be amazingly sustainable.[7]

[7] On Ghana's economic program and its politics, see Donald I. Ray, *Ghana: Politics, Economics and Society* (Boulder, Colo.: Lynne Rienner, 1986); Reginald Herbold Green, "Ghana: Stabilization and Structural Shifts" (Manuscript for the Lance Taylor WIDER project, Accra/Falmer, April–May 1987); Kwame A. Ninsin, "Ghanaian Politics After 1981: Revolution or Evolution?" *Ca-*

By the time Rawlings returned to power, Ghana had gone way, way down. The trough was deep, nasty, prolonged, and physically and psychologically devastating. Between 1970 and 1982, real per capita income declined 30 percent; real export earnings dropped 52 percent; and between 1974 and 1983, GDP fell by a fifth. From 1975 to 1983, the real minimun wage plummeted an astounding 86 percent, while per capita caloric intake, which had averaged about 92 percent of the minimum daily requirement during the 1970s, fell to only 65.4 percent by 1983. Infant mortality increased as a result. The 1964–1965 cocoa crop had been 557,000 tons; the 1983–1984 crop was only 158,000 tons. Much of the transportation infrastructure had seriously deteriorated.

The years 1982 and 1983 were unbelievably bad—little water and electrical power due to a severe drought, little food, no cigarettes, no beer, no fuel, no spare parts, nothing in the stores, and widespread hoarding. Real GDP dropped 4.6 percent in 1983 alone, and real GDP per capita fell 7.1 percent. Inflation, which had averaged just above 40 percent in the 1970s, shot up to 123 percent. The cedi, the national currency which had been pegged at 2.75 to the U.S. dollar since 1978, was selling for more than thirty times that rate on the parallel market. On top of all this, severe brush fires raged across much of the land, and Nigeria expelled over a million Ghanaians who were forced to return to this ravaged land.

Well-being, dignity, integrity, and self-image were shattered. The vivid, searing memories of these two years and the legitimacy of the new military regime helped to get Ghana through the early years of the economic reform effort. Something had to be done. Ghanaians remembered how very bad it was, and they did not want to go through it again. Many understood the counterfactual of inaction; they had lived it.[8]

To cope with this disastrous situation, the Rawlings government, the Provisional National Defense Council (PNDC), used a series of radical mass mobilization techniques, especially student task forces, to gather and collect the cocoa crop, grow food, repair roads, control smuggling, and root out black market operations. Popular committees were used to distribute essential commodities and enforce price and rent controls. While some of these efforts had positive results, key regime officials realized that such methods would be dif-

nadian Journal of African Studies, 21, 1 (1987): 17–37; Donald Rothchild and E. Gyimah-Boadi, "Ghana's Decline and Development Strategies" in Ravenhill, Africa in Economic Crisis, pp. 254–85; Tony Hodges, "Ghana's Strategy for Adjustment with Growth," Africa Recovery, 2, 3 (August 1988): 16–20, 27; Sheetal K. Chand and Reinold van Til, "Ghana: Toward Successful Stabilization and Recovery," Finance & Development 25, 1 (March 1988): 32–35; Jon Kraus, "Revolution and the Military in Ghana," Current History 82, 482 (March 1983): 115–19, 131–32; idem, "Ghana's Radical Populist Regime," Current History 85, 501 (April 1985): 164–68, 186; idem, "Ghana's Shift from Radical Populism," Current History 86, 520 (May 1987): 205–8, 227.

[8] Interviews, Accra, Ghana, January 1987 and Nairobi, Kenya, October 1987.

ficult to sustain over time and were not likely to become the basis for a rebuilt economy. The main missing incredient was capital. In the hope of becoming a client socialist state on the Cuban model, the government asked the Soviets for assistance. The Soviets replied with a polite but firm "nyet," suggesting that Ghana turn instead to the IMF and the World Bank.[9]

Believing that they had no other choice, the government opened discussions with the IMF in late summer 1982. This action precipitated two badly organized coup attempts in October and November supported by radical leftists and junior elements of the military. These were not the first plots against the new regime from both the left and right, nor were they to be the last. The most serious coup attempt came in June 1983 after the beginning of the formal IMF agreement and the Economic Recovery Program (ERP) in April. Despite its diffuse popular legitimacy, the new Rawling's regime was lucky to survive its first eighteen months. It might not have save for the ambivalence, utopian visions, and poor organization of the political left and radical labor.

Out of the enormous policy chaos, confusion, and contradictions of 1982 came the increasing influence and political protection of a small, but quite remarkable and stable economic team. At the center of this effort were Joe Abbey and Kwesi Botchwey, a former radical teacher at the University of Ghana, who became the secretary for Finance and Economic Planning. Over time the team also included key members of the PNDC itself, especially P. V. Obeng. The coherence, continuity, and ongoing political insulation of this economic team explains a good deal of the sustainablity of the economic reform effort in Ghana.

Abbey and Botchwey came to believe that, above all, they had to have access to external resources and that meant working and bargaining with the IMF and the World Bank. It also required explaining the economic logics involved to key political players in Ghana and the sociopolitical context of the economic logics in Ghana to the Fund, the Bank, and other external actors. As Botchwey put it, "We had to maneuver our way around the naivités of leftism and the crudities and rigidities of monetarism."[10] Rawlings understood the need to do something and the necessity of economic logic, even if he did not understand the details of the policies themselves. When asked about these reforms, he responded, "I don't understand all these theories, all this economic blah blah blah."[11] But he did comprehend their importance and the need to give them consistent political protection and insulation over time.

The economic reform program was designed to attack key elements of the postcolonial syndrome, especially the overvalued exchange rate. Through a series of small devaluations between 1983 and 1986, the cedi rate dropped to

[9] Interviews with Ghanaian and international officials, Accra, January 1987.

[10] James Brooke, "Ghana, Once 'Hopeless,' Gets At Least the Look of Success," *New York Times*, 3 January 1989, p. A8.

[11] Ibid., 11 December 1988, p. 28.

90 to the U.S. dollar. To regularize this process and help defuse its political implications, a weekly foreign exchange auction was introduced in September 1986. At first there were two rates, a fixed rate for certain key transactions and the auction rate. In February 1987, the two rates were unified. By late 1988, the cedi rate had fallen to 227 to the dollar. Because the parallel market did not disappear, an attempt was made in 1988 to "legalize" it by allowing the opening of licensed foreign exchange bureaus.

In an effort to reverse the urban-rural terms of trade, control smuggling, and boost export earnings, the price paid to cocoa producers was progressively raised from 12,000 cedis per ton in 1982 to 150,000 by 1987. The Ghana Cocoa Board was restructured, and 40 percent of its employees trimmed in an effort to increase efficiency, cut costs, and control political rents. The latter entailed removing 25,000 "ghost workers" from the payroll. The other two main export sectors, gold and timber, were rehabilitated, while some incentives for nontraditional exports were introduced. The import licensing system was greatly restructured, linking it to the auction and making it nearly automatic.

Overall state expenditure was cut, subsidies diminished, user fees for health services and education introduced, taxes increased, and tax collection improved. Interest rates were raised, and most price controls were removed. About 12,000 civil servants were cut in 1987 in a very complicated political and economic process. Real wages were held down, and debt service was improved. Major rehabilitation of the transportation infrastructure was undertaken, and initial, halting steps were taken to privatize some parastatal enterprises and reform others.

By late 1988, this economic recovery effort was in its seventh year and second phase. It had what one observer described as "fragile strength."[12] Given Ghana's political history and dismal economic record, this was quite an achievement and a tribute to the sustained courage, commitment, and luck of its leaders. In 1984, real GDP rose an amazing 8.7 percent, largely because of greatly increased food production due to the end of the drought. But in 1985 it rose again, this time by 5.1 percent, and in 1986 it increased yet again by 5.3 percent—the first time since the 1950s that GDP per capita had increased in three consecutive years. In 1987, the growth continued again at a little over 4 percent. The growth was quite evenly distributed by sector, but undergirded primarily by larger cocoa, timber, and gold exports.

Contradictions and serious disagreements within the PNDC led many to see the regime as having a "split personality." Most of these conflicts had to do with the thrust of the ERP, its impact on social groups, and its implications for Ghana's sovereignty and dependence on external actors. For both Ghanaian and external observers, the regime generated conflicting "schizophrenic" and

[12] Interview, international official, Accra, January 1987.

"patient revolutionary" images. In the schizophrenic image, the regime was seen as having two quite different but coexisting aspects—its radical populism reflected in its rhetoric and foreign policy and its neoclassical economic pragmatism. In this view, both aspects were presumed to be real, managing somehow to commingle and survive.In the patient revolutionary image, the regime was seen to be thoroughly radical, with the neoclassical recovery program being a mere tactical feint. According to this view, these patient revolutionaries realized that socializing a collapsed economy was senseless. The economy must recover first and then they would strike.

In the early years, serious tensions existed both within the PNDC and between it and its labor, student, and leftist supporters. Rawlings worked hard to keep these tensions under control, while allowing the membership of the PNDC to change. Over time the social base of the regime shifted away from its initial urban, labor, radical, and populist roots toward the diffuse and precarious support of rural groups that benefited from the reforms. These groups were hard to mobilize politically, however. During all this time, Rawlings maintained his support for the economic team and allowed it to work and bargain hard with external actors.[13]

How does one account for the sustainability of this economic reform effort despite these difficulties? The "trough factor" played a major role. With its series of ineffective and corrupt regimes since the fall of Nkrumah in 1966 and the near total disintegration of the economy, Ghana had suffered a great deal, both physically and mentally. People were tired, and Rawlings appeared to care and was not corrupt. In and of itself, however, this might not have been enough without the influence of a second, related factor. Ghana's debilitating regime change cycles had telling political consequences. They had seriously shredded the fabric of Ghanaian political life, decimated coalitions, wiped out leaders, altered political patterns and norms, and weakened the cohesiveness and clout of major sociopolitical groups. Under this new and different military regime, with its built-in authoritarian autonomy, these underlying changes manifested themselves clearly for the first time.

A key characterisitic of the Rawlings regime was its relatively narrow organizational base. What might appear at first to be a handicap for a regime undertaking major economic reform turned out, in fact, to be one of its fragile strengths. Insulation from important sociopolitical veto groups, themselves weakened by the shredding of the previous fifteen years, allowed the PNDC to do more than other more constrained regimes. This is not to say that there were no serious security challenges or important internal opposition to the Rawlings regime; there were both. But the institutionalized resistance of a

[13] See Ray, *Ghana*, chaps. 4, 7; interviews, Ghanaian and international officials, Accra, January 1987; also see an interview with Botchwey in "Ghana: High Stakes Gambles," *Africa News* 31, 2 (23 January 1989): 1–4, 9–11.

deeply rooted, single-party regime, as in Zambia, or a multiparty democratic regime, as in Shagari's Nigeria, did not exist. The Rawlings regime has maintained some social and political distance, some autonomy.

This form of fragile strength had a negative side, however. Initially the regime had quite real but diffuse legitimacy. As a result, the PNDC engaged in periodic, often vague and confused attempts to mobilize and institutionalize this diffuse support. Early in the regime the radical mobilizational efforts led to the creation of the Committees for the Defence of the Revolution and Workers' Defence Committees. Eventually they had to be reined in. The PNDC began searching for a nonparty electoral formula that would allow it to tap its support without creating coherent opposition groups, especially in the urban areas, or resurrecting old parties and power blocs.

The major beneficiaries of the economic recovery program were rural farmers because of the increases in producer prices for cocoa and other commodities and the major infrastructure rehabilitation efforts. A substantial reversal of the urban-rural terms of trade favored rural producers, while key urban groups shouldered much of the cost of the reform program. For example, the ratio of the price of a metric ton of cocoa to the urban minimum wage (a rough indicator of the relative pay of Ghana's rural producer to that of the urban worker) rose sharply, reversing the decline of the late 1960s and 1970s and bringing about a historic shift in the postcolonial syndrome.

The urban-rural terms of trade shift created a dilemma for the PNDC. What the regime desired, but had difficulty finding, was a way to tap and institutionalize rural support without giving urban opposition an effective mechanism for mobilizing its discontent. In July 1987, the PNDC finally announced long promised elections for 109 district assemblies, to be held in late 1988. Even this relatively limited political opening was fraught with enormous uncertainties for the PNDC and its ERP. Despite its populist rhetoric and promises of a "debate" about the reform effort, the PNDC allowed very little popular input into its policies. The vehemence of student and public response to an open discussion of World Bank-supported educational reforms in early 1987 took the regime by surprise. In anticipation of the elections, the government announced that it would increase social spending, especially for those most affected by the reforms. The elections were duly held in late 1988, but their implications for the PNDC's dilemma remained unclear. Pressures for full democratization continued to be very strong from a great diversity of groups.

Opposition to the reforms increased over time, particularly from the urban population that bore the great bulk of the costs. Ordinary urban people were squeezed on a number of fronts simultaneously—low incomes, higher prices via auction devaluations, the psychological factor of seeing things in the stores again but being unable to buy them, increased tax collection, an end to key subsidies, and the introduction of user fees for education and medical services. The potential benefits of the economic reforms for the urban population depended on new investment and thus were quite some way down the road, if they were to materialize at all.

This situation created for the government what could be called the "politics of counterfactuals" dilemma—that is, how to explain to people that without the reforms their situation would be much worse. This and other key political dilemmas of the ERP were graphically illustrated by a January 1986 exchange between Kwesi Pratt, a leading critic of the ERP, and Botchwey. After a speech on the ERP by Botchwey, Pratt asked the following "question":

> In fact, a lot of statistics have been pushed down our throat this morning, and I am only hoping that the answer to my question would not be loaded with statistics because it is always irrelevant to the suffering that the people of this country are faced with.
>
> It is strange that at this time when sick people are running away from our hospitals instead of going into the hospital; it is strange that at this time when the majority of our people are dropping out of schools because of the imposition of not "cut-throat" but "crush-head" school fees, we are talking of economic recovery in this society of ours.
>
> We are talking as if everything has improved, but the real condition on the ground is that people are dying, people are starving . . . because of the senseless policy of devaluation, retrenchment of labour etc.
>
> I would like the Secretary to react to this situation on the ground. The suffering of the ordinary people in the streets. I am not talking of the profits of the big companies . . . , I am not talking of the praises which come from the imperialist controlled IMF and the World Bank.

Botchwey responded as follows:

> This is a very good question. It is not put in the most agreeable way but I think it summarises a certain sort of tendency in this country which I find to be disagreeable for many reasons. . . . [T]o be positive such criticism must at least have at its point of departure facts about our national situation. Emotional outbursts we are all capable of.
>
> The question is, how are the very concrete problems . . . going to be addressed, leaving aside the external resource mobilization. Let's start from say: we don't want any money from the IMF. . . . It does not take the imagination of a genius therefore to see that without those inflows, our national situation and the state of the poverty of the majority of our people would have been much weaker than what Mr. Kwesi Pratt has just spoken about here. So let's start from the factual situation.
>
> I get amused when people bemoan statistics. . . . Now, if you don't want statistics how are we to measure the improvement or deterioration in this economy. Do we take a vote of everybody? Subjection?
>
> If we decide to live within our means, the standard of our people will sink to levels we have never seen before in this country. . . . You can beat your breast and swear

to heavens that you are against the IMF, therefore, you are not taking any devaluation but you are doing something actually crazy.[14]

Pratt was eventually arrested in July 1987 and held in detention until the end of the year.

The battle of the counterfactuals, of contending economic and political logics, was difficult to wage effectively. It was a battle that the PNDC appeared to be winning with less frequency as the memories of 1982–1983 faded a little while current troubles remained cruel and vivid. Botchwey later noted that, "We must measure the success of this program not against the background of everybody's wishes, but against what was possible under the circumstances." In late 1988, Rawlings echoed this counterfactual comment: "Living conditions are still tough for our people. I am not happy. But they could have been worse."[15] In response to this grim situation, a "culture of silence," of quiet resignation, emerged among the urban population, punctuated occasionally by outbursts of protest.

These outbursts and their suppression increased from 1986 on. Mounting opposition came mostly from labor, students, and the small but still active political left. Workers were a major concern of the PNDC, the major issues being wage and benefits restraint, layoffs linked to cutting the size of the state, the abolition of subsidies, and the creation of user fees. State layoffs were tried to pay the remaining workers more, thereby raising productivity. By 1982, the average amount of time worked by a state or parastatal employee was only between fifteen and twenty hours a week, and productivity was very low. This reinforced the already low level of state administrative capability, with enormous implications for the implementation of the more difficult economic reforms.

Most workers engaged in "straddling," that is, maintaining one foot in the formal economy and the other in the informal one. Only in this way was survival possible, especially as the government played games over wages and benefits. In April 1986, for example, to soften the blow of the devaluations, wage and benefit increases were announced. But the government had not adequately calculated their effect on the budget. The increases destroyed the IMF targets, leading to intense external pressure to rescind them. When the government announced the rollback of the increases, red flags (traditional symbols of mourning) went up all over Accra, the capital, and there were demonstrations in the city and in neighboring Tema. The regime responded with force and arrests; some officials believed the regime was within forty-eight hours of fall-

[14] Kwesi Botchwey, "The State of the Economy," Information Service Department, Accra, Ghana (January 1986), pp. 13–15, 20.

[15] *Africa Report*, 32, 6 (November–December 1987): 49; Brooke, "Ghana Once 'Hopeless,' " p. A8.

ing. The government formally reinstated the increases, but subsequently tried quietly to recoup the losses in other ways.

Another round came in June 1987 when pro-PNDC groups twice attacked the Trade Union Congress (TUC) offices in Accra. The TUC responded with a statement very hostile to the government. It warned the PNDC about harassment, detentions, and other human rights abuses, called for a halt to layoffs unless properly planned and for national, not just district, elections, condemned the PNDC's neglect of existing mechanisms for consulting with labor, and bitterly attacked the IMF and the World Bank. The biggest union in Ghana, the Industrial and Commercial Workers Union, demanded that the PNDC publish its agreements with the IMF and the World Bank, disclose the cost of maintaining foreign advisors, and restrict debt service to 10 percent of foreign exchange earnings.

After these events the government tried to use less clumsy techniques to control labor, but the tensions persisted. In March 1988, the newly elected, relatively moderate head of the Trade Union Congress called for the minimum wage to be tripled, the reintroduction of subsidies, and the end of the IMF program. He also rejected the upcoming district elections and demanded a representative constituent assembly that would draft a new constitution for the country.

Tensions were definitely rising with students and the political left as well. Student leaders were arrested and university campuses closed in 1987 due to protests, which at first aimed at the educational reforms but broadened considerably. Leaders of the small but vocal political left, who had close ties with radical student and labor groups, were detained in May after two groups—the New Democratic Movement and the Kwame Nkrumah Revolutionary Guards—published a vehement assault on the PNDC's relations with the IMF and the World Bank and issued a call for real elections. The government defended its relations with these two institutions and ridiculed the "infantile leftism" of its critics. In June, the government announced that it had uncovered another plot to overthrow it. A year later the government closed the universities again as students protested low food allowances and education user fees. Student leaders had recently supported labor's rejection of the district elections and the call for a consitutent assembly. Clearly the PNDC was walking an increasingly delicate political and social tightrope. Government officials worried that political clumsiness could bring the remarkably sustained efforts of the ERP to an end.

Some urban groups did have the potential to benefit from the ERP, however. A striking fact about the Ghanaian case was the ambivalence of its sizable urban middle class, one of the oldest and most sophisticated in Africa. A once relatively vibrant indigenous private sector was now moribund. Due to its resources and ability to understand the liberalization changes, the middle class could have taken advantage of the ERP to invest in productive activity, but it was unwilling to get involved. It did not want to give even tacit support to a regime it disliked intensely and wished to see replaced. Because it shared many of the split personality perceptions about the Rawlings regime, it refused to invest. The middle class vividly recalled early attacks by Rawlings on the wealthy, was uncertain about reform sustainability, and had its own political aspirations to hold power directly. It repatriated very little capital, and many people in exile refused to return at all, while those in Ghana were hesitant to lay scarce resources on the line. By 1988, owners of existing enterprises were also calling for protection from import competition resulting from the liberalization measures. Both Ghanaian and external observers began to worry about the viability of a strong private sector response to the reforms, a fear directly linked to the very slow movement toward some privatization.

One business group did respond aggressively to the ERP. Resident foreigners—Indians, Lebanese, Syrians, Taiwanese, and some Europeans—constituted one group which clearly took advantage of the liberalization measures. They had infrastructure in place, resources to invest, understanding of the changes and how to take advantage of them, good personnel, access to technology and information about local and international markets, political ties and external linkages, and the ability to borrow. Indignation was considerable that these people benefited so easily from the changes. Because they were quite visible, they became handy targets of resentment. In late 1987, a government-owned newspaper wrote about growing impatience "with those who abuse our hospitality by flouting our laws, vaunting their conspicious affluence and insulting our dignity . . . unless they take firm steps to curb the excesses of their countrymen, the anger of Ghanaians may spill over to the good and bad alike."[16]

In fact, a variety of external actors was central to the continuation of the economic reform effort. The split personality images about the PNDC also generated very complicated external actor confidence problems. The key political fact was not which of the two images was more accurate, but rather who believed which one and what this led them to do. For the first several years of the ERP, Western governments, banks, and businesses tended to believe the patient revolutionary version; the result was hedged aid commitments, limited lending, and marginal new investment. There was some respect for the achievements of the program, but also great caution and suspicion. The regime made matters worse by what key Western governments considered to be intemperate foreign policy rhetoric and behavior. One Western official described Ghana's behavior as "biting the hand that feeds it."[17] Announcing, for example, that AIDS was an American genocidal plot to wipe out Africans, maintaining close ties to Libya and Iran, and insulting high-ranking visiting offi-

[16] *Daily Graphic* quoted in Economist Intelligence Unit, "Ghana Country Report," 1 (1988): 11.

[17] Interview, Western official, Accra, January 1987.

cials did not endear the Rawlings regime to the Reagan administration. Even when aid was committed, it was often disbursed very slowly. Ghana also did not have a strategic advantage to use as leverage.

The World Bank and, to a lesser extent, the IMF were inclined to believe the schizophrenic version. The hope was that ultimately the neoclassical pragmatism would predominate. One World Bank official noted that by disposition and institutional inclination the Bank tended to be more optimistic than the donor countries and the IMF. Until 1987, however, the Bank was unable to obtain commitments from donor countries and others to match even its own estimates of the ERP's minimum needs. Clearly the World Bank's reputation was very much on the line in Ghana. The Bank believed that all external actors should support efforts such as those in Ghana with substantially more resources. With Ghana in mind, the senior World Bank official for Africa put the position bluntly and honestly:

> The alternative—a series of failed programs in Africa—is not worth thinking about, and not only because of the human suffering. . . . The basic idea of moving to a market economy, shifting policies out of grandiosity to step-by-step solid progress will be discredited, and we can't afford to have those ideas discredited. If they fail in a series of countries . . . then it is a failure of our approach to the economy, a failure of our institutions, a failure of our political will, and there's no way that we'll be able to say that it is just the failure of Africa! So we have a very, very big stake in this.[18]

Ghanaian officials intensely felt both their need for and their dependence on external resources to get them out of their no-man's-land between their weak state and their weak private sector. As one Ghanaian official vividly put it:

> We need two legs to walk—a strong and effective state and a strong private sector; we have neither and are not likely to have either anytime soon. We are like a cripple I saw recently with no legs, pushing himself around on a crude board with wheels, surviving only by begging and trying to look sympathetic to the potential alms giver.[19]

The early hesitancy of major Western actors created real sustainability problems for Ghana's economic recovery program. It meant very heavy dependence on the IMF and the World Bank and, in the initial period, the repeated use of costly and increasingly less effective private bank bridge loans. This double dependency created very high debt service ratios, especially to the Fund and the Bank. While Ghana's roughly $2.8 billion external debt in 1987 was relatively modest, even by African standards, the debt service ratio for that year was estimated to be 55.2 percent. Half of it was owed to the IMF alone, with

---

[18] *Africa Report*, 32, 6 (November–December 1987): 32.
[19] Interview, Ghanaian official, Accra, January 1987.

some arrears still remaining, and monies owed to the Fund and the Bank are not subject to formal rescheduling either. The estimated debt service for 1988 approached 70 percent. Despite these problems, Ghana struggled very hard to maintain a decent debt service record.

Just as internal opposition to the ERP was beginning to intensify, key external actors decided in 1987 to become more supportive. Up to this point, only the IMF and the World Bank had supported the ERP with substantial resources. A sizable World Bank structural adjustment credit of $115 million was approved in April to back up its previous sectoral loan programs which had totaled about $800 million over four years. IMF support up to 1987 came to $750 million via three stand-by agreements. The first real indication of broader Western support came at a Consultative Group meeting in Paris in May. The Bank and the PNDC had hoped to get about $575 million in commitments. Instead Ghana was offered more than $800 million. This decision may well have been affected by the dramatic collapse of the economic recovery program in Zambia on May 1, leaving Ghana as one of the last remaining "success stories" in Africa. Slow disbursement of bilateral support was still an issue, however.

In November 1987, the IMF committed considerably larger resources to Ghana and on more concessional terms. The Fund granted a rare extended fund facility (EFF) for SDR 245.4 million, the first since August 1985, and one of the new structural adjustment facilities (SAF) for SDR 40.9, also over three years. A year later, in November 1988, the Fund consolidated this support into one of the first of its enhanced structural adjustment facilities (ESAF) for SDR 368.1 million on very concessional terms. These new funds were one way of coping with the Fund and Bank rescheduling problem. Cases of dedicated and genuine effort at broad-scale economic reform were quite rare in Africa, and the "terrible twins" felt that Ghana deserved considerable support. With internal opposition mounting, it was hoped that this increased support would allow Ghana to continue and broaden its structural adjustment efforts.

Ghana was likewise on the cutting edge of efforts to deal with the social impact of economic reform programs, what is commonly referred to as "adjustment with a human face." Given the sensitivity of its urban dilemma, the PNDC had long been aware of these problems, and, starting in 1983, it began to work with UNICEF on these issues. But only in June 1987 did the World Bank begin a strong effort by dispatching a major mission to Ghana. The result was the Program of Action and Measures to Address the Social Costs of Adjustment (PAMSCAD). At a special donor meeting in February 1988, Ghana secured pledges of $85 million for PAMSCAD. The original intent of UNICEF was to protect the most vulnerable groups, but it clearly had political uses as well, by both domestic and external actors. Highly visible action was meant to increase sustainability. The PNDC hoped that PAMSCAD would help them in the 1988 elections. PAMSCAD was, however, a fragile playing field for contending social, political, economic, and technical logics, and it was not clear which would eventually predominate.

The increased resources flows from the Fund, the Bank, and the donor countries had to compensate for very modest direct foreign investment and a very serious drop in the world price for cocoa. In 1986, direct foreign investment was only one-quarter of its 1981 level, and much of that went into the rehabilitation of the gold sector, not into the development of nontraditional exports. Low levels of domestic and foreign private investment threatened the slowly emerging privatization plans.

By August 1988, world cocoa prices had reached their lowest nominal level in twelve years and possibly their lowest real level ever. Third World production of cocoa had soared over the previous decade, raising the "fallacy of composition" issue inherent in the recovery strategy. If a number of old and new producers simultaneously increased production, the world market price was likely to drop. Due to renewed drought in Ghana, production declined in 1987–1988, so the country was doubly hurt. The fall in cocoa revenue was partly compensated by increased gold and timber exports, but if the trend continued, it might begin to threaten the urban-rural terms of trade shift and affect the PNDC's diffuse but important rural support.

Two other issues involving external actors affected the sustainablity of the ERP. First was the fact that many Ghanaians believed that expatriates were a key group to benefit from the ERP, and this was a source of considerable resentment. While one of the strengths of the reform effort in Ghana was the quite striking stability of the key senior officials involved in it, the pervasive administrative weakness of the Ghanaian state greatly limited the economic recovery program. It affected policy formulation and, above all, implementation. Medium- and long-term government planning was almost nonexistent. Even basic data gathering and analysis capabilities and accounting skills were very rudimentary. The most effective reform policies were those that did not involve direct administration on a continuous basis. As noted in regard to the labor benefits fiasco of 1986, this administrative weakness could have dangerous political consequences.

Due to this state weakness, the ERP generated a real and quite visible reexpatriatization of Ghana—the near constant presence of IMF and World Bank personnel, visiting missions, hired consultants, and seconded bureaucrats and managers. The whole recovery effort was a high conditionality process, and the Fund, Bank, and donors felt that expatriate personnel and their skills were necessary to ensure that their funds were used wisely. The World Bank, for example, had over forty missions to Ghana in 1987. Without much of this expatriate work, the ERP would not have progressed very far, but a real political problem was created in the process. These difficulties were also directly linked to whether Ghana had the ability to absorb effectively its newly increased amounts of external resources.[20]

The second issue regarding external actors had do with the contending po-

[20] Interviews, Ghanaians and expatriates, Accra, January 1987.

litical or organizational logics at work. On the African side, Ghanaian officials complained about what they called the "macho-policy school"—that the IMF, the World Bank, and the donor countries were always pushing, always desiring more change and conditionality. Once a change was made, they immediately wanted four more, and for the same amount of money. Speaking of the IMF in particular, one Ghanaian official ascribed this behavior to internal Fund politics in which officials concerned with their own careers wanted to "look tough" by leaning hard on African countries. Ghanaian officials argued that such pushing jeopardized the political and administrative viability of the reform efforts. On the other side, officials from the Fund, the Bank, and the donor countries argued that if they did not push, little would get done, especially since these reform efforts needed simultaneous movement in multiple sectors. It was difficult to find the precarious middle ground between these contending logics.[21]

That Ghana's ERP managed to survive at all was a remarkable feat. By the end of 1988, however, it still had only "fragile strength," a strength that could easily be upset by clumsy action on the part of the PNDC or by external actors. While Ghana had attained quite striking growth by African standards of the 1980s, this growth had dampened opposition only marginally.

ZAMBIA: THE POLITICS OF COLLAPSE

The Zambian Syndrome

At independence in 1964, Zambia had great wealth and very weak state capability. The wealth came primarily from copper, and the low level of state capability came from the strong influence of white settlers over the colonial state. This influence resulted in very low African presence in the administrative apparatus and almost no preparation of Africans to take control of it. The first ten years of independence came to be known later as the "fat decade" due to the abundant revenue provided by copper. From 1964 to 1974, copper and related minerals accounted on average for more than 90 percent of foreign exchange earnings, about 40 percent of GDP, and about 70 percent of total government revenue. Average annual GDP growth for the period 1965–1973 was 2.4 percent. The "fat decade" was succeeded by the "lean decade" following the oil price increases and the collapse of the copper market in 1973–1974. Positive growth rates evaporated as a result. Both decades were dominated by political rather than economic logic. During the "fat decade," political logic allowed the typical African postcolonial syndrome to sink deeper roots in Zambia than in much of the rest of the continent. During the "lean

[21] Interviews, Ghanaian and international officials, Accra, January 1987.

decade,'' political logic encouraged an unproductive defense of this syndrome.[22]

Several factors account for the intensity of the postcolonial syndrome in Zambia: the political opportunity structures created by easily obtained copper wealth; the political dominance, but concomitant insecurity, of the party and leadership that brought Zambia to independence; the great importance of organized labor; and the very high rate of urbanization. Kenneth Kaunda and his United National Independence Party (UNIP) dominated politics but felt constantly on the defensive. Kaunda and his old guard used control of the state and the copper wealth to consolidate political preeminence. This process culminated in May 1972 when Zambia became a single-party state. The powerful labor movement long predated the rise of UNIP as an anticolonial movement and had different ethnic, regional, and class roots. Despite much effort over the years, Kaunda had never been able to control it fully. Zambia started out with a high urbanization rate of 24 percent. By the end of the "fat decade" it had reached 34 percent, and by 1986 had grown to an astounding 48 percent—the highest rate in black-ruled Africa. Zambia's nonmultinational private sector was small and comprised primarily of Asian, Greek, and other expatriate businesses and large-scale white farms. Consequently, there was little countervailing force to the statist, urban, and labor biases of the syndrome and the political logics that drove them.

The political class that emerged out of UNIP and the anticolonial struggle used the state and the rents derived from it to consolidate political control. The size of the state was greatly expanded; a huge parastatal sector, even by African standards, was created; and an extensive system of services and subsidies was created to help control labor and the more general urban population. As the state was quickly enlarged and Zambianized during the "fat decade," the number of state employees increased sixfold. Equivalent increases in state capability did not appear, however.

The parastatal sector dominated the Zambian economy. The country inherited fourteen parastatals at independence, including four agricultural marketing boards, the railroad and airways companies, and four electric companies. The new government quickly expanded its role in the economy to achieve its social, economic, and political goals. In 1968 and 1969, major nationaliza-

[22] On Zambia's version of the syndrome, see Nelson, "Zambia: 1978–82," in "Political Economy of Stabilization"; Cherry Gertzel, ed., *The Dynamics of the One-Party State in Zambia* (Manchester: Manchester University Press, 1984); Klaas Woldring, ed., *Beyond Political Independence: Zambia's Development Predicament in the 1980s* (Berlin: Mouton, 1984); William Tordoff, ed., *Administration in Zambia* (Manchester: Manchester University Press, 1980); idem, *Politics in Zambia* (Manchester: Manchester University Press, 1974); Ben Turok, ed., *Development in Zambia* (London: Zed Press, 1979); Richard L. Sklar, *Corporate Power in an African State* (Berkeley: University of California Press, 1975); Robert H. Bates, *Unions, Parties and Political Development: A Study of Mineworkers in Zambia* (New Haven: Yale University Press, 1971).

tions took place in all key sectors, including the dominant copper sector. By 1985, there were 147 parastatals—121 state-owned companies organized under a single holding company, the Zambia Industrial and Mining Corporation (ZIMCO), and 26 corporations and boards under direct ministerial control, including the National Agricultural Marketing Board (NAMBOARD). The two largest units of ZIMCO were ZCCM, the mining parastatal, and INDECO, the industrial holding company subsidiary. Of ZIMCO's 121 companies 82 were wholly state owned, the state had a majority share in 28, and a minority share in only 10. The parastatal sector long accounted for more than 30 percent of Zambia's GDP, a figure high even by African standards. It accounted for roughly 66 percent of total investment and about 37 percent of nonagricultural employment. The ZCCM mining group represented about 30 percent of ZIMCO's turnover. The performance of most of Zambia's parastatals was quite mediocre.

In addition to those from copper, rents were also extracted from the traditional and smallholder agricultural sectors via a state marketing board, NAMBOARD, and provincial cooperatives. Despite considerable development rhetoric about agriculture, it was largely ignored, except to extract rents from it. The huge hemorrhage of private rents from the entire state apparatus was used largely to lubricate the patron-client networks that held the system together. Kaunda became the main arbiter between the contending factions of this personalized and increasingly authoritarian political structure. Because the "fat decade" did not require hard choices, this syndrome took particularly intense root. It was reinforced by Kaunda's loose and eclectic ideology of Humanism, which had its ancestry largely in Fabian socialism.

A very small Zambian technocratic stratum existed from the beginning, but it had very little influence. It was supported by a number of expatriate staff on short-term contracts. Early in the independence period, this small technocratic cadre began to argue quietly for significant structural change. The main suggestions were to diversify the economy away from copper through agricultural development, labor-intensive manufacturing, and export diversification. At the same time, technocratic officials "warned repeatedly against diversion of resources from productive purposes through, for example, too rapid a growth in social welfare spending and recurrent expenditures, pursuit of capital (and so import) intensive projects, and subsidization of production or consumption."[23] Such suggestions and warnings were issued periodically throughout the "fat decade," but the power of the political logics was such that nobody listened. By the early 1970s, external actors were issuing similar suggestions.

To maintain his control of this political economy, Kaunda employed various

---

[23] D. Michael Shafer, "Getting Ahead: A Sectoral Approach to Third World Mobility" (Paper for the Annual Meeting of the American Political Science Association, Chicago, 3–6 September 1987), p. 23.

statecraft strategies, which had contradictory results. One of the most important of his techniques was "rotating senior officials at short, irregular intervals. This raised the president's autonomy and reduced threats to him, but demoralized administrators, impaired efficiency, and frustrated efforts to *improve state capacity and insulate its institutions from outside pressures.*"[24] Again, political logic prevailed, and while Kaunda's state became increasingly authoritarian, it also became less and less insulated. This control measure had a particularly negative impact on the fledging technocratic apparatus. Between 1964 and 1970, for example, the National Commission for Development Planning (NCDP) had seven permanent secretaries, including four in one twelve-month period.

The double shock of the collapse of copper prices and the enormous increase in oil prices in 1973–1974 was a rude awakening to this cozy system. It affected all of the principal underpinnings of the Zambian system. During the course of the "lean decade" from 1974 to 1984, per capita income dropped by 44 percent, state revenue was cut by more than half, and average growth rates turned negative. Despite the objective severity of the economic trough, most Zambians did not see the crisis as deeply rooted or even partially internal. It was perceived to be temporary, cyclical, and external, the result of the world capitalist system. A very important regional dimension also existed. A revolutionary struggle was being waged against the white regime next door in Rhodesia (now Zimbabwe), and Zambia was one of the military staging grounds for the opponents of the Ian Smith government. South Africa greatly disliked Zambia's strong support for Smith's opponents and for the African National Congress, and it engaged in political, economic, and military destabilization efforts against Zambia. This was particularly devastating because many of Zambia's transportation and communications lines ran through Rhodesia and South Africa.

Zambia attempted to adjust to the "lean decade" through periodic efforts at stabilization, but no real structural change. The Kaunda government cut spending, but on an ad hoc and politically determined basis, incurred considerable debt, ran up arrears, ran down reserves, and tried to increase copper output without protecting existing productive capacity. All of the major elements of the postcolonial syndrome remained untouched, however—the expanded state, the parastatal sector, the subsidies, political control over imports and foreign exchange, and the huge informal rents. In the "fat decade," Zambia had the resources to restructure its political economy and did not do so; then in the "lean decade" it tried to adjust without touching the sacred turf of the political kingdom.

The "lean decade" brought periodic reliance on what there was of the small technocratic stratum when external resources were desperately needed. This

24 Ibid., p. 26.

was the case for two stand-by agreements with the IMF in 1976 and 1978. Both were technical stabilization successes, but did not seek to address the underlying structural problems. Between 1976 and 1979, for example, the budget deficit was cut by about 50 percent, but this was achieved only by chopping recurrent and capital expenditure by 25 and 75 percent respectively.

The austerity actions were portrayed by the government and seen by the public as wartime measures brought on by the turmoil in the region and by world market forces. Thus, with Zimbabwe's independence in April 1980 and an earlier partial recovery of copper prices, elite and mass expectations soared. Most people believed that the temporary, cyclical, and external crisis was over and that Zambia would return to the days of the "fat decade." The small technocratic team in the Central Bank and elsewhere argued vainly against such a view. But, once again, political logic prevailed over economic logic. The dominance of political logic was vividly demonstrated by the views of Dr. Leonard Chivuno, a young and ideological Soviet-trained engineer who became the head of NCDP in January 1980. Representing the political half of the dualistic decision-making structure, he vigorously argued for an expansionary program that would reinforce and extend the existing system. His views prevailed because they were fully congruent with the rest of the resurgent political logics. The technocratic head of the Bank of Zambia, Luke Mwananshiku argued against this position, but to no avail. A major budgetary expansion took place in 1980 without the revenue to back it up, and near financial chaos ensued as the budget was overshot by 75 percent. State and labor unrest during the year, based on the new high expectations, led to significant pay increases, which also aggravated the problem.

In December 1980, Mwananshiku, as the leader of the embattled technocratic team, responded in public. In a dramatic press conference, he vividly sketched the disastrous condition of the economy. His views directly contradicted the widely publicized views of Chivuno and Zambia's political "old guard." Mwananshiku and several other members of the very small technocratic cadre were dismissed within a month.

Based on the technical success of the 1976 and 1978 stand-by agreements, the IMF tried to help Zambia out of its corner by agreeing to a generous three-year EFF in May 1981. It was very generous, "front-end loaded" (most of the resources to come early in the agreement period), and without preconditions. Despite these favorable terms, however, it was canceled in early 1982 because many of the performance targets were not met. After desperate attempts to find other sources of external assistance, including the Arabs, the Kaunda government eventually had to return to the IMF. The cycles of grudging partial stabilization and rhetorical structural change continued into 1983 and 1984 with two new stand-by agreements. In October 1983, six months after the beginning of the 1983 agreement, Luke Mwananshiku returned to the government as finance minister with greatly consolidated control over economic policy. NCDP was placed under his control, and he was given authority to coordinate policy with other key actors. Despite his valiant efforts, economic performance improved very little under the 1983 and 1984 agreements as resistance was strong, capacity was weak, and implementation was marginal. In fact, the twenty-two-month July 1984 stand-by was suspended in April 1985 for noncompliance as the political logics of the postcolonial syndrome continued to prevail.

The Program and the Politics

Despite its series of IMF agreements, Zambia's economic crisis continued to gather momentum. By mid-1985 the country was in terrible economic shape. As with Ghana, Zambia's average annual GNP per capita growth rate between 1965 and 1985 was − 1.7 percent. In 1980, GNP per capita was $600; by 1985, it was about $300 in constant dollars. Real wages were one-third of their 1975 levels. Surpisingly, and in contrast to Ghana, per capita caloric intake levels dropped only marginally from the 1970s average of 97.9 percent of the United Nations minimum requirement to 92 percent in 1985. The GDP growth rates for the previous three years (1982–1984) had all been negative: − 2.8, − 2.0, and − 0.4 percent, respectively. Foreign exchange was so scarce that the commercial line of credit for oil imports was threatened, while debt service arrears increased enormously, especially in 1984. Scheduled debt service for 1985 was 70 percent of export earnings, a fact that directly affected foreign aid levels and increased external pressure for change. Imports had declined 22 percent in 1982, 15.6 percent in 1983, and a further 2.5 percent in 1984. By 1985, import levels were 50 percent below those of 1980 and 75 percent below 1974 levels. Capacity utilization levels in the huge parastatal sector were well below 50 percent. After serious labor unrest in April 1985, the government permitted an 18 percent pay increase for union workers that was retroactive to the previous November. Exports had declined 9.7 percent in 1983 and another 6.8 percent in 1984. Copper production continued its decline, 10 percent in 1984 alone, with no prospect of an upturn. Finally, between 1983 and 1985 inflation jumped from 20 percent to about 60 percent.[25]

Given the severity of Zambia's economic crisis by 1985, the country had a strong objective need for major economic reform. While little perception of such a need existed, external pressure from the IMF, the World Bank, and the

[25] On Zambia's economic program and its politics, see Helen O'Neill, *Transforming A Single-Product Economy: An Examination of the First Stage of Zambia's Economic Reform Program, 1982–86* (Washington, D.C.: World Bank, 1987); Neva Seidman Maketla, "Theoretical and Practical Implications of I.M.F. Conditionality in Zambia," *Journal of Modern African Studies*, 24 (September 1986): 395–42; Manenga Ndulo and Martin Sakala, "Stabilization Policies in Zambia: 1976–85," World Employment Programme, working paper no. 13 (Geneva: Intenational Labour Office, May 1987).

principal donor countries to engage in significant and rapid structural change was considerable.

A serious attempt at reform finally began in 1985. After the collapse of the 1984 agreement, Mwananshiku became convinced that the reforms had to be substantially broadened and intensified. He worked very closely with the "terrible twins," David Phiri at the Bank of Zambia and presidential advisor Dominic Mulaisho at the State House, to put together a "shadow program," which if implemented, would lead to another IMF agreement. Despite Mwananshiku's talents and the commitment of the other two, the domestic analytic support staff behind the new economic team was still extremely weak. As a result, the IMF and the World Bank conducted the necessary studies and analysis, established the framework, and guided the negotiations. Without the IMF and the World Bank, the extremely thin Zambian technocratic team could not have put together a coherent neoorthodox reform package. As one Zambian official put it, "The IMF and the World Bank have become the Ministry of Finance in Zambia."[26] In the process, the economic team received uneven support from Kaunda and was perceived by the general public to be the instrument of the "terrible twins."

The 1985 "shadow program" was designed to attack central elements of the postcolonial syndrome. It sought to "intensify" the implementation of policies announced since 1983 while introducing several new ones. The three most important new policies were: (1) the liberalization and decontrol of bank interest rates in September 1985, and (2) the creation of a foreign exchange auction in October and the resulting abolition of the rent-riddled import licensing system, and (3) the planned complete elimination of the subsidies on maize meal (the staple food) and fertilizer. The government had devalued the national currency, the kwacha, by 20 percent in January 1983 and established a crawling-peg system to establish exchange rates. The auction was meant to substantially improve foreign exchange management. After the implementation of these new policies began, the "shadow program" was transformed into a twenty-four-month stand-by agreement with the IMF in February 1986.

The rest of the reform package reaffirmed previously announced, but unimplemented, policies. They included the following: progressively eliminating subsidies on more than fifty commodities by decontrolling prices in the state sector (except for maize meal and fertilizer); reducing the budgetary deficit by cutting expenditure rather than by domestic and international borrowing or by running down reserves; improving state economic management, especially for budgetary control and debt service; dismantling import restrictions; reforming the import tariff structure to decrease protection and increase domestic sourcing; restructuring the parastatal sector to cut costs, improve efficiency, and diminish rent seeking; rehabilitating the copper sector, which the

[26] O'Neill, *Transforming*, p. 66.

government had been starving of the very foreign exchange it produced; increasing producer prices for maize and other agricultural crops; ending NAMBOARD's interprovincial trading monopoly on maize and fertilizer; progressively reducing the size of the civil service by 25 percent; increasing export incentives via a foreign exchange retention scheme; compiling a new investment code; and reforming the tax system.

By mid-1985 President Kaunda was convinced that the proposed reform package, although difficult, was absolutely necessary. He had to ram it through the cabinet, however. Afterwards he sent top party and government officials out to explain the reforms, especially the auction, to the public, but most of them did not understand the reforms, were opposed to them, or both. The minuscule technocratic core of convinced officials was always politically weak and became increasingly isolated; the president gave it very little political protection. In fact, even Kaunda himself was becoming isolated, a new phenomenon in Zambian politics. More and more he appeared to be preoccupied by personal and regional matters such as the death of his son, the death of President Machel of Mozambique, and other ominous events in Southern Africa.[27]

The significant reforms of 1985 were extremely unpopular among nearly all strata of the population, from senior cabinet and party figures right down to the unemployed urban worker. Senior officials feared a social and political backlash; bureaucrats and parastatal managers worried about job security and their power, prestige, and standard of living; labor leaders were seriously disturbed about the grave social consequences of the price increases, stagnant wages, "capitalist exploitation," and layoffs resulting from these reforms, as well as their own power and standard of living; the very small domestic business community feared for its ability to compete in a liberalized economic environment; and urban workers and the unemployed feared for their very survival. All of these groups believed that the benefits of the reforms would go to external actors and resident foreigners, especially white farmers, Greeks, and Asians. In sharp contrast to Ghana, virtually no one beyond the small economic team viewed the crisis as systemic or caused by domestic factors.

Opposition to the liberalization was so powerful in Zambia, so institutionalized, pervasive and deeply rooted largely because the same people had controlled the Zambian state and politics since independence. Kaunda's "old guard" was still firmly in place. In this sense, Zambia's often touted stability worked against reform, not for it. Despite being an authoritarian single-party state, Kaunda's government had almost no insulation, and Zambia had not undergone any of the sociopolitical shredding so characteristic of Ghana. Not

[27] Interviews, Zambian and international officials, Lusaka, October–December 1986; Nairobi, January, February, July, October 1987; and Washington, D.C., January, May, September 1988.

only were dominant interests directly threatened, but so were key tenets of Kaunda's political philosophy of Humanism, which both the Zambian elite and labor had long used to defend their interests. Its statist, anticapitalist, antimarket, and antiforeign aspects and its powerful welfare, "common man" thrust helped to activate popular opposition. It gave the opposition something to organize around, a weapon to brandish. In addition, the government had neither the capability nor the will to use coercion.

A brief review of three specific areas of reform will illustrate how a combination of broad political opposition, administrative weakness, and sabotage destroyed Zambia's adjustment program. The three policy areas are: (1) the foreign exchange auction, (2) the collection of the large maize harvests that resulted from increases in producer prices, and (3) the elimination of the subsidy on maize meal, the staple food. A fourth, and equally important, area is not discussed here—the failure of the government to sustain the copper sector's rehabilitation program.

With the start of the foreign exchange auction in October 1985, opposition to the reforms became increasingly apparent within the government and the party, from labor leaders, and among the general public. By April 1986, it had reached a point where President Kaunda felt compelled to do something to blunt it. In a surprise move, he replaced Mwananshiku, Phiri, and Mulaisho with three vocal critics of the program. The unusual step seems to have been motivated by the hope that exposure to the hard realities would convert criticism into support. Mwananshiku's old nemesis, Leonard Chivuno, became governor of the Bank of Zambia, and Basil Kabwe, a former education and culture minister and union leader, became minister of finance. Both Chivuno and Kabwe were protégés of Grey Zulu, secretary general of UNIP and a key member of the old guard. Mulaisho was replaced as State House economics advisor by James Mapoma, a former head of ZIMCO. Since neither Kabwe nor Mapoma had strong backgrounds in economics and finance, Chivuno became the key player.

While Kaunda's ploy appeared to work for Kabwe, the other two publicly supported the reforms while working with other opponents in the party and the government to undermine them. Above all, Chivuno started to manipulate the auction, thereby reducing existing confidence in it. Since the auction was the centerpiece of the recovery program, Chivuno's actions weakened the larger reform effort as well. The kwacha had fallen from 2.2 to the dollar in October 1985 to about 7.0 to the dollar by the time of the personnel changes in April 1986. The auction was severely undermined by the fact that all key players knew that the most important economic officials were against it. Then in July and August 1986, Chivuno significantly increased the amount that could be bid for in the weekly auctions without adequate foreign exchange to pay the successful bidders. As a result, a payments "pipeline" was created; by November $40 million had been auctioned but not provided. Successful bidders had to wait ten weeks for their foreign exchange. It was not surprising that the rate quickly fell to more than K15 to the dollar by the end of the year. Rather than removing politics from exchange rate adjustment and reforms in general, the way the Zambian auction was handled put politics front and center. Foreign exchange auctions worked well in Ghana and Nigeria, but not in Zambia where political manipulation destroyed the auction.[28]

Generally, the auction was a disaster for those who relied heavily on the political rents derived from the old import licensing system. In addition, the sectoral impact was uneven. Broadly, the auction favored manufacturing over agriculture, private firms over the parastatals, and large private, especially foreign, firms over smaller, mostly Zambian-owned ones. More specifically, it was a very mixed blessing for the parastatal sector. For relatively healthy firms that were quite dependent on imported inputs and had good equipment and some liquidity, the auction greatly eased their foreign exchange problems and thus allowed them to function relatively well for both the domestic and the export markets. Despite enormously increased kwacha costs, they could function better than in years. For firms without these advantages, however, the auction had devastating effects. Fears of widespread closures, many of them unfounded, spread throughout the parastatal apparatus. The new import and tariff rules also meant that state firms had to contend with cheaper and often higher quality foreign goods. For urban consumers the effect on prices was very serious. Politically, this was a real cause for concern in a country with a 48 percent urbanization figure.

The functioning of the auction was made more difficult by the limited amount of foreign exchange provided for it by external actors. Even the little support that was given was often slow to be disbursed. Limited external support reflected doubts among the donor countries in particular about the seriousness with which the Zambians would pursue this latest attempt at reform. External actors had been disappointed by earlier efforts, which they had supported more generously. Given the degree and location of domestic opposition to the auction, it was not at all clear that substantially increased support would have saved it or the reform effort in general.

The second major reform examined in this chapter is the increase in the producer price of maize, which, despite incredible administrative incompetence, led to significantly larger harvests. Between 1982 and January 1986, NAMBOARD and the Provincial Cooperative Unions divided up the responsibility for purchasing the maize crop. After several years of intense governmental effort, however, they were still unable to settle their differences, establish clear procedures, and provide the necessary equipment and transportation needed to collect all the harvest. More than 20 percent of the bumper 1985 harvest of maize went uncollected. Allowing some private competition for

[28] Ibid.

collection of the 1986 crop only marginally improved the performance, once more because the government was unable to work out the administrative details and provide the necessary inputs. Again more than 20 percent of the harvest went uncollected, despite external pressure and help. The agricultural marketing tale was a prime example of the extreme administrative weakness of the Zambian state.[29]

The third example deals with the subsidy on maize meal, which had become a significant fiscal drain. The World Bank and the IMF urged cuts in the subsidy, but counseled gradualism. Nevertheless, in December 1986 the government raised the consumer price on the higher quality maize meal by 120 percent, but sought to buffer the poorer consumers by continuing to subsidize a lower grade of maize meal. Private millers would lose money on the lower grade unless the government compensated them properly, but compensation details remained very unclear. Therefore, the private millers increased production of the decontrolled meal causing shortages of the lower priced meal. Serious rioting broke out in the Copperbelt in which fifteen people died. The outbursts in Lusaka itself were less serious, but still frightening. Badly shaken by the riots, President Kaunda immediately reversed the maize price increase and nationalized all the large private maize mills, most of which were owned by Greeks, and accused the millers of capitalist exploitation. Again a combination of political manipulation and administrative weakness sabotaged the reform effort.[30]

Over the next four months, President Kaunda wavered over whether to continue the reform effort or to end it. External actors and small and isolated technocratic elements argued for continuing the adjustment program, while everybody else wanted to terminate it. An important background factor was growing concern about the public's response to elections scheduled for 1988. Already there were indications that people might refuse to vote as a protest against rising prices. Zambian officials believed that the elections were crucial to the legitimacy, and thus the stability, of the single-party state. A severe embarrassment in the elections might foster divisive and centrifugal political and social tendencies.

The first round came in January 1987 right after the maize meal riots. Kaunda suspended the auction, removed Kabwe (the one critic who had become a proponent of the reforms) from the finance ministry, and backed away from several other reform measures, pushing the IMF and World Bank programs into suspension. He announced new foreign exchange rate and alloca-

[29] See Kenneth Good, "The Reproduction of Weakness in the State and Agriculture: Zambian Experience," *African Affairs*, 85, 339 (April 1986): 239–65; idem, "Systematic Agricultural Mismanagement: The 1985 'Bumper' Harvest in Zambia," *Journal of Modern African Studies*, 24, 1 (June 1986): 257–84.

[30] Interviews, Zambian and international officials, Lusaka and Nairobi, January–February, May, and October 1987; and Washington, D.C., August 1988.

tion mechanisms which were internally contradictory and not well thought-out. Chivuno even asked the donor countries, the IMF, and the World Bank for suggestions on how to make the new measures work. The new changes essentially reestablished a fixed exchange rate of 8 kwacha to the dollar and reintroduced the administrative allocation of foreign exchange.

As Frederick Chiluba, the powerful and vocal head of the Congress of Trade Unions noted, "A government gets into power by making promises to look after its people. Once it reneges on these, the people begin to question the legitimacy of it continuing."[31] Most people blamed the IMF and felt that because Zambia was paying out more in debt service than it was getting in aid, foreigners were benefiting while the misery of Zambia increased. As one writer to the *Zambia Daily Mail* put it, "To finance and build our bridge, socialism, we go to the IMF, a red-eyed neocolonialist monster. Where on earth has the IMF financed socialism?"[32] At a three-day conference on "Zambia's Economic Adjustment and Reform Programme" organized by the World Bank in January 1987, just prior to the suspension of the auction, a member of the party's research bureau issued an implicit warning:

> The [1968] Reforms established state control of major sectors of the economy. But, as it turned out, the socialization objectives of the Party were not necessarily in accord with internal and external forces and consequently the Party and its Government were forced to strategically compromise some socialist ground to economic liberalisation. However, caution must be exercised in assessing liberalisation vis-à-vis Zambian Humanism. The fact of the matter is that the ideology and philosophy as a long-term programme of the Party is still intact.[33]

It turned out to be a prophetic warning.

In the next couple of months, teachers, nurses, and postal employees carried out a series of public sector strikes and unrest among mine workers increased. One former government official noted that, "The government has opened up a Pandora's box. People are going to feel that popular resistance can change government plans."[34] After considerable external pressure, however, including the intervention of very senior World Bank officials who happened to be in Lusaka and extensive discussions with an IMF team that came to Lusaka, the government restored the auction in late March. The exchange rate fell immediately to K21.01 to the dollar.

Discussions with the IMF to get the program back on track then shifted to

---

[31] "An Overdose of the IMF Medicine," *South* 76 (February 1987): 20.

[32] *Zambia Daily Mail* (Lusaka), 7 February 1987, p. 4.

[33] Bernard Chisanga, "Zambia—The Historical Perspective: From Capitalism to Humanism through Socialism—From State Control to Liberalization," (Paper presented to the "Seminar on Zambia's Economic Adjustment and Reform Programme" organized by the World Bank, 12–15 January 1987), p. 34.

[34] *South* (February 1987): 19.

Washington, D.C. and focused on the budget deficit, which by then was about 30 percent of GDP. It had been seriously aggravated by the policy reversals of December and January. These discussions were carried out by technocratic Zambian officials relatively committed to the reform effort. The major critics, including Chivuno, remained in Lusaka and used the absence of their colleagues to convince Kaunda that resurrecting the reforms was not a good idea.[35] Finally, on May Day 1987, President Kaunda announced that Zambia was suspending its IMF reform effort, abolishing the auction, freezing prices, reintroducing price controls, resurrecting the import licensing system of allocating foreign exchange, and limiting debt service to well under 10 percent of foreign exchange earnings.

The reform effort was over, and throwing the IMF out proved to be very popular. A carnival atmosphere seized Lusaka after the announcement. On 12 May rioting and looting took place in the Copperbelt as party activists demanded that traders reduce their prices now that the IMF reform program was gone. Chiluba observed that "the IMF had set the Government on a collision course with the people."[36] It was now gone, and Zambia seemed destined to wander ineffectively between a weak state and an incomplete market.

President Kaunda asserted that:

> We are witnessing a situation where our social fabric is slowly disintegrating, thereby sowing seeds of unrest and undermining the spirit and unity of the nation. This situation cannot and will not be allowed to continue. It is patently clear that far from improving our condition, we are not succeeding; hence the need for a fresh look. . . .
>
> The party and its government have therefore decided to reverse the negative impact of the system which we tried with such honesty of purpose, sincerity, and determination, all without success. . . .
>
> [W]e chose the way of the IMF of our own free will. Then, again of our own free will, we have decided to try another way.[37]

The effect of the resurgence of political over economic logic was to move the weak state even more emphatically back to center stage. Crony statism reasserted itself with a vengeance. President Kaunda asserted that the "Government's capacity for economic management is manifest." According to him, bringing the state back in meant that:

> The success of these measures will depend on each of us individually as well as collectively, but greater responsibility lies on those of us who have a direct role to play as . . . public officers and leaders. More responsibility shall devolve upon the

[35] Interviews, Zambian and international officials, Lusaka and Nairobi, May and October 1987; and Washington, D.C., January, August, September, and December 1988.

[36] *New York Times*, 17 June 1987, p. A18.

[37] Foreign Broadcast Information Service, 4 May 1987, pp. U9, 10, 12.

public service, which must implement these measures. However, the public service has the most able officials because of its competitive conditions of service, and this should be actively considered.[38]

The demise of the economic recovery program was largely due to the coherence, pervasiveness, and institutionalization of the opposition to it. Unlike Ghana, Zambia's political culture had not been shredded by years of political instability, and the government thus had little distance or autonomy. Major potential veto groups were very active, to the point of getting their people into key positions of formal power over the economic reforms. It was President Kaunda who increasingly found himself isolated and outmaneuvered. The events of December 1986 were a major psychological shock to him. He was no longer leading, but instead was being led. The ideology he had helped to create was being used against a major policy initiative to which he had committed himself, even if ambivalently. Another striking feature of the Zambian case was the sense of protest rather than governance exhibited by senior officials. They saw the crisis as temporary and did not appreciate its severity even though copper would run out within two decades. They hoped for a bailout because of Zambia's alleged strategic importance in Southern Africa or from greatly increased copper prices or a major oil find. Therefore, they viewed the reforms as unnecessary and externally imposed.[39]

Domestic opposition interacted with limited external actor confidence to further weaken the adjustment program. The IMF and the World Bank admitted that they did not "till the political soil" very well or have a very sophisticated understanding of the ongoing internal politics of the economic reform effort. Given the coherence of the opposition, however, "tilling the political soil" might not have altered the outcome. Too much weight was placed on President Kaunda's perceived commitment to the program. Given his long dominance of the Zambian political arena, the Fund and the Bank assumed that it would continue.[40]

Without a doubt, opposition to the economic recovery program was aided by the fact that its payoff was quite uncertain and far down the road. Both the IMF and World Bank admitted that even if all elements of the program were fully implemented, the real turnaround would not come until the middle of the 1990s. Zambia's nearly intolerable debt situation and limited external resource flows greatly aggravated this problem; no financial slack existed.

The collapse of the reform effort was also abetted by the lack of donor country, international bank, and foreign investor confidence in Zambia's will-

---

[38] Ibid., p. 12.

[39] Interviews, Zambian and international officials, Lusaka and Nairobi, May and October 1987; and Washington, D.C., January, August, September, and December 1988.

[40] Interviews, international officials, Lusaka, February 1987; and Washington, D.C., August–September and December 1988.

ingness or ability to implement the reforms. Donor confidence was badly shaken by the April 1986 personnel changes and their aftermath, the government's persistent inability to manage its agricultural harvest, its failure to keep the essential ZCCM rehabilitation on track, its weak budgetary restraint efforts, its clumsy handling of the maize price increase, and its very limited movement toward systematic parastatal reform and privatization. Correctly or incorrectly, the donors simply did not believe that Zambia was meeting them halfway. As a result external financial support was not high.

The World Bank noted that "the financing and sustainability of adjustment programs are mutually reinforcing. Inadequate funding was partly the reason for the policy reversal in Zambia [and] Ghana's effort has been helped by the availability of finance."[41] The IMF and the World Bank were the primary source of support, but disbursement was often slow. Despite quite generous Paris Club rescheduling in May 1983, July 1984, and February 1987, the Consultative Group meetings in May 1984, June 1985, and December 1986 produced only modest results. This greatly aggravated Zambia's severe foreign exchange scarcity, resulting in large part from its $5.7 billion debt. The debt per capita figure for 1987 was $840, while Brazil's was $798. Zambia's debt service ratio was high. In fact, Zambia was paying out more in debt service than it was getting back in new assistance. The projected debt service ratio for 1987 was 125 percent, much of it to the IMF and the World Bank. Arrears to the "terrible twins" had become considerable by 1987.

Zambia's program did not last long enough for external actors to respond to sustained and positive efforts, as they had in Ghana where the upturn in resource flows did not come until five years into the program. Timing and lack of sustained effort were both important. As changes in Paris Club procedures in 1987 and 1988 showed, movement within major donor governments, between them, and within the World Bank and the IMF, aimed at changing international debt management and structural adjustment norms and mechanisms was finally underway. Battles were fought, for example, between the U.S. State Department and Treasury Department over these issues using Zambia as an example. Ghana's reform effort was sustained long enough to take advantage of the IMF's new SAF and ESAF facilities and augmented World Bank resources. The serious part of Zambia's program (September 1985 to December 1986) lasted a mere sixteen months and ended before the new resources and mechanisms were available. More resources might have helped in Zambia, as they did in Ghana, but there was no assurance that the program would not have collapsed anyway for the reasons already mentioned. Ghana showed that sustained reform needs some strong combination of most of the following: understanding, commitment, insulation, luck, external advice and assistance

---

[41] World Bank, *Adjustment Lending* (Washington, D.C.: World Bank, 1988), p. 6.

to alleviate state capacity difficulties, *and* significant levels of external resource flows.

In August 1987, President Kaunda finally announced a "make or break"
interim national development plan (INDP) to replace the abandoned IMF program. With the theme of "growth with our own resources," the eighteen-
month program was meant to direct the country's scarce resources to priority
sectors in order to achieve a 2.2 percent GDP growth rate while protecting the
most vulnerable members of society. All the major policy measures announced in May were retained. The program stipulated that Zambia would not
enter into aid agreements that had policy conditionality. President Kaunda got
advice from a group of economists at the University of Zambia, all of whom
were critics of the IMF/World Bank recovery effort. Prime Minister Kebby
Musokotwane traveled to Europe in an attempt to explain the new plan. He
indicated that partial debt cancellation had to be one element of any solution
to Zambia's problems. Western officials believed that many of the new program's key assumptions and projections were faulty or based on dubious data.
The plan did not gain much donor country support, although the Scandinavian
countries continued their assistance programs and offered to pay part of Zambia's arrears to the World Bank if Zambia would also contribute. The rest of
the donors shifted funds to other countries. Ghana may well have been one of
the beneficiaries of these shifts. The Bank stopped disbursing new money as
of 1 May, and the IMF declared Zambia ineligible to use its resources in September. This was partly compensated for by a quite remarkable doubling of
world copper prices to near record levels and by the ceiling on debt service.

Nevertheless, the negative consequences of this resurrected crony statism
became obvious very quickly. Corruption and other forms of rent seeking reemerged overnight as people tried to adjust to the new situation. Shortages of
staple foods and basic consumer goods appeared as the blackmarket and smuggling thrived, while teams of UNIP youth roamed the streets attempting to enforce price controls. Foreign exchange became very scarce, and import stran-
gulation set in with a vengeance, affecting parastatal production levels, the
transportation and health infrastructure, and agriculture. Maize meal shortages
hit urban areas. Inflation increased to 60 percent again, as per capita income
finally dropped down to $200. In response to this situation, state and party
personnel received significant salary and allowance increases in September
1987 and again in June 1988. The GDP growth rate for 1987 was −0.2, and
subsidies were projected to account for 15 percent of budgetary expenditure
for 1988.

The old guard and its political logics were back. The general perception was
that Zambia was following the correct path after its tangle with the "terrible
twins." Prime Minister Kebby Musokotwane was "hoping that in a year or so
they will see that our own restructuring program is as effective, maybe more
effective, than the IMF program." "The only admission I make," President

Kaunda asserted, "where I went wrong, is that we subsidized consumption for too long."[42] In essence, his dilemma was that he was now hostage to an urban population he could neither subsidize nor control. Yet the crisis was still seen, in public at least, as temporary and caused by external factors or by capitalism. Blame was put on South Africa and external or domestic capitalists, especially Asians. When the situation reached a pressure point, Kaunda allowed a major confiscation of Asian businesses in February 1988, only to be forced to return most of them in October because of the negative economic consequences. Illusions died hard. When in March 1988 Placid Oil, a U.S. firm, announced the end of its oil exploration efforts, Zambian politicians expressed anger and outrage. They had been counting on oil to help bail Zambia out of its difficulties.

Weak state capacity remained a serious problem. Despite four attempts in five years to reorganize NAMBOARD and the Provincial Cooperative Unions, only two-thirds of the 1987 harvest was collected. The result was the same again the next year. In March 1988, Prime Minister Musokotwane actually issued a partial apology to the private millers involved in the events of December 1986, saying that they were not fully at fault after all. The state kept their mills, however.

With presidential and parliamentary elections now rapidly approaching, President Kaunda and the UNIP old guard spent much of 1988 consolidating their political position. Major efforts were made to tame parliament and to co-opt or intimidate labor leaders and their unions, especially Chiluba. Changes were made in both constitutional and party structure and personnel. Kaunda even threatened to make parliament a part-time institution to save money. The elections were duly held on 26 October 1988 with Kaunda the sole candidate for president. He won 95.5 percent of the vote, 2.5 percent more than in 1983, and the voter turnout was 55 percent, down 10 percent from 1983.

Zambia was again at a possible turning point. A former high Zambian official had predicted in October 1987 that Kaunda would seek to go back to the "terrible twins" after the elections.[43] Certainly Kaunda's political moves in 1988 could lead in that direction. Informal talks with the IMF and the World Bank began as early as late summer 1987 and continued periodically thereafter. The key issues that concerned the Fund and the Bank were devaluation, reduction of the budget deficit, elimination of subsidies, and debt service. A number of Zambian economic officials argued quietly that a return to externally supported economic reform was necessary and could not be avoided indefinitely. At one point, Kaunda wrote letters to major Western leaders asking them to help obtain more favorable terms from the IMF. In the summer of

---

[42] Steve Askin, "Taking on the IMF," *Africa News*, 28, 2 (5 October 1987): 9; Blaine Harden, "Kenneth Kaunda of Zambia Governs in Classic 'Big Man' Style," *Washington Post*, 11 September 1988, p. A34.

[43] Interview, Nairobi, October 1987.

1988, moves were announced to end price controls on a good number of consumer commodities, but when Chiluba and other union leaders reacted strongly, the government backed off. In September 1988, the government confirmed that the Dutch, Norwegian and Swedish governments were assisting it in a major evaluation of INDP and assessment of new options.

Immediately after the October 1988 elections, Kaunda announced a number of measures that could, if fully implemented, be transformed into a "shadow" economic reform program in preparation for renewed agreements with the IMF and the World Bank. He devalued the kwacha by 20 percent, pegging it to the SDR rather than the dollar, and raised interest rates substantially. He announced a much smaller and reshaped cabinet whose mission would be to cut public spending, reduce the deficit, and eventually trim the size of the parastatal sector through limited privatization. By early 1989, an opening existed for Zambia to get out of the "stop" phase of its latest stop-go cycle of attempted reform. It remained unclear, however, whether elite and mass attitudes and the weak administrative apparatus could sustain yet another attempt to alter the postcolonial syndrome and its powerful political logics in order to find a way out of the no-man's-land between state and market.

NIGERIA: WILL CLEVER POLITICS PREVAIL?

The Nigerian Syndrome

The Nigerian story deals with the relationship between oil and Africa's post-colonial syndrome. Rather than mitigating or eliminating key characteristics of the syndrome, as some had predicted, the oil bonanza only intensified it. Under both military and civilian regimes, and fueled by massive oil revenues after 1973, Nigeria developed powerful forms of both crony statism and crony capitalism. They emerged under a series of military governments between 1966 and 1979, only to be greatly strengthened after the partial and rather modest insulation of these military regimes was removed under the democratic government of the Second Republic from 1979 to 1983.[44]

Oil extraction began in Nigeria in 1958, well before independence under a

[44] On Nigeria's version of the syndrome, see Richard A. Joseph, *Democracy and Prebendalism in Nigeria* (New York: Cambridge University Press, 1987); Larry Diamond, *Class, Ethnicity and Democracy in Nigeria* (Syracuse: Syracuse University Press, 1988); Thomas J. Biersteker, *Multinationals, the State, and Control of the Nigerian Economy* (Princeton: Princeton University Press, 1987); Sayre Schatz, *Nigerian Capitalism* (Berkeley: University of California Press, 1977); idem, "Pirate Capitalism and the Inert Economy of Nigeria," *Journal of Modern African Studies*, 22, 1 (March 1984): 45–58; Sandra T. Barnes, *Patrons and Power* (Bloomington: Indiana University Press, 1986); Henry Bienen, "Oil Revenues and Policy Choice in Nigeria," World Bank staff working papers, no. 592 (Washington, D.C., 1983); Henry Bienen and V. P. Diejomaoh, eds. *The Political Economy of Income Distribution in Nigeria* (New York: Holmes and Meier, 1981); Berry, *Fathers*.

democratic govenment in 1964. From around 1 percent of GDP in 1960, oil reached 27 percent of GDP by 1977 and remained at about 25 percent into the 1980s. From 1974 on, oil accounted for at least four-fifths of total government revenue. By the early 1980s, it constituted more than 90 percent of total exports.

The military first seized power in 1966 (twice that year, in fact). Between July 1967 and January 1970, Nigeria fought a very bloody civil war as the Eastern Region attempted to secede from the country. After the leader of a 1975 intramilitary coup was assassinated early in 1976, General Olusegun Obasanjo came to power. He supervised a return to democratic rule in October 1979, as Shehu Shagari became the first president of the Second Republic. After being reelected in August 1983, Shagari was overthrown by General Muhammadu Buhari in December of that year. Finally, in August 1985 General Ibrahim Babangida seized power.

After the end of the civil war in 1970, the Nigerian state expanded greatly in both size and role. Income from oil rose dramatically from $700 million in 1970 to $26 billion fifteen years later. The state controlled the acquisition and use of this astounding increase in resources. The parastatal sector expanded in all directions, and a massive system of subsidies on food, fuel, education, health, and credit flowered, dispensing benefits to almost all social groups. Parallel to this crony statism, mostly commercial crony forms of capitalism developed. They fed on the rents derived from an overvalued exchange rate and the political control of foreign exchange and imports. Power was centralized in the federal government despite the creation of many new states; a major effort was undertaken to indigenize the economy; and the agricultural sector contracted greatly.

Under a process that has been termed "prebendalization," the rentier state was penetrated by complex patron-client networks that distributed state revenue and favors along ethnic and regional as well as emerging class lines. An "implicit moral economy" guided by political rather than economic logic began to dominate Nigerian life: "All major groups in a highly factionalized system expect roughly equal opportunities for access to state bounty, and the state contends with private interests over control of such wealth."[45] As a result, the military governments between 1966 and 1979 had only modest levels of insulation, and the Shagari civilian government had none at all. The modest insulation of the military government had very little positive impact on economic policy, however. The domestic and foreign "leakage" from this prebendal rentier state reached astounding proportions. One estimate put the external "leakage" alone between 1973 and 1983 at about $15 billion, a figure

[45] Peter Lewis, "Notes on Structural Adjustment and Public/Private Sector Relations in Nigeria" (Paper for the Annual Meeting of the African Studies Association, Denver, November 21, 1987), p. 11; Joseph, *Democracy*, on "prebendalization."

close to the country's official medium- and long-term debt.[46] Nigeria, thus, had its own "fat decade," after which it was left with a serious economic crisis and a sizeable debt hangover.[47]

The crunch came late in the Shagari period. With the advent of the world oil surplus, oil production dropped from 2.4 million barrels a day in 1979 to 1.2 million in 1982. Oil exports dropped substantially further, from 1 million barrels a day in 1982 to only 370,000 barrels a day in February 1983. Despite the enormous revenue loss, spending continued to increase. The economic policies of the Shagari government were largely ad hoc and based on political expediency. Out of desperation, the government approached the IMF in April 1983, despite the fact that all major sociopolitical groups were vehemently opposed to doing so. After six months, the negotiations stalemated over three key issues that were to plague the two succeeding military governments as well: devaluation, the elimination of petroleum subsidies, and trade liberalization. Each of these was central to the Nigerian version of the postcolonial syndrome.

The military under Buhari fared little better. It first responded with stabilization, launching austerity measures that reduced the fiscal and current account deficits, froze public sector wages, laid off 250,000 state workers, and slashed imports. These responses brought no medium-term relief, much less any viable restructuring. Buhari attempted to go around the IMF and get rescheduling relief from the Paris Club countries, but they sent him back to the Fund. After another year of negotiations, deadlock was reached yet again, essentially over the same three issues. By 1985, Nigeria was in a serious economic trough. That year GDP was about 15 percent lower than at the beginning of the decade, and real per capita GDP and consumption were well below the levels of the early 1970s. Between 1981 and 1985, public investment was halved, dropping to 14 percent of GDP. Private investment dropped even faster. Thus, in August 1985, General Babangida moved from behind the scenes to take his turn confronting the powerful political logics of Nigeria's version of Africa's postcolonial syndrome.

The Program and the Politics

The immediate dilemma of the new military government was that the debt service on Nigeria's roughly $25 billion external debt amounted to between 70 and 80 percent of total export earnings and was badly bunched, with much of it already in arrears. No new money was coming in and no London Club or

[46] Interviews, Nigerian and international officials, Lagos, January 1987.
[47] See Chinwiezu, "Debt Trap Peonage," *Monthly Review*, 33, 6 (November 1985): 21–35, for a vivid account of the moral economy of debt in Nigeria.

Paris Club reschedulings were in prospect because Nigeria did not have an agreement with the IMF.[48]

Long a sensitive political issue in Nigeria, the IMF posed a serious political problem for the Armed Forces Ruling Council (AFRC). How could Nigeria get around the rescheduling deadlock without going to the IMF? In September 1985, the military regime surprised almost everybody by announcing a "national debate" on the question of whether Nigeria should come to terms with the IMF. Although General Babangida had been seriously considering coming to terms with the IMF and the World Bank, he was also under considerable pressure from his military and civilian advisors to put the matter to public debate. In a very vociferous, emotional, and mostly one-sided public thrashing of the issue, the answer was clearly a resounding "*NO.*" This editorial view appeared in *Newswatch*, Nigeria's leading news periodical:

> Apologists of the IMF have given us the gospel: take the loan or perish. These apologists, consisting largely of conservative economists and monetarists, commission agents and middlemen and errand boys of multi-nationals, have insisted, as the debate gathers fire, that the only path that leads away from perdition for Nigeria is for the country to swallow the IMF pill. That, according to this textbook wisdom, is the answer, the only answer, to our current predicament. . . .
>
> [Nigeria] has discovered that the IMF loan is a Trojan horse, the kind of horse through which the Greeks entered and captured Troy. The three outstanding Trojan horses otherwise called the IMF "conditionalities" which Nigeria has to meet before the loan can be granted are devaluation, trade liberalization and the removal of petroleum subsidies. The first two will facilitate the admission of the Greeks into Troy and the last will ensure that Troy does not recover from the pandemonium that will come.[49]

The head of the Nigeria Labour Congress warned Babangida that he would call a nationwide strike if the government concluded an agreement with the IMF. As a result of his population's emphatic answer, President Babangida broke off talks with the IMF in December. This "debate" showed the general level of understanding of the main issues to be extremely low. Now the Babangida regime really was in a political corner—one of its own creation.

Efforts by the government in late 1985 and early 1986 to get the London

[48] On Nigeria's economic program and its politics, see Lewis, "Notes"; Thomas J. Biersteker, "The Prospects for Structural Adjustment in Nigeria" (Paper for the Annual Meeting of the African Studies Association, Denver, November 21, 1987); "Survey: Nigeria," *Financial Times*, 2 March 1987 and 8 March 1988; Stephen Wright, *Nigeria: The Dilemmas Ahead*, Economist Intelligence Unit Special Report 1072 (London: Economist Publications, 1986); Douglas Rimmer, "The Overvalued Exchange Currency and Over-Administered Economy of Nigeria," *African Affairs*, 84, 336 (July 1985): 435–46; Nils Borge Tallroth, *Finance & Development*, September 1987, pp. 20–22.

[49] *Newswatch* (Lagos), 14 October 1985, p. 10.

Club banks and the major Western creditor countries to reschedule without an IMF agreement by introducing some economic reforms on its own failed. Then the price of oil plummeted from $28 to about $10 a barrel before slowly recovering to $18 a barrel. Government revenue dropped by 50 percent, and imports declined by 60 percent. Nigeria was suffering from severe import strangulation as inflation increased. Babangida's corner had just become a good deal smaller. His sense of urgency was intensified by an attempted coup d'état in December.

Enter the World Bank, specifically its Lagos resident representative, Ishrat Husain, and his staff. Husain was often referred to as "the Nigerian who cared." He and senior Bank officials were to play an extraordinary role. Babangida created an interministerial committee in which both Nigerian and Bank officials participated fully to put together a quite comprehensive economic reform program, one certainly unprecedented in the Nigerian context. It was, in effect, the equivalent of an IMF stabilization and structural change package. In fact, in some areas it probably went further than the IMF would have. It was approved by the AFRC, presented informally to the donor countries and other external actors, and announced by General Babangida in June 1986 as Nigeria's own homespun indigenous solution taken at its own volition and its own pace. The IMF then very quietly sent a team to Lagos to negotiate a stand-by agreement based on the economic recovery program announced by President Babangida. Just as quietly, a letter of intent with the Fund was signed by the Nigerian government on 5 September 1986. It was ratified by the IMF Executive Board on 12 December. A one-year stand-by agreement, potentially worth SDR 650 million, officially went into effect on 30 January 1987.[50]

The December decision by the IMF board allowed London and Paris Club reschedulings to take place that month. Both of them would bring considerable relief when finalized. The Nigerians were unhappy that the London Club did not see fit to provide them with the same terms as the recent relatively generous Mexican rescheduling. In large part, this was the result of intransigence by Japanese banks unhappy about the generous terms extended to Mexico. A mostly symbolic bridge loan was arranged by the British with the direct help of U.S. Federal Reserve Chairman Paul A. Volcker. The U.S. Treasury also helped by holding off the private banks until the whole package could be put together.

Although not stressed publicly by the Babangida government, the IMF agreement was like any other, including quarterly targets and performance reviews, with one major exception—the government of Nigeria had decided not to use any of the SDR 650 million. This was a more formal IMF monitoring

[50] Interviews, Nigerian and international officials, Lagos and London, October and December 1986; and Washington, D.C., January, February, and May 1987.

agreement than the controversial informal one used in Colombia (see chapter 4). Although Nigeria was not going to take any IMF money, the World Bank was to make available a package of $4.28 billion over three years, mostly via structural adjustment loans.

Despite the earlier highly emotional and combative reaction to the IMF, there was no major negative reaction in Nigeria itself, even though the program included a foreign exchange auction that would bring about a devaluation of the naira (the national currency) and allow regular changes in its value thereafter. Devaluation had been one of the most contentious topics during the IMF debate. In short then, the military regime had gotten out of its self-created political corner with striking adroitness.

Although the World Bank had for several years been moving in the direction of dealing with debt, stabilization, and structural adjustment issues, both Nigerian and external actors showed considerable creativity by using it in such an original manner. The Bank had already done most of the key background studies that made assembling the package possible, especially in such a short period of time. In fact, the Bank probably would not have been able to play such a role if it had not had such a long-standing presence in Nigeria. In short, the Bank played, and continued to play, a major role in both the economics and politics of Nigeria's Structural Adjustment Program (SAP).[51]

The Structural Adjustment Program was meant to attack central characteristics of the postcolonial syndrome. An auction (SFEM or Second Tier Foreign Exchange Market) was introduced, resulting in a 66 percent devaluation of the naira and the effective abolition of the old import licensing system and of import restrictions; the growth of the budget and borrowing were to be controlled; inflation was to be cut; all but a few price controls were to be abolished; subsidies on petroleum and fertilizer were to be slashed; imports of wheat and rice were to be banned; the country's agricultural commodity boards were to be abolished and producer prices decontrolled; trade was to be liberalized; and numerous parastatal companies were to be abolished, privatized, or commercialized.

Babangida assembled a small but relatively unified and technically competent economic team, then kept it quite stable over time. He insulated and protected it politically yet kept it politically informed. Its principal members were Chu Okongwu, the finance minister; Alhaji Abdulkadir Ahmed, governor of the Central Bank of Nigeria; Chief Olu Falae, secretary to the federal government; and Kalu I. Kalu, the planning minister. In December 1987, Babangida further centralized economic decision making. Both the Central Bank and the Budget Office were removed from the Ministry of Finance and placed under the office of the president, while the Ministry of National Planning was consolidated with Finance. In the process, Kalu was transferred to the Ministry of

[51] Ibid.

Transport. The government's economic team was supported by an emerging technocratic stratum in Nigeria's increasingly sophisticated private banking and finance sector. Within the state itself, however, administrative depth was limited.

As in Ghana, and in contrast to Zambia, the foreign exchange auction, which began in September 1986, functioned quite well. The Nigerians had studied the operation of the Zambian auction before introducing their own and were assured of substantial financial support from the World Bank. The government "managed" the auction, but on the whole intelligently so. Occasional political flaps and modifications of the rules occurred, but nothing of major importance. The naira dropped from 1.6 to the dollar to 4.62 to the dollar at the first auction, while the first tier, which was used mostly for debt service, remained at 1.6. The second tier rate then slowly appreciated again until it settled down in the 3.5 to 4.0 range by early 1987. The Bank and the Fund wanted a rate of between 4.0 and 4.5 but were willing to accept the higher rate. The main problem in the functioning of the auction was, despite the external help, the scarcity of foreign exchange available for it. Although not eliminated, the blackmarket rate narrowed significantly at first. In July 1987, the government merged the nonauction exchange rate into the auction rate, thereby creating a single foreign exchange market (FEM). The expanded auction and the increasing scarcity of foreign exchange in late 1987 and 1988 led to the fall of the naira rate and a larger gap between the formal and parallel markets. By October 1988, the auction rate was 4.62 to the dollar.

Many Nigerians had hailed the economic recovery program as a major perceptual and attitudinal shift for the country; allegedly they now understood that major changes had to be made if Nigeria were to survive and prosper. Commitment to the program, however, and even basic understanding of its key elements and rationale remained very thin among most groups, including the political and socioeconomic elite. There was no immediate overt opposition as most people waited to see what the full consequences of SAP would be for them. Foreign exchange, the lifeblood of the dominant elites, was still very scarce. Inflation and frozen wage levels hurt urban working and partially working strata. Most people seemed to be waiting for oil prices to rise again and viewed the economic recovery program as merely a clever way of getting out of the rescheduling dilemma, keeping external actors at bay, and bringing in some new resources.

The major early political battles about SAP were fought over its impact on Nigeria's modest but heavily import-dependent manufacturing sector (8 percent of GDP). About 60 percent of inputs were imported. A good number of those who defended the IMF during the debate in September 1985 had been representatives of this sector. Their major hope was that the auction would allow them access to the foreign exchange they needed to import the capital goods and factors of production necessary to raise their low levels of capacity utilization. These owners and managers of very fixed assets quickly discovered, however, that the new tariff rate structure hastily proposed by the World Bank and accepted by the government in September 1986 allowed the easy entry of foreign finished goods that competed very effectively with the higher priced, sometimes lower quality Nigerian-produced goods. In addition, the auction greatly increased the naira costs of foreign exchange and thus of their import needs. The government's tight money and credit policies (M2—broad money—grew by only 2 percent in 1986) often made it difficult for these firms to get credit. It also quite effectively dampened domestic demand, forcing production cuts, worker layoffs (the sector accounted for 30 percent of formal sector employment), and eventually price cuts. The position of the government, at least in public, and of the World Bank was that any firm that could not restructure itself so that it used less than 50 percent imported inputs should be allowed to fail.

The Manufacturers Association of Nigeria (MAN) took the lead in the battles with the government, and indirectly with the World Bank, by calling for increased protection and at least a partial reflation of the economy. In early 1987, the government agreed to undertake, along with the World Bank, a review of the tariff structure and promised resolution within six months. MAN responded that it might be too late because much of the sector would be in very serious trouble by then. It reported that capacity utilization had actually gone down from 30 to 25 percent and that employment had dropped 14 percent. Automobile assembly firms were the hardest hit. Volkswagen of Nigeria, for example, sold only 147 of the 777 vehicles it produced in the first quarter of 1987. The World Bank contended that with proper restructuring 80 percent of the firms in the industrial sector could survive.

MAN, on the other hand, was worried about a widespread deindustrialization of Nigeria. Much of the politics of this battle was fought out in a "skull and crossbones" media battle in the newspapers as well as in the intricate patron-client networks so important to Nigerian politics. Full-page ads from local manufacturers urged Nigerians to buy Nigerian and lobbied the government for lower interest rates and other relevant policies.[52] Despite MAN's claims, however, there was some evidence that a number of firms were restructuring successfully, especially in textiles and food processing. In fact, manufacturing output increased 9.9 percent in 1987 and capacity utlization rose to about 40 percent. These increases were central to the GDP growth rate of 1.2 percent for the year. The government had promised its new tariff structure by June 1987, but World Bank concerns plus the large number of petitions delayed it. The new tariff structure was finally announced in January 1988. It provided relief to the automobile industry and established a basic level of protection for the manufacturing sector as a whole.

[52] Interviews, Nigerian businessmen, Lagos, January 1987.

Labor played an initially more muted but slowly intensifying role in the politics of SAP. The Nigeria Labour Congress (NLC) had long been considered a "toothless bulldog."[53] Its more than forty unions were badly factionalized, and it had not been able to carry through its threats of national strikes. Initially, the unions took a defensive rather than an offensive stance, particularly given the memories of the Buhari regime's harsh response to strikes. The AFRC also showed that it would not allow labor to get out of line. It arrested NLC leaders in June 1986 when they announced a solidarity demonstration on behalf of students at Ahmadu Bello University.

The main bones of contention were the wage freeze and auction-related price increases. Ali Chiroma, the president of the NLC, pointed out that "this structural adjustment programme allows everything else to go to the market and find its level except wages which have been frozen. In any country wages should be allowed to meet the rising costs of living."[54] Other sources of tension with labor included layoffs resulting from SAP's industrial sector policies, rising youth unemployment, intense antipathy for the government's privatization plans, and the refusal of the AFRC to accept its Political Bureau's recommendation to make socialism the official ideology of Nigeria. In an unusually bellicose move on May Day 1987, the NLC demonstrated vigorously against SAP policies during a celebration in the national stadium in Lagos. Shortly thereafter the government rescinded its decision to abolish the minimum wage in firms employing less than 500 workers. The government had already backed away from a decision to raise petroleum prices after intense NLC protest. Babangida went out of his way, however, to remind labor leaders not to step too far out of line.

The petroleum subsidy became the flashpoint. In December 1987, the government again proposed to eliminate it, and the NLC again launched a vigorous national protest campaign. This time it clearly tapped significant mass discontent; despite considerable IMF and World Bank pressure, the AFRC again backed away from eliminating the subsidy and released arrested NLC leaders after only a week. Still under strong external pressure, the AFRC tried a third time in April 1988. It cut the subsidy for a wide range of petroleum products by between 6 and 500 percent. Major strikes and violent protests emerged across the country, joined by students and workers of all kinds, which lasted into early May. There were several deaths, and over twenty university campuses were closed. The government eventually negotiated an end to the protests, but it did not reverse the partial cuts in the subsidy.

Beyond the opposition of key social groups, three issues dominated the future of SAP: (1) implementation, (2) the uncertain consequences of the return to civilian rule, and (3) external finance, especially oil revenue, debt resched-

[53] Wright, *Nigeria*, p. 41.
[54] *Financial Times*, 2 March 1987.

uling, commercial lending, and direct foreign investment. These issues concerned state capacity, insulation and the dominance of political logics, and the role and perceptions of external actors.

First, the steady, consistent, and effective implementation of the package was of major concern to the AFRC, the IMF, and the World Bank. Nigeria was characterized by quite chaotic and uneven policy implementation. While it had better administrative capabilities than many African countries, they were still quite thin. On the whole, the Nigerian "bureaucracies," both federal and state, were also quite demoralized. Beginning in January 1988, Babangida announced a series of administrative reforms meant to increase ministerial and financial accountability. The impact of these measures was quite uncertain, and they would be severely tested in two areas of slow and limited change— privatization and agriculture.

The second major issue was the transition back to democratic rule. In March 1987, the AFRC's Political Bureau, or Cookey Commission, made its long-awaited report on the various options for a third try at democratic rule.[55] After considering the report, President Babangida announced on July 1 a complex, five-year, multistaged return to complete civilian rule by 1992. The intricate timetable established a form of military-civilian diarchy for the transition period. The AFRC subsequently issued a White Paper that laid out the scenario and its position on the recommendations of the Political Bureau. The Cookey Commission had surveyed possible socioeconomic systems for Nigeria and recommended a socialist one. This surprised many people, including important external actors. In rejecting the recommendation, Babangida neatly sidestepped the issue by saying that the "government does not consider it necessary to attach any ideological label to our sociopolitical order."[56] The AFRC also rejected recommendations to fully nationalize the oil and banking sectors and to terminate the privatization process.

The rejection of socialism was not a popular move in leftist union, intellectual, and student circles. As one leftist monthly journal put it, "Again the reactionary foxes or forces of Dodan barracks have turned down the people's choice and are sticking us where we were—in the mire of peripheral capitalism. The Dodan foxes, like most bourgeois generals in reactionary Third World armies, are determined to sustain and protect capitalism even at the cost of destroying everything human in the country."[57] Although the military had

[55] On the prospects for democracy in Nigeria and its impact on economic change, see Thomas M. Callaghy, "Politics and Vision in Africa" in Patrick Chabal, ed., *Political Domination in Africa* (Cambridge: Cambridge University Press, 1986), pp. 30–51; Larry Diamond, "Nigeria: Pluralism, Statism, and the Struggle for Democracy" in Larry Diamond, Juan J. Linz, and Seymour Martin Lipset, eds., *Democracy in Developing Countries: Africa* (Boulder, Colo.: Lynne Rienner, 1988), pp. 33–91.

[56] Summary of World Broadcasts, 4 July 1987, p. B/6.

[57] *New Horizon* quoted in *African Analysis*, 24 July 1987, p. 7.

established some temporary insulation to protect the economic reform program, it was given a hint of what a return to democratic rule might mean for the reforms.

This type of debate was likely to continue. The mandate for only two political parties might lead to the emergence of ideological rather than the expected ethnoregional parties—one "liberal/capitalist," one "populist/socialist." Indications of such an emerging division in the late Shagari period might take on renewed momentum. Such an eventuality would concern important external actors and might increase hesitancy to invest in long-term productive enterprise in Nigeria. Whatever the outcome, the jockeying for power and position was clearly already underway despite a ban on political activity, and it was definitely being affected by the economic reforms and by the emergence of powerful new religious tensions.

The enormous uncertainty about how the transition process would be played out had serious implications for the effective, consistent and lasting implementation of the economic recovery program. Government officials argued that by delaying the return to civilian rule from the original October 1990 date to 1992 the AFRC had given the economic recovery program enough time to become well rooted before the civilians returned. Others were much less sanguine, including important external actors. Most people hedged their economic bets and were likely to continue doing so. The north of the country in particular had enormous reservations about the program. Long fearful about their ability to compete effectively in a liberalized economy with southerners, especially the Yoruba and the Ibo, many northerners resisted any major loosening of state control of the economy. Control of the state and state control of the economy had long been central linchpins of the northern worldview. How the democratization process affected northern control of the federal government would directly impinge on the future of the economic recovery program.

Elections were scheduled in each of the following transition years: 1987, 1989, 1990, and 1992. The first round—nonparty elections for local councillors—was held in December 1987. They were chaotic and badly organized, and voter registration rolls were greatly inflated. In some areas the elections were invalidated and reheld in March 1988. This first round vividly demonstrated the resurgence of the unruly vigor of the Second Republic, indicating that little sociopolitical shredding had taken place under the post-Shagari military regimes. The political insulation of economic policy established by the AFRC was likely to be temporary.

In April 1988, the newly elected councillors chose 75 percent of the members of a Constituent Assembly; the AFRC appointed the rest. The Assembly met for the first time in June and became a platform for attacks on the AFRC and the economic recovery program, clearly demonstrating that the political logics of the postcolonial syndrome were beginning to surge to the surface again. Of particular concern were the petroleum subsidy, the ban on all former politicians and military officers from participating in the transition elections, and the decision to limit the new regime to two political parties. According to the transition schedule, parties would be allowed again in mid-1989. Babangida had proved himself to be very adept at politics, one reason why he was referred to as the Pelé of Nigerian politics—all that fancy footwork. Clever politics by him and the other "foxes of Dodan barracks" would be essential if SAP were to survive the transition back to civilian rule.

As the transition continued and opposition to SAP increased, one of the principal temptations would be to reflate the economy. By mid-1987, there were already indications of both technocratic pressure for a selective reflation on economic grounds and of political pressure for a much larger and less controlled reflation that might threaten the viability of the SAP. Such a wobble, and a more general sense of slippage, did come at the very end of the year. The causes of it were complex; they included the following: a technical desire for a carefully moderated reflation to stimulate growth without inflation; stinging criticism from Olusegun Obasanjo, the very popular former military president, about the impact of SAP on the poor; apprehension over accumulating labor and student unrest; the lack of an urban-rural terms of trade shift comparable to the one in Ghana that helped Rawlings to counterbalance urban protest; the end to the low food prices that had cushioned much of the early impact of SAP; and concern about the accelerating political transition.

The wobble came in the form of the 1988 budget, which contained a 38 percent nominal increase in spending. This included a $600 million Special Reflationary Package for special projects for roads, transport systems, hospitals, schools, and job creation. It also included large civil service pay increases (later rescinded). The revenue estimates upon which the budget was based assumed the elimination of the petroleum subsidy, and the budget was accompanied by the lifting of the wage freeze. The reflationary measures were seen by many as the approaching end of SAP, and they sent expectations soaring. This clearly intensified popular reaction to the cuts in the petroleum subsidy in April 1988. The IMF and the World Bank expressed considerable concern about the reflationary measures. Nigeria had already overshot the 1987 budget targets with a deficit equal to 11 percent of GDP. In fact, the IMF stand-by agreement formally ended in January 1988 without a favorable review from the Fund.[58]

The third major issue facing the Structural Adjustment Program was related to this action by the IMF: the role and perceptions of external actors, especially as they affected resource flows. External banking and investor confidence in Nigeria was still low. Outside of the oil sector, there had been no real net

[58] See Stephan Haggard and Robert Kaufman, "The Politics of Stabilization and Structural Adjustment" in Jeffrey D. Sachs, ed., *Developing Country Debt and Economic Performance*, vol. 1 (Chicago: University of Chicago Press, 1989), pp. 209–54; and chaps. 3, 4, and 6, this volume, on military regimes and reflationary pressures.

foreign investment since the 1977 indigenization decree.[59] Very little private domestic investment in productive enterprise or capital repatriation had taken place. External actors were cautious, with real concerns about sustainability. Most Nigerians did not understand the degree to which the country had a very nasty reputation among the international business community. As a result, many Nigerians had enormously false expectations about what the economic recovery program would do for them. They had great visions of Nigeria as a NIC, a Newly Industrializing Country. By announcing SAP and instituting the auction, they felt that Nigeria had done its part; so, where was all the new money, all the new investment, all the new loans? The World Bank had compounded this problem. In selling the reform package to the AFRC, it had overestimated the resources that Nigeria would get by adopting the program.[60] During the 1985 IMF debate, a *Newswatch* editor made a statement that was fully applicable here: "Given the reality of the Nigerian situation and of the Nigerian population who are by nature impatient, the IMF loan may not work, because Nigerians would expect a miracle as soon as the loan is announced."[61]

As a 1987 IMF article on Nigeria made clear, "The adjustment strategy is based on the assumption that external financing will permit Nigeria to run current account deficits and thereby achieve higher import levels and growth rates than would otherwise be possible."[62] By the government's own estimates at the time, Nigeria would have a financing gap of $3.75 billion a year for 1988–1990. These projections *assumed* oil production of 1.5 million barrels a day against an existing OPEC quota of 1.23 billion, *assumed* a doubling of nonoil exports over the three years, and *assumed* investment inflows of about $500 million annually. None of this was likely to happen.

Thus, at the end of 1988, the Babangida government found itself in the same dilemma as in 1985—the vicious circle of the financing gap. Roughly sketched, this vicious circle is as follows: you need to close a debt service and financing gap; so you need rescheduling and new loans; thus you need an IMF agreement; to get it you must make internal policy changes, such as abolishing the petroleum subsidy; this causes internal unrest, which can be blunted most easily with new resources; so you need more external resource flows and rescheduling. In early 1988, Nigeria confronted an external debt of about $25 billion and $5.4 billion in debt service due that year (80 percent of expected foreign exchange earnings). The 1986–1987 London Club agreement had been signed only recently in November 1987, without the earlier promised additional monies. New arrears were accumulating, the long-running uninsured trade credit controversy had only just been resolved, and export trade cover

---

[59] See Biersteker, *Multinationals*, on external capital in Nigeria.

[60] Interviews, Nigerian and international officials, Nigerian and foreign businessmen, and journalists, Lagos, London, New York, and Washington, D.C.

[61] *Newswatch* (Lagos), 14 October 1985, p. 9.

[62] Tallroth, "Structural Adjustment," p. 21.

was not yet reestablished. The 1987 IMF agreement had just ended without a favorable review. The Babangida government thus needed another IMF agreement to get additional rescheduling. The Fund and the Bank, however, were demanding movement on the budget deficit and a number of other important issues. In the course of 1988, the London and Paris Clubs were cooperative while waiting for agreement with the IMF and the Bank. But by the end of 1988, such agreement had not yet come and foreign exchange remained extremely scarce, threatening to undermine the reforms already in place.

In early February 1989, Nigeria began yet another round of its financing gap vicious circle when the IMF finally approved a fifteen-month stand-by agreement for SDR 475 million. Once again the government expressed its intention not to draw on the funds. As with the 1986 stand-by agreement, this IMF agreement paved the way for more World Bank assistance, additional rescheduling relief from the Paris Club and London Club, and increased bilateral support. Despite this new help, however, Nigeria still appeared unable to break out of its vicious circle.

In sum, Nigeria's crisis was serious, but less so than those faced by Ghana and Zambia. Its social and political fabric had been shredded much less than Ghana's. Its technocratic team was better protected than Zambia's, but that insulation was likely to erode with the transition to democracy. External advice and support were extensive and creative, but external resource flows were smaller than for Ghana and Zambia relative to population and the scale of the economy. The result was an important but wobbly reform effort with uncertain prospects. Because the economic reform effort did not indicate a major perceptual and attitudinal shift for the country, much less a behavioral shift, Nigeria's "trough" might have been too shallow to sustain structural adjustment. If oil prices were to go much above $20 a barrel for any length of time, with or without a return to democracy, the major characteristics of the postcolonial syndrome and its political logics would likely return with a vengeance. Clever politics might not be able to cope with such an onslaught.

CONCLUSION

These three cases present a few surprises for the conventional wisdom about the politics of economic adjustment. First, as in Zambia, a stable authoritarian regime may well not make a good candidate for adjustment. In weakly authoritarian states such as Zambia, the opposition can be coherent, highly organized, and well placed to carry on its struggle. Clearly the caliber and effectiveness of top leadership is important, as in Ghana, but not all determining; structural factors have a significant impact on the sustainability of reform efforts. Second, a country with a recent history of great political instability and economic decline may not necessarily be a bad candidate for sustained economic reform. Third, a country that has suffered a great deal and has an enormous adjustment to make may be a more promising candidate than one that has suffered less. Both structural shredding and clear crisis perception may be required. The three cases also support some of the conventional wisdom. Above all, this applies to the centrality of external actors and resources to economic adjustment. From the perspective of the adjusting country, great external resources are needed to carry out reforms and cushion their impact on the population.

External and internal actors alike have asked: How can serious attempts at economic stabilization and structural change be prevented from collapsing? How can the enormous burdens of such efforts be softened, ameliorated? In a very real sense, these are classic issues of statecraft, at both the national and international levels.

Some learning may be taking place on both sides. External actors are learning that more resources and debt relief are desperately needed in Africa. Whether they will come or not is another matter. The new special facilities of the IMF and the World Bank are steps in that direction, but major support for them will be needed from all major donor countries. Conditionality can still be attached to these resource flows, but it needs to be more limited and targeted. The capacity of African states can easily be overloaded. Some actors on both sides have come to understand that even if Africa's debt problems were greatly diminished or eliminated, major structural adjustment would still have to be made; Africa's postcolonial syndrome would still be there. Both sides have become more attuned to the need for "the politics of fine-tuning"—the calibration of policy measures, instruments, pace, timing, and sequencing, especially for the politically sensitive issues of food, health, fuel, and wages—to modulate the socioeconomic and political impact of adjustment measures.[63] The two sets of lessons about resources and fine-tuning are linked because African countries need the former to help them do the latter. Zambia's economic reform program might have survived if the auction had received larger and more timely resource flows and the maize price changes had been handled with more finesse. Ghana has had both fine-tuning and resources; Nigeria has had more fine-tuning than resources.

These lessons are being learned, slowly and unevenly, but Africa's problems are larger still. Even if proper policy lessons are derived and resources are found to support them, it is not clear they would result in a large number of sustained reform efforts in Africa. The task of confronting the postcolonial syndrome is enormous; the challenges of reform are much greater than in almost all of the other cases in this volume. External actors have learned that Africa is a special case, a special situation because of its postcolonial syndrome.[64] Much of the continent really is lost between state and market. In a

---

[63] World Bank, *Adjustment Lending*, chaps. 3, 4; also see chap. 5, this volume.

[64] World Bank, *Adjustment Lending*, chap. 2 and Annex.

discussion of "institutional reform and sub-Saharan Africa" (SSA), the World Bank has noted that

> The supply response to adjustment lending in low-income countries, especially in SSA has been slow because of the legacy of deep-seated structural problems. Inadequate infrastructure, poorly developed markets, rudimentary industrial sectors, and severe institutional and managerial weaknesses in the public *and* the private sectors have proved *unexpectedly* serious as constraints to better performance—especially in the poorer countries of SSA. Greater recognition thus needs to be given to the time and attention needed for structural changes, especially institutional reforms and their effects.[65]

Note the revealing use of "unexpectedly"; it indicates a changed perception—the lesson that Africa is a special case. The reason for that special case is the postcolonial syndrome and its dominating political logics.

It is not just a question of reordering policies, but one of constructing a whole new context.[66] After roughly thirty years of independence, most of Africa is neither effectively socialist nor capitalist, not even statist. Socialist and statist efforts have come to very little; modern capitalism hardly exists. Current liberalization efforts may not have a major impact in many places, and the rest of the world increasingly passes the continent by. As Kahler has shown in chapter 2, neoorthodoxy, as was structuralism before it, is now explicitly linked to economic development concerns. Its two central tenets are export-led growth and a minimalist state. The new orthodoxy views the state itself as a key obstacle to development, whereas for the structuralists the key obstacles are to be found in internal and external socioeconomic structures. In a sense, for Africa both sides are right: as the structuralists maintain, economic and social structure obstacles to development, internal and external, are enormous; and, as the adherents of neoorthodoxy maintain, the state is also an obstacle. In addition, both sets of obstacles inhibit both import substitution industrialization and export-oriented economic activity, public and private. The structuralists are correct that socioeconomic obstacles prevent "mono-economics" from being fully operative in Africa, as the World Bank has discovered, and the proponents of neoorthodoxy are correct in their belief that the nature of the state in Africa makes import substitution industrialization ineffective and wasteful, as many African structuralists still have not discovered.

The orthodox paradox is real for Africa's postcolonial syndrome: "How does one convince governments to change policies that are economically damaging or irrational but politically rational?"[67] In Africa, the IMF, the World

---

[65] Ibid., p. 3, emphases added.
[66] See Callaghy, "State and the Development of Capitalism."
[67] Chap. 2, this volume, pp. 33–61.

Bank, and other external actors are attempting to use the state to implement neoorthodox policies of liberalization and export-oriented development while trying to restrict the role of the state, to remove it from the economy, to let economic rather than political logics dominate. The East Asian cases demonstrate a further orthodox irony: contrary to neoorthodox myths, the effective implementation of liberalization and export-oriented development cannot be carried out without at least a semistrong and capable state.[68] Structuralists do have a "theory of reform"; it is just a weak one because its instrument of reform, the state, is terribly weak in Africa. As Kahler pointed out, the adherents of neoorthodoxy do not have a theory of state reform, and Africa, where the burdens of neoorthodoxy weigh so heavily, is where such a theory is needed most. In addition, the adherents of neoorthodoxy are learning that their own proclaimed instrument of reform, the market, is also terribly weak in Africa. Nobody understands the functioning of African political economies very well; even the basic data set is extremely limited.

Because of the postcolonial syndrome and its powerful political logics, African states are still lost between state and market. As the three cases described in this chapter have demonstrated, it takes an extraordinary confluence of forces to begin to make a dent in it. Chinua Achebe captured the past thirty years in Africa all too well: "We sought the 'political kingdom' and nothing has been added unto us; a lot has been taken away."[69]

[68] See Frederic C. Deyo, ed., *The Political Economy of the New Asian Industrialism* (Ithaca, N.Y.: Cornell University Press, 1987); Stephan Haggard and Chung-in Moon, "The South Korean State in the International Economy: Liberal, Dependent, or Mercantile?" in John G. Ruggie, ed., *The Antinomies of Interdependence* (New York: Columbia University Press, 1983), pp. 131–89; Alice H. Amsden, "The State and Taiwan's Economic Development" in P. B. Evans, D. Rueschemeyer, and T. Skocpol, eds., *Bringing the State Back In* (New York: Cambridge University Press, 1985), pp. 78–106.

[69] Achebe, interview in *African Events*, p. 77.

CHAPTER EIGHT

Conclusions

Joan M. Nelson

WE RETURN in this concluding chapter to the questions posed at the outset. Our cases spanned a wide range of responses to the economic pressures of the 1980s, with respect to timing, scope, and content of policy choices and actual action. We seek to distill from the kaleidoscope of specific country experiences some broader explanations for these varied responses.

Table 8.1 provides a rough typology of adjustment decisions and implementation by nineteen governments in the thirteen countries examined in this volume. Decisions are classified mainly by their scope, ranging from failure to adopt any coherent and potentially adequate set of measures to adoption of both short-run stabilization policies and a broad agenda of structural reforms. While the great majority of programs in our sample were largely neoorthodox in content, the table indicates the three that were heterodox.

Each program is also classified by the extent to which it was actually implemented, ranging from efforts that fairly clearly stalled or collapsed, through an intermediate category, to those that were largely carried through. Because governments always pursue the various elements in adjustment packages unevenly, gauging implementation raises tricky issues of weighting. Assessments also vary depending on the time frame. Some governments, especially those holding office for many years, went through several phases of adjustment policy during the time span of our study. The table indicates the most important phases, but does not try to reflect all phases for every government.[1] The problems of and criteria for classifying the cases are considered in more detail in the course of the discussion.

Limann in Ghana and Guzmán in the Dominican Republic were unable to adopt a coherent stabilization program. All the other governments sooner or later adopted stabilization measures, but implementation varied. The program announced by Carazo in Costa Rica in early 1981 was abandoned before it began. The effort under Belaunde in Peru disintegrated during 1984; the Cruzado plan under Sarney in Brazil was collapsing by late 1986 or early 1987; and Kaunda definitively abandoned Zambia's stabilization-cum-reform program on May Day 1987. In three other cases—Betancur in Colombia, Jorge Blanco in the Dominican Republic, and Marcos in the Philippines—measures

---

[1] Some phases are clearly demarcated by changes in government, policy announcements, etc. Other phases evolve, so that it is difficult to assign precise beginning and ending dates.

TABLE 8.1
Adjustment Decisions and Implementation: A Rough Typology

Government	Periods to which Table Refers	No Coherent Program	Stabilization	Structural Change — Partial, Little Strategy	Structural Change — Broad, Clear Strategy
Limann (Ghana)	Sep. 1979–Dec. 1981	X			
Guzman (Dominican Republic)	Aug. 1978–Jul. 1982	X			
Carazo (Costa Rica)	Mid-1979–Apr. 1982	X			
Belaúnde (Peru)	Jan. 1983–Mar. 1984		C		
	Apr. 1984–Jul. 1985	X			
Kaunda (Zambia)	Jan. 1980–Nov. 1982	X			
	Dec. 1982–May 1987		C		C
	May 1987–end 1988[a]	X			
Sarney (Brazil)	Feb. 1986–Jan. 1987		C[b]		
	Feb. 1987–Mar. 1988	(moratorium)			
Jorge Blanco (Dominican Republic)	Aug. 1982–Jun. 1984	X			
	Jul. 1984–Apr. 1986		I		
Betancur (Colombia)	Jul. 1982–Jun. 1984	(mildly expansionist program)			
	Jul. 1984–Jun. 1986		I		
Marcos (Philippines)	1980–Jul. 1984	X			
	Aug. 1984–late 1985		I		
	Late 1985–Feb. 1986	X			
Babangida (Nigeria)	Sep. 1985–May 1986	X			
	Jun. 1986–end 1988[a]		I	M	

Leader	Period	Classification
Monge (Costa Rica)	Jun. 1982–Feb. 1984	I
	Mid-1983–Apr. 1986	M
Arias (Costa Rica)	Jun. 1986–end 1988[a]	M
Alfonsin (Argentina)	Dec. 1983–late 1984 (expansionist program)	I[h]
	Jun. 1985–mid-1987	M
Seaga (Jamaica)	Oct. 1980–Dec. 1983	I
	Apr. 1984–Oct. 1985	M
	Oct. 1985–Feb. 1989	I
Aquino (Philippines)	Feb. 1986–Jul. 1987	I
Rawlings (Ghana)	Jan. 1982–Mar. 1983	X
	Apr. 1983–end 1988[a]	I
de la Madrid (Mexico)	Dec. 1982–Dec. 1988	I
Pinochet (Chile)	Mid-1975–mid-1982	I
	Mid-1982–Mar. 1984	
	Apr. 1984–Feb. 1985	(retrenchment of some market-oriented measures)
	Feb. 1985–end 1988[a]	I
García (Peru)	Mid-1985–mid-1987	C[h]

Key: X = No coherent program
C = Program largely or wholly collapsed
M = Mixed record of implementation
I = Program substantially implemented
[h] = Heterodox program
[a] Program still under way as of late 1988.

to stabilize the economy eventually were largely carried through (and did result in at least temporary macroeconomic improvements), but virtually no longer-term structural reforms were attempted. The tales of these nine governments, then, are almost wholly concerned with adoption (or nonadoption) and implementation (or nonimplementation) of short-run stabilization measures.

The remaining ten governments all undertook not only short-run crisis management measures, but also medium-term reforms. The classification of such reforms as partial and piecemeal, or broad and integrated, is inevitably fuzzy and controversial. We believe that those familar with the particular cases would agree with enough of the assignments to preserve the utility of the classification as a framework for discussion. The number and scope (across sectors) of reforms undertaken is one obvious dimension of comparison.

Table 8.1 also tries to take into account a second dimension: the degree to which reforms are ad hoc responses to perceived problem areas or integrated components of an overarching reform strategy. As we suggested in chapter 1, such a strategy entails fairly clear-cut decisions regarding the role of the state in the economy, the degree and pace of integration into world markets, and the priorities and principles guiding public sector social programs and transfers. The governments listed as having undertaken broad adjustment reforms made fairly explicit choices on these issues. The governments adopting more piecemeal, partial measures debated the same issues, but have yet to reach decisions.

The table highlights a series of questions regarding adjustment decisions and follow-through.

1. Timing of adjustment decisions: Why were the Limann and Guzmán governments incapable of formulating coherent policy responses to economic crises? What factors influenced the prompt or delayed timing of adjustment decisions in the other seventeen cases?
2. Scope: What distinguishes the top nine countries in table 8.1, which adopted only stabilization measures, from the remaining ten, which adopted broader programs? Among the latter group, what determined the adoption of more partial versus more comprehensive reform efforts?
3. Content: Why did Sarney, Alfonsín, and García opt for heterodox stabilization programs, in García's case as an integral part of a longer-term heterodox strategy for resuming growth?
4. Implementation: What major factors explain the extent to which governments followed through on their adjustment decisions?

In sections 1 and 2 of this chapter we pursue these questions, focusing in turn on decision making and implementation in terms of the five sets of causal variables outlined in the introductory chapter.

1. *Nature of the economic crisis*—its severity, gradual or sudden emergence, and long or short duration, *and how it was interpreted*, in particular its expected

persistence and perceived roots in mainly external or substantially domestic problems

2. *State capacity—technical and administrative capabilities of the state*—especially the technical capacity and unity of the economic team, and the depth of managerial capacity
3. *Political structures*—regime type, and variation in more specific political institutions, especially electoral cycles and the autonomy of the chief executive
4. *Political circumstances*—leadership and coalitions of support and opposition
5. *Role of external agencies*

All these factors obviously are important, but the analysis seeks to single out those that best explain why governments followed similar or different adjustment paths.

The third section of the chapter turns from explaining variation in adjustment responses among our cases to direct examination of interest groups and other political forces that play key roles in the politics of adjustment.

EXPLAINING INITIAL ADJUSTMENT DECISIONS

The Timing and Scope of Adjustment Decisions

Adjustment measures by their nature arouse considerable opposition and win few immediate friends. Virtually no government is eager to take such measures. Stabilization and adjustment decisions are always in some degree forced by circumstances. But why do some governments take preemptive action to ward off danger in response to economic signals most others would view as no more than blinking yellow lights, while others postpone decisions long after it seems obvious that action is imperative?

Our cases represent almost the full range of variation in timing. Betancur's austerity measures in Colombia in late 1984 and early 1985 are close to the preemptive end of the scale. At the other extreme, Guzmán failed to take decisive adjustment action throughout his term of office, while Limann's paralysis in the face of deepening crisis led to his overthrow and Jerry Rawlings' "Second Coming," and Carazo, after delaying for two years, finally announced stabilization measures only to almost immediately retract them.

As we trace factors that affect the timing of adjustment decisions, we will try to identify determinants of scope. Among those governments able to formulate a coherent response to economic pressures, responses ranged from strictly short-run crisis management to far-reaching programs of structural reform. With the exceptions of Aquino and Arias, both of whom inherited largely stabilized economies, all programs included short-run macroeconomic stabilization elements. Therefore, what calls for explanation is variation in the degree to which governments also undertook longer-run structural reforms as part of their original schemes or as a second phase.

The *nature of the crisis* itself—its sudden or gradual emergence, its largely exogenous or substantially internal causes, even its severity—has little clear relation to the timing of policy response in many of our cases. By definition, preemptive action responds to warning signals rather than full-blown crisis. As Stallings made clear, when the new Colombian minister of finance announced in 1984 that the economy was in crisis and austerity was imperative, many aspects of the economy looked healthy. The nature of the crisis also fails to explain those cases at the other extreme of the timing spectrum, which postponed responding for years. Carazo delayed and wavered in the face of a startlingly sudden crisis; indeed, one reason for ineffective reactions was the speed of deterioration, which ran far ahead of data collection and analysis. In contrast, when Limann entered office, Ghana's economy had been unraveling for twenty years, yet he too could not formulate a program to cope with immediate pressures, much less a longer-term recovery plan.

Popular sayings notwithstanding, facts do not speak for themselves. Decisions are based on interpretations of the facts. Voices always are arguing that action should be taken and, conversely, that action should be delayed. Though Colombia is generally regarded as having taken early or preemptive action in 1984, some had been urging austerity measures in 1982, and even in 1980. In Chile, with its strong domestic analytic capabilities and sophisticated foreign advisors, expert opinions differed up to the very brink of the precipitous economic crash of 1982.

Understandably, politicians tend to choose the interpretations that require the least painful actions. This is particularly true where problems can plausibly be interpreted as externally caused and probably self-correcting. Thus Carazo in Costa Rica in 1979 focused on falling coffee prices and initially assumed the problem was cyclical and self-correcting. Similarly, after a decade's brisk growth in the Dominican Republic, structural problems were emerging by the mid-1970s, but the Guzmán government focused on the damage from the hurricanes of 1979 and pursued reconstruction through deficit finance. Governments can cling for surprisingly long times to interpretations that avoid difficult reforms. Throughout the 1960s and early 1970s copper financed Zambia's growth. Copper prices began their long slide in 1973, but hope of a recovery persisted for at least a decade. Until 1980, regional conflict added to Zambia's economic troubles, and hopes for a "peace dividend" further obscured the need for adjustment. In these and other cases, governments sought to finance gaps rather than shrink them. When concessional aid was not adequate, they turned to long- or short-term borrowing, ran down reserves, and built up arrears.

Interpretations of economic trends and policy options are often shaped by national historical experience or the accepted interpretations of that experience. For example, Limann's paralysis in Ghana in 1981 was partly due to the accepted view, dating from events of a decade earlier, that in Ghana "devaluations cause coups."

Interpretations of the nature of the crisis also shaped the scope of adjustment responses. Where ruling elites were confident that the economy was basically sound, little beyond stabilization was attempted. In Colombia, economic difficulties were assessed as largely due to external factors, including the drop in coffee prices in the late 1970s and the commercial banks' refusal to continue lending despite the absence of a severe debt problem. In the Dominican Republic, prevailing elite opinion viewed the troubles of the mid-1980s as a largely externally caused interruption in a record of satisfactory progress. They were not persuaded by IMF, World Bank and AID analyses pointing to more basic problems and urging structural reforms. The dominant view in Brazil was also that the economy was basically strong and did not require far-reaching changes.

At the other end of the spectrum, the broad reform programs adopted by Aquino, Seaga, Rawlings, Pinochet (starting in the mid-1970s) and García all responded to protracted economic and political difficulties; many of the public as well as political leaders were convinced that the problems were due to major structural weaknesses.

State capacity—more narrowly, economic analytic capabilities—may affect the timing of stabilization measures by providing accurate or faulty assessments. A divided economic team is also likely to lead to indecisive action or to permit political leaders to choose the more optimistic interpretation. But divisions within the team, as distinct from its experience and skill and the quality of information available to it, reflect political rather than technical and administrative factors; a split team is usually associated with weak leadership and/or deep divisions within the government.

Analytic capabilities affect the scope as well as the timing of adjustment decisions; limited capacity is likely to produce narrow responses. Where a small handful of economic staff are struggling to keep abreast of fast-evolving crises, they have little time or energy to consider medium-term strategy and reforms. This is a reasonable description of the situation in the Dominican Republic in 1984–1985, Costa Rica from 1979 through 1983, and Argentina during and after the Austral program. In Peru during the last year of Belaunde's government, already limited capacity was further undermined by the deep split between top economic officials. These governments largely confined their efforts to stabilization.

At the other end of the scale, among those governments that adopted broad adjustment programs, the strength of technical staffing varied widely. In Chile, Mexico, and the Philippines under Aquino, design and adoption of broad reforms were facilitated by strong technical economic staff. But state capacity cannot be described as strong in Ghana under Rawlings, Peru under García, or Jamaica under Seaga. In Ghana, external agencies' analysis and advice crucially bolstered the very small number of senior Ghanaian advisors pressing for reform. García and Seaga devised their own strategies, the former in consulation with Peruvian research analysts and the younger wing of his own party, and Seaga drawing on his own experience and convictions and on the example of Puerto Rico, with considerable analytic input from the World Bank and from AID. Limited state capability is no absolute bar to choosing a broad strategy.

More important than either interpretations of the nature of the crisis or state capacities as explanations for the timing and scope of adjustment decisions are *political institutions and circumstances*. Regime type in general explains little about the timing and scope of adjustment decisions; we found instances of speed and delay, narrow and broad responses among established democracies, transitional democracies and authoritarian systems. But electoral cycles clearly affected the timing of adjustment decisions in many of our cases. Most cases of extreme delay were associated with unusually fragile political support. And the governments that adopted broad-gauged adjustment programs shared a common syndrome of strong and autonomous central executive authority based on permanent or temporary institutions and on broad support coalitions.

It is hardly news that political leaders are reluctant to take austerity measures shortly before elections. Belaunde was early advised to take adjustment measures and blame the previous military government for the hardship, but chose to wait until after municipal elections scheduled some months after he took office. In Brazil, Sarney delayed urgently needed steps to cool the overheated economy until after the congressional elections of November 1986, thus sealing the fate of the Cruzado Plan. Marcos postponed stabilization measures until after the important legislative elections of May 1984. Conversely, immediately after elections may be an optimal moment to take adjustment measures. Monge launched Costa Rica's initial and effective stabilization program shortly after taking office in 1982, as did de la Madrid in Mexico.

A parliamentary system may permit politicians to time elections to facilitate adjustment. Seaga, recognizing by mid-1983 that austerity was unavoidable, seized an opportune moment to call a snap election at year's end, positioning himself to announce sharply tightened economic policies the following spring.

Quite apart from electoral cycles, extremely weak governments are particularly likely to procrastinate. Among our cases, Carazo, Guzmán, and Limann were severely handicapped by deeply divided parties or coalitions unresponsive to their leadership. Carazo's was also a minority government, whereas Guzman's party held a minority in the Senate. Such fragile governments are also likely, when they react at all, to adopt narrow and piecemeal measures rather than a more coherent stabilization package, far less a broader program of structural change. Indecisive and inadequate policies feed into a vicious circle of collapsing political support and further policy paralysis.

Conversely, broad scope, though not necessarily rapid response, is associated among our cases with strong executives. Six governments in our study adopted particularly broad programs of structural change; in chronological order these were Pinochet, Seaga, de la Madrid, Rawlings, García, and Aquino. All were new governments (although Rawlings did not adopt a neoorthodox program for some sixteen months after taking office, he did undertake earlier reforms). All except de la Madrid took office after periods of acute political turbulence in which the previous government was increasingly isolated and ineffective or, alternatively, the polity as a whole was polarized to or beyond the brink of civil war. Partly due to the political turbulence, long-standing economic problems had not been effectively addressed. More fundamentally, in Chile in the mid-1970s, Jamaica in 1980, Ghana in 1982, and the Philippines in 1986, many of the public viewed previous governments' poor economic records as intrinsic results of those governments' ideologies and/or their political structure. Rawlings, Pinochet, and Aquino represented not just new leadership and directions but changes of regime. Seaga, García, and Aquino were voted into office with massive public support, in Aquino's case accompanied by a broad urban uprising. Rawlings and Pinochet seized power in military coups, but both had the support of large segments of the population. Except in Mexico, opposition groups were splintered and in disarray; in Chile they were further repressed. The result was a high degree of autonomy and freedom of action for the political leaders in each case.

As already indicated, the de la Madrid government in Mexico fits the pattern only partially. De la Madrid took office with a reform agenda defined in reaction to the statist and populist leanings of the two previous administrations. But the political and economic situation was far less turbulent than in the other five cases of broad structural reform. Popular support (as usual in Mexican elections) was less for the man or the program than the party, and groups opposed to the new policy direction (particularly those within the party) were subdued, but not in total disarray. In this case, established political institutions were the key to the autonomy and power needed to adopt broad reforms, though shifts in the relative strength of elements within the ruling coalition also played a role.

Alfonsín's government in Argentina, which did not adopt broad reforms, resembles the five just described (other than Mexico) in most respects. The main contrast is in the continuing strength of opposition groups. The military were largely discredited when Alfonsín took power, but elements within the military remained a potential threat, as in the Philippines and Ghana. More importantly, the Peronist unions remained adamantly opposed to liberalizing reforms and quite capable of blocking government action. Attempts to deal separately with non-Peronist unions and to draw closer to labor produced only small victories. Union opposition, coupled with thin and overstrained technical economic staffing and the need to simultaneously address noneconomic reforms, led the Alfonsín government to focus mainly on stabilization and to undertake only limited and piecemeal structural changes. Like Alfonsín, Aquino and García also faced powerful opposition groups in the form of guerilla movements, but these challenged the governments from outside the political system and were a stimulus rather than an obstacle to structural change.

In most of our other cases, where political institutions and coalitions limited the autonomy of chief executives, adjustment decisions were confined to stabilization plus, perhaps, piecemeal, medium-term reforms. In Costa Rica, both constitutional arrangements and strong interest groups limit presidential power. In Zambia, Kaunda is politically dependent on precisely the groups most threatened by orthodox reforms; Marcos was in the same position vis-à-vis the cronies on whom he had become increasingly dependent. Sarney, having become president essentially by accident, had to maneuver with limited and unreliable support from the majority party (the PMDB), sporadic strong opposition from increasingly aggressive unions, and contingent support from the military. The scope of adjustment action undertaken by these governments reflected their leaders' limited autonomy.

Broadly, *external agencies* were less important than domestic political forces in determining the timing and scope of adjustment decisions. Concerted pressure from the international financial institutions, bilateral donors, and commercial banks and the providing or withholding of financial relief play prominent roles in the tales of all our cases. But the degree to which such pressures actually induced decisions that would not otherwise have been taken varied greatly. External pressures and offers of support contingent on stabilization measures failed to induce decisions from the weakest and most divided governments—Limann, Guzmán, and Carazo.

At the other end of the spectrum, the initiative for stabilization programs under de la Madrid, Pinochet, Monge, Seaga, and less clearly, Betancur was largely internal. So too was impetus for the Austral and Cruzado efforts. And domestic political forces were the main source of structural reforms under Pinochet, de la Madrid, Seaga, García, and Aquino. External pressures had greatest influence on the timing and scope of adjustment decisions not with the most fragile governments nor with those that had strong ideas of their own, but with an intermediate category: governments that were divided or indecisive but had sufficient authority to take action. Thus Kaunda at the end of 1983, Jorge Blanco in spring 1984, and Marcos in late 1984 almost surely would not have acted without outside pressure. In Rawlings' case, domestic factors created conditions permitting bold reforms, but it is impossible to imagine the same set of decisions in the absence of external advice, pressure, and support. Roughly the same holds for Babangida in Nigeria.

One further, more subtle channel of external agencies' influence on adjustment decisions (and on implementation) bears noting. By the 1980s, in almost all developing countries some senior economic officials (and/or influential private economists) had spent some time as staff members of the IMF, the World

Bank, or the regional international development banks. At a minimum, that experience introduced a broader perspective, some familiarity with adjustment efforts in other countries, and an understanding of (if not agreement with) perspectives in international financial circles. Often, alumni of the international financial institutions played key roles in the dual political game of adjustment. They interpreted external pressures and attempted to persuade their colleagues in domestic decision-making circles, and they interpreted internal constraints and attempted to persuade their former associates in dialogue with external agencies. Both state capacity and interpretations of economic problems are influenced by these alumni of the international agencies.

The Content of Adjustment Decisions

Of the seventeen adjustment efforts this volume reviews, fourteen were basically neoorthodox in content. Those undertaken by Sarney, Alfonsín, and García, by contrast, rejected demand constraint as the key element of short-run stabilization. García's strategy, which alone among these three incorporated longer-run structural reforms, turned away from the neoorthodox keystones of internal and external liberalization to attempt a more state-guided approach.[2] Given the dominance of neoorthodoxy, it is perhaps most interesting to explain these few but striking deviations from the norm.

In most respects the *nature of the immediate economic crises* and the broader economic trends of the previous decades differed sharply in Argentina, Brazil, and Peru. From the mid-1970s, Peru and Argentina had both grown at best slowly and sporadically. Brazil, by contrast, had done well save for the 1981–1983 period and had resumed brisk growth in 1984 and 1985. Both Brazil and Peru held strong reserve positions when they opted for heterodox plans; by contrast, Argentina's external financial situation was precarious. But all three countries confronted runaway inflation; their triple-digit rates just prior to adopting heterodox programs were far higher than those in any of the other countries in this study (appendix table A–13). In common, also, was the interpretation that inflation and related problems did not stem from excess demand and, therefore, would not be contained effectively through demand restraint.

State capabilities played little direct role in shaping initial heterodox deci-

---

[2] The fact that García's attempted heterodox adjustment strategy, which encompassed both short-run and longer-range elements, stands alone among our cases reflects broader trends in the 1980s. In longer historical perspective, of course, many governments have pursued development strategies that were heterodox, in the sense that they relied heavily on state direction and emphasized protection rather than trade liberalization. But in almost all countries during the 1980s, to the extent that any longer-term adjustment measures (as distinct from short-run stabilization measures) were adopted, the broad *direction* of adjustment has been towards reduced state intervention and towards liberalization of trade, even in highly statist and inward-oriented economies.

sions. The intellectual impetus for the heterodox programs in all three countries originated outside of the governments, in academic and private research organizations. But in a larger sense, the ability to formulate and adopt such programs did reflect domestic analytic talent able to formulate coherent alternatives to orthodoxy.

Regime type and aspects of political circumstance, particularly coalitions of support in the three countries shared certain features. All three governments were working within systems in transition to democracy.[3] All were basically centrist, but were formulating economic (and other) policies in reaction to markedly more conservative predecessors and placed high priority on support from popular sectors. The military had largely stepped (or stumbled) out of the political arena, but remained in the background to varying degrees. While business interests in both Brazil and Peru were politically powerful, both Sarney and García at the times of their heterodox choices saw their major opportunities for broadened political support among the popular sectors. Pressures on Alfonsín were more evenly balanced between traditionally powerful and aggressive unions and particularly liquid and skeptical financial and industrial interests; his room for maneuver depended largely on broad support among the middle sectors of society.

While similar patterns of coalition politics contributed to heterodox decisions, *external agencies* played very different roles in the three cases. In both Brazil and Peru, heterodox choices followed breaks with the IMF. Both governments felt they could act independently of or even oppose the international financial community. In the short run this reflected relatively strong reserves, but in the longer run the two had different reasons; Brazil was confident of its strong bargaining power, and Peru concluded that it had more to lose than gain by continuing to play by international rules. In contrast, the Argentine Austral Plan was designed in consultation with, and was ultimately endorsed by, the IMF and key representatives of the U.S. government. This reflected Argentina's shaky external financial situation and the sensitivity of Argentine industrial and financial interests to international respectability. At least partly because of the need to win external agencies' approval, the Austral Plan departed from neoorthodoxy much less than either the Cruzado Plan or García's program and was accompanied by quite conservative fiscal and monetary measures.

The heterodox experiments, in summary, were designed by sophisticated analysts in response to particularly acute and intractable inflations. They were adopted by regimes in transition to democracy, reacting to earlier, more ortho-

---

[3] In Peru, Belaunde's government was the immediate successor to military rule. But under García, general agreement on the rules of the political game remained limited and the possibility of reversion to military rule remained considerable, in contrast to situations in the governments listed as established democracies in table 1.3.

dox policies viewed as unsuccessful[4] and pursuing coalitional opportunities lying to their left. Two of the three governments also felt in a position to challenge the external agencies. The third, less strong in this dimension, was also less heterodox in its choices.

Does the combination of factors that helps explain the few heterodox choices among our cases also shed light on the prevalence of orthodoxy? Obviously, where the problems were different, attempted solutions were also different. Where runaway inflation was not a key aspect of the crisis, one would not expect the particular kind of heterodox shock adopted in Argentina, Brazil, and Peru. In Jamaica, much more moderate inflation thought to be caused by rapid devaluation led Seaga to depart from orthodoxy by freezing the exchange rate. Other mainly neoorthodox programs modified or abandoned orthodoxy in specific respects reflecting their specific problems; even Pinochet, for example, temporarily took control of the banks rather than permitting a massive collapse. But in many of our cases, at least the acute phase of the economic crisis of the 1980s was regarded by the chief executive and/or his key advisors as calling for basically neoorthodox solutions.

The neoorthodox thrust of stabilization and structural reform programs under Pinochet, de la Madrid, Seaga, Aquino, and less clearly Betancur also reflected coalitional politics contrasting with the patterns in the heterodox cases. Pinochet in the mid-1970s, de la Madrid, and Seaga designed their economic policies in reaction to what they viewed as their predecessors' damaging populist programs. All three saw greater opportunities for political and economic support to their right than their left. Anticipated foreign private and official responses reinforced this assessment. They were, in short, coalitions moving right.

The picture in the Philippines was only subtly different. Aquino had been swept into office with support from the middle classes and the majority of the business community excluded from Marcos' circle of cronies. The left hesitated to extend wholehearted support. Though Aquino sought to define her coalition inclusively, the center-left was clearly less important on economic policy than the center-right, which pressed some reforms but vetoed others such as land reform. Betancur's case showed some partial parallels. He too originally hoped to reduce pressure or even gain some support from the left by stimulating growth and undercutting the appeal of the guerillas. But the positive results of his early measures failed to translate into broader political support, while the economic costs—increased fiscal deficits and inflation, and

---

[4] As Kaufman notes, Argentine policy during Alfonsín's first year, while Grinspun was in charge, used highly stimulative wage and credit policies. The military governments immediately preceding both Alfonsín and Sarney had also relaxed austerity measures in response to populist pressures. But the Austral and Cruzado experiments are probably best viewed as designed in reaction to the longer history of efforts to stabilize the economy, including repeated orthodox packages that did not have enduring results.

falling reserves—alarmed conservatives. The upshot was a swing towards orthodoxy.

Several of our other cases illustrated a different combination of factors leading to a similar result: mainly neoorthodox adjustment programs. Jorge Blanco by mid-1984, Rawlings by early 1983, Kaunda by late 1983, and Babangida upon entering office all confronted serious economic problems. Moreover, in all these cases the same or a previous government had pursued "nonpolicies" of drift, or experimented with controls, punishment of speculators (Ghana, Dominican Republic), or mass mobilization (Ghana). It was clear such measures were not adequate. All were being offered strong orthodox advice from some internal advisors, while the opponents of conventional stabilization offered no plausible or coherent alternative. In all cases external agencies were pressing hard, offering financial support but insisting on difficult measures. Coalitional politics were not particularly supportive, nor were political leaders necessarily convinced that orthodox measures would work. Orthodoxy was simply the most promising or least unpromising course of action available.

Our cases broadly support Kaufman's and Stallings' thesis that strongly orthodox programs, especially those including both stabilization and longer-run structural changes, are more likely to be adopted by authoritarian governments, whereas heterodox efforts are most likely to be adopted by regimes in transition to democracy.[5] But the links are loose: all our heterodox programs were adopted by transitional regimes, but only three of the six transitional regimes adopted heterodox programs.

Level of development and to some extent scale also seem roughly associated with program content. Countries at relatively low levels of development and perhaps more advanced small countries may have less scope for deviating from orthodoxy than larger and more advanced nations. Particularly in sub-Saharan Africa, limited analytic capacity thus far has constrained ability to formulate detailed and realistic alternative approaches to adjustment. Most of the sub-Saharan countries and some poor non-African nations are finding growth strangled by lack of foreign exchange. In many, close to all investment is externally financed. Unlike Peru in 1985 or Brazil in 1986, reserves are at rock bottom; challenging the external agencies is an unacceptable risk. More broadly, small size and low levels of development constrain short- and medium-run economic options. To illustrate with only two of many possible points—internal markets are too small to support efficient production of most manufactured goods; and governments dependent on trade taxes for most of their revenue cannot readily shift to more inward-oriented strategies. There

<hr/>

[5] Robert Kaufman and Barbara Stallings, "Debt and Democracy in the 1980s: The Latin American Experience," in Barbara Stallings and Robert Kaufman, eds., *Debt Democracy in Latin America* (Boulder, Colo.: Westview, 1988), pp. 201–23.

may be an economic and administrative floor below which heterodox options are unrealistic.

Determinants of Adjustment Decisions Summarized

Before turning to implementation, it may be useful to summarize the clearest points regarding determinants of adjustment decisions.

The most important factors that determine the *timing* of adjustment decisions include

> The perceived nature of the economic difficulties, as influenced by prior experience and the cohesion of the economic team
>
> Electoral cycles
>
> A basic minimum of political support for the chief executive. Strength in a chief executive is no guarantee of quick decision, but acute weakness and inability to command support from party and/or legislature or other key support groups virtually guarantees delay or paralysis.

Broad *scope* of adjustment programs among our cases usually reflected

> A long history of economic (and often political) troubles, leading to widespread agreement that basic reforms were needed (though not necessarily to agreement on the design of those reforms)
>
> Concentrated and autonomous executive authority, as a result of varying combinations of durable political structure, temporary institutional arrangements, and coalitional politics
>
>> Recent military coups, with considerable popular backing (Pinochet, Rawlings)
>>
>> Recent sweeping electoral victories (Seaga, García, Aquino)
>>
>> An institutionalized strong executive (de la Madrid)
>>
>> Temporary institutional arrangements heightening executive autonomy (Aquino's first eighteen months; Seaga after the 1983 elections)
>>
>> Discredited and disorganized, or repressed opposition groups

Regarding *content* of adjustment choices, heterodoxy among our cases reflected

> high inflation and failed earlier orthodox efforts
>
> sophisticated analytic abilities
>
> transitional democratic regimes, based on "coalitions moving left."

Neoorthodox programs resulted from

> New governments reacting to prior populist or exclusive crony-based regimes
>
> Authoritarian governments, or nonauthoritarian governments based on coalitions moving right

Alternatively, in a few cases, old or new governments convinced that previous policies (their own, or predecessors') of drift or controls were inadequate, who saw little coherent alternative to orthodoxy.

IMPLEMENTING STABILIZATION AND STRUCTURAL CHANGES

Once governments have decided to launch adjustment measures, what factors determine the extent to which they follow through? Any effort to address the question promptly enters a thorny thicket of definitional and interpretive issues.

We noted in chapter 1 that we seek to explain the degree to which policy decisions were carried out rather than economic outcomes of the measures taken. More precisely, we do not attempt to assess the degree to which actual economic performance resulted from the policies adopted rather than from other factors. But we do take into account that economic outcomes, whatever their main causes, feedback to second- and third-round governmental choices and action.

How will "implementation" be gauged? A virtually universal goal of orthodox stabilization efforts is reduction of the fiscal (and often the broader public sector) deficit. A government may sharply slash expenditures, vigorously tighten tax collection, and increase tax and utility tariff rates, yet fail to shrink the public sector deficit because recession and foreign exchange shortages have dried up trade-dependent revenues, while increased interest rates and/or devaluation have swollen domestic and foreign public debt service obligations. Meeting specific goals is not an accurate measure of serious effort.

Implementation may also look more or less effective depending on the time frame. IMF stand-by agreements usually cover twelve to eighteen months. A government may miss targets and a stand-by may collapse—an apparent failure—yet over a longer period of time may pursue reasonably responsible macroeconomic policies and maintain considerable stability. The description applies to Costa Rica under Monge (where a stand-by was cancelled in 1986 with only half the funds drawn), and more arguably to Jamaica (where two stand-bys failed to be completed between 1983 and 1986). Conversely, a weak government with great difficulties maintaining responsible macroeconomic management may summon discipline for a strong but brief effort: examples are Marcos and Jorge Blanco, both in late 1984 and 1985. The appropriate time frame for assessing longer-run structural changes is still less clearcut.

No assessment of implementation can escape these ambiguities, nor find wholly objective ways to rank governments' adjustment efforts.[6] In this sec-

---

[6] See World Bank, *Adjustment Lending: An Evaluation of Ten Years of Experience*, Policy and Research Series no. 1 (Washington, D.C., 1988), a recent report that includes assessments of implementation of several major categories of adjustment measures in a sample of fifteen countries that receive sizable adjustment loans and compares economic performances of countries with

tion, we group cases according to our judgments that stabilization and structural change programs were implemented in substantial degree during the government's tenure (or, for long-lived governments, during the 1980s), were implemented only partially, or were largely abandoned. Because different types of adjustment packages can be expected to present different kinds of implementation problems and to generate different political dynamics, we examine separately the variation between our cases in pursuing neoorthodox stabilization and structural change, and heterodox adjustment programs.

Implementing Neoorthodox Adjustment Programs

The introduction to this volume noted the difficulties of carrying through macroeconomic stabilization measures, as indicated in the high proportion of agreements with the IMF that break down before completion. Seven of our cases are not relevant to a consideration of implementing orthodox stabilization programs. Limann and Guzmán failed entirely to adopt stabilization measures. Arias and Aquino inherited reasonably stabilized economies. Sarney, Alfonsín, and García adopted heterodox stabilization efforts that will be considered later.

Among the remaining twelve, it is useful to compare those that clearly failed to carry through stabilization programs (Carazo, Belaunde, Kaunda) with those that were largely successful, whether or not their histories include some failed stand-by agreements. In the latter group are Monge, Seaga, Pinochet, de la Madrid, Rawlings, more tenatively Babangida, and (with no formal IMF agreement) Betancur. Two other governments—Jorge Blanco and Marcos—are intermediate cases. Both first failed to implement agreements, then carried through major measures for roughly eighteen months and a year, respectively. Both then somewhat eroded the hard-won economic gains prior to elections in which they were resoundingly defeated.

It is still harder to assess implementation of structural changes than of stabilization decisions. This is partly because many structural changes must proceed in stages. If progress is delayed or apparently halted at one stage, it is difficult to know whether the reform is actually derailed or simply taking longer than expected. Structural change programs also contain many elements only loosely or indirectly interlinked. Some components move ahead much faster than others. Observers' judgments about overall progress inevitably will be colored by the priority each places on specific measures.

Despite these ambiguities, most observers would concur that, five among our cases moved ahead substantially with broad programs of neoorthodox structural change, at least relative to the other governments considered in this

and without adjustment lending. The Bank's assessments of implementation rely, in varying degrees for different types of measures, on qualitative judgments.

volume. Seaga, de la Madrid, Pinochet, Rawlings, and Aquino all significantly contracted government intervention in the economy, reduced major
price and nonprice disincentives to efficient production, promoted exports,
and moved towards import liberalization to increase ability to compete in international markets. Some backtracked on aspects of this agenda at times (for
example, Pinochet in 1984; Seaga in 1985–1986), but the overall shifts in the
economies were substantial.

Other governments either adopted much more partial agendas of change or
failed to follow through with broad programs. In early 1984, Kaunda announced an ambitious program of reforms, but very little was actually implemented. Marcos, under heavy pressure from external agencies, adopted a limited program of reform in 1984, but little action followed. Costa Rica and
Argentina are intermediate cases: both undertook piecemeal but significant
reforms; both followed through on some measures while others stalled or
aborted. It is early to assess Babangida's program in Nigeria. The reform program is fairly broad, but follow-through seems likely to be limited as a result
of pressure group resistance, general lack of recognition of need for change,
and preoccupation with the transition to democracy. Brazil, Colombia, and
the Dominican Republic attempted still less, at bottom because influential
elites in all three countries did not feel much structural change was needed for
sustained growth.

In attempting to explain adjustment decisions, we considered prior economic trends and factors influencing decision-makers' interpretations of their
economic problems. To understand implementation, we need to assess how
evolving economic trends (resulting only partly from the government's own
measures) play back on the vigor and persistence of stabilization efforts.

The simplest expectation is that economic improvement should help sustain
adjustment programs, whereas deterioration should undercut them. But the
relationship is more ambiguous, for several reasons. First, indices of economic performance that are central to outsiders' or central economic officials'
assessments of progress may not be the indicators of greatest interest to major
political groups. Reduced arrears, a smaller fiscal deficit, and sharp increases
(often from a very small base) in nontraditional exports may not persuade
labor and business groups confronting continued scarcities, unemployment,
and tight credit.

Second, even if there is agreement on the general trend of economic performance, the effects on continued implementation are not clear-cut. Two
mechanisms are at work. Economic improvements or deterioration affect confidence: among decision makers about whether they are on the right course;
and among domestic and foreign investors, interest groups, and the public as
to whether the government is in control of the situation. Changing economic
circumstances also affect both decision maker and public perceptions of the
need to continue painful measures. Continued stagnation or decline, therefore,

can prompt protest, or can (at least for a while) underscore the need for extraordinary measures already under way. Conversely, an economic upturn may generate support or undermine continued implementation by convincing politicans and the public that the need for austerity has passed.

Our cases provide instances of all these effects. The most common scenario is that of stagnation or decline eroding confidence in government economic management. Thus in Peru and Chile in 1983 and 1984, Jamaica in 1985, the Dominican Republic in winter 1984 and again in 1985, Zambia in late 1986 and early 1987, Nigeria in 1988, continued economic deterioration prompted growing protests. As a result, adjustment efforts crumbled in Peru under Belaunde, the Dominican Republic in spring 1984, and Zambia in 1987. Jointly with technical reassessments, protests spurred program modifications in Jamaica and Chile.

In contrast, in Ghana the "trough effect" not only prompted acceptance of the initial 1983 decision to attempt a drastic neoorthodox adjustment program, but also damped opposition to that program throughout an extraordinarily difficult two years (compounded by drought) before it began to produce some improvements. In Colombia, austerity measures introduced in late 1984 were continued by the new government taking office in 1986, which interpreted improved economic performance as evidence that the country was on the right track. But in Costa Rica in 1984, rapid economic improvements resulting from strong stabilization measures had the opposite effect, leading both the public and much of the government to conclude that austerity was over. Similarly, signs of recovery in Mexico in mid-1984, coupled with anticipation of mid-1985 gubernatorial elections, led to fiscal relaxation later criticized as premature.

Actual economic trends, in sum, have varying effects on sustainability of orthodox adjustment programs, depending on how those trends are interpreted by the government and the public. Even where economic crisis has convinced much of the public that drastic measures are required, however, the tacit mandate is normally temporary; some relief from economic hardships within, perhaps, a year usually is necessary to sustain confidence.

The earlier discussion of determinants of adjustment decisions noted the importance of unity or divisions in the economic team. This same aspect of *state capacity* has an important influence on implementation. It is striking that in all three cases of clearly failed conventional stabilization efforts, severe splits in the economic team crippled implementation. Under Carazo, Minister of Finance Sáenz was essentially alone in pressing for stabilization and negotiating with the IMF. Under Belaunde, Minister of Finance Carlos Rodríguez-Pastor and Central Bank Governor Richard Webb pursued direct and explicit contradictory measures. And under Kaunda, support from the Central Bank was partly countervailed by footdragging in the Ministry of Finance during 1984 and 1985; the new economic team appointed in mid-1986 solidly opposed the effort. The initial unsuccessful stabilization effort (1982–1983) under Jorge Blanco in the Dominican Republic was very similar to the pattern in Costa Rica under Carazo. The governor of the Central Bank rather than the minister of Finance played a lonely (and not wholly consistent) role in pressing for stabilization. Only after the economic team was changed, coupled perhaps with low-key shifts in the stance of the business community, was the more successful effort of 1984–1985 possible.

Many longer-term structural reforms are more complex administratively, and require coordinated action by more agencies than do most of the elements of short-run stabilization programs. Therefore, not only central economic staff able to fine-tune ongoing policies, but also the scope of central government authority and the depth of managerial talent in the public sector become crucial to implementation. Moreover, as discussed in more detail later, the bureaucracy is not merely an instrument but also a protagonist in conflicts generated by neoorthodox structural changes. Opposition from within the state may cripple implementation.

Several of the countries that followed through on broad structural changes rank high among developing countries in terms of competence and depth of the relevant administrative cadres. This is clearly the case in Chile and in Mexico, and to a lesser extent in the Philippines. But Jamaica's public services had deteriorated during the 1970s as a result of seriously eroded real wages, among other factors. Still more clearly, Ghana's civil service, probably the strongest in sub-Saharan Africa in the late 1950s, had been decimated by twenty years of falling real salaries, political turnover, and resulting emigration. Rawlings compensated for weak state capacity by extensive use of expatriates. He was free to do so because many positions were vacant when he took power; moreover, he distrusted many of the holdover officials. Seaga found a similar though less severe situation and used the same solution more modestly. In both countries, extensive use of expatriates eased the limits on state capabilities, but was also a source of growing criticism.

When Kaunda announced a program of fairly ambitious reforms in early 1984, he too faced limited state capabilities. But positions were not vacant, and he could not readily dismiss key officials because the public service was a major component of his political support. Zambia, therefore, did not use large numbers of expatriates. Simple administrative incompetence destroyed some key elements of the reform program. For example, farmers responded to higher producer prices, but the National Agricultural Marketing Board and the provincial cooperatives were unable to collect the increased maize crop for several successive years. In addition to incompetence, much of the Zambian state apparatus strongly resisted reforms.

To echo the findings with respect to adjustment decisions, broad regime type is not helpful, but more specific *institutional features*, particularly *electoral cycles and the scope of executive authority*, are important in explaining persistent and effective implementation of stabilization and structural change programs. Just as many of these governments delayed the adoption of adjustment measures until after important elections, many eased implementation of austerity measures as new elections approached. The pattern applied in Argentina prior to the 1983 presidential election and the October 1987 congressional election (though not the 1985 midterms); the approach of the November 1986 elections played a key role in the history of the Brazilian Cruzado effort; Costa Rica eased its drive to shrink the fiscal deficit in the months before the 1986 presidential election; Seaga similarly announced big budget increases before the local elections in mid-1986. The same tendencies were clearly evident even in much less competitive systems: Mexico in 1982 and 1985, Zambia in 1987–1988, Chile in 1988.

Executive autonomy also plays a central role in implementing adjustment decisions. As already noted, a variety of circumstances can produce at least temporary executive autonomy. Pinochet and Rawlings, as authoritarian rulers in nondemocratic systems, were essentially unconstrained by legislatures or party councils. De la Madrid controlled powerful and disciplined party machinery, and his selection as president had reflected a shift of opinion within the Mexican governing elite in favor of orthodox reforms. Aquino was presiding over a transition to democracy, but for her first eighteen months governed without a legislature and retained extraordinary powers. Seaga's personality combined with Westminster parliamentary institutions (somewhat stretched after 1983) to grant the prime minister unusual autonomy. He strongly dominated his own party and his cabinet, and after the snap elections of late 1983 the opposition was not represented in Parliament.

Coalitions and patterns of political support reinforced permanent or temporary institutional arrangements to grant these same leaders an unusual degree of autonomy. Most fundamentally, the groups benefiting from the policies and programs of the previous regimes were disempowered under the new governments: dramatically so under Pinochet, Rawlings, and Aquino, but only slightly less definitively in the two cases where governments changed while regime type persisted (Seaga and de la Madrid).

Broad support for the governments did not consistently translate into support for the reform programs. Pinochet and de la Madrid had support for some measures from certain business groups. Aquino had support from both non-crony business groups and many other groups for measures designed to dismantle the crony system and clean up administration, but trade liberalization, privatization, and especially land reform prompted resistance. Rawlings and Seaga had little positive support from almost any group for any of their reforms. The key political factor affecting many of the reforms in these five cases was not positive support for specific measures, but diffuse support for the government and, above all, the political leader coupled with the disabling of most opposition groups.

By contrast, those governments that launched structural changes but were markedly less successful in following through were also much less autonomous. More specifically, they relied for much of their political support on precisely the groups most threatened by economic liberalization. In Zambia, high officials and politicians resisted the reforms from the outset, preventing some measures from ever getting off the ground and sabotaging others, like the foreign exchange auction.

The fate of Marcos' rather narrower list of structural reforms in 1984 and 1986 followed a similar pattern. The package included rehabiliation of the state-owned banks, reform of the sugar and copra monopolies, tax reforms, import liberalization, and some privatization of state-owned economic enterprises. Reform of the monopolies, in particular, would have directly attacked some of the cronies who constituted a major element of Marcos' political support. Other proposed measures, including tax and import reforms, were dropped from the agenda (if indeed they had ever been more than window dressing for the external agencies) as elections neared.

From the perspective of individual governments, *external agencies* often played a major, even a domineering role in implementation of orthodox stabilization programs. Not only did the IMF condition release of its resources on prior conditions and the subsequent meeting of quarterly targets, but the World Bank, the commercial banks, and in some countries the U.S. Agency for International Development also conditioned part or all of their financing informally or formally on the maintenance of an active agreement with the IMF. As it monitored performance, the Fund also consulted closely with countries' own economic analysts. Especially where analytic capabilities were limited, these consultations could make a significant (if not always welcome) contribution to the fine-tuning of policies as economic trends unfolded.

However, external pressure is not very helpful in explaining *variation* between our cases—why some countries implemented stabilization programs while others abandoned the effort—precisely because the IMF role was fairly similar in almost all our cases. Some contrasts were apparent between cases in the "tightness" or rigor of required performance targets, and some notably "soft" agreements (including extended fund facility arrangements with the Dominican Republic in 1983, and with Jamaica in 1981–1982) were not implemented. But some much tougher agreements also collapsed; variation in the rigor of conditions is not neatly linked to variation in countries' implementation of stabilization measures.

The World Bank normally took the lead role in structural reforms, providing its own funds and advice as well as orchestrating broader financial support. All the programs of orthodox structural change among our cases were supported by World Bank structural or sector adjustment loans. The U.S. Agency for International Development was heavily involved in Costa Rica, Jamaica, and the Philippines.

External finance directly supported certain reforms. For example, Argentine and outside analysts agreed that taxes on agricultural exports should be reduced, but implementing the reform required bridging finance because the taxes provided a major share of revenue and alternative sources would take time to develop. More broadly, nonproject funding supported implementation not only by providing imports for industries and activities strangled by lack of foreign exchange, but also by helping restore public confidence and providing political breathing space.

But the level of financial support, measured either as concessional aid or as net capital flows (relative to the size of the recipients' economies or populations), bears no consistent relationship to extent of implementation of reforms. Financing for governments that pursued broad reforms varied from large to modest (or negative, in terms of net capital flows for some cases). And some countries that got very heavy financial support, like Costa Rica, made only modest progress on structural reforms.

Similarly, the degree to which external agencies offered ongoing, detailed advice and guidance as reforms were implemented ranged from minimal to intense among our cases of broad-gauged adjustment programs, but intensity of outside involvement is not neatly tied to extent of implementation.

The cases can be fairly clearly ranked. The World Bank supported financial packages to assist Mexico's adjustment efforts, but took a back seat to the IMF in actual discussions and played a major role only in design of certain trade-related reforms. Its role in Chile was more active, reflected in negotiation of three SALs in 1985, 1986, and 1987, but mainly reinforced rather than significantly altered the direction and design of Chilean measures. The Bank had tried energetically to prompt reforms in the Philippines under Marcos, including negotiating two SALs (1980, 1983) and an agricultural sector loan (1984). Many of the reforms urged by the Bank and other donors but not implemented under Marcos were pursued much more successfully by Aquino. World Bank involvement was fairly continuous, even though the first nonproject loan negotiated with the Aquino government did not take effect until early 1987. In Jamaica, the World Bank arranged three consecutive SALs between 1982 and 1984, followed by two sector loans in 1987. Both AID and Bank staff were deeply involved in detailed design and promotion of a wide range of specific reforms. Finally, in both Ghana and Nigeria, design and step-by-step implementation were still more closely guided by Bank staff.

The degree and detail of World Bank involvement in ongoing policy fine-tuning and implementation (as distinct from financial support) thus was roughly inversely related to state capabilities, and (still more roughly) to the size and international political roles of the countries.[7] Bank advice and guid-

[7] See Joan M. Nelson, "The Diplomacy of Policy-Based Lending," in Richard E. Feinberg

ance in Jamaica and Ghana, along with direct hiring of expatriates, functioned to partly compensate for limited administrative capacity. But similar Bank efforts in Zambia could not prevail in the absence of autonomous political leadership. Philippine experience tells the same story still more clearly; the same external agencies promoted the same reforms, unsuccessfully under Marcos, and with considerable success under a new regime in an entirely different political context. External advice and pressure often stretched internal political constraints on structural change, contributing in important ways to implementation. But domestic politics set the basic parameters of government efforts to carry out adjustment programs.

Implementing Heterodox Adjustment Programs

The heterodox adjustment efforts of the Alfonsín, Sarney, and García governments shared important features, but also differed in crucial respects. The Austral and Cruzado plans focused on the immediate goal of breaking the inertia of very rapid inflation. Neither included a plan for transition to longer-run strategy. García, in contrast, was primarily concerned with shifting Peru onto a sustainable long-term growth path, oriented much more strongly to the needs of the urban and particularly the rural poor. Inflation was a concern, but was not central.

All three programs were dramatically successful in quickly slowing inflation. But the course of implementation thereafter diverged sharply. In Brazil, crucial follow-on measures were delayed until after the November elections; attempts to tighten fiscal and monetary policy thereafter met massive opposition. The program collapsed within ten months.

In Argentina, the effort was sustained much longer, but gradually eroded. More cautious fiscal and monetary policies had been built into the initial plan. When prices began to edge higher after some months, the government fought the tendency with incremental measures, though holding the line became increasingly difficult as the mid-term elections of October 1987 approached. Three years after the Austral was launched, 1988 inflation rates were high but, nevertheless, a third of pre-Austral plan levels. It can reasonably be argued that the Austral plan itself was substantially successful in its near-term goals; the failure was the inability to supplement Austral with an adequate program of medium-term reforms.

In Peru, García's longer-term goals called for broader measures. But the strategy lacked a coherent focus. An initial thrust towards the poorest sectors of society was replaced by a somewhat surprising alliance with Peru's largest business conglomerates, which was then torpedoed by the decision to nation-

and contributors, *Between Two Worlds: The World Bank's Next Decade* (New Brunswick, N.J.: Transaction Books, 1986) p. 73, for a fuller discussion on this point.

alize most financial institutions. Meanwhile failure to promote exports and declining capital inflows as a result of tensions or breaks with external creditors led to the exhaustion of reserves. By the end of 1988, there were signs of a turn towards a more orthodox approach.

How did evolving *economic trends* affect these different implementation records? The initial dramatic drops in inflation generated a wave of popular support in all three cases. But demand-led programs have inherent tendencies to overheat. They, therefore, require well-timed changes in macroeconomic management. García's program also hinged essentially on a gamble that production would expand, initially by using previously underutilized capacity and later through investment, rapidly enough to start rebuilding dwindling reserves before they were exhausted. That gamble failed, but it is difficult to tell whether it was unrealistic from the outset, or whether it was forfeited by policy mistakes.

Stallings points out that heterodox programs make heavy demands on *state capacity*, precisely because they rely more on government controls and guidance and less on market mechanisms. Some of the measures necessary in the short run are diametrically opposed to those required for long-run sustainability, so that accurate gauging of turning points is crucial. Limits on analytic capabilities did affect implementation in all three cases, but in different degrees and ways. In Brazil, technical analysis must share responsibility with political pressures for flaws in the original design: overly stimulative monetary and wage measures. But by mid-1986, the economic team was urging Sarney to tighten fiscal and monetary policy. Political considerations governed Sarney's response. The same scenario was virtually replayed a year later, when new Minister of Finance Bresser attempted a modified heterodox formula: again Sarney refused to back his technical team for political reasons.

In Argentina, the initial design was sounder. But the small and overstrained economic team lacked time and energy to design and launch a program of longer-term reforms. In Peru, thin initial staffing was further weakened by sectarian splits and resignations. Overstrained capacity contributed to the policy inconsistencies that destroyed fragile business confidence.

Regime type does not help explain the different implementation records among the three. All three governments were in part preoccupied with problems of political transition, though García's was not the immediate successor of an authoritarian regime. All three, as discussed earlier, were also based on "coalitions moving left," reacting to earlier conservative or repressive regimes. But *support coalitions* do explain much of the contrast in performance between Alfonsín and Sarney. Alfonsín had recently won a landslide election. Sarney, in contrast, was president by accident, with shaky support from the majority party. This clearly contributed to his reluctance to follow technical advice and put on fiscal and monetary brakes.

The role of coalitions and political pressures in explaining the Peruvian story is less clear. By late 1986, growth was up spectacularly, inflation was down, and García was immensely popular. These successes, however, were based on using idle capacity. To move into a medium-term strategy, it was necessary to obtain investment in general and in exports in particular, given the lack of foreign capital inflows. These problems added to the antistatist ideology of APRA led to the alliance with the business groups. The apparent failure of business to fulfill its part of the bargain may have been one reason for the subsequent decision to nationalize the banks and increase the state's role, but the abrupt change certainly did not reflect strong political pressures.

Brazilian experience suggests a tentative broader point regarding heterodox demand-led programs and political dynamics. Such programs can generate prompt and tangible popular benefits. These short-term results produce widespread euphoria, a misleading belief that adjustment is truly possible without further pain added to the hardships of the economic crisis. The euphoria constitutes an intrinsic political obstacle to the requirement of tightened fiscal and monetary controls implicit in any sustainable version of the heterodox approach.

This political dynamic was clearly at work in the Brazilian experience. But the Peruvian effort foundered for reasons other than popular protest. Peruvian advisors, focused more on long-term growth than on inflation, did not advise García to tighten fiscal and monetary policy. However, it is a fair guess that any attempt to do so would have prompted considerable popular protest. In Argentina, by contrast, the design and presentation of the program made clear from the outset that it was a supplement, not a substitute for more conventional economic management. In contrast to the other two heterodox efforts, the initial effort did not try to combine income redistribution with inflation control. Union and other popular pressures caused the Alfonsín government to slowly lose its battle for fiscal and monetary restraint, but those pressures predated and were not particularly strengthened by the Austral experience.

As noted earlier, *external agencies*—the IMF, the World Bank, and the U.S. government—supported the Austral Plan; they opposed both the Cruzado plan and García's program.[8] But the collapse of the Cruzado plan had nothing to do with external finance or lack thereof. In Peru, the program wavered and began to stall well before reserves ran out, because of inconsistent policy decisions. In Argentina, some external finance was a crucial element in the gov-

---

[8] Net IMF finance was strongly positive in Argentina in 1985 and reasonably positive in 1986, while it was strongly negative in Brazil in the same years and even more negative on a per capita basis in Peru (World Bank, *World Debt Tables*, vol. 2, Country Tables [Washington, D.C., World Bank, 1988–1989], pp. 6, 42, 306). The World Bank approved major agricultural and trade sector loans for Argentina in Spring 1986 and 1987, respectively, totaling $850 million, but also approved a $500 million agricultural sector loan to Brazil in mid-1986 (see table 1.6 in this volume). The World Bank and Inter-American Bank also continued project assistance in Peru, and the ILO and other external agencies provided important technical assistance.

ernment's ability to maintain tight monetary policy during the first year. Put differently, external finance played the same role for the Austral plan as it can play in more orthodox stabilization efforts. As with many such efforts, it was a necessary but far from sufficient ingredient of reasonably effective implementation.

Factors Affecting Implementation Summarized

Among the factors influencing implementation of adjustment measures, a few broad generalizations stand out. When governments tried to implement orthodox stabilization packages,

- The cases of clear failure all traced collapse in large part to deeply divided economic teams. But other governments also were handicapped by divided teams for a period and then replaced them. Fragile support bases and inept leadership, preventing appointment of more unified teams, were more fundamental factors and contributed to a vicious circle of indecisiveness, eroding confidence, and rising protest.
- Governments that followed through effectively varied in the sophistication and depth of economic staffing, and their political institutions and circumstances. But in most cases, either broad public opinion or one or a few influential interest groups were pressing for firm action.

Clearer patterns emerged as governments tried to implement programs of orthodox structural change.

- The same key feature of concentrated executive authority and autonomy associated with the decision to adopt broad reform agendas also facilitated implementation.
- The greater complexity of such changes placed a premium on administrative capabilities. Governments with limited capabilities, but nevertheless committed to reform, were able to use direct-hire expatriates and advisors seconded from external agencies plus technical analysis and advice directly from external agency staff as partial substitutes for internal capacity. These solutions provoked criticism, raising some question about how long they can be relied on heavily.
- External agencies' financial support and technical guidance facilitated both stabilization and structural change in many of the cases of relatively successful implementation. Their degree of detailed involvement in implementation varied roughly inversely with state capacity. In the countries with very limited capacity, external guidance played a crucial role. But since similar guidance and financial support were being offered to the governments that failed to follow through, external support emerges as a sometimes necessary, but far from sufficient, condition for implementation.

Perhaps because of the small number of cases and the varied scope and design of the programs, generalizing about implementation of *heterodox adjustment efforts* is more difficult. The Cruzado plan collapsed because of policy mistakes, largely as the result of a politically weak chief executive confronting powerful interests. The relative success of the Austral plan reflected more cautious initial design and Alfonsín's strong initial political position (comparable to García's). The gradual erosion of the gains from the effort, and the failure to formulate a broader medium-term reform program, were results of the enduring Argentine dilemma: consensus that change is imperative but conflict among its powerful interest groups on direction of reforms and on allocation of costs. Peru's heterodox program was distinguished and complicated by its longer-run focus. Lack of consistent strategy flowed mainly from limited state capacity. García's initial political strength could not compensate for this weakness.

INTEREST GROUPS AND THE POLITICS OF ADJUSTMENT

These conclusions thus far have focused on major determinants of governments' adjustment choices and their persistence in pursuing those decisions. The implicit or explicit focal point has been the perceptions, priorities, and constraints of political leadership. That approach sheds considerable light on the course of adjustment in our cases. A different perspective focuses on the political roles of major interest groups in the process of adjustment. This perspective takes more fully and explicitly into account the perceptions, priorities, and constraints affecting various groups in their interactions with political authorities.

Political leaders concerned with the political feasibility of adjustment measures are likely to start with an implicit or explicit assessment of who wins and who loses. Technical staff, in the governments concerned or in external agencies seeking to promote adjustment, use the same starting point to the degree that they consider politics. But such an analysis is not easy. Interests defined in terms of sector (industry, commerce, agriculture) or factors of production (labor, capital) embrace subcategories with sharply different concerns and degrees of political organization.

Moreover, the complex mosaic of economic interests is often overlaid with other politically relevant affiliations, including regional, religious, and ethnic status. Where such ties cut across lines of economic interest, they often mute political action in defense of strictly economic concerns. In contrast, where ethnic lines coincide with economic cleavages, ethnic hostilies inflame economic decisions: for example, where measures that might benefit the private sector are resisted because of minority domination of business interests. Sometimes whole regions see their prospects as affected by adjustment programs. In Nigeria, for example, the powerful northern region has dominated the federal government and benefited from state control of the economy. Northerners fear they will lose heavily to southern regions and ethnic groups in a more competitive environment.

Political action motivated by economic interest may not be what economic or political analysts expect, because it is often hard for groups to gauge the multiple and often conflicting impacts of different components of policy packages, or to foresee longer-term effects as distinct from immediate effects. Especially where inflation is high and variable, as Kaufman noted, "There is often enormous confusion about who is winning or losing the distributional struggle, even among the participants themselves."[9]

Countries contrast enormously in the number and variety of well-organized, active groups and the degree to which they have long-established orientations, clearly identified constituencies, and well-understood relationships with the government. Among our cases, Argentina, Brazil, Costa Rica, and Mexico are towards the well-established end of the spectrum; Ghana and, perhaps, the Philippines during the transition from the Marcos period are towards the opposite, fluid extreme. Zambia illustrates an intermediate case, with three strongly entrenched interest groups (miners, party, and civil service) dominating politics. Nigeria has a considerably wider range of vocal interests, some of which are highly organized.

Strongly institutionalized groups, as Mancur Olson argued,[10] are likely to become highly rigid as a result both of dynamics within individual groups and interactions among them and between the groups and the state. The state may have sufficient autonomy to break the stalemate (Mexico); where it does not, the result may be semiparalysis (Argentina; less clearly, Costa Rica). Although the absence of highly organized interests apparently gives political leaders a freer hand, it also removes potential bases of support and leaves them vulnerable to pressures from institutional interests (particularly the military) or the unorganized popular urban sector. Rawlings' recent position in Ghana illustrates the pattern.

With these general points in mind, we turn to a closer examination of the roles of various types of interest groups in influencing the course of adjustment efforts.

Labor and the Popular Sectors

The introductory chapter noted the conventional wisdom that organized labor is the most probable source of protest and potential derailment of adjustment programs. Evidence from our cases suggests a rather different proposition.

[9] Robert Kaufman, *The Politics of Debt in Argentina, Brazil, and Mexico: Economic Stabilization in the 1980s*, monograph (Berkeley, Institute of International Studies, University of California, 1988), p. 109.

[10] Mancur Olson, *The Rise and Decline of Nations* (New Haven: Yale University Press, 1982).

Labor alone rarely can stall or drastically modify adjustment programs, although it may win limited concessions. Even in countries where unions are large and well-organized, governments have often faced down their opposition. But where union opposition combines with much broader protest, most commonly from the urban popular sectors but sometimes also from business, programs have indeed been drastically modified or abandoned.

Our cases did provide instances in line with the conventional wisdom, most clearly the sizable wage increases granted at the outset of Brazil's Cruzado plan, which deliberately sought to redistribute income in favor of workers as a preemptive tactic and contributed substantially to the eventual collapse of the program. Across this set of cases, however, the prevailing experience was supression of wage demands or their containment within bounds that did not too seriously erode the programs.[11]

In many of the cases, unions are fragmented and poorly organized. Even where they are large and well organized, they may be weak relative to other social groups or have limited autonomy from ruling parties or the government. Governments sometimes simply faced down union pressures, as in Jamaica in mid-1985, the Philippines in late 1984, and Nigeria in early 1988. Other governments resorted to tougher tactics. In Mexico, strike leaders were dismissed, plants were closed, and massive layoffs were threatened. In Brazil, the military broke a strike in early 1987.

Other governments relied more on negotiation and compromise to contain union pressures. In Argentina, Alfonsín worked out sector-by-sector agreements with powerful industrial unions in mid-1986. The government made some wage concessions, but in general the agreements stayed within guidelines and provided the government with a six-month no strike commitment. In Colombia, although unions in general are not viewed as politically powerful, the Betancur government gained union acquiescence to austerity measures through a combination of discussion and persuasion, partial compensation in the form of a sliding scale wage increase (weighted strongly in favor of the lowest-paid workers), and appointment of a top union leader as minister of Labor. The Monge government in Costa Rica skillfully combined persuasion, partial compensation, and firmness in the early months of its stabilization effort; the rapid economic turnaround and drop in inflation then permitted rapid real wage increases. It is worth noting that these governments were established or transitional democracies—though other governments in those categories used less consultative and conciliatory tactics.

In most instances where union pressures led governments to substantially

[11] Latin America, more than Africa or Asia, might be expected to be the region of greatest union influence. But Ian Roxborough reaches a conclusion similar to ours, for Latin America more generally, in "Organized Labor: A Major Victim of the Debt Crisis," in Stallings and Kaufman, eds., *Debt and Democracy*, pp. 91–108.

modify or to abandon adjustment programs, labor had joined forces with other "popular sector" groups. It is often pointed out that the interests of organized and unorganized labor conflict; high wages and fringe benefits in organized sectors discourage labor-intensive investment. But the two categories also share important interests as consumers of similar goods and as users of public services. Their interests are also intertwined in other ways: small-scale enterprises often do special lot assignments or are otherwise linked to the formal sector, and market venders and own-account service workers sell to formal sector customers. In short, a broad swath of the "popular sectors," including industrial and informal sector workers, small merchants, and the large and growing body of poorly paid public and private sector service and white collar workers share many interests. Moreover, many households include both formal and informal sector workers, further intermingling their concerns.

These shared interests prompted large-scale protest in several of the cases. In Zambia, the December 1986 maize price riots were spearheaded by mine workers but joined by many from the popular classes in the cities. The riots in Santo Domingo in April 1984 over increased food prices were a broad popular uprising with union involvement. In Chile, copper miners initiated the monthly days of protest between March and August 1983 that led Pinochet to shuffle his cabinet and temporarily ease his austerity policies, but those protests soon spread far beyond the miners.

Two broad situational factors obviously and strongly affect governments' sensitivity to popular pressures. The first, already discussed in this chapter, is the approach of elections. The second is the possibility that serious and sustained popular protests will trigger a coup. In Brazil, for instance, Sarney's precarious political support coupled with the lingering military self-image as arbiter of the political process gave the president ample grounds for pursuing union support or seeking to minimize their opposition. Jorge Blanco was under somewhat similar constraints in the Dominican Republic. In Ghana, Rawlings faced a chronic threat of dissident coups, triggered partly by factional and personal hostilities within the military and partly by corporate military concern about social unrest that might result from economic policies and trends. In contrast, in Chile Pinochet appeared to be in firm control of the military establishment; elections at that time were not a binding concern, yet even Pinochet yielded ground to broad and insistent popular pressures in league with much of the business community.

Business Interests and Responses to Adjustment

The roles of labor and business in adjustment offer a fundamental contrast. During conventional stabilization programs, workers are called upon to endure reduced real wages, increased prices, and often unemployment. During structural changes, they must shift from declining to emerging lines of activity and endure any transitional unemployment that results. Business, in contrast, is asked not only to acquiesce (for example, in tightened credit or increased taxes) but to cooperate. Stabilization requires a halt, and better still a reversal, in capital flight. For longer-term structural change, investment and production must increase and shift towards foreign exchange earning or saving activities, while the efficiency of old and new lines of production is increased. Businessmen, in short, are called on to be flexible and inventive, to take risks and be aggressive. Legal restrictions and capital controls can inhibit financial abuse and raise the costs of capital flight, and tax policy can influence patterns of investment. But the general levels of investment, energy, and innovation cannot be commanded; they can only be induced.

It is important to distinguish between direct political pressures by business interests regarding adjustment policies and their investment responses. Their political roles reflect industrial and commercial structure and business perceptions of their access to political authorities. Investment responses depend on perceived economic opportunities, which are only partly shaped by government policies.

The structure of business interests, of course, varies widely. Broadly, in more advanced middle-income countries business sectors are larger and more diverse, with greater flexibility and also deeper within-sector conflicts. The most obvious lines of cleavage are between export-oriented and import-substituting interests. Jeffrey Frieden suggests a second important distinction: the liquidity of capital assets. Liquid asset holders are likely to profit from policies such as devaluation and financial deregulation; they press for favorable measures using the threat of capital flight. In contrast, fixed-asset holders—smaller import-substituting manufacturers, enterprises with large fixed investments, companies tied closely to state-owned enterprise—tend to oppose devaluation, restrictions on domestic credit, and liberalizing reforms.

The distinction says more about the direction of various business interests' pressures than their probable political influence. Highly liquid firms gain leverage through the threat of capital flight, but more rooted interests may also be highly organized and powerful. In Mexico, large-scale, export-oriented, financial-industrial elites centered mainly in the north took a very hard-line position in favor of orthodoxy, pressing for devaluation, trade liberalization, high interest rates, and limited exchange controls. They largely prevailed over other elements of the business sector that opposed these measures. In Brazil, however, São Paulo industrialists with more "rooted" interests were highly successful in pressing their point of view.

In countries in early stages of industrialization, import-substitution interests usually far outweigh embryonic export-oriented industry. In most sub-Saharan African countries, moreover, medium-scale and the few large-scale industries are usually in the public sector or tightly linked to it. Precious little support comes from such business sectors for deregulation, devaluation, trade liberalization, or, of course, high interest rates. In Nigeria, the National Association of Manufacturers was the sole group that spoke in favor of an IMF-supported stabilization program during the public debates in September 1985, but the same group vehemently protested the import liberalization that accompanied the stabilization measures introduced in 1986. Even in some small middle-income countries, including Costa Rica and Jamaica, export-oriented business is mainly directed to protected regional markets. Business interests may support deregulation and export promotion, but not trade liberalization or reductions in the direct and indirect subsidies from which they benefit.

The structure of business interests determines their policy preferences, but the nature and channels of their political activities are shaped by their relationships with political authorities. In many countries, informal access is facilitated by overlap between business and political elites. As the business community itself becomes larger and more diverse, and particularly if business feels informal access is dwindling, organization and direct political action will increase. Kaufman describes the growing sense of alienation and reduced access in orthodox Mexican business circles during the 1970s as changes in the key economic appointments produced policies business viewed as adverse. Business groups shifted from relying mainly on informal access to the highest policy circles towards more formal organization and action. A major new peak association was formed, and the concerned groups sought to seize control of existing associations, to expand their influence within the PRI and the PAN, and to conduct aggressive media campaigns. In Peru, also, economic crisis and political uncertainty prompted a new peak association, Confederation of Private Business Institutions (CONFIEP), to increase business influence in economic policy. Similarly, when Guzmán was elected president of the Dominican Republic, larger businessmen, fearing lack of access, organized the National Chamber of Businessmen (CNHE). The Private Sector Organization of Jamaica was founded in 1976, when most of the business community strongly opposed the policies of the Manley government. And as business opposition to Marcos mounted, Philippine noncrony businessmen organized, starting with the formation of the Makati Business Club in 1981.

In other countries, such as Nigeria, business has continued to rely mainly on informal channels of influence. It has sought less to shape broad policy than to seek exceptions, modifications, delays, or other concessions in application of policies to their specific firms. Particularly in smaller and poorer countries, many businessmen have informal kinship or old school ties with prominent officials. The opportunities and rationale for low-key manuevering are increased by the complex interactions between parastatal organizations and private firms. Where changes such as tariff reduction or import liberalization are introduced in a phased and flexible manner, which would appear sensible both on economic and political grounds, the predictable response is to pick away at implementation through myriad administrative and political channels.

In countries where much business is controlled by ethnic minorities or alien residents, as in much of sub-Saharan Africa, this line of defense may be more effective than collective political efforts to block or alter general policies.

Business pressures on governments normally focus sharply on their economic interests, but sometimes merge with noneconomic goals. In Chile, business concerns over the financial crisis and acute depression merged with desire for a democratic opening and spurred businessmen to join with labor and popular sectors in the Days of Protest of 1983. Still more clearly in the Philippines, increasingly intense opposition to Marcos (and later, support for Aquino) among noncrony businessmen flowed from their exclusion and disadvantages vis-à-vis the cronies, concern over the increasingly inefficient and financially precarious public sector as a whole, and the increasing threat of the guerillas; ultimately they became convinced that only a major political overhaul could address these concerns.

Business agendas and political pressures on adjustment programs vary, but in the 1980s their investment responses have been far more uniform. Even though the thrust of adjustment efforts in almost all our cases was decidedly probusiness, in almost all cases private investment has yet to respond strongly.

Business confidence, the prerequisite to investment, hinges on expectations about the continuity of the new rules of the game. Skepticism about the durability of the reforms in Ghana inhibited middle-class responses. Jamaican businessmen delayed positive reactions not only because many of them opposed major aspects of Seaga's programs, but also because some feared the return of Michael Manley and a PNP administration. The increase in investment in 1987 and 1988, despite approaching elections, is probably the most convincing indicator of narrowing basic differences between the two parties. In Argentina, old and still unsettled conflicts continue to chill investment. More broadly, confidence is undermined to the degree that politics is polarized and lack of consensus across party lines on economic priorities and rules of the game creates fears of sharp policy discontinuities.

Failure of investment to respond to adjustment also testifies, in some countries, to the pervasiveness of import-substituting, high-subsidy and high-state-intervention patterns of business evolution over the past quarter century or longer. Lack of confidence and opposition to reforms are sometimes indices of the need for reforms. But more widely, in the second half of the 1980s reluctance to invest has reflected unsettled and rapidly shifting international trends, including recession and later slow growth in the industrialized world and, in many countries, the albatross of heavy debt.

Agricultural Interests and Rural versus Urban Balance

Much of the neoorthodox adjustment agenda favors agriculture, particularly to the degree that urban biases have previously distorted policies and investment. Realistic exchange rates hurt import-dependent and inefficient import-substituting industries and import-consuming urbanites, but help export-oriented and efficient import-substituting agriculture. "Getting prices right" usually means raising procurement prices to permit a reasonable return to the farmer, even if urban food prices increase as a result. Proponents of neoorthodox adjustment often assume their programs will be strongly supported by rural groups—who may be a majority—even if urban interests oppose reforms. The cases in this volume underscore a different assumption:

> Rural interests are usually politically weak, and rural approval may not translate into effective political support for adjustment.

Successful adjustment experience in the nineteen sixties and seventies was facilitated in Taiwan and to a lesser extent in Korea by strong rural political support for governments interacting with prorural government policies.[12] But in much of the developing world, political institutions and informal practices give rural interests relatively little weight. Small holders and agricultural workers are usually unorganized and lack good access to decision makers.

Even large-scale commercial farmers may lack influence. In some African countries, large farmers are almost nonexistent (Ghana) or are politically handicapped because many are settlers or expatriates (Zambia). In some Latin American countries, large-scale growers of traditional export crops are populist targets because they are the traditional elite and/or because they are foreign (coffee "barons" and banana interests in Costa Rica). In the Dominican Republic at the beginning of 1985, stiff resistance from the sugar interests could not prevent adoption of a steep temporary surcharge on windfall gains of sugar exports to cushion the fiscal shock of shifting to the market exchange rate. In some countries, the historical political clout of large export-oriented farmers was diminished as mineral exports came to account for the overwhelming share of foreign exchange earnings and government revenue: Chile, Peru, and Jamaica are examples.

Where large farmers do swing considerable political weight, they are often tied into the very political/economic system that orthodox structural reforms seek to dismantle. Thus rice growers in Costa Rica—a mere handful of large growers, plus a fair number of medium farmers who market small quantities— benefited from extraordinary subsidies and fought every reform step. The sugar and coconut monopolies in the Philippines under Marcos were still more extreme examples.[13]

---

[12] See, for example, Jeffrey D. Sachs, "Trade and Exchange Rate Policies in Growth-Oriented Adjustment Programs," Vittorio Corbo, Morris Goldstein, and Moshin Khan, eds., *Growth-Oriented Adjustment Programs* (Washington, D.C.: International Monetary Fund and World Bank, 1987), pp. 291–325. It bears noting that even in these Asian cases, while pro-rural measures generated rural support, they were not, for the most part, the result of pressure from powerful agricultural interests.

[13] Another source of resistance to orthodox prescriptions for agricultural development should be noted. In many countries that import much of their food, including most sub-Saharan African

Among the cases, the clearest instance of agricultural interests sufficiently strong to contend for influence on general economic policies is Argentina, despite the fact that only 13 percent of the labor force is engaged in agriculture. Argentine agriculture's role owes much to the combination of continued high dependence on agricultural exports (77 percent in the mid-1980s, compared to 44 percent for Brazil and 9 percent for Mexico)[14] plus well-developed political organization among farmers. Argentina's long history of political instability is closely related to a sectoral stalemate.

In a few countries, militant revolutionaries that seek to mobilize poor cultivators' support, as in Peru, Colombia, and the Philippines, are a countervailing force to urban bias. Plans to stimulate traditional agriculture were a major element in García's initial economic strategy. Betancur's original mildly expansionist program was intended to undercut the appeal of the guerillas with economic reforms. While resistance from landed interests has greatly diluted steps toward land reform in the Philippines, Aquino has considerably expanded programs to improve rural conditions, especially in distressed areas where the guerillas are strong, such as Negros.

In many countries, neither small and medium nor large-scale agriculture exercises much influence on general economic policies. The point has important implications for the political prospects of orthodox adjustment efforts. The easy assumption that liberalizing reforms (including maintaining a realistic exchange rate) will benefit agriculture, and therefore, generate political support from the rural majority, fails to consider how agricultural interests are actually represented in the political process. Particularly where the major beneficiaries are small cultivators, one or more vigorous mass parties is essential to convert economic benefit into political support. Rawlings' situation in Ghana vividly illustrates the point. Cocoa farmers have probably gained from the wrenching reforms of the past several years, but thus far, no political vehicle exists to mobilize them as a counterweight to urban groups opposed to the reforms.

The State as Protagonist

The state is often assumed to be the chief instrument of structural change. But state agencies and officials are also deeply engaged protagonists in adjustment

---

nations and, among our cases, Costa Rica and particularly Jamaica, "food self-sufficiency" or, at any rate, reduced reliance on imports is a strong driving force. This was a major argument in Costa Rica against cutting expensive subsidies for domestic rice production. In many countries the same argument is used against too strong a push to stimulate agricultural exports, lest producers shift to more lucrative export crops and away from growing food. In many sub-Saharan African nations, a deep reluctance to recreate the economic patterns of the colonial era works in the same direction. The result is opposition from outside agriculture to some major aspects of the neoorthodox agenda.

[14] World Bank, "The Structure of Merchandise Exports," Statistical app. tab. 12 in *World Development Report 1988* (Washington, D.C.: World Bank, 1988), pp. 244–45.

efforts. The strong "minimal state" thrust of orthodox reform strategy in the 1980s directly confronts an array of vested individual and institutional interests in existing arrangements within the very governments urged to implement reforms. In some of the cases, particularly in Africa, government or semipublic agencies dominate large-scale manufacturing and mining, foreign trade, the financial sector, distribution of inputs to agriculture, and collection and export of crops. In most of the cases, intricate networks link government, parastatal, and private agencies and activities.

The issue is partly corruption; opportunities for bribery and diversion of funds are threatened by reforms that substitute efficiency criteria or automatic allocation mechanisms for official discretion and control. But corruption is often not the most important part of the picture. In many countries, most higher civil servants hold extensive interests, personally or through their families, in private enterprises benefiting from existing arrangements; these holdings are fully legal, but constitute a major conflict of interest. Still more obviously, public employees at all levels see their jobs at stake in efforts to trim the public rolls or rationalize or privatize parastatals. Their unions are among the most powerful in the country.

At the highest levels of the state machinery, political leaders often also have vested political (as distinct from personal economic) interests in existing administrative arrangements, which further constrain state capacity to implement reforms. Especially in less institutionalized political systems (including many in sub-Saharan Africa), heads of state rely on control over major spending decisions to discipline and control their own lieutenants, as well as to maintain and build popular support. Tightened budgeting and public sector investment procedures, and other reforms that reduce or remove political discretion (elimination of import licensing; privatization of credit programs) reduce their ability to reward political friends and discipline enemies. At a different level, links between state or provincial (that is, subnational) financial institutions and political parties in both Brazil and Argentina have proved a major stumbling block to central bank efforts to maintain monetary discipline.

For many politicians and officials, not only vested interests but genuine convictions regarding the appropriate role of the state pose obstacles to sharp reductions in that role. And here their views often converge with those of intellectuals and much of the public, who generally harbor strong doubts that unbridled market forces will serve national interests. Identifying the most appropriate areas and modalities of state regulation and guidance of markets is a continuing, complex, and often bitter topic of political debate in almost all nations. The relevant point is that basic unresolved issues of public priorities merge with narrower vested interests to obstruct change.

External agencies usually have little direct influence on public or semipublic agencies and institutions beyond the narrow circle of the economic team. The benefits of nonproject external support are evident to those responsible for macroeconomic policy, but are not the direct concern of other agencies. Outsiders' usual means of pressing governments to comply with agreements involve threats or losses to the government and the nation, but not necessarily to the agencies causing the difficulty. In Costa Rica, for example, when one agency failed to meet conditions for release of the second tranche of the World Bank SAL, the government was plunged into a morass of cross-conditioned delays in funding worth far more than the $40 million sum directly at stake. But the "delinquent" agency had little to gain and a good deal to lose by complying.

Even within the confines of the state machinery, then, Kahler's point is telling: market-oriented reformers have not seriously addressed the paradox of using the state to change policy in a less statist direction. More heterodox reform programs with less strong antistatist overtones might provoke somewhat less ideological resistance from within the state machinery. But even heterodox reforms designed to move towards a more efficient and productive state are likely to prompt resistance from public sector vested interests and to upset broader networks of political patronage and influence.

The Politics of Stabilization and Structural Change Contrasted

Decision makers considering the political implications of adjustment choices must weigh not only the probable reactions of specific groups but also the aggregate effects of these reactions. A set of stylized contrasts can be drawn between the politics of short-run macroeconomic stabilization packages and the political dynamics of medium-term structural change. The contrasts are deliberately overdrawn, intended to draw attention to implications of different types of policy packages rather than to describe reality accurately. In the real world, boundaries between the categories of policy blur; some measures, most notably devaluation, often serve both ends. Despite this intertwining, it can plausibly be argued that stabilization packages pose different threats to established interests and have different patterns of political impact than do medium-term reforms.

Regarding threat, many stabilization measures (budget cuts, monetary management measures) are intended and presented as temporary. They are taken in response to national crises. In contrast, medium-term reforms are explicitly permanent, or long-term. Because they normally are expected to produce benefits only after a delay, they cannot usually claim crisis priority.

Regarding pattern of impact, stabilization measures are usually announced and carried out as a package. They feature macroeconomic measures, each of which affects many in the population simultaneously and transparently. (A "transparent" effect is one the affected groups think they understand, whether or not an economist would agree with the analysis.) Moreover, the measures are applied roughly simultaneously. In contrast, even where the strategy of structural change is explicit, most reform programs unfold as a series of measures announced at different times and carried out on varying timetables. And many reform measures are of immediate and obvious concern only to specific groups.

Reflecting these contrasts, stabilization packages are much more likely to prompt mass protest than are structural programs. But if the crisis is widely perceived and the government can present its program as a plausible solution, many people and groups may be willing to undergo short-term sacrifices for their own and the national benefit. Structural reforms, however, are likely to prompt determined opposition precisely because they are billed as permanent. Resistance will normally come from specific groups, and will less often take the form of mass demonstrations. Because reforms like trade liberalization or parastatal restructuring require many stages, resistance is likely to be spread over long periods and to change forms over time.

Just as the timing and distribution of losses has implications for the pattern of opposition, the timing and distribution of gains has implications for actual and potential political support. If benefits of structural changes are often delayed and accrue to individuals and groups who are not politically organized and may not even recognize their potential gains when the policy is launched, prospects for coalitions in support of the reforms are poor. It is sound economics to point to entrepreneurs "over the horizon" who will benefit from reduced regulations, freer imports, and more available (because it is unsubsidized) credit. But it is hard to build a political alliance with them.

These stereotypical contrasts between stabilization and adjustment emerge less clearly where, as in so many countries in the 1980s, governments have had to combine reform efforts with ongoing austerity. Interest groups and the public react to the overall economic effects. Even when they focus on specific measures, their responses are shaped by the broader economic situation and by their confidence or lack of confidence in the government's economic management as a whole. But contrasts in the nature of the threat or costs and in the timing and incidence of impact do help to unravel varying political reactions to adjustment in different countries and in the same countries over time.

Learning from Experience

Carlos Diaz-Alejandro once suggested that "the longer the history of failed stabilization plans, the smaller the chances of success (and/or the greater the costs of success of any new plan.)"[15] Diaz-Alejandro based his hypothesis on experience among the countries of the southern cone of Latin America. Chris-

[15] Carlos Diaz-Alejandro, "Southern Cone Stabilization Plans," in William R. Cline and Sidney Weintraub, eds., *Economic Stabilization in Developing Countries* (Washington, D.C.: Brookings Institution, 1981), p. 120, cited in Karen Remmer, "The Politics of Economic Stabilization: IMF Standby Programs in Latin America, 1954–1984," *Comparative Politics* 19, no. 1 (October 1986): 3.

tine Bogdanowicz-Bindert, examining the history of stabilization efforts in Portugal, Turkey, and Peru, arrived at a contradictory hypothesis. Several failed efforts, she concluded, may be necessary to pave the way for measures vigorous and coordinated enough to produce success.[16] Is there a cumulative learning process that tends toward more rational and realistic adjustment policy?

The mechanism behind Diaz-Alejandro's pessimism is that failure erodes confidence in the sustainability of subsequent efforts; each sequential failure does greater damage. Bindert more optimistically assumes more complex learning. Policy makers, and perhaps politically potent groups as well, learn not only that adjustment is difficult but what is necessary to succeed.

Our case studies offer only scattered clues on processes of learning about adjustment policy within countries confronting severe problems. Some obvious and discouraging tendencies are clear. Politicians tend towards interpretations of economic events with the easiest implications for immediate action. Economic staff may sometimes tend, like military strategists, to fight the last war: seeking to avoid the mistakes and repeat the successes of previous policy, without carefully considering whether changed circumstances call for different strategies.

Nevertheless, as Kahler indicates, there has been a good deal of general learning during the 1980s, reflected to varying degrees in policy circles of specific countries. In sub-Saharan Africa recognition of the distortions and costs of certain kinds of state economic intervention is wider now than a decade ago, and appreciation of the importance of "getting prices right" is greater. Costs of long-continued reliance on import substitution as the engine of industrialization were provoking growing debate in Latin America long before the crisis of the 1980s; the crisis has accelerated the revision of assumptions. On the other hand, the more ardent proponents of the magic of the marketplace have gained at least some recognition of the limits of private sector capabilities.

Because appropriate structural changes vary with each country's economic problems and potential and its institutional and social constraints and opportunities, the most useful form of learning from experience is a much more detailed and realistic appreciation of the mechanisms at work within the economy and the feasible options for that economy—an implicit modifying of "monoeconomics." The intensive analysis (by governments, private groups, and external agencies) and the public debate and experimentation of the 1980s without question have contributed to this process.

International trends have also pressed both officials and the public in each

---

[16] Christine A. Bogdanowicz-Bindert, "Portugal, Turkey, and Peru: Three Successful Stabilization Programs under the Auspices of the IMF," *World Development*, 11, no. 1 (January 1983): 65–70.

country to sort temporary problems from enduring ones. In 1981, Seaga, the Bretton Woods institutions, and most of the Jamaican public still believed that bauxite would again become the engine of Jamaican growth. In 1988, all parties' strategic thinking excludes this hope. In Costa Rica, recognition is now widespread that future development cannot rely substantially on the recovery of the Central American Common Market. Casting the same point in the terms that Kahler suggests, the political and economic viability within a country of imported economic ideas increases as those ideas are filtered through and modified by domestic experience and increasingly refined analysis.

Such learning obviously does not solve strategic dilemmas. Still more clearly, it leaves open the issue of how adjustment burdens should be allocated among groups. But by confining debate and conflict within realistic parameters, it can make a major contribution to the forging of adjustment programs that are both economically feasible and politically sustainable.

A broader lesson emerging from the experience of the 1980s is that answers to problems of adjustment with growth in specific countries are only partly "in the books," available to be learned—if necessary in the "school of hard knocks." The answers to many crucial questions are not ready at hand but must be invented for each country individually, often with support and suggestions from abroad, but primarily by domestic analysis, debate, conflict, and compromise. That lesson, most clearly, is not only one for politicians and publics in developing nations but also for the wealthy nations and the international community.

Statistical Appendix: Thirteen Countries, 1979–1988

DATA for these tables are drawn almost wholly from standard international statistical sources such as the International Monetary Fund's *International Financial Statistics Yearbook* and the World Bank's *World Debt Tables*. These data may differ not only from series produced by other organizations, including the governments of the countries concerned, but also from data on specific items calculated by operating staff of the IMF or the World Bank. Specific items, therefore, may not correspond precisely with data used in the case studies in this volume. The tables should be used primarily to gain perspective on broad contrasts or similarities among the countries in our study and trends in those countries during the 1980s.

TABLE A.1
Real GDP Growth[a]

	1979	1980	1981	1982	1983	1984	1985	1986	1987
Argentina	11.1	1.5	(6.7)	(5.0)	2.9	2.5	(4.4)	5.4	—
Brazil	7.2	9.1	(3.3)	0.9	(2.5)	5.7	8.3	8.2	—
Mexico	9.2	8.3	7.9	(0.6)	(5.3)	3.7	2.8	(3.7)	—
Chile	8.3	7.8	5.5	(14.1)	(0.7)	6.3	2.4	5.7	—
Peru	4.3	2.9	3.0	0.9	(12.0)	4.8	1.6	8.5[b]	—
Colombia	5.4	4.1	2.3	0.9	1.6	3.4	3.1	5.1	5.4
Costa Rica	4.9	0.8	(2.3)	(7.3)	2.9	8.0	.7	5.4	3.9
Jamaica	(1.7)	(5.8)	2.5	1.0	2.0	(0.4)	(4.6)	2.3	5.5
Dominican Republic	4.5	6.1	4.1	1.6	4.9	1.0	(3.6)	3.2	8.1
Ghana	(3.2)	0.0	(1.8)	(7.2)	0.7	8.7[b]	5.4[b]	4.3[b]	—
Nigeria	2.5	5.3	(8.4)	(3.2)	(6.3)	(5.2)	5.3	(3.3)	—
Zambia	(3.0)	3.0	6.2	(2.8)	(2.0)	(1.3)	4.4	0.5	—
Philippines	6.3	5.2	3.9	2.9	0.9	(6.0)	5.3	(7.7)	5.1

Source: International Monetary Fund, *International Financial Statistics Yearbook* (Washington, D.C.: International Monetary Fund, 1988), pp. 164–67, except where noted.

[a] Based on 1980 local currency.

[b] Data from World Bank, *Adjustment Lending: An Evaluation of Ten Years of Experience*, Policy and Research series no. 1 (Washington D.C., 1988), p. 89.

TABLE A.2
Real Per Capita GDP Growth

	1979	1980	1981	1982	1983	1984	1985	1986	1979–1986
Argentina	4.9	0.2	(8.6)	(5.4)	0.4	1.5	(6.4)	4.4	(9.1)
Brazil	4.8	4.3	(5.6)	(1.3)	(4.8)	3.4	6.1	10.2	1.4
Mexico	6.4	5.5	5.2	(3.2)	(7.8)	1.3	0.4	(5.1)	0.9
Chile	6.8	6.3	3.8	(15.8)	(2.4)	(4.6)	(0.7)	4.6	0.5
Peru	1.6	0.2	0.4	(2.2)	(14.6)	2.2	(1.0)	5.4	(0.4)
Colombia	3.4	2.1	0.2	(1.1)	(0.4)	1.4	0.4	3.1	5.6
Costa Rica	2.5	(3.1)	(3.2)	(9.5)	(2.3)	5.8	(1.9)	(3.2)	(10.7)
Jamaica	(3.1)	(6.7)	1.1	(0.4)	0.2	(1.7)	(6.3)	1.0	(13.2)
Dominican Republic	2.0	3.5	1.5	(1.2)	0.1	(1.9)	(4.5)	(0.9)	(3.9)
Ghana	(6.4)	(4.1)	(5.3)	(9.7)	(3.1)	6.0	3.3	—	(21.7)[a]
Nigeria	0.4	(0.6)	(6.3)	(3.4)	(11.9)	(8.9)	(2.1)	(6.2)	(26.7)
Zambia	(6.3)	(0.2)	6.2	(6.2)	(5.5)	(4.7)	1.0	(2.9)	(8.9)
Philippines	3.6	2.3	1.4	0.4	(1.6)	(8.5)	(6.9)	(1.4)	(13.6)

Source: International Monetary Fund, *International Financial Statistics Yearbook*, 1987.
Note: Real per capita GDP growth based on 1980 local currency.
[a] Data are for 1979–1985.

TABLE A.3
Current Account Balance as Percentage of GDP

	1979	1980	1981	1982	1983	1984	1985	1986	1987
Argentina	(0.5)	(3.1)	(3.8)	(4.1)	(3.8)	(3.2)	(1.4)	(3.6)	—
Brazil	(4.7)	(5.3)	(4.4)	(6.1)	(3.3)	0.0	(0.1)	(1.7)	—
Mexico	4.1)	(4.4)	(5.8)	(3.7)	3.8	2.5	0.7	(1.3)	—
Chile	(5.7)	(7.1)	(14.5)	(9.5)	(5.7)	(10.7)	(8.3)	6.7	—
Peru	5.3	0.4	(8.6)	(7.9)	(5.4)	(1.3)	0.9	(4.3)	—
Colombia	1.6	(0.6)	(5.4)	(7.8)	(7.8)	(3.7)	(5.3)	0.9	0.7
Costa Rica	(13.8)	(13.7)	(15.6)	(10.4)	(10.3)	7.0	(7.5)	(3.7)	—
Jamaica	(5.7)	(6.2)	(11.4)	(12.5)	(10.0)	(14.1)	(15.0)	(1.6)	—
Dominican Republic	(6.0)	(10.9)	(5.4)	(5.6)	(4.8)	(1.6)	(2.4)	2.2	—
Ghana	1.2	0.2	(1.6)	(0.3)	(0.8)	(0.5)	(2.1)	—	—
Nigeria	1.9	5.6	(7.4)	(8.8)	(5.7)	0.2	1.7	—	—
Zambia	1.1	(13.8)	(18.5)	(14.6)	(8.2)	(5.6)	(9.0)	(18.2)	—
Philippines	(5.1)	(5.4)	(5.4)	(8.1)	(8.0)	(3.9)	(0.1)	3.2	(1.6)

Source: International Monetary Fund, *International Financial Statistics Yearbook*, 1988, pp. 154–55.

TABLE A.4
Terms of Trade (Index, 1980 = 100)

	1979	1980	1981	1982	1983	1984	1985	1986
Argentina	108.0	100.0	98.9	91.5	97.3	98.8	91.4	79.9
Brazil	122.9	100.0	93.5	97.8	99.4	101.1	103.7	128.3
Mexico	86.0	100.0	106.5	103.2	96.5	97.2	96.3	63.8
Chile	109.1	100.0	85.8	78.7	84.7	79.5	78.3	75.0
Peru	97.0	100.0	91.9	83.7	83.9	83.9	80.5	66.4
Colombia	113.9	100.0	91.5	97.9	96.1	100.9	99.0	98.0
Costa Rica	111.8	100.0	93.6	94.2	97.5	96.5	96.3	105.5
Jamaica	111.3	100.0	94.2	93.6	94.5	94.8	93.9	108.6
Dominican Republic	106.5	100.0	88.2	81.9	86.9	88.3	82.6	103.9
Philippines	115.0	100.0	92.0	89.1	97.1	104.0	93.7	101.4
Nigeria	70.7	100.0	108.8	101.0	96.6	97.1	88.5	44.3
Ghana	132.6	100.0	81.4	73.1	88.1	98.1	90.3	88.0
Zambia	108.3	100.0	79.8	70.9	77.9	70.1	71.5	70.0

Source: World Bank, *World Tables 1987* (Washington, D.C.: World Bank and International Finance Corporation, 1988).

TABLE A.5
Real Effective Exchange Rate (Index, 1980 = 100)

	1979	1980	1981	1982	1983	1984	1985	1986	1987
Argentina	77	100	91	52	43	50	44	44	41
Brazil	113	100	121	128	104	104	100	94	95
Mexico	89	100	114	82	72	84	86	60	56
Chile	86	100	118	107	87	85	69	58	54
Peru	90	100	119	123	114	114	94	106	125
Colombia	98	100	108	115	114	105	91	68	61
Costa Rica	91	100	63	73	83	82	81	73	66
Jamaica	90	100	107	111	104	73	64	69	68
Dominican Republic	98	100	101	103	97	71	78	73	61
Philippines	95	100	103	107	90	89	98	76	70
Nigeria	94	100	111	114	134	185	166	91	29
Ghana	77	100	222	278	187	72	52	30	23
Zambia	102	100	102	114	106	91	84	40	43

Source: World Bank, macroeconomic indicators developed as background for *Adjustment Lending: An Evaluation of Ten Years of Experience* (Washington, D.C.: World Bank, 1989). The annex to *Adjustment Lending* provided the data for a sample of fifteen countries that included Brazil, Chile, Colombia, Ghana, Mexico, Philippines, and Zambia.

TABLE A.6
Trade Ratio[a]

	1980–1982 Average[a]	1984–1986 Average[a]
Argentina	49.4	31.6
Brazil	25.4	26.3
Mexico	34.8	37.8
Chile	54.3	74.2
Peru	44.9	39.6
Colombia	44.5	45.2
Costa Rica	102.9	85.2
Jamaica	127.5	162.8
Dominican Republic	53.3	69.4
Ghana	48.8	34.2
Nigeria	52.7	29.4
Zambia	83.8	135.2
Philippines	51.2	53.8

Sources: World Bank, World Development Report 1982 (New York: Oxford University Press, 1982), pp. 114, 124. World Bank, World Debt Tables, vol. 2, 1987–1988.
[a] Exports plus imports as a percentage of GNP, three-year average.

TABLE A.7
Service on Public and Publicly Guaranteed Debt as Percentage of Exports of Goods and Services

	1980	1981	1982	1983	1984	1985	1986	1987
Argentina	16.6	17.3	23.1	24.5	24.9	40.6	51.8	45.3
Brazil	34.6	33.7	43.3	28.8	25.0	26.7	34.1	26.7
Mexico	32.1	28.1	34.1	40.0	34.8	35.7	37.2	30.1
Chile	21.9	29.6	19.8	18.1	25.7	26.3	28.6	21.1
Peru	31.1	44.8	36.3	19.8	15.9	17.8	14.4	12.5
Colombia	8.9	13.1	17.3	21.9	20.1	29.9	26.4	30.7
Costa Rica	16.8	16.6	11.7	51.6	25.0	35.2	26.6	12.1
Jamaica	14.0	15.1	16.7	19.2	19.2	29.1	29.7	25.8
Dominican Republic	10.3	13.4	19.2	15.3	10.1	12.7	16.3	—
Ghana	8.3	7.2	9.6	23.3	16.4	15.6	16.7	—
Nigeria	1.8	4.6	10.8	17.5	25.5	30.7	17.9	10.0
Zambia	17.8	25.1	16.3	12.2	11.8	10.9	19.1	13.5
Philippines	7.1	9.7	12.3	14.4	13.7	15.4	22.4	22.7

Source: World Bank, World Debt Tables, vol. 2, 1988–1989. Calculated from country tables.

TABLE A.8

Interest on Public and Publicly Guaranteed Debt as Percentage of Exports of Goods and Services

	1980	1981	1982	1983	1984	1985	1986	1987
Argentina	7.0	8.5	13.1	14.8	20.2	32.6	35.2	39.4
Brazil	18.0	19.1	25.4	20.5	17.0	19.3	23.9	16.4
Mexico	15.8	15.9	22.3	23.1	22.8	25.3	26.3	19.2
Chile	7.7	8.6	10.6	11.4	19.2	21.4	23.2	18.2
Peru	11.3	12.5	13.1	10.4	9.3	8.6	6.2	5.5
Colombia	4.7	8.0	11.3	12.5	10.1	16.2	12.5	14.4
Costa Rica	10.6	9.7	6.8	42.7	16.9	25.4	13.6	8.1
Jamaica	7.8	6.7	9.5	11.0	13.6	15.4	14.6	13.4
Dominican Republic	6.2	7.0	8.1	7.4	6.3	8.1	10.4	—
Ghana	2.5	3.2	4.1	9.4	4.8	4.6	5.2	—
Nigeria	1.6	2.8	6.0	8.8	9.2	9.7	4.3	6.9
Zambia	6.6	8.0	7.8	7.3	6.0	4.9	8.8	5.9
Philippines	4.5	5.9	6.4	7.9	9.7	9.9	13.7	14.5

Source: World Bank, *World Debt Tables*, vol. 2, 1988–1989.

TABLE A.9

Total External Debt as Percentage of GNP

	1980	1981	1982	1983	1984	1985	1986	1987
Argentina	48.4	63.8	83.8	77.3	67.5	81.5	66.8	73.9
Brazil	30.4	31.8	35.7	50.1	52.6	49.1	42.0	39.4
Mexico	30.4	32.5	52.6	66.4	57.2	54.9	82.5	77.5
Chile	45.3	50.2	77.1	100.2	115.1	144.6	135.5	124.1
Peru	50.8	42.4	49.6	63.7	66.2	82.1	60.1	40.5
Colombia	20.9	24.1	26.9	30.1	32.3	42.0	45.6	50.2
Costa Rica	59.5	141.2	166.8	148.0	117.0	121.8	110.1	115.7
Jamaica	76.5	88.8	101.4	105.6	160.7	222.0	186.3	175.9
Dominican Republic	33.6	35.3	38.1	47.5	65.1	83.0	70.8	79.8
Ghana	29.6	34.7	34.7	39.8	43.7	49.1	47.5	63.3
Nigeria	8.9	13.0	14.1	21.1	20.5	22.1	53.1	122.6
Zambia	90.5	92.9	101.9	120.3	151.5	195.2	398.6	334.4
Philippines	49.4	54.0	61.9	70.8	77.1	81.9	95.0	86.5

Source: World Bank, *World Debt Tables*, vol. 2, 1988–1989.

TABLE A.10
Short-term Debt as Percentage of Total Debt

	1980	1981	1982	1983	1984	1985	1986	1987
Argentina	38.2	36.2	37.8	19.4	21.9	13.6	7.3	4.7
Brazil	19.1	19.0	18.9	14.6	10.9	10.3	8.2	11.2
Mexico	28.1	31.9	30.4	10.9	6.8	5.6	5.8	5.4
Chile	21.2	19.1	19.3	14.4	9.6	8.2	7.3	8.3
Peru	20.8	24.1	24.6	11.9	12.9	12.6	16.4	18.2
Colombia	33.7	31.8	30.3	28.6	23.8	21.8	10.4	9.7
Costa Rica	21.0	18.9	21.4	11.9	8.5	8.7	10.4	14.3
Jamaica	5.1	4.0	3.4	7.5	6.5	4.4	3.7	4.5
Dominican Republic	23.9	27.8	21.0	10.2	12.0	10.5	8.8	9.2
Ghana	10.0	19.6	14.7	5.6	12.5	8.4	6.8	3.5
Nigeria	40.0	36.7	19.5	27.2	30.8	25.5	14.3	9.3
Zambia	18.0	16.9	17.5	13.6	11.3	14.6	18.1	17.0
Philippines	43.5	45.4	46.6	39.9	38.9	13.6	18.6	16.5

Source: World Bank, *World Debt Tables*, vol. 2, 1988–1989.

TABLE A.11
Public and Publicly Guaranteed Debt as Percentage of Long-term Debt

	1980	1981	1982	1983	1984	1985	1986	1987
Argentina	60.7	46.5	58.6	71.0	72.1	88.6	89.5	94.3
Brazil	70.9	69.6	68.7	73.3	78.4	81.1	85.2	86.4
Mexico	82.3	80.9	86.4	81.9	81.1	82.2	83.4	85.4
Chile	50.1	35.5	37.5	45.4	62.5	73.2	83.8	86.3
Peru	83.0	81.5	80.7	84.1	86.4	88.5	89.4	89.7
Colombia	88.8	85.4	83.4	84.3	84.3	85.9	88.5	90.1
Costa Rica	80.4	85.5	86.2	89.9	90.9	92.1	92.1	92.6
Jamaica	94.9	98.6	97.7	96.9	97.3	97.8	98.0	98.4
Dominican Republic	82.8	85.7	86.8	92.4	93.8	94.6	95.0	95.7
Ghana	99.1	99.1	98.6	98.3	97.3	97.0	97.8	98.7
Nigeria	79.4	82.3	87.4	90.4	89.2	90.3	98.1	98.7
Zambia	96.2	97.8	98.2	99.1	99.2	100.0	100.0	100.0
Philippines	72.7	73.4	73.4	77.3	80.8	81.9	91.5	93.6

Source: World Bank, *World Debt Tables*, vol. 2, 1988–1989.

TABLE A.12

Money plus Quasi-money: Annual Growth (Percentage Change over Four Quarters)

	1979	1980	1981	1982	1983	1984	1985	1986	1987
Argentina	178.9	127.7	91.1	141.9	288.2	564.9	631.3	126.5	—
Brazil	58.4	68.4	67.7	99.7	118.0	215.7	305.3	—	—
Mexico	32.7	35.7	45.1	63.6	59.6	71.8	46.3	57.5	126.5
Chile	76.7	56.5	57.0	27.3	3.2	25.7	—	—	—
Peru	79.3	95.9	63.7	72.1	89.0	117.4	166.4	81.8	—
Colombia	23.2	29.1	44.4	31.6	18.3	24.9	25.3	—	—
Costa Rica	29.4	22.0	52.1	43.2	45.7	19.4	18.6	18.9	17.6
Jamaica	16.6	19.3	23.4	31.6	26.6	21.5	24.4	22.6	22.6
Dominican Republic	2.2	14.6	2.4	19.8	12.5	18.0	17.5	48.1	41.4
Ghana	30.9	35.7	36.2	32.8	47.4	33.7	43.7	51.9	60.6
Nigeria	18.6	30.8	19.8	8.8	13.3	13.3	10.5	5.9	—
Zambia	7.4	18.8	7.5	19.0	21.5	13.6	18.3	59.5	—
Philippines	15.5	17.1	18.1	23.0	19.8	17.5	14.0	9.1	12.7

Source: International Monetary Fund, *International Financial Statistics Yearbook*, 1988, pp. 94–97.

TABLE A.13

Consumer Price Changes (CPI, Percentage Change over Previous Year)

	1979	1980	1981	1982	1983	1984	1985	1986
Argentina	159.5	100.8	104.5	164.8	343.8	626.7	672.1	90.1
Brazil	52.7	82.8	105.6	97.8	142.1	197.0	226.9	145.2
Mexico	18.2	26.4	27.9	58.9	101.8	65.5	57.7	86.2
Chile	33.4	35.1	19.7	9.9	27.3	19.9	30.7	19.5
Peru	66.7	59.2	75.4	64.4	111.2	110.2	163.4	77.9
Colombia	24.7	26.5	27.5	24.5	19.8	16.1	24.0	18.9
Costa Rica	9.2	18.1	37.1	90.1	32.6	12.0	15.1	11.8
Jamaica	29.1	27.3	12.7	6.5	11.6	27.8	25.7	15.1
Dominican Republic	9.2	16.8	7.5	7.6	4.8	27.0	37.5	9.7
Ghana	54.4	50.1	116.5	22.3	122.9	39.7	10.3	24.6
Nigeria	11.7	10.0	20.8	7.7	23.2	39.6	5.5	1.1
Zambia	9.7	11.7	14.0	12.5	19.6	20.0	37.4	51.6
Philippines	17.5	18.2	13.1	10.2	10.0	50.3	23.1	0.8

Source: International Monetary Fund, *International Financial Statistics Yearbook*, 1988, pp. 116–17.

Index

Africa: adjustment policies, implementation of, 263–64; agricultural export, 257; colonial traditions, 259; crony statism, 258; debt forgiveness, 9; distribution of rents, 258; exchange rates, 259; foreign businessmen, 265; foreign exchange control and licensing systems, 259; and IMF, 262, 318–19; import controls, 259; mineral exports, 257; multinational firms, 265; and Paris Club, 262; postcolonial syndrome, 260–61, 317; property rights, 260; regime type, 263, 264, 316; "shredding," 263; state capacity, 265; structural change, 12, 263; subsidies, 258; sub-Saharan, 8; welfare services, 258; and World Bank, 262, 318–19
agricultural interests, 32, 354–56
A.I.D. *See* U. S. Agency for International Development
Akuffo, Fred, 271
Alfonsín, Raul, 73
Allende, Salvador, 117
analytic capabilities, of governments, 345
Andean Pact, 115
Aquino, Corazon, 31, 76, 215, 233
Argentina, 7, 9, 12, 13, 30, 45, 49, 57, 59, 63–112; agrarian exports, 68; Alfredo Concepción, 89; Argentine Central Bank, 59, 89; Austral decree, 30, 66, 76, 79–83, 88–91; Bignone government, 74; capital flows, 72; currency reform, 50; devaluation, 88; electoral politics, 74; expansionist policies, 74; Figuerido government, 74; General Confederation of Labor (CGT), 89; Bernardo Grinspun, 74; hard currency savings, 72; and IMF, 82, 89–90; impact of changing political regimes, 66; import-substituting industrialization, 65, 67; inflation, 71, 72, 76; interest rates, 72, 91; labor unions, 66, 79, 88, 328; Jóse Luis Machinea, 89; Malvina Falkland, 72–73, 82; Martinez de Hoz, 67, 70; Marxist terrorist groups, 69; official terrorism, 70; political liberalization, 70; political vulnerability, 82; popular support vs. military authority, 75; recession, 78; regime type, 68–69; short-term money mar-

ket activities, 82; Juan Sourroville, 78; tax revenues, 90; transitional governments, 76; wage-price freezes, 50; and World Bank, 89–90
Arias, Oscar, 187, 188
authority: of central government, 329–30, 335, 340, 340–41; centralization of, 340; of economic team, 198–99; of military, 24

Babangida, Ibrahim, 269, 304
Baker, James, III, 7, 52, 57, 86
Baker Plan, 7, 8, 47
Balaguer, Joaquin, 174, 176
balance-of-payments, 11
Balassa, Bela, 19
bank nationalization, 333
Barco, Virgilio, 159
Belaunde Terry, Fernando, 74, 114, 118, 321
Bernstein, Edward M., 37
Betancur, Belisario, 153–54, 321–22
Bogdanowicz-Bindert, Christine, 359–60
Bolivia, 10
Brazil, 7, 9, 10, 12, 13, 30, 49, 57, 63–112; Pérsio Arida, 83; Luiz Carlos Bresser Pereira, 86; business protests, 85; capital flight, 64, 82; coffee, 68; "compulsory savings" fees, 84; conclave in Carajas, 83–84; Cruzado decree, 30, 66, 76–77, 79–83, 321; currency reform, 50; Maílson Pereira da Nóbrega, 87; Francisco Dornelles, 74–75; economic liberalization, 76; electoral politics, 74; Estado Nôvo, 67; expansionist policies, 74, 79; Dilson Funaro, 75, 78; Getulio Vargas Institute, 83; illegal surcharges, 83; and IMF, 75, 86, 87; impact of changing political regimes, 66; import-substituting industrialization, 65, 67; income redistribution, 49; inflation and hyperinflation, 71, 76–77; labor unions, 85; André Lara-Resende, 83; military-backed regimes, 69; Plano do Metas, 76; political reform, 71–72; political vulnerability, 82; popular support vs. military authority, 75; São Paulo Industrial Federation (FIESP), 85; João Sayad, 75; tax increases, resistance to,

Brazil (*cont.*)
  87; trade balances, 83; transitional govern-
    ments, 76; United Confederation of Labor
    (CUT), 85; *Veja*, 86; wage increase, 79;
    wage-price freezes, 50
Bretton Woods agencies, 8, 11, 26, 39, 41,
    43, 47, 48, 53, 54, 59, 361. *See also* IMF;
    World Bank
Broad, Robin, 230
Buhari, Muhammadu, 304
business confidence, 354
business interests, 351–54

Callaghy, Thomas, 31, 56, 59
Camdessus, Michel, 52
Campos, Roberto, 38
Canitrot, Adolfo, 70
capital controls, 352
capital flight, 352
capital flow, 3, 25; and influence on reforms,
    343
Carazo, Rodrigo, 57, 183, 321
Cárdenas, Cuauhtémoc, 102, 107
Central American Common Market (CACM),
    170, 187, 198, 361
Chenery, Hollis, 41
Chile, 13, 22, 30, 40, 45, 113–68; agrarian
    reforms, 117; Jorge Alessandri, 117; bal-
    ance-of-payments crisis, 116, 119; Banco
    de Chile, 130; bank sales, 138–39; Hernán
    Büchi, 136–37; Carlos Cáceres, 130; Cath-
    olic University in Santiago, 118, 137;
    Christian Democrats, 114, 117; Confedera-
    tion of Production and Commerce (CPC),
    131; copper industry, 117, 122; Sergio de
    Castro, 118, 129; debt-equity swaps, 141;
    devaluation, 122, 130; export revenues,
    139; Extended Fund Facility (EFF), 140;
    GDP trends, 115; human rights, 141; and
    IMF, 131, 139; import-substitution industri-
    alization, 117; inflation, 116, 119, 126; in-
    terest rates, 128; Sergio Onofre Jarpa, 132;
    labor unions, 124, 132, 163; mineral ex-
    ports, 115; plebiscite, 141–42, 165–66;
    Popular Unity, 117, 122; private-sector
    wages, 137; privatization, 139; regime
    type, 118, 124–26, 135, 163; small busi-
    ness protests, 131; social expenditure, 137;
    Structural Adjustment Loans (SALs), 140;
    tariffs, reduction of, 128; tax reforms, 139;

  trade policy, 137–38; wage indexation, 46;
    and World Bank, 139
civil service, 34, 356. *See also* public sector,
    state agencies
Colombia, 22, 30, 38, 113–68; Banco de Co-
    lombia, 115; Banco de la República, 159;
    capital flight, 155; Edgar Gutiérrez Castro,
    154; coffee export, 115, 153, 166; devalua-
    tion, 154; exchange rate policy, 55; falling
    reserves, 166; Jorge Eliécer Gaitán, 150;
    GDP trends, 115; and IMF, 155, 157–59; im-
    port controls, 155; inflation, 151; insur-
    gency, 149; Roberto Junguito, 155; Liberal
    Party, 114; National Agricultural Society,
    156; National Front, 115, 150; Hugo Pala-
    cios, 159; stabilization, 151; tax reform,
    155; trade credits, 155; trade policy, 159;
    Turbay government, 152–53; unemploy-
    ment, 156; wage increase, 157; and World
    Bank, 151
commercial bank credit, 6
Conable, Barber, 53
conditionality, criticisms of, 57
Corden, Max, 61
corruption, 357
Costa Rica, 7, 10, 18–19, 25, 25–26, 26, 30,
    169–213; agricultural subsidies, 187; and
    A.I.D., 186; business and agricultural asso-
    ciations, 202; business and agricultural sub-
    sidies, 173; capital flight, 172, 183, 184,
    185; Carlos Manuel Castillo, 184, 186; and
    Central American Common Market (CACM),
    172, 187; CODESA, 187; debt moratorium,
    184; debt service, 188; Emergency Eco-
    nomic Law, 186, 204; exchange rate, 184,
    185; exports, 172, 176, 183; external debt,
    173; GDP trends, 172; and IMF, 202, 203–7;
    import controls, 184; import surcharges,
    188; inflation, 183; international interest
    rates, influence of, 176; Eduardo Lizano,
    187; manufacturing, 172; National Libera-
    tion Party (PLN), 173, 184; National Pro-
    duction Council (CNP), 187; oil prices, 176,
    183; and Paris Club, 185, 188; privatiza-
    tion, 187; public sector, 173, 205; real
    wages, 185; reform, resistance to, 183; rice
    subsidies, 187; Hernando Sáenz, 184; so-
    cial expenditures, 172, 188; social welfare,
    172; stabilization, 176, 183, 185; tariff pro-
    tection, 187; trade and fiscal deficits, 172–

73; and U.S., 172, 206–7; wage freeze, 208
Council of Economic Advisors, 106
credit policies, 338
crony-based regimes, reaction to, 202, 335. *See* Philippines

de la Madrid, Miguel, 14, 63, 91
debt bargaining, 18
debt forgiveness. *See* Africa
debt-for-equity swaps, 8–9
deflation, 34–35
democracy: constraints of, 197, 201; transition to, 335, 338; and adjustment tactics, 208–10; small democracies, 206–7
deregulation, 39
devaluation, 336, 352. *See also* Argentina; Chile; Colombia; Ghana; Mexico; Nigeria; Peru; Philippines; Zambia
Diaz-Alejandro, Carlos, 35, 359
Dominican Republic, 10, 14, 18–19, 22, 30, 169–213; and A.I.D., 182, 203–7; April 1984 riots, 209; balance-of-payments support, 181; borrowing, 178; business interests, 201; capital flight, 172; Central Bank, 178; debt service, 182–83; deficit spending, 178; Democratic Revolutionary Party (PRD), 178; Carlos Despradel, 178; economic recession, rate of, 181; elections, 182; exchange rate policy, 179–80, 181; export earnings, 172; Extended Fund Facility, 179; GDP trends, 172; Hugo Guiliani, 180; and IMF, 182, 203–7; import-substituting industrialization, 174; inflation, 179; interest rates, 17; labor unions, 201; manufacturing, 172; military, 178; oil prices, 178; and Paris Club, 181; petroleum imports, 180; property tax, 179; public sector employment, 178; real wages, 181; Reformist Party (PR), 175; revenues from import taxes, 181; Revolutionary Democratic Party (PRD), 175; rice subsidy, 182; stabilization, 176; strikes and protests, 181; sugar and other primary exports, 172, 178, 181; tax base, erosion of, 174–75; and U.S., 172; value-added tax (VAT), 179; Bernardo Vega, 178; and World Bank, 182
Drake, Paul, 58–59

Echeverría, Luis, 94
Economic Commission for Africa, 38

Economic Commission for Latin America (ECLA), 35, 38, 59
Ecuador, 10
elections; and economic adjustment, 24; timing of, 201, 207–8. *See also* Argentina; Brazil; Dominican Republic; Jamaica; Zambia
electoral cycles, 110–11, 207, 325, 328–30, 335, 340–41; affecting time horizons, 64
elites, 338
exchange rate policies, 41, 46, 333; flexible exchange rates, 9; over-valued exchange rates, 12
export earnings, 6
export policies: orientation, 352; promotion, 9, 338; strategies, 12; subsidies, neostructuralist views of, 49
export volume, 175–76
external agencies, influence of, 325, 330–31, 332, 342–44, 346–47, 357–58

Feinberg, Richard, 27
financial deregulation, 352
fiscal policy, 63, 64, 336
foreign exchange scarcities, 334, 336
Foxley, Alejandro, 5
Frei, Eduardo, 38, 114, 117
Frenkel, Jacob, 52

García, Alan, 30, 60, 142
Gardiner, Robert, 38
G-5 governments, 43, 47
Ghana, 13, 19, 22, 25–26, 31, 257–319; Joseph Abbey, 272, 275; abolition of subsidies, 280; Accra, 280; J. K. Acheampong, 271; blackmarket, 274; Kwesi Botchwey, 275; K. A. Busia, 271; cocoa, 266, 274, 276, 278, 285; Committees for the Defense of the Revolution, 278; corruption, 271; crony statism, 271; devaluation, 272, 275; drought, 274; economic growth, rate of, 276; economic recession, rate of, 274; education, 276, 278; exchange rate reform, 275–76; export earnings, 274, 276; foreign investment, 285; Ghana Cocoa Board, 276; gold exports, 276, 285; health services, 276; human rights abuses, 281; and IMF, 266, 275; Industrial and Commercial Workers Union, 281; inflation, 274; Kwame Nkrumah Revolutionary Guards, 281; labor organizations, 277, 280; leftist activities,

Ghana (*cont.*)
277, 280; Hilla Limann, 271, 321; military, 266; National Liberation Council, 271, 271–72; neoorthodox reform, 266; New Democratic Movement, 281; Amon Nikoi, 273; P. V. Obeng, 275; postcolonial syndrome, 271, 275–76; private sector, 266; Program of Action and Measures to Address the Social Costs of Adjustment (PAMSCAD), 284; Provisional National Defense Council (PNDC), 274; real wage, 272; resident foreigners, 282; rural support, 278; "shredding," 266, 277; Soviet assistance, appeal for, 275; stabilization, 272; state layoffs, 280; student organizations, 277, 280; tax collection, 276; Trades Union Congress (TUC), 281; transportation infrastructure, 276; and UNICEF, 284; University of Ghana, 275; urban middle class, 281; user fees, 280; wage and benefit increases, 280; Worker's Defense Committees, 278; and World Bank, 266, 275
Great Depression, 59; impact of, 35
Group of 24 Report, 51
guerilla movements, 330
Guzman, Antonio, 57, 175, 178, 321

Haggard, Stephan, 5, 21, 22, 25, 75
Hall, Peter, 57–58, 60
heterodox adjustment programs, 63, 335, 344–47, 348
Hirschman, Albert O., 4, 38
Honduras, 10

import-substituting industrialization, 352. *See also* Argentina; Brazil; Chile; Dominican Republic; Mexico; Peru; Philippines
Indonesia, 54, 215
inflation, 4, 35, 39, 49, 54, 331, 335, 344; hyperinflation, 9; in Southern Cone economies, 46. *See also* Argentina; Brazil; Chile; Colombia; Costa Rica; Dominican Republic; Ghana; Jamaica; Mexico; Peru; Zambia
Interamerican Development Bank, 147
interest groups: agriculture, 348; capital, 348; commerce, 348; ethnic, 348; industry, 348; labor, 348; regional, 348; religious, 348; rural, 355
interest rates, 9, 336; increases in, 175–76
international financial institutions, 331, 342–44

International Monetary Fund (IMF), 7, 8, 10, 15, 16, 25, 31, 33, 35, 42, 47, 51, 64, 69, 70, 71, 74, 80, 105, 109, 122, 158, 205, 330–31; Compensatory Financing Facility, 38–39; Enhanced Structural Adjustment Facility (ESAF), 8, 54; Extended Fund Facility (EFF), 16–17, 22, 25, 42; stand-bys, 16–17, 25; Structural Adjustment Facility, 8, 54. *See also* Africa; Argentina; Brazil; Chile; Colombia; Costa Rica; Dominican Republic; Ghana; Jamaica; Mexico; Nigeria; Peru; Philippines; Zambia
Israel, 49, 54; currency reform, 50; wage-price freezes, 50
Ivory Coast, 10

Jamaica, 19, 25–26, 26, 30, 169–213, 174; Alcoa, 192; and Baker Plan, 193; Bank of Jamaica, 193; bauxite/alumina, 172, 174, 176, 190, 191, 192, 194, 197, 213; and Bretton Woods agencies, 190; Bustamente Industrial Trade Union (BITU), 209–10; capital flight, 172; capital inflows, 191; Caribbean Economic Community (CARICOM), 195; debt service, 192; economic management, 196; elections, 190, 191–92; export earnings, 172; Extended Fund Facility, 174; GDP trends, 172; and IMF, 174; import liberalization, resistance to, 195; imports, 190; inflation, 191, 194; Jamaica Commodities Trading Corporation (JCTC), 210; Jamaica Labour Party (JLP), 190; Joint Trade Union Center, 210; labor union protest, 196; labor union strikes, 192–93; manufacturing, 172; oil prices, 176, 192, 194; People's National Party (PNP), 174; price controls, 210; private capital, 191; Private Sector Organization of Jamaica (PSOJ), 203; public sector deficit, 192; real wages, 174; Reynolds Aluminum Company, 192; Hugh Shearer, 210; social expenditures, 172, 196; stabilization, 191; state monopolies, 194; subsidies, 192; taxes, 192, 194; tourism, 194; and U.S., 172, 190, 206–7; utility rates, 194
Japan, Dodge Plan, 38
Jorge Blanco, Salvador, 178, 321–22

Kahler, Miles, 11, 29–30
Katzenstein, Peter, 211
Kaufman, Robert, 23, 25, 30, 59

Kaunda, Kenneth, 268, 287, 321
Kemmerer, Edwin, 58
Keynesian ideas, influence of, 58
Killick, Tony, 51
Klein-Saks mission, 46
Korea, 21, 60–61, 215, 220, 355
Kubitschek, Juscelino, 68

labor unions, 24, 25, 32, 329; combined with urban popular sectors, 350. *See also* Argentina; Brazil; Chile; Dominican Republic; Ghana; interest groups; Jamaica; Peru; Philippines; Zambia
laissez-faire policies, 34–35
Larosière, Jacques de, 52–53
Lessard, Donald R., 19
liquidity of capital assets, 352
Little, Ian, 36

McCarthy, F. Desmond, 19
Malaysia, 215
Manley, Michael, 174
Marcos, Ferdinand, 31, 76, 215, 222–24, 321–22
Mexico, 13, 30, 37, 38, 63–112; Aeromexico, 105; Altos Hornos, 105; bank nationalization, 98–99; business interests, 96; capital flight, 100; Central Bank, 92; Consejo Coordinador Empresarial (CCE), 96–97; democratic reform, 108; devaluation, 107; electoral turnout, decline in, 94; external debt, 7; Fundidora, 105; guerilla activity, 94; Jesus Silva Herzog, 98; and IMF, 95, 100; import-substituting industrialization, 65; inflation, 92; Institutional Revolutionary Party (PRI), 91; Keynesian influence, 96; Miguel Mancera, 98; Mexican Worker's Confederation (CTM), 92; Minetas Cananea, 105; oil exports, 97; outflow of capital, 97; PEMEX, 104–5; privatization, 104–5; public expenditure, 95; real wages, 92; recession, 106; rural land seizures, 94; Secretaría de Programacíon Presupuesto (SPP), 96; stabilization policy, 100–104; structural reform, 100; student protest, 94; tax rates, 95; trade liberalization, 104–5; Treasury Department, 92; wage/price controls, 103
Military coups, 335
Monge Alvarez, Alberto, 14, 183, 184
Moon, Chung-in, 21
Morales Bermúdez, Francisco, 119

Nelson, Joan, 5, 30
neoorthodox programs, 9, 335–36, 337–44. *See also* stabilization policies
neostructuralists, 48–49, 54
Neves, Tancredo, 72, 83
Nigeria, 10, 25, 31, 257–319; agricultural commodity boards abolished, 308; Ahmadu Bello University, 311; Alhaji Abdulkadir Ahmed, 308; Ali Chiroma, 311; Armed Forces Ruling Council (AFRC), 306; Central Bank of Nigeria, 308; civil service, 314; crony statism, 304; devaluation, 308; Olu Falae, 308; foreign exchange, 309–10; Ishrat Husain, 307; and IMF, 270; investment, 315; Kalu I. Kalu, 308; and London Club, 306–7; Manufacturers Association of Nigeria (MAN), 310; Nigeria Labour Congress (NLC), 306, 311; Olusegan Obasanjo, 304; oil, 262, 269, 303, 305; Chu Okongwu, 308; and Paris Club, 305; postcolonial syndrome, 269, 303, 308; price controls, 308; private sector, 270; regime type, 269, 303; subsidies on fertilizer, 308; subsidies on petroleum, 308, 311; tariff structure, 310; trade liberalization, 308; transition to democratic rule, 270, 312; and World Bank, 270
Nkrumah, Kwame, 271
North, Douglass, 260

oil crisis of 1973, and 1979, 71
oil price increases, 6
Onganía, Juan Carlos, 70
opposition groups, 329, 335
organized labor, 349–51
orthodox policies. *See* neoorthodox programs

Paris Club, 80. *See also* Africa; Costa Rica; Dominican Republic; Nigeria; Philippines; Zambia
patronage systems, 24, 357
per capita income, in indebted countries, 10
Perón, Juan, 59, 66–67
Peru, 9, 10, 12, 13, 22, 30, 40, 57, 113–68; agrarian reforms, 118; balance-of-payments crisis, 116, 119, 128, 142, 144, 166; Banco de Crédito, 145; bank nationalization, 145–46, 163; Alfonso Barrantes, 142; capital outflow, 143; Daniel Carbonetto, 142–43; Centro de Estudios para el Desarrollo y la Participación (CEDEP), 142–43;

Peru (*cont.*)

Confederation of Private Business Institutions (CONFIEP), 134; debt-service cap, 147; devaluation, 122; education, 118; exchange rate, 144; export promotion, 143; food prices, 144; Fund for Investment and Employment (FIE), 145; GDP trends, 115; housing, 118; and IMF, 133, 147; import substitution, 143; inflation, 116, 119, 128; interest rates, 144; international trade, 118; labor union strikes, 125, 134; Sendero Luminoso, 126, 143, 149, 164; mineral exports, 115; National Investment Council, 145; Popular Action Party, 114, 118; Manuel Prado, 117–18; price freeze, 144; public utility prices, 144; regime type, 118, 125–26, 135; Carlos Rodríguez-Pastor, 133; short-term stabilization, 143–44; Standard Oil subsidiary (IPC), 122; tax evasion, 144; tax reforms, 118; trade deficit, 128–29; unemployment, 128, 144; wage increases, 143; welfare payments, 144

Philippines, 60–61, 75, 202, 215–55; accountability, 247; agricultural monopolies, 232, 247; Benigno Aquino, 219, 235, 239; Joker Arroyo, 245, 250; auditing, 218; banking, rehabilitation of, 215; Roberto Benedicto, 238; blackmarket, 239; Board of Investments (BOI), 222; and George Bush, 241; capital flight, 218, 233–34, 239; Central Bank, 240, 243; centralized power, 223; Chinese entrepreneurs, 222; Church hierarchy, 219; civil service, 228; closing of Congress, 224; coconut sector, 232, 240, 243; Community Employment and Development Program (CEDP), 249; Comprehensive Agrarian Reform Program (CARP), 253; José Concepción, 252; José Concepción, Jr., 246; Construction and Development Corporation of the Philippines (CDCP), 236; control of media, 228; "Convenor Group," 246; cronyism, 216, 231–34, 243–44; decentralization, 247; Dewey Dee, 235; "democratization," 220, 254–55; deregulation of agricultural markets, 215; devaluation, 239; Development Bank of the Philippines (DBP), 236, 240, 252; discretionary "taxation," 218; Herminio Disini, 233; Juan Ponce Enrile, 245; exchange rate policy, 247; export promotion, 230, 247; José Fernandez, 246; financial institutions, 234, 239; foreign ownership, 251; GDP trends, 230–31; government contracts, 232; heavy industry, 230; human rights activists, 219; and IMF, 76, 219, 226; import-substituting industrialization, 215; institutional reform, 247; Interim National Assembly (Batasang Pambasa), 228; Kilusang Bagong Lipunan (KBL), 225; labor unions, 223, 242; land reform, 215, 224, 225, 248, 252; Jaime Laya, 236; leftist insurgency, 223; Makati Business Club, 237; Imelda Marcos, 238, 242; martial law, 216, 223; middle classes, 219; military, 219, 225, 245; Ministry of Human Settlements, 238, 242; misallocation of resources, 218; monopolies, elimination of, 250; Solita Monsod, 247; National Economic Development Authority (NEDA), 225; National Sugar Trading Corporation (NASUTRA), 232; Jaime Ongpin, 237, 246; Roberto Ongpin, 226, 230; and Paris Club, 242; patronage system, 217, 221, 254–55; "People's Livelihood Program," 238, 242; petroleum, 239; Philippine Coconut Authority, 232; Philippine National Bank (PNB), 236, 240, 252; Philippine National Oil Company, 252; Philippines Export Guarantee Corporation (PGC), 240; plebiscite, 228, 236; preferential loans, 218; privatization, 247, 252; promotion of domestic industry, 224; property rights, 218; public enterprises, 215, 240; Fidel Ramos, 245; Reagan administration, relation with Marcos, 241; rice sector, 232; rural insurgency, 245; rural-based elites, 221; Augusto Sanchez, 245; Girardo P. Sicat, 225, 230; Ricardo Silverio, 236; stabilization, 219, 244; state capacity, 217; student protests, 223; sugar sector, 221–22, 232, 240, 243; tax reform, 228, 240, 247, 250; trade liberalization, 76, 222, 247, 250; trade tax revenues, 225–26; United Coconut Oil Millers (UNICOM), 232; United Coconut Planters Bank (UCPB), 232; and U.S., 219; Cesar Virata, 228, 230, 233, 236; and World Bank, 219, 230; Enrique Zobel, 237

Pinochet, Augusto, 60, 124, 129

Polak model, 37

Portillo, José López, 94

Prebisch, Raul, 35, 58–59

privatization, 9, 205

public enteprises, 352; reform, 39, 64, 359
public sector employment, 9, 351
public sector social programs, 324

Quick, Stephen, 102

Ramos, Fidel, 47
Rawlings, Jerry, 266, 271
recession, 336
regime change, 224; and policy choices, 73–79
regime type, 18, 22, 63, 64, 111, 169, 208, 325, 332, 345; authoritarian governments, 22; democracies, 22. See also Africa; Argentina; Chile; Nigeria; Peru
Remmer, Karen, 22
repression, 209
Restrepo, Carlos Lleras, 114

Sachs, Jeffrey, 51; and income redistribution, 51
Salinas, Carlos, 98, 99
Sarney, José, 64, 72, 321
Seaga, Edward, 31, 189
Shagari, Shehu, 304
Sikkink, Kathryn, 58
size (population), and adjustment, 170
Skidmore, Thomas, 4
socialist economies, 33
Southern Cone, 45–47, 53, 55
stabilization policies, 3, 136, 321, 337, 347, 358–59; domestic prices, 64; external accounts, 64
Stallings, Barbara, 22–23, 30, 60
state, role of, 324
state agencies, 356–57
state capacity, 21–22, 325, 327–28, 331–32, 339, 345
state-owned enterprises, 352. See also public enterprises
Stauffer, Robert, 223
structural change, 4, 321, 337, 347, 359; v. crisis management, 13–14
subsidies, 9, 12; utility rates, 336
Sunkel, Osvaldo, 35–36

Taiwan, 215, 220, 355
Tanzania, 10
tax collection, 9, 336
tax reforms, 9

Taylor, Lance, 48
Thailand, 215
Thorp, Rosemary, 144
timing of adjustment decisions, 324, 325, 335
timing of elections. See elections
trade policy, 11, 39, 49; import liberalization, 205, 338; trade liberalization, 9, 40, 46–47, 64, 359. See also export policies
Turkey, 54

unemployment, 338, 351
UNICEF, 50, 56
United Nations, 39, 42, 48
Uruguay, 45
U.S. Agency for Internal Development (A.I.D.), 26, 342

Vargas, Getulio, 66–67
Velasco Alvarado, Juan, 74, 118
Volcker, Paul, 158, 307

wage policies and trends, 351
weather, influence on economic performance, 9, 174, 178
Whitehead, Laurence, 5
Williamson, John, 19
Williamson, Mary, 27
World Bank, 7, 10, 15, 25, 31, 33, 42, 47, 53, 60, 158, 205, 330–31; list of seventeen "highly indebted countries," 19; Sectoral Adjustment Loans, 7, 25; Structural Adjustment Loans (SALs), 42–43, 54
World Institute for Development Economics Research, 48
world markets, integration into, 324

Zaire, 10
Zambia, 10, 13, 19, 22, 31, 257–319; and African National Congress, 289; agricultural development, 288; Bank of Zambia, 292; blackmarket, 301; Frederick Chiluba, 297; Leonard Chivuno, 290; civil service, 293; copper production, 268, 286, 291; corruption, 301; crony statism, 298, 301; devaluation, 292; economic recession, rate of, 291; economic reform, resistance to, 268; elections, 269, 302; exports, 286, 288, 295, 301; Fabian socialism, 288; fertilizer subsidy cuts, 292; foreign businessmen, 269; foreign exchange auction, 292, 294; and IMF, 268; import licensing system, 292;

Zambia (*cont.*)
import tariff structure, 292; inflation, 301; interest rate decontrol, 292; Basil Kabwe, 294; labor organizations, 287; labor unrest and strikes, 291, 297; labor-intensive manufacturing, 288; maize meal riots, 296; maize subsidy, 292, 295, 296; James Mapoma, 294; Dominic Mulaisho, 292; Kebby Musokotwane, 301; Luke Mwananshiku, 290; National Agricultural Marketing Board (NAMBOARD), 288, 293; National Commission for Development Planning (NCDP), 289; neoorthodox reform, 292–300; oil prices, 289; parastatal sector, 287; and Paris Club, 300; David Phiri, 292; postcolonial syndrome, 287, 303; public sector strikes, 297; and Rhodesia (now Zimbabwe), 289; riots, 269; "shredding," 268–69, 299; single-party regime, 268; social welfare spending, 288; and South Africa, 289; stabilization, 289; state capacity, 286, 289, 302; tax reform, 293; United National Independence Party (UNIP), 287; urbanization, 268, 287, 295; and World Bank, 268; Zambia Industrial and Mining Corporation (ZIMCO), 288; Grey Zulu, 294